KWIKSCAN™

New Testament

COMPLETE AUTHORIZED KING JAMES VERSION

KWIKSCAN™ EDITORIAL STAFF

Editor In Chief: M.F. Morris, D.D.
Editor: Nila Vae Morris
Executive Editor: Scott M. Morris
Managing Editor: Scott Jones
Statistical Editor: Julianne Morris
Senior Scan Editors:
Karl David, Ph.D.
Walter Humphrey, Ph.D.
Scan Review Editor:
George Overby, Ph.D.
Editor of Introductions:
Scott M. Morris

Scan Editorial Staff:
Senior Coordinator:
Lee E. Davis
Assistants: Grace Taylor,
George Truitt
Computer Scan Editor:
Scott Jones
Typesetting Editor:
Arthur E. Janz
Computer Systems Editor:
Maggi Honda

Micro-Books, Incorporated
Windermere, Florida 32786

Library of Congress Cataloging - in - Publication Data:
BS2085 1986.w56 1987   220.5'2034   87-1515

ISBN 0-941485-01-3

Published in the United States of America

II

HOW KWIKSCAN™ BENEFITS YOU

Try a simple experiment and immediately you will see the tremendous benefits of **KWIKSCAN™**. First, read every word in the text below. Secondly, go back through the text reading only those words in bold type. Once you read a couple of columns, you will never want to read anything printed the traditional way again.

- **KWIKSCAN™ words** (The words printed in bold type) **comprise about 50% of a** total **Text,** and often much less. **And,** as you are about to find out, **by reading the bold words only, you** will **reduce reading time by up to Two Thirds!** (Much less time for some people and a little more for others.) **This is true because** of two reasons. The first is obvious. **You simply eliminate** the necessity of **reading about half the words** – words that can be left out without changing the overall meaning of the text. **Secondly,** and less obvious until you think about it, **you eliminate left to right head and or eye movement – a big problem** many have **in reading and** also **a consumer of** large chunks of your valuable

- **time. Besides** the benefits of **saving** huge amounts of **time, KWIKSCAN™** also **increases the understanding** of most readers **by making the text** less complicated and **easier to follow. It helps retention too.** (You will remember more of what you read!) **If right now, you are reading just the bold words** when you finish, **you will read only 119 out of** a total of **256 words,** and you will do it **in about one-third the time required to read the entire text. Yes, after** reading the exciting new **KWIKSCAN™ way, you will never want to go back to the old** and ordinary **ways of reading** and you will know why KWIKSCAN™ is called "The greatest step forward in reading since the invention of the printing press."

TABLE OF CONTENTS

IMPORTANT MESSAGE TO THE READERS

"All scripture is given by inspiration of God..." (II Timothy 3:16).

The text of the KWIKSCAN™ New Testament includes every word of The Authorized King James Version. Not a single word has been eliminated or altered. Highlighting (placing certain words in bold faced type), does not indicate that they have greater importance. Rather, the bold words assist readers in quickly reviewing the text. For a thorough understanding of the scripture, readers should study the complete text. However, the SCAN represents thousands of hours of intensive research and work by dedicated Bible scholars, proof editors, computer systems analyst, and typesetting specialists, all of whom are committed to assisting readers in understanding the Holy Scriptures.

THE GOSPEL ACCORDING TO MATTHEW

BACKGROUND INFORMATION

Author – Matthew, a tax collector who became **one of The Twelve Disciples** of Jesus.
Date Written – probably **between 61** and **70** A.D.

Number of:
Verses -   1,071
Chapters -   28
Total Words - 23,684
Scan Words - 11,770
Scan Words represent 49 % of Total Words.

Theme – showing that **Jesus Christ is the Fulfillment of** The Old Testament **prophecies** concerning the promised Messiah.

OUTLINE OF THE GOSPEL

I.   **The birth and childhood** of Jesus Christ.
     Chapters 1:1—2:23
II. **The beginning of the ministry** of Jesus Christ.
     Chapters 3:1—4:11
III. **The public ministry** of Jesus Christ in fulfillment of Old Testament prophecy.
     Chapters 4:12—25:46
IV. **The passion** of Jesus Christ in fulfillment of Old Testament prophecy.
     Chapters 26:1—27:66
V.   **The resurrection** of Jesus Christ.
     Chapter 28:1—20

CHAPTER 1

1. **The book** of the generation **of Jesus Christ, the son of David, the son of Abraham.**

2. Abraham begat Isaac; and Isaac begat Jacob; and Jacob begat Judas and his brethren;

3. And Judas begat Phares and Zara of Thamar; and Phares begat Esrom; and Esrom begat Aram;

4. And Aram begat Aminadab; and Aminadab begat Naasson; and Naasson begat Salmon;

5. And Salmon begat Booz of Rachab; and Booz begat Obed of Ruth; and Obed begat Jesse;

6. And Jesse begat David the king; and David the king begat Solomon of her *that had been the wife* of Urias;

7. And Solomon begat Roboam; and Roboam begat Abia; and Abia begat Asa;

8. And Asa begat Josaphat; and Josaphat begat Joram; and Joram begat Ozias;

9. And Ozias begat Joatham; and Joatham begat Achaz; and Achaz begat Ezekias;

10. And Ezekias begat Manasses; and Manasses begat Amon; and Amon begat Josias;

11. And Josias begat Jechonias and his brethren, about the time they were carried away to Babylon:

12. And after they were brought to Babylon, Jechonias begat Salathiel; and Salathiel begat Zorobabel;

13. And Zorobabel begat Abiud; and Abiud begat Eliakim; and Eliakim begat Azor;

14. And Azor begat Sadoc; and Sadoc begat Achim; and Achim begat Eliud;

15. And Eliud begat Eleazar; and Eleazar begat Matthan; and Matthan begat Jacob;

16. And Jacob begat Joseph the husband of Mary, of whom was born Jesus, who is called Christ.

17. So all the generations **from Abraham to David** *are* **fourteen generations; and from David until the carrying away into Babylon** *are* **fourteen generations; and from** the carrying away into **Babylon unto Christ** *are* **fourteen generations.**

18. **Now** the birth of Jesus Christ was on this wise: **When** as his mother **Mary was espoused to Joseph, before they came together, she was found with child of the Holy Ghost.**

19. **Then Joseph** her husband, **being a just** *man,* and not willing to make her a public example, **was minded to put her away** privily.

20. **But** while he thought on these things, behold, **the angel of the LORD appeared** unto him in a dream, **saying, Joseph,** thou son of David, **fear not to take** unto thee **Mary** thy wife: **for that which is conceived in her is of the Holy Ghost.**

21. **And she shall bring forth a son, and** thou shalt **call his name JESUS: for he shall save his people** from their sins.

22. **Now all this** was done, that it might be fulfilled which **was spoken** of the Lord **by the prophet, saying,**

23. **Behold, a virgin shall** be with child, and shall **bring forth a son, and they shall call his name Emmanuel, which** being interpreted **is, God with us.**

24. **Then Joseph** being raised from sleep did as the angel of the Lord had bidden him, and **took unto him his wife:**

25. **And knew her not till she had brought forth** her firstborn son: and he called his name **JESUS.**

CHAPTER 2

■ 1. **Now** when Jesus was born in Bethlehem of Judaea **in the days of Herod** the king, behold, **there came wise men from the east** to Jerusalem, 2. **Saying, Where is he** that is **born King of the Jews? for we have seen his star** in the east, **and are come to worship him.** 3. **When Herod** the king had **heard** *these things,* **he was troubled,** and all Jerusalem with him. 4. **And when he had gathered all the chief priests and scribes** of the people together, **he demanded** of them **where Christ should be born.** 5. **And they said** unto him, **In Bethlehem** of Judaea: **for thus it is written by the prophet,** 6. And thou Bethlehem, *in* the land of Juda, art not the least among the princes of Juda: for out of thee shall come a Governor, that shall rule my people Israel. 7. **Then Herod,** when he had privily called the wise men, **inquired** of them diligently **what time the star appeared.** 8. **And he** sent them to Bethlehem, and **said, Go and search** diligently **for the young child;** and when ye have found *him* , bring me word again, **that I may** come and **worship him** also. 9. When they had heard the king, **they departed; and, lo, the star,** which they saw in the east, **went before them,** till it came **and stood** over **where the** young **child was.**

10. When they saw the star, they rejoiced with exceeding great joy. ■ 11. **And** when they were come into the house, **they saw the** young **child** with Mary his mother, and fell down, **and worshipped him: and** when they had opened their treasures, they **presented** unto him **gifts; gold,** and **frankincense and myrrh.** 12. **And being warned of** God in a dream that they **should not return to Herod, they departed into their own country** another way. 13. **And** when they were departed, behold, **the angel** of the Lord **appeareth to Joseph in a dream, saying,** Arise, and **take the young child and his mother, and flee into Egypt,** and be thou there until I bring thee word: **for Herod will seek** the young child **to destroy him.** 14. When he arose, **he took the young child** and his mother by night, **and departed into Egypt:** 15. And was there until the death of Herod: **that it might be fulfilled which was spoken of** the Lord by **the prophet, saying, Out of Egypt have I called my son.** 16. **Then Herod,** when he saw that he was mocked of the wise men, was exceeding wroth, and sent forth, and **slew all the children** that were **in Bethlehem, and in all the coasts** thereof, **from two years old and under,** according to the time which he had diligently inquired of the wise men. ■ 17. **Then was fulfilled that** which was

- spoken by Jeremy
the prophet, saying,
- 18. In Rama was there a voice
- heard, lamentation, and weeping,
and great
- mourning, Rachel weeping
- *for* her children, and would not
be comforted, because they are not.
- 19. But when Herod was
- dead, behold,
- an angel of the Lord
- appeareth in a dream
- to Joseph in Egypt,
- 20. Saying, Arise, and
- take the young child and
- his mother, and go into
the land of
- Israel: for they are dead which
sought the young child's life.
21. And he arose, and took the young
child and his mother, and came into
the land of Israel.
- 22. But when he heard that
- Archelaus did reign in
- Judaea in the room of
his father Herod,
- he was afraid
to go thither: notwithstanding,
- being warned of God
in a dream,
- he turned aside into
the parts of
- Galilee:
23. And he came
- and dwelt in a city called
- Nazareth: that it might
- be fulfilled
which was spoken by the prophets,
- He shall be called
- a Nazarene.

CHAPTER 3
- 1. In those days came John
- the Baptist, preaching
in the wilderness of Judaea,
- 2. And saying, Repent ye:
- for the kingdom of heaven
- is at hand.
- 3. For this is he that was
- spoken of by the prophet
- Esaias, saying, The voice
- of one crying in the
- wilderness, Prepare ye the

- way of the Lord,
make his paths straight.
4. And the same John had his raiment
of camel's hair, and a leathern girdle
about his loins; and his meat was
locusts and wild honey.
- 5. Then went out to him
- Jerusalem, and all
- Judaea, and all
the region round about
- Jordan,
- 6. And were baptized
of him in Jordan,
- confessing their sins.
- 7. But when he saw many of
- the Pharisees and
- Sadducees come to his baptism,
- he said unto them,
- O generation of vipers,
- who hath warned you to
- flee from the wrath
- to come?
- 8. Bring forth therefore
- fruits meet
- for repentance:
- 9. And think not
to say within yourselves,
- We have Abraham to *our*
- father: for I say unto you, that
- God is able of these
- stones to raise up children
- unto Abraham.
10. And now also the axe is laid unto
the root of the trees: therefore every
tree which bringeth not forth good fruit
is hewn down, and cast into the fire.
- 11. I indeed baptize you
- with water unto repentance.
- but he that cometh after me
- is mightier than I, whose
- shoes I am not worthy to
- bear: he shall baptize you
- with the Holy Ghost, and *with*
- fire:
12. Whose fan *is* in his hand, and he
will throughly purge his floor, and
gather his wheat into the garner; but
he will burn up the chaff with
unquenchable fire.
- 13. Then cometh Jesus
from Galilee to Jordan
- unto John, to be baptized
of him.

14. But John forbad him, saying, I have need to be baptized of thee, and comest thou to me? **15. And Jesus** answering **said** unto him, **Suffer** *it to be so* now: for thus it becometh us **to fulfil all righteousness.** Then he suffered him. **16. And Jesus, when he was baptized, went** up straightway **out of the water: and, lo, the heavens** were **opened** unto him, **and he saw the Spirit of God descending like a dove, and lighting upon him: 17. And lo a voice from heaven, saying, This is my beloved Son, in whom I am well pleased.**

CHAPTER 4

1. Then was Jesus led up of the Spirit into the wilderness to be **tempted of the devil. 2. And when he had fasted forty days and** forty **nights, he was** afterward an **hungered.** 3. And when **the tempter** came to him, he **said, If thou be the Son of God, command that these stones be made bread. 4. But he answered** and said, **It is written, Man shall not live by bread alone, but by every word** that proceedeth out of the mouth **of God. 5. Then the devil** taketh him up into the holy city, and **setteth him on a pinnacle of the temple, 6. And saith** unto him, If thou be the Son of God, **cast thyself down: for it is written,** He shall give his **angels** charge concerning thee: and in *their* hands they **shall bear thee up,** lest at any

time thou dash thy foot against a stone. **7. Jesus said** unto him, **It is written again, Thou shalt not tempt** the Lord thy **God. 8. Again, the devil taketh him up into an** exceeding **high mountain, and sheweth him all the kingdoms of the world,** and the glory of them; **9. And saith** unto him, **All these** things will **I give thee, if thou wilt** fall down and **worship me. 10. Then saith Jesus** unto him, **Get thee hence, Satan: for it is written, Thou shalt worship the Lord** thy God, **and him only** shalt thou serve. **11. Then the devil leaveth him, and,** behold, **angels** came and **ministered unto him. 12. Now when Jesus had heard that John was cast into prison, he departed into Galilee;** 13. And leaving Nazareth, he came and dwelt in Capernaum, which is upon the sea coast, in the borders of Zabulon and Nephthalim: 14. That it might be fulfilled which was spoken by Esaias the prophet, saying, 15. The land of Zabulon, and the land of Nephthalim, *by* the way of the sea, beyond Jordan, Galilee of the Gentiles; 16. The people which sat in darkness saw great light; and to them which sat in the region and shadow of death light is sprung up. **17. From that time Jesus began to preach, and** to say, **Repent: for the kingdom of heaven is at hand. 18. And Jesus,** walking by the sea of Galilee, **saw** two brethren, Simon called **Peter, and Andrew his**

■ **brother,** casting a net into the sea: for they were fishers.

■ 19. **And he saith** unto them,

■ **Follow me, and I will make**

■ **you fishers of men.**

■ 20. **And they** straightway left *their* nets, and

■ **followed him.**

■ 21. **And** going on from thence,

■ **he saw** other two brethren,

■ **James** *the son* of Zebedee,

■ **and John his brother,** in a ship with Zebedee their father, mending their nets;

■ **and he called them.**

■ 22. **And they immediately** left the ship and their father, and

■ **followed him.**

■ 23. **And Jesus went about**

■ **all Galilee, teaching in their**

■ **synagogues,** and

■ **preaching** the gospel of the kingdom,

■ **and healing all** manner of

■ **sickness and all** manner of

■ **disease** among the people.

24. And his fame went throughout all Syria:

■ **and they brought** unto him

■ **all sick people** that were taken with divers diseases and torments,

■ **and those** which were

■ **possessed with devils,**

■ **and those which**

■ **were lunatic,** and those that had the palsy;

■ **and he healed them.**

■ 25. **And there followed him**

■ **great multitudes** of people from Galilee, and *from* Decapolis, and *from* Jerusalem, and *from* Judaea, and *from* beyond Jordan.

■ **CHAPTER 5**

■ 1. **And seeing the**

■ **multitudes, he went up into**

■ **a mountain:** and when he was set, his disciples came unto him:

■ 2. **And** he opened his mouth, and

■ **taught them, saying,**

■ 3. **Blessed are the poor in**

■ **spirit: for theirs is the**

■ **kingdom** of heaven.

■ 4. **Blessed are they that**

■ **mourn: for they shall**

■ **be comforted.**

■ 5. **Blessed are the meek: for**

■ **they shall inherit the earth.**

■ 6. **Blessed are they which**

■ **do hunger and thirst after**

■ **righteousness: for they**

■ **shall be filled.**

■ 7. **Blessed are the merciful:**

■ **for they shall obtain mercy.**

■ 8. **Blessed are the pure in**

■ **heart: for they shall**

■ **see God.**

■ 9. **Blessed are the**

■ **peacemakers: for they**

■ **shall be called the children**

■ **of God.**

■ 10. **Blessed are they which**

■ **are persecuted for**

■ **righteousness' sake: for**

■ **theirs is the kingdom** of heaven.

■ 11. **Blessed are ye, when**

■ *men* **shall revile you, and**

■ **persecute** *you,* **and** shall

■ **say** all manner of

■ **evil against you falsely,**

■ **for my sake.**

■ 12. **Rejoice,** and be exceeding glad:

■ **for great** *is* **your reward** in heaven: for so persecuted they the prophets which were before you.

■ 13. **Ye are the salt of the**

■ **earth: but if the salt have**

■ **lost his savour,** wherewith shall it be salted?

■ **it is** thenceforth

■ **good for nothing,** but to be cast out, and to be trodden under foot of men.

■ 14. **Ye are the light of the**

■ **world.** A city that is set on an hill cannot be hid.

15. Neither do men light a candle, and put it under a bushel, but on a candlestick; and it giveth light unto all that are in the house.

■ 16. **Let your light so shine**

■ **before men, that they may**

■ **see your good works, and**

■ **glorify your Father**

which is in heaven.

■ 17. **Think not that I am come**
■ **to destroy the law,**
■ **or the prophets:**

I am not come to destroy,

■ **but to fulfil.**

18. For verily I say unto you,

■ **Till heaven and earth pass,**
■ **one jot**

or one tittle

■ **shall in no wise pass**

from the law,

■ **till all be fulfilled.**

19. **Whosoever therefore**
■ **shall break one of these**
■ **least commandments, and**
■ **shall teach men so, he**
■ **shall be** called the
■ **least in the kingdom**

of heaven:

■ **but whosoever shall do**
■ **and teach** *them,* the same
■ **shall be called great**

in the kingdom of heaven.

20. For I say unto you, That

■ **except your righteousness**
■ **shall exceed** *the*
■ *righteousness* **of the**
■ **scribes and Pharisees, ye**
■ **shall in no case enter into**
■ **the kingdom** of heaven.

21. **Ye have heard**

that it was said by them of old time,

■ **Thou shalt not kill;**

and whosoever shall kill shall be in
danger of the judgment:

■ 22. **But I say** unto you, That
■ **whosoever is angry with**
■ **his brother without a cause**
■ **shall be in danger of the**
■ **judgment: and** whosoever shall

say to his brother, Raca, shall be in
danger of the council: but

■ **whosoever shall say, Thou**
■ **fool, shall be in danger of**
■ **hell** fire.

23. **Therefore if thou bring**
■ **thy gift to the altar, and** there
■ **rememberest that thy**
■ **brother hath aught**
■ **against thee;**
■ 24. **Leave there thy gift**

before the altar,

■ **and** go thy way;
■ **first be reconciled**
■ **to thy brother,**

and then come and offer thy gift.

■ 25. **Agree with thine**
■ **adversary quickly,** whiles

thou art in the way with him; lest at
any time the adversary deliver thee to
the judge, and the judge deliver thee
to the officer, and thou be
cast into prison.

26. Verily I say unto thee, Thou shalt
by no means come out thence, till
thou hast paid the uttermost farthing.

■ 27. **Ye have heard** that it was

said by them of old time,

■ **Thou shalt not**
■ **commit adultery:**
■ 28. **But I say** unto you, That
■ **whosoever looketh on a**
■ **woman to lust** after her
■ **hath committed adultery**

with her already

■ **in his heart.**
■ 29. **And if thy right eye**
■ **offend thee, pluck it out,**

and cast *it* from thee:

■ **for it is profitable for thee**
■ **that one of thy members**
■ **should perish, and not** *that*
■ **thy whole body should be**
■ **cast into hell.**

30. And if thy right hand offend thee,
cut it off, and cast *it* from thee: for it is
profitable for thee that one of thy
members should perish, and not *that*
thy whole body should be
cast into hell.

31. It hath been said, Whosoever
shall put away his wife, let him give
her a writing of divorcement:

32. But I say unto you, That

■ **whosoever shall put away**
■ **his wife, saving for**

the cause of

■ **fornication, causeth her to**
■ **commit adultery: and**
■ **whosoever shall marry her**

that is divorced

■ **committeth adultery.**
■ 33. **Again, ye have heard** that

it hath been said by them of old time,

■ **Thou shalt not forswear**

thyself, but shalt perform unto the Lord thine oaths:

34. **But I say** unto you, **Swear not at all;** neither by heaven; for it is God's throne:

35. Nor by the earth; for it is his footstool: neither by Jerusalem; for it is the city of the great King.

36. Neither shalt thou swear by thy head, because thou canst not make one hair white or black.

37. **But let your communication be, Yea, yea; Nay, nay: for whatsoever is more** than these **cometh of evil.**

38. **Ye have heard** that it hath been said, **An eye for an eye,** and a tooth for a tooth:

39. **But I say** unto you, That ye resist not evil: but **whosoever shall smite thee on thy right cheek, turn to him the other** also.

40. **And if any man will sue thee** at the law, **and take away thy coat, let him have** *thy* **cloak** also.

41. **And whosoever shall compel thee to go a mile, go with him twain.**

42. **Give to him that asketh thee, and from him that would borrow** of thee **turn not thou away.**

43. **Ye have heard** that it hath been said, **Thou shalt love thy neighbour, and hate thine enemy.**

44. **But I say** unto you, **Love your enemies,** bless them that curse you, do good to them that hate you, and pray for them which despitefully use you, and persecute you;

45. **That ye may be the children of your Father** which is in heaven: **for he maketh his sun to rise on the evil and on the good,** and sendeth rain on the just and on the unjust.

46. **For if ye love them which love you,** what reward have ye? **do not even the publicans the same?**

47. **And if ye salute your brethren only, what do ye more** *than others?* do not even the publicans so?

48. **Be ye therefore perfect, even as your Father** which is in heaven **is perfect.**

CHAPTER 6

1. Take heed that ye **do not your alms before men,** to be seen of them: **otherwise ye have no reward** of your Father which is in heaven.

2. Therefore when thou doest *thine* alms, do not sound a trumpet before thee, as the hypocrites do in the synagogues and in the streets, that they may have glory of men. Verily I say unto you, They have their reward.

3. **But when thou doest alms, let not thy left hand know what thy right hand doeth:**

4. That thine alms may be in secret: **and thy Father which seeth in secret** himself **shall reward thee openly.**

5. **And when thou prayest, thou shalt not be as the hypocrites** *are:* for they love to pray standing in the synagogues and in the corners of the streets, that they may be seen of men. Verily I say unto you, They have their reward.

6. But thou, **when thou prayest, enter into thy closet,** and when thou hast shut thy door, pray to thy Father which is **in secret; and thy Father** which seeth in secret **shall reward thee openly.**

7. But when ye pray, **use not vain repetitions,** as the heathen *do* : for they think that

they shall be heard for their much speaking.

8. Be not ye therefore like unto them: for **your Father knoweth what** things **ye** have **need** of, before ye ask him.

9. **After this manner** therefore **pray ye: Our Father which art in heaven, Hallowed be thy name.**

10. **Thy kingdom come, Thy will be done in earth, as** *it is* **in heaven.**

11. **Give us this day our daily bread.**

12. **And forgive us our debts, as we forgive our debtors.**

13. **And lead us not into temptation, but deliver us from evil: For thine is the kingdom, and the power, and the glory, for ever. Amen.**

14. **For if ye forgive men** their trespasses, **your heavenly Father will also forgive you:**

15. But if ye forgive not men their trespasses, neither will your Father forgive your trespasses.

16. **Moreover when ye fast, be not, as the hypocrites, of a sad countenance:** for they disfigure their faces, that they may appear unto men to fast. Verily I say unto you, They have their reward.

17. **But** thou, when thou fastest, **anoint thine head, and wash thy face;**

18. **That thou appear not unto men to fast,** but unto thy Father which is in secret: **and thy Father, which seeth in secret, shall reward thee openly.**

19. **Lay not up for yourselves treasures upon earth,** where moth and rust doth corrupt, and where thieves break through and steal:

20. **But lay up** for yourselves **treasures in heaven,** where neither moth nor rust doth corrupt, and where thieves do not break through nor steal:

21. **For where your treasure is, there will your heart be also.**

22. The light of the body is the eye: if therefore thine eye be single, thy whole body shall be full of light.

23. But if thine eye be evil, thy whole body shall be full of darkness. If therefore the light that is in thee be darkness, how great *is* that darkness!

24. **No man can serve two masters:** for either he will hate the one, and love the other; or else he will hold to the one, and despise the other. **Ye cannot serve God and mammon.**

25. **Therefore I say unto you, Take no thought for your life, what ye** shall **eat, or** what ye shall **drink; nor** yet for your body, **what ye** shall **put on.** Is not the life more than meat, and the body than raiment?

26. **Behold the fowls** of the air: for **they sow not, neither do they reap,** nor gather into barns; **yet your** heavenly **Father feedeth them. Are ye not much better than they?**

27. **Which of you by taking thought can add** one cubit **unto his stature?**

28. **And why take** ye **thought for raiment? Consider the lilies** of the field, how they grow; **they toil not,** neither do they spin:

29. **And yet** I say unto you, That even **Solomon** in all his glory **was not arrayed like one of these.**

30. **Wherefore, if God so clothe the grass** of the field, which to-day is, and to-morrow is cast

into the oven,
■ *shall he* not much more
■ *clothe* you, O ye
■ of little faith?
■ 31. **Therefore take no**
■ **thought, saying, What shall**
■ **we eat? or,** What shall we
■ **drink? or, Wherewithal**
■ **shall we be clothed?**
32. (For after all these things do the Gentiles seek:) for
■ **your** heavenly
■ **Father knoweth** that
■ **ye have need** of all these things.
■ 33. **But seek ye first the**
■ **kingdom of God, and his**
■ **righteousness; and all**
■ **these things shall be**
■ **added** unto you.
■ 34. **Take therefore no**
■ **thought for the morrow:**
for the morrow shall take thought for the things of itself. Sufficient unto the day *is* the evil thereof.

CHAPTER 7
■ 1. **Judge not, that ye be**
■ **not judged.**
2. For with what judgment ye judge, ye shall be judged: and with what measure ye mete, it shall be measured to you again.
■ 3. **And why beholdest** thou
■ **the mote** that is
■ **in thy brother's eye, but**
■ **considerest not the beam**
that is
■ **in thine own eye?**
4. Or how wilt thou say to thy brother, Let me pull out the mote out of thine eye; and, behold, a beam *is* in thine own eye?
■ 5. **Thou hypocrite, first cast**
■ **out the beam** out
■ **of thine own eye; and then**
shalt thou see clearly to
■ **cast out the mote** out
■ **of thy brother's eye.**
6. Give not that which is holy unto the dogs, neither cast ye your pearls before swine, lest they trample them under their feet, and turn again and rend you.

■ 7. **Ask, and it shall be given**
you;
■ **seek, and ye shall find;**
■ **knock, and it shall be**
■ **opened** unto you:
8. For every one that asketh receiveth; and he that seeketh findeth; and to him that knocketh it shall be opened.
■ 9. **Or what man**
is there of you, whom
■ **if his son ask bread, will** he
■ **give him a stone?**
10. Or if he ask a fish, will he give him a serpent?
■ 11. **If ye then, being evil,**
■ **know how to give good**
■ **gifts** unto your children,
■ **how much more shall your**
■ **Father** which is in heaven
■ **give good things to them**
■ **that ask** him?
12. Therefore all things
■ **whatsoever ye would that**
■ **men should do to you, do**
ye even so
■ **to them:** for this is the law
and the prophets.
■ 13. **Enter ye in at the strait**
■ **gate: for wide** *is* **the gate,**
■ **and broad** *is* **the way, that**
■ **leadeth to destruction,** and
many there be which go in thereat:
■ 14. **Because strait** *is* **the**
■ **gate, and narrow** *is* **the**
■ **way, which leadeth unto**
■ **life, and few** there be that
■ **find it.**
■ 15. **Beware of false**
■ **prophets, which come** to you
■ **in sheep's clothing, but**
inwardly they
■ **are** ravening
■ **wolves.**
■ 16. **Ye shall know them by**
■ **their fruits.** Do men gather grapes of thorns, or figs of thistles?
17. Even so every good tree bringeth forth good fruit; but a corrupt tree bringeth forth evil fruit.
■ 18. **A good tree cannot bring**
■ **forth evil fruit,** neither *can* a
corrupt tree bring forth good fruit.

19. Every tree that bringeth not forth good fruit is hewn down, and cast into the fire.

20. Wherefore by their fruits ye shall know them.

21. **Not every one that saith unto me, Lord, Lord, shall enter into the kingdom** of heaven; **but he that doeth the will of my Father** which is in heaven.

22. **Many will say** to me in that day, **Lord, Lord, have we not prophesied in thy name? and in thy name** have **cast out devils?** and in thy name done many wonderful works?

23. **And then will I profess unto them, I never knew you:** depart from me, ye that work iniquity.

24. **Therefore whosoever heareth these sayings** of mine, **and doeth them, I will liken** him **unto a wise man, which built his house upon a rock:**

25. **And the rain** descended, **and the floods** came, **and the winds** blew, and **beat upon that house; and it fell not:** for it was founded upon a rock.

26. **And every one that heareth these sayings** of mine, **and doeth them not, shall be likened unto a foolish man, which built his house upon the sand:**

27. **And the rain** descended, **and the floods** came, **and the winds** blew, and **beat upon that house; and it fell: and great was the fall** of it.

28. **And** it came to pass, when Jesus had ended these sayings, **the people were astonished at his doctrine:**

29. **For he taught** them **as** *one* **having authority,** and not as the scribes.

CHAPTER 8

1. **When he was come down** from the mountain, great **multitudes followed** him.

2. **And,** behold, there came **a leper and worshipped him, saying,** Lord, if thou wilt, **thou canst make me clean.**

3. **And Jesus** put forth *his* hand, and **touched him, saying, I** will; **be thou clean. And** immediately **his leprosy was cleansed.**

4. **And Jesus saith** unto him, **See thou tell no man; but go** thy way, **shew thyself to the priest,** and offer the gift that Moses commanded, **for a testimony** unto them.

5. **And when Jesus** was **entered** into **Capernaum, there came** unto him **a centurion, beseeching him,**

6. And **saying, Lord, my servant lieth** at home **sick of** the **palsy,** grievously tormented.

7. **And Jesus saith** unto him, **I will come and heal him.**

8. **The centurion** answered and **said, Lord, I am not worthy that thou shouldest come under my roof: but speak the word only, and my servant shall be healed.**

9. For I am a man under authority, having soldiers under me: and I say to this *man,* Go, and he goeth; and to another, Come, and he cometh; and to my servant, Do this, and he doeth *it.*

10. **When Jesus heard** *it,* **he** marvelled, and **said** to them that followed, Verily I say unto you **I have not found so great faith, no, not in Israel.**

11. And I say unto you, That many shall come from the east and west, and shall sit down with Abraham, and Isaac, and Jacob, in the kingdom of heaven.

12. But the children of the kingdom shall be cast out into outer darkness: there shall be weeping and gnashing of teeth.

13. **And Jesus said unto the centurion,** Go thy way; and **as thou hast believed,** *so* **be it done** unto thee. **And his servant was healed** in the selfsame hour.

14. **And when Jesus was come into Peter's house, he saw his wife's mother** laid, and **sick of a fever.**

15. **And he touched her hand, and the fever left** her: and she arose, and ministered unto them.

16. When the even was come, they brought unto him many that were possessed with devils: **and he cast out the spirits with** *his* **word, and healed all** that were sick:

17. **That it might be fulfilled** which was spoken by Esaias the prophet, saying, **Himself took our infirmities,** and bare *our* sickness.

18. Now when Jesus saw great multitudes about him, he gave commandment to depart unto the other side.

19. **And a certain scribe** came, and **said** unto him, Master, **I will follow thee** whithersoever thou goest.

20. **And Jesus saith** unto him, The foxes have holes, and the birds of the air *have* nests; but **the Son of man hath not where to lay** *his* **head.**

21. **And another** of his disciples **said** unto him, **Lord, suffer me first to go and bury my father.**

22. **But Jesus said** unto him, Follow me; and **let the dead bury their dead.**

23. **And when he was entered** into **a ship, his disciples followed** him.

24. **And, behold, there arose a great tempest** in the sea, insomuch that the ship was covered with the waves: **but he was asleep.**

25. **And his disciples** came to *him,* and **awoke him, saying, Lord, save us:** we perish.

26. **And he saith** unto them, Why are ye fearful, **O ye of little faith? Then he** arose, and **rebuked the winds** and the sea; **and there was a great calm.**

27. **But the men marvelled, saying, What manner of man is this,** that **even the winds and** the **sea obey him!**

28. **And when he was come** to the other side **into the country of the Gergesenes, there met him two possessed with devils,** coming out of the tombs, exceeding fierce, so that no man might pass by that way.

29. **And, behold, they cried out, saying, What have we to do with thee, Jesus, thou Son of God? art thou come** hither **to torment us before the time?**

30. And there was a good way off from them an herd of many swine feeding.

31. So the devils besought him, saying, If thou cast us out, **suffer us to go** away **into the herd of swine.** 32. **And he said** unto them, **Go. And** when they were come out, **they went into the herd** of swine: **and,** behold, the whole herd of swine **ran violently down** a steep place **into the sea, and perished** in the waters. 33. **And they that kept them fled,** and went their ways into the city, **and told every thing,** and what was befallen to the possessed of the devils. 34. **And, behold, the whole city came** out to meet Jesus: **and** when they saw him, they **besought** *him* **that he would depart** out of their coasts.

CHAPTER 9

1. **And he** entered into a ship, and passed over, and **came into his own city.** 2. **And,** behold, **they brought** to **him a man sick of** the **palsy,** lying on a bed: **and Jesus seeing their faith said** unto the sick of the palsy; **Son,** be of good cheer; **thy sins be forgiven** thee. 3. **And, behold,** certain of **the scribes said within themselves, This** *man* **blasphemeth.** 4. **And Jesus knowing their thoughts said, Wherefore think ye evil** in your hearts? 5. **For whether is easier, to say,** *Thy* **sins be forgiven** thee; **or** to say, **Arise, and walk?** 6. **But that ye may know** that **the Son** of man **hath power** on earth **to forgive sins, (then saith he to the sick** of the palsy,) **Arise,** take up thy bed, and go unto thine house. 7. **And he arose,** and departed to his house. 8. But when the multitudes saw *it,* they marvelled, and glorified God, which had given such power unto men. 9. **And as Jesus passed** forth from thence, **he saw** a man, named **Matthew,** sitting at the receipt of custom: **and he saith** unto him, **Follow me. And he** arose, and **followed him.** 10. **And** it came to pass, **as Jesus sat at meat in the house,** behold, **many publicans and sinners** came and **sat down with him** and his disciples. 11. **And when the Pharisees saw** *it,* **they said** unto his disciples, **Why eateth your Master with** publicans and **sinners?** 12. **But** when **Jesus** heard *that,* he **said** unto them, **They that be whole need not a physician,** but they that are sick. 13. But go ye and learn what *that* meaneth, I will have mercy, and not sacrifice: for **I am not come to call the righteous, but sinners to repentance.** 14. **Then came** to him **the disciples of John, saying, Why do we and the Pharisees fast** oft, **but thy disciples fast not?** 15. **And Jesus said** unto them, **Can the children of the bridechamber mourn, as long as the bridegroom is with them?** but the days will come, when the bridegroom shall be taken from them, and then shall they fast.

16. No man putteth a piece of new cloth unto an old garment, for that which is put in to fill it up taketh from the garment, and the rent is made worse.
17. Neither do men put new wine into old bottles: else the bottles break, and the wine runneth out, and the bottles perish: but they put new wine into new bottles, and both are preserved.
18. **While he spake** these things unto them, behold, **there came a certain ruler, and worshipped him, saying, My daughter is** even now **dead: but come** and lay thy hand upon her, **and she shall live.**
19. And Jesus arose, and followed him, and *so did* his disciples.
20. **And, behold, a woman,** which was diseased **with an issue of blood** twelve years, came behind *him,* and **touched** the hem of **his garment:**
21. **For she said** within herself, **If I may but touch his garment, I shall be whole.**
22. **But Jesus turned** him about, **and** when he saw her, he **said, Daughter,** be of good comfort; **thy faith hath made thee whole.** And the woman was made whole from that hour.
23. **And when Jesus came into the ruler's house,** and saw the minstrels and the people making a noise,
24. **He said** unto them, Give place: for **the maid is not dead, but sleepeth. And they laughed him to scorn.**
25. **But** when the people were put forth, **he** went in, and **took her by the hand, and the maid arose.**
26. And the fame hereof went abroad into all that land.
27. **And when Jesus departed** thence, **two blind men followed him,** crying, and saying, *Thou* son of David, have mercy on us.
28. And when he was come **into the house,** the blind men came to him: **and Jesus saith** unto them, **Believe ye that I am able to do this? They said** unto him, **Yea, Lord.**
29. **Then touched he their eyes, saying, According to your faith be it unto you.**
30. **And their eyes were opened;** and Jesus straitly charged them, saying, See *that* no man know *it* .
31. But they, when they were departed, spread abroad his fame in all that country.
32. **As they went out,** behold, **they brought** to him **a dumb man possessed with a devil.**
33. **And when the devil was cast out, the dumb spake:** and the multitudes marvelled, saying, It was never so seen in Israel.
34. **But the Pharisees said, He casteth out devils through the prince of the devils.**
35. **And Jesus went about** all the cities and villages, **teaching** in their synagogues, **and preaching** the gospel of the kingdom, **and healing** every sickness and every disease among the people.
36. **But when he saw the multitudes, he was moved with compassion** on them, **because they** fainted, and **were** scattered abroad, **as sheep having no shepherd.**
37. **Then saith he** unto his disciples, **The harvest truly** *is* **plenteous, but the**

■ **labourers** *are* **few;**
■ 38. **Pray ye** therefore
■ **the Lord** of the harvest,
■ **that he will send forth**
■ **labourers** into his harvest.

CHAPTER 10
■ 1. **And** when he had called
■ **unto** *him*
■ **his twelve disciples, he**
■ **gave** them
■ **power** *against* **unclean**
■ **spirits,** to cast them out,
■ **and to heal all** manner of
■ **sickness** and all
manner of disease.
2. Now the names of the twelve
apostles are these; The first, Simon,
who is called Peter, and Andrew his
brother; James *the son* of Zebedee,
and John his brother;
3. Philip, and Bartholomew; Thomas,
and Matthew the publican; James *the*
son of Alphaeus, and Lebbaeus,
whose surname was Thaddaeus;
4. Simon the Canaanite, and Judas
Iscariot, who also betrayed him.
■ 5. **These twelve Jesus**
sent forth, and
■ **commanded** them,
■ **saying, Go not into** the way of
■ **the Gentiles, and into**
any city of
■ **the Samaritans** enter ye not:
■ 6. **But go rather to the lost**
■ **sheep** of the house
■ **of Israel.**
■ 7. **And** as ye go,
■ **preach, saying, The**
■ **kingdom of heaven**
■ **is at hand.**
■ 8. **Heal** the sick, cleanse the lepers,
■ **raise the dead, cast out**
■ **devils: freely ye have**
■ **received, freely give.**
■ 9. **Provide neither gold,**
■ **nor silver, nor brass in**
■ **your purses,**
10. Nor scrip for *your* journey,
■ **neither two coats, neither**
■ **shoes, nor yet staves: for**
■ **the workman is worthy of**
■ **his meat.**

■ 11. **And into whatsoever city**
or town
■ **ye shall enter,**
■ **inquire who** in it
■ **is worthy; and there abide**
till ye go thence.
12. And when ye come into an house,
salute it.
■ 13. **And if the house be**
■ **worthy, let your peace**
■ **come upon it:** but if it be not
worthy, let your peace return to you.
■ 14. **And whosoever shall**
■ **not receive you,**
nor hear your words,
■ **when ye depart**
out of that house or city,
■ **shake off the dust of**
■ **your feet.**
15. Verily I say unto you,
■ **It shall be more tolerable**
■ **for** the land of
■ **Sodom and Gomorrha in**
■ **the day of judgment, than**
■ **for that city.**
■ 16. **Behold, I send you forth**
■ **as sheep in the midst of**
■ **wolves: be** ye therefore
■ **wise as serpents, and**
■ **harmless as doves.**
■ 17. **But beware** of men: for
■ **they will** deliver you up to the
councils, and they will
■ **scourge you**
in their synagogues;
■ 18. **And ye shall be brought**
■ **before governors and**
■ **kings for my sake,**
■ **for a testimony**
against them and the Gentiles.
19. But when they deliver you up,
■ **take no thought** how or
■ **what ye shall speak:**
■ **for it shall be given you**
in that same hour what ye shall speak.
■ 20. **For it is** not ye that speak, but
■ **the Spirit of your Father**
■ **which speaketh** in you.
■ 21. **And the brother shall**
■ **deliver** up the
■ **brother to death, and the**
■ **father the child: and the**
■ **children** shall rise up against

■ *their* parents, and cause
■ them to be put to death.
■ 22. And ye shall be hated
of all *men*
■ for my name's sake: but he
■ that endureth to the end
■ shall be saved.

23. But when they persecute you in this city, flee ye into another: for verily I say unto you, Ye shall not have gone over the cities of Israel, till the Son of man be come.

24. The disciple is not above *his* master, nor the servant above his lord.

25. It is enough for the disciple that he be as his master, and the servant as his lord. If they have called the master of the house Beelzebub, how much more *shall they call* them of his household?

■ 26. Fear them not therefore:
■ for there is nothing covered,
■ that shall not be revealed;
and hid, that shall not be known.
■ 27. What I tell you in
■ darkness, *that* speak ye in light:
and what ye hear in the ear,
■ *that* preach ye upon
■ the housetops.
■ 28. And fear not them which
■ kill the body,
but are not able to kill the soul:
■ but rather fear him which is
■ able to destroy both soul
■ and body in hell.
■ 29. Are not two sparrows
■ sold for a farthing? and
■ one of them shall not fall
on the ground
■ without your Father.
■ 30. But the very hairs of your
■ head are all numbered.
■ 31. Fear ye not therefore,
■ ye are of more value
than many sparrows.
■ 32. Whosoever therefore
■ shall confess me before
■ men, him will I confess also
■ before my Father
which is in heaven.
■ 33. But whosoever shall
■ deny me before men,

■ him will I also deny before
■ my Father which is in heaven.
■ 34. Think not that I am come
■ to send peace
on earth: I came not to send peace,
■ but a sword.
■ 35. For I am come to set a
■ man at variance
■ against his father, and the
■ daughter against her
■ mother, and the daughter in law
against her mother in law.

36. And a man's foes *shall be they* of his own household.

■ 37. He that loveth father or
■ mother more than me is not
■ worthy of me: and he that
■ loveth son or daughter
■ more than me is not worthy
of me.
■ 38. And he that taketh not
■ his cross, and followeth after me,
■ is not worthy of me.

39. He that findeth his life shall lose it: and
■ he that loseth his life for my
■ sake shall find it.
■ 40. He that receiveth you
■ receiveth me, and he that
■ receiveth me receiveth him
■ that sent me.

41. He that receiveth a prophet in the name of a prophet shall receive a prophet's reward; and he that receiveth a righteous man in the name of a righteous man shall receive a righteous man's reward.

42. And whosoever shall give to drink unto one of these little ones a cup of cold *water* only in the name of a disciple, verily I say unto you, he shall in no wise lose his reward.

CHAPTER 11

1. And it came to pass, when Jesus had made an end of commanding his twelve disciples, he departed thence to teach and to preach in their cities.
■ 2. Now when John had
■ heard in the prison
■ the works of Christ, he sent
■ two of his disciples,
■ 3. And said unto him,

Art thou he that should come, or do we look for another? 4. **Jesus answered** and said unto them, **Go and shew John again those things which ye do hear and see:** 5. The blind receive their sight, and the lame walk, the lepers are cleansed, and the deaf hear, the dead are raised up, and the poor have the gospel preached to them. 6. **And blessed is he, whosoever shall not be offended in me.** 7. **And** as they departed, **Jesus began to say unto the multitudes concerning John, What went ye** out into the wilderness **to see?** A reed shaken with the wind? 8. But what went ye out for to see? A man clothed in soft raiment? behold, they that wear soft *clothing* are in kings' houses. 9. But what went ye out for to see? **A prophet? yea,** I say unto you, **and more than a prophet.** 10. **For this is he, of whom it is written, Behold, I send my messenger** before thy face, **which shall prepare thy way** before thee. 11. Verily I say unto you, Among them that are born of women **there hath not risen a greater than John the Baptist: notwithstanding he that is least in the kingdom** of heaven **is greater** than he. 12. And from the days of John the Baptist until now the kingdom of heaven suffereth violence, and the violent take it by force. 13. For all the prophets and the law prophesied until John. 14. **And if ye will receive it, this is Elias, which was** for **to come.** 15. He that hath ears to hear, let him hear.

16. **But whereunto shall I liken this generation?** It is like unto children sitting in the markets, and calling unto their fellows, 17. And saying, We have piped unto you, and ye have not danced; we have mourned unto you, and ye have not lamented. 18. **For John came neither eating nor drinking, and they say, He hath a devil.** 19. **The Son of man came eating and drinking, and they say, Behold a man gluttonous, and** a winebibber, **a friend of** publicans and **sinners.** But wisdom is justified of her children. 20. Then began he to upbraid the cities wherein most of his mighty works were done, because they repented not: 21. **Woe unto thee, Chorazin! woe unto thee, Bethsaida!** for if the mighty works, which were done in you, had been done in Tyre and Sidon, they would have repented long ago in sackcloth and ashes. 22. But I say unto you, **It shall be more tolerable for Tyre and Sidon at the** day of **judgment, than for you.** 23. **And thou, Capernaum,** which art exalted unto heaven, shalt be brought down to hell: for **if the mighty works, which have been done in thee, had been done in Sodom, it would have remained** until this day. 24. **But** I say unto you, That **it shall be more tolerable for** the land of **Sodom in** the day of **judgment, than for thee.** 25. At that time Jesus answered and **said, I thank thee, O Father,** Lord of heaven and earth, **because thou hast hid**

these things
from the wise
and prudent,
and hast
revealed them unto babes.
26. Even so, Father: for so it seemed
good in thy sight.
27. All things are delivered
unto me of my Father:
and no man knoweth
the Son, but the Father; neither
knoweth any man
the Father, save the Son,
and he to whomsoever the
Son will reveal him.
28. Come unto me, all ye that
labour and are heavy laden,
and I will give you rest.
29. Take my yoke upon you,
and learn of me;
for I am meek and lowly in heart:
and ye shall find rest
unto your souls.
30. For my yoke is easy, and
my burden is light.

CHAPTER 12

1. At that time
Jesus went on the sabbath
day through the corn; and
his disciples
were an hungered, and
began to pluck the ears of
corn and to eat.
2. But when the Pharisees
saw it, they said
unto him, Behold,
thy disciples do that which
is not lawful to do
upon the sabbath day.
3. But he said
unto them, Have ye not read what
David did, when he was an
hungered, and they that
were with him;
4. How he entered into the house of
God, and
did eat the shewbread,
which was not lawful for
him to eat,
neither for them which were with him,
but only for the priests?
5. Or have ye not read in the law, how

that on the sabbath days the priests
in the temple profane the sabbath,
and are blameless?
6. But I say unto you, That
in this place is one greater
than the temple.
7. But if ye had known what this
meaneth, I will have mercy, and not
sacrifice, ye would not have
condemned the guiltless.
8. For the Son of man
is Lord even
of the sabbath day.
9. And when he was departed thence,
he went into their synagogue:
10. And, behold, there was
a man which had his hand
withered. And they asked
him, saying,
Is it lawful to heal on the
sabbath days? that they
might accuse him.
11. And he said unto them,
What man
shall there be among you, that
shall have one sheep,
and if it
fall into a pit on the
sabbath day,
will he
not lay hold on it, and
lift it out?
12. How much then is a man
better than a sheep?
Wherefore it is lawful to do well on the
sabbath days.
13. Then saith he to the man,
Stretch forth thine hand. And
he stretched it forth;
and it was restored
whole, like as the other.
14. Then the Pharisees
went out, and
held a council against him,
how they might
destroy him.
15. But when Jesus knew it,
he withdrew himself from thence:
and great multitudes
followed him,
and he healed them all;
16. And charged them that
they should not make him

known:
17. That it might be fulfilled which was spoken by Esaias the prophet, saying,
18. Behold my servant, whom I have chosen; my beloved, in **whom** my soul is well pleased: **I will put my spirit upon** him, and he shall shew judgment to the Gentiles.
19. He shall not strive, nor cry; neither shall any man hear his voice in the streets.
20. A bruised reed shall he not break, and smoking flax shall he not quench, till he send forth judgment unto victory.
21. And in his name shall the Gentiles trust.
22. Then was brought unto him **one** possessed **with a devil, blind, and dumb: and he healed him,** insomuch that the blind and dumb both spake and saw.
23. And all the people were amazed, and said, Is not this the son of David?
24. But when the Pharisees heard *it,* **they said, This** *fellow* **doth not cast out devils, but by Beelzebub** the prince of the devils.
25. And Jesus knew their thoughts, and said unto them, Every kingdom divided against itself is brought to desolation; and every city or house divided against itself shall not stand:
26. And if Satan cast out Satan, he is divided against himself; **how shall then his kingdom stand?**
27. And if I by Beelzebub cast out devils, by whom do your children cast *them* out? therefore they shall be your judges.
28. But if I cast out devils by the Spirit of God, then the kingdom of God is come

unto you.
29. Or else how can one enter into a strong man's house, and spoil his goods, except he first bind the strong man? and then he will spoil his house.
30. He that is not with me is against me; and he that gathereth not with me scattereth abroad.
31. Wherefore I say unto you, **All manner of sin and blasphemy shall be forgiven** unto men: **but the blasphemy** *against* **the** *Holy* **Ghost** shall not be forgiven unto men.
32. And whosoever speaketh a word **against the Son of man, it shall be forgiven** him: **but whosoever speaketh against the Holy Ghost, it shall not be forgiven** him, neither **in this world, neither in the** *world to come.*
33. Either make the tree good, and his fruit good; or else make the tree corrupt, and his fruit corrupt: for the tree is known by *his* fruit.
34. O generation of vipers, how **can ye, being evil, speak good** things? for out of the abundance of the heart the mouth speaketh.
35. A good man out of the good treasure of the heart bringeth forth good things: and an evil man out of the evil treasure bringeth forth evil things.
36. But I say unto you, **That every idle word that men** shall **speak, they shall give account** thereof in the day of judgment.
37. For by thy words thou shalt be justified, and by thy words thou shalt be **condemned.**
38. Then certain of the scribes and of the

Pharisees answered, saying,
Master, we would see a
sign from thee.
39. **But he answered**
and said unto them,
An evil and adulterous
generation seeketh after
a sign; and there shall no
sign be given to it,
but the sign of the prophet
Jonas:
40. **For as Jonas was three**
days and three nights in the
whale's belly;
so shall the Son of man be
three days and three nights
in the heart of the earth.
41. **The men of Nineveh shall**
rise in judgment with this
generation, and
shall condemn it:
because they repented at the
preaching of Jonas; and,
behold, a greater than
Jonas is here.
42. The queen of the south shall rise
up in the judgment with this
generation, and shall condemn it: for
she came from the uttermost parts of
the earth to hear the wisdom of
Solomon; and, behold, a greater than
Solomon is here.
43. **When the unclean spirit**
is gone out of a man, he
walketh through dry places,
seeking rest, and
findeth none.
44. **Then he saith, I will return**
into my house
from whence I came out;
and when he is come,
he findeth it empty,
swept, and garnished.
45. **Then goeth he, and**
taketh with himself
seven other spirits
more wicked than himself,
and they enter in and dwell there:
and the last state of that
man is worse than the first.
Even so shall it be also
unto this wicked
generation.

46. While he yet talked to the people,
behold, *his* mother and his brethren
stood without, desiring to
speak with him.
47. **Then one said** unto him,
Behold, thy mother and thy
brethren stand without,
desiring to speak
with thee.
48. But he answered and said unto
him that told him, Who is my mother?
and who are my brethren?
49. **And he stretched forth**
his hand toward his
disciples, and said,
Behold my mother
and my brethren!
50. **For whosoever shall do**
the will of my Father
which is in heaven,
the same is my brother, and
sister, and mother.

CHAPTER 13

1. **The same day** went Jesus out
of the house, and sat by the sea side.
2. And great multitudes were gathered
together unto him, so that
he went into a ship, and sat;
and the whole multitude
stood on the shore.
3. **And he spake**
many things unto them in
parables, saying, Behold,
a sower went forth to sow;
4. **And when he sowed,**
some *seeds* **fell by the way**
side, and the
fowls came and
devoured them up:
5. **Some fell upon stony**
places, where they had not much
earth: and forthwith they sprung up,
because they had no
deepness of earth:
6. **And when the sun**
was up, they were
scorched; and because
they had no root, they
withered away.
7. **And some fell among**
thorns; and the thorns
sprung up, and

■ choked them:
■ 8. But other fell into good
■ ground, and brought forth
■ fruit, some an hundredfold, some
sixtyfold, some thirtyfold.
9. Who hath ears to hear, let him hear.
■ 10. And the disciples
came, and
■ said unto him,
■ Why speakest thou unto
■ them in parables?
■ 11. He answered
and said unto them,
■ Because it is given unto
■ you to know the mysteries
of the kingdom of heaven,
■ but to them it is not given.
■ 12. For whosoever hath, to
■ him shall be given, and he
shall have more abundance:
■ but whosoever hath not,
■ from him shall be taken
away even that he hath.
■ 13. Therefore speak I to them
■ in parables: because they
■ seeing see not; and
■ hearing they hear not,
neither do they understand.
■ 14. And in them is fulfilled
■ the prophecy of Esaias,
which saith,
■ By hearing ye shall hear,
■ and shall
■ not understand; and
■ seeing ye shall see, and
■ shall not perceive:
■ 15. For this people's heart is
■ waxed gross, and
■ their ears are dull of hearing,
■ and their eyes they have
■ closed; lest at any time they
should see with *their* eyes, and hear
with *their* ears, and should understand
with *their* heart, and should be
converted, and I should heal them.
■ 16. But blessed *are* your
■ eyes, for they see:
■ and your
■ ears, for they hear.
■ 17. For verily I say unto you, That
■ many prophets and righteous *men*
■ have desired to see those
■ things which ye see,

and have not seen *them;*
■ and to hear *those*
■ things which ye hear
and have not heard *them.*
18. Hear ye therefore the parable of
the sower.
■ 19. When any one heareth
■ the word of the kingdom,
■ and understandeth *it* not,
then cometh
■ the wicked *one,* and
■ catcheth away that which
■ was sown in his heart.
■ This is he which received seed
■ by the way side.
■ 20. But he that received the
■ seed into stony places,
the same
■ is he that heareth the word,
■ and anon with joy receiveth it;
■ 21. Yet hath he not root in
himself, but dureth for a while:
■ for when tribulation
or persecution
■ ariseth because of the word,
by and by
■ he is offended.
■ 22. He also that received
■ seed among the thorns
is he that heareth the word;
■ and the care of this world,
■ and the deceitfulness of
■ riches, choke the word,
and he becometh unfruitful.
■ 23. But he that received
■ seed into the
■ good ground is he that
■ heareth the word,
■ and understandeth
it; which also
■ beareth fruit, and bringeth
■ forth, some
■ an hundredfold,
some sixty, some thirty.
24. Another parable put he forth unto
them, saying,
■ The kingdom of heaven
■ is likened unto a man
■ which sowed good seed
in his field:
25. But while men slept,
■ his enemy came and
■ sowed tares among the wheat,

and went his way.

26. But when the blade was sprung up, and brought forth fruit, then appeared the tares also.

27. **So the servants** of the householder came and **said** unto him, **Sir, didst not thou sow good seed** in thy field? **from whence** then **hath it tares?**

28. **He said** unto them, **An enemy hath done this.** The servants said unto him, Wilt thou then that we go and gather them up?

29. But he said, Nay; lest while ye gather up the tares, ye root up also the wheat with them.

30. **Let both grow together until the harvest: and in** the time of **harvest I will say** to the reapers, **Gather ye** together **first the tares, and** bind them in bundles to **burn them: but gather the wheat into my barn.**

31. **Another parable put he forth** unto them, **saying, The kingdom** of heaven **is like** to **a** grain of **mustard seed, which a man** took, and **sowed in his field:**

32. **Which indeed is** the **least of all seeds: but when** it is **grown, it is** the **greatest among herbs, and becometh a tree,** so that the birds of the air come and lodge in the branches thereof.

33. Another parable spake he unto them; **The kingdom** of heaven **is like** unto **leaven, which a woman** took, and **hid in three measures of meal, till the whole**

was leavened.

34. **All these things spake Jesus** unto the multitude in parables; and without a parable spake he not unto them:

35. **That it might be fulfilled** which was spoken by the prophet, saying, **I will** open my mouth **in parables;** I will **utter things which have been kept secret from the foundation of the world.**

36. Then Jesus sent the multitude away, and went into the house: and **his disciples came** unto him, **saying, Declare** unto us **the parable of the tares** of the field.

37. **He answered** and said unto them, **He that soweth** the good seed **is the Son of man;**

38. **The field is the world; the good seed are the children of the kingdom; but the tares are the children of the wicked** *one;*

39. **The enemy** that sowed them **is the devil; the harvest is the end** of the world; **and the reapers are the angels.**

40. **As therefore the tares are gathered and burned** in the fire; **so shall it be in the end** of this world.

41. **The Son of man shall send** forth **his angels, and they shall gather** out of his kingdom **all things** that offend, and them **which do iniquity;**

42. **And shall cast them into a furnace of fire:** there shall be wailing and gnashing of teeth.

43. **Then shall the righteous shine forth** as the sun in the kingdom of their Father. Who hath ears to hear, let him hear.

44. **Again, the kingdom** of heaven

■ is like unto treasure hid in a
■ field; the which when a man
■ hath found, he hideth, and
for joy thereof goeth and
■ selleth all that
■ he hath,
■ and buyeth that field.
■ 45. Again, the kingdom
of heaven
■ is like unto
■ a merchant man,
■ seeking goodly
■ pearls:
■ 46. Who, when he had
■ found one pearl of great
■ price, went and
■ sold all that
■ he had, and bought it.
■ 47. Again, the kingdom
of heaven
■ is like unto a net, that was
■ cast into the sea, and
■ gathered of every kind:
48. Which, when it was full, they drew
to shore, and sat down,
■ and gathered the good
into vessels,
■ but cast the bad away.
■ 49. So shall it be at the end
of the world:
■ the angels shall come forth, and
■ sever the wicked from among
■ the just,
■ 50. And shall cast them into
■ the furnace of
■ fire: there shall be wailing and
gnashing of teeth.
51. Jesus saith unto them, Have ye
understood all these things? They say
unto him, Yea, Lord.
52. Then said he unto them, Therefore
every scribe *which is* instructed unto
the kingdom of heaven is like unto a
man *that is* an householder, which
bringeth forth out of his treasure
things new and old.
■ 53. And it came to pass, *that* when
■ Jesus had finished these
parables, he
■ departed thence.
■ 54. And when he was come
■ into his own country, he
■ taught them in their synagogue,

■ insomuch that they were
■ astonished, and said,
■ Whence hath this *man* this
■ wisdom, and these mighty
■ works?
55. Is not this the
carpenter's son? is not his
mother called Mary? and his brethren,
James, and Joses,
and Simon, and Judas?
56. And his sisters, are they not all
with us? Whence then hath this *man* all
these things?
■ 57. And they were offended
in him.
■ But Jesus said unto them,
■ A prophet is not without
■ honour, save in his own
■ country, and in his own house.
58. And he did not many mighty works
there because of their unbelief.

CHAPTER 14

1. At that time
■ Herod the tetrarch heard of
■ the fame of Jesus,
■ 2. And said unto his servants,
■ This is John the Baptist; he is
■ risen from the dead; and therefore
mighty works do shew forth
themselves in him.
■ 3. For Herod had laid hold on
John, and bound him, and
■ put *him* in prison for
■ Herodias' sake, his brother
■ Philip's wife.
■ 4. For John said unto him, It
■ is not lawful for thee to
■ have her.
5. And when he would have put him to
death, he feared the multitude,
because they counted him as a
prophet.
■ 6. But when Herod's
■ birthday was kept, the
■ daughter of Herodias
■ danced before them,
■ and pleased Herod.
■ 7. Whereupon he promised
with an oath to give
■ her whatsoever she
■ would ask.
■ 8. And she, being before

■ **instructed of her mother,**
■ **said, Give me** here
■ **John Baptist's head**
in a charger.
■ 9. **And the king** was sorry:
nevertheless for the oath's sake, and
them which sat with him at meat,
he commanded *it* to be given *her.*
10. And he sent, and
■ **beheaded John** in the prison.
■ 11. **And his head was**
■ **brought in a charger,**
and given to the damsel: and she
brought *it* to her mother.
■ 12. **And his disciples came,**
■ **and took** up
■ **the body, and buried it,**
■ **and** went and
■ **told Jesus.**
■ 13. **When Jesus heard** *of it,*
■ **he departed** thence
■ **by ship into a**
■ **desert place** apart:
■ **and** when the
■ **people** had heard *thereof,* they
■ **followed him on foot**
out of the cities.
■ 14. **And Jesus** went forth, and
saw a great multitude, and was
■ **moved with compassion**
toward them, and he
■ **healed their sick.**
15. And when it was evening,
■ **his disciples came** to him,
■ **saying, This is a desert**
■ **place,** and the time is now past;
■ **send the multitude away,**
■ **that they may**
go into the villages, and
■ **buy themselves victuals.**
■ 16. **But Jesus said**
unto them, They need not depart;
■ **give** ye
■ **them to eat.**
■ 17. **And they say** unto him,
■ **We have** here
■ **but five loaves,**
■ **and two fishes.**
18. He said, Bring them hither to me.
■ 19. **And he** commanded the
multitude to sit down
on the grass, and
■ **took the five loaves, and**

■ **the two fishes, and**
looking up to heaven,
■ **he blessed, and** brake, and
■ **gave the loaves to** *his*
■ **disciples, and the**
■ **disciples to the multitude.**
■ 20. **And they did all eat,**
and were filled: and they took up of
the fragments that remained twelve
baskets full.
21. And they that had eaten were
■ **about five thousand men,**
■ **beside women**
■ **and children.**
■ 22. **And straightway Jesus**
■ **constrained his disciples**
■ **to get into a ship,** and to go
before him unto the other side, while
he sent the multitudes away.
■ 23. **And when he had sent**
■ **the multitudes away, he**
■ **went** up into a mountain apart
■ **to pray:** and when the evening was
come, he was there
■ **alone.**
■ 24. **But the ship was**
now in the midst of the sea,
■ **tossed with waves:**
for the wind was contrary.
■ 25. **And** in the fourth
watch of the night
■ **Jesus went unto them,**
■ **walking on the sea.**
■ 26. **And when the disciples**
■ **saw** him walking on the sea,
■ **they were troubled,**
■ **saying, It is a spirit;**
and they cried out for fear.
■ 27. **But straightway**
■ **Jesus spake**
unto them, saying, Be of good cheer;
■ **it is I; be not afraid.**
■ 28. **And Peter** answered him and
■ **said, Lord,** if it be thou,
■ **bid me come unto thee**
on the water.
■ 29. **And he said, Come. And**
when
■ **Peter** was come down
out of the ship, he
■ **walked on the water,**
to go to Jesus.
■ 30. **But when he saw the**

wind boisterous,
he was afraid; and
beginning to sink, he cried,
saying,
Lord, save me.
31. **And immediately Jesus**
stretched forth *his* hand, and
caught him, and said
unto him,
O thou of little faith,
wherefore didst thou doubt?
32. And when they were come into the
ship, the wind ceased.
33. **Then they**
that were in the ship came and
worshipped him, saying,
Of a truth
thou art the Son of God.
34. **And** when they were gone over,
they came into the land of
Gennesaret.
35. **And** when the men of that place
had knowledge of him,
they sent out into all that country
round about, and
brought unto him all that
were diseased;
36. **And besought him that**
they might only touch
the hem of
his garment: and
as many as touched
were made perfectly
whole.

CHAPTER 15
1. **Then came** to Jesus
scribes and Pharisees,
which were of Jerusalem,
saying,
2. **Why do thy disciples**
transgress the tradition of
the elders? for they wash not their
hands when they eat bread.
3. **But he answered**
and said unto them,
Why do ye also transgress
the commandment of God
by your tradition?
4. For God commanded, saying,
Honour thy father and mother: and, He
that curseth father or mother, let him
die the death.

5. But ye say, Whosoever shall say to
his father or *his* mother, It is a gift, by
whatsoever thou mightest be profited
by me;
6. And honour not his father or his
mother, *he shall be free.* Thus have ye
made the commandment of God of
none effect by your tradition.
7. *Ye* **hypocrites, well did**
Esaias prophesy of you,
saying,
8. **This people** draweth nigh unto
me with their mouth, and
honoureth me with *their*
lips; but their heart is far
from me.
9. But in vain they do worship me,
teaching *for* doctrines the
commandments of men.
10. **And he called the**
multitude, and said
unto them, Hear, and understand:
11. **Not that which goeth into**
the mouth defileth a man;
but that which cometh out
of the mouth, this
defileth a man.
12. **Then came his disciples,**
and said
unto him, Knowest thou that
the Pharisees
were offended,
after they heard this saying?
13. **But he answered** and said,
Every plant, which my
heavenly
Father hath not planted,
shall be rooted up.
14. **Let them alone: they be**
blind leaders of the blind.
And if the blind lead the
blind, both shall fall
into the ditch.
15. Then answered Peter and said
unto him, Declare unto us this
parable.
16. **And Jesus said,** Are ye also
yet without understanding?
17. Do not ye yet understand, that
whatsoever entereth in at
the mouth goeth into the belly, and
is cast out into
the draught?

18. **But those things which proceed out of the mouth come** forth **from the heart;** and they defile the man.
19. **For out of the heart proceed evil** thoughts, murders, adulteries, fornications, thefts, false witness, blasphemies:
20. These are *the things* **which defile** a man: **but to eat with unwashen hands defileth not** a man.
21. **Then Jesus went** hence, and departed **into** the coasts of **Tyre and Sidon.**
22. **And, behold, a woman of Canaan** came out of the same coasts, and **cried** unto him, saying, **Have mercy** on me, **O Lord,** *thou* son of David; **my daughter** *is* grievously **vexed with a devil.**
23. **But he answered her not** a word. **And his disciples** came and **besought him, saying, Send her away;** for she crieth after us.
24. **But he answered** and said, **I am not sent but unto** the lost sheep of the house of **Israel.**
25. **Then came she and worshipped him, saying, Lord, help me.**
26. **But he answered** and said, **It is not meet to take the children's bread, and to cast** *it* **to dogs.**
27. **And she said,** Truth, Lord: **yet the dogs eat of the crumbs** which fall from their masters' table.
28. **Then Jesus** answered and **said** unto her, O woman, **great** *is* **thy faith: be it** unto thee even **as thou wilt. And her daughter was made whole** from that very hour.

29. **And Jesus** departed from thence, and **came** nigh **unto** the sea of **Galilee; and went** up **into a mountain,** and sat down there.
30. **And great multitudes came** unto him, having with them *those that were* lame, blind, dumb, maimed, and many others, and cast them down at Jesus' feet; **and he healed them:**
31. Insomuch that the multitude wondered, when they saw the dumb to speak, the maimed to be whole, the lame to walk, and the blind to see: **and they glorified the God of Israel.**
32. **Then Jesus** called his disciples *unto him,* and **said, I have compassion on the multitude,** because they continue with me now three days, and have nothing to eat: **and I will not send them away fasting,** lest they faint in the way.
33. And his disciples say unto him, Whence should we have so much bread in the wilderness, as to fill so great a multitude?
34. And Jesus saith unto them, **How many loaves have ye? And they said, Seven, and a few** little **fishes.**
35. And he commanded the multitude to sit down on the ground.
36. **And he took the seven loaves and** the **fishes, and gave thanks,** and brake *them,* **and gave to his disciples, and the disciples to the multitude.**
37. **And they did all eat,** and were filled: **and they** took up of the broken *meat* that was **left seven baskets** full.
38. **And they that did eat were four thousand men,**

beside women and children. 39. **And he** sent away the multitude, and took ship, and **came into** the coasts of **Magdala.**

CHAPTER 16

1. **The Pharisees** also **with the Sadducees came,** and **tempting** desired **him that he** would **shew them a sign** from heaven. 2. **He answered** and said unto them, When it is evening, ye say, *It will be* fair weather: for the sky is red. 3. And in the morning, *It will be* foul weather to-day: for the sky is red and lowering. **O** *ye* **hypocrites, ye can discern the face of the sky; but** can ye **not** *discern* **the signs of the times?** 4. **A wicked** and adulterous **generation seeketh after a sign; and there shall no sign be given** unto it, **but the sign of** the prophet **Jonas.** And he left them, and departed. 5. **And when his disciples were come** to the other side, **they had forgotten** to take **bread.** 6. **Then Jesus said** unto them, Take heed and **beware of the leaven of the Pharisees and** of the **Sadducees.** 7. **And they reasoned** among themselves, **saying,** *It is* **because we have taken no bread.** 8. *Which* **when Jesus perceived, he said** unto them, O ye of little faith, why reason ye among yourselves, because ye have brought no bread? 9. Do ye not yet understand, neither remember the five loaves of the five thousand, and how many baskets ye took up? 10. Neither the seven loaves of the four thousand, and how many baskets ye took up? 11. How is it that ye do not understand that **I spake** *it* **not to you concerning bread,** that ye should beware of the leaven of the Pharisees and of the Sadducees? 12. **Then understood they** how **that he bade** *them* **not beware** of the leaven of bread, but **of the doctrine of the Pharisees and** of the **Sadducees.** 13. **When Jesus came into** the coasts of **Caesarea Philippi, he asked his disciples,** saying, **Whom do men say that I** the Son of man **am?** 14. **And they said, Some** *say* *that thou art* **John the Baptist: some, Elias;** and **others, Jeremias,** or one of the prophets. 15. **He saith** unto them, **But whom say ye that I am?** 16. **And** Simon **Peter** answered and **said, Thou art the Christ, the Son of the living God.** 17. **And Jesus answered** and said unto him, **Blessed art thou,** Simon Barjona: **for flesh** and blood **hath not revealed** *it* unto thee, **but my Father** which is in heaven. 18. And I say also unto thee, That **thou art Peter, and upon this rock I will build my church; and the gates of hell shall not prevail against it.** 19. **And I will give unto thee the keys of the kingdom** of heaven: **and whatsoever thou** shalt

bind on earth shall be
bound in heaven: and
whatsoever thou shalt
loose on earth shall be
loosed in heaven.
20. Then charged he his disciples that
they should tell no man that he was
Jesus the Christ.
21. **From that time** forth
began Jesus to shew unto
his disciples, how that
he must go unto Jerusalem, and
suffer many things of the elders and
chief priests and scribes,
and be killed, and be
raised again the third day.
22. **Then Peter** took him, and
began to rebuke him,
saying, Be it far from thee,
Lord: this shall not be
unto thee.
23. **But he** turned, and
said unto Peter, Get thee
behind me, Satan:
thou art an offence unto me: for thou
savourest not the things that be of
God, but those that be of men.
24. **Then said Jesus**
unto his disciples,
If any *man* will
come after me, let him deny
himself, and take up his
cross, and follow me.
25. **For whosoever will save**
his life shall lose it: and
whosoever will lose his life
for my sake shall find it.
26. **For what is a man**
profited, if he shall
gain the whole
world, and lose his own
soul? or what shall a man give in
exchange for his soul?
27. **For the Son of man shall**
come in the glory of his
Father with his angels;
and then he shall reward
every man according
to his works.
28. Verily I say unto you, There be
some standing here, which shall not
taste of death, till they see the Son of
man coming in his kingdom.

CHAPTER 17
1. **And after six days Jesus**
taketh Peter, James,
and John
his brother, and bringeth them up
into an high mountain apart,
2. **And was transfigured**
before them: and his face did
shine as the sun, and his raiment was
white as the light.
3. **And, behold, there**
appeared unto them
Moses and Elias talking
with him.
4. **Then answered Peter,**
and said unto Jesus,
Lord, it is good for us to be here: if
thou wilt,
let us make here
three tabernacles; one
for thee, and one for
Moses, and one for
Elias.
5. **While he yet spake,** behold,
a bright
cloud overshadowed
them: and behold
a voice out of the cloud,
which
said, This is my beloved
Son, in whom I am well
pleased; hear ye him.
6. And when the disciples heard *it,*
they fell on their face,
and were sore afraid.
7. **And Jesus** came and
touched them, and said,
Arise, and
be not afraid.
8. **And** when they had
lifted up their eyes,
they saw no man, save
Jesus only.
9. And as they came down from the
mountain, Jesus charged them,
saying, Tell the vision to no man, until
the Son of man be risen again from the
dead.
10. **And his disciples asked**
him, saying,
Why then
say the scribes that Elias
must first come?

11. And Jesus answered and said unto them, Elias truly shall first come, and restore all things. 12. But I say unto you, That **Elias is come already,** and they knew him not, but have done unto him whatsoever they listed. Likewise shall also the Son of man suffer of them. **13. Then the disciples understood that he spake** unto them **of John the Baptist. 14. And** when they were come to the multitude, **there came** to him **a** *certain* **man, kneeling** down to him, **and saying, 15. Lord, have mercy on my son: for he is lunatic,** and sore vexed: for ofttimes he falleth into the fire, and oft into the water. **16. And I brought him to thy disciples, and they could not cure him.** 17. Then Jesus answered and said, O faithless and perverse generation, how long shall I be with you? how long shall I suffer you? bring him hither to me. **18. And Jesus rebuked the devil;** and he departed out of him: **and the child was cured** from that very hour. **19. Then came the disciples** to Jesus apart, **and said, Why could not we cast him out? 20. And Jesus said** unto them, **Because of your unbelief:** for verily I say unto you, **If ye have faith as a** grain of **mustard seed, ye shall say unto this mountain, Remove** hence to yonder place; **and it shall remove; and nothing shall be impossible** unto you. 21. **Howbeit this kind goeth** not out but **by prayer and fasting.** 22. **And while** they abode

in Galilee, Jesus said unto them, **The Son of man shall be betrayed** into the hands of men: 23. **And they shall kill him, and the third day he shall be raised** again. And they were exceeding sorry. 24. **And when they were come to Capernaum, they that received tribute** *money* **came to Peter, and said, Doth not your master pay tribute?** 25. **He saith, Yes. And when he was come into the house, Jesus prevented him, saying, What thinkest thou, Simon? of whom do the kings** of the earth **take** custom or **tribute? of their** own **children, or** of **strangers?** 26. **Peter saith** unto him, **Of strangers. Jesus saith** unto him, **Then are the children free.** 27. **Notwithstanding, lest we should offend** them, **go** thou **to the sea, and cast** an hook, **and take** up **the fish that first cometh** up; **and when thou hast opened his mouth, thou shalt find** a piece of **money:** that **take, and give unto them** for me and thee.

CHAPTER 18
1. **At the same time came the disciples** unto Jesus, **saying, Who is the greatest in the kingdom** of heaven? 2. **And Jesus called a little child** unto him, and set him in the midst of them, 3. **And said,** Verily I say unto you, **Except ye be converted, and become** as little

children, ye shall not enter into the kingdom of heaven.

4. Whosoever therefore shall humble himself as this little child, the same is greatest in the kingdom of heaven.

5. And whoso shall receive one such little child in my name receiveth me.

6. But whoso shall offend one of these little ones which believe in me, it were better for him that a millstone were hanged about his neck, and *that* he were drowned in the depth of the sea.

7. Woe unto the world because of offences! for it must needs be that offences come; but woe to that man by whom the offence cometh!

8. Wherefore if thy hand or thy foot offend thee, cut them off, and cast *them* from thee: it is better for thee to enter into life halt or maimed, rather than having two hands or two feet to be cast into everlasting fire.

9. And if thine eye offend thee, pluck it out, and cast *it* from thee: it is better for thee to enter into life with one eye, rather than having two eyes to be cast into hell fire.

10. Take heed that ye despise not one of these little ones; for I say unto you, That in heaven their angels do always behold the face of my Father which is in heaven.

11. For the Son of man is come to save that which was lost.

12. How think ye? if a man have an hundred sheep, and one of them be gone astray, doth he not leave the ninety and nine, and goeth into the mountains, and seeketh that which is gone astray?

13. And if so be that he find it, verily I say unto you, he rejoiceth more of that *sheep*, than of the ninety and nine which went not astray.

14. Even so it is not the will of your Father which is in heaven that one of these little ones should perish.

15. Moreover if thy brother shall trespass against thee, go and tell him his fault between thee and him alone: if he shall hear thee, thou hast gained thy brother.

16. But if he will not hear *thee, then* take with thee one or two more, that in the mouth of two or three witnesses every word may be established.

17. And if he shall neglect to hear them, tell *it* unto the church: but if he neglect to hear the church, let him be unto thee as an heathen man and a publican.

18. Verily I say unto you, Whatsoever ye shall bind on earth shall be bound in heaven: and whatsoever ye shall loose on earth shall be loosed in heaven.

19. Again I say unto you, That if two of you shall agree on earth as touching any thing that they shall ask, it shall be done for them of my Father which is in heaven.

20. For where two or three are gathered together in my name, there am I in the midst of them.

21. Then came Peter to him,

and said, Lord,
how oft shall my brother
sin against me,
and I forgive him? till
seven times?
22. **Jesus saith**
unto him, I say not unto thee, Until
seven times: but, Until
seventy times seven.
23. **Therefore is the kingdom**
of heaven
likened unto a certain
king, which would
take account of
his servants.
24. And when he had begun to reckon,
one was brought unto him, which
owed him ten thousand
talents.
25. But forasmuch as he had not to
pay,
his lord commanded
him to be sold, and his wife, and
children, and all that he had, and
payment to be made.
26. **The servant** therefore
fell down, and worshipped him,
saying, Lord,
have patience with me,
and I will pay thee all.
27. **Then the lord** of that servant
was moved with
compassion, and loosed him,
and forgave him
the debt.
28. **But the same servant**
went out, and
found one of his fellow-
servants, which owed him
an hundred pence:
and he laid hands on him, and
took *him* **by the throat,**
saying, Pay me that thou owest.
29. **And his fellow-servant**
fell down
at his feet, and besought him,
saying, Have patience
with me,
and I will pay thee all.
30. **And he would not: but**
went and
cast him into prison,
till he should pay the debt.

31. **So when his fellow-**
servants saw what was done,
they were very sorry, and came and
told unto
their lord all that was done.
32. **Then his lord,**
after that he had called him,
said unto him, O
thou wicked servant, I
forgave thee all that debt,
because thou desiredst me:
33. **Shouldest not thou also**
have had compassion on
thy fellow-servant,
even as I had pity on thee?
34. **And his lord** was wroth, and
delivered him to the
tormentors, till he should
pay all that was due unto him.
35. **So likewise shall my**
heavenly
Father do also uno you,
if ye from your hearts
forgive not every one his brother
their trespasses.

CHAPTER 19

1. **And** it came to pass, *that* when
Jesus had finished these sayings,
he departed from Galilee, and
came into the coasts of
Judaea beyond Jordan;
2. And great multitudes followed him;
and he healed them there.
3. **The Pharisees also came**
unto him, tempting him, and
saying unto him,
Is it lawful for a man to put
away his wife for
every cause?
4. **And he answered**
and said unto them,
Have ye not read, that he
which made *them* at the beginning
made them male and female,
5. And
said, For this cause shall a man
leave father and mother, and shall
cleave to his wife: and
they twain shall be
one flesh?
6. **Wherefore** they are no more
twain, but one flesh.

What therefore
God hath joined together,
let not man put asunder.
7. They say unto him,
Why did Moses
then command to
give a writing of
divorcement,
and to put her away?
8. He saith unto them,
Moses because of the
hardness of your hearts
suffered you to put away
your wives: but
from the beginning it was not so.
9. And I say unto you,
Whosoever shall put away
his wife, except it be
for fornication, and shall
marry another, committeth
adultery: and whoso marrieth her
which is put away doth
commit adultery.
10. His disciples say
unto him, If the case of the man be so
with his wife,
it is not good to marry.
11. But he said unto them,
All men cannot receive this
saying, save they to whom
it is given.
12. For there are some eunuchs,
which were so born from their mother's
womb: and there are some eunuchs,
which were made eunuchs of men:
and there be eunuchs, which have
made themselves eunuchs for the
kingdom of heaven's sake.
He that is able to receive it,
let him receive it.
13. Then were there brought
unto him
little children, that he should put
his hands on them, and pray:
and the disciples
rebuked them.
14. But Jesus said, Suffer
little children,
and forbid them not,
to come unto me: for of
such is the kingdom
of heaven.
15. And he laid his hands on them,

and departed thence.
16. And, behold, one came and
said unto him,
Good Master, what good
thing shall I do, that I may
have eternal life?
17. And he said unto him,
Why callest thou
me good? there is none
good but one, that is,
God: but if thou wilt enter
into
life, keep the
commandments.
18. He saith unto him,
Which? Jesus said, Thou
shalt do no murder,
Thou shalt
not commit adultery,
Thou shalt
not steal, Thou shalt
not bear false witness,
19. Honour thy father and thy
mother: and, Thou shalt
love thy neighbour
as thyself.
20. The young man saith
unto him,
All these things
have I kept from my youth up:
what lack I yet?
21. Jesus said
unto him, If thou wilt be perfect,
go and sell that thou hast,
and give to the poor, and thou
shalt have treasure in heaven:
and come and
follow me.
22. But when the young man
heard that saying,
he went away sorrowful:
for he had great
possessions.
23. Then said Jesus unto his
disciples, Verily I say unto you, That a
rich man shall hardly enter into the
kingdom of heaven.
24. And again I say unto you,
It is easier for a camel to
go through the eye of a
needle, than for a rich man
to enter into the kingdom
of God.

25. **When his disciples heard** *it,* **they were** exceedingly **amazed, saying, Who** then **can be saved?** 26. **But Jesus** beheld *them,* and **said** unto them, With men this is impossible; but **with God all things are possible.** 27. **Then answered Peter** and said unto him, Behold, **we have** forsaken all, and **followed thee; what shall we have** therefore? 28. **And Jesus said** unto them, Verily I say unto you, That ye which have followed me, in the regeneration when the Son of man shall sit in the throne of his glory, **ye** also **shall sit upon twelve thrones, judging** the twelve tribes of **Israel.** 29. **And every one that hath forsaken houses,** or **brethren,** or **sisters,** or **father,** or **mother,** or **wife,** or **children, or lands, for my name's sake, shall receive an hundredfold, and shall inherit everlasting life.** 30. But many *that are* first shall be last; and the last *shall be* first.

CHAPTER 20

1. **For the kingdom** of heaven **is like unto a man** *that is* an householder, **which went out early** in the morning **to hire labourers** into his vineyard. 2. And when he had agreed with the labourers **for a penny a day,** he sent them into his vineyard. 3. **And** he went out **about the third hour,** and **saw others standing idle** in the marketplace, 4. **And said** unto them; **Go** ye also **into the vineyard, and whatsoever is right I will give you.** And they went their way. 5. **Again he went out about the sixth and ninth hour, and did likewise.** 6. **And about the eleventh hour he** went out, and **found others** standing idle, **and saith** unto them, **Why stand ye** here all the day **idle?** 7. **They say** unto him, Because **no man hath hired us. He saith** unto them, **Go** ye also **into the vineyard; and whatsoever is right,** *that* **shall ye receive.** 8. **So when even was come, the lord** of the vineyard **saith** unto his steward, **Call the labourers, and give them** *their* **hire,** beginning from the last unto the first. 9. **And when they came that** *were hired* **about the eleventh hour, they received every man a penny.** 10. **But when the first came, they supposed that they should have received more; and they likewise received every man a penny.** 11. **And** when they had received *it,* **they murmured** against the goodman of the house, 12. **Saying, These last have wrought** *but* **one hour, and thou hast made them equal** unto us, which have borne the burden and heat of the day. 13. **But he answered** one of them, and said, Friend, I do thee no wrong: **didst not thou agree with me for a penny?** 14. Take *that* thine *is,* and go thy way: I will give unto this last,

even as unto thee.

■ 15. **Is it not lawful** for me
■ **to do what I will with mine**
■ **own?** Is thine eye evil,
because I am good?
■ 16. **So the last shall be first,**
and the first last:
■ **for many be called,**
■ **but few chosen.**
■ 17. **And Jesus**
going up to Jerusalem
■ **took the twelve disciples**
■ **apart** in the way,
■ **and said** unto them,
■ 18. **Behold, we go** up
■ **to Jerusalem; and the Son**
of man
■ **shall be betrayed** unto the
chief priests and unto the scribes,
■ **and they shall condemn**
him to death,
■ 19. **And shall deliver him**
to the Gentiles to mock,
and to scourge, and
■ **to crucify** *him:* **and** the third
day
■ **he shall rise again.**
■ 20. **Then came** to him
■ **the mother of Zebedees**
■ **children** with her sons,
worshipping *him,* and desiring a
certain thing of him.
■ 21. **And** he said unto her,
What wilt thou?
■ **She saith** unto him,
■ **Grant that** these
■ **my two sons may sit, the**
■ **one on thy right hand, and**
■ **the other on the left,**
■ **in thy kingdom.**
■ 22. **But Jesus answered**
and said, Ye know not what ye ask.
■ **Are ye able to drink of the**
■ **cup that I shall drink**
of, and to be baptized with the
baptism that I am baptized with?
■ **They say** unto him,
■ **We are able.**
■ 23. **And he saith** unto them,
■ **Ye shall drink indeed**
of my cup, and be baptized with the
baptism that I am baptized with:
■ **but to sit on my right hand,**

■ **and on my left, is not mine**
■ **to give,** but *it shall be given to them*
for whom it is prepared of my Father.
■ 24. **And when the**
■ **ten heard** *it,*
■ **they were moved with**
■ **indignation**
against the two brethren.
■ 25. **But Jesus**
called them unto *him,* and
■ **said,** Ye know that the princes of
the Gentiles exercise dominion over
them, and they that are great exercise
authority upon them.
26. But it shall not be so
among you: but
■ **whosoever will be great**
■ **among you, let him be**
■ **your minister;**
27. And whosoever will be chief
among you, let him be your servant:
■ 28. **Even as the Son** of man
■ **came not to be ministered**
■ **unto, but to minister, and to**
■ **give his life a ransom**
■ **for many.**
29. And as they departed from
Jericho, a great multitude
followed him.
■ 30. **And, behold, two blind**
■ **men** sitting by the way side, when
they heard that Jesus passed by,
■ **cried** out, saying,
■ **Have mercy on us,**
O Lord, *thou* son of David.
■ 31. **And the multitude**
■ **rebuked them,** because they
should hold their peace:
■ **but they cried the more,**
saying, Have mercy on us, O Lord,
thou son of David.
■ 32. **And Jesus**
stood still, and called them, and
■ **said, What will ye that I**
■ **shall do** unto you?
■ 33. **They say** unto him, Lord,
■ **that our eyes may**
■ **be opened.**
■ 34. **So Jesus**
had compassion *on them,* and
■ **touched their eyes: and**
immediately
■ **their eyes received sight,**

and they followed him.

CHAPTER 21

■ 1. **And when they** drew nigh unto Jerusalem, and
■ **were come to Bethphage,** unto the mount of Olives,
■ **then sent Jesus two**
■ **disciples,**
■ 2. **Saying** unto them,
■ **Go** into the village over against you,
■ **and** straightway
■ **ye shall find an ass tied,**
■ **and a colt** with her: loose *them,* and
■ **bring *them* unto me.**
3. And if any *man* say aught unto you, ye shall say, The Lord hath need of them; and straightway he will send them.
■ 4. **All this** was done, that it might be fulfilled which
■ **was spoken by the**
■ **prophet, saying,**
5. Tell ye the daughter of Sion, Behold,
■ **thy King cometh** unto thee, meek, and
■ **sitting upon an ass,** and a colt the foal of an ass.
■ 6. **And the disciples** went, and
■ **did as Jesus commanded** them,
■ 7. **And brought the ass,** and the colt, and put on them their clothes,
■ **and they set *him* thereon.**
■ 8. **And a very great**
■ **multitude spread** their
■ **garments** in the way;
■ **others cut** down
■ **branches** from the trees,
■ **and strawed *them***
■ **in the way.**
■ 9. **And** the multitudes that went before, and that followed,
■ **cried,** saying,
■ **Hosanna** to the son of David:
■ **Blessed *is* he that cometh in**
■ **the name of the Lord;** Hosanna in the highest.
10. And when he was come into Jerusalem, all the city was moved,

saying, Who is this?
11. And the multitude said, This is Jesus the prophet of Nazareth of Galilee.
■ 12. **And Jesus went into the**
■ **temple** of God,
■ **and cast out all** them
■ **that sold and bought** in the temple,
■ **and overthrew the tables** of the moneychangers, and the seats of them that sold doves,
■ 13. **And said** unto them,
■ **It is written, My house shall**
■ **be called the house of**
■ **prayer; but ye have made it**
■ **a den of thieves.**
■ 14. **And the blind and the**
■ **lame came** to him in the temple;
■ **and he healed them.**
■ 15. **And when the chief**
■ **priests and scribes saw**
■ **the** wonderful
■ **things** that
■ **he did, and the children**
■ **crying** in the temple, and saying,
■ **Hosanna** to the son of David;
■ **they were** sore
■ **displeased,**
■ 16. **And said** unto him,
■ **Hearest** thou
■ **what these say?** And
■ **Jesus saith** unto them,
■ **Yea; have ye never read,**
■ **Out of the mouth of babes** and sucklings
■ **thou hast**
■ **perfected praise?**
■ 17. **And he left** them,
■ **and went** out of the city
■ **into Bethany; and** he
■ **lodged** there.
■ 18. **Now in the morning** as he returned into the city,
■ **he hungered.**
■ 19. **And when he saw a fig**
■ **tree** in the way, he came to it,
■ **and found nothing thereon,** but leaves only,
■ **and said** unto it,
■ **Let no fruit grow on thee** henceforward for ever.
■ **And** presently

the fig tree withered away.

20. And when the disciples saw it, they marvelled, saying, How soon is the fig tree withered away !

21. Jesus answered and said unto them, Verily I say unto you, If ye have faith, and doubt not, ye shall not only do this *which is done* to the fig tree, but also if ye shall say unto this mountain, Be thou removed, and be thou cast into the sea; it shall be done.

22. And all things, whatsoever ye shall ask in prayer, believing, ye shall receive.

23. And when he was come into the temple, the chief priests and the elders of the people came unto him as he was teaching, and said, By what authority doest thou these things? and who gave thee this authority?

24. And Jesus answered and said unto them, I also will ask you one thing, which if ye tell me, I in like wise will tell you by what authority I do these things.

25. The baptism of John, whence was it? from heaven, or of men? And they reasoned with themselves, saying, If we shall say, From heaven; he will say unto us, Why did ye not then believe him?

26. But if we shall say, Of men; we fear the people; for all hold John as a prophet.

27. And they answered Jesus, and said, We cannot tell. And he said unto them, Neither tell I you by what authority I do these things.

28. But what think ye? A *certain* man had two sons; and he came to the first, and said, Son, go work to day in my vineyard.

29. He answered and said, I will not: but afterward he repented, and went.

30. And he came to the second, and said likewise. And he answered and said, I *go,* sir: and went not.

31. Whether of them twain did the will of *his* father? They say unto him, The first. Jesus saith unto them, Verily I say unto you, That the publicans and the harlots go into the kingdom of God before you.

32. For John came unto you in the way of righteousness, and ye believed him not: but the publicans and the harlots believed him: and ye, when ye had seen *it,* repented not afterward, that ye might believe him.

33. Hear another parable: There was a certain householder, which planted a vineyard, and hedged it round about, and digged a winepress in it, and built a tower, and let it out to husbandmen, and went into a far country:

34. And when the time of the fruit drew near, he sent his servants to the husbandmen, that they might receive the fruits of it.

35. And the husbandmen took his servants, and beat one, and killed another, and stoned another.

36. Again, he sent other servants more than the first: and they did unto them likewise.

37. **But last** of all **he sent** unto them **his son,** saying, They will reverence my son.
38. **But when the husbandmen saw the son, they** said among themselves, This is the heir; come, let us kill him, and let us seize on his inheritance.
39. And they caught *him*, and cast *him* out of the vineyard, and **slew *him.***
40. **When the lord** therefore **of the vineyard cometh, what will he do** unto those husbandmen?
41. **They say** unto him, **He will** miserably **destroy those wicked men and will let out *his* vineyard unto other husbandmen,** which shall render him the fruits in their seasons.
42. **Jesus saith** unto them, **Did ye never read** in the scriptures, **The stone which the builders rejected,** the same **is become the head of the corner:** this is the Lord's doing, and it is marvellous in our eyes?
43. **Therefore say I unto you, The kingdom** of God **shall be taken from you, and given to a nation bringing forth** the **fruits** thereof.
44. **And whosoever shall fall on this stone shall be broken:** but on whomsoever it shall fall, it will grind him to powder.
45. And when the chief priests and Pharisees had heard his parables, **they perceived that he spake of them.**
46. But when they sought to lay hands on him, they feared the multitude, because they took him for a prophet.

CHAPTER 22

1. **And Jesus** answered and **spake** unto them **again by parables,** and said,
2. The kingdom of heaven is like unto **a** certain **king,** which **made a marriage for his son,**
3. **And sent** forth his **servants to call them** that were **bidden to the wedding: and they would not come.**
4. **Again, he sent forth** other **servants, saying, Tell them** which are bidden, Behold, **I have prepared my dinner:** my oxen and *my* fatlings *are* killed, **and all things *are* ready:** come unto the marriage.
5. **But they made light of *it,* and went their ways,** one to his farm, another to his merchandise:
6. **And the remnant took his servants,** and entreated *them* spitefully, **and slew *them.***
7. **But when the king heard** *thereof,* he was wroth: and **he sent** forth **his armies, and destroyed those murderers,** and burned up their city.
8. **Then saith he to his servants, The wedding is ready,** but they which were bidden were not worthy.
9. **Go** ye therefore **into the highways, and as many as ye** shall **find, bid to the marriage.**
10. **So those servants** went out into the highways, and **gathered** together all **as many as they found,** both bad and good: **and the wedding was furnished with guests.**
11. **And when the king came** in to see the guests, **he saw** there **a man which had not on a wedding garment:**
12. **And he saith** unto him, Friend, **how camest thou in** hither **not having a wedding**

garment? And he
was speechless.
13. Then said the king
to the servants,
Bind him hand and foot, and
take him away,
and cast *him* into outer
darkness, there shall be weeping
and gnashing of teeth.
14. For many are called, but
few *are*
chosen.
15. Then went the Pharisees,
and took counsel how they
might entangle him in *his* talk.
16. And they sent out unto him
their disciples
with the Herodians,
saying, Master,
we know that thou art true,
and teachest the way of God in truth,
neither carest thou for any *man:* for
thou regardest not the person of men.
17. Tell us therefore,
What thinkest thou?
Is it lawful to give tribute
unto Caesar, or not?
18. But Jesus perceived their
wickedness, and
said, Why tempt ye me,
ye hypocrites?
19. Shew me the tribute
money. And they brought
unto him
a penny.
20. And he saith unto them,
Whose *is* this image
and superscription?
21. They say unto him,
Caesar's. Then saith he
unto them,
Render therefore
unto Caesar the things
which are Caesar's; and
unto God the things
that are God's.
22. When they had heard *these words,*
they marvelled, and left him,
and went their way.
23. The same day came to him
the Sadducees, which say
that
there is no resurrection,

and asked him,
24. Saying, Master,
Moses said, If a man die,
having no children, his
brother shall marry his
wife, and raise up seed
unto his brother.
25. Now there were with us
seven brethren: and
the first, when he had married a
wife, deceased, and,
having no issue, left his
wife unto his brother:
26. Likewise the second
also, and the third,
unto the seventh.
27. And last of all the
woman died also.
28. Therefore in the
resurrection whose wife
shall she be of the seven?
for they all had her.
29. Jesus answered
and said unto them,
Ye do err, not knowing the
scriptures, nor the power
of God.
30. For in the resurrection
they neither marry,
nor are given in marriage,
but are as the angels of God
in heaven.
31. But as touching the
resurrection of the dead,
have ye not read that which
was spoken unto you by God, saying,
32. I am the God of
Abraham, and the God of
Isaac, and the God of
Jacob? God is not
the God of the dead, but
of the living.
33. And when the multitude heard *this,*
they were astonished at his doctrine.
34. But when the Pharisees
had heard that he had put the
Sadducees to silence, they were
gathered together.
35. Then one of them, *which was*
a lawyer, asked *him a question,*
tempting him, and saying,
36. Master, which *is* the
great commandment

in the law?

37. **Jesus said** unto him, **Thou shalt love the Lord thy God** with all thy heart, and with all thy soul, and with all thy mind.

38. This is the first and great commandment.

39. **And the second** *is* like unto it, **Thou shalt love thy neighbour as thyself.**

40. **On these** two commandments **hang all the law and the prophets.**

41. While the Pharisees were gathered together, **Jesus asked** them,

42. **Saying, What think ye of Christ? whose son is he? They say** unto him, *The son* **of David.**

43. **He saith** unto them, **How then doth David** in spirit **call him Lord,** saying,

44. The LORD said unto my Lord, Sit thou on my right hand, till I make thine enemies thy footstool?

45. **If David then call him Lord, how is he his son?**

46. **And no man was able to answer** him a word, neither durst any *man* from that day forth ask him any more *questions* .

CHAPTER 23

1. **Then spake Jesus** to the multitude, and to his disciples,

2. **Saying The** scribes and the **Pharisees sit in Moses' seat:**

3. All therefore **whatsoever they bid you observe,** that observe and do; **but do not ye after their works:** for they say, and do not.

4. **For they bind heavy burdens** and grievous to be borne, **and lay** *them* **on men's shoulders; but they** *themselves* **will not move** them with **one of their fingers.**

5. But all their works

they do for **to be seen** of men: they make broad their phylacteries, and enlarge the borders of their garments,

6. **And love** the uppermost rooms at feasts, and the chief seats in the synagogues,

7. And greetings in the markets, and **to be called** of men, **Rabbi,** Rabbi.

8. **But be not ye called Rabbi:** for **one is your Master,** *even* **Christ;** and all ye are brethren.

9. **And call no** *man* your **father** upon the earth: **for** one is **your Father,** which **is in heaven.**

10. Neither be ye called masters: for one is your Master, *even* Christ.

11. **But he that is greatest** among you **shall be your servant.**

12. And whosoever shall exalt himself shall be abased; and he that shall humble himself shall be exalted.

13. **But woe unto you,** scribes and **Pharisees,** hypocrites! **for ye shut up the kingdom** of heaven **against men:** for ye neither go in *yourselves*, neither suffer ye them that are entering to go in.

14. Woe unto you, scribes and Pharisees, hypocrites! for **ye devour widows' houses, and** for a pretence **make long prayer: therefore ye shall receive the greater damnation.**

15. Woe unto you, scribes and Pharisees, hypocrites! for **ye** compass sea and land to **make one proselyte, and** when he is made, ye **make him twofold more the child of hell than yourselves.**

16. **Woe unto you,** *ye* blind guides, **which say, Whosoever**

shall swear by the temple, it is nothing; but whosoever shall swear by the gold of the temple, he is a debtor!

17. *Ye* fools and blind: for whether is greater, the gold, or the temple that sanctifieth the gold?

18. And, Whosoever shall swear by the altar, it is nothing; but whosoever sweareth by the gift that is upon it, he is guilty.

19. *Ye* fools and blind: for whether *is* greater, the gift, or the altar that sanctifieth the gift?

20. Whoso therefore shall swear by the altar, sweareth by it, and by all things thereon.

21. And whoso shall swear by the temple, sweareth by it, and by him that dwelleth therein.

22. And he that shall swear by heaven, sweareth by the throne of God, and by him that sitteth thereon.

23. Woe unto you, scribes and Pharisees, hypocrites! for ye pay tithe of mint and anise and cummin, and have omitted the weightier *matters* of the law, judgment, mercy, and faith: these ought ye to have done, and not to leave the other undone.

24. *Ye* blind guides, which strain at a gnat, and swallow a camel.

25. Woe unto you, scribes and Pharisees, hypocrites! for ye make clean the outside of the cup and of the platter, but within they are full of extortion and excess.

26. *Thou* blind Pharisee, cleanse first that *which is* within the cup and platter, that the outside of them may be clean also.

27. Woe unto you, scribes and Pharisees, hypocrites! for

ye are like unto whited sepulchres, which indeed appear beautiful outward, but are within full of dead *men's* bones, and of all uncleanness.

28. Even so ye also outwardly appear righteous unto men, but within ye are full of hypocrisy and iniquity.

29. Woe unto you, scribes and Pharisees, hypocrites! because ye build the tombs of the prophets, and garnish the sepulchres of the righteous,

30. And say, If we had been in the days of our fathers, we would not have been partakers with them in the blood of the prophets.

31. Wherefore ye be witnesses unto yourselves, that ye are the children of them which killed the prophets.

32. Fill ye up then the measure of your fathers.

33. *Ye* serpents, *ye* generation of vipers, how can ye escape the damnation of hell?

34. Wherefore, behold, I send unto you prophets, and wise men, and scribes: and *some* of them ye shall kill and crucify; and *some* of them shall ye scourge in your synagogues, and persecute *them* from city to city:

35. That upon you may come all the righteous blood shed upon the earth, from the blood of righteous Abel unto the blood of Zacharias son of Barachias, whom ye slew between the temple and the altar.

36. Verily I say unto you, All these things shall come upon this generation.

37. O Jerusalem, Jerusalem, *thou* that killest the

prophets, and stonest them which are sent unto thee,

how often would I have gathered thy children together, even **as a hen gathereth her chickens** under *her* wings, **and ye would not!**

38. Behold, your house is left unto you desolate.

39. For I say unto you, Ye shall not see me henceforth, till ye shall say, Blessed *is* he that cometh in the name of the Lord.

CHAPTER 24

1. **And Jesus** went out, and **departed** from the temple: **and his disciples came to** *him* for to **shew him the buildings of the temple.**

2. **And Jesus said** unto them, See ye not all these things? verily I say unto you, **There shall not be left** here **one stone upon another,** that shall not be thrown down.

3. **And as he sat** upon the mount of Olives, **the disciples came** unto him privately, **saying,** Tell us, **when shall these things be? and** what *shall be* **the sign of thy coming, and of the end** of the world?

4. **And Jesus answered** and said unto them, **Take heed that no man deceive you.**

5. **For many shall come** in my name, **saying, I am Christ;** and shall deceive many.

6. **And ye shall hear of wars** and rumours of wars: see that ye **be not troubled:** for all *these things* must come to pass, but **the end is not yet.**

7. **For nation shall rise against nation,** and kingdom against kingdom:

and there shall be famines, and **pestilences, and earthquakes,** in divers places.

8. **All these** *are* **the beginning of sorrows.**

9. **Then shall they** deliver you up to be afflicted, and shall **kill you: and ye shall be hated** of all nations **for my name's sake.**

10. **And then shall many** be offended, and shall **betray one another,** and shall hate one another.

11. **And many false prophets** shall rise, and **shall deceive** many.

12. **And** because iniquity shall abound **the love of many shall wax cold.**

13. **But he that shall endure** unto the end, the same **shall be saved.**

14. **And this gospel** of the kingdom **shall be preached in all the world** for a witness unto all nations; **and then shall the end come.**

15. **When ye therefore shall see the abomination of desolation,** spoken of by Daniel the prophet, stand in the holy place, (whoso readeth, let him understand:)

16. Then let them which be in Judaea **flee into the mountains:**

17. Let him which is on the housetop not come down to take any thing out of his house:

18. Neither let him which is in the field return back to take his clothes.

19. And woe unto them that are with child, and to them that give suck in those days!

20. But pray ye that your flight be not in the winter, neither on the sabbath day:

21. **For then shall be great tribulation, such as was not since the beginning** of the world to this time, no,

nor ever shall be.

■ 22. **And except those days**
■ **should be shortened, there**
■ **should no flesh be saved:**
but for the elect's sake those days
shall be shortened.

■ 23. **Then if any man** shall
■ **say** unto you,
■ **Lo, here** *is* **Christ,** or there;
■ **believe** *it* **not.**

■ 24. **For there shall arise**
■ **false Christs,**
and false prophets,
■ **and** shall
■ **shew** great
■ **signs** and wonders;
■ **insomuch that, if** *it were*
■ **possible, they shall**
■ **deceive the** very
■ **elect.**

25. Behold, I have told you before.

■ 26. **Wherefore if they** shall
■ **say** unto you,
■ **Behold, he is in the desert;**
go not forth: behold,
he is in the secret chambers;

■ **believe** *it*
■ **not.**

■ 27. **For as the lightning**
■ **cometh** out of the east, and
shineth even unto the west;

■ **so shall also the coming**
■ **of the Son** of man
■ **be.**

28. For wheresoever the carcase is,
there will the eagles be gathered
together.

■ 29. **Immediately after the**
■ **tribulation** of those days shall the
sun be darkened, and the moon shall
not give her light, and the stars shall
fall from heaven, and the powers of
the heavens shall be shaken:

30. And then shall appear the sign of
the Son of man in heaven: and then
shall all the tribes of the
earth mourn, and

■ **they shall see the Son of**
■ **man coming**
in the clouds of heaven
■ **with power and**
■ **great glory.**

■ 31. **And he shall send his**

■ **angels** with a great sound of a
trumpet,
■ **and they shall gather** together
■ **his elect** from the four winds, from
one end of heaven to the other.

■ 32. **Now learn** a parable
■ **of the fig tree; When his**
■ **branch is** yet
■ **tender, and putteth**
■ **forth leaves,**
ye know that
■ **summer** *is* **nigh:**

■ 33. **So likewise** ye,
■ **when ye shall see all these**
■ **things, know that it is near,**
even at the doors.

34. Verily I say unto you,
This generation shall not pass,
till all these things be fulfilled.

■ 35. **Heaven and earth shall**
■ **pass** away,
■ **but my words shall not**
■ **pass** away.

■ 36. **But of that day** and hour
■ **knoweth no** *man,* no, not the
angels of heaven,
■ **but my Father only.**

■ 37. **But as the days of Noe**
■ *were,* **so shall also the**
■ **coming** of the Son of man
■ **be.**

38. For as in the days that were
■ **before the flood they were**
■ **eating and** drinking,
■ **marrying** and giving in marriage,
■ **until** the day that
■ **Noe entered into the ark,**

■ 39. **And** knew not until
■ **the flood** came, and
■ **took them** all away;
■ **so shall also the coming**
■ **of the Son** of man
■ **be.**

■ 40. **Then shall two be in the**
■ **field; the one shall be**
■ **taken, and the other left.**

41. Two *women shall be* grinding at the
mill; the one shall be taken, and the
other left.

■ 42. **Watch** therefore: for
■ **ye know not what hour your**
■ **Lord doth come.**

43. But know this, that if the goodman

of the house had known in what watch the thief would come, he would have watched, and would not have suffered his house to be broken up.

44. Therefore be ye also ready: **for in such an hour as ye think not the Son** of man **cometh.**

45. Who then is a faithful and wise servant, whom his lord hath made ruler over his household, to give them meat in due season?

46. **Blessed** *is* **that servant, whom his lord when he cometh shall find** so **doing.**

47. Verily I say unto you, That **he shall make him ruler** over all his goods.

48. **But** and if **that evil servant shall say** in his heart, **My lord delayeth his coming;**

49. And shall begin to smite *his* fellow servants, and to eat and drink with the drunken;

50. **The lord** of that servant **shall come** in a day **when he looketh not for** *him,* and in an hour that he is not aware of,

51. **And shall cut him asunder, and** appoint *him* his portion with the hypocrites: **there shall be weeping and gnashing of teeth.**

CHAPTER 25

1. Then shall the kingdom of heaven be likened unto **ten virgins, which took** their **lamps,** and went forth **to meet the bridegroom.**

2. **And five** of them **were wise, and five** *were* **foolish.**

3. **They that** *were* **foolish took** their lamps, and took **no oil** with them:

4. **But the wise took oil** in their vessels with their lamps.

5. **While the bridegroom tarried, they** all slumbered and **slept.**

6. **And at midnight there was a cry** made, **Behold, the bridegroom cometh;** go ye out to meet him.

7. **Then all those virgins** arose, and **trimmed** their **lamps.**

8. **And the foolish said unto the wise, Give us** of your **oil; for our lamps are** gone **out.**

9. **But the wise answered,** saying, *Not so;* lest there be not enough for us and you: **but go** ye rather to them that sell, **and buy for yourselves.**

10. **And while they went to buy, the bridegroom came; and they that were ready went in with him** to the marriage: **and the door was shut.**

11. **Afterward came also the other virgins, saying, Lord,** Lord, **open to us.**

12. **But he answered** and said, Verily I say unto you, **I know you not.**

13. **Watch therefore, for ye know neither the day nor the hour** wherein **the Son** of man **cometh.**

14. For *the kingdom of heaven is* as **a man travelling** into a far country, *who* **called his own servants,** and delivered unto them his goods.

15. **And unto one he gave five talents, to another two, and to another one;** to every man according to his several ability; **and** straightway **took his journey.**

16. **Then he that had received the five talents** went and traded with the same, and **made** *them* **other**

five talents.

17. And likewise he that *had received* two, he also gained other two.

18. But he that had received one went and digged in the earth, and hid his lord's money.

19. After a long time the lord of those servants cometh, and reckoneth with them.

20. And so he that had received five talents came and brought other five talents, saying, Lord, thou deliveredst unto me five talents: behold, I have gained beside them five talents more.

21. His lord said unto him, Well done, *thou* good and faithful servant: thou hast been faithful over a few things, I will make thee ruler over many things: enter thou into the joy of thy lord.

22. He also that had received two talents came and said, Lord, thou deliveredst unto me two talents: behold, I have gained two other talents beside them.

23. His lord said unto him, Well done, good and faithful servant; thou hast been faithful over a few things, I will make thee ruler over many things: enter thou into the joy of thy lord.

24. Then he which had received the one talent came and said, Lord, I knew thee that thou art an hard man, reaping where thou hast not sown, and gathering where thou hast not strawed:

25. And I was afraid, and went and hid thy talent in the earth: lo, *there* thou hast *that is* thine.

26. His lord answered and said unto him, *Thou* wicked and slothful servant, thou knewest that I reap where I sowed not, and gather where I have not strawed:

27. Thou oughtest therefore to have put my money to the exchangers, and *then* at my coming I should have received mine own with usury.

28. Take therefore the talent from him, and give *it* unto him which hath ten talents.

29. For unto every one that hath shall be given, and he shall have abundance: but from him that hath not shall be taken away even that which he hath.

30. And cast ye the unprofitable servant into outer darkness: there shall be weeping and gnashing of teeth.

31. When the Son of man shall come in his glory, and all the holy angels with him, then shall he sit upon the throne of his glory:

32. And before him shall be gathered all nations: and he shall separate them one from another, as a shepherd divideth *his* sheep from the goats:

33. And he shall set the sheep on his right hand, but the goats on the left.

34. Then shall the King say unto them on his right hand, Come, ye blessed of my Father, inherit the kingdom prepared for you from the foundation of the world:

35. For I was an hungered, and ye gave me meat: I was thirsty, and ye gave me drink: I was a stranger, and ye took me in:

36. Naked, and ye clothed me: I was sick, and ye visited me: I was in

prison, and ye came unto me.

37. Then shall the righteous answer him, saying, Lord, **when saw we thee** an hungred, and fed *thee?* or thirsty, and gave *thee* drink?

38. When saw we thee a stranger, and took *thee* in? or naked, and clothed *thee?*

39. Or when saw we thee sick, or in prison, and came unto thee?

40. And the King shall answer and say unto them, Verily I say unto you, **inasmuch as ye have done** *it* **unto one of the least of these my brethren, ye have done** *it* **unto me.**

41. Then shall he say also unto them on the left hand, Depart from me, ye cursed, into everlasting fire, prepared for the devil and his angels:

42. For I was an hungered, and ye gave me no meat: I was thirsty, and ye gave me no drink:

43. I was a stranger, and ye took me not in: naked, and ye clothed me not: sick, and in prison, and ye visited me not.

44. Then shall they also answer him, saying, Lord, when saw we thee an hungred, or athirst, or a stranger, or naked, or sick, or in prison, and did not minister unto thee?

45. Then shall he answer them, saying, Verily I say unto you, Inasmuch as ye did *it* not to one of the least of these, ye did *it* not to me.

46. And these shall go away into everlasting punishment: but the righteous into life eternal.

CHAPTER 26

1. And it came to pass, **when Jesus had finished** all these sayings, **he said** unto his disciples,

2. Ye know that **after two days** is *the feast of* the passover, and

the Son of man **is betrayed to be crucified.**

3. Then assembled together the chief priests, and the scribes, and the elders of the people, **unto the palace of** the high priest, who was called **Caiaphas,**

4. And consulted that they might take Jesus by subtilty, **and kill** *him.*

5. But they said, Not on the feast *day,* lest there be an uproar among the people.

6. Now when Jesus was in Bethany, in the house of Simon the leper,

7. There came unto him **a woman having** an alabaster box of very precious **ointment, and poured it on his head,** as he sat *at meat.*

8. But when his disciples saw *it,* **they had indignation,** saying, To what purpose *is* this waste?

9. For this ointment might have been sold for much, **and given to the poor.**

10. When Jesus understood *it,* **he said** unto them, Why trouble ye the woman? for **she hath wrought a good work** upon me.

11. For ye have the poor always with you; but me ye have not always.

12. For in that **she hath poured this ointment on my body,** she did *it* **for my burial.**

13. Verily I say unto you, **Wheresoever this gospel shall be preached** in the whole world, *there* **shall also this, that this woman hath done, be told for a memorial of her.**

14. Then one of the twelve, called **Judas** Iscariot, **went unto the chief priests,**

■ 15. **And said** *unto them,*
■ **What will ye give** me,
■ **and I will deliver him**
unto you?
■ **And they covenanted**
with him for
■ **thirty pieces of silver.**
16. And from that time he sought
opportunity to betray him.
17. Now the first *day* of the *feast of*
unleavened bread
■ **the disciples came to**
■ **Jesus, saying** unto him,
■ **Where wilt thou that we**
■ **prepare for** thee to eat
■ **the passover?**
■ 18. **And he said, Go into the**
■ **city to** such
■ **a man, and say** unto him,
■ **The Master saith,**
My time is at hand;
■ **I will keep the passover at**
■ **thy house** with my disciples.
19. And the disciples did as Jesus
had appointed them; and they made
ready the passover.
■ 20. **Now** when the even was come,
■ **he sat down with**
■ **the twelve.**
■ 21. **And** as they did eat,
■ **he said,** Verily I say unto you, that
■ **one of you shall betray me.**
■ 22. **And they were** exceeding
■ **sorrowful, and began**
every one of them
■ **to say** unto him,
■ **Lord, is it I?**
■ 23. **And he answered** and said,
■ **He that dippeth** *his* hand
■ **with me** in the dish,
■ **the same shall betray me.**
24. The Son of man goeth as it is
written of him: but woe unto that man
by whom the Son of man is betrayed!
it had been good for that man if he had
not been born.
■ 25. **Then Judas,** which betrayed
him, answered and
■ **said,** Master,
■ **is it I? He said** unto him,
■ **Thou hast said.**
26. And as they were eating,
■ **Jesus took bread, and**

■ **blessed** *it,*
■ **and brake** *it,* **and**
gave *it* to the disciples, and
■ **said, Take, eat;**
■ **this is my body.**
■ 27. **And he took the cup, and**
■ **gave thanks,** and gave *it* to them,
■ **saying, Drink** ye all of
■ **it;**
■ 28. **For this is my blood**
of the new testament, which is
■ **shed for** many for
■ **the remission of sins.**
29. But I say unto you, I will not drink
henceforth of this fruit of the vine,
until that day when I drink it new with
you in my Father's kingdom.
■ 30. **And when they had sung**
an hymn
■ **they went out**
into the mount of Olives.
■ 31. **Then saith Jesus** unto them,
■ **All ye shall be offended**
■ **because of me this night:**
for it is written, I will smite the
shepherd, and the sheep of the flock
shall be scattered abroad.
■ 32. **But after I am risen**
■ **again, I will go before you**
■ **into Galilee.**
■ 33. **Peter answered**
and said unto him,
■ **Though all** *men* shall
■ **be offended** because of thee,
■ *yet* **will I never be offended.**
■ 34. **Jesus said** unto him, Verily I
say unto thee, That this night,
■ **before the cock crow, thou**
■ **shalt deny me thrice.**
35. Peter said unto him, Though I
should die with thee, yet will I not deny
thee. Likewise also said
all the disciples.
■ 36. **Then cometh Jesus with**
■ **them unto** a place called
■ **Gethsemane, and saith**
unto the disciples,
■ **Sit** ye here,
■ **while I go and pray** yonder.
■ 37. **And he took** with him
■ **Peter and the two sons of**
■ **Zebedee,** and began to be
sorrowful and very heavy.

38. Then saith he unto them, **My soul is** exceeding **sorrowful, even unto death: tarry** ye here, **and watch with me.** 39. **And he went** a little **farther,** and fell on his face, **and prayed,** saying, O my **Father, if it be possible, let this cup pass** from me: **nevertheless not as I will, but as thou** *wilt.* 40. **And he cometh** unto the disciples, **and findeth them asleep, and saith unto Peter,** What, **could ye not watch** with me **one hour?** 41. Watch and pray, that ye enter not into temptation: **the spirit** indeed *is* **willing, but the flesh** *is* **weak.** 42. **He went** away again **the second time, and prayed,** saying, O my Father, **if this cup may not pass** away from me, **except I drink** it, **thy will be done.** 43. **And he** came and **found them asleep again:** for their eyes were heavy. 44. **And he** left them, and went away again, and **prayed the third time,** saying **the same words.** 45. **Then cometh he to his disciples, and saith** unto them, **Sleep on now,** and take *your* rest: behold, the hour is at hand, and the Son of man is betrayed into the hands of sinners. 46. Rise, let us be going: behold, he is at hand that doth betray me. 47. **And while he yet spake,** lo, **Judas,** one of the twelve, **came,** and **with him a great multitude** with swords and staves, **from the chief priests**

and elders of the people. 48. **Now he** that betrayed him **gave them a sign, saying, Whomsoever I shall kiss,** that same **is he:** hold him fast. 49. **And forthwith he** came to Jesus, and said, Hail, master; and **kissed him.** 50. And Jesus said unto him, Friend, wherefore art thou come? **Then** came **they,** and **laid hands on Jesus and took him.** 51. **And, behold, one** of them which were **with Jesus** stretched out *his* hand, and **drew his sword, and struck a servant of the high priest's, and smote off his ear.** 52. **Then said Jesus** unto him, **Put up again thy sword** into his place: **for** all **they that take the sword shall perish with the sword.** 53. **Thinkest thou that I cannot now pray to my Father, and he shall** presently **give me** more than **twelve legions of angels?** 54. **But how then shall the scriptures be fulfilled, that thus it must be?** 55. In that same hour said Jesus to the multitudes, Are ye come out as against a thief with swords and staves for to take me? I sat daily with you teaching in the temple, and ye laid no hold on me. 56. But all this was done, that the scriptures of the prophets might be fulfilled. **Then all the disciples** forsook him, and **fled.** 57. **And they** that had laid hold on Jesus **led** *him* away **to Caiaphas the high**

- **priest,** where the scribes and the elders were assembled.
- 58. **But Peter followed** him
- **afar off** unto the high priest's palace, and went in,
- **and sat with the servants,** to see the end.
- 59. **Now** the chief priests, and elders, and all
- **the council, sought false**
- **witness against Jesus,** to put him to death;
- 60. **But found none:** yea, though many false witnesses came, yet found they none.
- **At the last came two** false witnesses,
- 61. **And said, This *fellow***
- **said, I am able to destroy**
- **the temple** of God,
- **and** to
- **build it in three days.**
- 62. **And the high priest** arose, and
- **said unto him, Answerest**
- **thou nothing?** what *is it which* these witness against thee?
- 63. **But Jesus held his**
- **peace, And the high priest** answered and
- **said** unto him, I adjure thee by the living God, that thou
- **tell us whether thou be the**
- **Christ,** the Son of God.
- 64. **Jesus saith** unto him, Thou hast said: nevertheless I say unto you,
- **Hereafter shall ye see the**
- **Son** of man
- **sitting on the right hand of**
- **power, and coming in the**
- **clouds** of heaven.
- 65. **Then the high priest rent**
- **his clothes, saying, He hath**
- **spoken blasphemy;** what further need have we of witnesses? behold, now ye have heard his blasphemy.
- 66. **What think ye? They** answered and
- **said, He is guilty of death.**
- 67. **Then** did
- **they spit in his face, and**

buffeted him; and others
- **smote *him*** with the palms of their hands,
- 68. **Saying, Prophesy unto**
- **us, thou Christ, Who** is he that
- **smote thee?**
- 69. **Now Peter sat** without in the palace:
- **and a damsel came** unto him,
- **saying, Thou** also
- **wast with Jesus** of Galilee.
- 70. **But he denied** before *them* all, saying, I know not what thou sayest.
- 71. **And** when he was gone out into the porch,
- **another *maid* saw him, and**
- **said** unto them that were there,
- **This *fellow* was** also
- **with Jesus** of Nazareth.
- 72. **And again he denied** with an oath, I do not know the man.
- 73. **And** after a while came unto *him*
- **they that stood by, and**
- **said** to Peter,
- **Surely thou** also
- **art *one* of them**; for thy speech bewrayeth thee.
- 74. **Then began he to**
- **curse and** to
- **swear, *saying,* I know not**
- **the man. And** immediately
- **the cock crew.**
- 75. **And Peter remembered**
- **the word of Jesus,** which said unto him, Before the cock crow, thou shalt deny me thrice.
- **And he went out,**
- **and wept bitterly.**

CHAPTER 27

1. When the morning was come, all
- **the chief priests and elders** of the people
- **took counsel against**
- **Jesus** to put him to death:
- 2. **And** when they had bound him,
- **they** led *him* away, and
- **delivered him to** Pontius
- **Pilate the governor.**
- 3. **Then Judas,** which had betrayed him, when he saw that he was condemned,
- **repented** himself,

■ **and brought** again
■ **the** thirty pieces of
■ **silver to the chief priests**
and elders,
■ 4. **Saying, I have**
sinned in that I have
■ **betrayed the innocent**
■ **blood. And they said, What**
■ *is that* **to us?** see thou *to that.*
■ 5. **And he cast down the**
pieces of
■ **silver** in the temple, and departed,
■ **and** went and
■ **hanged himself.**
■ 6. **And the chief priests took**
■ **the silver** pieces, and said, It is
not lawful for to put them into the
treasury, because it is the
price of blood.
7. And they took counsel,
■ **and bought** with them
■ **the** potter's
■ **field,** to bury strangers in.
8. Wherefore that field was
■ **called, The field of blood,**
unto this day.
■ 9. **Then was fulfilled that**
■ **which was spoken by**
■ **Jeremy** the prophet, saying, And
they took the thirty pieces of silver,
the price of him that was valued,
whom they of the children of
Israel did value;
10. And gave them for the potter's
field, as the Lord appointed me.
■ 11. **And Jesus stood before**
■ **the governor: and the**
■ **governor asked him,** saying,
■ **Art thou the King of the**
■ **Jews? And Jesus said**
unto him,
■ **Thou sayest.**
■ 12. **And when he**
■ **was accused**
of the chief priests and elders,
■ **he answered nothing.**
13. Then said Pilate unto him, Hearest
thou not how many things they
witness against thee?
■ 14. **And** he answered him to never a
word; insomuch that
■ **the governor marvelled**
greatly.

■ 15. **Now at** *that* **feast the**
■ **governor was wont to**
■ **release** unto the people
■ **a prisoner,** whom they would.
16. And they had then a notable
prisoner, called Barabbas.
17. Therefore when they were
gathered together,
■ **Pilate said** unto them,
■ **Whom will** ye that
■ **I release** unto you?
■ **Barabbas, or Jesus**
which is called Christ?
18. For he knew that for envy they had
delivered him.
19. When he was set down on the
judgment seat,
■ **his wife sent unto him,**
■ **saying, Have** thou
■ **nothing to do with that just**
■ **man:** for
■ **I have suffered**
many things this day
■ **in a dream because of him.**
■ 20. **But the chief priests**
and elders
■ **persuaded the multitude**
■ **that they should ask**
■ **Barabbas, and**
■ **destroy Jesus.**
21. The governor answered and said
unto them, Whether of the twain will ye
that I release unto you?
They said, Barabbas.
■ 22. **Pilate saith** unto them,
■ **What shall I do then with**
■ **Jesus** which is called Christ?
■ *They* **all say** unto him,
■ **Let him be crucified.**
■ 23. **And the governor said,**
■ **Why, what evil hath he**
■ **done? But they cried**
■ **out** the
■ **more, saying, Let him**
■ **be crucified.**
24. **When Pilate saw that he**
■ **could prevail nothing,** but
that rather a tumult was made,
■ **he** took water, and
■ **washed** *his* **hands**
before the multitude,
■ **saying, I am innocent of the**
■ **blood of this just person:**

see *ye to it.*
25. **Then** answered all
the people, and
said, His blood *be* **on us,**
and on
our children.
26. Then released he
Barabbas unto them:
and when he had scourged
Jesus, he delivered *him* **to**
be crucified.
27. **Then the soldiers**
of the governor
took Jesus into the common hall,
and gathered unto him the whole band
of soldiers.
28. **And they stripped him,**
and put on him a
scarlet robe.
29. **And** when they had platted
a crown of thorns, they put *it*
upon his head,
and a reed in his right hand:
and they
bowed the knee before him,
and mocked him,
saying, Hail, King
of the Jews!
30. **And they spit upon him,**
and took the reed,
and smote him on the head.
31. **And after that**
they had mocked him,
they took the robe off from him, and
put his own raiment on him,
and led him away to
crucify *him.*
32. **And** as they came out,
they found
a man of Cyrene,
Simon by name: him
they compelled to
bear his cross.
33. **And when they were**
come unto a place called
Golgotha, that is to say, a place
of a skull,
34. **They gave him vinegar**
to drink mingled
with gall: and
when he had tasted *thereof,*
he would not drink.
35. **And they crucified him,**

and parted his garments,
casting lots: that it might be
fulfilled which was
spoken by the prophet,
They parted my garments among
them, and upon my vesture did they
cast lots.
36. And sitting down they
watched him there;
37. **And set up over his head**
his accusation written, THIS
IS JESUS THE KING
OF THE JEWS.
38. **Then were there two**
thieves crucified with him,
one on the right hand,
and another on the left.
39. **And they that passed by**
reviled him, wagging their heads,
40. **And saying,** Thou that
destroyest the temple, and buildest *it*
in three days, save thyself.
If thou be the Son of God,
come down from the cross.
41. **Likewise also the chief**
priests mocking
him, with the scribes and elders,
said,
42. He saved others; himself he
cannot save.
If he be the King of Israel,
let him now come down
from the cross,
and we will believe him.
43. He trusted in God; let him deliver
him now, if he will have him: for he
said, I am the Son of God.
44. The thieves also, which were
crucified with him, cast the
same in his teeth.
45. Now from the sixth hour there was
darkness over all the land unto the
ninth hour.
46. **And about the ninth hour**
Jesus cried with a loud voice,
saying, Eli, Eli, lama sabachthani?
that is to say,
My God, my God, why hast
thou forsaken me?
47. Some of them that stood there,
when they heard *that,* said, This *man*
calleth for Elias.
48. **And straightway one**

of them ran, and

■ **took a sponge,** and
■ **filled** *it*
■ **with vinegar, and**
put *it* on a reed, and
■ **gave him to drink.**
■ 49. **The rest said,** Let be,
■ **let us see whether Elias will**
come to
■ **save him.**
■ 50. **Jesus, when he had**
■ **cried** again
■ **with a loud voice, yielded**
■ **up the ghost.**
■ 51. **And, behold, the veil of**
■ **the temple was rent**
in twain from the top to the bottom;
■ **and the earth did quake,**
and the rocks rent;
■ 52. **And** the graves were
opened; and
■ **many bodies of the saints**
which slept
■ **arose,**
■ 53. **And came out of the**
■ **graves** after his resurrection, and
went into the holy city,
■ **and appeared unto many.**
■ 54. **Now when the centurion,**
■ **and they** that were
■ **with him,** watching Jesus,
■ **saw** the earthquake, and
■ **those things** that were done,
■ **they feared** greatly,
■ **saying, Truly this was the**
■ **Son of God.**
■ 55. **And many women were**
there beholding afar off, which
followed Jesus from Galilee,
■ **ministering unto him:**
56. Among which was Mary
Magdalene, and Mary the mother of
James and Joses, and the mother of
Zebedees children.
57. When the even was come,
there came
■ **a rich man** of Arimathaea,
■ **named Joseph,** who also
himself was Jesus' disciple:
■ 58. **He went to Pilate, and**
■ **begged the body** of Jesus.
Then Pilate commanded the body to
be delivered.

■ 59. **And when Joseph had**
■ **taken the body, he**
■ **wrapped it in** a clean
■ **linen** cloth,
■ 60. **And laid it in his own** new
■ **tomb,** which he had hewn
out in the rock:
■ **and he rolled a** great
■ **stone to the door** of the
sepulchre, and departed.
61. And there was Mary Magdalene,
and the other Mary, sitting over
against the sepulchre.
■ 62. **Now the next day,** that
followed the day of the preparation,
■ **the chief priests and**
■ **Pharisees came** together
■ **unto Pilate,**
■ 63. **Saying, Sir, we remem-**
■ **ber that that deceiver said,**
while he was yet alive,
■ **After three days I will rise**
again.
■ 64. **Command therefore that**
■ **the sepulchre be made**
■ **sure** until the third day,
■ **lest his disciples**
come by night, and
■ **steal him away,** and say unto
the people, He is risen from the dead:
so the last error shall be worse
than the first.
■ 65. **Pilate said** unto them,
■ **Ye have a watch:** go your way,
■ **make** *it* **as sure as ye can.**
■ 66. **So they went,**
and made the sepulchre sure,
■ **sealing the stone, and**
■ **setting a watch.**

CHAPTER 28
1. In the end of the sabbath, as it
began to dawn toward
■ **the first** *day* **of the week,**
■ **came Mary Magdalene**
■ **and the other Mary to see**
■ **the sepulchre.**
■ 2. **And, behold, there was a**
■ **great earthquake: for the**
■ **angel of the Lord**
■ **descended**
from heaven, and came
■ **and rolled back the stone**

from the door, and sat upon it.
3. His countenance was like lightning, and his raiment white as snow:
■ 4. **And for fear** of him
■ **the keepers did shake, and**
■ **became as dead** *men.*
■ 5. **And the angel** answered and
■ **said unto the women, Fear**
■ **not** ye: for I know that
■ **ye seek Jesus,**
which was crucified.
■ 6. **He is not here: for he is**
■ **risen,** as he said. Come, see the place where the Lord lay.
■ 7. **And go quickly, and tell**
■ **his disciples**
that he is risen from the dead;
■ **and, behold, he goeth**
■ **before you into Galilee;**
there shall ye see him: lo, I have told you.
■ 8. **And they** departed quickly from the sepulchre with fear and great joy; and
■ **did run to bring his**
■ **disciples word.**
■ 9. **And as they went to tell**
his disciples, behold,
■ **Jesus met them,** saying, All hail.
■ **And they**
came and held him by the feet, and
■ **worshipped him.**
10. Then said Jesus unto them, Be not afraid: go tell my brethren that they go into Galilee, and there shall they see me.
■ 11. **Now** when they were going, behold,
■ **some of the watch came**
into the city,
■ **and shewed** unto
■ **the chief priests** all

■ **the things that were done.**
■ 12. **And** when they were assembled with
■ **the** elders, and had taken
■ **counsel,** they
■ **gave** large
■ **money unto the soldiers,**
■ 13. **Saying, Say ye, His**
■ **disciples** came by night, and
■ **stole him** *away*
■ **while we slept.**
14. And if this come to the governor's ears, we will persuade him, and secure you.
■ 15. **So they** took the money, and
■ **did as they were taught:**
and this saying is commonly reported among the Jews until this day.
■ 16. **Then the eleven** disciples
■ **went away into Galilee,**
into a mountain where Jesus had appointed them.
17. And when they saw him, they worshipped him: but some doubted.
■ 18. **And Jesus came and**
■ **spake** unto them,
■ **saying, All power is given**
■ **unto me** in heaven and in earth.
■ 19. **Go** ye therefore,
■ **and teach all nations,**
■ **baptizing them** in the name of the Father, and of the Son, and of the Holy Ghost:
■ 20. **Teaching them to**
■ **observe** all things
■ **whatsoever I have**
■ **commanded** you:
■ **and, lo, I am with**
■ **you alway,** *even*
■ **unto the end**
of the world.
■ **Amen.**

THE GOSPEL ACCORDING TO MARK

BACKGROUND INFORMATION

Author – Mark, a missionary
Date Written – probably
between 57 and **65** A.D.

Number of:
Verses -   678
Chapters -   16
Total Worlds -15,171
Scan Words -7,290
Scan Words represent 48 %
of Total Words.

Theme – written to
Christians to inform them
of the ministry of Jesus on
earth as the Son of God.

OUTLINE OF THE GOSPEL

I.   **Christ's early ministry,**
     baptism and temptation,
     including healings,
     conflicts with Pharisees
     and early travels.
     Chapters 1—8
II. **Christ's predictions of**
     his death, doctrine of
     discipleship
     and transfiguration.
     Chapters 8—10
III. **Christ's** entry into
     Jerusalem and
     Crucifixion.
     Chapters 10—16
IV. **Christ's Resurrection**
     and appearances to his
     disciples.
     Chapters 16—20

CHAPTER 1

1. **The beginning of the gospel of Jesus Christ,** the Son of God;

2. **As it is written** in the prophets, Behold, I send **my messenger** before thy face, which **shall prepare thy way** before thee.

3. **The voice of one crying in the wilderness, Prepare ye the way of the Lord,** make his paths straight.

4. **John did baptize** in the wilderness, **and preach** the baptism of **repentance** for the remission **of sins.**

5. **And there went out** unto him **all** the land of **Judaea, and** they of **Jerusalem, and were all baptized** of him in the river of Jordan, **confessing their sins.**

6. **And John was clothed with camel's hair,** and with a girdle of a skin about his loins; and he did eat locusts and wild honey;

7. **And preached, saying, There cometh one mightier** than I after me, the latchet of **whose shoes I am not worthy to** stoop down and **unloose.**

8. I indeed have baptized you with water: but **he shall baptize you with the Holy Ghost.**

9. **And** it came to pass in those days, that **Jesus** came from Nazareth of Galilee, and **was baptized of John** in Jordan.

10. **And straightway coming up out of the water, he saw** the heavens opened, and **the Spirit like a dove descending upon him:**

11. **And there came a voice** from heaven, **saying, Thou art my beloved Son,** in whom I am well pleased.

12. **And immediately the spirit driveth him into** the wilderness.

13. And he was there in **the wilderness forty days, tempted of Satan;** and was with the wild beasts; **and the angels ministered unto him.**

14. **Now after that John was put in prison, Jesus came** into Galilee, **preaching the gospel** of the kingdom of God,

15. **And saying,** The time is fulfilled, and the kingdom of God is at hand: **repent ye, and believe the gospel.**

16. **Now** as he walked by the sea of Galilee, he saw **Simon and Andrew** his brother casting a net into the sea: for they **were fishers.**

17. **And Jesus said** unto them, **Come** ye after me, **and I will make you** to become **fishers of men.**

18. **And straightway they** forsook their nets, and **followed him.**

19. **And** when he had gone a little farther thence, **he saw James** the *son* of Zebedee, **and John** his brother, who also were in the ship **mending their nets.**

20. **And straightway he called them: and they left** their father Zebedee in **the ship** with the hired servants, **and went after him.**

21. **And** they went into Capernau m; and straightway **on the sabbath day he entered into the synagogue, and taught.**

22. And they were astonished at his

doctrine: for he taught them
- **as one that had authority,**
- **and not as the scribes.**
- 23. **And** there was in their synagogue
- **a man with an unclean**
- **spirit;** and he
- **cried out,**
- 24. **Saying, Let** *us* **alone;** what have we to do with thee,
- **thou Jesus of Nazareth?** art thou come to destroy us? I know thee who thou art, the Holy One of God.
- 25. **And Jesus rebuked him,**
- **saying,** Hold thy peace, and
- **come out of him.**
- 26. **And when the unclean**
- **spirit** had torn him, and
- **cried** with a loud voice,
- **he came out of him.**
- 27. **And they were all**
- **amazed,** insomuch that they questioned among themselves,
- **saying, What** thing is this? what
- **new doctrine** *is* **this?** for with authority commandeth he
- **even the unclean spirits,**
- and they do
- **obey him.**
- 28. **And immediately his**
- **fame spread abroad**
- throughout all the region round about Galilee.
- 29. **And** forthwith, when they were come out of the synagogue,
- **they entered into the house**
- **of Simon and Andrew,** with James and John.
- 30. **But Simon's wife's**
- **mother lay sick** of a fever, and anon they tell him of her.
- 31. **And he** came and took her by the hand, and
- **lifted her up; and** immediately
- **the fever left her,** and she ministered unto them.
- 32. **And** at even, when the sun did set,
- **they brought** unto him
- **all that were diseased, and**
- them that were
- **possessed with devils.**
- 33. And all the city was gathered

together at the door.
- 34. **And he healed many** that were sick of divers diseases, and cast out many devils; and suffered not the devils to speak, because they knew him.
- 35. **And in the morning,**
- rising up a great while
- **before day, he went**
- out, and departed
- **into a solitary place, and**
- **there prayed.**
- 36. **And Simon and they that**
- **were with him followed**
- after him.
- 37. **And when they had**
- **found him, they said** unto him,
- **All** *men* **seek for thee.**
- 38. **And he said** unto them,
- **Let us go** into the next towns,
- **that I may preach** there also:
- for therefore came I forth.
- 39. **And he preached**
- in their synagogues
- **throughout all Galilee,**
- **and cast out devils.**
- 40. **And there came a leper**
- to him, beseeching him, and kneeling down to him, and
- **saying** unto him, If thou wilt,
- **thou canst make me clean.**
- 41. **And Jesus,** moved with compassion, put forth *his* hand, and
- **touched him, and saith**
- unto him, I will;
- **be thou clean.**
- 42. **And** as soon as he had spoken,
- **immediately** the leprosy
- departed from him, and
- **he was cleansed.**
- 43. **And he** straitly charged him, and forthwith
- **sent him away;**
- 44. **And saith** unto him, See thou
- **say nothing to any man:**
- **but go** thy way, shew thyself
- **to the priest, and offer**
- for thy cleansing
- **those things which Moses**
- **commanded, for a**
- **testimony** unto them.
- 45. **But he** went out, and
- **began** to publish *it* much, and

to blaze abroad the matter, insomuch that Jesus could no more openly enter into the city, but was without in desert places: and they came to him from every quarter.

CHAPTER 2

1. And again he entered into Capernaum after *some* days; and it was noised that he was in the house.

2. And straightway many were gathered together, insomuch that there was no room to receive *them,* no, not so much as about the door: and he preached the word unto them.

3. And they come unto him, bringing one sick of the palsy, which was borne of four.

4. And when they could not come nigh unto him for the press, they uncovered the roof where he was: and when they had broken *it* up, they let down the bed wherein the sick of the palsy lay.

5. When Jesus saw their faith, he said unto the sick of the palsy, Son, thy sins be forgiven thee.

6. But there was certain of the scribes sitting there, and reasoning in their hearts,

7. Why doth this *man* thus speak blasphemies? who can forgive sins but God only?

8. And immediately when Jesus perceived in his spirit that they so reasoned within themselves, he said unto them, Why reason ye these things in your hearts?

9. Whether is it easier to say to the sick of the palsy, *Thy* sins be forgiven thee; or to say, Arise, and take up thy bed, and walk?

10. But that ye may know that the Son of man hath power on earth to forgive sins, (he saith to the sick of the palsy,)

11. I say unto thee, Arise, and take up thy bed, and go thy way into thine house.

12. And immediately he arose, took up the bed, and went forth before them all; insomuch that they were all amazed, and glorified God, saying, We never saw it on this fashion.

13. And he went forth again by the sea side; and all the multitude resorted unto him, and he taught them.

14. And as he passed by, he saw Levi the *son* of Alphaeus sitting at the receipt of custom, and said unto him, Follow me. And he arose and followed him.

15. And it came to pass, that, as Jesus sat at meat in his house, many publicans and sinners sat also together with Jesus and his disciples: for there were many, and they followed him.

16. And when the scribes and Pharisees saw him eat with publicans and sinners, they said unto his disciples, How is it that he eateth and drinketh with publicans and sinners?

17. When Jesus heard *it,* he saith unto them, They that are whole have no need of the physician, but they that are sick: I came not to call the righteous, but sinners to repentance.

18. And the disciples of John and of the Pharisees used to fast: and

they come and
say unto him, Why do the
disciples of John and of the Pharisees
fast, but
thy disciples fast not?
19. **And Jesus said** unto them,
Can the children of the bridechamber
fast, while the bridegroom is
with them?
as long as they have the
bridegroom with them,
they cannot fast.
20. **But** the days will come,
when the bridegroom shall
be taken away from them, and
then shall they fast
in those days.
21. **No man also seweth**
a piece of
new cloth on an old
garment: else
the new piece that filled it up
taketh away from the old,
and the rent is made worse.
22. **And no man putteth new**
wine into old bottles: else
the new wine doth burst the
bottles, and the wine is spilled, and
the bottles will be marred:
but new wine must be put
into new bottles.
23. **And** it came to pass, that
he went through the corn
fields on the sabbath day;
and his disciples began,
as they went,
to pluck the ears of
corn.
24. **And the Pharisees said**
unto him, Behold,
why do they on the sabbath day
that which is not lawful?
25. **And he said** unto them,
Have ye never read what
David did, when he
had need, and was an
hungered, he, and they that
were with him?
26. **How he went into the**
house of God in the days of
Abiathar the high priest,
and did eat the
shewbread, which is not

lawful to eat but for the priests, and
gave also to them which
were with him?
27. And he said unto them, The
sabbath was made for man, and not
man for the sabbath:
28. Therefore
the Son of man is Lord also
of the sabbath.

CHAPTER 3

1. And he entered again into the
synagogue; and
there was a man there
which had a
withered hand.
2. **And they watched him,**
whether he would heal him
on the sabbath day;
that they might accuse him.
3. **And he saith unto the man**
which had the withered hand,
Stand forth.
4. And he saith unto them,
Is it lawful to do good on
the sabbath days, or to do
evil? to save life, or to kill? But they
held their peace.
5. **And** when he had looked round
about on them
with anger, being grieved
for the hardness of their
hearts, he saith unto the
man, Stretch forth thine
hand. And he stretched *it* out:
and his hand was restored
whole as the other.
6. **And the Pharisees**
went forth, and straightway
took counsel
with the Herodians against him,
how they might
destroy him.
7. **But Jesus withdrew**
himself with his disciples
to the sea:
and a great multitude from Galilee
followed him, and from Judaea,
8. And from Jerusalem, and from
Idumaea, and *from* beyond Jordan;
and they about Tyre and Sidon, a
great multitude,
when they had heard what

■ **great things he did, came**
■ **unto him.**
■ 9. **And he spake to his**
■ **disciples, that a small ship**
■ **should wait on him**
because of the multitude,
■ **lest they should throng him.**
■ 10. **For he had healed many;**
insomuch that they pressed upon him
for to touch him,
as many as had plagues.
■ 11. **And unclean spirits,**
when they saw him,
■ **fell down before him,**
and cried,
■ **saying, Thou art the**
■ **Son of God.**
■ 12. **And he straitly charged**
■ **them that they should not**
■ **make him known.**
■ 13. **And he goeth up into a**
■ **mountain,** and calleth *unto him*
whom he would: and they
came unto him.
■ 14. **And he ordained twelve,**
■ **that they should be with**
■ **him, and that he might send**
■ **them forth to preach,**
■ 15. **And** to have power
■ **to heal** sicknesses,
■ **and to cast out devils:**
16. And Simon he surnamed Peter;
17. And James the *son* of Zebedee,
and John the brother of James; and
he surnamed them Boanerges, which
is, The sons of thunder:
18. And Andrew, and Philip, and
Bartholomew, and Matthew, and
Thomas, and James the *son* of
Alphaeus, and Thaddaeus, and Simon
the Canaanite,
19. And Judas Iscariot, which also
betrayed him: and they went into an
house.
■ 20. **And the multitude**
■ **cometh together again,** so
that they could not so much
as eat bread.
■ 21. **And** when
■ **his friends** heard *of it,* they
■ **went out to lay hold on him:**
■ **for they said, He is**
■ **beside himself.**

■ 22. **And the scribes** which came
down from Jerusalem
■ **said,** He hath Beelzebub, and
■ **by the prince of the devils**
■ **casteth he out devils.**
■ 23. **And he** called them
unto him, and
■ **said** unto them
■ **in parables, How can**
■ **Satan cast out Satan?**
24. And if a kingdom be divided
against itself, that kingdom
cannot stand.
25. And if a house be divided against
itself, that house cannot stand.
■ 26. **And if Satan** rise up against
himself, and
■ **be divided, he cannot**
■ **stand,** but hath an end.
■ 27. **No man can enter** into
■ **a strong man's house,**
and spoil his goods,
■ **except he will first bind the**
■ **strong man;** and then he will spoil
his house.
28. Verily I say unto you,
■ **All sins shall be forgiven**
unto the sons of men, and
blasphemies wherewith soever they
shall blaspheme:
■ 29. **But he that shall**
■ **blaspheme against the**
■ **Holy Ghost hath never**
■ **forgiveness, but** is in danger of
■ **eternal damnation.**
30. Because they said, He hath an
unclean spirit.
31. There came
■ **then his brethren and his**
■ **mother,** and, standing without,
■ **sent** unto him,
■ **calling him.**
■ 32. **And the multitude** sat about
him, and they
■ **said** unto him, Behold,
■ **thy mother and thy brethren**
without
■ **seek for thee.**
33. And he answered them, saying,
Who is my mother, or my brethren?
■ 34. **And he looked** round about
■ **on them which sat about**
■ **him, and said, Behold my**

■ mother and my brethren!
■ 35. For whosoever shall do
■ the will of God, the same
■ is my brother, and my
■ sister, and mother.

CHAPTER 4
■ 1. And he began again to teach by
the sea side: and there was gathered
unto him a great multitude, so that he
■ entered into a ship,
and sat in the sea;
■ and the whole
■ multitude was by the sea
■ on the land.
■ 2. And he taught them
many things
■ by parables, and said
unto them in his doctrine,
3. Hearken; Behold,
■ there went out a
■ sower to sow:
■ 4. And it came to pass, as he sowed,
■ some fell by the way side,
■ and the fowls of the air came and
■ devoured it up.
■ 5. And some fell on stony
■ ground, where it had
not much earth;
■ and immediately it sprang up,
■ because it had no depth
of earth:
6. But when
■ the sun was up, it was
■ scorched; and
because it had no root,
■ it withered away.
■ 7. And some fell among
■ thorns, and the thorns
grew up, and
■ choked it, and it yielded no fruit.
■ 8. And other fell on good
■ ground, and did yield fruit
that sprang up and increased; and
brought forth, some thirty, and some
sixty, and some an hundred.
9. And he said unto them, He that hath
ears to hear, let him hear.
■ 10. And when he was
■ alone, they that were about him
with the twelve
■ asked of him the parable.
■ 11. And he said unto them,

■ Unto you it
■ is given to know
■ the mystery of the kingdom
■ of God: but unto them
that are without, all *these*
■ things are done
■ in parables:
■ 12. That seeing they may
see, and
■ not perceive; and hearing
they may hear, and
■ not understand; lest
at any time
■ they should
■ be converted, and *their* sins
should be forgiven them.
13. And he said unto them,
■ Know ye not
■ this parable? and how then will
ye know all parables?
■ 14. The sower soweth
■ the word.
■ 15. And these are they
■ by the way side, where the word
is sown; but
■ when they have
■ heard, Satan cometh
immediately,
■ and taketh away the word
that was sown in their hearts.
■ 16. And these
are they likewise which are
■ sown on stony ground; who,
■ when they have heard
the word, immediately
■ receive it with gladness;
■ 17. And have no root
in themselves, and
■ so endure but for a time: afterward,
■ when affliction or
■ persecution ariseth for the
word's sake, immediately
■ they are offended.
■ 18. And these are they which are
■ sown among thorns; such as
■ hear the word,
■ 19. And the cares of this world,
■ and the deceitfulness of
■ riches, and the lusts of other things
entering in,
■ choke the word,
and it becometh unfruitful.
■ 20. And these are they which are

■ **sown on good ground;** such as hear the word, and
■ **receive** *it,* **and bring forth**
■ **fruit,** some thirtyfold, some sixty, and some an hundred.
■ 21. **And he said** unto them,
■ **Is a candle** brought to be
■ **put under a bushel, or** under a bed? and not to be
■ **set on a candlestick?**
■ 22. **For there is nothing hid,** which shall not be manifested;
■ **neither** was any thing
■ **kept secret, but that it**
■ **should come abroad.**
23. If any man have ears to hear, let him hear.
24. And he said unto them, Take heed what ye hear: with what measure ye mete, it shall be measured to you: and
■ **unto you that hear shall**
■ **more be given.**
■ 25. **For he that hath,** to him
■ **shall be given: and he that**
■ **hath not,** from him
■ **shall be taken** even that which he hath.
26. And he said,
■ **So is the kingdom of God,** as
■ **if a man** should
■ **cast seed into the ground;**
■ 27. **And should sleep,** and rise night and day,
■ **and the seed should** spring and
■ **grow up, he knoweth**
■ **not how.**
■ 28. **For the earth bringeth**
■ **forth fruit of herself;** first the blade, then the ear, after that the full corn in the ear.
■ 29. **But** when the fruit is brought forth,
■ **immediately he putteth in**
■ **the sickle, because the**
■ **harvest is come.**
30. And he said,
■ **Whereunto shall we liken**
■ **the kingdom** of God? or with what comparison shall we compare it?
■ 31. *It is* **like a grain of**
■ **mustard seed, which,** when it

is sown in the earth,
■ **is less than all the seeds** that be in the earth:
■ 32. **But when it is sown,** it groweth up, and
■ **becometh greater than all**
■ **herbs,** and shooteth out great branches; so that the fowls of the air may lodge under the shadow of it.
■ 33. **And with** many such
■ **parables spake he the**
■ **word** unto them, as they were able to hear *it.*
34. But without a parable spake he not unto them:
■ **and when they were alone,**
■ **he expounded** all things
■ **to his disciples.**
■ 35. **And** the same day, when the even was come, he
■ **saith** unto them,
■ **Let us pass over unto the**
■ **other side.**
■ 36. **And** when they had sent away the multitude, they took him even as he was
■ **in the ship.** And there were also
■ **with** him
■ **other little ships.**
37. And
■ **there arose a great storm** of wind, and the waves beat into the ship, so that it was now full.
■ 38. **And he was** in the hinder part of the ship,
■ **asleep** on a pillow:
■ **and they awake him, and**
■ **say** unto him, Master,
■ **carest thou not that**
■ **we perish?**
■ 39. **And he** arose, and
■ **rebuked the wind,** and said unto the sea, Peace, be still. And the wind ceased,
■ **and there was a**
■ **great calm.**
■ 40. **And he said** unto them,
■ **Why** are ye so fearful? how
■ **is it that ye have no faith?**
■ 41. **And they feared**
■ **exceedingly, and said** one to another,
■ **What manner of man is this,**

that even the wind and the
sea obey him?

CHAPTER 5

1. **And they came**
over unto the other side of the sea,
**into the country of
the Gadarenes.**
2. **And** when he was come out of the
ship, immediately
**there met him out of the
tombs a man with an
unclean spirit,**
3. **Who** had *his* dwelling among the
tombs; and
no man could bind
him, no, not with chains:
4. Because that he had been often
bound with fetters and chains, and the
chains had been plucked asunder by
him, and the fetters broken in pieces:
**neither could any *man*
tame him.**
5. **And always,** night and day, he
was in the mountains,
and in the tombs,
**crying, and cutting himself
with stones.**
6. **But when he saw Jesus**
afar off,
**he ran and
worshipped him,**
7. And cried with a loud voice,
**and said, What have I to do
with thee, Jesus, *thou* Son
of** the most high
God? I adjure thee
by God, that thou
torment me not.
8. For he said unto him, Come out of
the man, *thou* unclean spirit.
9. **And he asked him, What
is thy name? And he
answered,** saying, My name *is*
Legion: for we are many.
10. **And he besought him**
much that he would
**not send them away out of
the country.**
11. **Now there was** there nigh
unto the mountains
**a great herd of
swine feeding.**

12. **And all the devils
besought him,** saying,
Send us into the swine,
that we may enter into them.
13. And forthwith
Jesus gave them leave.
And the unclean spirits went out, and
entered into the swine:
and the herd ran violently
down a steep place
into the sea,
(they were about two thousand;)
and were choked in the sea.
14. **And they**
that fed the swine fled, and
told *it* in the city, and in the
**country. And they went out
to see** what it was that was done.
15. And they come to
Jesus, and see him that
was possessed with the devil, and
had the legion, sitting,
and clothed,
and in his right mind:
and they were afraid.
16. And they that saw *it* told them how
it befell to him that was possessed
with the devil, and *also* concerning the
swine.
17. **And they began** to pray him
to depart out of their coasts.
18. **And** when he was
come into the ship,
**he that had been
possessed** with the devil
**prayed him that he might
be with him.**
19. Howbeit
Jesus suffered him not, but
saith unto him, Go home
to thy friends,
**and tell them how great
things the Lord hath done**
for thee, and hath had
compassion on thee.
20. **And he** departed, and
began to publish in Decapolis
**how great things Jesus had
done** for him:
and all *men* did marvel.
21. **And** when
Jesus was
passed over again

by ship unto the other side, much people gathered unto him: and he was nigh unto the sea.

22. **And,** behold, there cometh **one of the rulers** of the synagogue, **Jairus** by name; and when he saw him, he **fell at his feet,**

23. And besought him greatly, **saying, My little daughter lieth at the point of death:** *I pray thee,* **come** and lay thy hands on her, **that she may be healed;** and she shall live.

24. And *Jesus* went with him; and much people followed him, and thronged him.

25. **And a certain woman, which had an issue of blood twelve years,**

26. **And had suffered many things** of many physicians, and had spent all that she had, and was nothing bettered, but rather grew worse,

27. **When she had heard of Jesus, came** in the press behind, **and touched his garment.**

28. For she said, If I may touch but his clothes, I shall be whole.

29. **And straightway** the fountain of her blood was dried up; and she felt in *her* body that **she was healed** of that plague.

30. **And Jesus,** immediately **knowing** in himself **that virtue had gone out of him,** turned him about in the press, and **said, Who touched my clothes?**

31. **And his disciples said** unto him, **Thou seest the multitude thronging thee,** and sayest thou, Who touched me?

32. **And he looked round** about **to see her** that had done this thing.

33. **But the woman fearing** and trembling, knowing what was done

in her, **came** and fell down before him, **and told him all the truth.**

34. **And he said** unto her, Daughter, **thy faith hath made thee whole; go in peace,** and be whole of thy plague.

35. **While he yet spake, there came from the ruler of the synagogue's** *house certain* **which said, Thy daughter is dead:** why troublest thou the Master any further?

36. **As soon as Jesus heard** the word that was spoken, **he saith** unto the ruler of the synagogue, **Be not afraid, only believe.**

37. And he suffered no man to follow him, save Peter, and James, and John the brother of James.

38. **And he cometh to the house** of the ruler of the synagogue, and seeth the tumult, and them that wept and wailed greatly.

39. **And** when he was come in, he **saith** unto them, **Why** make ye this ado, and **weep? the damsel is not dead, but sleepeth.**

40. **And they laughed** him to scorn. **But when he had put them all out, he taketh the father and the mother** of the damsel, and them that were with him, **and entereth in where the damsel was lying.**

41. **And he took the damsel by the hand, and said** unto her, Talitha cumi; which is, being interpreted, **Damsel, I say unto thee, arise.**

42. **And straightway the damsel arose,** and walked; for she was *of the age* of twelve years. **And they were astonished** with a great astonishment.

43. **And he** charged them straitly that no man should know it; and **commanded that**

something should be given her to eat.

CHAPTER 6

1. **And he** went out from thence, and **came into his own country;** and his disciples follow him.

2. **And** when the sabbath day was come, **he began to teach in the synagogue: and many hearing** *him* **were astonished, saying,** From whence hath this *man* these things? and what wisdom *is* this which is given unto him, that even such mighty works are wrought by his hands?

3. **Is not this the carpenter, the son of Mary,** the brother of James, and Joses, and of Juda, and Simon? and are not his sisters here with us? **And they were offended** at him.

4. **But Jesus, said** unto them, **A prophet is not without honour, but in his own country,** and among his own kin, and in his own house.

5. **And he could** there **do no mighty work, save** that he laid his hands **upon a few sick folk,** and healed *them.*

6. **And he marvelled because of their unbelief.** And he went round about the villages, teaching.

7. **And he called** *unto him* **the twelve, and began to send them forth by two and two; and gave them power** over unclean spirits;

8. **And commanded them that they should take nothing for** *their* **journey,** save a staff only; no scrip, no bread, no money in *their* purse:

9. But *be* shod with sandals; and not put on two coats.

10. **And he said** unto them, In what place soever ye enter into an house, there abide till ye depart from that place.

11. **And whosoever shall not receive you,** nor hear you, when ye depart thence, **shake off the dust under your feet for a testimony against them.** Verily I say unto you, **It shall be more tolerable for Sodom and Gomorrha in the day of judgment, than for that city.**

12. **And they** went out, and **preached that men should repent.**

13. **And they cast out many devils, and anointed with oil many** that were **sick, and healed** *them.*

14. **And king Herod** heard *of him;* (for his name was spread abroad:) and he **said, That John the Baptist was risen** from the dead, and therefore mighty works do shew forth themselves in him.

15. **Others said, That it is Elias.** And others said, That it is a prophet, **or** as **one of the prophets.**

16. **But** when **Herod** heard *thereof,* he **said, It is John, whom I beheaded:** he is risen from the dead.

17. **For Herod himself had** sent forth and laid hold upon John, and **bound him in prison for Herodias' sake,** his brother Philip's wife: for he had married her.

18. **For John had said** unto Herod, **It is not lawful** for thee **to have thy brother's wife.**

19. **Therefore Herodias** had a quarrel against him, and **would have killed him; but she could not:**

20. **For Herod feared John,** knowing that he was a just man and an holy, and observed him; and when he

heard him, he did many things, and
heard him gladly.

21. **And** when a convenient day was
come, that

**Herod on his birthday
made a supper**
to his lords, high captains,
and chief *estates* of Galilee;

22. **And when the daughter
of** the said

Herodias came in, and

**danced, and pleased
Herod** and them that sat with him,
the king said unto the damsel,
Ask of me

**whatsoever thou wilt, and I
will give** *it* **thee.**

23. And he sware unto her,
Whatsoever thou shalt ask of me, I
will give *it* thee, unto the half
of my kingdom.

24. **And she went** forth, and said
**unto her mother, What shall
I ask? And she said, The
head of John the Baptist.**

25. **And she came** in straightway
with haste unto the king,
and asked, saying, I will that thou
give me by and by in a charger
**the head of
John the Baptist.**

26. **And the king was** exceeding
sorry; *yet* **for his oath's
sake,** and for their sakes which sat
with him,

he would not reject her.

27. **And** immediately
the king sent

an executioner,
and commanded his head to be
brought: and he went and

beheaded him in the prison,

28. **And brought his head** in a
charger, and gave it to the damsel:
**and the damsel gave it to
her mother.**

29. And when his disciples heard *of it,*
they came and took up his corpse,
and laid it in a tomb.

30. **And the apostles
gathered** themselves together
unto Jesus, and told him
all things, both

what they had done,
and what they had taught.

31. **And he said** unto them,
Come ye yourselves
apart into a desert place,
and rest a while: for there were
many coming and going, and they had
no leisure so much as to eat.

32. **And they departed** into a
desert place
by ship privately.

33. **And the people saw
them** departing, and many knew him,
and ran afoot thither out of all
cities, and outwent them,
and came together
unto him.

34. **And Jesus,** when he came
out, saw much people, and
**was moved with
compassion** toward them,
**because they were as
sheep not having a
shepherd:** and he began to teach
them many things.

35. **And when the day was
now far spent, his
disciples** came unto him, and
**said, This is a desert
place,** and now the
time *is* far passed:

36. **Send them away, that
they may** go into the country round
about, and into the villages, and
buy themselves
bread: for they have
nothing to eat.

37. **He answered**
and said unto them,
**Give ye them to eat. And
they say** unto him,
Shall we go and buy
two hundred pennyworth of
bread, and give them to eat?

38. **He saith** unto them,
**How many loaves have
ye?** go and see.
And when they knew,
**they say, Five,
and two fishes.**

39. **And he commanded
them to** make all
sit down by companies upon the

green grass.
40. And they sat down
in ranks,
by hundreds, and by fifties.
41. **And when he had taken the five loaves and the two fishes, he**
looked up to heaven, and
blessed, and brake the loaves,
and gave *them*
to his disciples to set before
them; and the two fishes divided he among them all.
42. **And they** did all eat, and **were filled.**
43. **And they took up twelve baskets full of the fragments,** and of the fishes.
44. **And they that did eat**
of the loaves
were about five thousand men.
45. **And straightway he constrained his disciples to get into the ship, and to go to** the other side before unto **Bethsaida,** while he sent
away the people.
46. **And** when he had
sent them away,
he departed into a mountain to pray.
47. And when even was come, the ship was in the midst of the sea, and he alone on the land.
48. **And he saw them toiling in rowing; for the wind was contrary** unto them: **and** about the fourth
watch of the night
he cometh unto them, **walking upon the sea, and would have passed by**
them.
49. **But** when they saw him walking upon the sea, **they** supposed it had been a spirit, and **cried out:**
50. For they all saw him, and were troubled.
And immediately he
talked with them, and

saith unto them,
Be of good cheer: it is I; be not afraid.
51. **And he went** up unto them **into the ship; and the wind ceased: and they were sore amazed** in themselves
beyond measure, and wondered.
52. For they considered not *the miracle* of the loaves: for their heart was hardened.
53. **And** when they had passed over, **they came into the land of Gennesaret,**
and drew to the shore.
54. **And when they**
were come out of the ship, straightway they knew him,
55. And ran through that whole region round about, and
began to carry about in beds those that were sick,
where they heard he was.
56. And whithersoever he entered, into villages, or cities, or country, **they laid the sick in the streets,** and besought him **that they might touch**
if it were but the border of **his garment: and**
as many as touched him **were made whole.**

CHAPTER 7
1. **Then came** together unto him **the Pharisees, and**
certain of the **scribes,**
which came from Jerusalem.
2. **And** when they **saw** some of **his disciples eat bread**
with defiled, that is to say, **with unwashen hands,**
they found fault.
3. **For the Pharisees,**
and all the Jews, **except they wash**
their hands oft, **eat not,**
holding the tradition of the elders.
4. **And** *when they* come from the market, except they wash, they eat

not. And many other things there be, which they have received to hold, *as* the washing of cups, and pots, brasen vessels, and of tables.

5. Then the Pharisees and scribes **asked him, Why walk not thy disciples according to the tradition** of the elders, **but eat bread with unwashen hands?**

6. **He answered** and said unto them, Well hath Esaias prophesied of **you hypocrites,** as **it is written, This people honoureth me with** *their* **lips, but their heart is far from me.**

7. **Howbeit in vain do they worship me,** teaching *for* doctrines the commandments of men.

8. **For** laying aside the commandment of God, ye hold the tradition of men, *as* the washing of pots and cups: and many other such like things ye do.

9. And he said unto them, Full well **ye reject the command- ment of God, that ye may keep your own tradition.**

10. **For Moses said, Honour thy father and thy mother;** and, Whoso curseth father or mother, let him die the death:

11. **But ye say,** If a man shall say to his father or mother, *It is* Corban, that is to say, **a gift,** by whatsoever **thou mightest be profited by me;** *he shall be free.*

12. **And** ye suffer him **no more to do aught for his father or his mother;**

13. **Making the word of God of none effect** through your tradition, which ye have delivered: and many such like things do ye.

14. **And when he had called all the people** unto him, **he said** unto them, **Hearken** unto me every one *of you,* **and understand:**

15. **There is nothing from without a man, that** entering into him

can defile him: but the things which come out of him, those are they that **defile the man.**

16. If any man have ears to hear, let him hear.

17. And when he was entered into the house from the people, **his disciples asked him concerning the parable.**

18. **And he saith** unto them, Are ye so without understanding also? Do ye not perceive, that **whatsoever thing from without entereth** into the **man,** *it* **cannot defile him;**

19. **Because it entereth** not into his heart, but **into the belly, and goeth out into the draught,** purging all meats?

20. **And he said, That which cometh out of the man, that defileth the man.**

21. **For from within,** out of the heart of men, **proceed evil** thoughts, adulteries, fornications, murders,

22. Thefts, covetousness, wickedness, deceit, lasciviousness, an evil eye, blasphemy, pride, foolishness:

23. All these evil things come from within, and defile the man.

24. **And** from thence **he** arose, and **went into the borders of Tyre and Sidon,** and entered into an house, **and would have no man know** *it:* **but he could not be hid.**

25. **For a** *certain* **woman,** whose young daughter had an unclean spirit, heard of him, and came and fell at his feet:

26. The woman was a Greek, **a Syrophenician** by nation; and she **besought him that he would cast forth the devil out of her daughter.**

27. **But Jesus said** unto her, Let

the children first be filled: for
■ **it is not meet to take the**
■ **children's bread, and to**
■ **cast** *it* **unto the dogs.**
■ 28. **And she answered** and
said unto him, Yes, Lord:
■ **yet the dogs** under the table
■ **eat** of the children's
■ **crumbs.**
■ 29. **And he said** unto her,
■ **For this saying** go thy way;
■ **the devil is gone out**
■ **of thy daughter.**
30. And when she was come to her
house, she found the devil gone out,
and her daughter laid upon the bed.
■ 31. **And** again, departing from the
coasts of Tyre and Sidon,
■ **he came unto** the sea of Galilee,
through the midst of the coasts of
■ **Decapolis.**
■ 32. **And they bring unto**
■ **him one that was deaf,**
■ **and had an impediment**
■ **in his speech;**
and they beseech him to
put his hand upon him.
■ 33. **And he took him aside**
from the multitude,
■ **and put his fingers into his**
■ **ears, and he spit, and**
■ **touched his tongue;**
34. And looking up to heaven,
he sighed,
■ **and saith** unto him,
Ephphatha, that is,
■ **Be opened.**
■ 35. **And straightway his**
■ **ears were opened,** and the
string of his tongue was loosed,
■ **and he spake** plain.
■ 36. **And he charged them**
■ **that they should tell no**
■ **man: but** the more he charged
them, so much the more a great deal
■ **they published** *it;*
■ 37. **And were** beyond measure
■ **astonished, saying,** He hath
done all things well:
■ **he maketh** both
■ **the deaf to hear,**
■ **and the dumb**
■ **to speak.**

CHAPTER 8

1. In those days the multitude being
very great, and having nothing to eat,
■ **Jesus called his disciples**
unto him,
■ **and saith** unto them,
2. I have compassion on
■ **the multitude,** because they
have now been with me
three days, and
■ **have nothing to eat:**
■ 3. **And if I send them away**
■ **fasting** to their own houses,
■ **they will faint** by the way: for
divers of them came from far.
■ 4. **And his disciples**
■ **answered** him,
■ **From whence can a man**
■ **satisfy these** *men* **with**
■ **bread** here in the wilderness?
■ 5. **And he asked** them,
■ **How many loaves have**
■ **ye? And they said, Seven.**
6. And he commanded the people to
sit down on the ground: and
■ **he took the seven loaves,**
■ **and gave thanks, and**
■ **brake,** and gave to his disciples to
set before *them;*
■ **and** they did
■ **set** *them* **before the people**
7. And they had a few small fishes:
and he blessed, and commanded to
set them also before *them.*
■ 8. **So they** did eat, and
■ **were filled: and** they took up of
■ **the** broken
■ *meat* **that was left**
■ **seven baskets.**
■ 9. **And they** that had eaten
■ **were about four thousand:**
and he sent them away.
■ 10. **And** straightway
■ **he entered** into
■ **a ship** with his disciples,
■ **and came into** the parts of
■ **Dalmanutha.**
■ 11. **And the Pharisees came**
forth, and began
■ **to question** with
■ **him, seeking** of him
■ **a sign** from heaven,
■ **tempting him.**

12. **And he** sighed deeply in his spirit, and

saith, Why doth this generation seek after a sign? verily I say unto you,

There shall no sign be given unto this generation.

13. **And he** left them, and entering into the ship again **departed** to the other side.

14. **Now** *the disciples* **had forgotten to take bread,** neither had they in the ship with them more than one loaf.

15. **And he charged them,** saying, Take heed,

beware of the leaven of the Pharisees, and *of* the leaven of **Herod.**

16. **And they reasoned** among themselves, saying,

It is **because we have no bread.**

17. And when **Jesus** knew *it,* he **saith** unto them,

Why reason ye, because ye have no bread?

perceive ye not yet, neither understand? have ye your heart yet hardened?

18. Having eyes, see ye not? and having ears, hear ye not? and

do ye not remember?

19. **When I brake the five loaves among five thousand,** how many baskets full of fragments took ye up? They say unto him, Twelve.

20. **And** when the **seven among four thousand,** how many baskets full of fragments took ye up? And they said, Seven.

21. **And he said unto them, How is it that ye do not understand?**

22. **And he cometh to Bethsaida; and they bring a blind man unto him,** and besought him to touch him.

23. **And he** took the blind man by the hand, and led him out of the town;

and when he had **spit on his eyes, and** put his hands upon him, he **asked** him **if he saw aught.**

24. **And he** looked up, and **said, I see men as trees, walking.**

25. **After that he put** *his* **hands again upon his eyes,** and made him look up: **and he** was restored, and **saw every man clearly.**

26. And he sent him away to his house, saying, Neither go into the town, nor tell *it* to any in the town.

27. **And Jesus** went out, and his disciples, into the towns of Caesarea Philippi: and by the way he **asked his disciples,** saying unto them,

Whom do men say that I am?

28. And **they answered, John the Baptist; but some** *say,* **Elias; and others, One of the prophets.**

29. **And he saith** unto them, **But whom say ye that I am? And Peter answereth** and saith unto him,

Thou art the Christ.

30. And he charged them that they should tell no man of him.

31. **And he began to teach them, that the Son of man must suffer** many things, and be rejected of the elders, and *of* the chief priests, and scribes,

and be killed, and after three days rise again.

32. And he spake that saying openly.

And Peter took him, and **began to rebuke him.**

33. **But** when he had turned about and looked on his disciples,

he rebuked Peter, saying, Get thee behind me, Satan: for thou savourest not the things that be of God, but the things that be of men.

34. **And when he had called**

the people *unto him* with his disciples also,

he said unto them,

Whosoever will come after me, let him deny himself, and take up his cross, and follow me.

35. For whosoever will save his life shall lose it; but whosoever shall lose his life for my sake and the gospel's, the same shall save it.

36. **For what shall it profit a man, if he shall gain the whole world, and lose his own soul?**

37. **Or what shall a man give in exchange for his soul?**

38. **Whosoever** therefore **shall be ashamed of me** and of my words in this adulterous and sinful generation; **of him also shall the Son of man be ashamed,** when he cometh in the glory of his Father with the holy angels.

CHAPTER 9

1. **And he said** unto them, Verily I say unto you, That **there be some** of them that stand **here, which shall not taste of death, till they have seen the kingdom of God come** with power.

2. And after six days **Jesus taketh** *with him* **Peter, and James, and John,** and leadeth them up **into an high mountain apart** by themselves: **and he was transfigured** before them.

3. **And his raiment became** shining, exceeding **white as snow;** so as no fuller on earth can white them.

4. **And there appeared** unto them **Elias with Moses:** and they were **talking with Jesus.**

5. **And Peter answered** and said to Jesus,

Master, it is good for us to be here: and **let us make three tabernacles;** one for thee, and one for Moses, and one for Elias.

6. For he wist not what to say; for they were sore afraid.

7. **And** there was **a cloud** that **overshadowed them: and** a voice came out of the cloud, **saying, This is my beloved Son: hear him.**

8. **And suddenly,** when they had looked round about, **they saw** no man any more, save **Jesus only** with themselves.

9. **And** as they came down from the mountain, **he charged them that they should tell no man** what things they had seen, **till the Son of man were risen** from the dead.

10. **And they** kept that saying with themselves, **questioning one** with **another what the rising from the dead should mean.**

11. And they **asked** him, saying, **Why say the scribes that Elias must first come?**

12. **And he answered** and told them, **Elias verily cometh first,** and restoreth all things; **and** how it is written of **the Son of man,** that he **must suffer many things,** and be set at nought.

13. **But I say** unto you, That **Elias is indeed come, and they have done** unto him **whatsoever they listed,** as it is written of him.

14. **And when he came to** *his* **disciples, he saw** a great multitude about them, and **the scribes questioning with them.**

15. And straightway all the people, when they beheldd him, were greatly amazed, and running to *him* saluted him.

16. **And he asked** the scribes, **What question ye** with them?

17. **And one** of the multitude **answered** and said, Master, **I have brought** unto thee **my son, which hath a dumb spirit;**

18. And wheresoever he taketh him, he teareth him: and he foameth, and gnasheth with his teeth, and pineth away:

and I spake to thy disciples that they should cast him out; and they could not.

19. **He answereth** him, and saith, O faithless generation, how long shall I be with you? how long shall I suffer you?

bring him unto me.

20. And they brought him unto him:

and when he saw him, straightway **the spirit tare him; and he fell** on the ground, **and wallowed foaming.**

21. **And he asked his father, How long** is it ago **since this came unto him? And he said, Of a child.**

22. And ofttimes it hath cast him into the fire, and into the waters, to destroy him:

but if thou canst do any thing, have compassion on us, and **help us.**

23. **Jesus said** unto him, If thou canst believe,

all things *are* **possible to him that believeth.**

24. And straightway **the father** of the child **cried** out, and said with tears, **Lord, I believe;** help thou mine unbelief.

25. **When Jesus saw** that **the people** came running together,

he rebuked the foul spirit,

saying unto him, **Thou** dumb **and deaf spirit,** I charge thee, **come out of him,** and enter no more into him.

26. **And** *the spirit* cried, and rent him sore, and **came out of him: and he was as one dead;** insomuch that many said, He is dead.

27. **But Jesus** took him by the hand, and **lifted him up; and he arose.**

28. And when he was come into the house,

his disciples asked him privately, **Why could not we cast him out?**

29. **And he said** unto them, **This kind can come forth by nothing, but by prayer and fasting.**

30. And they departed thence, and passed through Galilee;

and he would not that any man should know *it.*

31. **For he taught his disciples,** and said unto them, **The Son of man is delivered into the hands of men, and they shall kill him; and** after that he is killed, **he shall rise the third day.**

32. But they understood not that saying, and were afraid to ask him.

33. **And he** came to Capernaum: and being in the house he **asked them, What was it that ye disputed among yourselves** by the way?

34. But they held their peace: for by the way **they had disputed** among themselves, **who** *should be* **the greatest.**

35. **And he** sat down, and called the twelve, and **saith unto them, If any man desire to be first,** *the same* **shall be** last of all, and **servant of all.**

36. **And he took a child, and** set him in the midst of them: and when he had taken him in his arms, he **said** unto them,

37. **Whosoever shall receive one** of such children **in my name, receiveth me: and** whosoever shall receive me, receiveth not me, but **him that sent me.**

38. **And John answered** him, saying, Master, **we saw one casting out devils in thy name,** and he followeth not us: **and we forbad him, because he followeth not us.**

39. **But Jesus said, Forbid him not:** for there is no man which shall do a miracle in my name, that can lightly speak evil of me.

40. For he that is not against us is on our part.

41. **For whosoever shall give** you a cup of **water** to drink **in my name,** because ye belong to Christ, verily I say unto you, he **shall not lose his reward.**

42. **And whosoever shall offend** one of **these little ones** that believe in me, **it is better** for him that a millstone were hanged about his neck, and **he were cast into the sea.**

43. **And if thy hand offend thee, cut it off: it is better** for thee **to enter into life maimed, than having two hands to go into hell,** into the fire that never shall be quenched:

44. Where their worm dieth not, and the fire is not quenched.

45. **And if thy foot offend thee, cut it off: it is better** for thee to enter halt into life, **than having two feet to be cast into hell,** into the fire that never shall be quenched:

46. Where their worm dieth not, and the fire is not quenched.

47. **And if thine eye offend thee, pluck it out: it is better** for thee to enter into the kingdom of God with one eye, **than having two eyes to be cast into hell fire:**

48. **Where their worm dieth not, and the fire is not quenched.**

49. For every one shall be salted with fire, and every sacrifice shall be salted with salt.

50. Salt *is* good: but if the salt have lost his saltness, wherewith will ye season it? Have salt in yourselves, and have peace one with another.

CHAPTER 10

1. **And** he arose from thence, and cometh into the coasts of Judaea **by the** farther side of **Jordan:** and the people resort unto him again; and, as he was wont, **he taught** them again.

2. **And the Pharisees** came to him, and **asked him, Is it lawful for a man to put away** *his* **wife?** tempting him.

3. **And he answered** and said unto them, **What did Moses command you?**

4. **And they said,** Moses suffered **to write a bill of divorcement,** and to put *her* away.

5. **And Jesus answered** and said unto them, **For the hardness of your heart he wrote** you this precept.

6. **But from the beginning** of the creation **God made them male and female.**

7. For this cause shall a man leave his father and mother, and cleave to his wife;

8. **And they twain shall be one flesh:** so then they are no more twain, but one flesh.

9. What therefore God hath joined together, let not man put asunder.

10. And in the house his disciples asked him again of the same *matter*.

11. And he saith unto them, **Whosoever shall put away his wife, and marry another, committeth adultery** against her.

12. And if a woman shall put away her husband, and be married to another, she committeth adultery.

13. And they brought young children to him, that he should touch them: **and *his* disciples rebuked those that brought *them*.**

14. **But** when **Jesus** saw *it*, he was much displeased, and **said** unto them, **Suffer the little children to come unto me,** and forbid them not: **for of such is the kingdom** of God.

15. Verily I say unto you, **Whosoever shall not receive the kingdom** of God **as a little child, he shall not enter** therein.

16. **And he** took them up in his arms, put *his* hands upon them, and **blessed them.**

17. And when he was gone forth into the way, **there came one** running, and kneeled to him, **and asked him,** Good Master, **what shall I do that I may inherit eternal life?**

18. **And Jesus said** unto him, Why callest thou me good? *there is* none good but one, *that is,* God.

19. Thou knowest the commandments, **Do not commit adultery,** Do not **kill,** Do not **steal,** Do not **bear false witness, Defraud** not, **Honour thy father and mother.**

20. **And he** answered and **said** unto him, **Master, all these have I observed** from my youth.

21. **Then Jesus** beholding him loved him, and **said** unto him, **One thing thou lackest:** go thy way, **sell whatsoever thou hast, and give to the poor,** and thou shalt have treasure in heaven: and come, take up the cross, **and follow me.**

22. **And he was sad** at that saying, and went away grieved: **for he had great possessions.**

23. **And Jesus** looked round about, and **saith** unto his disciples, How hardly shall they that have riches enter into the kingdom of God!

24. And the disciples were astonished at his words. But Jesus answereth again, and saith unto them, Children, **how hard is it for them that trust in riches to enter into the kingdom of God!**

25. It is easier for a camel to go through the eye of a needle, than for a rich man to enter into the kingdom of God.

26. **And they were astonished** out of measure, **saying** among themselves, **Who then can be saved?**

27. **And Jesus** looking upon them **saith, With men *it is* impossible, but** not with God: for **with God all things are possible.**

28. **Then Peter** began to **say** unto him, Lo, **we have left all, and have followed thee.**

29. **And Jesus answered** and said, Verily I say unto you, **There is no man that hath left house, or brethren,**

or sisters, or father, or mother,
or wife, or children,
or lands, for my sake,
and the gospel's,
30. But he shall receive an
hundredfold now in this
time, houses, and brethren, and
sisters, and mothers,
and children, and lands,
with persecutions; and in
the world to come
eternal life.
31. But many *that are* first shall be
last; and the last first.
32. And they were
in the way going up
to Jerusalem; and Jesus went
before them: and they were amazed;
and as they followed, they were
afraid. And
he took again the twelve, and
began to tell them what
things should happen
unto him,
33. *Saying*, Behold, we go up to
Jerusalem; and
the Son of man shall be
delivered unto the chief
priests, and unto the
scribes; and they shall
condemn him to death,
and shall deliver him to the Gentiles:
34. And they shall mock him, and shall
scourge him, and shall spit upon him,
and shall kill him:
and the third day he shall
rise again.
35. And James and John,
the sons of Zebedee,
come unto him,
saying, Master,
we would that thou shouldest
do for us whatsoever we
shall desire.
36. And he said unto them,
What would ye that I
should do for you?
37. They said unto him,
Grant unto us
that we may sit, one
on thy right hand,
and the other on thy
left hand, in thy glory.

38. But Jesus said unto them,
Ye know not what ye ask:
can ye drink of the cup that
I drink of? and be baptized with
the baptism that I am baptized with?
39. And they said unto him,
We can.
And Jesus said unto them,
Ye shall indeed drink of the
cup that I drink of; and with the
baptism that I am baptized withal shall
ye be baptized:
40. But to sit on my right hand
and on my
left hand is not mine to
give; but *it shall be given*
to them for whom
it is prepared.
41. And when
the ten heard *it*, they
began to be much
displeased with
James and John.
42. But Jesus
called them *to him*, and
saith unto them, Ye know that they
which are accounted to rule over the
Gentiles exercise lordship over them;
and their great ones exercise
authority upon them.
43. But so shall it not be
among you: but
whosoever will be great
among you, shall be
your minister:
44. And whosoever of you will be
the chiefest, shall be
servant of all.
45. For even the Son of man
came not to be ministered unto, but
to minister, and to give his
life a ransom for many.
46. And they came to
Jericho: and as he went out of
Jericho with his disciples and a great
number of people,
blind Bartimaeus,
the son of Timaeus,
sat by the highway
side begging.
47. And when he heard that it was
Jesus of Nazareth,
he began to cry out, and say,

Jesus, *thou* son of David, **have mercy on me.** 48. And many charged him that he should hold his peace: but he cried the more a great deal, *Thou* son of David, have mercy on me. 49. **And Jesus** stood still, and **commanded him to be called.** And they call the blind man, saying unto him, Be of good comfort, rise; he calleth thee. 50. **And he,** casting away his garment, rose, and **came to Jesus.** 51. **And Jesus** answered and **said** unto him, **What wilt thou that I should do** unto thee? **The blind man said** unto him, **Lord, that I might receive my sight.** 52. **And Jesus said** unto him, Go thy way; **thy faith hath made thee whole. And immediately he received his sight,** and followed Jesus in the way.

CHAPTER 11

1. **And when they came nigh to** Jerusalem, unto Bethphage and Bethany, at **the mount of Olives, he sendeth** forth **two** of his **disciples,** 2. **And saith** unto them, **Go** your way **into the village** over against you: **and** as soon as ye be entered into it, **ye shall find a colt tied,** whereon never man sat; **loose him, and bring** *him.* 3. And if any man say unto you, Why do ye this? say ye that the Lord hath need of him; and straightway he will send him hither. 4. **And they** went their way, and **found the colt** tied by the door without in a place where two ways met; **and they loose him.**

5. **And certain** of them **that stood there said** unto them, **What do ye,** loosing the colt? 6. **And they said** unto them **even as Jesus** had **commanded:** and they let them go. 7. **And they brought the colt to Jesus,** and cast their garments on him; **and he sat upon him.** 8. **And many spread their garments** in the way: **and** others cut down **branches off the trees,** and strawed *them* **in the way.** 9. **And they** that went before, and they that followed, **cried,** saying, **Hosanna; Blessed** *is* **he that cometh in the name of the Lord:** 10. Blessed *be* the kingdom of our father David, that cometh in the name of the Lord: Hosanna in the highest. 11. **And Jesus entered** into Jerusalem, and **into the temple: and** when he had **looked round** about upon all things, **and** now the eventide was come, he **went** out **unto Bethany** with the twelve. 12. **And on the morrow,** when they were come from Bethany, **he was hungry:** 13. **And seeing a fig tree** afar off having leaves, **he came,** if haply he might find any thing thereon: **and** when he came to it, he **found nothing but leaves;** for the time of figs was not *yet.* 14. **And Jesus** answered and **said unto it, No man eat fruit of thee hereafter** for ever. And his disciples heard *it.* 15. **And they come to Jerusalem: and Jesus** went into the temple, and

■ **began to cast out them that**
■ **sold and bought in the**
■ **temple,** and overthrew the tables of
the moneychangers, and the seats of
them that sold doves;
16. And would not suffer that any man
should carry *any* vessel
through the temple.
■ 17. **And he taught, saying**
unto them, Is it not written,
■ **My house shall be called**
of all nations
■ **the house of prayer? but ye**
■ **have made it a den**
■ **of thieves.**
■ 18. **And the scribes and**
■ **chief priests** heard *it,* and
■ **sought how they might**
■ **destroy him: for they**
■ **feared him,** because all the
people were astonished
at his doctrine.
19. And when even was come, he
went out of the city.
■ 20. **And in the morning,**
as they passed by,
■ **they saw the fig tree dried**
■ **up** from the roots.
■ 21. **And Peter**
calling to remembrance
■ **saith** unto him,
■ **Master,** behold,
■ **the fig tree which thou**
■ **cursedst is withered** away.
■ 22. **And Jesus** answering
■ **saith** unto them,
■ **Have faith in God.**
■ 23. **For** verily I say unto you, That
■ **whosoever shall say unto**
■ **this mountain,**
Be thou removed, and
■ **be thou cast into the sea;**
■ **and shall not doubt** in his
heart, but shall believe that those
things which he saith shall come to
pass; he
■ **shall have whatsoever**
■ **he saith.**
■ 24. **Therefore I say** unto you,
■ **What things soever ye**
■ **desire, when ye pray,**
■ **believe** that ye receive *them,*
■ **and ye shall have *them.***

■ 25. **And when** ye stand
■ **praying, forgive,** if ye have
aught against any: that your Father
also which is in heaven may forgive
you your trespasses.
■ 26. **But if ye do not forgive,**
■ **neither will your Father**
which is in heaven
■ **forgive** your trespasses.
■ 27. **And they come again to**
■ **Jerusalem: and**
as he was walking in the temple,
■ **there come** to him
■ **the chief priests, and the**
■ **scribes, and the elders,**
■ 28. **And say** unto him,
■ **By what authority doest**
■ **thou these things?** and who
gave thee this authority
to do these things?
■ 29. **And Jesus answered**
and said unto them,
■ **I will also ask of you one**
■ **question,** and answer me, and I
will tell you by what authority I do
these things.
■ 30. **The baptism of John,**
■ **was** *it* **from heaven, or of**
■ **men?** answer me.
■ 31. **And they reasoned** with
themselves, saying,
■ **If we shall say, From**
■ **heaven; he will say, Why**
■ **then did ye not**
■ **believe him?**
■ 32. **But if we shall say, Of**
■ **men; they feared** the people:
■ **for all** *men* **counted John,**
that he was
■ **a prophet** indeed.
■ 33. **And they answered**
and said unto Jesus,
■ **We cannot tell. And Jesus**
■ **answering** saith unto them,
■ **Neither do I tell you by what**
■ **authority I do these things.**

CHAPTER 12
■ 1. **And he began to speak**
unto them
■ **by parables. A** *certain*
■ **man planted a vineyard,**
and set an hedge about *it,*

■ and digged *a* place *for* the
■ winevat and built a tower,
■ and let it out
■ to husbandmen,
and went into a far country.
■ 2. And at the season
■ he sent to the husbandmen
■ a servant, that he might
■ receive from the husbandmen of
■ the fruit of the vineyard.
■ 3. And they caught *him,* and
■ beat him, and sent *him*
■ away empty.
■ 4. And again he sent unto them
■ another servant; and at him
■ they cast stones, and
■ wounded *him* in the head,
and sent *him* away
shamefully handled.
■ 5. And again he sent
■ another; and him they
■ killed, and many others;
■ beating some, and
■ killing some.
■ 6. Having yet therefore
■ one son, his wellbeloved,
■ he sent him also last unto them,
■ saying, They will
■ reverence my son.
■ 7. But those husbandmen
■ said among themselves,
This is the heir; come,
■ let us kill him, and the
■ inheritance shall be our's.
■ 8. And they took him, and
■ killed *him,* and cast *him*
out of the vineyard.
■ 9. What shall therefore the
■ lord of the vineyard do? he
■ will come and
■ destroy the husbandmen,
■ and will give the vineyard
■ unto others.
10. And have ye not read this
scripture; The stone which the
builders rejected is become the head
of the corner:
11. This was the Lord's doing, and it is
marvellous in our eyes?
■ 12. And they sought to lay
■ hold on him,
but feared the people:
■ for they knew that he had

■ spoken the parable
■ against them:
and they left him, and went their way.
■ 13. And they send
unto him certain of the
■ Pharisees and of the Herodians,
■ to catch him in *his* words.
■ 14. And when they were come,
■ they say unto him,
■ Master, we know that thou
■ art true, and carest for no man: for
thou regardest not the person of men,
but teachest the way of God in truth:
■ Is it lawful to give tribute to
■ Caesar, or not?
15. Shall we give, or shall we not give?
■ But he, knowing their
■ hypocrisy, said unto them,
■ Why tempt ye me? bring me
■ a penny, that I may see *it.*
■ 16. And they brought *it.* And
■ he saith unto them,
■ whose *is* this image and
■ superscription? And they
■ said unto him,
■ Caesar's.
■ 17. And Jesus answering
■ said unto them,
■ Render to Caesar the
■ things that are Caesar's,
■ and to God the things that
■ are God's.
And they marvelled at him.
■ 18. Then come unto him
■ the Sadducees,
which say there is no resurrection;
■ and they asked him, saying,
■ 19. Master, Moses wrote
unto us,
■ If a man's brother die, and
■ leave *his*
■ wife *behind him,*
■ and leave
■ no children, that his
■ brother should take his
■ wife, and raise up seed
unto his brother.
■ 20. Now there were seven
■ brethren: and the first took a wife,
and dying left no seed.
21. And the second took her, and
died, neither left he any seed: and the
third likewise.

22. **And the seven had her, and left no seed:** last of all the woman died also.
23. **In the resurrection** therefore, when they shall rise, **whose wife shall she be** of them? for the seven had her to wife.
24. **And Jesus answering** said unto them, Do ye not therefore err, because ye know not the scriptures, neither the power of God?
25. For **when they shall rise** from the dead, **they neither marry, nor are given in marriage; but are as the angels** which are in heaven.
26. **And as touching the dead,** that they rise: **have ye not read** in the book of Moses, how in the bush God spake unto him, saying, I *am* the God of Abraham, and the God of Isaac, and the God of Jacob?
27. **He is not the God of the dead, but** the God **of the living:** ye therefore do greatly err.
28. **And one of the scribes** came, and having heard them reasoning together, and perceiving that he had answered them well, **asked him, Which is the first commandment** of all?
29. **And Jesus answered** him, The first of all the commandments *is*, Hear, O Israel; **The Lord our God is one Lord:**
30. **And thou shalt love the Lord thy God with all thy heart,** and with all thy **soul,** and with all thy **mind, and** with all thy **strength:** this *is* the first commandment.
31. **And the second *is*** like, *namely* this, **Thou shalt love thy neighbour as thyself.** There is none other commandment greater than these.

32. **And the scribe said** unto him, Well, Master, **thou hast said the truth: for there is one God;** and there is none other but he:
33. **And to love him** with all the heart, and with all the understanding, and with all the soul, and with all the strength, **and to love *his* neighbour** as himself, **is more than all whole burnt offerings** and sacrifices.
34. And when **Jesus** saw that he answered discreetly, he **said** unto him, **Thou art not far from the kingdom** of God. And no man after that durst ask him *any question.*
35. **And Jesus** answered and **said,** while he taught in the temple, **How say the scribes that Christ is the son of David?**
36. **For David** himself **said** by the Holy Ghost, **The LORD said to my Lord, Sit thou on my right hand,** till I make thine enemies thy footstool.
37. **David** therefore himself **calleth him Lord; and whence is he** *then* **his son?** And the common people heard him gladly.
38. **And he said** unto them in his doctrine, **Beware of the scribes, which love** to go in long **clothing, and** *love* **salutations** in the marketplaces,
39. **And the chief seats** in the synagogues, **and the uppermost rooms at feasts:**
40. **Which devour widows' houses, and** for a pretence **make long prayers: these shall receive greater damnation.**
41. **And Jesus sat** over against the treasury, **and beheld how the people cast money into the**

- **treasury:** and many that were rich cast in much.
42. And there came
- **a certain poor widow,** and she
- **threw in two mites,** which make a farthing.
- 43. **And he** called *unto him* his disciples, and
- **saith** unto them, Verily I say unto you, That
- **this poor widow hath cast**
- **more in, than all** they which have cast into the treasury:
- 44. **For all** *they* **did cast in of**
- **their abundance; but she** of her want did
- **cast in all that she had,** *even* all her living.

CHAPTER 13
- 1. **And** as he went out of the temple,
- **one of his disciples saith** unto him,
- **Master, see what manner**
- **of** stones and what
- **buildings** *are here!*
- 2. **And Jesus answering**
- **said** unto him,
- **Seest thou these great**
- **buildings? there shall not**
- **be left one stone upon**
- **another,** that shall not be thrown down.
3. And as he sat upon the mount of Olives over against the temple,
- **Peter and James and John**
- **and Andrew asked him** privately,
- 4. **Tell us, when shall these**
- **things be?** and what *shall be* the sign when all these things shall be fulfilled?
- 5. **And Jesus** answering them
- **began to say,** Take heed lest any *man* deceive you:
- 6. **For many shall come in**
- **my name,** saying, I am *Christ;*
- **and shall deceive many.**
- 7. **And when ye shall hear of**
- **wars** and rumours of wars,
- **be ye not troubled: for** *such* things must needs be; but

- **the end** *shall* **not** *be* **yet.**
- 8. **For nation shall rise**
- **against nation,** and kingdom against kingdom:
- **and there shall be**
- **earthquakes** in divers places,
- **and** there shall be
- **famines** and troubles:
- **these** *are* **the beginnings**
- **of sorrows.**
- 9. **But take heed** to yourselves:
- **for they shall deliver you**
- **up to councils;** and in the synagogues ye shall be beaten: and ye shall be brought before rulers and kings
- **for my sake,** for a testimony against them.
- 10. **And the gospel must first**
- **be published among**
- **all nations.**
- 11. **But** when they shall lead *you,* and deliver you up,
- **take no thought** beforehand
- **what ye shall speak,** neither do ye premeditate: but whatsoever shall be given you in that hour, that speak ye:
- **for it is not ye that speak,**
- **but the Holy Ghost.**
- 12. **Now the brother shall**
- **betray the brother** to death, and the father the son;
- **and children** shall rise up against
- **their** **parents, and shall**
- **cause them to be**
- **put to death.**
- 13. **And ye shall be hated** of all *men*
- **for my name's sake: but he**
- **that shall endure** unto the end, the same
- **shall be saved.**
- 14. **But when ye shall see the**
- **abomination of**
- **desolation,** spoken of by Daniel the prophet, standing where it ought not, (let him that readeth understand,)
- **then** let them that be in Judaea
- **flee to the mountains:**
- 15. **And let him that is on the**
- **housetop not go down** into the house, neither enter *therein,* to

take any thing out of his house:

■ 16. **And let him that is in the**
■ **field not turn back again**
■ **for** to take up
■ **his garment.**
■ 17. **But woe to them** that are
■ **with child,** and to them that give
suck in those days!
■ 18. **And pray** ye that
■ **your flight be not**
■ **in the winter.**
■ 19. **For** *in* **those days shall**
■ **be affliction,** such as was not
from the beginning of the creation
which God created unto this time,
neither shall be.
■ 20. **And except that the Lord**
■ **had shortened those days,**
■ **no flesh should be saved:**
but for the elect's sake, whom he hath
chosen, he hath shortened the days.
21. And then
■ **if any man** shall
■ **say** to you, Lo,
■ **here** *is* **Christ;** or, lo, *he is* there;
■ **believe** *him* **not:**
■ 22. **For false Christs**
and false prophets
■ **shall rise,** and shall shew signs
and wonders,
■ **to seduce, if** *it were*
■ **possible, even the elect.**
23. But take ye heed: behold,
■ **I have foretold you**
■ **all things.**
■ 24. **But** in those days,
■ **after that tribulation, the**
■ **sun shall be darkened,** and
the moon shall not give her light,
■ 25. **And the stars** of heaven
■ **shall fall, and the**
powers that are in
■ **heaven** shall be
■ **shaken.**
■ 26. **And then shall they see**
■ **the Son of man coming** in the
clouds with great power and glory.
■ 27. **And** then shall he send
■ **his angels,** and
■ **shall gather** together
■ **his elect** from the four winds, from
the uttermost part of the earth to the
uttermost part of heaven.

■ 28. **Now learn a parable of**
■ **the fig tree; When her**
■ **branch** is yet tender, and
■ **putteth forth leaves,**
ye know that
■ **summer is near:**
■ 29. **So ye in like manner,**
■ **when ye shall see these**
■ **things** come to pass,
■ **know that it is nigh,**
even at the doors.
■ 30. **Verily I say** unto you, that
■ **this generation shall not**
■ **pass, till all these**
■ **things be done.**
■ 31. **Heaven and earth shall**
■ **pass away: but my words**
■ **shall not** pass away.
■ 32. **But of that day and** *that*
■ **hour knoweth no man,** no, not
the angels which are in heaven,
■ **neither the Son,**
■ **but the Father.**
33. Take ye heed, watch and pray: for
ye know not when the time is.
■ 34. *For the Son of Man is* as
■ **a man taking a far journey,**
■ **who** left his house, and
■ **gave** authority to his servants, and
■ **to every man his work,** and
commanded the porter to watch.
■ 35. **Watch ye therefore: for**
■ **ye know not when the**
■ **master** of the house
■ **cometh,** at even, or at midnight, or
at the cockcrowing, or in the morning:
■ 36. **Lest coming suddenly he**
■ **find you sleeping.**
37. And what I say unto you I say unto
all, Watch.

CHAPTER 14
■ 1. **After two days was**
the feast of
■ **the passover,**
and of unleavened bread:
■ **and the chief priests and**
■ **the scribes sought how**
■ **they might** take him by craft, and
■ **put** *him* **to death.**
2. But they said, Not on the feast *day,*
lest there be an uproar of the people.
■ 3. **And being in Bethany**

in the house of Simon the leper,
as he sat at meat,
there came a woman
having an alabaster box of
ointment of spikenard very
precious; and she brake the box,
and poured *it* on his head.
4. And there were
some that had indignation
within themselves, and
said, Why was this waste of
the ointment made?
5. For it might have
been sold
for more than three hundred pence,
and have been
given to the poor.
And they murmured against her.
6. And Jesus said,
Let her alone; why trouble ye her?
she hath wrought a good
work on me.
7. For ye have the poor
with you
always, and whensoever ye will ye
may do them good:
but me ye have not always.
8. She hath done what she could:
she is come aforehand
to anoint my body
to the burying.
9. Verily I say unto you,
Wheresoever this gospel
shall be preached throughout
the whole world,
this also that she hath done
shall be spoken of for a
memorial of her.
10. And Judas Iscariot,
one of the twelve,
went unto the chief priests,
to betray him unto them.
11. And when they heard *it,*
they were glad, and
promised to give
him money. And he sought how
he might conveniently betray him.
12. And the first day of unleavened
bread, when they killed
the passover, his
disciples said unto him,
Where wilt thou that we
go and

prepare that thou mayest eat
the passover?
13. And he sendeth forth two
of his disciples, and saith
unto them,
Go ye into the city, and there shall
meet you
a man bearing
a pitcher of water:
follow him.
14. And wheresoever he shall go in,
say ye to the goodman of the house,
The Master saith,
Where is the
guestchamber, where I
shall eat the passover with
my disciples?
15. And he will shew you a
large upper room
furnished *and* prepared:
there make ready for us.
16. And his disciples went forth, and
came into the city, and found as he
had said unto them: and they made
ready the passover.
17. And in the evening
he cometh with the twelve.
18. And as
they sat and did eat, Jesus
said, Verily I say unto you,
One of you which eateth with me
shall betray me.
19. And they began
to be sorrowful, and
to say
unto him one by one,
Is it I? and another *said, Is* it I?
20. And he answered
and said unto them,
It is one of the twelve,
that dippeth with me
in the dish.
21. The Son of man indeed goeth,
as it is written of him: but
woe to that man by whom the
Son of man is betrayed!
good were it for that man
if he had never been born.
22. And as they did eat,
Jesus took bread, and
blessed, and brake *it,*
and gave to them,
and said, Take, eat:

this is my body.
23. And he took the cup, and when he had given thanks, he gave *it* to them: and they all drank of it.
24. And he said unto them, This is my blood of the new testament, which is shed for many.
25. Verily I say unto you, I will drink no more of the fruit of the vine, until that day that I drink it new in the kingdom of God.
26. And when they had sung an hymn, they went out into the mount of Olives.
27. And Jesus saith unto them, All ye shall be offended because of me this night: for it is written, I will smite the shepherd, and the sheep shall be scattered.
28. But after that I am risen, I will go before you into Galilee.
29. But Peter said unto him, Although all shall be offended, yet *will* not I.
30. And Jesus saith unto him, Verily I say unto thee, That this day, *even* in this night, before the cock crow twice, thou shalt deny me thrice.
31. But he spake the more vehemently, If I should die with thee, I will not deny thee in any wise. Likewise also said they all.
32. And they came to a place which was named Gethsemane: and he saith to his disciples, Sit ye here, while I shall pray.
33. And he taketh with him Peter and James and John, and began to be sore amazed, and to be very heavy;
34. And saith unto them, My soul is exceeding sorrowful unto death: tarry ye here, and watch.
35. And he went forward a little, and fell on the ground, and prayed that, if it were possible, the hour might pass from him.
36. And he said, Abba, Father, all things *are* possible unto thee; take away this cup from me: nevertheless not what I will, but what thou wilt.
37. And he cometh, and findeth them sleeping, and saith unto Peter, Simon, sleepest thou? couldest not thou watch one hour?
38. Watch ye and pray, lest ye enter into temptation. The spirit truly *is* ready, but the flesh *is* weak.
39. And again he went away, and prayed, and spake the same words.
40. And when he returned, he found them asleep again, (for their eyes were heavy,) neither wist they what to answer him.
41. And he cometh the third time, and saith unto them, Sleep on now, and take *your* rest: it is enough, the hour is come; behold, the Son of man is betrayed into the hands of sinners.
42. Rise up, let us go; lo, he that betrayeth me is at hand.
43. And immediately, while he yet spake, cometh Judas, one of the twelve, and with him a great multitude with swords and staves, from the chief priests and the scribes and the elders.
44. And he that betrayed him had given them a token, saying, Whomsoever I shall kiss, that same is he; take him, and lead *him* away safely.
45. And as soon as he was come, he goeth straightway to him, and

saith, Master, master; and
- **kissed him.**
- 46. **And they**
laid their hands on him, and
- **took him.**
- 47. **And one** of them that stood by
- **drew a sword, and smote a**
- **servant of the high priest,**
- **and cut off his ear.**
- 48. **And Jesus** answered and
- **said** unto them,
- **Are ye come out, as**
- **against a thief,**
with swords and *with* staves
- **to take me?**
- 49. **I was daily** with you
- **in the temple teaching,**
and ye took me not:
- **but the scriptures**
- **must be fulfilled.**
- 50. **And they all** forsook him, and
- **fled.**
51. And there followed him a certain
young man, having a linen cloth cast
about *his* naked *body;* and the young
men laid hold on him:
52. And he left the linen cloth, and fled
from them naked.
- 53. **And they led Jesus**
- **away to the high priest:** and
with him were assembled all the chief
priests and the elders
and the scribes.
- 54. **And Peter followed him**
- **afar off,** even into the palace of the
high priest:
- **and he sat with the**
- **servants, and warmed**
- **himself at the fire.**
- 55. **And the chief priests** and
all the council
- **sought for witness against**
- **Jesus** to put him to death;
- **and found none.**
- 56. **For many bare false**
- **witness** against him,
- **but their witness agreed**
- **not** together.
- 57. **And there arose certain,**
and bare false witness against him,
- **saying,**
- 58. **We heard him say, I will**
- **destroy this temple** that is

made with hands,
- **and within three days I will**
- **build another made**
- **without hands.**
59. But neither so did their witness
agree together.
- 60. **And the high priest**
stood up in the midst, and
- **asked Jesus,** saying,
- **Answerest thou nothing?**
what *is it which* these
witness against thee?
- 61. **But he held his peace,**
and answered nothing.
- **Again the high priest asked**
- **him,** and said unto him,
- **Art thou the Christ,**
the Son of the Blessed?
- 62. **And Jesus said, I am:**
- **and ye shall see the Son of**
- **man sitting on the right**
- **hand of power, and**
- **coming in the clouds**
of heaven.
- 63. **Then the high priest rent**
- **his clothes, and saith,** What
need we any further witnesses?
- 64. **Ye have heard the**
- **blasphemy:** what think ye?
- **And they all condemned**
- **him to** be guilty of
- **death.**
- 65. **And some began** to spit on
him, and to cover his face, and
- **to buffet him,** and to say unto
him, Prophesy:
- **and** the servants did
- **strike him**
with the palms of their hands.
- 66. **And** as Peter was beneath in the
palace, there cometh
- **one of the maids of**
- **the high priest:**
67. And when she
- **saw Peter warming himself,**
she looked upon him,
- **and said,** And
- **thou** also
- **wast with Jesus** of Nazareth.
- 68. **But he denied,** saying, I know
not, neither understand I what thou
sayest. And he went out
into the porch;

and the cock crew.

69. **And a maid saw him again,** and began to say to them that stood by,

This is *one* of them.

70. **And he denied it again.** And a little after, **they that stood by said again** to Peter, **Surely thou art *one* of them:** for thou art a Galilaean, and thy speech agreeth *thereto.*

71. **But he began to curse** and to swear, *saying,* **I know not this man** of whom ye speak.

72. **And the second time the cock crew. And Peter called to mind the word that Jesus said** unto him, Before the cock crow twice, thou shalt deny me thrice.

And when he thought thereon, **he wept.**

CHAPTER 15

1. **And** straightway in the morning **the chief priests** held a consultation with the elders and scribes **and the whole council, and bound Jesus,** and carried *him* away, **and delivered *him* to Pilate.**

2. **And Pilate asked** him, **Art thou the King of the Jews? And** he answering **said** unto him, **Thou sayest *it.***

3. **And the chief priests accused him of many things:** but he answered nothing.

4. And Pilate asked him again, saying, Answerest thou nothing? behold how many things they witness against thee.

5. **But Jesus** yet **answered nothing; so that Pilate marvelled.**

6. **Now at *that* feast he released** unto them

one prisoner, whomsoever they desired.

7. **And there was *one* named Barabbas,** *which lay* bound with them that had made insurrection with him, **who had committed murder** in the insurrection.

8. And the multitude crying aloud began to desire *him to do* as he had ever done unto them.

9. But **Pilate answered** them, saying, **Will ye that I release** unto you **the King of the Jews?**

10. For he knew that the chief priests had delivered him for envy.

11. **But the chief priests moved the people, that he should** rather **release Barabbas** unto them.

12. **And Pilate answered and** said again unto them, **What will ye then that I** shall **do *unto*** him whom ye call **the King of the Jews?**

13. **And they cried** out again, **Crucify him.**

14. **Then Pilate said** unto them, **Why, what evil hath he done? And they cried out** the more exceedingly, **Crucify him.**

15. **And *so*** Pilate, willing to content the people, **released Barabbas** unto them, **and delivered Jesus,** when he had scourged *him,* to be crucified.

16. **And the soldiers led him** away **into the hall, called Praetorium;** and they call together the whole band.

17. **And they clothed him with purple, and platted a crown of thorns,** and put it **about his *head,***

18. And began to salute him, Hail, King of the Jews!

19. And they smote him on the head with a reed, and did spit upon him, and bowing *their* knees worshipped him.

20. **And when they had mocked him, they** took off the purple from him, and put his own clothes on him, and **led him out to crucify him.**

21. **And they compel one Simon a Cyrenian,** who passed by, coming out of the country, the father of Alexander and Rufus, **to bear his cross.**

22. **And they bring him unto** the place **Golgotha,** which is, being interpreted, The place of a skull.

23. **And they gave him** to drink **wine mingled with myrrh: but he received** *it* **not.**

24. **And when they had crucified him, they parted his garments, casting lots** upon them, what every man should take.

25. **And** it was the third hour, and **they crucified him.**

26. **And the superscription** of his accusation **was** written over, **THE KING OF THE JEWS.**

27. **And with him they crucify two thieves;** the one on his right hand, and the other on his left.

28. **And the scripture was fulfilled, which saith, And he was numbered with the transgressors.**

29. **And they that passed by railed on him,** wagging their heads, and **saying,** Ah, thou that destroyest the temple, and buildest *it* in three days,

30. **Save thyself, and come down from the cross.**

31. **Likewise also the chief priests mocking said** among themselves with the scribes, **He saved others; himself he cannot save.**

32. Let Christ the King of Israel descend now from the cross, that we may see and believe. And they that were crucified with him reviled him.

33. And when **the sixth hour** was come, **there was darkness over the whole land until the ninth hour.**

34. **And at the ninth hour Jesus cried** with a loud voice, saying, Eloi, Eloi, lama sabachthani? which is, being interpreted, **My God, my God, why hast thou forsaken me?**

35. And some of them that stood by, when they heard *it,* said, Behold, he calleth Elias.

36. **And one ran and filled a sponge full of vinegar,** and put *it* on a reed, **and gave him to drink, saying,** Let alone; **let us see whether Elias will** come to **take him down.**

37. **And Jesus cried with a loud voice, and gave up the ghost.**

38. **And the veil of the temple was rent in twain** from the top to the bottom.

39. **And when the centurion,** which stood over against him, **saw that he** so **cried** out, and gave up the ghost, **he said, Truly this man was the Son of God.**

40. **There were also women looking on afar off:** among whom was **Mary Magdalene,** and **Mary the mother of James** the less and of **Joses, and Salome;**

41. **(Who** also, when he was in Galilee, **followed him, and ministered unto him;)** and many other women which came up with him unto Jerusalem.

42. And now when the even was come, because it was the preparation, that is, the day before the sabbath,

43. **Joseph** of Arimathaea, **an honourable counsellor,** which also waited for the kingdom of God, came, and

went in boldly
unto Pilate, and craved the body of Jesus.
44. **And Pilate** marvelled if he were already dead: and calling *unto him* the centurion, he asked him whether he had been any while dead.
45. And when he knew *it* of the centurion, he
gave the body to Joseph.
46. **And he bought fine linen,** and took him down,
and wrapped him in the linen,
and laid him in a sepulchre which was hewn out of a rock,
and rolled a stone unto the door of the sepulchre.
47. And Mary Magdalene and Mary *the mother* of Joses beheld where he was laid.

CHAPTER 16
1. And when the sabbath was past,
Mary Magdalene, and Mary the *mother* of James, and Salome, had bought sweet spices, that they might come and anoint him.
2. And very early in the morning the first *day* of the week, they
came unto the sepulchre at the rising of the sun.
3. **And they said** among themselves,
Who shall roll us away the stone from the door of the sepulchre?
4. **And** when they looked,
they saw that the stone was rolled away: for it was very great.
5. **And entering** into the sepulchre,
they saw a young man sitting on the right side,
clothed in a long white garment; and they were affrighted.
6. **And he saith** unto them, Be not affrighted:
Ye seek Jesus of Nazareth, which was crucified:
he is risen; he is not here: behold the place where they laid him.

7. But go your way,
tell his disciples and Peter
that he goeth before you
into Galilee: there shall ye see him, as he said unto you.
8. **And they went out quickly,** and fled from the sepulchre; for they trembled and were amazed: neither said they any thing to any *man;*
for they were afraid.
9. Now when
Jesus was risen early the first *day* of the week, he
appeared first to Mary Magdalene, out of whom he had cast seven devils.
10. *And* **she** went and
told them that had been with him, as they mourned and wept.
11. **And they,** when they had heard that he was alive, and had been seen of her, and had
believed not.
12. **After that he appeared in another form unto two of them,** as they walked, and went into the country.
13. **And they** went and
told *it* unto
the residue: neither believed they them.
14. **Afterward he appeared unto the eleven** as they sat at meat,
and upbraided them with their unbelief and hardness of heart,
because they believed not them which had seen him after he was risen.
15. **And he said** unto them,
Go ye into all the world, and preach the gospel to every creature.
16. He that believeth and is baptized
shall be saved; but he that believeth not shall be damned.
17. And these
signs shall follow them that believe; In my name shall they cast out devils; they shall speak with

new tongues;
18. They shall take up serpents; and if they drink any deadly thing, it shall not hurt them; they shall lay hands on the sick, and they shall recover.

■ 19. **So then after the Lord had spoken** unto them, **he was received up** into heaven,

■ **and sat on the right hand of God.**
■ 20. **And they went forth,** and **preached every where,** the Lord working with *them,* and **confirming the word with signs** following. **Amen.**

THE GOSPEL ACCORDING TO LUKE

BACKGROUND INFORMATION

Author – Luke, physician and Gentile companion of Paul
Date Written – probably **between 60** and **80** A.D.

Number of:
Verses -   1,151
Chapters -   24
Total Words - 25,944
Scan Words - 12,707
Scan Words represent 48 % of Total Words.

Theme – written to reveal that Jesus is **The Son of God** in a way that would appeal **to the Gentile world.**

OUTLINE OF THE GOSPEL

I. **Christ's birth narratives** and early years.
Chapters 1—2

II. **Christ's preparation for his ministry.**
Chapters 3—4

III. **Christ's Galilaean ministry** including sermon at Nazareth.
Chapters 4—9

IV. **Christ's journey to Jerusalem** including resurrection of Lazarus and conversion of Zacchaeus.
Chapters 9—19

V. **Christ's crucifixion, resurrection, and ascension.**
Chapters 19—24

CHAPTER 1

■ 1. **Forasmuch as many have** taken in hand to **set forth** in order **a declaration of those things** which are most surely **believed among us,**

■ 2. **Even** as they delivered **them** unto us, **which** from the beginning **were eyewitnesses, and ministers of the word;**

■ 3. **It seemed good** to me also, having had perfect understanding of all things from the very first, **to write unto thee** in order, **most excellent Theophilus,**

■ 4. **That thou mightest know the certainty of those things, wherein thou hast been instructed.**

■ 5. **There was** in the days of Herod, the king of Judaea, **a certain priest named Zacharias,** of the course of Abia: **and his wife** *was* of the daughters of Aaron, and her name *was* **Elisabeth.**

■ 6. **And they were both righteous** before God, walking in all the commandments and ordinances of the Lord blameless.

■ 7. **And** they had no child, because that **Elisabeth was barren, and** they both were *now* **well stricken in years.**

■ 8. **And** it came to pass, that **while he executed the priest's office** before God in the order of his course,

9. According to the custom of the priest's office, **his lot was to burn incense when he went into the temple** of the Lord.

■ 10. **And the whole multitude** of the people **were praying without** at the time of incense.

■ 11. **And there appeared** unto him **an angel** of the Lord standing on the right side of the altar of incense.

■ 12. **And when Zacharias saw** *him,* he was troubled, and **fear fell upon him.**

■ 13. **But the angel said** unto him, **Fear not,** Zacharias: for thy prayer is heard; and **thy wife Elisabeth shall bear thee a son, and thou shalt call his name John.**

■ 14. **And** thou shalt have joy and gladness; and **many shall rejoice at his birth.**

■ 15. **For he shall be great** in the sight of the Lord, and shall drink neither wine nor strong drink; **and** he shall be **filled with the Holy Ghost,** even from his mother's womb.

■ 16. **And many** of the children of Israel **shall he turn to the Lord** their God.

■ 17. **And he shall go before him in the spirit and power of Elias,** to turn the hearts of the fathers to the children, and the disobedient to the wisdom of the just; **to make ready a people prepared for the Lord.**

■ 18. **And Zacharias said** unto the angel, **Whereby shall I know this?** for I am an old man, and my wife well stricken in years.

■ 19. **And the angel** answering **said** unto him, **I am Gabriel,** that stand in the presence of God; **and am sent to speak** unto thee, and to shew thee **these glad tidings.**

■ 20. **And, behold, thou shalt be dumb,** and not able to speak, until the day that these things shall be performed, **because thou believest not my words,** which shall be fulfilled in their season.

■ 21. **And the people** waited for Zacharias, and **marvelled that he tarried**

■ **so long in the temple.**
■ 22. **And when he came out,**
he could not speak unto them: and
■ **they perceived that he had**
■ **seen a vision** in the temple:
■ **for he beckoned unto them,**
■ **and remained speechless.**
23. And it came to pass, that, as soon
as the days of his ministration were
accomplished, he departed to his own
house.
■ 24. **And** after those days his wife
■ **Elisabeth conceived, and**
■ **hid herself five months,**
saying,
25. Thus hath the Lord dealt with me in
the days wherein he looked on *me*, to
take away my reproach among men.
■ 26. **And in the sixth month**
the angel
■ **Gabriel was sent** from God
■ **unto** a city of Galilee, named
■ **Nazareth,**
■ 27. **To a virgin** espoused to a man
■ **whose** name was Joseph, of the
house of David; and the virgin's
■ **name** *was* **Mary.**
■ 28. **And the angel**
came in unto her, and
■ **said, Hail,** *thou that art* highly
favoured, the Lord *is* with thee:
■ **blessed** *art* **thou**
■ **among women.**
■ 29. **And** when she saw *him*,
■ **she was troubled at his**
saying, and cast in her mind what
manner of
■ **salutation** this should be.
■ 30. **And the angel said**
unto her,
■ **Fear not, Mary: for thou**
■ **hast found favour**
■ **with God.**
■ 31. **And,** behold,
■ **thou shalt conceive**
in thy womb,
■ **and bring forth a son, and**
■ **shalt call his name JESUS.**
■ 32. **He shall be** great, and shall be
■ **called the Son of the**
■ **Highest:** and the Lord God shall
give unto him the throne
of his father David:

■ 33. **And** he shall reign over the
house of Jacob for ever; and
■ **of his kingdom there shall**
■ **be no end.**
■ 34. **Then said Mary**
unto the angel,
■ **How shall this be, seeing I**
■ **know not a man?**
■ 35. **And the angel answered**
and said unto her,
■ **The Holy Ghost shall come**
■ **upon thee,** and the power of the
Highest shall overshadow thee:
■ **therefore** also
■ **that** holy thing
■ **which shall be born of thee**
■ **shall be called the Son of**
■ **God.**
■ 36. **And, behold, thy cousin**
■ **Elisabeth,** she
■ **hath also conceived**
a son in her old age: and this is the
sixth month with her,
who was called barren.
37. For with God nothing
shall be impossible.
■ 38. **And Mary said,** Behold the
handmaid of the Lord;
■ **be it unto me according to**
■ **thy word.** And the angel
departed from her.
■ 39. **And Mary arose**
in those days,
■ **and went into** the hill country
with haste, into a city of
■ **Juda;**
■ 40. **And entered** into
■ **the house of Zacharias,**
and saluted Elisabeth.
■ 41. **And** it came to pass, that,
■ **when Elisabeth heard the**
■ **salutation of Mary, the**
■ **babe leaped in her womb;**
and Elisabeth was filled
with the Holy Ghost:
■ 42. **And she spake**
out with a loud voice, and said,
■ **Blessed** *art* **thou**
■ **among women,**
and blessed *is* the fruit of thy womb.
■ 43. **And whence** *is* **this to me,**
■ **that the mother of my Lord**
■ **should come to me?**

44. For, lo, as soon as the voice of thy salutation sounded in mine ears, the babe leaped in my womb for joy.
45. And blessed *is* she that believed: for there shall be a performance of those things which were told her from the Lord.

■ 46. **And Mary said, My soul**
■ **doth magnify the Lord,**
■ 47. **And my spirit hath**
■ **rejoiced in God**
■ **my Saviour.**

48. For he hath regarded the low estate of his handmaiden: for, behold,

■ **from henceforth all**
■ **generations shall**
■ **call me blessed.**

49. For he that is mighty hath done to me great things; and holy *is* his name.

■ 50. **And his mercy *is* on them**
■ **that fear him**

from generation to generation.
51. He hath shewed strength with his arm; he hath scattered the proud in the imagination of their hearts.

■ 52. **He hath** put down the mighty

from *their* seats, and

■ **exalted them of**
■ **low degree.**

53. He hath filled the hungry with good things;

■ **and the rich he hath sent**
■ **empty away.**

54. He hath holpen his servant Israel, in remembrance of *his* mercy;
55. As he spake to our fathers, to Abraham, and to his seed for ever.

■ 56. **And Mary abode with**
■ **her about three months,**

and returned to her own house.

■ 57. **Now Elisabeth's full time**
■ **came** that she should be delivered;
■ **and she brought**
■ **forth a son.**
■ 58. **And her neighbours**

and her cousins heard how the Lord had shewed great mercy upon her; and they

■ **rejoiced with her.**

59. *And* it came to pass, that

■ **on the eighth day they**
■ **came to circumcise the**
■ **child; and they**

■ **called him Zacharias,**

after the name of his father.

■ 60. **And his mother**

answered and

■ **said, Not *so*; but he shall**
■ **be called John.**

61. And they said unto her, There is none of thy kindred that is called by this name.

■ 62. **And they made signs to**
■ **his father, how he would**
■ **have him called.**
■ 63. **And he asked for a**
■ **writing table, and wrote,**

saying,

■ **His name is John.**

And they marvelled all.

■ 64. **And his mouth was**
■ **opened** immediately, and his

tongue *loosed*,

■ **and he spake,**
■ **and praised God.**
■ 65. **And** fear came on all that dwelt

round about them: and all

■ **these sayings were noised**
■ **abroad throughout**

all the hill country of

■ **Judaea.**

66. And all they that heard *them* laid *them* up in their hearts, saying,

■ **What manner of child shall**
■ **this be!** And the hand

of the Lord was with him.

■ 67. **And** his father
■ **Zacharias** was filled with

the Holy Ghost, and

■ **prophesied, saying,**
■ 68. **Blessed *be* the Lord**

God of Israel;

■ **for he hath visited and**
■ **redeemed his people,**
■ 69. **And hath raised up an**
■ **horn of salvation** for us in the

house of his servant David;

■ 70. **As he spake by** the mouth of
■ **his holy prophets,** which have

been since the world began:

■ 71. **That we should be**
■ **saved** from our enemies, and from

the hand of all that hate us;
72. To perform the mercy *promised* to our fathers,

■ **and to remember**

■ **his holy covenant;**
73. The oath which he sware to our father Abraham,
74. That he would grant unto us,
■ **that we** being delivered out of the hand of our enemies
■ **might serve him**
■ **without fear,**
■ 75. **In holiness and**
■ **righteousness** before him,
■ **all the days of our life.**
■ 76. **And thou, child,**
shalt be called the prophet of the Highest: for thou
■ **shalt go before** the face of
■ **the Lord to prepare**
■ **his ways;**
■ 77. **To give knowledge of**
■ **salvation** unto his people
■ **by the remission of**
■ **their sins,**
78. Through the tender mercy of our God; whereby the dayspring from on high hath visited us,
■ 79. **To give light to them** that sit
■ **in darkness and**
in the shadow of death,
■ **to guide our feet**
into the way of peace.
■ 80. **And the child grew, and**
■ **waxed strong in spirit, and**
■ **was in the deserts till**
the day of
■ **his shewing unto Israel.**

CHAPTER 2
■ 1. **And** it came to pass in those days, that
■ **there went out a decree**
■ **from Caesar Augustus that**
■ **all the world should**
■ **be taxed.**
2. (*And* this taxing was first made when Cyrenius was governor of Syria.)
■ 3. **And all went to be taxed,**
every one
■ **into his own city.**
■ 4. **And Joseph also went**
up from Galilee, out of the city of Nazareth, into Judaea,
■ **unto the city of**
David, which is called

■ **Bethlehem;** (because he was of the house and lineage of David:)
■ 5. **To be taxed with Mary**
his espoused wife,
■ **being great with child.**
■ 6. **And** so it was, that,
■ **while** they were
■ **there,** the days were accomplished that
■ **she** should be delivered.
7. And she
■ **brought forth her**
■ **firstborn son,** and wrapped him in swaddling clothes,
■ **and laid him in a manger;**
because there was no room for them in the inn.
■ 8. **And there were**
in the same country
■ **shepherds** abiding in the field,
■ **keeping watch over their**
■ **flock by night.**
■ 9. **And, lo, the angel of the**
■ **Lord came upon them,** and the glory of the Lord shone round about them: and they were sore afraid.
■ 10. **And** the angel
■ **said** unto them,
Fear not: for, behold,
■ **I bring you good tidings**
■ **of great joy,**
which shall be to all people.
■ 11. **For unto you is born**
this day in the city of David
■ **a Saviour,**
which is Christ the Lord.
■ 12. **And** this *shall be* a sign unto you;
■ **Ye shall find the babe**
wrapped in swaddling clothes,
■ **lying in a manger.**
■ 13. **And suddenly**
there was with the angel a multitude of
■ **the heavenly host praising**
■ **God, and saying,**
■ 14. **Glory to God in the**
■ **highest, and on earth**
■ **peace, good**
■ **will toward men.**
■ 15. **And** it came to pass, as the angels were gone away from them into heaven,
■ **the shepherds said**

one to another,
Let us now go
even unto Bethlehem,
and see this thing
which is come to pass,
which the Lord hath made
known unto us.
16. **And they came** with haste,
and found Mary, and Joseph, and
the babe lying in a manger.
17. **And** when they had seen *it*,
they made known abroad
the saying which was
told them concerning
this child.
18. **And all they that heard** *it*
wondered at those things which
were told them by the shepherds.
19. **But Mary kept all these**
things, and pondered *them*
in her heart.
20. **And the shepherds**
returned, glorifying and
praising God for all the things
that they had heard and seen, as it
was told unto them.
21. **And when eight days**
were accomplished for the
circumcising of the child,
his name was called
JESUS, which was so named
of the angel before he was
conceived in the womb.
22. **And** when the days of her
purification according to the law of
Moses were accomplished,
they brought him to
Jerusalem, to present *him*
to the Lord;
23. (As it is written in the law of the
LORD, Every male that openeth the
womb shall be called holy to the Lord;)
24. **And to offer a sacrifice**
according to that which
is said in the law
of the Lord,
A pair of turtledoves, or
two young pigeons.
25. **And, behold, there was**
a man in Jerusalem, whose
name *was* **Simeon;** and the
same man *was* just and devout,
waiting for the consolation of Israel:

and the Holy Ghost was upon him.
26. And it was revealed unto him by
the Holy Ghost, that he should not
see death, before he had seen the
Lord's Christ.
27. **And he came by the**
Spirit into the temple: and
when the parents brought
in the child Jesus, to do for him
after the custom of the law,
28. **Then took he him up in**
his arms, and blessed
God, and said,
29. **Lord, now lettest thou thy**
servant depart in peace,
according to thy word:
30. **For mine eyes have seen**
thy salvation,
31. Which thou hast prepared before
the face of all people;
32. A light to lighten the Gentiles, and
the glory of thy people Israel.
33. **And Joseph and his**
mother marvelled at those
things which were spoken of him.
34. **And Simeon**
blessed them, and
said unto Mary his mother,
Behold, this *child* **is set for**
the fall and rising again of
many in Israel; and for a sign which
shall be spoken against;
35. (Yea, a sword shall pierce through
thy own soul also,)
that the thoughts of many
hearts may be revealed.
36. **And there was one Anna,**
a prophetess, the daughter of
Phanuel, of the tribe of Aser: she was
of a great age, and had lived with
an husband seven years from
her virginity;
37. And she *was* a widow of about
fourscore and four years,
which departed not from
the temple, but served *God*
with fastings and prayers
night and day.
38. **And she** coming in that instant
gave thanks
likewise unto the Lord,
and spake of him to all
them that looked for

redemption in Jerusalem.
39. And when they had performed all things according to the law of the Lord,
they returned into Galilee,
to their own city Nazareth.
40. And the child grew, and waxed strong in spirit, filled with wisdom: and the grace of God was upon him.
41. Now his parents went to Jerusalem every year at the feast of the passover.
42. And when he was twelve years old, they went up to Jerusalem after the custom of the feast.
43. And when they had fulfilled the days, as they returned, the child Jesus tarried behind in Jerusalem; and Joseph and his mother knew not *of it*.
44. But they, supposing him to have been in the company, went a day's journey; and they sought him among *their* kinsfolk and acquaintance.
45. And when they found him not, they turned back again to Jerusalem, seeking him.
46. And it came to pass, that after three days they found him in the temple, sitting in the midst of the doctors, both hearing them, and asking them questions.
47. And all that heard him were astonished at his understanding and answers.
48. And when they saw him, they were amazed: and his mother said unto him, Son, why hast thou thus dealt with us? behold, thy father and I have sought thee sorrowing.
49. And he said unto them, How is it that ye sought me?

wist ye not that I must be about my Father's business?
50. And they understood not the saying which he spake unto them.
51. And he went down with them, and came to Nazareth, and was subject unto them: but his mother kept all these sayings in her heart.
52. And Jesus increased in wisdom and stature, and in favour with God and man.

CHAPTER 3
1. Now in the fifteenth year of the reign of Tiberius Caesar, Pontius Pilate being governor of Judaea, and Herod being tetrarch of Galilee, and his brother Philip tetrarch of Ituraea and of the region of Trachonitis, and Lysanias the tetrarch of Abilene,
2. Annas and Caiaphas being the high priests, the word of God came unto John the son of Zacharias in the wilderness.
3. And he came into all the country about Jordan, preaching the baptism of repentance for the remission of sins;
4. As it is written in the book of the words of Esaias the prophet, saying, The voice of one crying in the wilderness, Prepare ye the way of the Lord, make his paths straight.
5. Every valley shall be filled, and every mountain and hill shall be brought low; and the crooked shall be made straight, and the rough ways *shall be* made smooth;
6. And all flesh shall see the salvation of God.
7. Then said he to the multitude that came forth to be baptized of him, O generation of vipers, who hath warned you to flee from the

wrath to come?

■ 8. **Bring forth** therefore
■ **fruits worthy of repentance,**
and begin not to say within
yourselves, We have Abraham
to *our* father:
■ **for** I say unto you, That God is able
of these stones to raise up children
unto Abraham.

9. And now also the axe is laid unto
the root of the trees:
■ **every tree therefore which**
■ **bringeth not forth good fruit**
■ **is hewn down, and cast**
■ **into the fire.**
■ 10. **And the people asked**
■ **him,** saying,
What shall we do then?
■ 11. **He answereth**
and saith unto them,
He that hath two coats,
let him
■ **impart to him that hath**
■ **none;** and he that hath meat,
let him do likewise.
■ 12. **Then came also**
■ **publicans** to be baptized,
■ **and said** unto him,
Master, what shall we do?
■ 13. **And he said** unto them,
Exact no more than that
which is appointed you.
■ 14. **And the soldiers**
■ **likewise demanded**
of him, saying, And
what shall we do? And he
■ **said** unto them,
Do violence to no man,
neither accuse *any* falsely; and be
content with your wages.
■ 15. **And as the people were**
■ **in expectation,** and all men
mused in their hearts of John,
■ **whether he were the Christ,**
■ **or not;**
■ 16. **John answered,** saying
unto *them* all, I indeed baptize
you with water; but
■ **one mightier than I cometh,**
the latchet of
■ **whose shoes I am not**
■ **worthy to unloose: he shall**
■ **baptize you with the Holy**

■ **Ghost** and with fire:
17. Whose fan *is* in his hand,
■ **and he will**
throughly purge his floor, and will
■ **gather the wheat into his**
■ **garner; but the chaff he will**
■ **burn** with fire unquenchable.
18. And many other things in his
exhortation preached
he unto the people.
■ 19. **But Herod** the tetrarch,
■ **being reproved by him for**
Herodias
■ **his brother Philip's wife,**
■ **and for** all the
■ **evils which Herod had**
■ **done,**
20. Added yet this above all, that he
■ **shut up John in prison.**
■ 21. **Now** when all the people
were baptized,
■ **it came to pass, that Jesus**
■ **also being baptized,**
and praying, the
■ **heaven** was
■ **opened,**
■ 22. **And the Holy Ghost**
■ **descended** in a bodily shape
■ **like a dove upon him, and**
■ **a voice** came from heaven, which
■ **said, Thou art my beloved**
■ **Son; in thee I am**
■ **well pleased.**
23. And Jesus himself began to be
about thirty years of age, being (as
was supposed) the son of Joseph,
which was *the son* of Heli,
24. Which was *the son* of Matthat,
which was *the son* of Levi, which was
the son of Melchi, which was *the son*
of Janna, which was *the son* of
Joseph,
25. Which was *the son* of Mattathias,
which was *the son* of Amos, which was
the son of Naum, which was *the son* of
Esli, which was *the son* of Nagge,
26. Which was *the son* of Maath,
which was *the son* of Mattathias,
which was *the son* of Semei, which
was *the son* of Joseph, which was *the*
son of Juda,
27. Which was *the son* of Joanna,
which was *the son* of Rhesa, which

was *the son* of Zorobabel, which was *the son* of Salathiel, which was *the son* of Neri,

28. Which was *the son* of Melchi, which was *the son* of Addi, which was *the son* of Cosam, which was *the son* of Elmodam, which was *the son* of Er,

29. Which was *the son* of Jose, which was *the son* of Eliezer, which was *the son* of Jorim, which was *the son* of Matthat, which was *the son* of Levi,

30. Which was *the son* of Simeon, which was *the son* of Juda, which was *the son* of Joseph, which was *the son* of Jonan, which was *the son* of Eliakim,

31. Which was *the son* of Melea, which was *the son* of Menan, which was *the son* of Mattatha, which was *the son* of Nathan, which was *the son* of David,

32. Which was *the son* of Jesse, which was *the son* of Obed, which was *the son* of Booz, which was *the son* of Salmon, which was *the son* of Naasson,

33. Which was *the son* of Aminadab, which was *the son* of Aram, which was *the son* of Esrom, which was *the son* of Phares, which was *the son* of Juda,

34. Which was *the son* of Jacob, which was *the son* of Isaac, which was *the son* of Abraham, which was *the son* of Thara, which was *the son* of Nachor,

35. Which was *the son* of Saruch, which was *the son* of Ragau, which was *the son* of Phalec, which was *the son* of Heber, which was *the son* of Sala,

36. Which was *the son* of Cainan, which was *the son* of Arphaxad, which was *the son* of Sem, which was *the son* of Noe, which was *the son* of Lamech,

37. Which was *the son* of Mathusala, which was *the son* of Enoch, which was *the son* of Jared, which was *the son* of Maleleel, which was *the son* of Cainan,

38. Which was *the son* of Enos, which was *the son* of Seth, which was *the son* of Adam, which was *the son* of God.

CHAPTER 4

1. **And Jesus** being full of the Holy Ghost returned from Jordan, and **was led by the Spirit into the wilderness,**

2. **Being forty days tempted of the devil. And** in those days he **did eat nothing: and** when they were ended, **he** afterward **hungered.**

3. **And the devil said** unto him, **If thou be the Son of God, command this stone** that it **be made bread.**

4. **And Jesus answered** him, saying, It is written, That **man shall not live by bread alone, but by every word of God.**

5. **And the devil,** taking him up into an high mountain, **shewed** unto **him all the kingdoms of the world** in a moment of time.

6. **And the devil said** unto him, **All this power will I give thee,** and the glory of them: for that is delivered unto me; and to whomsoever I will I give it.

7. **If thou therefore wilt worship me,** all shall be thine.

8. **And Jesus answered** and said unto him, **Get thee behind me, Satan: for** it is written, **Thou shalt worship the Lord thy God,** and him **only** shalt thou serve.

9. **And he brought him to Jerusalem,** and set him **on a pinnacle of the temple, and said** unto him, **If thou be the Son of God, cast thyself down** from hence:

10. **For** it is written, **He shall give his angels charge over thee,** to keep thee:

11. **And** in *their* hands **they shall bear thee up,** lest at any time thou dash thy foot

against a stone.
12. And Jesus answering said unto him, It is **said, Thou shalt not tempt the Lord thy God.** **13. And when the devil had ended all the temptation, he departed** from him for a season. **14. And Jesus returned** in the power of the Spirit **into Galilee: and there went out a fame of him** through all the region round about. 15. And he taught in their synagogues, being glorified of all. **16. And he came to Nazareth,** where he had been brought up: **and,** as his custom was, he **went into the synagogue on the sabbath day,** and stood up for to read. **17. And there was delivered** unto him **the book of the prophet Esaias.** And when he had opened the book, he found the place **where it was written,** **18. The Spirit of the Lord** *is* upon me, because he **hath anointed me to preach the gospel** to the poor; he hath sent me **to heal** the brokenhearted, to preach deliverance to the captives, **and recovering of sight to the blind, to set at liberty them that are bruised,** 19. To preach the acceptable year of the Lord. **20. And he closed the book,** and he gave *it* again to the minister, **and sat down.** And the eyes of all them that were in the synagogue were fastened on him. **21. And he began to say** unto them, **This day is this scripture fulfilled** in your ears. **22. And all bare him witness, and wondered** at the gracious words which proceeded

out of his mouth. And they said, **Is not this Joseph's son?** 23. And he said unto them, Ye will surely say unto me this proverb, Physician, heal thyself: whatsoever we have heard done in Capernaum, do also here in thy country. **24. And he said,** Verily I say unto you, **No prophet is accepted in his own country.** 25. **But** I tell you of a truth, **many widows were in Israel in the days of Elias,** when the heaven was shut up three years and six months, **when great famine was throughout all the land;** 26. **But unto none of them was Elias sent, save** unto Sarepta, *a city* of Sidon, unto **a woman** *that was* a widow. **27. And many lepers** were in Israel in the time of Eliseus the prophet; **and none of them was cleansed, saving Naaman** the Syrian. **28. And all they in the synagogue,** when they heard these things, **were filled with wrath,** 29. **And** rose up, and thrust him out of the city, and **led him unto the brow of the hill** whereon their city was built, **that they might cast him down** headlong. 30. **But he passing through the midst of them went his way,** 31. **And came** down **to** Capernaum, a city of **Galilee, and taught** them on the sabbath days. **32. And they were astonished at his doctrine:** for his word was with power. 33. **And** in the synagogue there was **a man, which had** a spirit of **an unclean devil, and cried out** with a loud voice, **34. Saying, Let** *us* **alone;**

what have we to do with thee,
thou Jesus of Nazareth? art thou come to destroy us? I know thee who thou art; the
Holy One of God.
35. **And Jesus rebuked him,** saying,
Hold thy peace, and come out of him. And when the devil had thrown him in the midst,
he came out of him, and hurt him not.
36. **And they were all amazed,** and spake among themselves,
saying, What a word *is* **this! for** with authority and power **he commandeth the unclean spirits, and they come out.**
37. And the fame of him went out into every place of the country round about.
38. **And he** arose out of the synagogue, and **entered into Simon's house. And Simon's wife's mother was taken with a great fever;** and they besought him for her.
39. **And he** stood over her, and **rebuked the fever;** and it left her:
and immediately she arose and ministered unto them.
40. **Now when the sun was setting, all they that had any sick** with divers diseases **brought them unto him; and he** laid his hands on every one of them, and **healed them.**
41. **And devils also came out of many, crying out,** and saying,
Thou art Christ the Son of God. **And he** rebuking *them* **suffered them not to speak:** for they knew that he was Christ.
42. **And** when it was day, **he departed** and went **into a desert place: and the**

people sought him, and **came unto him, and stayed him, that he should not depart** from them.
43. **And he said** unto them, **I must preach** the kingdom of God **to other cities also: for therefore am I sent.**
44. And he preached in the synagogues of Galilee.

CHAPTER 5

1. **And** it came to pass, that, **as the people pressed upon him** to hear the word of God, **he stood by the lake** of Gennesaret,
2. **And saw two ships** standing by the lake: but the fishermen were gone out of them, and were washing *their* nets.
3. **And he entered** into one of the ships, which was **Simon's, and prayed him that he would thrust out** a little from the land. **And he** sat down, and **taught the people out of the ship.**
4. **Now when he had left speaking, he said unto Simon, Launch out** into the deep, **and let down your nets** for a draught.
5. **And Simon answering** said unto him,
Master, we have toiled all the night, and have taken nothing: nevertheless at thy word I will let down the net.
6. **And** when they had this done, **they enclosed a great multitude of fishes:** and their net brake.
7. **And they beckoned** unto *their* **partners,** which were **in the other ship,** that they should come and help them. **And they** came, and **filled both the ships,** so that they began to sink.

8. **When Simon Peter saw** it, **he fell down at Jesus' knees, saying, Depart** from me; for **I am** a **sinful** man, O Lord. 9. **For he was astonished,** and all that were with him, at the draught of the fishes which they had taken: 10. **And so** was also James, and John, the sons of Zebedee, which **were partners with Simon. And Jesus said** unto Simon, **Fear not; from henceforth thou shalt catch men.** 11. **And** when they had brought their ships to land, **they forsook all, and followed him.** 12. **And** it came to pass, when he was in a certain city, behold **a man full of leprosy: who seeing Jesus** fell on *his* face, and **besought him, saying, Lord, if thou wilt,** thou canst **make me clean.** 13. **And he** put forth *his* hand, and **touched him, saying, I will: be thou clean. And** immediately **the leprosy departed** from him. 14. **And he charged him to tell no man: but go,** and shew thyself **to the priest, and offer** for thy cleansing, **according as Moses commanded, for a testimony** unto them. 15. But so much the more went there a fame abroad of him: **and great multitudes came together to hear, and to be healed by him** of their infirmities. 16. And he withdrew himself into the wilderness, and prayed. 17. And it came to pass on a certain day, as he was teaching, that there were Pharisees and doctors of the law sitting by, which were come out of every town of Galilee, and Judaea, and Jerusalem: and the power of the Lord was *present* to heal them. 18. **And, behold, men brought in a bed a man** which was taken **with a palsy: and they sought** *means* to bring him in, and to lay *him* before him. 19. And when they could not find **by what** *way* **they might bring him in because of the multitude, they went upon the housetop, and let him down through the tiling** with *his* couch into the midst **before Jesus.** 20. **And when he saw their faith, he said** unto him, **Man, thy sins are forgiven thee.** 21. **And the scribes and the Pharisees began to reason,** saying, Who is this which speaketh blasphemies? **Who can forgive sins, but God** alone? 22. **But when Jesus perceived** their thoughts, **he** answering **said** unto them, What reason ye in your hearts? 23. **Whether is easier, to say, Thy sins be forgiven thee; or** to say, **Rise up and walk?** 24. **But** that ye may **know that the Son of man hath power** upon earth **to forgive sins, (he said unto the sick of the palsy,)** I say unto thee, **Arise,** and take up thy couch, **and go into thine house.** 25. **And** immediately **he rose up** before them, and took up that whereon he lay, **and departed** to his own house, glorifying God. 26. **And they were all amazed,** and they glorified God, and were filled with fear, saying, We have seen strange things to-day.

27. **And** after these things **he went forth, and saw** a publican, named **Levi, sitting at the receipt of custom: and** he **said** unto him, **Follow me.** 28. **And he left all,** rose up, **and followed him.** 29. **And Levi made him a great feast** in his own house: **and** there was a great company of **publicans** and of others that **sat** down **with them.** 30. **But their scribes and Pharisees murmured** against his disciples, **saying, Why do ye eat** and drink **with** publicans and **sinners?** 31. **And Jesus** answering **said** unto them, They that are whole need not a physician; but they that are sick. 32. **I came not to call the righteous, but sinners to repentance.** 33. **And they said** unto him, **Why do the disciples of John fast** often, and make prayers, and likewise *the disciples* of the Pharisees; **but thine eat and drink?** 34. **And he said** unto them, **Can** ye make **the children of the bridechamber fast, while the bridegroom is with them?** 35. **But** the days will come, when **the bridegroom shall be taken away** from them, and **then shall they fast** in those days. 36. **And he spake also a parable** unto them; **No man putteth a piece of a new garment upon an old;** if otherwise, then both the new maketh a rent, and the piece that was *taken* out of

the new agreeth not with the old. 37. **And no man putteth new wine into old bottles;** else the new wine will burst the bottles, and be spilled, and the bottles shall perish. 38. But new wine must be put into new bottles; and both are preserved. 39. **No man also having drunk old** *wine* straightway **desireth new:** for he saith, The old is better.

CHAPTER 6

1. **And** it came to pass on the second sabbath after the first, that **he went through the corn fields; and his disciples plucked** the ears of **corn, and did eat,** rubbing *them* in *their* hands. 2. **And** certain of **the Pharisees said** unto them, **Why do ye that which is not lawful** to do **on the sabbath** days? 3. **And Jesus answering** them said, **Have ye not read** so much as this, **what David did,** when himself was an hungred, and they which were with him; 4. **How he went into the house of God, and did take** and eat **the shewbread,** and gave also to them that were with him; **which it is not lawful to eat but for the priests** alone? 5. And he said unto them, That **the Son of man is Lord also of the sabbath.** 6. **And** it came to pass also on another sabbath, that he entered into the synagogue and taught: and **there was a man whose right hand was withered.** 7. And the scribes and **Pharisees watched him, whether he would heal on the sabbath day;** that they might find an accusation against him.

8. **But he** knew their thoughts, and **said to the man** which had the withered hand, **Rise up,** and stand forth in the midst. And he arose and stood forth.

9. **Then said Jesus unto them,** I will ask you one thing; **Is it lawful on the sabbath days to do good, or** to do **evil?** to save life, or to destroy *it?*

10. **And** looking round about upon them all, **he said unto the man, Stretch forth thy hand.** And he did so: **and his hand was restored** whole as the other.

11. **And they** were filled with madness; and **communed** one with another **what they might do to Jesus.**

12. **And** it came to pass in those days, that **he went out into a mountain** to pray, **and continued all night in prayer to God.**

13. **And when it was day, he called** *unto him* **his disciples: and** of them he **chose twelve, whom** also **he named apostles;**

14. **Simon,** (whom he also named Peter,) **and Andrew** his brother, **James and John, Philip and Bartholomew,**

15. **Matthew and Thomas, James** the *son* of Alphaeus, **and Simon** called Zelotes,

16. **And Judas** *the brother* **of James, and Judas Iscariot, which also was the traitor.**

17. **And** he came down **with** them, and stood in the plain, and the company of **his disciples,** and **a great multitude** of people out of all Judaea and Jerusalem, and from the sea coast of Tyre and Sidon, which

came to hear him, and to be healed of their diseases;

18. And they that were vexed with unclean spirits: and they were healed.

19. **And the** whole **multitude sought to touch him: for there went virtue out of him, and healed** *them* **all.**

20. **And he** lifted up his eyes on his disciples, and **said, Blessed** *be ye* **poor: for yours is the kingdom of God.**

21. **Blessed** *are ye* **that hunger** now: **for ye shall be filled. Blessed** *are ye* **that weep** now: **for ye shall laugh.**

22. **Blessed are ye, when men** shall hate you, and when they shall separate you *from their company,* and **shall reproach** *you,* and cast out your name as evil, **for the Son of man's sake.**

23. **Rejoice** ye in that day, and leap for joy: for, behold, **your reward** *is* **great in heaven:** for in the like manner did their fathers unto the prophets.

24. **But woe unto you that are rich!** for **ye have** received **your consolation.**

25. **Woe unto you that are full!** for **ye shall hunger. Woe unto you that laugh now!** for **ye shall mourn** and weep.

26. **Woe unto you, when** all **men** shall **speak well of you! for so did their fathers to the false prophets.**

27. **But I say** unto you which hear, **Love your enemies,** do good to them which hate you,

28. **Bless** them that curse you, **and pray for them which despitefully use you.**

29. **And unto him that**

smiteth thee on the *one* cheek offer also the other; and him that taketh away thy cloak forbid not *to take* *thy* coat also.

30. Give to every man that asketh of thee; and of him that taketh away thy goods ask *them* not again.

31. And as ye would that men should do to you, do ye also to them likewise.

32. For if ye love them which love you, what thank have ye? for sinners also love those that love them.

33. And if ye do good to them which do good to you, what thank have ye? for sinners also do even the same.

34. And if ye lend *to them* of whom ye hope to receive, what thank have ye? for sinners also lend to sinners, to receive as much again.

35. But love ye your enemies, and do good, and lend, hoping for nothing again; and your reward shall be great, and ye shall be the children of the Highest: for he is kind unto the unthankful and *to* the evil.

36. Be ye therefore merciful, as your Father also is merciful.

37. Judge not, and ye shall not be judged: condemn not, and ye shall not be condemned: forgive, and ye shall be forgiven:

38. Give, and it shall be given unto you; good measure, pressed down, and shaken together, and running over, shall men give into your bosom. For with the same measure that ye mete withal it shall be measured to you again.

39. And he spake a parable unto them, Can the blind lead the blind? shall they not both fall into the ditch?

40. The disciple is not above his master: but every one that is perfect shall be as his master.

41. And why beholdest thou the mote that is in thy brother's eye, but perceivest not the beam that is in thine own eye?

42. Either how canst thou say to thy brother, Brother, let me pull out the mote that is in thine eye, when thou thyself beholdest not the beam that is in thine own eye? Thou hypocrite, cast out first the beam out of thine own eye, and then shalt thou see clearly to pull out the mote that is in thy brother's eye.

43. For a good tree bringeth not forth corrupt fruit; neither doth a corrupt tree bring forth good fruit.

44. For every tree is known by his own fruit. For of thorns men do not gather figs, nor of a bramble bush gather they grapes.

45. A good man out of the good treasure of his heart bringeth forth that which is good; and an evil man out of the evil treasure of his heart bringeth forth that which is evil: for of the abundance of the heart his mouth speaketh.

46. And why call ye me, Lord, Lord, and do not the things which I say?

47. Whosoever cometh to me, and heareth my sayings, and doeth them, I will shew you to whom he is like:

48. He is like a man which built an house, and digged deep, and laid the foundation

- on a rock: and when
- the flood arose, the stream
beat vehemently upon that house,
- and could not shake it: for it
was founded upon a rock.
- 49. But he that heareth, and
- doeth not, is like a man that
without a foundation
- built an house upon the
- earth; against which
- the stream did beat
- vehemently, and immediately
- it fell; and the ruin of that house
- was great.

CHAPTER 7
- 1. Now when he had ended all his
sayings in the audience of the people,
- he entered into
- Capernaum.
- 2. And a certain centurion's
- servant, who was dear unto him,
- was sick, and ready to die.
- 3. And when he heard of
- Jesus, he sent
unto him the elders of the Jews,
- beseeching him that he
- would come and
- heal his servant.
- 4. And when they came to
- Jesus, they besought him instantly,
saying, That he was worthy for whom
he should do this:
- 5. For he loveth our nation, and he
hath built us a synagogue.
- 6. Then Jesus went with them.
And when he
- was now not far from the
- house, the centurion sent
- friends to him,
- saying unto him, Lord,
- trouble not thyself:
- for I am not worthy that
- thou shouldest enter
- under my roof:
- 7. Wherefore neither thought I myself
worthy to come unto thee:
- but say in a word, and my
- servant shall be healed.
- 8. For I also am a man set under
authority, having under me soldiers,
and I say unto one, Go, and he goeth;
and to another, Come, and he cometh;

and to my servant, Do this,
and he doeth *it*.
- 9. When Jesus heard
these things,
- he marvelled
at him, and turned him about,
- and said unto the people that
followed him, I say unto you,
- I have not found so great
- faith, no, not
- in Israel.
- 10. And they that were sent,
- returning to the house,
- found the servant whole
that had been sick.
- 11. And it came to pass
- the day after, that
- he went into a city called
- Nain; and many of his disciples
went with him, and much people.
- 12. Now when he came nigh
- to the gate of the city, behold,
- there was a dead man
- carried out, the only son of
his mother, and she was
- a widow: and much people of the
city was with her.
- 13. And when the Lord saw
- her, he had compassion
- on her, and said unto her,
- Weep not.
- 14. And he came and
- touched the bier: and they that
bare *him* stood still.
- And he
- said, Young man,
I say unto thee,
- Arise.
- 15. And he that was dead
- sat up, and began to
- speak. And he delivered
him to his mother.
- 16. And there came a fear on all: and
- they glorified God, saying,
- That a great prophet is
- risen up among us;
and, That God hath visited his people.
- 17. And this rumour of him
- went forth
- throughout all Judaea,
and throughout all
- the region round about.
- 18. And the disciples of

John shewed him of all
these things.
19. And John calling *unto him*
two of his
disciples sent *them* to
Jesus, saying, Art thou he that
should come? or look we for another?
20. When the men were
come unto him,
they said, John Baptist hath sent
us unto thee, saying,
Art thou he that should
come? or look
we for another?
21. And in that same hour
he cured many of *their*
infirmities and plagues, and of
evil spirits; and unto many
that were blind he
gave sight.
22. Then Jesus answering
said unto them,
Go your way, and
tell John what things
ye have seen and heard;
how that the blind see, the lame walk,
the lepers are cleansed, the deaf
hear, the dead are raised, to the poor
the gospel is preached.
23. And blessed is *he*, whosoever
shall not be offended in me.
24. And when the
messengers of John were
departed, he began to
speak unto the people
concerning John, What
went ye out into the
wilderness for to see?
A reed shaken with the wind?
25. But what went ye out for to see?
A man clothed in soft
raiment? Behold, they
which are gorgeously apparelled,
and live delicately,
are in kings' courts.
26. But what went ye out for to see? A
prophet? Yea, I say unto you, and
much more than a prophet.
27. This is *he*, of whom it is written,
Behold, I send my
messenger before thy face,
which shall prepare thy
way before thee.

28. For I say unto you,
Among those that are
born of women there is not
a greater prophet than
John the Baptist:
but he that is least in the
kingdom of God is greater
than he.
29. And all the people that
heard *him*, and the publicans,
justified God, being
baptized with the baptism
of John.
30. But the Pharisees
and lawyers
rejected the counsel
of God against themselves,
being not baptized of him.
31. And the Lord said,
Whereunto then shall I liken the men
of this generation? and to what are
they like?
32. They are like unto
children sitting
in the marketplace,
and calling one to another, and
saying, We have piped
unto you,
and ye have not danced;
we have
mourned to you,
and ye have not wept.
33. For John the Baptist
came neither eating bread
nor drinking wine; and ye
say, He hath a devil.
34. The Son of man is come
eating and drinking; and ye
say, Behold a gluttonous
man, and
a winebibber, a friend of
publicans and
sinners!
35. But wisdom is justified
of all her children.
36. And one of the Pharisees
desired him that he would
eat with him. And he went into the
Pharisee's house, and sat down to
meat.
37. And, behold, a woman
in the city,
which was a sinner,

when she knew that *Jesus* sat at meat in the Pharisee's house,

■ **brought** an alabaster box of
■ **ointment,**
■ 38. **And** stood at his feet behind *him*
■ **weeping, and**
■ **began to wash his feet with**
■ **tears, and** did
■ **wipe** *them* **with the hairs of**
■ **her head, and kissed**
his feet,
■ **and anointed** *them*
with the ointment.
■ 39. **Now when the Pharisee**
which had bidden him
■ **saw** *it,* **he spake within**
himself,
■ **saying, This man, if he were**
■ **a prophet, would have**
■ **known** who and what manner of
woman *this is* that toucheth him: for
■ **she is a sinner.**
■ 40. **And Jesus** answering
■ **said** unto him,
■ **Simon,** I have somewhat to say
unto thee. And he saith,
Master, say on.
■ 41. **There was a certain**
■ **creditor which had two**
■ **debtors: the one owed five**
■ **hundred pence, and the**
■ **other fifty.**
■ 42. **And** when they had
nothing to pay,
■ **he** frankly
■ **forgave them both.**
Tell me therefore,
■ **which of them will**
■ **love him most?**
■ 43. **Simon answered**
and said, I suppose that
■ *he,* **to whom he forgave**
■ **most. And he said** unto him,
■ **Thou hast rightly judged.**
■ 44. **And he**
turned to the woman, and
■ **said unto Simon, Seest**
■ **thou this woman?**
I entered into thine house,
■ **thou gavest me no water**
■ **for my feet: but she** hath
■ **washed my feet with tears,**
and wiped *them* with the

hairs of her head.
■ 45. **Thou gavest me no kiss:**
■ **but this woman**
since the time I came in
■ **hath not ceased to kiss**
■ **my feet.**
46. My head with oil thou didst not anoint: but this woman hath anointed my feet with ointment.
■ 47. **Wherefore** I say unto thee,
■ **Her sins, which are many,**
■ **are forgiven; for she loved**
■ **much:** but to whom little is forgiven,
the same loveth little.
48. And he said unto her, Thy sins are forgiven.
■ 49. **And they that sat at meat**
with him
■ **began to say** within themselves,
■ **Who is this that forgiveth**
■ **sins** also?
■ 50. **And he said to the**
■ **woman, Thy faith hath**
■ **saved thee;** go in peace.

CHAPTER 8

1. And it came to pass afterward, that he went throughout every city and village, preaching and shewing the glad tidings of the kingdom of God: and the twelve *were* with him,
2. And certain women, which had been healed of evil spirits and infirmities,
■ **Mary called Magdalene,**
out of whom went seven devils,
3. And Joanna the wife of Chuza Herod's steward, and Susanna,
■ **and** many
■ **others,** which
■ **ministered unto him of**
■ **their substance.**
■ 4. **And when much people**
■ **were gathered** together, and
were come to him out of every city,
■ **he spake by a parable:**
■ 5. **A sower went out to sow**
his seed:
■ **and** as he sowed,
■ **some fell by the way side;**
and it was trodden down,
■ **and the fowls** of the air
■ **devoured it.**
■ 6. **And some fell upon a**

rock; and
as soon as it was sprung up,
it withered away,
because it lacked
moisture.
7. **And some fell among**
thorns; and the thorns
sprang up with it, and
choked it.
8. **And other fell on good**
ground, and sprang up,
and bare fruit an
hundredfold. And when he had
said these things, he cried, He that
hath ears to hear, let him hear.
9. **And his disciples asked**
him, saying,
What might this parable
be?
10. **And he said,** Unto you it is
given to know the mysteries of the
kingdom of God: but to others in
parables; that seeing they might not
see, and hearing they might not
understand.
11. **Now the parable is this:**
The seed is the word of God.
12. **Those by the way side**
are they that hear; then
cometh
the devil, and
taketh away the word out
of their hearts, lest they
should
believe and be saved.
13. **They on the rock**
are they, which, when they hear,
receive the word with joy;
and these
have no root,
which for a while believe,
and in time of temptation
fall away.
14. **And that which fell**
among thorns are they, which,
when they have heard, go forth, and
are choked with cares and
riches and pleasures of
this **life, and bring no fruit**
to perfection.
15. **But that on the good**
ground are they, which in an
honest and good heart, having heard

the word, keep *it,* and
bring forth fruit
with patience.
16. **No man, when he hath**
lighted a candle, covereth
it with a vessel,
or putteth *it* under a bed;
but setteth *it* **on a**
candlestick, that they
which enter in
may see the light.
17. **For nothing is** secret, that
shall not be made manifest; neither
any thing
hid, that shall not be known
and come abroad.
18. Take heed therefore how ye hear:
for whosoever hath, to him
shall be given; and
whosoever hath not, from
him shall be taken even that
which he seemeth to have.
19. **Then came** to him
his mother and his
brethren, and could not come at
him for the press.
20. **And it was told him**
by certain which said,
Thy mother and thy
brethren stand without,
desiring to see thee.
21. **And he answered**
and said unto them,
My mother and my brethren
are these which hear the
word of God,
and do it.
22. **Now** it came to pass on a certain
day, that
he went into a ship
with his disciples:
and he
said unto them,
Let us go over
unto the other side
of the lake. And they launched forth.
23. **But as they sailed he fell**
asleep: and there came
down
a storm of wind on the lake;
and they were filled *with*
water, and were in jeopardy.
24. **And they came to him,**

and awoke him,
■ **saying, Master,** master,
■ **we perish. Then he** arose, and
■ **rebuked the wind** and the
raging of the water: and they ceased,
■ **and there was a calm.**
■ 25. **And he said** unto them,
■ **Where is your faith? And**
■ **they** being afraid
■ **wondered, saying**
one to another,
■ **What manner of man is this!**
for he commandeth
■ **even the winds and water,**
and they
■ **obey him.**
■ 26. **And** they arrived
■ **at the country of**
■ **the Gadarenes,**
which is over against Galilee.
27. And when he went forth to land,
■ **there met him** out of the city
■ **a** certain
■ **man, which had devils**
long time,
■ **and** ware no clothes, neither
■ **abode in** *any* house, but in
■ **the tombs.**
■ 28. **When he saw Jesus, he**
cried out, and
■ **fell down before him, and**
with a loud voice
■ **said,** What have I to do with thee,
■ **Jesus,** *thou* **Son of God**
most high? I beseech thee,
■ **torment me not.**
29. (For he had commanded the
unclean spirit to come out of the man.
■ **For** oftentimes it had caught him: and
■ **he was kept bound with**
■ **chains** and in fetters;
■ **and he brake the bands,**
■ **and was driven of the devil**
■ **into the wilderness.)**
■ 30. **And Jesus asked**
him, saying,
■ **What is thy name? And he**
■ **said, Legion: because**
■ **many devils were entered**
■ **into him.**
31. And they besought him that he
would not command them to go out
into the deep.

■ 32. **And there was**
there an herd of
■ **many swine feeding**
on the mountain:
■ **and they besought him**
that he would suffer them
■ **to enter into them.**
And he suffered them.
■ 33. **Then** went
■ **the devils** out of the man, and
■ **entered** into
■ **the swine: and** the herd
■ **ran violently** down a steep place
■ **into the lake,** and were choked.
■ 34. **When they that fed** *them*
■ **saw** what was done,
■ **they fled,** and went
■ **and told** *it* **in the city**
and in the country.
■ 35. **Then they went out to see**
what was done; and came to
■ **Jesus, and** found
■ **the man, out of whom the**
■ **devils were departed,**
sitting at the feet of Jesus,
■ **clothed, and in his right**
■ **mind:** and they were afraid.
■ 36. **They also** which saw *it*
■ **told them by what means**
■ **he** that was possessed of the devils
■ **was healed.**
■ 37. **Then the whole multitude**
of the country of the
Gadarenes round about
■ **besought him to depart**
from them;
■ **for they were taken with**
■ **great fear:** and he went up into the
ship, and returned back again.
■ 38. **Now the man** out of whom the
devils were departed
■ **besought him that he might**
■ **be with him: but Jesus sent**
■ **him away, saying,**
■ 39. **Return to thine own**
■ **house,** and shew how great things
God hath done unto thee.
■ **And he went** his way,
■ **and published**
throughout the whole city
■ **how great things Jesus**
■ **had done** unto him.
■ 40. **And** it came to pass, that,

■ **when Jesus was returned,**
■ **the people**
gladly received him: for they
■ **were** all
■ **waiting** for him.
■ 41. **And,** behold,
there came a man named
■ **Jairus,** and he was
■ **a ruler of the synagogue:**
and he fell down at Jesus' feet, and
■ **besought him that he would**
■ **come into his** *house:*
■ 42. **For he had one** only
■ **daughter,**
about twelve years of age,
■ **and she lay a-dying.** But as
he went the people thronged him.
■ 43. **And a woman having an**
■ **issue of blood twelve**
■ **years,** which had spent all her living
upon physicians, neither could be
healed of any,
■ 44. **Came behind** *him,* **and**
■ **touched** the border of
■ **his garment: and**
■ **immediately her issue of**
■ **blood stanched.**
■ 45. **And Jesus said, Who**
■ **touched me?** When all denied,
■ **Peter** and they that were with him
■ **said, Master, the multitude**
■ **throng thee** and press *thee,*
■ **and sayest thou, Who**
■ **touched me?**
■ 46. **And Jesus said,**
Somebody hath touched me: for
■ **I perceive that virtue is**
■ **gone out of me.**
■ 47. **And when the woman**
■ **saw** that
■ **she was not hid, she came**
trembling,
■ **and** falling down before him, she
■ **declared** unto him
before all the people
■ **for what cause she had**
■ **touched him, and how she**
■ **was healed** immediately.
■ 48. **And he said** unto her,
■ **Daughter,** be of good comfort:
■ **thy faith hath made thee**
■ **whole;** go in peace.
■ 49. **While he yet spake, there**

■ **cometh one from the ruler**
■ **of the synagogue's** *house,*
■ **saying** to him,
■ **Thy daughter is dead;** trouble
not the Master.
■ 50. **But when Jesus heard** *it,*
■ **he answered** him, saying,
■ **Fear not:** believe only, and
■ **she shall be made whole.**
■ 51. **And when he came into**
■ **the house,** he suffered no man to
go in, save Peter, and James, and
John, and the father and the mother of
the maiden.
52. And all wept, and bewailed her: but
■ **he said, Weep not; she**
is not dead, but
■ **sleepeth.**
■ 53. **And they laughed him to**
■ **scorn,** knowing that she was dead.
■ 54. **And he** put them all out, and
■ **took her by the hand,**
and called,
■ **saying, Maid, arise.**
■ 55. **And** her spirit came again, and
■ **she arose** straightway: and he
commanded to give her meat.
56. And her parents were astonished:
but he charged them that they should
tell no man what was done.

CHAPTER 9
■ 1. **Then he called his twelve**
■ **disciples** together,
■ **and gave them power**
and authority over all devils,
and to cure diseases.
■ 2. **And he sent them to**
■ **preach** the kingdom of God,
■ **and to heal the sick.**
■ 3. **And he said** unto them,
■ **Take nothing for** *your*
■ **journey,** neither staves, nor scrip,
neither bread, neither money; neither
have two coats apiece.
■ 4. **And whatsoever house**
■ **ye enter** into,
■ **there abide,** and thence depart.
■ 5. **And whosoever will not**
■ **receive you,**
when ye go out of that city,
■ **shake off the** very
■ **dust from your feet for a**

■ testimony against them.
■ 6. And they departed, and
■ went through the towns,
■ preaching the gospel, and
■ healing every where.
■ 7. Now Herod the tetrarch heard
of all that was done by him: and he
■ was perplexed,
■ because that
■ it was said of some,
■ that John was risen
■ from the dead;
8. And of some, that Elias had
appeared; and of others, that one of
the old prophets was risen again.
■ 9. And Herod said, John
■ have I beheaded: but who
■ is this, of whom I hear such things?
■ And he desired to see him.
■ 10. And the apostles, when
■ they were
■ returned, told him
■ all that
■ they had done. And he took
■ them, and went aside
■ privately into a desert
■ place belonging to the
city called Bethsaida.
■ 11. And the people,
when they knew *it,*
■ followed him: and he
received them, and
■ spake unto them of the
■ kingdom of God, and
■ healed them
that had need of healing.
■ 12. And when the day
began to wear away,
■ then came the twelve,
■ and said unto him,
■ Send the multitude away,
■ that they may go into the towns
and country round about,
■ and lodge, and get
■ victuals: for we are here in a
desert place.
■ 13. But he said unto them,
■ Give ye them to eat. And
■ they said, We have no more
■ but five loaves and two
■ fishes; except we should go and
buy meat for all this people.
■ 14. For they were about five

■ thousand men. And he said
to his disciples,
■ Make them sit down
by fifties in a company.
15. And they did so, and made them
all sit down.
■ 16. Then he took the five
■ loaves and the two fishes,
■ and looking up to heaven, he
■ blessed them, and brake,
■ and gave to the disciples to
■ set before the multitude.
■ 17. And they did eat,
and were all filled:
■ and there
was taken up of fragments that
■ remained to them
■ twelve baskets.
■ 18. And it came to pass,
■ as he was alone
■ praying, his disciples were
■ with him: and he asked
■ them, saying,
■ Whom say the people
■ that I am?
■ 19. They answering
■ said, John the Baptist; but
■ some *say,* Elias; and
■ others *say,* that
■ one of the old
■ prophets is risen again.
■ 20. He said unto them,
■ But whom say ye that I am?
■ Peter answering said,
■ The Christ of God.
■ 21. And he
straitly charged them, and
■ commanded *them* to tell no
■ man that thing;
■ 22. Saying, The Son of man
■ must suffer many things, and be
rejected of the elders and chief
priests and scribes,
■ and be slain, and be
■ raised the third day.
■ 23. And he said to *them all,*
■ If any *man* will come after
■ me, let him deny himself, and
■ take up his cross daily,
■ and follow me.
24. For whosoever will save his life
shall lose it: but whosoever will lose
his life for my sake, the same

shall save it.
25. **For what is a man advantaged, if he gain the whole world, and lose himself,** or be cast away?
26. **For whosoever shall be ashamed of me** and of my words, of him **shall the Son of man be ashamed, when he shall come in his own glory,** and *in his* Father's, and of the holy angels.
27. But I tell you of a truth, there be some standing here, which shall not taste of death, till they see the kingdom of God.
28. **And** it came to pass about an **eight days after** these sayings, **he took Peter and John and James,** and went up **into a mountain to pray.**
29. **And** as he prayed, **the fashion of his countenance was altered,** and his raiment *was* white *and* glistering.
30. **And, behold, there talked with him** two men, which were **Moses and Elias:**
31. **Who** appeared in glory, and **spake of his decease which he should accomplish** at Jerusalem.
32. **But Peter and they that were with him** were heavy with sleep: and when they were awake, they **saw his glory, and the two men that stood with him.**
33. **And** it came to pass, **as they departed** from him, **Peter said** unto Jesus, Master, it is good for us to be here: and **let us make three tabernacles; one for thee, and** one for **Moses, and** one for **Elias:** not knowing what he said.
34. **While he thus spake,** there came **a cloud,** and **overshadowed them:**

and they feared as they entered into the cloud.
35. **And there came a voice** out of the cloud, **saying, This is my beloved Son: hear him.**
36. And when the voice was past, Jesus was found alone. **And they** kept *it* close, and **told no man** in those days **any of those things** which they had seen.
37. **And** it came to pass, that on the next day, **when they were come down** from the hill, **much people met him.**
38. **And, behold, a man** of the company **cried out,** saying, **Master, I** beseech thee, **look upon my** son: for he is mine **only child.**
39. **And, lo, a spirit taketh him,** and he suddenly crieth out; **and** it **teareth him** that he foameth again, and **bruising him** hardly departeth from him.
40. **And I besought thy disciples to cast him out; and they could not.**
41. **And Jesus** answering **said, O faithless** and perverse **generation,** how long shall I be with you, and suffer you? **Bring thy son hither.**
42. **And** as he was yet a-coming, **the devil threw him down,** and tare *him.* **And Jesus rebuked the unclean spirit, and healed the child,** and delivered him again to his father.
43. **And they were all amazed at the mighty power of God.** But while they wondered every one at all things which **Jesus** did, he **said** unto his disciples,
44. Let these sayings sink

down into your ears: for
- **the Son of man shall be**
- **delivered into the hands**
- **of men.**
- 45. **But they understood not**
this saying, and it was hid from them,
that they perceived it not:
- **and** they
- **feared to ask him**
of that saying.
- 46. **Then there arose a**
- **reasoning among them,**
- **which** of them
- **should be greatest.**
- 47. **And Jesus,** perceiving the
thought of their heart,
- **took a child,** and set him by him,
- 48. **And said** unto them,
- **Whosoever shall receive**
- **this child in my name**
- **receiveth me:**
and whosoever shall receive me
receiveth him that sent me:
- **for he that is least**
- **among you** all, the same
- **shall be great.**
- 49. **And John** answered and
- **said,** Master,
- **we saw one casting out**
- **devils in thy name; and we**
- **forbad him,**
because he followeth not with us.
- 50. **And Jesus said** unto him,
- **Forbid** *him* **not: for he that**
- **is not against us is for us.**
- 51. **And** it came to pass,
- **when the time was come**
- **that he should be received**
- **up, he** stedfastly
- **set his face to**
- **go to Jerusalem,**
- 52. **And sent messengers**
before his face: and they went,
and entered
- **into a village of the**
- **Samaritans, to make**
- **ready for him.**
- 53. **And they did not receive**
- **him,** because his face was as
though he would go to Jerusalem.
- 54. **And when his disciples**
James and John
- **saw** *this***, they said, Lord,**

- **wilt thou that we command**
- **fire** to come down
- **from heaven, and consume**
- **them,** even as Elias did?
- 55. **But he** turned, and
- **rebuked them, and said,**
Ye know not what manner
of spirit ye are of.
- 56. **For the Son of man is not**
- **come to destroy men's**
- **lives, but to save** *them***.**
And they went to another village.
- 57. **And** it came to pass,
that, as they went in the way,
- **a certain** *man* **said** unto him,
- **Lord, I will follow thee**
whithersoever thou goest.
- 58. **And Jesus said**
unto him, Foxes have holes, and
birds of the air *have* nests; but
- **the Son of man hath not**
- **where to lay** *his* **head.**
- 59. **And he said unto**
- **another, Follow me. But he**
- **said, Lord, suffer me first to**
go and
- **bury my father.**
- 60. **Jesus said** unto him,
- **Let the dead bury their**
- **dead: but go** thou
- **and preach** the kingdom of God.
- 61. **And another** also
- **said, Lord,** I will follow thee;
- **but let me first** go
- **bid them farewell, which**
- **are** at home
- **at my house.**
- 62. **And Jesus said** unto him,
- **No man, having put his**
- **hand to the plough, and**
- **looking back, is fit for the**
- **kingdom** of God.

CHAPTER 10
- 1. **After these things the**
- **LORD appointed other**
- **seventy** also,
- **and sent them**
two and two before his face
into every city and place,
- **whither he himself**
- **would come.**
- 2. **Therefore said he** unto them,

- **The harvest** truly
- _is_ **great, but the labourers**
- _are_ **few: pray** ye therefore
- **the Lord** of the harvest,
- **that he** would
- **send forth labourers**
  into his harvest.
- 3. **Go** your ways: behold,
  I send you forth
- **as lambs among wolves.**
- 4. **Carry neither purse, nor**
- **scrip,** nor shoes: and
  salute no man by the way.
- 5. **And into whatsoever**
- **house ye enter, first say,**
- **Peace** _be_ **to this house.**
  6. And if the son of peace be there,
  your peace shall rest upon it: if not, it
  shall turn to you again.
- 7. **And** in the same house
- **remain, eating and**
- **drinking such things as**
- **they give: for the labourer**
- **is worthy of his hire.**
  Go not from house to house.
- 8. **And into whatsoever city**
- **ye enter,** and they receive you,
- **eat** such
- **things** as are
- **set before you:**
- 9. **And heal the sick**
  that are therein,
- **and say** unto them,
- **The kingdom of God is**
- **come nigh unto you.**
- 10. **But into whatsoever city**
- **ye enter, and they receive**
- **you not,** go your ways out into
  the streets of the same, and
- **say,**
- 11. **Even the very dust of**
- **your city,** which cleaveth on us,
- **we** do
- **wipe off against you:**
  notwithstanding be ye sure of
  this, that the kingdom of God is
  come nigh unto you.
  12. But I say unto you, that it shall be
  more tolerable in that day for Sodom,
  than for that city.
  13. Woe unto thee, Chorazin!
  woe unto thee, Bethsaida!
- **for if the mighty works had**

- **been done in Tyre and**
- **Sidon, which have been**
- **done in you, they had**
  a great while ago
- **repented,**
  sitting in sackcloth and ashes.
- 14. **But it shall be more**
- **tolerable for Tyre and**
- **Sidon at the judgment, than**
- **for you.**
  15. And thou, Capernaum, which art
  exalted to heaven, shalt be thrust
  down to hell.
  16. He that heareth you heareth me;
  and he that despiseth you despiseth
  me; and he that despiseth me
  despiseth him that sent me.
- 17. **And the seventy returned**
  again with joy,
- **saying, Lord, even the**
- **devils are subject unto us**
- **through thy name.**
- 18. **And he said** unto them,
- **I beheld Satan as lightning**
- **fall from heaven.**
- 19. **Behold, I give unto you**
- **power** to tread on serpents
  and scorpions, and over all
  the power of the enemy:
- **and nothing shall**
  by any means
- **hurt you.**
  20. Notwithstanding in this
- **rejoice not, that the spirits**
- **are subject unto you; but**
- **rather** rejoice,
- **because your names are**
- **written in heaven.**
- 21. **In that hour Jesus**
  rejoiced in spirit, and
- **said, I thank thee, O Father,**
  Lord of heaven and earth,
- **that thou hast hid these**
- **things from the wise and**
- **prudent, and hast revealed**
- **them unto babes:**
  even so, Father; for so it
  seemed good in thy sight.
- 22. **All things are delivered**
- **to me of my Father:**
  and no man knoweth who the
  Son is, but the Father; and
  who the Father is, but the Son,

and *he* to whom the
Son will reveal *him*.
23. And he turned him
unto *his* disciples,
and said privately,
Blessed *are* the eyes which
see the things that ye see:
24. For I tell you, that many
prophets and kings have
desired to see those things
which ye see, and have not seen
them; and to hear those things which
ye hear, and have not heard *them*.
25. And, behold, a certain
lawyer stood up, and
tempted him, saying, Master,
what shall I do to inherit
eternal life?
26. He said unto him,
What is written
in the law? how readest thou?
27. And he answering said,
Thou shalt love the Lord thy
God with all thy heart,
and with all thy
soul, and with all thy
strength, and with all thy
mind; and thy
neighbour as thyself.
28. And he said unto him,
Thou hast answered right:
this do, and thou shalt live.
29. But he, willing to justify
himself, said unto Jesus, And
who is my neighbour?
30. And Jesus answering
said,
A certain *man* went down
from Jerusalem to Jericho,
and fell among thieves,
which stripped him
of his raiment,
and wounded *him*,
and departed,
leaving *him* half dead.
31. And by chance there came down
a certain priest that way: and
when he saw him, he
passed by on the other side.
32. And likewise a Levite,
when he was at the place, came
and looked *on him*, and
passed by on the other side.

33. But a certain Samaritan,
as he journeyed, came
where he was: and when he
saw him,
he had compassion *on him*,
34. And went to *him*, and
bound up
his wounds, pouring in oil and
wine, and set him on his own beast,
and brought him to an inn,
and took care of him.
35. And on the morrow
when he departed,
he took out two pence,
and gave *them* to the host,
and said unto him,
Take care of him; and
whatsoever thou
spendest more,
when I come again,
I will repay thee.
36. Which now of these
three, thinkest thou,
was neighbour unto him
that fell among the thieves?
37. And he said, He that
shewed mercy on him.
Then said Jesus unto him,
Go, and do thou
likewise.
38. Now it came to pass,
as they went, that
he entered into a certain
village: and a certain
woman named
Martha received him into
her house.
39. And she had a sister called
Mary, which
also sat at Jesus' feet, and
heard his word.
40. But Martha was
cumbered about much
serving, and came to him,
and said, Lord, dost thou not
care that
my sister hath left me to
serve alone? bid her
therefore that she
help me.
41. And Jesus answered
and said unto her, Martha,
Martha, thou art careful and

■ **troubled about**
■ **many things:**
■ 42. **But** one thing is needful: and
■ **Mary hath chosen that**
■ **good part, which shall not**
■ **be taken away** from her.

CHAPTER 11

■ 1. **And** it came to pass, that,
■ **as he was praying**
in a certain place, when he ceased,
■ **one of his disciples said**
unto him,
■ **Lord, teach us to pray,**
as John also taught his disciples.
■ 2. **And he said** unto them,
■ **When ye pray, say, Our**
■ **Father** which art in heaven,
■ **Hallowed be thy name.**
■ **Thy kingdom come. Thy**
■ **will be done,** as
■ **in heaven, so in earth.**
■ 3. **Give us** day by day
■ **our daily bread.**
■ 4. **And forgive us our sins;**
■ **for we also forgive**
every one that is indebted to us.
■ **And lead us not into**
■ **temptation; but deliver**
■ **us from evil.**
■ 5. **And he said** unto them,
■ **Which of you shall have a**
■ **friend, and shall go unto**
■ **him at midnight, and say**
unto him, Friend,
■ **lend me three loaves;**
6. For a friend of mine in his
journey is come to me, and I have
nothing to set before him?
■ 7. **And he** from within
■ **shall answer** and say,
■ **Trouble me not:** the door
is now shut, and my children are
with me in bed;
■ **I cannot rise and give thee.**
■ 8. **I say** unto you,
■ **Though he will not rise**
and give him,
■ **because he is his friend,**
■ **yet because of his**
■ **importunity he will** rise and
■ **give him** as many as he needeth.
■ 9. **And I say** unto you,

■ **Ask, and it shall be given**
you;
■ **seek, and ye shall find;**
■ **knock, and it shall be**
■ **opened** unto you.
10. For every one that asketh
receiveth; and he that seeketh
findeth; and to him that knocketh it
shall be opened.
■ 11. **If a son** shall
■ **ask bread of** any of you that is
■ **a father, will he give** him
■ **a stone? or** if *he ask*
■ **a fish, will he** for a fish
■ **give** him
■ **a serpent?**
12. Or if he shall ask an egg, will he
offer him a scorpion?
■ 13. **If ye then, being evil,**
know how to
■ **give good gifts**
unto your children:
■ **how much** more
■ **shall *your* heavenly Father**
■ **give the Holy Spirit to them**
■ **that ask** him?
■ 14. **And he was casting out**
■ **a devil, and it was dumb.**
And it came to pass,
■ **when the devil was gone**
■ **out, the dumb spake;**
and the people wondered.
■ 15. **But some** of them
■ **said, He casteth out devils**
■ **through Beelzebub**
the chief of the devils.
■ 16. **And others,** tempting *him*,
■ **sought** of him
■ **a sign** from heaven.
■ 17. **But he,** knowing their thoughts,
■ **said** unto them,
■ **Every kingdom divided**
against itself is brought to desolation;
and a house *divided* against a house
■ **falleth.**
■ 18. **If Satan also be divided**
against himself,
■ **how shall his kingdom**
■ **stand?** because ye say that I cast
out devils through Beelzebub.
19. And if I by Beelzebub cast out
devils, by whom do your sons cast
them out? therefore shall they be your

judges.

■ 20. **But if I with the finger of**
■ **God cast out devils, no**
■ **doubt the kingdom of God**
■ **is come** upon you.
■ 21. **When a strong man** armed
■ **keepeth his palace, his**
■ **goods are in peace:**
■ 22. **But when a stronger**
than he shall come upon him, and
■ **overcome him, he taketh**
from him
■ **all** his armour wherein
he trusted, and divideth
■ **his spoils.**
■ 23. **He that is not with me is**
■ **against me:** and he that
gathereth not with me scattereth.
■ 24. **When the unclean spirit**
■ **is gone out of a man,**
he walketh through dry places,
■ **seeking rest;** and finding none,
■ **he saith, I will return unto**
■ **my house** whence I came out.
■ 25. **And** when he cometh,
■ **he findeth** *it* **swept**
■ **and garnished.**
■ 26. **Then goeth he, and**
■ **taketh** to him
■ **seven other spirits**
more wicked than himself; and they
enter in, and dwell there:
■ **and the last** *state* of that man
■ **is worse than the first.**
27. And it came to pass,
■ **as he spake** these things,
■ **a** certain
■ **woman** of the company
lifted up her voice, and
■ **said** unto him,
■ **Blessed** *is* **the womb that**
■ **bare thee,** and the paps which
thou hast sucked.
■ 28. **But he said,** Yea
■ **rather, blessed** *are* **they**
■ **that hear the word** of God,
■ **and keep it.**
29. And when the people were
gathered thick together, he began
to say,
■ **This** is an
■ **evil generation:** they
■ **seek a sign; and** there shall

■ **no sign be given it, but the**
■ **sign of Jonas** the prophet.
■ 30. **For as Jonas was a sign**
■ **unto the Ninevites, so shall**
■ **also the Son of man be**
to this generation.
31. The queen of the south shall rise
up in the judgment with the men of this
generation, and condemn them: for
she came from the utmost parts of the
earth to hear the wisdom of Solomon;
and, behold, a greater than Solomon
is here.
■ 32. **The men of Nineve**
shall rise up in the judgment with
this generation, and shall condemn
it: for they
■ **repented at the preaching**
■ **of Jonas; and,** behold,
■ **a greater than Jonas** *is*
■ **here.**
■ 33. **No man, when he hath**
■ **lighted a candle, putteth** *it*
in a secret place, neither
■ **under a bushel, but on a**
■ **candlestick, that they**
which come in
■ **may see the light.**
■ 34. **The light of the body is**
■ **the eye:** therefore
■ **when thine eye is single, thy**
■ **whole body** also is full of light;
but when *thine eye* is evil, thy body
also *is* full of darkness.
35. Take heed therefore that the light
which is in thee be not darkness.
36. If thy whole body therefore *be* full
of light, having no part dark, the whole
■ **shall be full of light,**
as when the bright shining of a
candle doth give thee light.
■ 37. **And** as he spake,
■ **a** certain
■ **Pharisee besought him to**
■ **dine with him:** and he went in,
and sat down to meat.
■ 38. **And** when the Pharisee saw *it*,
■ **he marvelled that he had**
■ **not** first
■ **washed** before dinner.
■ 39. **And the Lord said** unto him,
■ **Now do ye Pharisees make**
■ **clean the outside**

of the cup and the platter;
■ **but your inward part is full**
■ **of** ravening and
■ **wickedness.**
■ 40. *Ye* **fools, did not he that**
■ **made that which is without**
■ **make that which is within**
■ **also?**
41. But rather give alms of such
things as ye have; and, behold, all
things are clean unto you.
■ 42. **But woe unto you,**
■ **Pharisees! for ye tithe**
mint and rue and all manner of herbs,
■ **and pass over** judgment and
■ **the love of God:**
these ought ye to have done,
and not to leave the other undone.
43. Woe unto you, Pharisees! for
■ **ye love the uppermost**
■ **seats in the synagogues,**
■ **and greetings in**
■ **the markets.**
■ 44. **Woe unto you,**
scribes and Pharisees,
■ **hypocrites!** for ye are as graves
which appear not, and the men that
walk over *them* are not aware of *them.*
■ 45. **Then answered one of**
■ **the lawyers,** and said unto him,
■ **Master, thus saying thou**
■ **reproachest us also.**
■ 46. **And he said, Woe unto**
■ **you also,** *ye* lawyers!
■ **for ye lade men with**
■ **burdens** grievous to be borne,
■ **and ye** yourselves
■ **touch not the burdens with**
one of
■ **your fingers.**
47. Woe unto you! for
■ **ye build the sepulchres of**
■ **the prophets, and your**
■ **fathers killed them.**
48. Truly ye bear witness that
ye allow the deeds of your fathers:
for they indeed killed them,
and ye build their sepulchres.
49. Therefore also said the
wisdom of God,
■ **I will send them prophets**
■ **and apostles, and** *some*
of them

■ **they shall slay**
■ **and persecute:**
■ 50. **That the blood of all the**
■ **prophets,** which was shed from
the foundation of the world,
■ **may be required of this**
■ **generation;**
51. From the blood of Abel unto the
blood of Zacharias which perished
between the altar and the temple:
verily I say unto you, It shall be
required of this generation.
■ 52. **Woe unto you, lawyers!**
■ **for ye have taken away the**
■ **key of knowledge:**
ye entered not in yourselves,
and them that were entering
in ye hindered.
■ 53. **And as he said these**
■ **things** unto them,
■ **the scribes and the**
■ **Pharisees began to urge**
■ *him* vehemently, and to provoke him
■ **to speak of many things:**
54. Laying wait for him, and
■ **seeking to catch something**
out of his mouth,
■ **that they might accuse him.**

CHAPTER 12
1. In the mean time, when there were
gathered together an innumerable
multitude of people, insomuch that
they trode one upon another,
■ **he began to say unto his**
■ **disciples** first of all,
■ **Beware ye of the leaven of**
■ **the Pharisees, which is**
■ **hypocrisy.**
■ 2. **For there is nothing** covered,
that shall not be revealed; neither hid,
■ **that shall not be known.**
3. Therefore whatsoever ye have
spoken in darkness shall be heard in
the light; and that which ye have
spoken in the ear in closets shall be
proclaimed upon the housetops.
■ 4. **And I say** unto you my friends,
■ **Be not afraid of them that**
■ **kill the body,** and after that have
no more that they can do.
■ 5. **But** I will forewarn
you whom ye shall fear:

Fear him, which after he hath killed hath power to cast into hell; yea, I say unto you, Fear him. 6. Are not five sparrows sold for two farthings, and not one of them is forgotten before God? 7. But even the very hairs of your head are all numbered. Fear not therefore: ye are of more value than many sparrows.

8. Also I say unto you, Whosoever shall confess me before men, him shall the Son of man also confess before the angels of God: 9. But he that denieth me before men shall be denied before the angels of God.

10. And whosoever shall speak a word against the Son of man, it shall be forgiven him: but unto him that blasphemeth against the Holy Ghost it shall not be forgiven. 11. And when they bring you unto the synagogues, and *unto* magistrates, and powers, take ye no thought how or what thing ye shall answer, or what ye shall say: 12. For the Holy Ghost shall teach you in the same hour what *ye* ought to say. 13. And one of the company said unto him, Master, speak to my brother, that he divide the inheritance with me. 14. And he said unto him, Man, who made me a judge or a divider over you? 15. And he said unto them, Take heed, and beware of covetousness: for a man's life consisteth not in the abundance of the things which he possesseth.

16. And he spake a parable unto them, saying, The ground of a certain rich man brought forth plentifully: 17. And he thought within himself, saying, What shall I do, because I have no room where to bestow my fruits? 18. And he said, This will I do: I will pull down my barns, and build greater; and there will I bestow all my fruits and my goods. 19. And I will say to my soul, Soul, thou hast much goods laid up for many years; take thine ease, eat, drink, *and* be merry. 20. But God said unto him, *Thou* fool, this night thy soul shall be required of thee: then whose shall those things be, which thou hast provided? 21. So *is* he that layeth up treasure for himself, and is not rich toward God. 22. And he said unto his disciples, Therefore I say unto you, Take no thought for your life, what ye shall eat; neither for the body, what ye shall put on. 23. The life is more than meat, and the body *is more* than raiment. 24. Consider the ravens: for they neither sow nor reap; which neither have storehouse nor barn; and God feedeth them: how much more are ye better than the fowls? 25. And which of you with taking thought can add to his stature one cubit? 26. If ye then be not able to do that

thing which is least, why take ye thought for the rest?

■ 27. **Consider the lilies how**
■ **they grow: they toil not,**
they spin not; and
■ **yet** I say unto you, that
■ **Solomon** in all his glory
■ **was not arrayed like** one of
■ **these.**
■ 28. **If then God so clothe the**
■ **grass,** which is to day in the field, and to-morrow is cast into the oven;
■ **how much more** *will he*
■ *clothe* **you,** O ye of little faith?
■ 29. **And seek not ye what ye**
■ **shall eat, or** what ye shall
■ **drink,** neither be ye of doubtful mind.
30. For all these things do the nations of the world seek after: and
■ **your Father knoweth that ye**
■ **have need** of these things.
■ 31. **But rather seek ye the**
■ **kingdom of God; and all**
■ **these** things
■ **shall be added** unto you.
■ 32. **Fear not,** little flock; for
■ **it is your Father's good**
■ **pleasure to give you the**
■ **kingdom.**
■ 33. **Sell that ye have, and**
■ **give alms; provide**
■ **yourselves**
bags which wax not old,
■ **a treasure in the heavens**
■ **that faileth not,**
where no thief approacheth, neither moth corrupteth.
■ 34. **For where your treasure**
■ **is, there will your heart be**
■ **also.**
35. Let your loins be girded about, and *your* lights burning;
36. And ye yourselves like unto men that wait for their lord, when he will return from the wedding; that when he cometh and knocketh, they may open unto him immediately.
■ 37. **Blessed** *are* **those**
servants,
■ **whom the lord when he**
■ **cometh shall find watching:**
verily I say unto you, that he shall gird

himself, and make them to sit down to meat, and will come forth and serve them.
38. And if he shall come in the second watch, or come in the third watch, and find *them* so, blessed are those servants.
39. And this know, that if the goodman of the house had known what hour the thief would come, he would have watched, and not have suffered his house to be broken through.
■ 40. **Be ye therefore ready**
also:
■ **for the Son of man cometh**
at an hour
■ **when ye think not.**
41. Then Peter said unto him, Lord, speakest thou this parable unto us, or even to all?
42. And the Lord said,
■ **Who** then
■ **is that faithful and wise**
■ **steward, whom** *his* **lord**
■ **shall make ruler over his**
■ **household,** to give *them their* portion of meat in due season?
43. Blessed *is* that servant, whom his lord when he cometh shall find so doing.
44. Of a truth I say unto you, that he will make him ruler over all that he hath.
■ 45. **But and if that servant**
■ **say** in his heart,
■ **My lord delayeth his**
■ **coming; and shall begin**
to beat the menservants and maidens, and
■ **to eat and drink,**
and to be drunken;
■ 46. **The lord** of that servant
■ **will come** in a day when he looketh not for *him*, and at an hour when he is not aware, and will cut him in sunder,
■ **and will appoint him his**
■ **portion with the**
■ **unbelievers.**
■ 47. **And that servant, which**
■ **knew his lord's will, and**
■ **prepared not** *himself*, neither did according to his will,
■ **shall be beaten with many**

■ *stripes.*
■ 48. **But he that knew not, and**
■ **did** commit
■ **things worthy of stripes,**
■ **shall be beaten with few**
■ *stripes.* For unto
■ **whomsoever much is**
■ **given,** of him
■ **shall be much required:**
and to whom men have committed
much, of him they will ask the more.
49. I am come to send fire on the
earth; and what will I, if it be already
kindled?
50. But I have a baptism to be
baptized with; and how am I straitened
till it be accomplished!
■ 51. **Suppose ye that I am**
■ **come to give peace**
on earth? I tell you,
■ **Nay; but rather division:**
52. For from henceforth there shall be
five in one house divided, three
against two, and two against three.
■ 53. **The father shall be**
■ **divided against the son,**
and the son against the father;
■ **the mother against the**
■ **daughter,** and the daughter
against the mother; the mother in law
against her daughter in law, and the
daughter in law against her mother in
law.
■ 54. **And he said**
also to the people,
■ **When ye see a cloud rise**
■ **out of the west,** straightway
■ **ye say, There cometh a**
■ **shower;** and so it is.
55. And when *ye see* the south wind
blow, ye say, There will be heat;
and it cometh to pass.
56. *Ye* hypocrites,
■ **ye can discern the** face of the
■ **sky and** of the
■ **earth; but** how is it that
■ **ye do not discern**
■ **this time?**
57. Yea, and why even of yourselves
judge ye not what is right?
■ 58. **When thou goest with**
■ **thine adversary to**
■ **the magistrate,**

as thou art in the way,
■ **give diligence that thou**
mayest
■ **be delivered** from him;
■ **lest he** hale thee to the judge, and
the judge deliver thee to the officer,
and the officer
■ **cast thee into prison.**
59. I tell thee, thou shalt not depart
thence,
■ **till thou hast paid the very**
■ **last mite.**

CHAPTER 13
■ 1. **There were**
present at that season
■ **some that told him of the**
■ **Galilaeans, whose blood**
■ **Pilate had mingled with**
■ **their sacrifices.**
■ 2. **And Jesus answering**
said unto them,
■ **Suppose ye that these**
■ **Galilaeans were sinners**
above all the Galilaeans,
■ **because they suffered**
■ **such things?**
3. I tell you, Nay: but, except ye
repent, ye shall all likewise perish.
■ 4. **Or those** eighteen,
■ **upon whom the tower in**
■ **Siloam fell,**
and slew them, think ye
■ **that they were sinners**
■ **above all men**
that dwelt in Jerusalem?
■ 5. **I tell you, Nay: but, except**
■ **ye repent, ye shall all**
■ **likewise perish.**
■ 6. **He spake also this**
■ **parable; A certain** *man*
■ **had a fig tree**
planted in his vineyard;
■ **and he** came and
■ **sought fruit thereon,**
■ **and found none.**
■ 7. **Then said he unto the**
■ **dresser** of his vineyard, Behold,
these three years I come seeking fruit
on this fig tree, and find none:
■ **cut it down;**
why cumbereth it the ground?
■ 8. **And he answering said**

unto him,
Lord, let it alone this year also,
till I shall dig about it, and
dung *it*:
9. **And if it bear fruit,** *well*: and
if not, *then* after that thou shalt
cut it down.
10. **And** he was teaching
in one of the synagogues on the sabbath.
11. And, behold, there was
a woman which had a **spirit of infirmity** eighteen years,
and was bowed together, and could in no wise lift up *herself.*
12. **And when Jesus saw** **her, he** called *her to him*, and **said** unto her,
Woman, thou art loosed **from thine infirmity.**
13. **And** he laid *his* hands on her: and immediately
she was made straight, **and glorified God.**
14. **And the ruler** of the synagogue
answered with indignation, **because** that
Jesus had
healed on the sabbath day,
and said unto the people,
There are six days in which **men ought to work:** in them therefore come and be healed, and not on the sabbath day.
15. **The Lord then answered** him, and said,
Thou **hypocrite, doth not** **each one of you on the** **sabbath loose his ox or** *his* **ass** from the stall,
and lead *him* away
to watering?
16. **And ought not this** **woman,** being a daughter of Abraham, whom Satan hath bound, lo, these eighteen years,
be loosed from this bond on the sabbath day?
17. **And** when he had said these things,

all his adversaries were **ashamed:** and all the people rejoiced for all the glorious things that were done by him.
18. **Then said he, Unto what** **is the kingdom of God like?** and whereunto shall I resemble it?
19. **It is like a grain of** **mustard seed, which a man** took, and
cast into his garden; and it **grew, and waxed a great** **tree;** and the fowls of the air lodged in the branches of it.
20. **And again** he said, Whereunto shall I liken the kingdom of God?
21. **It is like leaven,** **which a woman** took and **hid in** three measures of **meal, till the whole** **was leavened.**
22. And he went through the cities and villages, teaching, and journeying toward Jerusalem.
23. **Then said one** unto him, Lord,
are there few that be **saved? And he said** unto them,
24. **Strive to enter** in at **the strait gate: for many,** I say unto you,
will seek to enter in, **and shall not be able.**
25. **When once the master** of the house is risen up, and **hath shut** to **the door, and ye** begin to stand without, and to **knock at the door, saying,** Lord,
Lord, open unto us; and he **shall answer** and say unto you, **I know you not** whence ye are:
26. **Then shall ye** begin to **say, We have eaten and** **drunk in thy presence,** and thou hast taught in our streets.
27. **But he shall say,** I tell you, I know you not whence ye are; **depart from me,** all *ye* **workers of iniquity.**
28. **There shall be weeping**

■ **and gnashing of teeth,**
when ye shall see Abraham, and Isaac, and Jacob, and all the prophets, in the kingdom of God, and you yourselves thrust out.
■ 29. **And they shall come**
■ **from the east,** and *from* the
■ **west,** and from the
■ **north, and** *from* the
■ **south, and shall sit down**
■ **in the kingdom** of God.
30. And, behold, there are last which shall be first, and there are first which shall be last.
■ 31. **The same day** there
■ **came** certain of
■ **the Pharisees, saying**
unto him, Get thee out, and
■ **depart** hence:
■ **for Herod will kill thee.**
■ 32. **And he said** unto them,
■ **Go** ye, and
■ **tell that fox,** Behold,
■ **I cast out devils, and I do**
■ **cures** to-day and to-morrow,
■ **and the third day I shall**
■ **be perfected.**
■ 33. **Nevertheless I must walk**
■ **to-day, and to-morrow,**
and the *day* following:
■ **for it cannot be that a**
■ **prophet perish out of**
■ **Jerusalem.**
■ 34. **O Jerusalem,** Jerusalem,
which killest the prophets, and stonest them that are sent unto thee;
■ **how often would I have**
■ **gathered thy children**
■ **together,** as a hen *doth gather*
her brood under *her* wings,
■ **and ye would not !**
■ 35. **Behold, your house is**
left unto you
■ **desolate: and**
verily I say unto you,
■ **Ye shall not see me, until**
the time come when
■ **ye** shall
■ **say, Blessed** *is*
■ **he that cometh**
■ **in the**
■ **name of**
■ **the Lord.**

CHAPTER 14

■ 1. **And** it came to pass, as
■ **he went into the house of**
■ **one of the chief Pharisees**
■ **to eat** bread
■ **on the sabbath**
day, that they watched him.
■ 2. **And, behold,**
■ **there was a** certain
■ **man** before him
■ **which had the dropsy.**
■ 3. **And Jesus** answering
■ **spake** unto the lawyers and
Pharisees, saying,
■ **Is it lawful to heal on the**
■ **sabbath** day?
■ 4. **And they held their**
■ **peace. And he** took *him,* and
■ **healed him,** and let him go;
5. And answered them, saying, Which of you shall have an ass or an ox fallen into a pit, and will not straightway pull him out on the sabbath day?
6. And they could not answer him again to these things.
■ 7. **And he put forth a**
■ **parable** to those which
were bidden,
■ **when he marked how they**
■ **chose** out
■ **the chief rooms;**
saying unto them.
■ 8. **When thou art bidden**
of any *man*
■ **to a wedding, sit not down**
■ **in the highest room; lest a**
■ **more honourable man**
than thou
■ **be bidden** of him;
■ 9. **And he** that bade thee and him
■ **come and say** to thee,
■ **Give this man place; and**
■ **thou** begin with shame to
■ **take the lowest room.**
10. **But** when thou art bidden,
■ **go and sit** down
■ **in the lowest room; that**
when he that bade thee cometh,
■ **he may say** unto thee,
■ **Friend, go up higher: then**
■ **shalt thou have worship**
in the presence

■ ■ **of them** that sit at meat **with thee.**

11. For whosoever exalteth himself shall be abased; and

■ ■ **he that humbleth himself shall be exalted.**

■ 12. **Then said he** also to him that bade him,

■ **When thou makest a dinner** or a supper,

■ **call not thy friends,** nor *thy* brethren, neither thy kinsmen,

■ **nor** *thy*
■ **rich neighbours; lest** they also bid thee again, and

■ **a recompence be made** thee.

■ 13. **But** when thou makest a feast,

■ **call the poor, the maimed,**
■ **the lame, the blind:**

■ 14. **And thou shalt be**
■ **blessed;** for they cannot recompense thee:

■ **for thou shalt be**
■ **recompensed at the**
■ **resurrection** of the just.

15. And when one of them that sat at meat with him heard these things, he said unto him, Blessed *is* he that shall eat bread in the kingdom of God.

■ 16. **Then said he** unto him,
■ **A** certain
■ **man made a great supper,**
■ **and bade many:**

■ 17. **And sent his servant** at supper time

■ **to say** to them that were bidden,

■ **Come; for all things are**
■ **now ready.**

■ 18. **And they** all with one *consent*
■ **began to make excuse.** The first said unto him, I have bought a piece of ground, and I must needs go and see it: I pray thee have me excused.

19. And another said, I have bought five yoke of oxen, and I go to prove them: I pray thee have me excused.

20. And another said, I have married a wife, and therefore I cannot come.

■ 21. **So that servant** came, and
■ **shewed his lord these**
■ **things. Then the master**

of the house

■ **being angry said** to his servant,

■ **Go** out quickly
■ **into the streets and lanes** of the city,

■ **and bring** in hither
■ **the poor, and the maimed,**
■ **and the halt, and the blind.**

■ 22. **And the servant said,** Lord,

■ **it is done** as thou hast commanded, and

■ **yet there is room.**

■ 23. **And the lord said** unto the servant,

■ **Go out into the highways**
■ **and hedges, and compel**
■ **them to come** in, that my house may be filled.

■ 24. **For I say** unto you,
■ **That none of those** men which were

■ **bidden shall taste of my**
■ **supper.**

25. And there went great multitudes with him: and he turned, and said unto them,

26. If any *man* come to me, and hate not his father, and mother, and wife, and children, and brethren, and sisters, yea, and his own life also, he cannot be my disciple.

■ 27. **And whosoever doth not**
■ **bear his cross, and come**
■ **after me, cannot be**
■ **my disciple.**

■ 28. **For which of you,**
■ **intending to build a tower,** sitteth not down

■ **first,** and
■ **counteth the cost,** whether he have *sufficient* to finish *it.*

■ 29. **Lest haply,** after
■ **he** hath laid the foundation, and
■ **is not able to finish it,** all that behold *it* begin to mock him,

30. Saying, This man began to build, and was not able to finish.

■ 31. **Or what king, going to** make

■ **war** against another king, sitteth not down

■ **first,** and
■ **consulteh wether he be**
■ **able** with ten thousand
■ **to meet him that cometh**
■ **against him**
with twenty thousand?
■ 32. **Or else,** while the other is
yet a great way off,
■ **he sendeth an ambassage,**
■ **and desireth** conditions of
■ **peace.**
■ 33. **So likewise,** whosoever
■ **he** be of you
■ **that forsaketh not all**
that he hath, he
■ **cannot be my disciple.**
■ 34. **Salt is good: but if the**
■ **salt have lost his savour,**
wherewith shall it be seasoned?
■ 35. **It is** neither fit for the land, nor
yet for the dunghill; *but* men
■ **cast** it
■ **out.** He that hath ears to hear, let
him hear.

CHAPTER 15
■ 1. **Then drew near** unto him all
■ **the publicans and sinners**
for to hear him.
■ 2. **And the Pharisees and**
■ **scribes murmured, saying,**
■ **This man receiveth sinners,**
and eateth with them.
■ 3. **And he spake this**
■ **parable** unto them, saying,
■ 4. **What man** of you,
■ **having an hundred sheep,**
■ **if he lose one** of them,
■ **doth not** leave the ninety and nine
in the wilderness, and
■ **go after that which is lost,**
until he find it?
■ 5. **And** when he hath found *it,* he
■ **layeth it on his shoulders,**
■ **rejoicing.**
■ 6. **And** when he cometh home, he
■ **calleth together his** friends and
■ **neighbours, saying** unto them,
■ **Rejoice with me; for I have**
■ **found my sheep**
which was lost.
■ 7. **I say** unto you, that likewise
■ **joy shall be in heaven over**

■ **one sinner that repenteth,**
more than over ninety and nine just
persons, which need no repentance.
■ 8. **Either what woman**
■ **having** ten pieces of
■ **silver, if she lose one**
■ **piece, doth not** light a candle,
and sweep the house, and
■ **seek diligently till**
■ **she find it?**
9. And when she hath found *it,* she
calleth *her* friends and *her* neighbours
together, saying, Rejoice with me; for
I have found the piece
which I had lost.
■ 10. **Likewise,** I say unto you,
■ **there is joy in the presence**
■ **of** the angels of
■ **God over one sinner**
■ **that repenteth.**
■ 11. **And he said, A** certain
■ **man had two sons:**
■ 12. **And the younger** of them
■ **said** to *his* father,
■ **Father, give me the portion**
■ **of goods that falleth to me.**
And he divided unto them *his* living.
■ 13. **And** not many days after
■ **the younger son**
gathered all together, and
■ **took his journey into a far**
■ **country, and there wasted**
■ **his substance with**
■ **riotous living.**
■ 14. **And** when he had spent all,
■ **there arose a** mighty
■ **famine** in that land;
■ **and he began to**
■ **be in want.**
■ 15. **And he went**
and joined himself
■ **to a citizen of that country;**
■ **and he sent him** into his fields
■ **to feed swine.**
■ 16. **And he** would fain have
■ **filled his belly with the**
■ **husks that the swine did**
■ **eat: and no man**
■ **gave unto him.**
■ 17. **And when he came to**
■ **himself, he said,** How many
hired servants of my father's have
bread enough and to spare, and

■ **I perish with hunger!**
■ 18. **I will** arise and
■ **go to my father, and will**
■ **say** unto him, Father,
■ **I have sinned**
against heaven, and before thee,
19. And am no more worthy to be
called thy son:
■ **make me as one of thy**
■ **hired servants.**
■ 20. **And he arose,**
and came to his father.
■ **But when he was yet a great**
■ **way off, his father saw him,**
and
■ **had compassion, and ran,**
and fell on his neck,
■ **and kissed him.**
■ 21. **And the son said**
unto him, Father,
■ **I have sinned** against heaven,
and in thy sight, and am no more
worthy to be called thy son.
■ 22. **But the father said**
to his servants,
■ **Bring forth the best robe,**
and put *it* on him;
■ **and put a ring on his hand,**
■ **and shoes on his feet:**
■ 23. **And** bring hither the
fatted calf, and kill *it*; and
■ **let us eat, and be merry:**
■ 24. **For this my son**
was dead, and is alive again; he
■ **was lost, and is found.**
And they began to be merry.
■ 25. **Now his elder son**
was in the field: and as he
■ **came and**
drew nigh to the house, he
■ **heard music and dancing.**
■ 26. **And** he called
one of the servants, and
■ **asked what these**
■ **things meant.**
■ 27. **And he said** unto him,
■ **Thy brother is come; and**
■ **thy father hath killed the**
■ **fatted calf,** because he hath
received him safe and sound.
■ 28. **And he was angry, and**
would not go in: therefore came his
father out, and entreated him.

29. And he answering
■ **said to his father,** Lo, these
■ **many years do I serve**
■ **thee, neither**
■ **transgressed I** at any time
■ **thy commandment: and yet**
■ **thou never gavest me a kid,**
that I might make merry
with my friends:
■ 30. **But** as soon as
■ **this thy son** was come,
■ **which hath devoured thy**
■ **living with harlots, thou**
■ **hast killed for him the**
■ **fatted calf.**
■ 31. **And he said** unto him,
■ **Son,** thou art ever with me, and
■ **all that I have is thine.**
32. It was meet that
■ **we should make merry,**
and be glad:
■ **for** this
■ **thy brother was dead, and**
■ **is alive** again; and was lost, and is
found.

CHAPTER 16

■ 1. **And he said also unto his**
■ **disciples, There was a**
certain
■ **rich man, which had a**
■ **steward;** and
■ **the same was accused**
unto him
■ **that he had wasted**
■ **his goods.**
■ 2. **And he** called him, and
■ **said** unto him, How is it that
I hear this of thee?
■ **give an account of thy**
■ **stewardship;** for thou
mayest be no longer steward.
■ 3. **Then the steward said**
■ **within himself, What shall I**
■ **do?** for my lord taketh away from me
the stewardship: I cannot dig; to beg I
am ashamed.
■ 4. **I am resolved what to do,**
that, when I am put out of the
stewardship, they may receive me
into their houses.
■ 5. **So he called** every one of
■ **his lord's debtors** *unto him,*

and said unto the first,
How much owest thou unto
my lord?
6. **And he said, An hundred
measures of oil. And he
said** unto him,
Take thy bill,
and sit down quickly,
and write fifty.
7. **Then said he to another,**
And
how much owest thou?
And he said,
**An hundred measures of
wheat. And he said** unto him,
**Take thy bill, and
write fourscore.**
8. **And the lord commended
the unjust steward,**
because he had done wisely:
**for the children of this
world are** in their generation
**wiser than the children
of light.**
9. **And I say** unto you,
Make to yourselves
friends of the mammon of
**unrighteousness; that,
when ye fail, they may
receive you**
into everlasting habitations.
10. **He that is faithful in that
which is least is** faithful
also in much: and he that is
unjust in the least is unjust also in
much.
11. **If therefore ye have not
been faithful**
in the unrighteous mammon,
**who will commit to your
trust the true riches?**
12. And if ye have not been faithful in
that which is another man's, who shall
give you that which is your own?
13. **No servant can serve
two masters:** for either he will
hate the one, and love the other; or
else he will hold to the one, and
despise the other.
**Ye cannot serve God
and mammon.**
14. **And the Pharisees**
also, who were covetous,

heard all these things:
**and they
derided him.**
15. **And he said** unto them, Ye
are they which justify yourselves
before men; but
**God knoweth your hearts:
for that which is highly
esteemed** among men
**is abomination in the sight
of God.**
16. **The law and the
prophets were until John:
since that time the kingdom
of God is preached,**
and every man presseth into it.
17. **And it is easier for
heaven and earth to pass,
than one tittle of the
law to fail.**
18. **Whosoever putteth
away his wife, and
marrieth another,**
committeth adultery:
**and whosoever marrieth
her that is put away**
from *her* husband
committeth adultery.
19. **There was a certain rich
man,** which was clothed in purple
and fine linen, and fared sumptuously
every day:
20. **And** there was
a certain
**beggar named Lazarus,
which** was
laid at his gate, full of sores,
21. **And desiring to be fed
with the crumbs** which fell
from the rich man's table:
moreover the dogs came and licked
his sores.
22. **And** it came to pass, that
**the beggar died, and was
carried** by the angels
**into Abraham's bosom: the
rich man also died,**
and was buried;
23. **And in hell he lift
up his eyes,** being
**in torments, and seeth
Abraham** afar off,
and Lazarus in his bosom.

24. **And he cried** and said,
Father Abraham,
have mercy on me, and
send Lazarus, that
he may dip the tip of
his finger in water, and
cool my tongue; for I am
tormented in this flame.
25. **But Abraham said,**
Son, remember that
thou in thy lifetime
receivedst thy good things,
and likewise
Lazarus evil things: but
now he is comforted, and
thou art tormented.
26. **And beside** all this,
between us and you
there is a great gulf fixed:
so that they which would pass
from hence to
you cannot; neither can they
pass to us, that *would come* from
thence.
27. **Then he said,** I pray thee
therefore, father, that thou wouldest
send him to my
father's house:
28. **For I have five brethren;**
that he may testify unto them,
lest they also come into
this place of torment.
29. **Abraham saith** unto him,
They have Moses and the
prophets; let them hear them.
30. **And he said,**
Nay, father Abraham: but
if one went unto them
from the dead, they
will repent.
31. **And he said** unto him,
If they hear not Moses and
the prophets, neither will
they be persuaded, though
one rose from the dead.

CHAPTER 17
1. **Then said he unto the**
disciples, It is impossible but that
offences will come: but
woe unto him, through
whom they come!
2. **It were better** for him

that a millstone were hanged
about his neck, and
he cast into the sea, than
that he should
offend one of these
little ones.
3. Take heed to yourselves:
If thy brother trespass
against thee,
rebuke him; and if he
repent, forgive him.
4. **And if he trespass**
against thee
seven times in a day, and
seven times in a day turn again to
thee, saying, I
repent; thou shalt
forgive him.
5. **And the apostles said**
unto the Lord,
Increase our faith.
6. **And the Lord said, If ye**
had faith as a grain of
mustard seed, ye might
say unto this sycamine
tree, Be thou plucked
up by the root, and be
thou planted in the sea;
and it should obey you.
7. But which of you, having a servant
plowing or feeding cattle, will say unto
him by and by, when he is come from
the field, Go and sit down to meat?
8. And will not rather say unto him,
Make ready wherewith I may sup, and
gird thyself, and serve me, till I have
eaten and drunken; and afterward
thou shalt eat and drink?
9. Doth he thank that servant
because he did the things that were
commanded him? I trow not.
10. So likewise ye, when ye shall have
done all those things which are
commanded you, say, We are
unprofitable servants: we have done
that which was our duty to do.
11. **And** it came to pass,
as he went to Jerusalem,
that he passed
through the midst of
Samaria and Galilee.
12. And as he entered into
a certain village,

- **there met him ten** men that were
- **lepers,** which stood afar off:
- 13. **And they**
  lifted up *their* voices, and
- **said, Jesus,** Master,
- **have mercy on us.**
- 14. **And** when he saw *them,*
- **he said** unto them,
- **Go shew yourselves unto**
- **the priests. And**
  it came to pass, that,
- **as they went, they**
- **were cleansed.**
- 15. **And one of them,**
  when he saw that he was healed,
- **turned back, and**
  with a loud voice
- **glorified God,**
- 16. **And fell** down on *his* face
- **at his feet, giving him**
- **thanks:** and he was a Samaritan.
- 17. **And Jesus** answering
- **said,** Were there not ten
  cleansed? but
- **where are the nine?**
- 18. **There are not** found that
- **returned** to give glory to God,
- **save this stranger.**
- 19. **And he said** unto him,
- **Arise,** go thy way:
- **thy faith hath made**
- **thee whole.**
- 20. **And when he was**
- **demanded of the**
- **Pharisees, when the**
- **kingdom** of God
- **should come, he answered**
  them and said, The kingdom of God
  cometh not with observation:
  21. Neither shall they say, Lo here! or,
  lo there! for, behold
- **the kingdom of**
- **God is within you.**
- 22. **And he said unto the**
- **disciples, The days will**
- **come, when ye shall desire**
- **to see** one of the days of
- **the Son** of man,
- **and ye shall not** see *it.*
  23. And they shall say to you, See
  here; or, see there: go not after *them,*
  nor follow *them.*
- 24. **For as the lightning,** that

lighteneth out of the one *part*
under heaven,
- **shineth** unto the other *part*
under heaven;
- **so shall** also
- **the Son of man be**
- **in his day.**
- 25. **But first must he suffer**
  many things,
- **and be rejected**
  of this generation.
- 26. **And as** it was
- **in the days of Noe, so shall**
- **it be** also
- **in the days of the Son** of man.
- 27. **They did eat,** they
- **drank,** they
- **married** wives,
  they were given in marriage,
- **until the day** that
- **Noe entered** into
- **the ark, and the flood**
  came, and
- **destroyed them** all.
- 28. **Likewise also as** it was in
  the days of Lot; they did eat, they
  drank, they bought, they sold, they
  planted, they builded;
  29. But the same day that
- **Lot went out of Sodom it**
- **rained fire** and brimstone
- **from heaven, and**
- **destroyed them** all.
- 30. **Even thus shall it be**
  in the day
- **when the Son** of man
- **is revealed.**
- 31. **In that day, he which**
- **shall be upon**
- **the housetop,**
  and his stuff in the house,
- **let him not come down**
  to take it away: and he that is in the
  field, let him likewise not return back.
  32. Remember Lot's wife.
  33. Whosoever shall seek to save his
  life shall lose it; and whosoever shall
  lose his life shall preserve it.
- 34. **I tell you,** in that night
- **there shall be two men**
  in one bed; the
- **one shall be taken, and the**
- **other** shall be

left.
35. Two *women* shall be grinding together; the one shall be taken, and the other left.
36. Two *men* shall be in the field; the one shall be taken, and the other left.
37. **And they** answered and **said** unto him,
Where, Lord? And he said unto them,
Wheresoever the body is, thither will the eagles be gathered together.

CHAPTER 18
1. **And he spake a parable** unto them to *this* end,
that men ought always to pray, and not to faint;
2. **Saying, There was** in a city **a judge, which feared not God,** neither regarded man:
3. **And** there was **a widow** in that city; and she **came unto him, saying, Avenge me of mine adversary.**
4. **And he would not** for a while: **but** afterward he **said within himself,** Though I fear not God, nor regard man;
5. Yet because this widow *troubleth* me,
I will avenge her, lest by her continual coming she weary me.
6. **And the Lord said,** Hear what the unjust judge saith.
7. **And shall not God avenge his own elect, which cry** day and night **unto him,** though he bear long with them?
8. I tell you that he will avenge them speedily. Nevertheless when the Son of man cometh, shall he find faith on the earth?
9. **And he spake this parable unto certain which trusted in themselves** that they were righteous,
and despised others:
10. **Two men went** up into the temple **to pray;** the one **a Pharisee, and** the other **a publican.**
11. **The Pharisee** stood and **prayed** thus with himself,
God, I thank thee, that I am not as other men *are*, extortioners, unjust, adulterers, or even as this publican.
12. **I fast** twice in the week, **I give tithes** of all that I possess.
13. **And the publican,** standing afar off, **would not lift up** so much as **his eyes** unto heaven, but smote upon his breast, **saying, God be merciful to me a sinner.**
14. I tell you, **this man went** down **to his house justified** *rather* than the other: for every one that exalteth himself shall be abased; and **he that humbleth himself shall be exalted.**
15. **And they brought** unto him also **infants, that he would touch them: but** when **his disciples** saw *it*, they **rebuked them.**
16. **But Jesus** called them *unto him*, and **said, Suffer little children to come unto me,** and forbid them not: **for of such is the kingdom** of God.
17. Verily I say unto you, **Whosoever shall not receive the kingdom** of God **as a** little **child shall in no wise enter** therein.
18. **And a certain ruler asked** him, saying, Good Master, **what shall I do to inherit eternal life?**
19. **And Jesus said** unto him, Why callest thou me good? none *is* good, save one, *that is*, God.
20. Thou knowest the

commandments,

Do not commit adultery,

Do not

kill, Do not

steal, Do not

bear false witness, Honour thy father and thy mother.

21. **And he said, All these have I kept** from my youth up.

22. **Now when Jesus heard** these things, **he said** unto him, Yet lackest thou one thing:

sell all that thou hast, and distribute unto the poor, and thou shalt have treasure in heaven: and come, follow me.

23. **And** when he heard this, **he was** very **sorrowful: for he was very rich.**

24. **And when Jesus saw** that he was very sorrowful, **he said, How hardly shall they that have riches enter into the kingdom** of God!

25. **For it is easier for a camel to go through a needle's eye,** than for a rich man to enter into the kingdom of God.

26. **And they that heard it said, Who then can be saved?**

27. **And he said, The things** which are **impossible with men are possible with God.**

28. **Then Peter said,** Lo, **we have left all, and followed thee.**

29. **And he said** unto them, Verily I say unto you, **There is no man that hath left house, or parents, or brethren, or wife, or children, for the kingdom of God's sake,**

30. **Who shall not receive manifold more** in this present time, **and** in the world to come **life everlasting.**

31. **Then he took** unto him **the twelve, and said** unto them, Behold, **we go up to Jerusalem, and all things** that are **written by the prophets** concerning the Son of man **shall be accomplished.**

32. **For he shall be delivered unto the Gentiles,** and shall be mocked, and spitefully entreated, and spitted on:

33. **And they shall** scourge him, and **put him to death: and the third day he shall rise** again.

34. And they understood none of these things: and this saying was hid from them, neither knew they the things which were spoken.

35. **And** it came to pass, that **as he was come** nigh **unto Jericho, a** certain **blind man sat** by the way side **begging:**

36. And hearing the multitude pass by, he asked what it meant.

37. And they told him, that Jesus of Nazareth passeth by.

38. **And he cried,** saying, **Jesus,** thou son of David, **have mercy on me.**

39. **And they** which went before **rebuked him,** that he should hold his peace: but he cried so much the more, Thou son of David, have mercy on me.

40. **And Jesus** stood, and **commanded him to be brought** unto him: and when he was come near, he asked him,

41. **Saying, What wilt thou that I shall do** unto thee? And he said, Lord, that I may receive my sight.

42. **And Jesus said** unto him, **Receive thy sight: thy faith hath saved thee.**

43. **And immediately he received his sight,** and followed him, glorifying God: and all the people, when they saw it, gave praise unto God.

CHAPTER 19

1. And *Jesus* entered and passed through Jericho.
2. And, behold, *there was* **a man named Zacchaeus,** which was **the chief among the publicans,** and he **was rich.**
3. **And he sought to see Jesus** who he was; **and could not** for the press, **because he was little of stature.**
 4. **And he** ran before, and **climbed up into a sycomore tree** to see him: for he was to pass that *way.*
5. **And when Jesus came** to the place, **he looked up,** and saw him, **and said** unto him, **Zacchaeus,** make haste, and **come down; for** to-day **I must abide at thy house.**
6. **And he** made haste, and **came down,** and received him joyfully.
7. **And when they saw** it, **they all murmured, saying, That he was** gone to be guest **with a man that is a sinner.**
8. **And Zacchaeus** stood, and **said** unto the Lord: Behold, Lord, the **half of my goods I give to the poor; and if I have taken any thing from any man** by false accusation, **I restore him fourfold.**
9. **And Jesus said** unto him, **This day is salvation come to this house,** forsomuch as he also is a son of Abraham.
10. **For the Son of man is come** to seek and **to save that which was lost.**
11. **And** as they heard these things, **he** added and **spake a parable,** because he was nigh to Jerusalem, and because they thought that the kingdom of God should immediately appear.
12. He said therefore, **A certain nobleman went into a far country to receive** for himself **a kingdom,** and to return.
13. **And he called his ten servants, and delivered them ten pounds, and said** unto them, **Occupy till I come.**
14. But his citizens hated him, and sent a message after him, saying, We will not have this *man* to reign over us.
15. **And** it came to pass, that **when he** was **returned,** having received the kingdom, then **he commanded these servants to be called** unto him, to whom he had given the money, **that he might know how much every man had gained** by trading.
16. **Then came the first, saying, Lord, thy pound hath gained ten pounds.**
17. **And he said** unto him, **Well, thou good servant: because thou hast been faithful** in a very little, **have thou authority over ten cities.**
18. **And the second** came, saying, Lord, thy pound hath **gained five pounds.**
19. **And he said** likewise to him, **Be thou also over five cities.**
20. **And another came,** saying, Lord, behold, **here is thy pound,** which I have kept laid up in a napkin:
21. **For I feared thee, because thou art an austere man:** thou takest up that thou layedst not down, and reapest that thou didst not sow.
22. **And he saith** unto him, Out of thine own mouth will I judge thee, **thou wicked servant.** Thou knewest that I was an austere man,

taking up that I laid not down, and reaping that I did not sow:

23. **Wherefore then gavest not thou my money into the bank, that** at my coming **I might have** required mine own with **usury?**

24. And he said unto them that stood by, **Take** from him **the pound, and give it to him that hath ten pounds.**

25. (And they said unto him, Lord, he hath ten pounds.)

26. **For I say** unto you, **That unto every one which hath shall be given;** and from him that hath not, even that he hath shall be taken away from him.

27. **But those mine enemies,** which would not that I should reign over them, **bring hither, and slay them** before me.

28. And when he had thus spoken, he went before, ascending up to Jerusalem.

29. **And** it came to pass, **when he was come** nigh **to** Bethphage and Bethany, at the mount called **the mount of Olives, he sent two** of his **disciples,**

30. **Saying, Go ye into the village** over against *you* ; in the which at your entering **ye shall find a colt tied,** whereon yet never man sat: loose him, and **bring him hither.**

31. **And if any man ask** you, **Why do ye loose him?** thus shall ye **say** unto him, Because **the Lord hath need of him.**

32. And they that were sent went their way, and found even as he had said unto them.

33. And as they were loosing the colt, the owners thereof said unto them, Why loose ye the colt?

34. And they said, The Lord hath need of him.

35. **And they brought him** to Jesus: **and** they **cast their garments upon the colt, and they set Jesus thereon.**

36. **And** as he went, they **spread their clothes in the way.**

37. **And** when he was come nigh, even now at the descent of the mount of Olives, **the whole multitude** of the disciples **began to** rejoice and **praise God** with a loud voice **for all the mighty works that they had seen;**

38. Saying, Blessed *be* the King that cometh in the name of the Lord: peace in heaven, and glory in the highest.

39. **And some of the Pharisees** from among the multitude **said** unto him, Master, **rebuke thy disciples.**

40. **And he answered** and said unto them, I tell you that, **if these should hold their peace, the stones would** immediately **cry out.**

41. **And** when he was come near, **he beheld the city, and wept over it,**

42. **Saying, If thou hadst known,** even thou, at least in this thy day, **the things** *which belong* **unto thy peace! but now they are hid** from thine eyes.

43. **For** the days shall come upon thee, that **thine enemies shall** cast a trench about thee, and **compass thee round,** and keep thee in on every side,

44. **And shall lay thee even with the ground,** and thy children within thee; **and they shall not leave**

in thee
one stone upon another;
because thou knewest not
the time of
thy visitation.
45. **And he went into the**
temple, and began to cast
out them that sold therein,
and them that
bought;
46. **Saying** unto them,
It is written, My house is the
house of prayer: but ye
have made it a den
of thieves.
47. **And** he taught daily
in the temple. But
the chief priests and the
scribes and the chief of the people
sought to destroy him,
48. And could not find what they might
do: for all the people were very
attentive to hear him.

CHAPTER 20

1. And it came to pass, *that* on one of
those days, as he taught the people in
the temple,
and preached the gospel,
the chief priests and the
scribes came
upon *him* with the elders,
2. And spake unto him,
saying, Tell us, by what
authority doest thou these
things? or who is he that gave thee
this authority?
3. **And he answered and**
said unto them, I will also ask you
one thing; and answer me:
4. **The baptism of John, was**
it from heaven, or of men?
5. **And they reasoned**
with themselves,
saying, If we shall say,
From heaven; he will say,
Why then believed ye
him not?
6. **But and if we say,**
Of men; all
the people will stone us:
for they be persuaded that
John was a prophet.

7. **And they answered, that**
they could not tell
whence *it was.*
8. **And Jesus said** unto them,
Neither tell I you by what
authority I do these things.
9. **Then began he to speak**
to the people
this parable; A certain
man planted a vineyard,
and let it forth
to husbandmen, and went
into a far country
for a long time.
10. **And** at the season
he sent a servant
to the husbandmen,
that they should give him of
the fruit of the vineyard:
but the husbandmen beat
him, and sent *him* away empty.
11. **And again he sent**
another servant:
and they beat him also, and
entreated *him* shamefully, and sent
him away empty.
12. **And again he sent a**
third: and they wounded
him also, and cast *him* out.
13. **Then said the lord**
of the vineyard, What shall I do?
I will send my beloved son:
it may be they will reverence *him* when
they see him.
14. **But** when the husbandmen
saw him,
they reasoned
among themselves, saying,
This is the heir: come,
let us kill him, that the
inheritance may be ours.
15. So they cast him out of the
vineyard, and killed *him.*
What therefore shall the
lord of the vineyard
do unto them?
16. **He shall** come and
destroy these
husbandmen, and shall
give the vineyard to others.
And when they heard *it*, they said,
God forbid.
17. **And he** beheld them, and

■ **said,** What is this then that is
written,
■ **The stone which the**
■ **builders rejected,** the same
■ **is become the head of**
■ **the corner?**
18. Whosoever shall fall upon that
stone shall be broken; but on
whomsoever it shall fall, it will grind
him to powder.
■ 19. **And the** chief
■ **priests and the scribes**
the same hour sought to lay hands
on him; and they feared the people:
for they
■ **perceived that he had**
■ **spoken** this parable
■ **against them.**
■ 20. **And they watched**
him, and sent forth spies, which
should feign themselves just men,
■ **that they might take hold of**
■ **his words,** that
■ **so they might deliver him**
■ **unto** the power and authority of
■ **the governor.**
■ 21. **And they asked him,**
saying,
■ **Master, we know that thou**
sayest and teachest rightly, neither
acceptest thou the person *of any*, but
■ **teachest the way of**
■ **God truly:**
■ 22. **Is it lawful** for us
■ **to give tribute unto Caesar,**
or no?
■ 23. **But he** perceived their
craftiness, and
■ **said** unto them,
■ **Why tempt ye me?**
■ 24. **Shew me a penny.**
■ **Whose image** and superscription
■ **hath it? They answered**
and said,
■ **Caesar's.**
■ 25. **And he said** unto them,
■ **Render** therefore
■ **unto Caesar the things**
■ **which be Caesar's, and**
■ **unto God the things which**
■ **be God's.**
■ 26. **And they** could not take hold of
his words before the people: and they

■ **marvelled at his answer,**
and held their peace.
■ 27. **Then came** to him certain of
■ **the Sadducees, which deny**
that there is
■ **any resurrection;**
and they asked him,
■ 28. **Saying, Master, Moses**
■ **wrote** unto us,
■ **If any man's brother die,**
■ **having a wife,** and he die
■ **without children, that his**
■ **brother should take his**
■ **wife, and raise up seed**
unto his brother.
■ 29. **There were** therefore
■ **seven brethren: and the**
■ **first took a wife, and died**
■ **without children.**
30. And the second took her to wife,
and he died childless.
■ 31. **And** the third took her; and
■ **in like manner the seven**
■ **also: and** they
■ **left no children,** and died.
■ 32. **Last of all the woman**
■ **died** also.
■ 33. **Therefore in the**
■ **resurrection whose wife**
of them
■ **is she?** for seven had her to wife.
■ 34. **And Jesus answering**
■ **said** unto them,
The children of this world marry,
and are given in marriage:
■ 35. **But they which shall**
be accounted worthy to
■ **obtain** that world, and
■ **the resurrection** from the dead,
■ **neither marry, nor are**
■ **given in marriage:**
■ 36. **Neither can they die**
any more: for they are
equal unto the angels;
■ **and are the children of**
■ **God,** being the children of the
resurrection.
37. Now that the dead are raised,
even Moses shewed at the bush,
when he calleth the Lord the God of
Abraham, and the God of Isaac, and
the God of Jacob.
■ 38. **For he is not a God of the**

■ **dead, but of the living:**
for all live unto him.
■ 39. **Then** certain of
■ **the scribes** answering
■ **said,** Master,
■ **thou hast well said.**
40. And after that they durst not ask
him any *question at all*.
■ 41. **And he said** unto them,
■ **How say they that Christ is**
■ **David's son?**
■ 42. **And David** himself
■ **saith** in the book of Psalms,
■ **The Lord said unto**
■ **my Lord, Sit** thou
■ **on my right hand,**
43. Till I make thine enemies
thy footstool.
■ 44. **David therefore calleth**
■ **him Lord, how is he**
■ **then his son?**
■ 45. **Then** in the audience
of all the people
■ **he said unto his disciples,**
■ 46. **Beware of the scribes,**
which desire to walk in long robes, and
love greetings in the markets, and the
highest seats in the synagogues, and
the chief rooms at feasts;
■ 47. **Which devour widows'**
■ **houses, and for a shew**
■ **make long prayers: the**
■ **same shall receive**
■ **greater damnation.**

CHAPTER 21
■ 1. **And he** looked up, and
■ **saw the rich men casting**
■ **their gifts into the treasury.**
■ 2. **And** he saw also
■ **a** certain
■ **poor widow casting in** thither
■ **two mites.**
■ 3. **And he said,** Of a truth
I say unto you, that
■ **this poor widow hath cast**
■ **in more than they all:**
■ 4. **For all these have of their**
■ **abundance cast in**
unto the offerings of God:
■ **but she** of her penury
■ **hath cast in all the living**
■ **that she had.**

■ 5. **And as some spake of**
■ **the temple,** how it was adorned
with goodly stones and gifts,
■ **he said,**
6. *As for* these things which ye
behold, the days will come, in the
which
■ **there shall not be left one**
■ **stone upon another,**
that shall not be thrown down.
■ 7. **And they asked** him,
saying, Master, but when shall
these things be? and
■ **what sign will there be** when
these things shall come to pass?
■ 8. **And he said,** Take heed
that ye be not deceived: for
■ **many shall come in my**
■ **name, saying, I am Christ;**
and the time draweth near:
■ **go** ye
■ **not** therefore
■ **after them.**
■ 9. **But when ye shall hear of**
■ **wars** and commotions,
■ **be not terrified:** for these things
must first come to pass;
■ **but the end is not** by and by.
10. Then said he unto them,
■ **Nation shall rise against**
■ **nation,** and kingdom against
kingdom:
■ 11. **And great earthquakes**
shall be in divers places,
■ **and famines,**
and pestilences; and fearful sights
■ **and great signs shall there**
■ **be from heaven.**
■ 12. **But before all these, they**
■ **shall** lay their hands on you, and
■ **persecute you,** delivering *you* up
to the synagogues, and into prisons,
being brought before kings and rulers
■ **for my name's sake.**
■ 13. **And it shall turn to you**
■ **for a testimony.**
■ 14. **Settle it** therefore in your hearts,
■ **not to meditate before what**
■ **ye shall answer:**
■ 15. **For I will give you**
a mouth and
■ **wisdom,** which all your
adversaries shall not be able to

gainsay nor resist.

16. **And ye shall be betrayed** both by parents, and brethren, and kinsfolks, and friends; **and some** of you **shall** they cause to **be put to death.**

17. **And ye shall be hated** of all *men* **for my name's sake.**

18. **But there shall not an hair of your head perish.**

19. In your patience possess ye your souls.

20. **And when ye shall see Jerusalem compassed with armies, then know that the desolation** thereof **is nigh.**

21. **Then let them** which are **in Judaea flee** to the mountains; and let them which are in the midst of it depart out; and let not them that are in the countries enter thereinto.

22. **For these be the days of vengeance, that all** things which are written **may be fulfilled.**

23. But woe unto them that are with child, and to them that give suck, in those days! for **there shall be great distress** in the land, and wrath upon this people.

24. And they shall fall by the edge of the sword, and shall be led away captive into all nations: **and Jerusalem shall be trodden down** of the Gentiles, **until the times of the Gentiles be fulfilled.**

25. **And there shall be signs in the sun,** and in the **moon, and** in the **stars; and upon the earth distress of nations,** with perplexity; the sea and the waves roaring;

26. **Men's hearts failing them for fear,** and for looking after those things which are coming on the earth: for the powers of heaven shall be shaken.

27. **And then shall they see the Son of man coming** in a cloud with power and great glory.

28. **And when these things** begin to **come to pass, then look up,** and lift up your heads; **for your redemption draweth nigh.**

29. **And he spake** to them **a parable; Behold the fig tree,** and all the trees;

30. **When they now shoot forth, ye** see and **know** of your own selves **that summer is** now **nigh** at hand.

31. **So likewise ye, when ye see these things** come to pass, **know** ye **that the kingdom of God is** nigh **at hand.**

32. Verily I say unto you, **This generation shall not pass away, till all be fulfilled.**

33. **Heaven and earth shall pass away: but my words shall not** pass away.

34. **And take heed** to yourselves, **lest** at any time **your hearts be overcharged with** surfeiting, and drunkenness, and **cares of this life, and so that day come upon you unawares.**

35. For as a snare shall it come on all them that dwell on the face of the whole earth.

36. **Watch** ye therefore, **and pray** always, **that ye may be accounted worthy** to escape all these things that shall come to pass, and **to stand before the Son** of man.

37. And in the day time he was teaching in the temple; and at night he went out, and abode in the mount that is called *the mount* of Olives.

38. And all the people came early in the morning to him in the temple, for to hear him.

CHAPTER 22

1. **Now the feast of unleavened bread drew nigh,** which is called the Passover. 2. **And the** chief **priests and scribes sought how they might kill him;** for they feared the people.

3. **Then entered Satan into Judas** surnamed Iscariot, being of the number of the twelve. 4. **And he went** his way, **and communed with the chief priests** and captains, **how he might betray him unto them.** 5. **And they** were glad, and **covenanted to give him money.** 6. **And he** promised, and **sought opportunity to betray him** unto them in the absence of the multitude.

7. **Then came the day of** unleavened bread, when **the passover** must be killed. 8. **And he sent Peter and John, saying, Go and prepare us the passover,** that we may eat. 9. And they said unto him, Where wilt thou that we prepare? 10. And he said unto them, Behold, when ye are entered into the city, there shall a man meet you, bearing a pitcher of water; follow him into the house where he entereth in. 11. And ye shall say unto the goodman of the house, The Master saith unto thee, Where is the guestchamber, where I shall eat the passover with my disciples? 12. And he shall shew you a large upper room furnished: there make ready. 13. **And they went, and** found as he had said unto them: and they **made ready the passover.** 14. **And** when the hour was come,

he sat down, and the twelve apostles with him. 15. **And he said** unto them, With desire **I have desired to eat this passover with you before I suffer:** 16. **For** I say unto you, **I will not any more eat** thereof, **until it be fulfilled in the kingdom** of God. 17. **And he took the cup, and gave thanks, and said, Take this,** and divide *it* among yourselves: 18. **For** I say unto you, **I will not drink of the fruit** of the vine, **until the kingdom of God shall come.** 19. **And he took bread,** and **gave thanks, and brake** *it*, and gave unto them, **saying, This is my body** which is **given for you: this do in remembrance of me.** 20. **Likewise also the cup** after supper, **saying, This cup** *is* **the new testament in my blood, which is shed for you.** 21. **But,** behold, the hand of **him that betrayeth me** *is* **with me on the table.** 22. **And truly the Son of man goeth,** as it was determined: **but woe unto that man by whom he is betrayed!** 23. **And they began to inquire** among themselves, **which of them** it was that **should do this thing.** 24. **And there was also a strife among them, which** of them **should be** accounted **the greatest.** 25. **And he said** unto them, The kings of the Gentiles exercise lordship over them; and they that exercise authority upon them are called benefactors.

26. But ye *shall* not *be* so: but
■ **he that is greatest** among you,
■ **let him** be as the younger; and he
that is chief, as he that doth
■ **serve.**

27. For whether *is* greater, he that
sitteth at meat, or he that serveth? *is*
not he that sitteth at meat? but
■ **I am among you as he**
■ **that serveth.**

■ 28. **Ye** are they which
■ **have continued with me**
in my temptations.

■ 29. **And I appoint** unto
■ **you a kingdom,** as my Father
hath appointed unto me;

■ 30. **That ye may eat** and drink
■ **at my table** in my kingdom,
■ **and sit** on thrones
■ **judging the twelve tribes**
■ **of Israel.**

■ 31. **And the Lord said,**
■ **Simon,** Simon, behold,
■ **Satan hath desired** *to have*
■ **you,** that he may sift *you* as wheat:

■ 32. **But I have prayed** for thee,
■ **that thy faith fail not:**
and when thou art converted,
strengthen thy brethren.

■ 33. **And he said** unto him,
■ **Lord, I am ready to go with**
■ **thee, both into prison, and**
■ **to death.**

■ 34. **And he said,** I tell thee,
■ **Peter, the cock shall not**
■ **crow** this day,
■ **before that thou shalt thrice**
■ **deny** that thou knowest
■ **me.**

35. And he said unto them, When I
sent you without purse, and scrip, and
shoes, lacked ye any thing? And they
said, Nothing.

36. Then said he unto them, But now,
he that hath a purse, let him take *it*,
and likewise *his* scrip: and he that
hath no sword, let him sell his
garment, and buy one.

37. For I say unto you, that this that is
written must yet be accomplished in
me, And he was reckoned among the
transgressors: for the things

concerning me have an end.

38. And they said, Lord, behold, here
are two swords. And he said unto
them, It is enough.

■ 39. **And he came**
out, and went, as he was wont,
■ **to the mount of Olives; and**
■ **his disciples also followed**
him.

40. And when he was at the place, he
said unto them, Pray that ye enter not
into temptation.

■ 41. **And he was withdrawn**
■ **from them** about a stone's cast,
■ **and kneeled down,**
■ **and prayed,**

■ 42. **Saying, Father,**
if thou be willing,
■ **remove this cup from me:**
■ **nevertheless not my will,**
■ **but thine, be done.**

■ 43. **And there appeared an**
■ **angel** unto him
■ **from heaven,**
■ **strengthening him.**

■ 44. **And being in an agony**
he prayed more earnestly: and
■ **his sweat was as it were**
■ **great drops of blood**
■ **falling** down
■ **to the ground.**

■ 45. **And when he**
rose up from prayer, and
■ **was come to his disciples,**
■ **he found them sleeping**
for sorrow,

■ 46. **And said** unto them,
Why sleep ye?
■ **rise and pray, lest ye enter**
■ **into temptation.**

■ 47. **And** while he yet spake,
■ **behold a multitude, and**
he that was called
■ **Judas,** one of the twelve,
■ **went before them, and**
■ **drew near** unto
■ **Jesus to kiss him.**

■ 48. **But Jesus said** unto him,
■ **Judas, betrayest thou the**
■ **Son** of man
■ **with a kiss?**

49. When they which were about him
saw what would follow, they said unto

him, Lord, shall we smite with the sword?

50. **And one** of them **smote the servant of the high priest, and cut off his right ear.**

51. **And Jesus** answered and said, Suffer ye thus far. And he **touched his ear, and healed him.**

52. **Then Jesus said** unto the chief priests, and captains of the temple, and the elders, which were come to him, **Be ye come** out, **as against a thief, with swords** and staves?

53. When I was daily with you in the temple, ye stretched forth no hands against me: but this is your hour, and the power of darkness.

54. **Then took they him,** and led *him*, **and brought him into the high priest's house. And Peter followed** afar off.

55. **And when they had kindled a fire** in the midst of the hall, and were set down together, **Peter sat** down **among them.**

56. **But a certain maid beheld him** as he sat by the fire, and earnestly looked upon him, **and said, This man was also with him.**

57. **And he denied** him, saying, Woman, I know him not.

58. **And** after a little while **another** saw him, and **said, Thou art also of them.** **And Peter said,** Man, **I am not.**

59. And about the space of one hour after **another** confidently **affirmed,** saying, Of a truth **this** *fellow* also **was with him:** for he is a Galilaean.

60. **And Peter said,** Man, **I know not what thou sayest. And immediately,**

while he yet spake, **the cock crew.**

61. **And the Lord** turned, and **looked upon Peter.** And Peter remembered the word of the Lord, how he had said unto him, Before the cock crow, thou shalt deny me thrice.

62. **And Peter went out, and wept bitterly.**

63. **And the men that held Jesus mocked him,** and smote *him.*

64. **And when they had blindfolded him, they struck him** on the face, and asked him, **saying, Prophesy, who** is that **smote thee?**

65. **And** many other things **blasphemously spake** they **against him.**

66. **And** as soon as it was day, **the elders** of the people and the chief priests and the scribes came together, and **led him into their council, saying,**

67. **Art thou the Christ?** tell us. **And he said** unto them, **If I tell you, ye will not believe:**

68. And if I also ask *you*, ye will not answer me, nor let *me* go.

69. **Hereafter shall the Son of man sit on the right hand of the power of God.**

70. **Then said they** all, **Art thou then the Son of God? And he said** unto them, **Ye say that I am.**

71. **And they said,** What **need we any further witness? for we** ourselves **have heard of his own mouth.**

CHAPTER 23

1. **And the whole multitude** of them arose, and **led him unto Pilate.**

2. And they began to accuse him, **saying, We found this**

- *fellow* perverting the nation, and
- **forbidding to give tribute to**
- **Caesar, saying** that
- **he** himself
- **is Christ a King.**
- 3. **And Pilate asked**
him, saying,
- **Art thou the King of the**
- **Jews? And he** answered him and
- **said, Thou sayest** *it.*
- 4. **Then said Pilate** to the chief
priests and *to* the people,
- **I find no fault in this man.**
- 5. **And they were the more**
- **fierce, saying, He stirreth**
- **up the people,** teaching
throughout all Jewry, beginning
- **from Galilee to this place.**
- 6. **When Pilate heard**
of Galilee, he asked whether
the man were a Galilaean.
- 7. And as soon as he knew
- **that he belonged unto**
- **Herod's jurisdiction, he**
- **sent him to Herod,** who himself
also was at Jerusalem at that time.
- 8. **And when Herod saw**
- **Jesus, he was exceeding**
- **glad:** for he was desirous to see him
of a long *season,*
- **because he had heard**
- **many things** of him;
- **and** he
- **hoped to have seen some**
- **miracle** done by him.
- 9. **Then he questioned** with
- **him** in many words;
- **but he answered** him
- **nothing.**
- 10. **And the chief priests and**
- **scribes** stood and
- **vehemently accused him.**
- 11. **And Herod** with his
men of war set him at nought,
and mocked *him,* and arrayed
him in a gorgeous robe, and
- **sent him again to Pilate.**
- 12. And the same day Pilate and
Herod were made friends together: for
before they were at enmity between
themselves.
- 13. **And Pilate,** when he had
- **called** together

- **the chief priests and**
the rulers and the people,
- 14. **Said** unto them,
- **Ye have brought this man**
unto me,
- **as one that perverteth the**
- **people: and,** behold,
- **I,** having examined *him* before you,
- **have found no fault in**
this man touching those things
whereof ye accuse
- **him:**
- 15. No, nor yet Herod: for I sent you to
him; and, lo, nothing worthy of death
is done unto him.
- 16. **I will therefore chastise**
- **him, and release** *him.*
- 17. (**For** of necessity
- **he must release one**
unto them
- **at the feast.**)
- 18. **And they cried** out all at
once, saying, Away with this *man,* and
- **release** unto us
- **Barabbas:**
- 19. (**Who for** a certain
- **sedition** made in the city,
- **and** for
- **murder, was cast**
- **into prison.**)
- 20. **Pilate** therefore,
- **willing to release Jesus,**
- **spake again** to them.
- 21. **But they cried,**
saying, Crucify *him,*
- **crucify him.**
- 22. **And he said** unto them
- **the third time, Why, what**
- **evil hath he done?** I have
found no cause of death in him: I will
therefore chastise him, and let *him* go.
- 23. **And they** were instant
- **with loud voices,** requiring that
he might be crucified. And the voices
of them and of the chief priests
- **prevailed.**
- 24. **And Pilate gave**
- **sentence** that it should be
- **as they required.**
- 25. **And** he released unto them
him that for sedition and murder
was cast into prison, whom they had
desired; but he

■ **delivered Jesus to**
■ **their will.**
■ 26. **And** as they led him away, they laid hold
■ **upon** one
■ **Simon, a Cyrenian,** coming out of the country, and on him
■ **they laid the cross,** that he might bear *it* after Jesus.
■ 27. **And** there followed him
■ **a great company** of people, and of women, which also bewailed and
■ **lamented him.**
■ 28. **But Jesus** turning unto them
■ **said,** Daughters of Jerusalem,
■ **weep not for me, but** weep
■ **for yourselves,** and for your children.
■ 29. **For, behold, the days**
■ **are coming, in** the
■ **which they shall say,**
■ **Blessed** *are* **the barren,** and the wombs that never bare, and the paps which never gave suck.
■ 30. **Then shall they** begin to
■ **say to the mountains, Fall**
■ **on us; and** to the hills,
■ **Cover us.**
31. For if they do these things in a green tree, what shall be done in the dry?
■ 32. **And there were also two** other,
■ **malefactors,** led with him
■ **to be put to death.**
■ 33. **And when they were**
■ **come to** the place, which is called
■ **Calvary,** there
■ **they crucified him, and the**
■ **malefactors,** one
■ **on the right** hand,
■ **and** the other on
■ **the left.**
■ 34. **Then said Jesus, Father,**
■ **forgive them; for they know**
■ **not what they do. And they**
■ **parted his raiment, and**
■ **cast lots.**
■ 35. **And the people** stood beholding. And the rulers also with them
■ **derided** *him,* **saying, He**

■ **saved others; let him save**
■ **himself,** if he be Christ, the chosen of God.
■ 36. **And the soldiers also**
■ **mocked him,** coming to him, and
■ **offering him vinegar,**
37. And saying, If thou be the king of the Jews, save thyself.
■ 38. **And a superscription** also
■ **was written over him** in letters of Greek, and Latin, and Hebrew,
■ **THIS IS THE KING OF THE**
■ **JEWS.**
■ 39. **And one of the**
■ **malefactors** which were hanged
■ **railed** on him,
■ **saying, If thou be Christ,**
■ **save thyself and us.**
■ 40. **But the other** answering
■ **rebuked him, saying, Dost**
■ **not thou fear God,** seeing thou art in the same condemnation?
41. And we indeed justly; for
■ **we receive the due reward**
■ **of our deeds: but this man**
■ **hath done nothing** amiss.
■ 42. **And he said** unto Jesus,
■ **Lord, remember me when**
■ **thou comest into**
■ **thy kingdom.**
■ 43. **And Jesus said** unto him, Verily I say unto thee,
■ **To-day shalt thou be with**
■ **me in paradise.**
■ 44. **And** it was about
■ **the sixth hour,** and
■ **there was a darkness** over all the earth
■ **until the ninth hour.**
45. And the sun was darkened,
■ **and the veil of the temple**
■ **was rent** in the midst.
■ 46. **And when Jesus had**
■ **cried** with a loud voice, he said,
■ **Father, into thy hands I**
■ **commend my spirit:** and having said thus,
■ **he gave up the ghost.**
■ 47. **Now when the centurion**
■ **saw** what was done,
■ **he glorified God, saying,** Certainly
■ **this was a righteous man.**

48. And all the people that came together to that sight, beholding the things which were done, smote their breasts, and returned.
49. And all his acquaintance, and the women that followed him from Galilee, stood afar off, beholding these things.
50. **And,** behold, *there was* a man named **Joseph,** a counsellor; *and he was* a good man, and a just:
51. (The same had not consented to the counsel and deed of them;) *he was* **of Arimathaea,** a city of the Jews: who also himself waited for the kingdom of God.
52. This *man* went unto Pilate, and **begged the body of Jesus.**
53. **And he** took it down, and **wrapped it in linen, and laid it in a sepulchre** that was hewn in stone, wherein never man before was laid.
54. And that day was the preparation, and the sabbath drew on.
55. **And the women** also, which came with him from Galilee, followed after, and beheld the sepulchre, and how his body was laid.
56. And they returned, and **prepared spices and ointments;** and rested the sabbath day according to the commandment.

CHAPTER 24

1. **Now upon the first** *day* **of the week,** very early in the morning, **they came unto the sepulchre, bringing the spices** which they had prepared, and certain *others* with them.
2. **And they found the stone rolled away** from the sepulchre.
3. **And they** entered in, and **found not the body of the Lord Jesus.**
4. **And** it came to pass, as they were much perplexed thereabout, behold, **two men stood by them in shining garments:**

5. **And** as they were afraid, and bowed down *their* faces to the earth, they **said** unto them, **Why seek ye the living among the dead?**
6. **He is not here, but is risen: remember how he spake** unto you when he was yet in Galilee,
7. **Saying, The Son of man must be** delivered into the hands of sinful men, and be **crucified, and the third day rise again.**
8. **And they remembered** his words,
9. **And returned** from the sepulchre, **and told** all these things unto **the eleven,** and to all the rest.
10. It was Mary Magdalene and Joanna, and Mary *the mother* of James, and other *women that were* with them, which told these things unto the apostles.
11. **And their words seemed** to them **as idle tales, and they believed them not.**
12. **Then arose Peter, and ran unto the sepulchre; and** stooping down, he **beheld the linen clothes laid by themselves,** and departed, wondering in himself at that which was come to pass.
13. **And, behold, two of them went** that same day **to** a village called **Emmaus,** which was from Jerusalem *about* threescore furlongs.
14. **And they talked** together **of all these things which had happened.**
15. **And** it came to pass, that, while they communed *together* and reasoned, **Jesus himself drew near,** and went with them.
16. **But their eyes were holden that they should not**

know him.
17. **And he said** unto them,
What manner of
communications *are* **these**
that ye have one to another, as
ye walk, and are sad?
18. **And the one** of them,
whose name was Cleopas,
answering
said unto him,
Art thou only a stranger
in Jerusalem,
and hast not known the
things which are come to
pass there in these days?
19. **And he said** unto them,
What things? And they said
unto him,
Concerning Jesus
of Nazareth, which was
a prophet mighty in deed
and word
before God and all the people:
20. **And how the chief**
priests and our rulers
delivered him to be
condemned to death, and have
crucified him.
21. **But we trusted**
that it had been
he which
should have redeemed
Israel: and beside all this, to-day is
the third day since these
things were done.
22. **Yea, and certain women**
also of our company made us
astonished, which were
early at the sepulchre;
23. And when they
found not his body,
they came,
saying, that they had also
seen a vision of angels,
which said that he
was alive.
24. And certain of them which were
with us went to the sepulchre, and
found *it* even so as the women had
said: but him they saw not.
25. **Then he said** unto them,
O fools, and slow of heart
to believe all that

the prophets have spoken:
26. **Ought not Christ to have**
suffered these things,
and to
enter into his glory?
27. **And beginning at Moses**
and all the prophets,
he expounded unto them in all
the scriptures the things
concerning himself.
28. And they drew nigh unto the
village, whither they went: and he
made as though he would have gone
further.
29. But they constrained him, saying,
Abide with us: for it is toward evening,
and the day is far spent. And he went
in to tarry with them.
30. **And** it came to pass,
as he sat at meat with them,
he took bread, and
blessed *it,* and brake,
and gave to them.
31. **And their eyes** were
opened, and they knew
him; and he vanished
out of their sight.
32. **And they said**
one to another,
Did not our heart burn
within us, while he talked
with us by the way, and
while he opened to
us the scriptures?
33. **And they**
rose up the same hour, and
returned to Jerusalem, and
found the eleven
gathered together, and them
that were with them,
34. Saying, The Lord is risen indeed,
and hath appeared to Simon.
35. **And they told** what things
were done in the way, and
how he was known of them
in breaking of bread.
36. **And** as they thus spake,
Jesus himself
stood in the midst of them,
and saith unto them,
Peace *be* **unto you.**
37. **But they were terrified**
and affrighted,

and supposed that they had seen a spirit.

38. And he said unto them, Why are ye troubled? and why do thoughts arise in your hearts?

39. Behold my hands and my feet, that it is I myself: handle me, and see; for a spirit hath not flesh and bones, as ye see me have.

40. And when he had thus spoken, he shewed them *his* hands and *his* feet.

41. And while they yet believed not for joy, and wondered, he said unto them, Have ye here any meat?

42. And they gave him a piece of a broiled fish, and of an honeycomb.

43. And he took *it*, and did eat before them.

44. And he said unto them, These *are* the words which I spake unto you, while I was yet with you, that all things must be fulfilled, which were written in the law of Moses, and *in* the prophets, and *in* the psalms, concerning me.

45. Then opened he their understanding, that they might understand the scriptures,

46. And said unto them, Thus it is written, and thus it behoved Christ to suffer, and to rise from the dead the third day:

47. And that repentance and remission of sins should be preached in his name among all nations, beginning at Jerusalem.

48. And ye are witnesses of these things.

49. And, behold, I send the promise of my Father upon you: but tarry ye in the city of Jerusalem, until ye be endued with power from on high.

50. And he led them out as far as to Bethany, and he lifted up his hands, and blessed them.

51. And it came to pass, while he blessed them, he was parted from them, and carried up into heaven.

52. And they worshipped him, and returned to Jerusalem with great joy:

53. And were continually in the temple, praising and blessing God. Amen.

THE GOSPEL ACCORDING TO JOHN

BACKGROUND INFORMATION

Author – John, one of The Twelve Disciples of Jesus.
Date written – probably **between 70** and **85** A.D.

Number of:
Versus -   879
Chapters -   21
Total Words - 19,099
Scan Words -9,115
Scan Words represent 47 % of Total Words.

Theme – The Eternal Word of God who **became a human** being in order **that we might have** the gift of **eternal life** through Him.

OUTLINE OF THE GOSPEL

I.   **The Introduction.**
Chapter 1

II. **Christ's glory and power** revealed.
Chapters 2—6

III. **Christ's conflicts** as He taught and continued to perform miracles.
Chapter 7—12

IV. **Christ's special revelations** to his disciples.
Chapters 13—17

V.   **Christ's arrest, trial, crucifixion and resurrection.**
Chapters 18—20

VI. **Christ's appearance to His disciples.**
Chapter 21

CHAPTER 1

1. In the beginning was the Word, and the Word was with God, and the Word was God.

2. The same was in the beginning with God.

3. All things were made by him; and without him was not any thing made that was made.

4. In him was life; and the life was the light of men.

5. And the light shineth in darkness; and the darkness comprehended it not.

6. There was a man sent from God, whose name *was* John.

7. The same came for a witness, to bear witness of the Light, that all *men* through him might believe.

8. He was not that Light, but was sent to bear witness of that Light.

9. *That* was the true Light, which lighteth every man that cometh into the world.

10. He was in the world, and the world was made by him, and the world knew him not.

11. He came unto his own, and his own received him not.

12. But as many as received him, to them gave he power to become the sons of God, *even* to them that believe on his name:

13. Which were born, not of blood, nor of the will of the flesh, nor of the will of man, but of God.

14. And the Word was made flesh, and dwelt among us, (and we beheld his glory, the glory as of the only begotten of the Father,) full of grace and truth.

15. John bare witness of him, and cried, saying, This was he of whom I spake, He that cometh after me is preferred before me: for he was before me.

16. And of his fulness have all we received, and grace for grace.

17. For the law was given by Moses, *but* grace and truth came by Jesus Christ.

18. No man hath seen God at any time; the only begotten Son, which is in the bosom of the Father, he hath declared *him.*

19. And this is the record of John, when the Jews sent priests and Levites from Jerusalem to ask him, Who art thou?

20. And he confessed, and denied not; but confessed, I am not the Christ.

21. And they asked him, What then? Art thou Elias? And he saith, I am not. Art thou that prophet? And he answered, No.

22. Then said they unto him, Who art thou? that we may give an answer to them that sent us. What sayest thou of thyself?

23. He said, I *am* the voice of one crying in the wilderness, Make straight the way of the Lord, as said the prophet Esaias.

24. And they which were sent were of the Pharisees.

25. And they asked him, and said unto him, Why baptizest thou then, if thou be not that Christ, nor Elias, neither that prophet?

26. John answered them, saying, I baptize with water: but there standeth one among you, whom ye know not;

27. He it is, who coming after me is preferred before me, whose shoe's latchet I am not worthy to unloose.

28. These things were done in

Bethabara beyond Jordan, where John was baptizing.

29. **The next day John seeth Jesus coming** unto him, **and saith, Behold the Lamb of God, which taketh away the sin of the world.**

30. **This is he** of whom I said, After me cometh a man which is **preferred before me:** for he was before me.

31. And I knew him not: but that he should be made manifest to Israel, therefore am I come baptizing with water.

32. **And John bare record, saying, I saw the Spirit descending** from heaven **like a dove, and** it abode **upon him.**

33. And I knew him not: but **he that sent me** to baptize with water, the same **said** unto me, **Upon whom thou shalt see the Spirit descending, and remaining** on him **the same** is he which **baptizeth with the Holy Ghost.**

34. And I saw, and bare record that this is the Son of God.

35. **Again the next day after John stood, and two of his disciples;**

36. **And looking upon Jesus** as he walked, **he saith, Behold the Lamb of God!**

37. **And the two disciples** heard him speak, and they **followed Jesus.**

38. **Then Jesus** turned, and saw them following, and **saith unto them, What seek ye? They said** unto him, Rabbi, (which is to say, being interpreted, Master,) **where dwellest thou?**

39. **He saith** unto them, **Come and see. They came** and saw where he dwelt, **and abode with him that**

day: for it was about the tenth hour.

40. **One of the two** which heard John *speak,* and followed him, **was Andrew,** Simon Peter's brother.

41. **He first findeth his own brother Simon, and saith** unto him, **We have found the Messias,** which is, being interpreted, the Christ.

42. **And he brought him to Jesus.** And when **Jesus** beheld him, he **said,** Thou art Simon the son of Jona: **thou shalt be called Cephas,** which is by interpretation, **A stone.**

43. **The day following Jesus** would go forth into Galilee, and **findeth Philip, and saith** unto him, **Follow me.**

44. Now Philip was of Bethsaida, the city of Andrew and Peter.

45. **Philip findeth Nathanael, and saith** unto him, **We have found him, of whom Moses** in the law, **and the prophets, did write,** Jesus of Nazareth, the son of Joseph.

46. **And Nathanael said** unto him, **Can there any good thing come out of Nazareth? Philip saith** unto him, **Come and see.**

47. **Jesus saw Nathanael** coming to him, **and saith** of him, Behold **an Israelite** indeed, **in whom is no guile!**

48. **Nathanael saith** unto him, **Whence knowest thou me? Jesus answered** and said unto him, Before that Philip called thee, **when thou wast under the fig tree, I saw thee.**

49. **Nathanael answered** and saith unto him,

Rabbi, thou art the Son of God; thou art the King of Israel.
50. **Jesus answered** and said unto him, **Because** I said unto thee, **I saw thee under the fig tree, believest thou? thou shalt see greater things than these.**
51. And he saith unto him, Verily, verily, I say unto you, **Hereafter ye shall see heaven open, and the angels of God ascending and descending upon the Son of man.**

CHAPTER 2

1. And the third day **there was a marriage in Cana** of Galilee; **and** the mother of Jesus was there:
2. And both Jesus was called, and his disciples, to the marriage.
3. And when they wanted wine, **the mother of Jesus saith unto him, They have no wine.**
4. Jesus saith unto her, Woman, what have I to do with thee? mine hour is not yet come.
5. **His mother saith unto the servants, Whatsoever he saith** unto you, **do** *it.*
6. **And there were** set there **six waterpots** of stone, after the manner of the purifying of the Jews, containing two or three firkins apiece.
7. **Jesus saith** unto them, **Fill the waterpots with water.** And they filled them up to the brim.
8. **And** he saith unto them, **Draw out now, and bear unto the governor** of the feast. And they bare *it.*
9. **When the ruler** of the feast had **tasted the water** that was made wine, and knew not whence it was: (but the servants which drew the water knew;) **the governor** of the feast

called the bridegroom,
10. **And saith** unto him, **Every man at the beginning doth set forth good wine;** and when men have well drunk, then that which is worse: *but* **thou hast kept the good wine until now.**
11. **This beginning of miracles did Jesus in Cana of Galilee, and** manifested forth his glory; and his disciples believed on him.
12. After this he went down to Capernaum, he, and his mother, and his brethren, and his disciples: and they continued there not many days.
13. **And the Jews' passover was at hand, and Jesus went up to Jerusalem.**
14. **And found in the temple those that sold** oxen and sheep and doves, **and the changers of money** sitting:
15. **And when he had made a scourge** of small cords, **he drove them all out** of the temple, and the sheep, and the oxen; and poured out the changers' money, **and overthrew the tables;**
16. **And said** unto them that sold doves, Take these things hence; **make not my Father's house an house of merchandise.**
17. And his disciples remembered that it was written, The zeal of thine house hath eaten me up.
18. **Then answered the Jews** and said unto him, **What sign shewest** thou unto us, **seeing that thou doest these things?**
19. **Jesus answered** and said unto them, **Destroy this temple, and in three days I will raise it up.**
20. Then said the Jews, Forty and six years was this temple in building, and

wilt thou rear it up in three days?

21. **But he spake of the temple of his body.**

22. **When therefore he was risen** from the dead, **his disciples remembered** that he had said this unto them; **and they believed** the scripture, and the word which Jesus had said.

23. **Now** when he was in Jerusalem **at the passover,** in the feast day, **many believed** in his name, **when they saw the miracles which he did.**

24. **But Jesus did not commit himself unto them, because** he knew all *men,*

25. And needed not that any should testify of man: for **he knew what was in man.**

CHAPTER 3

1. There was a man of the Pharisees, named **Nicodemus, a ruler** of the Jews:

2. The same **came to Jesus by night, and said** unto him, Rabbi, we know that **thou art a teacher come from God: for no man can do these miracles** that thou doest, **except God be with him.**

3. **Jesus** answered and **said unto him,** Verily, verily, I say unto thee, **Except a man be born again, he cannot see the kingdom of God.**

4. **Nicodemus saith** unto him, **How can a man be born** when he is old? can he enter **the second time** into his mother's womb, and be born?

5. **Jesus answered,** Verily, verily, I say unto thee, **Except a man be born of water and** *of* **the Spirit, he cannot enter into the kingdom** of God.

6. **That which is born of the flesh is flesh; and that** which is **born of the Spirit is spirit.**

7. **Marvel not that** I said unto thee, **Ye must be born again.**

8. **The wind bloweth** where it listeth, **and thou** hearest the sound thereof, but **canst not tell whence it cometh, and** whither it **goeth: so is every one** that is **born of the Spirit.**

9. **Nicodemus answered** and said unto him, **How can these things be?**

10. **Jesus answered** and said unto him, Art thou a master of Israel, and knowest not these things?

11. Verily, verily, I say unto thee, **We speak that we do know,** and testify that we have seen; and ye receive not our witness.

12. If I have told you earthly things, **and ye believe not,** how shall ye believe, if I tell you *of* heavenly things?

13. And no man hath ascended up to heaven, but he that came down from heaven, *even* the Son of man which is in heaven.

14. **And as Moses lifted up the serpent in the wilderness, even so must the Son of man be lifted up:**

15. **That whosoever believeth in him should not perish,** but have eternal life.

16. **For God so loved the world, that he gave his only begotten Son, that whosoever believeth in him should not perish, but have everlasting life.**

17. **For God sent not his Son** into the world **to condemn the world; but that the world through him might be saved.**

18. He that believeth on him is not condemned:

but he that believeth not is condemned already, because he hath not believed in the name of the only begotten Son of God. 19. **And this is the condemnation, that light is come** into the world, **and men loved darkness** rather than light, **because their deeds were evil.**

20. For every one that doeth evil hateth the light, neither cometh to the light, lest his deeds should be reproved. 21. **But he that doeth truth cometh to the light,** that his deeds may be made manifest, that they are wrought in God.

22. **After these things came Jesus** and his disciples **into** the land of **Judaea;** and there he tarried with them, and baptized.

23. **And John also was baptizing in Aenon** near to Salim, because there was much water there: and they came, and were baptized.

24. For John was not yet cast into prison.

25. **Then there arose a question** between *some* of John's disciples and the Jews **about purifying.**

26. **And they came unto John, and said** unto him, Rabbi, **he that was with thee** beyond Jordan, **to whom thou barest witness, behold,** the same baptizeth, and **all** *men* **come to him.**

27. **John answered** and said, A man can receive nothing, except it be given him from heaven.

28. Ye yourselves bear me witness, that I said, **I am not the Christ,** but that I am sent before him.

29. **He that hath the bride is the bridegroom: but the friend of the bridegroom,** which standeth and heareth him, **rejoiceth greatly** because of the bridegroom's voice: this **my joy therefore is fulfilled.**

30. **He must increase, but I** *must* **decrease.**

31. **He that cometh from above is above all:** he that is of the earth is earthly, and speaketh of the earth: he that cometh from heaven is above all.

32. And what he hath seen and heard, that he testifieth; and no man receiveth his testimony.

33. **He that hath received his testimony hath set to his seal that God is true.**

34. For he whom God hath sent speaketh the words of God: for God giveth not the Spirit by measure *unto him.*

35. **The Father loveth the Son, and hath given all things into his hand.**

36. **He that believeth on the Son hath everlasting life: and he that believeth not** the Son shall not see life; but **the wrath of God abideth on him.**

CHAPTER 4

1. When therefore the LORD knew how the Pharisees had heard that **Jesus** made and baptized more disciples than John,

2. (Though Jesus himself baptized not, but his disciples,)

3. He left Judaea, and **departed again into Galilee.**

4. And he must needs go **through Samaria.**

5. **Then cometh he to a city** of Samaria, which is **called Sychar,** near to the parcel of ground that Jacob gave to his son Joseph.

6. **Now Jacob's well was there. Jesus** therefore, being

wearied with *his* journey,

■ **sat thus on the well:** *and*

it was about the sixth hour.

■ 7. **There cometh a woman**

of Samaria

■ **to draw water: Jesus saith**

unto her,

■ **Give me to drink.**

8. (For his disciples were gone away unto the city to buy meat.)

■ 9. **Then saith the woman**

of Samaria unto him,

■ **How is it that** thou, being

■ **a Jew, askest drink of**

me, which am

■ **a woman of Samaria?** for the

Jews have no dealings with the Samaritans.

■ 10. **Jesus answered**

and said unto her,

■ **If thou knewest**

the gift of God, and

■ **who it is that saith** to thee,

■ **Give me to drink; thou**

■ **wouldest have asked of**

■ **him, and he would have**

■ **given thee living water.**

■ 11. **The woman saith**

unto him, Sir,

■ **thou hast nothing to draw**

■ **with,** and the well is deep: from

whence then hast thou that living water?

12. Art thou greater than our father Jacob, which gave us the well, and drank thereof himself, and his children, and his cattle?

■ 13. **Jesus answered**

and said unto her,

■ **Whosoever drinketh of this**

■ **water shall thirst again:**

■ 14. **But whosoever drinketh**

■ **of the water that I**

■ **shall give** him

■ **shall never thirst;**

but the water that

■ **I shall give him** shall be in him

■ **a well of water springing up**

■ **into everlasting life.**

■ 15. **The woman saith** unto him,

■ **Sir, give me this water,** that I

thirst not, neither come hither to draw.

■ 16. **Jesus saith** unto her, Go,

■ **call thy husband,**

and come hither.

■ 17. **The woman** answered and

■ **said, I have no husband.**

■ **Jesus said** unto her,

■ **Thou hast well said,**

I have no husband:

■ 18. **For thou hast had five**

■ **husbands;** and he whom thou now

hast is not thy husband: in that saidst thou truly.

■ 19. **The woman saith**

unto him, Sir, I perceive that

■ **thou art a prophet.**

■ 20. **Our fathers worshipped**

■ **in this mountain; and ye**

■ **say, that in Jerusalem is**

■ **the place** where men ought

■ **to worship.**

■ 21. **Jesus saith** unto her, Woman,

believe me, the hour cometh, when ye shall neither in this mountain, nor yet at Jerusalem, worship the Father.

■ 22. **Ye worship ye know not**

■ **what:** we know what we worship: for

salvation is of the Jews.

■ 23. **But the hour** cometh, and

■ **now is, when the true**

■ **worshippers shall worship**

■ **the Father in spirit and in**

■ **truth:** for the Father seeketh such to

worship him.

■ 24. **God** *is* **a Spirit: and they**

■ **that worship him must**

■ **worship** *him* **in spirit**

■ **and in truth.**

■ 25. **The woman saith** unto him,

■ **I know that Messias**

cometh, which is called Christ:

■ **when he is come,** he

■ **will tell us all things.**

■ 26. **Jesus saith** unto her,

■ **I** that speak unto thee

■ **am** *he.*

27. An upon this came his disciples, and marvelled that he talked with the woman: yet no man said, What seekest thou? or, Why talkest thou with her?

■ 28. **The woman**

then left her waterpot, and

■ **went** her way

■ **into the city, and saith**

to the men,

29. **Come, see a man, which told me all** things that ever **I did: is not this the Christ?**

30. Then they went out of the city, and came unto him.

31. **In the mean while his disciples prayed him, saying, Master, eat.**

32. **But he said** unto them, **I have meat to eat that ye know not of.**

33. **Therefore said the disciples** one to another, **Hath any man brought him *aught* to eat?**

34. **Jesus saith** unto them, **My meat is to do the will of him that sent me,** and to finish his work.

35. **Say not ye, There are yet four months, and *then* cometh harvest?** behold, I say unto you, **Lift up your eyes,** and look on **the fields;** for they **are white already to harvest.**

36. **And he that reapeth** receiveth wages, and **gathereth fruit unto life eternal:** that both he that soweth and he that reapeth may rejoice together.

37. And herein is that saying true, One soweth, and another reapeth.

38. I sent you to reap that whereon ye bestowed no labour: other men laboured, and ye are entered into their labours.

39. **And many of the Samaritans** of that city **believed** on him **for the saying of the woman,** which testified, He told me all that ever I did.

40. So when **the Samaritans** were come unto him, they **besought him that he would tarry** with them: **and he abode there two days.**

41. **And many more believed** because of his own word;

42. **And said unto the woman, Now we believe,** not because of thy saying: **for we have heard *him* ourselves, and know that this is indeed the Christ,** the Saviour of the world.

43. **Now** after two days **he** departed thence, and **went into Galilee.**

44. **For Jesus himself testified, that a prophet hath no honour in his own country.**

45. **Then** when he was come into Galilee, **the Galilaeans received him, having seen all the things that he did at Jerusalem** at the feast: for they also went unto the feast.

46. **So Jesus came again into Cana** of Galilee, where he made the water wine. **And** there was **a certain nobleman,** whose son was sick at Capernaum.

47. When he heard that Jesus was come out of Judaea into Galilee, he went unto him, and **besought him that he would** come down, and **heal his son:** for he was **at the point of death.**

48. Then said Jesus unto him, Except ye see signs and wonders, ye will not believe.

49. **The nobleman saith** unto him, **Sir, come down ere my child die.**

50. **Jesus saith** unto him, Go thy way; **thy son liveth. And the man believed** the word that Jesus had spoken unto him, and he went his way.

51. **And** as he was now going down, **his servants met him,**

and told *him,*

■ **saying, Thy son liveth.**

52. Then inquired he of them the hour when he began to amend. And they said unto him, Yesterday at the seventh hour the fever left him.

53. So the father knew that *it was* at the same hour, in the which Jesus said unto him, Thy son liveth: and himself believed, and his whole house.

■ 54. **This** *is* **again the second**
■ **miracle** *that* **Jesus did,**

when he was come out of Judaea into Galilee.

CHAPTER 5

■ 1. **After this** there was a feast of the Jews; and

■ **Jesus went up**
■ **to Jerusalem.**

2. Now there is at Jerusalem
■ **by** the sheep *market*
■ **a pool,** which is
■ **called** in the Hebrew tongue
■ **Bethesda, having five**
■ **porches.**
■ 3. **In these lay** a great multitude of
■ **impotent folk,**

of blind, halt, withered,

■ **waiting for the moving**
■ **of the water.**
■ 4. **For an angel went down**

at a certain season

■ **into the pool, and troubled**
■ **the water: whosoever then**
■ **first after the troubling of**
■ **the water stepped in**
■ **was made whole**

of whatsoever disease he had.

■ 5. **And a certain man**

was there, which

■ **had an infirmity thirty and**
■ **eight years.**
■ 6. **When Jesus saw him**

lie, and knew that he had been now a long time *in that case,*

■ **he saith** unto him,
■ **Wilt thou be made whole?**
■ 7. **The impotent man**
■ **answered** him, Sir,
■ **I have no man,**

when the water is troubled,

■ **to put me into the pool:** but

while I am coming, another steppeth down before me.

■ 8. **Jesus saith** unto him,
■ **Rise, take up thy bed,**
■ **and walk.**
■ 9. **And immediately the man**
■ **was made whole,** and took up

his bed, and walked: and on the same day was the sabbath.

■ 10. **The Jews therefore said**
■ **unto him** that was cured,
■ **It is the sabbath day: it is**
■ **not lawful for thee to**
■ **carry** *thy* **bed.**
■ 11. **He answered** them,
■ **He that made me whole,**

the same

■ **said** unto me,
■ **Take up thy bed,** and walk.
■ 12. **Then asked they him,**
■ **What man** is that which said unto

thee, Take up thy bed, and walk?

■ 13. **And he** that was healed
■ **wist not who it was:** for Jesus

had conveyed himself away, a multitude being in *that* place.

■ 14. **Afterward Jesus findeth**
■ **him** in the temple,
■ **and said** unto him, Behold,
■ **thou art made whole: sin**
■ **no more,**

lest a worse thing come unto thee.

■ 15. **The man** departed, and
■ **told the Jews that it was**
■ **Jesus,** which had made him whole.

16. **And** therefore did

■ **the Jews** persecute Jesus, and
■ **sought to slay him,**
■ **because he had done**
■ **these things**
■ **on the sabbath day.**
■ 17. **But Jesus answered** them,
■ **My Father worketh** hitherto,
■ **and I work.**
■ 18. **Therefore the Jews**
■ **sought the more to kill him,**
■ **because he** not only had broken

the sabbath, but

■ **said** also that
■ **God was his Father,**

making himself equal with God.

■ 19. **Then answered Jesus** and

said unto them, Verily, verily, I say unto you, **The Son can do nothing of himself, but what he seeth the Father do:** for what things soever he doeth, these also doeth the Son likewise. 20. **For the Father loveth the Son, and sheweth him all things that himself doeth:** and he will shew him greater works than these, that ye may marvel. 21. **For as the Father raiseth up the dead,** and quickeneth *them;* **even so the Son quickeneth whom he will.** 22. **For the Father** judgeth no man, but **hath committed all judgment unto the Son:** 23. That all *men* should honour the Son, even as they honour the Father. **He that honoureth not the Son honoureth not the Father** which hath sent him. 24. Verily, verily, I say unto you, **He that heareth my word, and believeth** on him that sent me, **hath everlasting life, and** shall not come into condemnation; but **is passed from death unto life.** 25. Verily, verily, I say unto you, **The hour** is coming, and **now is, when the dead shall hear the voice of the Son** of God: **and they that hear shall live.** 26. For as the Father hath life in himself; so hath he given to the Son to have life in himself; 27. And hath given him authority to execute judgment also, because he is the Son of man. 28. Marvel not at this: for **the hour is coming, in the which all that are in the graves shall**

hear his voice, 29. **And shall come forth;** they that have done good, **unto the resurrection of life; and** they that have done evil, unto the resurrection of **damnation.** 30. **I can** of mine own self **do nothing: as I hear, I judge:** and my judgment is just; because I seek not mine own will, but the will of the Father which hath sent me. 31. **If I bear witness of myself, my witness is not true.** 32. **There is another that beareth witness of me;** and I know that the witness which he witnesseth of me is true. 33. **Ye sent unto John, and he bare witness** unto the truth. 34. But I receive not testimony from man: but these things I say, that ye might be saved. 35. **He was** a burning and **a shining light:** and ye were willing for a season to rejoice in his light. 36. **But I have greater witness than** *that* of **John:** for the works which the Father hath given me to finish, **the same works that I do, bear witness of me, that the Father hath sent me.** 37. **And the Father** himself, which hath sent me, **hath borne witness of me.** Ye have neither heard his voice at any time, nor seen his shape. 38. **And ye have not his word** abiding in you: **for whom he hath sent, him ye believe not.** 39. **Search the scriptures; for** in them ye think ye have eternal life: and **they** are they which **testify of me.** 40. And ye will not come to me, that ye might have life. 41. I receive not honour from men.

42. **But** I know you, that **ye have not the love of God** in you.

43. **I am come in my Father's name, and ye receive me not:** if another shall come in his own name, him ye will receive.

44. How can ye believe, which receive honour one of another, and seek not the honour that *cometh* from God only?

45. **Do not think that I will accuse you** to the Father: **there is** *one* **that accuseth you,** *even* **Moses,** in whom ye trust.

46. For had ye believed **Moses,** ye would have believed me; for he **wrote of me.**

47. **But if ye believe not his writings, how shall ye believe my words?**

CHAPTER 6

1. After these things **Jesus went over the sea of Galilee,** which is *the sea* of Tiberias.

2. **And a great multitude followed him, because they saw his miracles** which he did on them that were diseased.

3. **And Jesus went up into a mountain,** and there he sat with his disciples.

4. And the passover, a feast of the Jews, was nigh.

5. **When Jesus** then lifted up *his* eyes, and **saw a great company come** unto him, **he saith unto Philip, Whence shall we buy bread,** that these may eat?

6. **And this he said to prove him:** for he himself knew what he would do.

7. **Philip answered him, Two hundred pennyworth of bread is not sufficient** for them, that every one of them may take a little.

8. One of his disciples, **Andrew,** Simon Peter's brother, **saith** unto him,

9. There is **a lad** here, which **hath five barley loaves, and two small fishes:** but what are they among so many?

10. **And Jesus said, Make the men sit down.** Now there was much grass in the place. So the men sat down, **in number about five thousand.**

11. **And Jesus took the loaves; and when he had given thanks, he distributed** to the disciples, and the disciples to them that were set down; **and likewise of the fishes** as much as they would.

12. **When they were filled, he said** unto his disciples, **Gather up** the fragments that remain, **that nothing be lost.**

13. **Therefore they gathered** *them* together, and filled **twelve baskets with the fragments** of the five barley loaves, **which remained** over and above unto them that had eaten.

14. **Then those men, when they had seen the miracle** that Jesus did, **said, This is** of a truth **that prophet that should come** into the world.

15. **When Jesus** therefore **perceived that they would** come and take him by force, to **make him a king, he departed** again into a mountain himself alone.

16. **And** when even was *now* come, **his disciples went** down unto the sea,

17. **And entered into a ship, and went** over the sea **toward Capernaum.** And it

was now dark, and Jesus was not come to them.

18. **And the sea arose** by reason **of a great wind** that blew. 19. **So when they had rowed about** five and twenty or **thirty furlongs, they see Jesus walking on the sea,** and drawing nigh unto the ship: **and they were afraid.** 20. **But he saith** unto them, **It is I; be not afraid.** 21. **Then they willingly received him** into the ship: **and** immediately **the ship was at the land** whither they went.

22. The day following, when the people which stood on the other side of the sea saw that there was none other boat there, save that one whereinto his disciples were entered, and that Jesus went not with his disciples into the boat, but *that* his disciples were gone away alone;

23. (Howbeit there came other boats from Tiberias nigh unto the place where they did eat bread, after that the Lord had given thanks:)

24. **When the people** therefore **saw that Jesus was not there,** neither his disciples, **they** also took shipping, and **came to Capernaum,** seeking for Jesus.

25. **And when they had found him** on the other side of the sea **they said** unto him, Rabbi, **when camest thou hither?** 26. **Jesus answered** them and said, Verily, verily, I say unto you, **Ye seek me,** not because ye saw the miracles, but **because ye did eat of the loaves,** and were filled.

27. **Labour** not for the meat which perisheth, but **for that meat which endureth unto everlasting life, which the Son** of man **shall give** unto you: for him hath

God the Father sealed. 28. **Then said they** unto him, **What shall we do,** that we might work the works of God? 29. **Jesus answered** and said unto them, **This is the work of God, that ye believe on him whom he hath sent.** 30. **They said** therefore unto him, **What sign shewest thou** then, that we may see, and believe thee? **what dost thou work?** 31. **Our fathers did eat manna** in the desert; **as it is written, He gave them bread from heaven** to eat. 32. **Then Jesus said** unto them, Verily, verily, I say unto you, **Moses gave you not that bread from heaven;** but my Father giveth you the true bread from heaven. 33. **For the bread of God is he which cometh down** from heaven, **and giveth life** unto the world. 34. **Then said they** unto him, Lord, evermore **give us this bread.** 35. **And Jesus said** unto them, **I am the bread of life:** he that cometh to me shall never hunger; and he that believeth on me shall never thirst. 36. **But** I said unto you, That **ye** also have seen me, and **believe not.** 37. **All that the Father giveth** me shall **come to me;** and him that cometh to me I will in no wise cast out. 38. **For I came** down from heaven, **not to do mine own will, but the will of him that sent me.** 39. And this is the Father's will which hath sent me, that of all which he hath given me I should lose nothing, but should raise it up again at the last day. 40. **And** this is the will of him that sent me, that every one which seeth the Son, and believeth on him, may have everlasting life: and I will raise him up at the last day.

41. **The Jews then murmured** at him, **because he said, I am the bread** which came down **from heaven.**

42. **And they said, Is not this Jesus, the son of Joseph,** whose father and mother we know? **how is it** then that **he saith, I came down from heaven?**

43. **Jesus therefore answered** and said unto them, Murmur not among yourselves.

44. **No man can come to me, except the Father** which hath sent me draw him: and I will raise him up at the last day.

45. It is written in the prophets, And they shall be all taught of God. **Every man therefore that** hath heard, and **hath learned of the Father, cometh unto me.**

46. Not that any man hath seen the Father, save he which is of God, he hath seen the Father.

47. Verily, verily, I say unto you, **He that believeth on me hath everlasting life.**

48. **I am that bread of life.**

49. **Your fathers did eat manna** in the wilderness, **and are dead.**

50. This is the bread which cometh down from heaven, that a man may eat thereof, and not die.

51. **I am the living bread** which came down from heaven: **if any man eat** of this bread, **he shall live for ever: and the bread that I will give is my flesh,** which I will give for the life of the world.

52. **The Jews therefore strove** among themselves, **saying, How can this man give us** *his* **flesh to eat?**

53. **Then Jesus said** unto them, Verily, verily, I say unto you, **Except ye eat the flesh of the Son of man, and drink his blood, ye have no life** in you.

54. **Whoso eateth my flesh, and drinketh my blood, hath eternal life; and** I will raise him up at the last day.

55. For my flesh is meat indeed, and my blood is drink indeed.

56. He that eateth my flesh, and drinketh my blood, **dwelleth in me, and I in him.**

57. As the living Father hath sent me, and **I live by the Father: so he that eateth me,** even he **shall live by me.**

58. This is that bread which came down from heaven: not as your fathers did eat manna, and are dead: **he that eateth of this bread shall live forever.**

59. These things said he in the synagogue, as he taught in Capernaum.

60. **Many therefore of his disciples,** when they had heard *this,* **said, This is an hard saying;** who can hear it?

61. **When Jesus knew** in himself that **his disciples murmured** at it, **he said** unto them, **Doth this offend you?**

62. *What* and if ye shall see the Son of man ascend up where he was before?

63. **It is the spirit that quickeneth;** the flesh profiteth nothing: **the words that I speak** unto you, *they* **are spirit, and** *they* are **life.**

64. **But** there are **some** of you that **believe not. For Jesus knew** from the beginning **who** they were that **believed not, and who**

should betray him.

65. **And he said,** Therefore said I unto you, that **no man can come unto me, except it were given** unto him **of my Father.**

66. **From that** *time* **many of his disciples** went back, and **walked no more with him.**

67. **Then said Jesus unto the twelve, Will ye also go away?**

68. Then Simon **Peter answered him, Lord, to whom shall we go? thou hast the words of eternal life.**

69. **And we believe** and are sure **that thou art** that Christ, **the Son of the living God.**

70. **Jesus answered** them, Have not I chosen you twelve, and **one of you is a devil?**

71. **He spake of Judas Iscariot** *the son* of Simon: for he it was that should betray him, being one of the twelve.

CHAPTER 7

1. After these things **Jesus walked in Galilee:** for he would not walk in Jewry, **because the Jews sought to kill him.**

2. Now the Jew's feast of tabernacles was at hand.

3. **His brethren therefore said** unto him, Depart hence, and **go into Judaea,** that thy disciples also may see the works that thou doest.

4. **For** *there is* **no man** *that* **doeth any thing in secret,** and he himself seeketh to be known openly. If thou do these things, **shew thyself to the world.**

5. For neither did his brethren believe in him.

6. **Then Jesus said** unto them, **My time is not yet come:** but your time is alway ready.

7. The world cannot hate you; but me it hateth, because I testify of it, that

the works thereof are evil.

8. **Go ye up unto this feast: I go not up yet** unto this feast: for my time is not yet full come.

9. **When he had said these words** unto them, **he abode** *still* **in Galilee.**

10. **But** when his brethren were gone up, **then went he also up** unto the feast, not openly, but as it were **in secret.**

11. **Then the Jews** sought him at the feast, and **said, Where is he?**

12. **And there was much murmuring** among the people concerning him: for **some said, He is a good man: others said, Nay;** but he deceiveth the people.

13. **Howbeit no man spake openly** of him **for fear** of the Jews.

14. **Now** about the midst of the feast **Jesus went up into the temple, and taught.**

15. **And the Jews marvelled, saying, How knoweth this man letters, having never learned?**

16. **Jesus answered** them, and said, **My doctrine is** not mine, but **his that sent me.**

17. **If any man will do his will, he shall know** of the doctrine, **whether it be of God,** or *whether* I speak of myself.

18. He that speaketh of himself seeketh his own glory: but he that seeketh his glory that sent him, the same is true, and no unrighteousness is in him.

19. **Did not Moses give you the law, and** *yet* **none** of you **keepeth the law? Why go ye about to kill me?**

20. **The people answered** and said, **Thou hast a devil:** who goeth about to kill thee?

21. **Jesus answered** and said unto them

I have done one work, and ye all marvel.

22. Moses therefore gave unto you circumcision; (not because it is of Moses, but of the fathers;) **and** ye on the sabbath day circumcise a man.

23. **If a man on the sabbath day receive circumcision, that the law** of Moses **should not be broken; are ye angry at me, because I have made a man** every whit **whole on the sabbath day?**

24. Judge not according to the appearance, but judge righteous judgment.

25. **Then said some** of them of Jerusalem,

Is not this he, whom they seek to kill?

26. **But, lo,** he speaketh boldly, and **they say nothing** unto him. **Do the rulers know** indeed that **this is** the very **Christ?**

27. Howbeit we know this man whence he is: but when Christ cometh, no man knoweth whence he is.

28. **Then cried Jesus in the temple** as he taught, saying, Ye both know me, and ye know whence I am: and

I am not come of myself, but he that sent me is true, whom ye know not.

29. **But I know him:** for I am from him,

and he hath sent me.

30. **Then they sought to take him: but no man laid hands on him,** because his hour was not yet come.

31. **And many** of the people **believed** on him,

and said, When Christ cometh, will he do more miracles than these which this *man* hath done?

32. The Pharisees heard that the people murmured such things concerning him; and

the Pharisees and the chief priests sent officers to take him.

33. **Then said Jesus** unto them, Yet a little while am I with you, and *then* I go unto him that sent me.

34. **Ye shall seek me, and shall not find** *me:* **and where I am,** *thither* **ye cannot come.**

35. **Then said the Jews** among themselves,

Whither will he go, that we shall not find him? will he go unto the dispersed among the Gentiles, and teach the Gentiles?

36. What *manner of* saying is this that he said, Ye shall seek me, and shall not find *me*: and where I am, *thither ye* cannot come?

37. **In the last day, that great day** of the feast, Jesus stood and **cried, saying, If any man thirst, let him come unto me, and drink.**

38. **He that believeth on me,** as the scripture hath said, **out of his belly shall flow rivers of living water.**

39. **(But this spake he of the Spirit,** which they that believe on him should receive: for the Holy Ghost was not yet *given*; because that Jesus was not yet glorified.)

40. **Many of the people** therefore, when they heard this saying, **said,** Of a truth **this is the Prophet.**

41. **Others said, This is the Christ. But some said, Shall Christ come out of Galilee?**

42. **Hath not the scripture said, That Christ cometh** of the seed of David, and **out of the town of Bethlehem, where David was?**

43. **So there was a division among the people**

because of him.

44. And some of them would
have taken him; but no man
laid hands on him.

45. **Then came the officers
to the chief priests**
and Pharisees; and
they said unto them,
**Why have ye not
brought him?**

46. **The officers answered,
Never man spake
like this man.**

47. **Then answered them the
Pharisees, Are ye
also deceived?**

48. Have any of the rulers or of the
Pharisees believed on him?

49. But this people who knoweth not
the law are cursed.

50. **Nicodemus saith** unto
them, (he that came to Jesus by
night, being one of them,)

51. **Doth our law judge**
any man,
before it hear him,
and know what he doeth?

52. **They answered** and said
unto him, Art thou also of Galilee?
Search, and look:
**for out of Galilee
ariseth no prophet.**

53. And every man went
unto his own house.

CHAPTER 8

1. Jesus went unto the mount
of Olives.

2. **And early in the morning
he came again into the
temple, and all the people
came** unto him;
and he sat down, and
taught them.

3. **And the scribes and
Pharisees brought** unto him
a woman taken in adultery;
and when they had
set her in the midst,

4. **They say** unto him,
**Master, this woman was
taken in adultery,**
in the very act.

5. Now Moses in
**the law commanded us,
that such should be
stoned: but what
sayest thou?**

6. This they said, tempting him, that
they might have to accuse him. But
**Jesus stooped down, and
with** *his* **finger wrote
on the ground,**
as though he heard them not.

7. **So when they continued
asking him, he**
lifted up himself, and
said unto them,
He that is without sin
among you,
**let him first cast a stone
at her.**

8. **And again he**
stooped down, and
wrote on the ground.

9. **And they** which heard *it,*
being convicted
by *their own* conscience,
went out one by one, beginning at
the eldest, *even* unto the last:
**and Jesus was left alone,
and the woman**
standing in the midst.

10. When Jesus had lifted up himself,
and saw none but the woman,
he said unto her, Woman,
where are those thine accusers?
**hath no man
condemned thee?**

11. **She said, No man, Lord.
And Jesus said** unto her,
Neither do I condemn thee:
go, and sin no more.

12. **Then spake Jesus**
again unto them,
**saying, I am the light of the
world:** he that followeth me shall
not walk in darkness, but shall have
the light of life.

13. **The Pharisees therefore
said** unto him,
**Thou bearest record of
thyself; thy record
is not true.**

14. **Jesus answered**
and said unto them,

■ **Though I bear record** of myself,

■ *yet* **my record is true:** for I know whence I came, and whither I go;

■ **but ye cannot tell whence I**
■ **come, and whither I go.**

■ **15. Ye judge after the flesh; I**
■ **judge no man.**

■ **16. And yet if I judge, my**
■ **judgment is true:** for I am not alone, but I and the Father that sent me.

■ **17. It is also written** in your law,
■ **that the testimony of two**
■ **men is true.**

■ **18. I** am one that
■ **bear witness of myself,**
■ **and the Father** that sent me beareth witness of me.

■ **19. Then said they** unto him,
■ **Where is thy Father? Jesus**
■ **answered,** Ye neither know me, nor my Father:

■ **if ye had known me, ye**
■ **should have known my**
■ **Father also.**

20. These words spake Jesus in the treasury, as he taught in the temple: and no man laid hands on him; for his hour was not yet come.

■ **21. Then said Jesus** again unto them, I go my way, and

■ **ye shall seek me, and shall**
■ **die in your sins: whither I**
■ **go, ye cannot come.**

■ **22. Then said the Jews, Will**
■ **he kill himself?** because he saith, Whither I go, ye cannot come.

■ **23. And he said** unto them, Ye are from beneath; I am from above:

■ **ye are of this world; I am**
■ **not of this world.**

24. I said therefore unto you, that ye shall die in your sins: for

■ **if ye believe not that I am**
■ *he,* **ye shall die in your**
■ **sins.**

■ **25. Then said they** unto him,
■ **Who art thou? And Jesus**
■ **saith** unto them,
■ **Even** *the same* **that I said** unto you

■ **from the beginning.**

26. I have many things to say and to judge of you: but

■ **he that sent me is true; and I**
■ **speak** to the world
■ **those things** which I have
■ **heard of him.**

■ **27. They understood not** that he spake to them of the Father.

■ **28. Then said Jesus** unto them,
■ **When ye have lifted up the**
■ **Son** of man,
■ **then shall ye know that I am**
■ *he,* and *that* I do nothing of myself; but as my Father hath taught me, I speak these things.

■ **29. And** he that sent me is with me:
■ **the Father hath not left me**
■ **alone; for I** do always those things that
■ **please him.**

■ **30. As he spake** these words,
■ **many believed on him.**

■ **31. Then said Jesus** to those Jews which believed on him,
■ **If ye continue in my word,**
■ *then* **are ye my disciples** indeed;

■ **32. And ye shall know the**
■ **truth, and the truth shall**
■ **make you free.**

■ **33. They answered him, We** be Abraham's seed, and
■ **were never in bondage** to any man:
■ **how sayest thou, Ye shall**
■ **be made free?**

■ **34. Jesus answered** them, Verily, verily, I say unto you,
■ **Whosoever committeth sin**
■ **is the servant of sin.**

35. And the servant abideth not in the house for ever: *but* the Son abideth ever.

■ **36. If the Son** therefore shall
■ **make you free, ye shall be**
■ **free indeed.**

37. I know that ye are Abraham's seed; but ye seek to kill me, because my word hath no place in you.

■ **38. I speak that which I have**
■ **seen with my Father: and ye**
■ **do that which ye have seen**

with your father.

39. **They answered**
and said unto him,
Abraham is our father.
Jesus saith unto them,
If ye were Abraham's
children, ye would do the
works of Abraham.
40. **But now ye seek to kill**
me, a man that hath told you the
truth, which I have heard of God:
this did not Abraham.
41. Ye do the deeds of your father.
Then said they to him, We be not
born of fornication;
we have one Father,
even God.
42. **Jesus said** unto them,
If God were your Father, ye
would love me: for I
proceeded forth and
came from God; neither came I
of myself, but he sent me.
43. Why do ye not understand my
speech? *even* because ye cannot
hear my word.
44. **Ye are of** *your* **father the**
devil, and the lusts of your father
ye will do.
He was a murderer
from the beginning,
and abode not in the truth,
because there is no truth in him. When
he speaketh a lie, he speaketh
of his own:
for he is a liar, and the
father of it.
45. And because I tell *you* the truth,
ye believe me not.
46. Which of you convinceth me of
sin? And if I say the truth, why do ye
not believe me?
47. **He that is of God heareth**
God's words: ye therefore hear
them not, because
ye are not of God.
48. **Then answered the**
Jews, and said unto him, Say we
not well that
thou art a Samaritan, and
hast a devil?
49. **Jesus answered, I have**
not a devil; but I honour my

Father, and ye do dishonour me.
50. And I seek not mine own glory:
there is one that seeketh and judgeth.
51. Verily, verily, I say unto you,
If a man keep my saying,
he shall never see death.
52. **Then said the Jews** unto
him, Now we know that
thou hast a devil.
Abraham is dead, and the
prophets; and thou sayest, If a man
keep my saying, he shall never taste
of death.
53. **Art thou greater than**
our father
Abraham, which is dead? and the
prophets are dead:
whom makest thou thyself?
54. **Jesus answered,** If I
honour myself, my honour is nothing:
it is my Father that
honoureth me; of whom ye say,
that he is your God:
55. **Yet ye have not known**
him; but I know him: and if I should
say, I know him not, I shall be a liar
like unto you:
but I know him, and keep
his saying.
56. **Your father Abraham**
rejoiced to see my day: and
he saw *it,* and was glad.
57. **Then said the Jews**
unto him,
Thou art not yet fifty years old,
and hast thou
seen Abraham?
58. **Jesus said** unto them, Verily,
verily, I say unto you,
Before Abraham was, I am.
59. **Then took they up stones**
to cast at him: but Jesus hid
himself, and went out of the temple,
going through the midst
of them, and so
passed by.

CHAPTER 9
1. And as *Jesus* passed by,
he saw a man which was
blind from *his* **birth.**
2. **And his disciples asked**
him, saying, Master,

■ who did sin, this man, or
■ his parents,
that he was born blind?
■ 3. **Jesus answered, Neither**
hath this man sinned, nor his parents:
■ but that the works of God
■ should be made manifest
in him.
■ 4. **I must work** the works of him
that sent me, while it is day:
■ the night cometh, when no
■ man can work.
5. As long as I am in the world,
■ I am the light of the world.
■ 6. When he had thus
■ spoken, he spat on the
■ ground, and made clay of
■ the spittle, and he anointed
■ the eyes of the blind man
■ with the clay,
■ 7. **And said** unto him,
■ Go, wash in the
■ pool of Siloam,
(which is by interpretation, Sent.)
■ He went his way therefore,
■ and washed,
■ and came seeing.
■ 8. **The neighbours** therefore,
and they which before had seen him
that he was blind,
■ said, Is not this he that sat
■ and begged?
9. Some said, This is he: others *said,*
He is like him: *but*
■ he said, I am *he.*
■ 10. **Therefore said they**
unto him,
■ How were thine
■ eyes opened?
■ 11. **He answered**
and said, A man that is called
■ Jesus made clay, and
■ anointed mine eyes, and
■ said unto me,
■ Go to the pool of
■ Siloam, and wash:
and I went and washed,
■ and I received sight.
12. Then said they unto him, Where is
he? He said, I know not.
13. They brought to the Pharisees him
that aforetime was blind.
■ 14. **And it was the sabbath**

■ day when Jesus made the clay, and
opened his eyes.
15. Then again
■ the Pharisees also asked
■ him how he had received
■ his sight. He said unto them, He
put clay upon mine eyes, and I
washed, and do see.
■ 16. **Therefore said some of**
■ the Pharisees, This man
is not of God, because he
■ keepeth not the sabbath
■ day. Others said, How can
a man that is
■ a sinner do such miracles?
And there was a division among them.
17. They say unto the blind man
again, What sayest thou of him, that
he hath opened thine eyes? He said,
He is a prophet.
■ 18. **But the Jews did not**
■ believe concerning him, that he
had been blind,
■ and received his sight, until they
■ called the parents of him
■ that had received his sight.
■ 19. **And they asked**
them, saying,
■ Is this your son,
who ye say was born blind?
■ how then doth he now see?
■ 20. **His parents answered**
them and said, We know that
■ this is our son,
and that he was born blind:
■ 21. **But by what means he**
■ now seeth, we know not; or
who hath opened his eyes,
we know not:
■ he is of age; ask him: he shall
speak for himself.
22. These *words* spake his parents,
because they feared the Jews: for the
Jews had agreed already, that if any
man did confess that he was Christ,
he should be put out
of the synagogue.
23. Therefore said his parents, He is
of age; ask him.
■ 24. **Then again called they**
■ the man that was blind,
■ and said
unto him, Give God the praise:

■ **we know that this man**
■ **is a sinner.**
■ 25. **He answered** and said,
■ **Whether he be a sinner** *or no,*
■ **I know not: one thing I**
■ **know, that, whereas I was**
■ **blind, now I see.**
■ 26. **Then said they** to him again,
What did he to thee?
■ **how opened he thine eyes?**
■ 27. **He answered them, I**
■ **have told you already,**
and ye did not hear: wherefore would
ye hear *it* again?
■ **will ye also be his**
■ **disciples?**
■ 28. **Then they reviled him,**
■ **and said,**
Thou art his disciple; but
■ **we are Moses' disciples.**
29. We know that God spake unto
Moses:
■ *as for* **this** *fellow,* **we know**
■ **not from whence he is.**
■ 30. **The man answered** and
said unto them, Why herein is a
marvellous thing, that
■ **ye know not** from whence he is,
■ **and** *yet* **he hath opened**
■ **mine eyes.**
■ 31. **Now we know that God**
■ **heareth not sinners:** but if any
man be a worshipper of God, and
doeth his will, him he heareth.
32. Since the world began was it not
heard that any man opened the eyes
of one that was born blind.
■ 33. **If this man were not of**
■ **God, he could do nothing.**
■ 34. **They answered** and said
unto him,
■ **Thou wast altogether born**
■ **in sins,** and dost thou teach us?
■ **And they cast him out.**
■ 35. **Jesus heard** that they had
cast him out;
■ **and when he had found**
■ **him,** he said unto him,
■ **Dost thou believe on the**
■ **Son of God?**
■ 36. **He answered** and said,
■ **Who is he, Lord,** that I might
believe on him?

■ 37. **And Jesus said** unto him,
Thou hast both seen him, and
■ **it is he that talketh**
■ **with thee.**
■ 38. **And he said, Lord, I**
■ **believe. And he**
■ **worshipped him.**
■ 39. **And Jesus said, For**
■ **judgment I am come**
into this world,
■ **that they which see not**
■ **might see; and that they**
■ **which see might**
■ **be made blind.**
■ 40. **And** *some* **of the**
■ **Pharisees** which were with him
heard these words, and
■ **said** unto him,
■ **Are we blind also?**
■ 41. **Jesus said** unto them,
■ **If ye were blind, ye should**
■ **have no sin: but now ye**
■ **say, We see; therefore your**
■ **sin remaineth.**

CHAPTER 10
1. Verily, verily, I say unto you,
■ **He that entereth not by the**
■ **door into the sheepfold,** but
climbeth up some other way
■ **the same is a thief**
and a robber.
■ 2. **But he that entereth in by**
■ **the door is the shepherd**
of the sheep.
3. To him the porter openeth;
■ **and the sheep hear his**
■ **voice:** and he calleth his own sheep
by name, and leadeth them out.
4. And when he putteth forth his own
sheep, he goeth before them,
■ **and the sheep follow**
him: for they know his voice.
■ 5. **And a stranger will they**
■ **not follow,** but will flee from him:
for they know not the
voice of strangers.
6. This parable spake Jesus unto
them: but they understood not what
things they were which he
spake unto them.
■ 7. **Then said Jesus** unto them
again, Verily, verily, I say unto you,

I am the door of the sheep.
8. All that ever came before me are thieves and robbers: but the sheep did not hear them.
9. I am the door:
by me if any man enter in, he shall be saved, and shall go in and out, and find pasture.
10. **The thief cometh** not, but for **to steal, and to kill, and to destroy: I am come that they might have life,** and that they might have *it* **more abundantly.**
11. **I am the good shepherd:** the good shepherd giveth his life for the sheep.
12. **But he that is an hireling,** and not the shepherd, whose own the sheep are not,
seeth the wolf coming, and leaveth the sheep, and fleeth: **and the wolf catcheth them, and scattereth the sheep.**
13. The hireling fleeth, because he is an hireling, and careth not for the sheep.
14. **I am the good shepherd, and know my *sheep,* and am known of mine.**
15. As the Father knoweth me, even so know I the Father:
and I lay down my life for the sheep.
16. **And other sheep I have,** which are **not of this fold:** them also I must bring, and they shall hear my voice; **and there shall be one fold, *and* one shepherd.**
17. Therefore doth my Father love me, because **I lay down my life,** that I might take it again.
18. **No man taketh it** from me, but I lay it down of myself. I have power to lay it down, and **I have power to take it again.** This commandment have I received of my Father.
19. There was a division therefore again among the Jews for these sayings.

20. **And many** of them **said, He hath a devil,** and is mad; why hear ye him?
21. **Others said,** These are not the words of him that hath a devil. **Can a devil open the eyes of the blind?**
22. And it was at Jerusalem the feast of the dedication, and it was winter.
23. **And Jesus walked** in the temple **in Solomon's porch.**
24. **Then came the Jews** round about him, **and said** unto him, How long dost thou make us to doubt? **If thou be the Christ, tell us plainly.**
25. **Jesus answered** them, **I told you, and ye believed not:** the works that I do in my Father's name, they bear witness of me.
26. But ye believe not, because ye are not of my sheep, as I said unto you.
27. **My sheep hear my voice,** and I know them, and they follow me:
28. **And I give unto them eternal life; and they shall never perish, neither shall any *man* pluck them out of my hand.**
29. My Father, which gave *them* me, is greater than all; **and no *man* is able to pluck *them* out of my Father's hand.**
30. **I and *my* Father are one.**
31. **Then the Jews took up stones** again to stone him.
32. **Jesus answered** them, **Many good works have I shewed** you from my Father; **for which** of those works **do ye stone me?**
33. **The Jews answered** him, saying, For a good work **we stone thee** not; but **for blasphemy; and because that thou,** being a man,

■ **makest thyself God.**
■ 34. **Jesus answered** them,
■ **Is it not written** in your law, I said,
■ **Ye are gods?**
35. If he called them gods, unto whom the word of God came, and the scripture cannot be broken;
■ 36. **Say ye of him,** whom the Father hath sanctified, and sent into the world,
■ **Thou blasphemest;**
■ **because I said, I am the**
■ **Son of God?**
■ 37. **If I do not the works of**
■ **my Father, believe me not.**
38. But if I do, though ye believe not me, believe the works: that ye may know, and believe, that the Father *is* in me, and I in him.
■ 39. **Therefore they sought**
■ **again to take him: but he**
■ **escaped** out of their hand,
40. And went away again
■ **beyond Jordan** into the place
■ **where John** at first
■ **baptized;** and there he abode.
■ 41. **And many**
resorted unto him, and
■ **said,** John did no miracle: but
■ **all things that John spake**
■ **of this man were true.**
■ 42. **And many believed**
on him there.

CHAPTER 11
■ 1. **Now a certain** *man* **was**
■ **sick,** *named* **Lazarus,** of
Bethany, the town of Mary and her sister Martha.
2. (It was *that* Mary which anointed the Lord with ointment, and wiped his feet with her hair, whose brother Lazarus was sick.)
■ 3. **Therefore his sisters sent**
■ **unto him, saying, Lord,**
■ **behold, he whom thou**
■ **lovest is sick.**
4. When Jesus heard *that,*
■ **he said, This sickness is**
■ **not unto death,** but for the glory of God, that the Son of God might be glorified thereby.
■ 5. **Now Jesus loved Martha,**

■ **and her sister,**
■ **and Lazarus.**
■ 6. **When he had heard**
therefore that
■ **he was sick, he abode two**
■ **days still in the same place**
where he was.
■ 7. **Then** after that
■ **saith he** to *his* disciples,
■ **Let us go into Judaea** again.
■ 8. *His* **disciples say**
unto him, Master,
■ **the Jews of late sought to**
■ **stone thee;**
and goest thou thither again?
9. Jesus answered, Are there not twelve hours in the day? If any man walk in the day, he stumbleth not, because he seeth the light of this world.
10. But if a man walk in the night, he stumbleth, because there is no light in him.
11. These things said he: and
■ **after that he saith** unto them,
■ **Our friend Lazarus**
■ **sleepeth; but I go, that I**
■ **may awake him** out of sleep.
■ 12. **Then said his disciples,**
■ **Lord, if he sleep, he shall**
■ **do well.**
13. Howbeit Jesus spake of his death: but they thought that he had spoken of taking of rest in sleep.
■ 14. **Then said Jesus** unto them
■ **plainly, Lazarus is dead.**
15. And I am glad for your sakes that I was not there, to the intent ye may believe; nevertheless let us go unto him.
16. Then said Thomas, which is called Didymus, unto his fellow disciples, Let us also go, that we may die with him.
■ 17. **Then when Jesus came,**
■ **he found that he had** *lain* **in**
■ **the grave four days** already.
18. Now Bethany was nigh unto Jerusalem, about fifteen furlongs off:
19. And many of the Jews came to Martha and Mary, to comfort them concerning their brother.
■ 20. **Then Martha,** as soon as she heard that Jesus was coming,

went and met him: but Mary sat *still* in the house.

21. Then said Martha unto Jesus,

Lord, if thou hadst been here, my brother had not died.

22. But I know, that even now, whatsoever thou wilt ask of God,

God will give *it* thee.

23. Jesus saith unto her,

Thy brother shall rise again.

24. Martha saith unto him,

I know that he shall rise again in the resurrection at the last day.

25. Jesus said unto her,

I am the resurrection, and the life: he that believeth in me, though he were dead, yet shall he live:

26. And whosoever liveth and believeth in me shall never die. Believest thou this?

27. She saith unto him,

Yea, Lord: I believe that thou art the Christ, the Son of God, which should come into the world.

28. And when she had so said, she went her way, and called Mary her sister secretly, saying, The Master is come, and calleth for thee.

29. As soon as she heard *that,* she arose quickly, and came unto him.

30. Now Jesus was not yet come into the town, but was in that place where Martha met him.

31. The Jews then which were with her in the house, and comforted her, when they saw Mary, that she rose up hastily and went out, followed her, saying, She goeth unto the grave to weep there.

32. Then when Mary was come where Jesus was, and saw him, she fell down at his feet, saying unto him,

Lord, if thou hadst been here, my brother had not died.

33. When Jesus therefore saw her weeping, and the Jews also weeping which came with her, he groaned in the spirit, and was troubled.

34. And said, Where have ye laid him? They said unto him, Lord,

come and see.

35. Jesus wept.

36. Then said the Jews,

Behold how he loved him!

37. And some of them said, Could not this man, which opened the eyes of the blind, have caused that even this man should not have died?

38. Jesus therefore again groaning in himself cometh to the grave.

It was a cave, and a stone lay upon it.

39. Jesus said, Take ye away the stone. Martha, the sister of him that was dead, saith unto him,

Lord, by this time he stinketh: for he hath been *dead* four days.

40. Jesus saith unto her, Said I not unto thee, that, if thou wouldest believe, thou shouldest see the glory of God?

41. Then they took away the stone *from the place* where the dead was laid.

And Jesus lifted up *his* eyes, and said, Father, I thank thee that thou hast heard me.

42. And I knew that thou hearest me always:

but because of the people which stand by I said *it,* that they may believe that thou hast sent me.

43. And when he thus had spoken, he cried with a loud voice, Lazarus, come forth.

44. And he that was dead came forth, bound hand and foot with graveclothes: and his

face was bound about with a napkin.
■ **Jesus saith** unto them,
■ **Loose him,** and let him go.
■ **45. Then many of the Jews**
which came to Mary, and had seen the
things which Jesus did,
■ **believed on him.**
■ **46. But some** of them
■ **went** their ways
■ **to the Pharisees, and told**
■ **them** what things Jesus had done.
■ **47. Then gathered** the chief
priests and the Pharisees
■ **a council, and said, What**
■ **do we?** for this man
doeth many miracles.
■ **48. If we let him thus alone,**
■ **all** *men* **will believe** on him:
and the Romans shall come and take
away both our place and nation.
■ **49. And** one of them, *named*
■ **Caiaphas, being the high**
■ **priest** that same year,
■ **said** unto them,
Ye know nothing at all,
50. Nor consider that
■ **it is expedient** for us,
■ **that one man should die for**
■ **the people,** and that the whole
nation perish not.
■ **51. And this spake he not of**
■ **himself: but**
being high priest that year,
■ **he prophesied that Jesus**
■ **should die for that nation;**
52. And not for that nation only,
■ **but that also he should**
■ **gather together in one the**
■ **children of God**
that were scattered abroad.
■ **53. Then** from that day forth
■ **they took counsel** together for
■ **to put him to death.**
■ **54. Jesus** therefore walked no more
openly among the Jews; but
■ **went** thence unto a country near to
the wilderness,
■ **into a city called Ephraim,**
and there continued with his
disciples.
■ **55. And the Jews' passover**
■ **was nigh** at hand:
■ **and many went**

out of the country up
■ **to Jerusalem**
before the passover,
■ **to purify themselves.**
56. Then sought they for Jesus, and
spake among themselves, as they
stood in the temple, What think ye,
that he will not come to the feast?
57. Now both the chief priests and the
Pharisees had given a commandment,
that, if any man knew where he were,
he should shew *it*, that they
might take him.

CHAPTER 12
■ **1. Then Jesus**
six days before the passover
■ **came to Bethany,** where
Lazarus was, which had been dead,
whom he raised from the dead.
■ **2. There they made him a**
■ **supper;** and Martha served: but
Lazarus was one of them that sat at
the table with him.
■ **3. Then took Mary** a pound of
■ **ointment of spikenard,**
very costly,
■ **and anointed the feet of**
■ **Jesus, and wiped his feet**
■ **with her hair:** and the house was
filled with the odour of the ointment.
■ **4. Then saith** one of his disciples,
■ **Judas** Iscariot, Simon's *son*,
■ **which should betray him,**
■ **5. Why was not this ointment**
■ **sold** for three hundred pence,
■ **and given to the poor?**
6. This he said, not that he cared for
the poor; but because he was a thief,
and had the bag, and bare what was
put therein.
■ **7. Then said Jesus, Let her**
■ **alone: against the day of**
■ **my burying hath**
■ **she kept this.**
■ **8. For the poor**
■ **always ye have**
with you; but me ye have not always.
■ **9. Much people**
of the Jews therefore
■ **knew that he was there:**
■ **and they came not for**
■ **Jesus' sake only, but that**

■ **they might see Lazarus** also, whom he had raised from the dead.

■ 10. **But the chief priests**
■ **consulted that they might**
■ **put Lazarus also to death;**
■ 11. **Because that by reason**
■ **of him many** of the Jews went away, and

■ **believed on Jesus.**

12. On the next day
■ **much people** that were come to the feast,

■ **when they heard that Jesus**
■ **was coming to Jerusalem,**
■ 13. **Took branches of palm**
■ **trees, and went forth** to meet him,

■ **and cried, Hosanna:**
■ **Blessed** *is* **the King of Israel** that cometh in the name of the Lord.

■ 14. **And Jesus,** when he had
■ **found a young ass, sat**
■ **thereon; as it is written,**

15. Fear not, daughter of Sion: behold,

■ **thy King cometh, sitting on**
■ **an ass's colt.**

16. These things understood not his disciples at the first: but when Jesus was glorified, then remembered they that these things were written of him, and *that* they had done these things unto him.

■ 17. **The people therefore**
■ **that was with him when he**
■ **called Lazarus** out of his grave,
■ **and raised him** from the dead,
■ **bare record.**
■ 18. **For this cause the**
■ **people also met him,** for that they heard that he had done this miracle.

19. The Pharisees therefore said among themselves, Perceive ye how ye prevail nothing? behold, the world is gone after him.

■ 20. **And** there were
■ **certain Greeks** among them that
■ **came up to worship**
■ **at the feast:**
■ 21. **The same came**
■ **therefore to Philip,** which was of Bethsaida of Galilee,

and desired him,
■ **saying, Sir, we would**
■ **see Jesus.**

22. Philip cometh
■ **and** telleth Andrew: and again
■ **Andrew and Philip**
■ **tell Jesus.**
■ 23. **And Jesus answered** them, saying,
■ **The hour is come, that the**
■ **Son of man should**
■ **be glorified.**

24. Verily, verily, I say unto you,
■ **Except a corn of wheat fall**
■ **into the ground and die, it**
■ **abideth alone: but if it die,**
■ **it bringeth forth much fruit.**
■ 25. **He that loveth his life**
■ **shall lose it;** and he that hateth his life in this world shall keep it unto life eternal.

■ 26. **If any man serve me, let**
■ **him follow me;** and where I am, there shall also my servant be: if any man serve me, him will *my* Father honour.

27. Now is my soul troubled; and
■ **what shall I say? Father,**
■ **save me from this hour: but**
■ **for this cause came I unto**
■ **this hour.**
■ 28. **Father, glorify thy name.**
■ **Then came there a voice**
■ **from heaven,** *saying,* **I**
■ **have** both
■ **glorified** *it,* **and will glorify**
■ *it* **again.**
■ 29. **The people** therefore,
■ **that** stood by, and
■ **heard** *it,* **said** that
■ **it thundered: others said,**
■ **An angel spake** to him.
■ 30. **Jesus answered** and said,
■ **This voice came** not because of me, but
■ **for your sakes.**
■ 31. **Now is the judgment of**
■ **this world: now shall the**
■ **prince** of this world
■ **be cast out.**
■ 32. **And I, if I be lifted up** from the earth,
■ **will draw all** *men* **unto me.**

33. This he said, signifying what death he should die.

34. **The people answered** him, We have heard out of the law that **Christ abideth for ever: and how sayest thou, The Son** of man **must be lifted up?** who is this Son of man?

35. **Then Jesus said** unto them, Yet a little while is the light with you. **Walk while ye have the light,** lest darkness come upon you: **for he that walketh in darkness knoweth not whither he goeth.**

36. While ye have light, **believe in the light, that ye may be the children of light.** These things spake Jesus, and departed, and did hide himself from them.

37. **But though he had done so many miracles** before them, **yet they believed not** on him:

38. **That** the saying of **Esaias** the prophet **might be fulfilled,** which he spake, **Lord, who hath believed our report?** and to whom hath the arm of the Lord been revealed?

39. Therefore they could not believe, because that **Esaias said again,**

40. **He hath blinded their eyes,** and hardened their heart; **that they should not see** with *their* eyes, **nor understand** with *their* heart, **and be converted,** and I should heal them.

41. These things said Esaias, when he saw his glory, and spake of him.

42. **Nevertheless among the chief rulers also many believed** on him; **but** because of the Pharisees they **did not confess *him*,** lest they should be put out of the synagogue:

43. **For they loved the praise of men** more than the praise of God.

44. **Jesus cried** and said, **He that believeth on me, believeth** not on me, but **on him that sent me.**

45. And he that seeth me seeth him that sent me.

46. **I am** come a **light** into the world, that **whosoever believeth on me should not abide in darkness.**

47. And if any man hear my words, and believe not, I judge him not: for **I came not to judge the world, but to save the world.**

48. **He that rejecteth me,** and receiveth not my words, **hath one that judgeth him: the word** that I have spoken, the same **shall judge him in the last day.**

49. **For I have not spoken of myself; but the Father** which sent me, he **gave me** a commandment, **what I should say,** and what I should speak.

50. And I know that his commandment is life everlasting: whatsoever I speak therefore, even as the Father said unto me, so I speak.

CHAPTER 13

1. **Now before the** feast of the **passover,** when Jesus knew that his hour was come that he should depart out of this world unto the Father, having loved his own which were in the world, he loved them unto the end.

2. **And supper being ended, the devil having now put into** the heart of **Judas** Iscariot, Simon's son, **to betray him;**

3. **Jesus** knowing that the Father had given all things into his hands, and that he was come from God, and went to God;

4. He riseth from supper, and laid aside his garments; and

■ **took a towel, and**
girded himself.
5. After that he
■ **poureth water into a basin,**
■ **and began to wash the**
■ **disciples' feet,** and to wipe *them*
with the towel wherewith
he was girded.
6. Then cometh he to
Simon Peter: and
■ **Peter saith** unto him,
■ **Lord, dost thou**
■ **wash my feet?**
7. Jesus answered and said unto him,
What I do thou knowest not now; but
thou shalt know hereafter.
8. Peter saith unto him, Thou shalt
never wash my feet.
■ **Jesus answered** him,
■ **If I wash thee not, thou hast**
■ **no part with me.**
■ 9. **Simon Peter saith** unto him,
■ **Lord, not my feet only, but**
also
■ *my* **hands and** *my* **head.**
■ 10. **Jesus saith** to him,
■ **He that is washed needeth**
■ **not save to wash**
■ *his* **feet,** but is clean every whit:
■ **and ye are clean,**
■ **but not all.**
■ 11. **For he knew who should**
■ **betray him;** therefore said he, Ye
are not all clean.
12. So after he had washed their feet,
and had taken his garments, and was
set down again,
■ **he said** unto them,
■ **Know ye what I have done**
to you?
13. Ye call me Master and Lord: and
ye say well; for *so* I am.
14. **If** I then,
■ *your* **Lord** and Master,
■ **have washed your feet; ye**
■ **also ought to wash one**
■ **another's feet.**
■ 15. **For** I have given
you an example, that
■ **ye should do as I have**
■ **done** to you.
16. Verily, verily, I say unto you,
■ **The servant is not greater**

■ **than his lord;** neither he that is
sent greater than he that sent him.
17. If ye know these things, happy are
ye if ye do them.
■ 18. **I speak not of you all:**
I know whom I have chosen: but that
the scripture may be fulfilled,
■ **He that eateth bread with**
■ **me hath lifted up his heel**
■ **against me.**
19. Now I tell you before it come, that,
when it is come to pass, ye may
believe that I am *he.*
20. Verily, verily, I say unto you, He
that receiveth whomsoever I send
receiveth me; and he that receiveth
me receiveth him that sent me.
21. When Jesus had thus said,
■ **he was troubled** in spirit,
■ **and testified,** and said, Verily,
verily, I say unto you, that
■ **one of you shall betray me.**
22. Then the disciples looked one on
another, doubting of whom he spake.
■ 23. **Now there was leaning**
■ **on Jesus' bosom one of his**
■ **disciples,** whom Jesus loved.
■ 24. **Simon Peter** therefore
■ **beckoned to him,**
■ **that he** should
■ **ask who it should be**
of whom he spake.
■ 25. **He** then lying on Jesus' breast
■ **saith** unto him,
■ **Lord, who is it?**
■ 26. **Jesus answered, He it is,**
■ **to whom I shall give a sop,**
when I have dipped *it.*
■ **And** when he had dipped the sop,
■ **he gave** *it* **to Judas**
Iscariot, *the son* of Simon.
■ 27. **And** after the sop
■ **Satan entered into him.**
■ **Then said Jesus** unto him,
■ **That thou doest,**
■ **do quickly.**
28. Now no man at the table knew for
what intent he spake this unto him.
29. For some *of them* thought,
because Judas had the bag, that
Jesus had said unto him, Buy *those*
things that we have need of against
the feast; or that he should give

something to the poor.

30. **He** then having received the sop **went immediately** out: and it was night.

31. Therefore, when he was gone out, **Jesus said, Now is the Son of man glorified, and God is glorified in him.**

32. If God be glorified in him, God shall also glorify him in himself, and shall straightway glorify him.

33. Little children, yet a little while I am with you. Ye shall seek me: and as I said unto the Jews, Whither I go, ye cannot come; so now I say to you.

34. **A new commandment I give** unto you, **That ye love one another;** as I have loved you, that ye also love one another.

35. **By this shall all *men* know that ye are my disciples,** if ye have love one to another.

36. **Simon Peter said** unto him, **Lord, whither goest thou? Jesus answered** him, Whither I go, **thou canst not follow me now; but thou shalt follow me afterwards.**

37. **Peter said** unto him, Lord, why cannot I follow thee now? **I will lay down my life for thy sake.**

38. **Jesus answered** him, Wilt thou lay down thy life for my sake? Verily, verily, I say unto thee, **The cock shall not crow, till thou hast denied me thrice.**

CHAPTER 14

1. **Let not your heart be troubled: ye believe in God, believe also in me.**

2. **In my Father's house are many mansions:** if *it were* not so, I would have told you. **I go to prepare a place for you.**

3. And if I go and prepare a place for you, **I will come again, and**

receive you unto myself; **that where I am, *there* ye may be also.**

4. And whither I go ye know, and the way ye know.

5. **Thomas saith** unto him, Lord, we know not whither thou goest; and **how can we know the way?**

6. **Jesus saith** unto him, **I am the way, the truth, and the life: no man cometh unto the Father, but by me.**

7. If ye had known me, ye should have known my Father also: and from henceforth ye know him, and have seen him.

8. **Philip saith** unto him, Lord, **shew us the Father,** and it sufficeth us.

9. **Jesus saith** unto him, Have I been so long time with you, and yet hast thou not known me, Philip? **he that hath seen me hath seen the Father;** and how sayest thou *then,* Shew us the Father?

10. **Believest thou not that I am in the Father, and the Father in me?** the words that I speak unto you **I speak not of myself: but the Father** that dwelleth **in me,** he **doeth the works.**

11. Believe me that I *am* in the Father, and the Father in me: or else believe me for the very works' sake.

12. Verily, verily, I say unto you, **He that believeth on me, the works that I do shall he do also; and greater *works* than these shall he do;** because I go unto my Father.

13. **And whatsoever ye shall ask in my name, that will I do,** that the Father may be glorified in the Son.

14. If ye shall ask any thing in my name, I will do *it.*

15. **If ye love me, keep my commandments.**

16. **And I will pray the Father, and he shall give you another Comforter,** that

he may abide with you for ever;

17. *Even* the Spirit of truth; whom the world cannot receive, because it seeth him not, neither knoweth him: but ye know him; for he dwelleth with you, and shall be in you. 18. I will not leave you comfortless: I will come to you.

19. Yet a little while, and the world seeth me no more; but ye see me: because I live, ye shall live also. 20. At that day ye shall know that I *am* in my Father, and ye in me, and I in you.

21. He that hath my commandments, and keepeth them, he it is that **loveth me: and** he that loveth me shall be loved of my Father, and **I will** love him, and will **manifest myself to him.** **22. Judas saith** unto him, **not Iscariot, Lord, how is it that thou wilt manifest thyself** unto us, and not unto the world?

23. Jesus answered and said unto him, **If a man love me, he will keep my words: and my Father will love him, and we will** come unto him, and **make our abode with him.** 24. He that loveth me not keepeth not my sayings: and the word which ye hear is not mine, but the Father's which sent me.

25. These things have I spoken unto you, **being *yet* present** with you. 26. **But the** Comforter, *which is the* **Holy Ghost,** whom the Father will send in my name, he **shall teach you all things, and bring all things to your remembrance,** whatsoever I have said unto you. **27. Peace I leave** with you, my **peace I give** unto you: not as the world giveth, give I unto you. **Let not your heart be troubled, neither**

let it be afraid. 28. Ye have heard how I said unto you, **I go away, and** come again unto you. **If ye loved me, ye would rejoice, because** I said, **I go unto the Father:** for my Father is greater than I. 29. And now I have told you before it come to pass, that, when it is come to pass, ye might believe. **30. Hereafter I will not talk much** with you: **for the prince of this world cometh,** and hath nothing in me. 31. But that the world may know that I love the Father; and as the Father gave me commandment, even so I do. Arise, let us go hence.

CHAPTER 15
1. I am the true vine, and my Father is the husbandman. 2. Every branch in me **that beareth not fruit he taketh away: and every** *branch* **that beareth fruit,** **he purgeth it, that it may bring forth more fruit.** **3. Now ye are clean through the word which I have spoken** unto you. 4. Abide in me, and I in you. As **the branch cannot bear fruit** of itself, **except** it abide **in the vine;** no more can ye, except ye abide in me. **5. I am the vine,** ye *are* the branches: **He that abideth in me,** and I in him, the same **bringeth forth much fruit:** for without me ye can do nothing. **6. If a man abide not in me, he is cast forth** as a branch, **and is** withered; and men gather them, and cast *them* into the fire, and they are **burned.** **7. If ye abide in me, and my words abide in you,** ye shall

■ ■ **ask what ye will, and it shall be done** unto you.

8. Herein is my Father glorified, that ye bear much fruit; so shall ye be my disciples.

9. As the Father hath loved me, so have I loved you: continue ye in my love.

10. If ye keep my commandments, ye shall abide in my love; even as I have kept my Father's commandments, and abide in his love.

■ ■ 11. **These things have I spoken** unto you, **that my joy might remain in you, and** *that* your joy **might be full.**

■ ■ 12. **This is my commandment, That ye love one another,** as I have loved you.

■ ■ 13. **Greater love hath no man than** this, that **a man lay down his life for his friends.**

14. Ye are my friends, if ye do whatsoever I command you.

■ 15. **Henceforth I call you not servants;** for the servant knoweth not what his lord doeth: **but** I have called you **friends; for all things** that I have heard of my Father **I have made known unto you.**

16. Ye have not chosen me, but **I have chosen you, and ordained you, that ye should go and bring forth fruit,** and *that* your fruit should remain: that **whatsoever ye shall ask of the Father in my name, he may give it you.**

17. These things I command you, that ye love one another.

■ 18. **If the world hate you, ye know that it hated me** before *it hated* you.

19. If ye were of the world, the world would love his own: but because ye are not of the world, but **I have chosen you out of the world,** therefore the world

hateth you.

20. Remember the word that I said unto you, The servant is not greater than his lord.

■ ■ ■ **If they have persecuted me, they will also persecute you;** if they have kept my saying, they will keep yours also.

■ ■ ■ 21. **But all these things will they do unto you for my name's sake,** because they know not him that sent me.

■ 22. **If I had not come** and spoken unto them, **they had not had sin: but now they have no cloak** for their sin.

■ 23. **He that hateth me hateth my Father also.**

24. If I had not done among them the works which none other man did, they had not had sin: but now have they both seen and hated both me and my Father.

■ 25. **But** *this cometh to pass,* **that the word might be fulfilled** that is written in their law, **They hated me without a cause.**

■ 26. **But when the Comforter is come,** whom I will send unto you from the Father, *even* the Spirit of truth, which proceedeth from the Father, **he shall testify of me:**

■ 27. **And ye also shall bear witness,** because ye have been with me from the beginning.

CHAPTER 16

1. These things have I spoken unto you, that ye should not be offended.

■ 2. **They shall put you out of the synagogues: yea, the time cometh, that whosoever killeth you will think that he doeth God service.**

3. And these things will they do unto you, because they have not known the Father, nor me.

■ 4. **But these things have I told you, that when the**

time shall come,
ye may remember that I told you of them. And these things I said not unto you at the beginning, because I was with you.
5. But now I go my way to him that sent me; and none of you asketh me, Whither goest thou?
6. **But because I have said these things** unto you, **sorrow hath filled your heart.**
7. Nevertheless I tell you the truth; **It is expedient** for you **that I go away: for if I go not** away, **the Comforter will not come** unto you; but if I depart, I will send him unto you.
8. **And** when he is come, **he will reprove the world of sin, and of righteousness, and of judgment:**
9. Of sin, because they believe not on me;
10. Of righteousness, because I go to my Father, and ye see me no more;
11. Of judgment, because the prince of this world is judged.
12. **I have yet many things to say** unto you, **but ye cannot bear them now.**
13. Howbeit **when** he, **the Spirit of truth, is come, he will guide you into all truth:** for he shall not speak of himself; but whatsoever he shall hear, *that* shall he speak: **and he will shew you things to come.**
14. **He shall glorify me:** for he shall receive of mine, and shall shew *it* unto you.
15. All things that the Father hath are mine: therefore said I, that he shall take of mine, and shall shew *it* unto you.
16. **A little while, and ye shall not see me: and again, a little while, and ye shall see me, because I go to the Father.**
17. **Then said** *some* **of his disciples** among themselves, **What is this that he saith unto us,** A little while, and ye shall not see me: and again, a little while, and ye shall see me: and, Because I go to the Father?
18. They said therefore, What is this that he saith, A little while? **we cannot tell what he saith.**
19. **Now Jesus knew that they were desirous to ask him, and said** unto them, Do ye inquire among yourselves of that I said, A little while, and ye shall not see me: and again, a little while, and ye shall see me?
20. Verily, verily, **I say unto you, That ye shall weep and lament,** but the world shall rejoice: and ye shall be sorrowful, **but your sorrow shall be turned into joy.**
21. **A woman** when she is **in travail hath sorrow,** because her hour is come: **but as soon as she is delivered of the child, she remembereth no more the anguish,** for joy that a man is born into the world.
22. **And ye now therefore have sorrow: but I will see you again,** and your heart shall rejoice, **and your joy no man taketh** from you.
23. And in that day ye shall ask me nothing. Verily, verily, I say unto you, **Whatsoever ye shall ask the Father in my name, he will give** *it* **you.**
24. Hitherto have ye asked nothing in my name: **ask, and ye shall receive, that your joy may be full.**
25. These things have I spoken unto you in proverbs: but the time cometh, when I shall no more speak unto you in proverbs, but I shall shew you

plainly of the Father.

26. At that day ye shall ask in my name: and I say not unto you, that I will pray the Father for you:

27. **For the Father himself loveth you, because ye have loved me,** and have believed that I came out from God.

28. I came forth from the Father, and am come into the world: again, **I leave the world, and go to the Father.**

29. **His disciples said** unto him, Lo, **now speakest thou plainly,** and speakest no proverb.

30. Now are we sure that **thou knowest all things,** and needest not that any man should ask thee: **by this we believe that thou camest forth from God.**

31. **Jesus answered** them, Do ye now believe?

32. **Behold, the hour cometh,** yea, is now come, **that ye shall be scattered,** every man to his own, **and shall leave me alone:** and yet I am not alone, because the Father is with me.

33. **These things I have spoken** unto you, **that in me ye might have peace. In the world ye shall have tribulation: but be of good cheer; I have overcome the world.**

CHAPTER 17

1. These words spake **Jesus,** and lifted up his eyes to heaven, and **said, Father, the hour is come; glorify thy Son,** that thy Son also may glorify thee:

2. As thou hast given him power over all flesh, **that he should give eternal life to as many as thou hast given him.**

3. **And this is life eternal,** **that they might know thee** the only true God, **and Jesus Christ,** whom thou hast sent.

4. I have glorified thee on the earth: **I have finished the work which thou gavest me** to do.

5. **And now, O Father, glorify thou me with** thine own self with **the glory which I had with thee before the world was.**

6. I have manifested thy name unto the men which thou gavest me out of the world: thine they were, and thou gavest them me; and they have kept thy word.

7. Now they have known that all things whatsoever thou hast given me are of thee.

8. **For I have given unto them the words which thou gavest me;** and they have received *them,* and have known surely that I came out from thee, and they have believed that thou didst send me.

9. I pray for them: **I pray not for the world, but for them which thou hast given me;** for they are thine.

10. And all mine are thine, and thine are mine; and I am glorified in them.

11. And now I am no more in the world, but these are in the world, and I come to thee. **Holy Father, keep through thine own name those whom thou hast given me, that they may be one, as we are.**

12. While I was with them in the world, I kept them in thy name: those that thou gavest me I have kept, and none of them is lost, but the son of perdition; that the scripture might be fulfilled.

13. **And now come I to thee;** and these things I speak in the world, **that they might have my joy fulfilled** in themselves.

14. I have given them thy word; and the world hath hated them, because they are not of the world, even as I am

not of the world.

■ 15. **I pray not that thou**
■ **shouldest take them out of**
■ **the world, but**
that thou shouldest
■ **keep them from the evil.**
16. They are not of the world, even as I am not of the world.

■ 17. **Sanctify them through**
■ **thy truth: thy word is truth.**
18. As thou hast sent me into the world, even so have I also sent them into the world.
19. And for their sakes I sanctify myself, that they also might be sanctified through the truth.

■ 20. **Neither pray I for these**
■ **alone, but for them also**
■ **which shall believe on me**
■ **through their word;**
■ 21. **That they all may be one;**
as thou, Father, *art* in me,
■ **and** I in thee,
■ **that they also may be one**
■ **in us: that the world may**
■ **believe that thou**
■ **hast sent me.**
22. And the glory which thou gavest me I have given them; that they may be one, even as we are one:
■ 23. **I in them, and thou in me,**
■ **that they may be made**
■ **perfect in one;**
and that the world may know that thou hast sent me, and hast loved them, as thou hast loved me.
■ 24. **Father, I will that**
they also, whom thou hast given me, be with me where I am; that
■ **they may behold my glory,**
which thou hast given me:
■ **for thou lovedst me before**
■ **the foundation**
■ **of the world.**
25. O righteous Father, the world hath not known thee: but I have known thee, and these have known that thou hast sent me.
■ 26. **And I have declared**
■ **unto them thy name,** and will declare *it:* that the love wherewith thou hast loved me may be in them, and I in them.

CHAPTER 18
1. When Jesus had spoken these words,
■ **he went forth with his**
■ **disciples** over the brook Cedron,
■ **where was a garden,** into the which he entered, and his disciples.
2. And Judas also, which betrayed him, knew the place: for Jesus ofttimes resorted thither with his disciples.
■ 3. **Judas then, having**
■ **received a band** *of men*
■ **and officers** from the chief priests and Pharisees,
■ **cometh thither** with lanterns and torches and weapons.
■ 4. **Jesus** therefore,
■ **knowing all things** that should come upon him, went forth, and
■ **said unto them,**
■ **Whom seek ye?**
■ 5. **They answered** him,
■ **Jesus of Nazareth.**
■ **Jesus saith** unto them,
■ **I am** *he.* **And Judas**
also, which betrayed him,
■ **stood with them.**
■ 6. **As soon then as he** had
■ **said** unto them,
■ **I am** *he,* **they** went backward, and
■ **fell to the ground.**
■ 7. **Then asked he them**
■ **again, Whom seek ye? And**
■ **they said, Jesus** of Nazareth.
■ 8. **Jesus answered, I have**
■ **told you that I am** *he:* if
■ **therefore ye seek me, let**
■ **these go their way:**
■ 9. **That the saying might be**
■ **fulfilled,** which he spake,
■ **Of them**
which thou gavest me have
■ **I lost none.**
10. Then Simon
■ **Peter having a sword**
drew it, and
■ **smote the high priest's**
■ **servant, and cut off his**
■ **right ear.**
The servant's name was Malchus.
■ 11. **Then said Jesus** unto Peter,
■ **Put up thy sword**

into the sheath:
the cup which my Father hath given me, shall I not drink it?
12. **Then** the band and the captain and officers of
the Jews took Jesus, and bound him,
13. **And led him away to Annas first; for he was father in law to Caiaphas,** which was the high priest that same year.
14. Now Caiaphas was he, which gave counsel to the Jews, that it was expedient that one man should die for the people.
15. **And Simon Peter followed Jesus, and** *so did* **another disciple:** that disciple was known unto the high priest, and went in with Jesus into the palace of the high priest.
16. But Peter stood at the door without.
Then went out that other disciple, which was known unto the high priest,
and spake unto her that kept the door, and brought in Peter.
17. **Then saith the damsel** that kept the door unto Peter,
Art not thou also *one* **of this man's disciples? He saith, I am not.**
18. **And the servants and officers** stood there, who had **made a fire** of coals; for it was cold:
and they **warmed themselves: and Peter** stood with them, and **warmed himself.**
19. **The high priest then asked Jesus** of his disciples, and **of his doctrine.**
20. **Jesus answered** him, **I spake openly** to the world; I ever taught in the synagogue, and in the temple, whither the Jews always resort;

and in secret have I said nothing.
21. Why askest thou me?
ask them which heard me, what I have said unto them: behold, they know what I said.
22. **And** when he had thus spoken, **one of the officers** which stood by **struck Jesus** with the palm of his hand, **saying, Answerest thou the high priest so?**
23. **Jesus answered** him, If I have spoken evil, bear witness of the evil: but if well, **why smitest thou me?**
24. **Now Annas had sent him** bound **unto Caiaphas the high priest.**
25. **And Simon Peter** stood and **warmed himself. They said** therefore unto him, **Art not thou also** *one* **of his disciples? He** denied *it,* and **said, I am not.**
26. **One of the servants of the high priest,** being *his* kinsman whose ear Peter cut off, **saith, Did not I see thee in the garden** with him?
27. **Peter then denied again: and** immediately **the cock crew.**
28. **Then led they Jesus from Caiaphas unto the hall of judgment:** and it was early; and they themselves went not into the judgment hall, lest they should be defiled; but that they might eat the passover.
29. **Pilate then** went out unto them, and **said, What accusation bring ye against this man?**
30. **They answered** and said unto him, **If he were not a malefactor, we would not have delivered him** up unto thee.
31. **Then said Pilate** unto them, Take ye him, and

judge him according to
your law. The Jews therefore
said unto him,
It is not lawful for us to put
any man to death:
32. That the saying of Jesus might be
fulfilled, which he spake, signifying
what death he should die.
33. Then Pilate entered into the
judgment hall again, and
called Jesus, and said
unto him,
Art thou the King
of the Jews?
34. Jesus answered him,
Sayest thou this thing
of thyself,
or did others tell it thee of me?
35. Pilate answered, Am I a
Jew? Thine own nation and the chief
priests have delivered thee unto me:
what hast thou done?
36. Jesus answered, My
kingdom is not of this
world: if my kingdom were of this
world, then would my servants fight,
that I should not be delivered to the
Jews: but now is my
kingdom not from hence.
37. Pilate therefore said
unto him,
Art thou a king then? Jesus
answered, Thou sayest
that I am a king. To this end
was I born, and for this cause
came I into the world;
that I should bear witness
unto the truth. Every one that is
of the truth heareth my voice.
38. Pilate saith unto him,
What is truth? And
when he had said this,
he went out again unto the
Jews, and saith unto them,
I find in him no fault *at all*.
39. But ye have a custom,
that I should release unto you
one at the passover: will ye
therefore that I release
unto you
the King of the Jews?
40. Then cried they
all again, saying,

Not this man, but
Barabbas. Now Barabbas was
a robber.

CHAPTER 19

1. Then Pilate
therefore took Jesus, and
scourged *him.*
2. And the soldiers platted
a crown of thorns, and put
it on his head, and they put
on him a purple robe,
3. And said, Hail, King of the
Jews! and they smote him
with their hands.
4. Pilate therefore went forth
again, and saith unto them,
Behold, I bring him forth to you,
that ye may know that
I find no fault in him.
5. Then came Jesus forth,
wearing the crown of thorns, and the
purple robe.
And *Pilate* saith unto them,
Behold the man!
6. When the chief priests
therefore
and officers saw him, they
cried out, saying,
Crucify *him,* crucify *him.*
Pilate saith unto them,
Take ye him, and crucify
him: for I find no fault in him.
7. The Jews answered
him, We have a law, and by our law
he ought to die, because he
made himself the
Son of God.
8. When Pilate therefore
heard that saying, he was
the more
afraid;
9. And went again into the judgment
hall, and
saith unto Jesus, Whence
art thou? But Jesus gave
him no answer.
10. Then saith Pilate unto him,
Speakest thou not
unto me? knowest thou not that
I have power to
crucify thee,
and have power to release thee?

11. **Jesus answered, Thou couldest have no power** *at all* against me, **except it were given thee from above:** therefore he that delivered me unto thee hath the greater sin.

12. And from thenceforth **Pilate sought to release him: but the Jews cried** out, saying,

If thou let this man go, thou art not Caesar's friend: whosoever maketh himself a king speaketh against Caesar.

13. **When Pilate** therefore **heard** that saying, **he brought Jesus forth,** and sat down in the judgment seat in a place that is called the Pavement, but in the Hebrew, Gabbatha.

14. And it was the preparation of the passover, and about the sixth hour: **and he saith** unto the Jews, **Behold your King!**

15. **But they cried** out, Away with *him,* **away with** *him,* **crucify him. Pilate saith** unto them, **Shall I crucify your King? The chief priests answered, We have no king but Caesar.**

16. **Then delivered he him** therefore unto them **to be crucified. And they took Jesus,** and led *him* away.

17. **And he bearing his cross went forth into a place** called *the place* of a skull, which is **called** in the Hebrew **Golgotha:**

18. **Where they crucified him, and two other with him,** on either side one, and Jesus in the midst.

19. **And Pilate wrote a title, and put** *it* **on the cross.** And the writing was **JESUS OF NAZARETH THE KING OF THE JEWS.**

20. This title then read many of the Jews: for the place where Jesus was crucified was nigh to the city: and it was written in Hebrew, *and* Greek, *and* Latin.

21. **Then said the chief priests** of the Jews to Pilate, **Write not, The King of the Jews; but that he said, I am King of the Jews.**

22. **Pilate answered, What I have written I have written.**

23. **Then the soldiers,** when they had crucified Jesus, **took his garments,** and made four parts, to every soldier a part; **and also** *his* **coat:** now the coat was **without seam,** woven from the top throughout.

24. **They said** therefore among themselves, **Let us not rend it, but cast lots for it,** whose it shall be: **that the scripture might be fulfilled,** which saith, **They parted my raiment** among them, **and for my vesture they did cast lots.** These things therefore the soldiers did.

25. **Now there stood by the cross of Jesus his mother,** and his mother's sister, Mary the *wife* of Cleophas, and Mary Magdalene.

26. **When Jesus therefore saw his mother, and the disciple** standing by, **whom he loved, he saith** unto his mother, **Woman, behold thy son!**

27. **Then saith he to the disciple, Behold thy mother!** And from that hour that disciple took her unto his own *home.*

28. **After this, Jesus** knowing that all things were now accomplished, that the scripture might be fulfilled, **saith, I thirst.**

29. Now there was set a vessel full of vinegar: **and they filled a sponge with vinegar,**

and put *it* upon hyssop,
■ **and put *it* to his mouth.**
■ 30. **When Jesus** therefore had
■ **received the vinegar, he**
■ **said, It is finished:**
and he bowed his head,
■ **and gave up the ghost.**
■ 31. **The Jews** therefore, because it
was the preparation, that the bodies
should not remain upon the cross on
the sabbath day, (for that sabbath
day was an high day,)
■ **besought Pilate that their**
■ **legs might be broken,**
and *that* they might be taken away.
■ 32. **Then** came
■ **the soldiers, and**
■ **brake the legs of the first,**
■ **and of the other which was**
■ **crucified with him.**
■ 33. **But** when they came to
■ **Jesus,** and saw that he
■ **was dead already,**
■ **they brake not his legs:**
■ 34. **But one**
of the soldiers with a spear
■ **pierced his side, and**
■ **forthwith came** there out
■ **blood and water.**
35. And he that saw *it* bare record,
and his record is true: and he knoweth
that he saith true, that ye might
believe.
■ 36. **For these things were**
■ **done, that the scripture**
■ **should be fulfilled, A bone**
■ **of him shall not be broken.**
■ 37. **And** again another
scripture saith,
■ **They shall look on him**
■ **whom they pierced.**
■ 38. **And** after this
■ **Joseph of Arimathaea,** being
a disciple of Jesus, but secretly for
fear of the Jews,
■ **besought Pilate that he**
■ **might take away the body**
of Jesus:
■ **and Pilate gave** *him* **leave.**
He came therefore,
and took the body of Jesus.
■ 39. **And there came also**
■ **Nicodemus,** which at the first

came to Jesus by night,
■ **and brought a mixture of**
■ **myrrh and aloes,**
about an hundred pound *weight.*
■ 40. **Then took they the body**
of Jesus,
■ **and wound it in linen** clothes
■ **with the spices,** as the manner
of the Jews is to bury.
■ 41. **Now** in the place
where he was crucified
■ **there was a garden;**
■ **and in the garden**
■ **a new sepulchre,**
wherein was never man yet laid.
■ 42. **There laid they Jesus**
therefore because of the Jews'
preparation *day;* for the sepulchre
was nigh at hand.

CHAPTER 20
■ 1. **The first** *day* **of the week**
■ **cometh Mary Magdalene**
early,
■ **when it was yet dark,**
unto the sepulchre,
■ **and seeth the stone taken**
■ **away** from the sepulchre.
■ 2. **Then she runneth,**
and cometh
■ **to Simon Peter, and to the**
■ **other disciple,**
whom Jesus loved,
■ **and saith** unto them,
■ **They have taken away the**
■ **LORD** out of the sepulchre, and we
know not where they have laid him.
■ 3. **Peter** therefore went forth,
■ **and that other disciple,** and
■ **came to the sepulchre.**
4. So they ran both together: and
■ **the other disciple did**
■ **outrun Peter,**
and came first to the sepulchre.
■ 5. **And he stooping down,**
and looking in,
■ **saw the linen clothes lying,**
yet went he not in.
■ 6. **Then cometh Simon Peter**
following him,
■ **and went into the**
■ **sepulchre, and seeth the**
■ **linen** clothes lie,

■ ■ 7. **And the napkin, that was about his head,** not lying with the linen clothes, but wrapped together **in a place by itself.**

8. Then went in also that other disciple, which came first to the sepulchre, and he saw, and believed.

9. For as yet they knew not the scripture, that he must rise again from the dead.

■ ■ 10. **Then the disciples went away again** unto their own home.

■ 11. **But Mary stood** without at the sepulchre weeping: ■ **and as she wept, she** stooped down, *and* ■ **looked into the sepulchre,**

■ 12. **And seeth two angels in** white sitting, the one at the head, and the other at the feet, where the body of Jesus had lain.

■ 13. **And they say** unto her, Woman, ■ **why weepest thou? She** ■ **saith** unto them, ■ **Because they have taken** ■ **away my LORD,** and I know not where they have laid him.

■ 14. **And when she had thus** ■ **said, she turned** herself back, ■ **and saw Jesus** standing, ■ **and knew not that it was** ■ **Jesus.**

15. **Jesus saith** unto her, Woman, ■ **why weepest thou?** whom seekest thou? ■ **She, supposing him to be** ■ **the gardener, saith** unto him, ■ **Sir,** if thou have borne him hence, ■ **tell me where thou** ■ **hast laid him,** ■ **and I will take him away.**

16. **Jesus saith** unto her, ■ **Mary. She turned** herself, ■ **and saith** unto him, ■ **Rabboni; which is** to say, ■ **Master.**

17. **Jesus saith** unto her, ■ **Touch me not;** for I am not yet ascended to my Father: ■ **but go to my brethren, and** ■ **say** unto them,

■ **I ascend unto my Father,** and your Father; and *to* my God, and your God.

■ 18. **Mary** Magdalene came and ■ **told the disciples that she** ■ **had seen the LORD, and** ■ *that* **he had spoken** these things ■ **unto her.**

■ 19. **Then the same day** ■ **at evening,** being the first *day* of the week, ■ **when the doors were shut** ■ **where the disciples were** assembled for fear of the Jews, ■ **came Jesus** and stood in the midst, ■ **and saith** unto them, ■ **Peace** *be* **unto you.**

■ 20. **And** when he had so said, ■ **he shewed unto them** *his* ■ **hands and his side.** Then were the disciples glad, when they saw the LORD.

■ 21. **Then said Jesus** to them ■ **again, Peace** *be* **unto you:** ■ **as** *my* **Father hath sent me,** ■ **even so send I you.**

■ 22. **And** when he had said this, ■ **he breathed on** *them,* ■ **and saith** unto them, ■ **Receive ye the Holy Ghost:** ■ 23. **Whose soever** *sins* **ye** ■ **remit,** they ■ **are remitted** unto them; ■ *and* **whose soever sins ye** ■ **retain,** they ■ **are retained.**

■ 24. **But Thomas,** one of the twelve, called Didymus, ■ **was not with them** when Jesus came.

■ 25. **The other disciples** therefore ■ **said unto him, We have** ■ **seen the LORD. But he said** unto them, ■ **Except I shall see in his** ■ **hands the print of the nails,** ■ **and put my finger into the** ■ **print** of the nails, ■ **and thrust my hand into his** ■ **side, I will not believe.**

26. **And after eight days again** his disciples were within, and Thomas with them: *then* came **Jesus,** the doors being shut, and **stood in the midst,** and said, Peace *be* unto you.

27. **Then saith he to Thomas, Reach hither thy finger, and behold my hands;** and reach hither thy hand, and thrust *it* into my side: and be not faithless, but believing.

28. **And Thomas answered** and said unto him, **My LORD and my God.**

29. **Jesus saith** unto him, Thomas, **because thou hast seen** me, **thou** hast **believed: blessed** *are* **they that have not seen, and** *yet* **have believed.**

30. **And many other signs truly did Jesus** in the presence of his disciples, **which are not written in this book:**

31. **But these are written, that ye might believe that Jesus is the Christ,** the Son of God; and that believing ye might have life through his name.

CHAPTER 21

1. After these things Jesus shewed himself again to the disciples at the sea of Tiberias; and on this wise shewed he *himself.*

2. **There were together Simon Peter, and Thomas** called Didymus, **and Nathanael** of Cana in Galilee, **and the** *sons* **of Zebedee, and two other** of his **disciples.**

3. **Simon Peter saith** unto them, **I go a fishing. They say** unto him, **We also go** with thee. **They went forth,** and entered into a ship immediately; **and** that night they

caught nothing.

4. **But when the morning was** now **come, Jesus stood on the shore:** but the disciples knew not that it was Jesus.

5. **Then Jesus saith** unto them, **Children, have ye any meat? They answered** him, **No.**

6. **And he said** unto them, **Cast** the net **on the right side** of the ship, and ye shall find. **They cast** therefore, **and** now they **were not able to draw** it for **the multitude of fishes.**

7. **Therefore that disciple whom Jesus loved saith** unto Peter, **It is the Lord. Now when** Simon **Peter heard that** it was the Lord, **he** girt *his* fisher's coat *unto him,* (for he was naked,) and did **cast himself into the sea.**

8. **And the other disciples came** in a little ship; (for they were not far from land, but as it were two hundred cubits,) **dragging the net with fishes.**

9. As soon then as they were come to land, **they saw a fire** of coals there, **and fish laid thereon, and bread.**

10. Jesus saith unto them, Bring of the fish which ye have now caught.

11. Simon Peter went up, and drew the net to land full of great fishes, an hundred and fifty and three: and for all there were so many, yet was not the net broken.

12. **Jesus saith** unto them, **Come** *and* **dine. And** none of the disciples durst ask him, Who art thou? knowing that it was the Lord.

13. **Jesus** then cometh, and **taketh bread, and giveth them, and fish** likewise.

14. This is now the third time that

Jesus shewed himself to his disciples, after that he was risen from the dead.

■ 15. **So when they had dined, Jesus saith** to **Simon** Peter, Simon, *son* of Jonas, **lovest thou me more than these? He saith** unto him, **Yea, Lord;** thou knowest that I love thee. **He saith** unto him, **Feed my lambs.**

16. **He saith** to him again **the second time, Simon,** *son* of Jonas, **lovest thou me? He saith** unto him, **Yea, Lord;** thou knowest that I love thee. **He saith** unto him, **Feed my sheep.**

17. **He saith** unto him the **third time, Simon,** *son* of Jonas, **lovest thou me? Peter was grieved** because he said unto him the third time, Lovest thou me? **And he said** unto him, **Lord,** thou knowest all things; **thou knowest that I love thee. Jesus saith** unto him, **Feed my sheep.**

18. Verily, verily, I say unto thee, **When thou wast young, thou** girdest thyself, and **walkedst whither thou wouldest: but when** thou shalt be **old,** thou shalt stretch forth thy hands, and **another shall gird thee,**

■ **and carry** *thee* **whither thou wouldest not.**

■ 19. **This spake he, signifying by what death he should glorify God.** And when he had spoken this, he saith unto him, Follow me.

■ 20. **Then Peter,** turning about, **seeth the disciple** whom **Jesus loved** following; which also leaned on his breast at supper, and said, Lord, which is he that betrayeth thee?

■ 21. **Peter** seeing him **saith** to Jesus, **Lord, and what** *shall* **this man** *do?*

■ 22. **Jesus saith** unto him, **If I will that he tarry till I come, what** *is that* **to thee? follow thou me.**

23. Then went this saying abroad among the brethren, that that disciple should not die: yet Jesus said not unto him, He shall not die; but, If I will that he tarry till I come, what *is that* to thee?

24. This is the disciple which testifieth of these things, and wrote these things: and we know that his testimony is true.

■ 25. **And there are also many other things which Jesus did,** the which, **if they should be written every one,** I suppose that even **the world itself could not contain the books that should be written. Amen.**

THE ACTS OF THE APOSTLES

BACKGROUND INFORMATION

Author – Luke, physician and Gentile companion of Paul. Date Written – probably **between 60** and **64** A.D.

Number of:
Verses -   1,007
Chapters -   28
Total Words - 24,250
Scan Words - 11,781
Scan Words represent 48 % of Total Words.

Theme – the ministry of the Holy Spirit in the early church as the gospel was spread in fulfillment of the Great Commission.

OUTLINE OF THE ACTS

I. **Christ's commission, the Promise of the Holy Spirit, and His ascension.**
Chapter 1

II. Activities of **Peter, John and the Church at Jerusalem**
Chapter 2—5

III. Activities of **"The Twelve" and** of **Stephen.**
Chapters 5—8

IV. Activities of Philip, Paul, Peter and other Christians. in **taking the Gospel to the Gentiles.**
Chapters 8—12

V. **Activities of Paul,** Barnabas and Silas until Paul's imprisonment in Rome.
Chapters 13—28

CHAPTER 1

1.**The former treatise have I made,** O Theophilus, **of all** that **Jesus began** both **to do and teach,** 2. **Until** the day in which **he was taken up, after that he** through the Holy Ghost **had given commandments unto the apostles** whom he had chosen: 3. **To whom also he shewed himself alive** after his passion **by many infallible proofs,** being seen of them forty days, and speaking of the things pertaining to the kingdom of God: 4. **And, being** assembled together **with *them*, commanded** them **that they should not depart from Jerusalem, but wait for the promise of** the Father, which, *saith he,* ye have heard of me. 5. For John truly baptized with water; but ye shall be baptized with **the Holy Ghost** not many days hence. 6. **When they** therefore **were** come **together, they asked of him,** saying, **Lord, wilt thou at this time restore** again **the kingdom** to Israel? 7. **And he said** unto them **It is not for you to know the times** or the seasons, **which the Father hath put in his own power.** 8. **But ye shall receive power, after that the Holy Ghost is come** upon you: **and ye shall be witnesses unto me** both in Jerusalem, and in all Judaea, and in Samaria, and **unto the uttermost part of the earth.** 9. **And** when he had spoken these things, **while they beheld,** he was taken up; and **a cloud received him out of their sight.** 10. **And while they looked** stedfastly toward heaven as he went up, behold, **two men stood** by them **in white apparel;** 11. **Which also said,** Ye men of Galilee, **why stand ye gazing** up **into heaven? this same Jesus,** which is taken up from you into heaven, **shall so come** in like manner **as ye have seen him go** into heaven. 12. **Then returned they unto Jerusalem** from the mount called Olivet, which is from Jerusalem a sabbath day's journey. 13. **And** when they were come in, they **went** up **into an upper room,** where abode both Peter, and James, and John, and Andrew, Philip, and Thomas, Bartholomew, and Matthew, James *the son* of Alphaeus, and Simon Zelotes, and Judas the brother of James. 14. **These all continued with one accord in prayer and supplication,** with the women, and Mary the mother of Jesus, and with his brethren. 15. **And** in those days **Peter stood** up in the midst of the disciples, **and said,** (the number of names together were about an hundred and twenty,) 16. Men *and* brethren, **this scripture must** needs **have been fulfilled,** which the Holy Ghost by the mouth of David spake before **concerning Judas,** which was guide to them that took Jesus. 17. For he was numbered with us, and had obtained part of this ministry. 18. **Now this man purchased a field with the**

reward of iniquity; and
falling headlong, he burst
asunder in the midst,
and all his bowels
gushed out.
19. And it was known unto
all the dwellers at
Jerusalem; insomuch as
that field is called
in their proper tongue, Aceldama,
that is to say,
The field of blood.
20. For it is written
in the book of Psalms,
Let his habitation
be desolate,
and let no man dwell therein:
and his bishopric let
another take.
21. Wherefore of these men
which have companied
with us all the time that the Lord
Jesus went in and out among us,
22. Beginning from the baptism of
John, unto that same day that he was
taken up from us,
must one be ordained to be a
witness with us of his resurrection.
23. And they appointed two,
Joseph called Barsabas, who was
surnamed Justus,
and Matthias.
24. And they prayed,
and said, Thou,
Lord, which knowest
the hearts of all *men*,
shew whether of these two
thou hast chosen,
25. That he may take part of
this ministry and
apostleship, from which
Judas by transgression
fell, that he
might go to his own place.
26. And they gave forth their lots;
and the lot fell upon
Matthias; and he was numbered
with the eleven apostles.

CHAPTER 2
1. And when the day of
Pentecost was fully
come, they were all with

one accord in one place.
2. And suddenly there came
a sound from heaven
as of a rushing mighty wind,
and it filled all the house
where they were sitting.
3. And there appeared
unto them
cloven tongues like as of
fire, and it sat upon each of
them.
4.And they were all filled
with the Holy Ghost, and
began to speak with other
tongues, as the Spirit gave
them utterance.
5. And there were dwelling
at Jerusalem
Jews, devout men,
out of every nation
under heaven.
6. Now when this was noised abroad,
the multitude
came together,
and were confounded,
because that every man
heard them speak in his
own language.
7. And they were all amazed
and marvelled,
saying one to another, Behold,
are not all these which speak
Galilaeans?
8. And how hear we every
man in our own tongue,
wherein we were born?
9. Parthians, and Medes, and
Elamites, and the dwellers in
Mesopotamia, and in Judaea, and
Cappadocia, in Pontus, and Asia,
10. Phrygia, and Pamphylia, in Egypt,
and in the parts of Libya about
Cyrene, and strangers of Rome, Jews
and proselytes,
11. Cretes and Arabians, we do hear
them speak in our tongues the
wonderful works of God.
12. And they were
all amazed, and were
in doubt, saying one to another,
What meaneth this?
13. Others mocking said,
These men are full

■ **of new wine.**
■ 14. **But Peter,**
standing up with the eleven,
■ **lifted up his voice, and**
■ **said** unto them, Ye men of Judaea,
and all *ye* that dwell at Jerusalem, be
this known unto you, and
■ **hearken to my words:**
■ 15. **For these are not**
■ **drunken,** as ye suppose, seeing it
is *but* the third hour of the day.
■ 16. **But this is that** which was
■ **spoken by** the prophet
■ **Joel;**
17. And it shall come to pass
■ **in the last days, saith God,**
■ **I will pour out of my Spirit**
■ **upon all flesh:** and your sons
and your daughters shall prophesy,
and your young men shall see visions,
and your old men shall dream dreams:
18. And on my servants and on my
handmaidens I will pour out in those
days of my Spirit; and they
shall prophesy:
■ 19. **And I will shew wonders**
in heaven above,
■ **and signs** in the earth beneath;
blood, and fire, and vapour of smoke:
20. The sun shall be turned into
darkness, and the moon into blood,
before the great and notable day of
the Lord come:
■ 21. **And** it shall come to pass, *that*
■ **whosoever shall call on**
■ **the name of the Lord shall**
■ **be saved.**
22. Ye men of Israel,
■ **hear these words; Jesus**
of Nazareth,
■ **a man approved of God**
among you
■ **by miracles**
and wonders and signs,
■ **which God did by him**
in the midst of you,
■ **as ye** yourselves also
■ **know:**
■ 23. **Him,** being delivered by the
determinate counsel and foreknowledge of God,
■ **ye have taken, and**
by wicked hands have

■ **crucified** and slain:
■ 24. **Whom God hath raised**
■ **up,** having loosed the pains of death:
because it was not possible that he
should be holden of it.
■ 25. **For David speaketh**
■ **concerning him,** I foresaw the
Lord always before my face, for he is
on my right hand, that I should not
be moved:
26. Therefore did my heart rejoice,
and my tongue was glad; moreover
also my flesh shall rest in hope:
■ 27. **Because thou wilt not**
■ **leave my soul in hell,**
■ **neither wilt thou suffer**
■ **thine Holy One to**
■ **see corruption.**
28. Thou hast made known to me the
ways of life; thou shalt make me full
of joy with thy countenance.
29 Men *and* brethren, let me freely
speak unto you of the patriarch
■ **David,** that he
■ **is both dead and buried,**
■ **and his sepulchre is with**
■ **us** unto this day.
■ 30. **Therefore being a**
■ **prophet, and knowing**
■ **that God had sworn**
with an oath to him,
■ **that of the fruit of his loins,**
according to the flesh,
■ **he would raise up Christ**
to sit on his throne;
■ 31. **He** seeing this before
■ **spake of the resurrection**
■ **of Christ,** that his soul was
not left in hell, neither his flesh
did see corruption.
■ 32. **This Jesus hath God**
■ **raised up,**
whereof we all are witnesses.
■ 33. **Therefore being**
by the right hand of God
■ **exalted,** and having received
of the Father the promise of the
Holy Ghost,
■ **he hath shed forth this,**
■ **which ye now see**
■ **and hear.**
■ 34. **For David is not**
■ **ascended into the**

■ **heavens:** but he saith himself,
The Lord said unto my Lord, Sit thou
on my right hand,
35. Until I make thy foes thy footstool.
■ 36. **Therefore** let all the house of
Israel know assuredly, that
■ **God hath made the same**
■ **Jesus, whom ye have**
■ **crucified, both Lord**
■ **and Christ.**
■ 37. **Now when they heard**
this,
■ **they were pricked**
in their heart,
■ **and said** unto Peter and to the
rest of the apostles,
Men *and* brethren,
■ **what shall we do?**
■ 38. **Then Peter said** unto them,
■ **Repent, and be baptized**
every one of you
■ **in the name of Jesus Christ**
■ **for the remission of sins,**
■ **and ye shall receive**
the gift of
■ **the Holy Ghost.**
■ 39. **For the promise is unto**
you, and to your children, and to all
that are afar off, *even*
■ **as many as the LORD** our God
■ **shall call.**
40. And with many other words did he
testify and exhort, saying, Save
yourselves from this untoward
generation.
■ 41. **Then they that** gladly
■ **received his word were**
■ **baptized: and** the same day
■ **there were added** *unto*
■ *them* **about three**
■ **thousand souls.**
■ 42. **And they continued**
stedfastly
■ **in the apostles' doctrine** and
■ **fellowship,** and in
■ **breaking** of
■ **bread, and** in
■ **prayers.**
43. And fear came upon every soul:
■ **and many wonders**
and signs
■ **were done by the apostles.**
■ 44. **And all that believed**

were together, and
■ **had all things common;**
■ 45. **And sold their**
■ **possessions** and goods,
■ **and parted them** to all *men*,
■ **as every man had need.**
■ 46. **And they, continuing**
■ **daily with one accord**
in the temple, and breaking bread
from house to house, did eat their
meat with gladness and singleness
of heart,
47. Praising God, and having favour
with all the people.
■ **And the Lord added to**
■ **the church daily**
such as should be saved.

CHAPTER 3
■ 1. **Now Peter and John went**
up together
■ **into the temple at the hour**
■ **of prayer,** *being* the ninth *hour*.
■ 2. **And a certain man lame**
■ **from his mother's womb**
■ **was** carried, whom they
■ **laid daily at the gate**
of the temple which is called
■ **Beautiful, to ask alms**
of them that entered into the temple;
■ 3. **Who seeing Peter and**
■ **John** about to go into the temple
■ **asked an alms.**
■ 4. **And Peter,** fastening his eyes
upon him with John,
■ **said, Look on us.**
5. And he gave heed unto them, expecting to receive something of them.
6. Then Peter said,
■ **Silver and gold have I**
■ **none; but such as I have**
■ **give I thee: In the name of**
■ **Jesus Christ** of Nazareth
■ **rise** up
■ **and walk.**
■ 7. **And he took him**
by the right hand,
■ **and lifted** *him* **up:**
and immediately his feet and ankle
bones received strength.
■ 8. **And he leaping up**
stood, and walked, and
■ **entered** with them into

■ **the temple, walking, and**
■ **leaping, and praising God.**
■ **9. And all the people**
saw him walking and praising God:
10. And they knew that it was he
which sat for alms at the Beautiful
gate of the temple: and they
■ **were filled with wonder**
and amazement
■ **at that which had**
■ **happened** unto him.
■ 11. **And** as the lame man which was
healed held Peter and John, all
■ **the people ran together**
unto them in the porch that is called
Solomon's, greatly wondering.
■ 12. **And when Peter saw** *it*,
■ **he answered**
unto the people, Ye men of Israel,
■ **why marvel ye at this?**
or why look ye so earnestly on us, as
though by our own power or holiness
we had made this man to walk?
■ 13. **The God of Abraham,**
and of
■ **Isaac, and** of
■ **Jacob,** the God of our fathers,
■ **hath glorified his Son**
■ **Jesus; whom ye delivered**
■ **up, and denied** him in the
presence of Pilate, when he was
determined to let *him* go.
■ 14. **But ye denied the Holy**
■ **One** and the Just,
■ **and desired a murderer to**
■ **be granted unto you;**
■ 15. **And killed the Prince of**
■ **life, whom God** hath
■ **raised** from the dead;
■ **whereof we are witnesses.**
■ 16. **And** his name
■ **through faith in his name**
■ **hath made this man strong,**
whom ye see and know: yea, the faith
which is by him hath given him this
perfect soundness in the presence of
you all.
■ 17. **And now,** brethren,
■ **I wot that through**
■ **ignorance ye did** *it,* as *did*
also your rulers.
■ 18. **But** those things, which
■ **God before had shewed by**

the mouth of all
■ **his prophets, that Christ**
■ **should suffer,**
he hath so fulfilled.
■ 19. **Repent ye therefore, and**
■ **be converted, that your**
■ **sins may be blotted out,**
when the times of refreshing shall
come from the presence of the Lord.
■ 20. **And he shall send**
■ **Jesus Christ,**
which before was preached unto you:
21. Whom the heaven must receive
until the times of restitution
of all things,
■ **which God hath spoken by**
■ **the mouth of** all his holy
■ **prophets since the**
■ **world began.**
■ 22. **For Moses truly said**
unto the fathers,
■ **A prophet shall the Lord**
your God
■ **raise up** unto you of your brethren,
like unto me; him shall ye hear in
all things whatsoever he shall say
unto you.
■ 23. **And it shall come to**
■ **pass,** *that* **every soul,**
■ **which will not hear that**
■ **prophet, shall**
■ **be destroyed**
from among the people.
24. Yea, and all the prophets from
Samuel and those that follow after, as
many as have spoken, have likewise
foretold of these days.
■ 25. **Ye are the children**
of the prophets, and
■ **of the covenant which God**
■ **made** with our fathers, saying
■ **unto Abraham,** And in thy seed
shall all the kindreds of the
earth be blessed.
■ 26. **Unto you first God,**
■ **having raised up his Son**
■ **Jesus, sent him to bless**
■ **you,** in turning away every one of
you from his iniquities.

CHAPTER 4
■ 1. **And** as they spake
unto the people,

the priests,
and the captain of the temple,
and the
Sadducees, came
upon them,
2. Being grieved that they
taught the people, and
preached through Jesus
the resurrection from the dead.
3. And they laid hands on
them, and put *them* in hold
unto the next day:
for it was now eventide.
4. Howbeit many of them
which heard the word
believed; and the number
of the
men was about
five thousand.
5. And it came to pass on the morrow,
that their rulers, and elders, and
scribes,
6. And Annas the high
priest, and
Caiaphas, and
John, and Alexander,
and as many as were of the kindred of
the high priest,
were gathered together
at Jerusalem.
7. And when
they had set them in the midst,
they ask By what power, or
by what
name, have ye done this?
8. Then Peter, filled with the
Holy Ghost, said
unto them, Ye rulers of the people,
and elders of Israel,
9. If we this day
be examined of the good
deed done to the
impotent man,
by what means he is made whole;
10. Be it known unto
you all, and to all the people of
Israel, that by the name of
Jesus Christ of Nazareth,
whom ye crucified, whom
God raised from the dead,
even by him doth this man
stand here before you whole.
11. This is the stone which was
set at nought of you builders,
which is become the head
of the corner.
12. Neither is there
salvation in any other: for
there is none other name
under heaven given among men,
whereby we must
be saved.
13. Now when they saw the
boldness of Peter and
John, and perceived that
they were unlearned and
ignorant men,
they marvelled; and they
took knowledge of them,
that they had been
with Jesus.
14. And beholding the man
which was
healed standing with them,
they could say nothing
against it.
15. But when they had commanded
them to go aside out of the council,
they conferred among
themselves,
16. Saying, What shall
we do
to these men? for that indeed
a notable
miracle hath been done
by them *is* manifest to all them that
dwell in Jerusalem;
and we cannot deny *it*.
17. But that it spread no
further among the people,
let us straitly
threaten them, that they speak
henceforth to no man in this name.
18. And they called them, and
commanded them not to
speak at all
nor teach in the
name of Jesus.
19. But Peter and John
answered and said unto them,
Whether it be right
in the sight of God
to hearken unto you more
than unto God, judge ye.
20. For we cannot but speak
the things which we have seen

and heard.
21. **So when they** had **further threatened them, they let them go, finding nothing how they might punish them, because of the people: for all** *men* **glorified God** for that which was done.
22. For the man was above forty years old, on whom this miracle of healing was shewed.
23. **And being let go, they went** to their own company, **and reported all that the chief priests and elders had said** unto them.
24 **And** when they heard that, **they lifted up their voice to God** with one accord, **and said, Lord, thou** *art* **God, which hast made** heaven, and earth, and the sea, and **all** that in them is:
25. Who by the mouth of thy servant David hast said, Why did the heathen rage, and the people imagine vain things?
26. The kings of the earth stood up, and the rulers were gathered together against the Lord, and against his Christ.
27. For of a truth against thy holy child Jesus, whom thou hast anointed, both Herod, and Pontius Pilate, with the Gentiles, and the people of Israel, were gathered together,
28. For to do whatsoever thy hand and thy counsel determined before to be done.
29. **And now, Lord, behold their threatenings: and grant** unto **thy servants, that with** all **boldness they may speak thy word,**
30. By stretching forth thine hand to heal; **and that signs and wonders may be done by the name of** thy holy child **Jesus.**
31. **And when they had prayed, the place was shaken** where they were assembled together; **and they were all filled with the Holy Ghost, and** they spake the word of God with boldness.
32. **And the multitude** of them **that believed were of one heart and** of one soul: neither said any *of them* that aught of the things which he possessed was his own; but they **had all things common.**
33. **And with great power gave the apostles witness of the resurrection** of the Lord Jesus: and great grace was upon them all.
34. **Neither was there any** among them **that lacked: for as many as were possessors of lands or houses sold them, and brought the prices** of the things that were sold,
35. **And laid** *them* **down at the apostles' feet: and distribution was made unto every man** according **as he had need.**
36. And Joses, who by the apostles was surnamed Barnabas, (which is, being interpreted, The son of consolation,) a Levite, *and* of the country of Cyprus,
37. Having land, sold *it*, and brought the money, and laid *it* at the apostles' feet.

CHAPTER 5

1. **But** a certain man named **Ananias, with Sapphira his wife, sold a possession,**
2. **And kept back** *part* **of the price,** his wife also being privy *to it,* **and brought** a certain **part, and laid** *it* **at the apostles' feet.**
3. **But Peter said, Ananias, why hath Satan filled thine heart to lie to the Holy Ghost, and to keep back** *part* **of the price** of the land?

4. Whiles it remained, was it not thine own? and after it was sold, was it not in thine own power? why hast thou conceived this thing in thine heart? **thou hast not lied unto men, but unto God.** 5. **And Ananias hearing these words fell down, and gave up the ghost:** and great fear came on all them that heard these things. 6. **And the young men** arose, wound him up, and carried *him* out, and **buried *him*.** 7. **And** it was about the space of **three hours after,** when **his wife, not knowing what was done, came in.** 8. **And Peter answered** unto **her, Tell me whether ye sold the land for so much? And she said, Yea,** for so much. 9. **Then Peter said** unto her, **How is it that ye have agreed together to tempt the Spirit of the Lord?** behold, the feet of them which have buried thy husband *are* at the door, and shall carry thee out. 10. **Then fell she down** straightway at his feet, **and yielded** up **the ghost:** and the young men came in, and found her dead, and, carrying *her* forth, buried *her* by her husband. 11. **And great fear came upon all the church,** and upon as many as heard these things. 12. **And by the hands of the apostles were many signs and wonders wrought** among the people; (and they were all with one accord in Solomon's porch. 13. And of the rest durst no man join himself to them: but the people magnified them. 14. **And believers were** the more **added to the Lord,** multitudes both of men and women.) 15. **Insomuch that they**

brought forth **the sick into the streets,** and laid *them* on beds and couches, **that at the least the shadow of Peter passing by might overshadow** some of **them.** 16. **There came** also **a multitude *out* of the cities** round about unto Jerusalem, **bringing sick** folks, **and them** which were vexed **with unclean spirits: and they were healed** every one. 17. **Then the high priest** rose up, **and all** they **that were with him, (**which is the sect of the Sadducees,) and **were filled with indignation,** 18. **And laid their hands on the apostles, and put them in** the common **prison.** 19. **But the angel of the Lord** by night **opened the prison doors,** and brought them forth, **and said,** 20. **Go, stand and speak in the temple** to the people all the words of this life. 21. **And** when they heard *that,* **they entered** into **the temple** early in the morning, **and taught. But the high priest came,** and they that were with him, **and called the council** together, and all the senate of the children of Israel, **and sent to the prison to have them brought.** 22. **But when the officers** came, and **found them not in** the **prison, they returned** and told, 23. **Saying, The prison** truly **found we shut with all safety**, and the keepers standing without before the doors: **but** when we had opened,

■ **we found no man within.**
24. Now when the high priest and the captain of the temple and the chief priests heard these things, they doubted of them whereunto this would grow.
■ 25. **Then came one**
and told them,
■ **saying,** Behold,
■ **the men** whom
■ **ye put in prison are**
standing in the temple, and
■ **teaching the people.**
■ 26. **Then went the captain**
with the officers,
■ **and brought them** without
violence: for they feared the people, lest they should have been stoned.
■ 27. **And** when they had brought them, they set *them* before the council: and
■ **the high priest asked them,**
■ 28. **Saying, Did not we** straitly
■ **command you that ye**
■ **should not teach in this**
■ **name?** and, behold, ye have filled Jerusalem with your doctrine, and intend to bring this man's blood upon us.
■ 29 **Then Peter and the** *other*
■ **apostles answered** and said,
■ **We ought to obey God**
■ **rather than men.**
■ 30. **The God of our fathers**
■ **raised up Jesus,**
whom ye slew and hanged on a tree.
■ 31. **Him hath God exalted**
with his right hand
■ *to be* **a Prince and a**
■ **Saviour,** for to give repentance to Israel, and forgiveness of sins.
■ 32. **And we are his**
■ **witnesses** of these things;
■ **and** *so is* **also the Holy**
■ **Ghost,** whom God hath given to them that obey him.
■ 33. **When they heard** *that,*
■ **they** were cut *to the heart,* and
■ **took counsel to slay them.**
■ 34. **Then stood**
there up one in the council,
■ **a Pharisee, named**
■ **Gamaliel, a doctor of the**

■ **law,** had
■ **in reputation among all the**
■ **people,** and commanded to put the apostles forth a little space;
■ 35. **And said unto them,**
Ye men of Israel,
■ **take heed to yourselves**
■ **what ye intend to do**
as touching these men.
■ 36. **For before these days**
■ **rose up Theudas,**
boasting himself to be somebody; to whom a number of men, about four hundred, joined themselves:
■ **who was slain; and all, as**
■ **many as obeyed him, were**
■ **scattered,** and brought to nought.
■ 37. **After this man rose** up
■ **Judas of Galilee**
in the days of the taxing, and drew away much people after him:
■ **he also perished;**
and all, *even* as many as obeyed him, were dispersed.
■ 38. **And now I say** unto you,
■ **Refrain from these men,**
and let them alone:
■ **for if** this counsel or
■ **this work be of men, it will**
■ **come to nought:**
■ 39. **But if it be of God, ye**
■ **cannot overthrow it; lest**
■ **haply ye** be found even to
■ **fight against God.**
■ 40. **And to him they agreed:**
■ **and when they had called**
■ **the apostles, and beaten**
■ *them,* **they commanded**
■ **that they should not speak**
in the name
■ **of Jesus, and let them go.**
■ 41. **And they departed**
from the presence of the council,
■ **rejoicing that they were**
■ **counted worthy to suffer**
■ **shame for his name.**
■ 42. **And daily in the temple,**
■ **and in every house, they**
■ **ceased not to teach and**
■ **preach Jesus Christ.**

CHAPTER 6
1. And in those days, when the

number of the disciples was multiplied,

■ **there arose a murmuring of** the

■ **Grecians against** the **Hebrews, because their widows were neglected in the daily ministration.**

■ 2. **Then the twelve** called the multitude of the disciples *unto them,* and

■ **said,** It is not reason that we should leave the word of God, and serve tables.

■ 3. **Wherefore, brethren, look**

■ **ye out** among you

■ **seven men of honest report, full of the Holy Ghost and wisdom, whom we may appoint over this business.**

4. But we will give ourselves continually to prayer, and to the ministry of the word.

5. And the saying pleased the whole multitude:

■ **and they chose Stephen,** a man full of faith and of the Holy Ghost, and

■ **Philip, and**

■ **Prochorus, and**

■ **Nicanor, and**

■ **Timon, and**

■ **Parmenas, and Nicolas** a proselyte of Antioch:

■ 6. **Whom they set before the**

■ **apostles: and when they** had

■ **prayed, they laid**

■ **their hands on them.**

■ 7. **And the word** of God

■ **increased; and the number**

■ **of** the

■ **disciples multiplied in**

■ **Jerusalem** greatly; and a great company of the priests were obedient to the faith.

■ 8. **And Stephen, full of faith**

■ **and power, did great**

■ **wonders** and miracles among the people.

■ 9. **Then there arose certain**

■ **of** the synagogue, which is called

■ *the synagogue* **of the**

■ **Libertines, and Cyrenians,**

■ **and Alexandrians,** and of them of Cilicia and of Asia,

■ **disputing with Stephen.**

■ 10. **And they were not able**

■ **to resist the wisdom and**

■ **the spirit by which**

■ **he spake.**

■ 11. **Then they** suborned men, which

■ **said, We have heard him**

■ **speak blasphemous**

■ **words** against Moses, and *against* God.

■ 12. **And they stirred up the**

■ **people,** and the elders, and the scribes, and came upon *him,* and caught him,

■ **and brought** *him*

■ **to the council,**

■ 13. **And set up false**

■ **witnesses, which said,** This man ceaseth not to speak blasphemous words against this holy place, and the law:

■ 14. **For we have heard him**

■ **say, that** this

■ **Jesus** of Nazareth

■ **shall destroy this place,**

■ **and** shall

■ **change the customs** which

■ **Moses delivered** us.

■ 15. **And all** that sat in the council, looking stedfastly on him,

■ **saw his face as** it had been

■ **the face of an angel.**

CHAPTER 7

■ 1. **Then said the high priest,**

■ **Are these things so?**

■ 2. **And he said,** Men, brethren, and fathers, hearken;

■ **The God of glory appeared**

■ **unto** our father

■ **Abraham,** when he was in Mesopotamia, before he dwelt in Charran,

■ 3. **And said** unto him, Get thee out of thy country, and from thy kindred, and

■ **come into the land which I**

■ **shall shew thee.**

4. **Then** came he out of the land of the Chaldaeans, and dwelt in Charran: and from thence, when his father was dead, **he removed him into this land, wherein ye now dwell.**

5. And he gave him none inheritance in it, no, not *so much* as to set his foot on: yet he promised that he would give it to him for a possession, and to his seed after him, when *as yet* he had no child.

6. **And God spake** on this wise, **That his seed should sojourn in a strange land; and that they should bring them into bondage,** and entreat *them* evil four hundred years.

7. And the nation to whom they shall be in bondage will I judge, said God: **and after that shall they** come forth, and **serve me in this place.**

8. **And he gave him the covenant of circumcision: and so *Abraham* begat Isaac,** and circumcised him the eighth day; **and Isaac** *begat* **Jacob; and Jacob** *begat* **the twelve patriarchs.**

9. **And the patriarchs,** moved with envy, **sold Joseph into Egypt: but God** was with him,

10. And delivered him out of all his afflictions, and **gave him favour and** wisdom in the sight of **Pharaoh** king of Egypt; and he **made him governor over Egypt** and all his house.

11. **Now there came a dearth** over all the land of Egypt and Chanaan, and great affliction: and our fathers found no sustenance.

12. **But when Jacob heard that there was corn in Egypt, he sent out our fathers first.**

13. And at the second *time* Joseph was made known to his brethren; and Joseph's kindred was made known unto Pharaoh.

14. **Then sent Joseph, and called his father Jacob to him, and all his kindred,** threescore and fifteen souls.

15. **So Jacob** went down into Egypt, and **died,** he, **and our fathers,**

16. **And were** carried over into Sychem, and **laid in the sepulchre that Abraham bought** for a sum of money of the sons of Emmor *the father* of Sychem.

17. **But when the time of** the **promise drew nigh,** which God had sworn to Abraham, **the people grew and multiplied in Egypt,**

18. **Till another king arose, which knew not Joseph.**

19. **The same dealt subtilly with our kindred,** and evil entreated our fathers, so that they cast out their young children, to the end they might not live.

20. **In which time Moses was born,** and was exceeding fair, and nourished up in his father's house three months:

21. **And** when he was cast out, **Pharaoh's daughter** took him up, and **nourished him for her own son.**

22. **And Moses was learned in all the wisdom of the Egyptians,** and was mighty in words and in deeds.

23. **And when he was** full **forty** years old, **it came into his heart to visit his brethren** the children of Israel.

24. **And seeing one** *of them* **suffer wrong, he defended** *him,* and avenged him that was oppressed, **and smote the Egyptian:**

25. **For he supposed his brethren** would have

understood how that
God by his hand would
deliver them: but they
understood not.

26. And the next day he shewed himself unto them as they strove, and would have set them at one again, saying, Sirs, ye are brethren; why do ye wrong one to another?

27. But he that did his neighbour wrong thrust him away, saying, Who made thee a ruler and a judge over us?

28. Wilt thou kill me, as thou diddest the Egyptian yesterday?

29 Then fled Moses
at this saying,
and was a stranger in
the land of
Madian, where he
begat two sons.

30. And when forty years were expired, there appeared to him in the wilderness of mount Sina an angel of the Lord in a flame of fire in a bush.

31. When Moses saw *it*, he wondered at the sight: and as he drew near to behold *it*,
the voice of the LORD came
unto him,

32. *Saying, I am* the God of thy fathers, the God of Abraham, and the God of Isaac, and the God of Jacob. Then Moses trembled, and durst not behold.

33. Then said the Lord to him, Put off thy shoes from thy feet: for the place
where thou standest
is holy ground.

34. I have seen,
I have seen the affliction of
my people which is
in Egypt, and I have heard their groaning, and am come down to deliver them.
And now come,
I will send thee into Egypt.

35. This Moses whom they refused, saying, Who made thee a ruler and a judge? the same

did God send *to be* a ruler and a deliverer by the hand of the angel which appeared to him in the bush.

36. He brought them out,
after that he had shewed
wonders and signs
in the land of Egypt, and in the Red sea, and in the wilderness forty years.

37. This is that Moses, which
said unto the children of Israel,
A prophet shall the Lord
your God raise up
unto you of your brethren,
like unto me; him
shall ye hear.

38. This is he, that was in the church in the wilderness with the angel which spake to him in the mount Sina, and *with* our fathers: who received the lively oracles to give unto us:

39. To whom our fathers
would not obey,
but thrust *him* from them,
and in their hearts
turned back again into Egypt,

40. Saying unto Aaron,
Make us gods to go before
us: for *as for* this
Moses, which brought *us* out of the land of Egypt, we wot not what is become of him.

41. And they made a calf
in those days,
and offered sacrifice unto
the idol, and rejoiced in the works
of their own hands.

42 Then God turned,
and gave them up to
worship the host of
heaven; as it is written in the book of the prophets, O ye house of Israel, have ye offered to me slain beasts and sacrifices *by the space* of forty years in the wilderness?

43 Yea, ye took up the tabernacle of Moloch, and the star of your god Remphan, figures which ye made to worship them: and I will carry you away beyond Babylon.

44 Our fathers had the
tabernacle of witness in the

wilderness, as he
had appointed, speaking
unto Moses, that he should
make it according to the
fashion that he had seen.
45 Which also our fathers that came
after brought in with Jesus into the
possession of the Gentiles, whom
God drave out before the face of our
fathers, unto the days of
David;
46 Who found favour before God, and
desired to find a
tabernacle for the God
of Jacob.
47 But Solomon built
him an house.
48 Howbeit the most High
dwelleth not in temples
made with hands;
as saith the prophet,
49 Heaven *is* my throne,
and earth *is* my footstool:
what house will ye build
me? saith the Lord: or what *is* the
place of my rest?
50 Hath not my hand made
all these things?
51 Ye stiffnecked and
uncircumcised in heart
and ears,
ye do always
resist the Holy Ghost: as
your fathers *did, so do* ye.
52 Which of the prophets
have not your fathers
persecuted? and they have
slain them which shewed
before of
the coming of the Just One;
of whom ye have been
now the betrayers
and murderers:
53 Who have received the law by the
disposition of angels, and have not
kept *it.*
54 When they heard these
things, they were cut to the
heart, and they
gnashed on him with *their* teeth.
55 But he,
being full of the Holy Ghost,
looked up stedfastly into

heaven, and saw the glory of God,
and Jesus standing on the right hand
of God,
56 And said, Behold, I see
the heavens opened, and the
Son of man
standing on the right hand
of God.
57 Then they cried out with
a loud voice,
and stopped their ears,
and ran upon him
with one accord,
58 And cast *him* out
of the city, and stoned *him:*
and the witnesses laid
down their clothes at a
young man's feet, whose
name was Saul.
59 And they stoned
Stephen, calling upon *God,* and
saying, Lord Jesus, receive my spirit.
60 And he kneeled down, and
cried with a loud voice,
Lord, lay not this sin to their
charge. And
when he had said this,
he fell asleep.

CHAPTER 8
1. And Saul was consenting
unto his death. And at that
time there was a great
persecution against the
church which was at Jerusalem;
and they were all scattered abroad
throughout the regions of Judaea and
Samaria, except the apostles.
2. And devout men carried Stephen *to*
his burial, and made great
lamentation over him.
3. As for Saul, he made
havock of the church,
entering into every house,
and haling men and
women committed
them to prison.
4. Therefore they that were scattered
abroad went every where preaching
the word.
5. Then Philip went down to
the city of
Samaria, and preached

Christ unto them.
6. And the people
with one accord
gave heed unto those
things which Philip spake,
hearing and seeing the miracles which
he did.
7. For unclean spirits,
crying with loud voice,
came out of many
that were possessed *with them*:
and many taken with palsies,
and that were lame,
were healed.
8. And there was great
joy in that city.
9. But there was a certain
man, called
Simon, which beforetime
in the same city used sorcery, and
bewitched the people of
Samaria, giving out that
himself was some
great one:
10. To whom they all gave
heed, from the least to the greatest,
saying, This man is the
great power of God.
11. And to him they had regard,
because that of long time he had
bewitched them with sorceries.
12. But when they believed
Philip preaching the things
concerning the
kingdom of God, and
the name of
Jesus Christ, they were
baptized, both men and women.
13. Then Simon himself
believed also: and when
he was baptized, he
continued with Philip,
and wondered, beholding the miracles
and signs which were done.
14. Now when the apostles
which were at Jerusalem
heard that Samaria had received
the word of God,
they sent unto them Peter
and John:
15. Who, when they
were come down
prayed for them,

that they might receive
the Holy Ghost:
16. (For as yet he was fallen
upon none of them: only
they were baptized
in the name of the Lord Jesus.)
17. Then laid they *their*
hands on them, and they
received the Holy Ghost.
18. And when Simon saw
that through laying on of the apostles'
hands the Holy Ghost was given,
he offered them money,
19. Saying, Give me also
this power,
that on whomsoever I lay hands, he
may receive the Holy Ghost.
20. But Peter said unto him,
Thy money perish with thee,
because thou hast thought that the
gift of God may be purchased
with money.
21. Thou hast neither part
nor lot in this matter: for thy
heart is not right
in the sight of God.
22. Repent therefore
of this thy wickedness,
and pray God, if perhaps
the thought of thine heart
may be forgiven thee.
23. For I perceive that thou art in the
gall of bitterness, and *in* the
bond of iniquity.
24. Then answered Simon,
and said,
Pray ye to the LORD for me,
that none of these things
which ye have spoken
come upon me.
25. And they,
when they had testified and
preached the word of the Lord,
returned to Jerusalem,
and preached the gospel
in many villages of
the Samaritans.
26. And the angel of the Lord
spake unto Philip, saying,
Arise, and
go toward the south unto the way
that goeth down from Jerusalem
unto Gaza, which is desert.

27. **And he arose and went:
and,** behold,
**a man of Ethiopia, an
eunuch of great authority
under Candace queen of
the Ethiopians,** who had the
charge of all her treasure, and had
come to Jerusalem for to worship,
28. **Was returning, and** sitting
in his chariot read Esaias
the prophet.
29 **Then the Spirit said unto
Philip, Go near,** and join thyself
to this chariot.
30. **And Philip**
ran thither to *him*, and
**heard him read the prophet
Esaias, and said,
Understandest** thou
what thou readest?
31. **And he said, How can I,
except some man should
guide me?** And he desired Philip
that he would come up
and sit with him.
32. **The** place of the
**scripture which he read
was this, He was led as a
sheep to the slaughter;**
and like a lamb dumb before his
shearer, so opened he not his mouth:
33. In his humiliation his judgment was
taken away: and who shall declare
his generation? for his life is taken
from the earth.
34. **And the eunuch**
answered Philip, and
**said, I pray thee, of whom
speaketh the prophet this?**
of himself, or of some other man?
35. **Then Philip** opened his mouth,
and began at the same scripture, and
preached unto him Jesus.
36. **And** as they went on *their* way,
they came unto a certain
**water: and the eunuch
said, See,** *here is* **water;
what doth hinder me
to be baptized?**
37. **And Philip said, If thou
believest** with all thine heart,
**thou mayest and he
answered** and said,

**I believe that Jesus Christ
is the Son of God.**
38. And he commanded the chariot to
stand still:
and they went down both
into the water, both Philip and
the eunuch;
and he baptized him.
39. **And** when they were come up out
of the water,
the Spirit of the Lord
**caught away Philip, that the
eunuch saw him no more:**
and he went on his way rejoicing.
40. **But Philip was found at
Azotus: and** passing through
he preached in all the cities,
till he came to Caesarea.

CHAPTER 9

1. **And Saul,** yet breathing out
threatenings and slaughter against
the disciples of the Lord,
went unto the high priest,
2. **And desired** of him
letters to Damascus
to the synagogues,
**that if he found any of this
way,** whether they were
men or women,
**he might bring them
bound unto Jerusalem.**
3. **And as** he journeyed,
he came near Damascus:
and
suddenly there shined
round about him
a light from heaven:
4. **And he fell** to the earth,
and heard a voice saying
unto him,
**Saul, Saul, why persecutest
thou me?**
5. **And he said, Who art
thou, Lord? And the Lord
said, I am Jesus whom
thou persecutest:** *it is* hard for
thee to kick against the pricks.
6. **And he** trembling and astonished
**said, Lord, what wilt thou
have me to do? And the
Lord** *said* unto him, Arise, and
go into the city, and it shall be

told thee what thou must do.

7. And the men which journeyed with him stood speechless, hearing a voice, but seeing no man.

8. **And Saul arose** from the earth; **and when his eyes were opened, he saw no man: but they led him** by the hand, and brought *him* **into Damascus.**

9. **And he was three days without sight, and neither did eat nor drink.**

10. **And there was a certain disciple** at Damascus, **named Ananias; and to him said the Lord in a vision, Ananias.** And he said, Behold, I *am here*, Lord.

11. And the Lord *said* unto him, **Arise, and go into the street** which is called Straight, **and inquire** in the house of Judas **for** *one* **called Saul,** of Tarsus: **for,** behold, **he prayeth,**

12. **And hath seen in a vision a man named Ananias coming** in, and putting *his* hand on him, **that he might receive his sight.**

13. **Then Ananias answered, Lord, I have heard** by many of this man, **how much evil he hath done** to thy saints at Jerusalem:

14. And here he hath authority from the chief priests to bind all that call on thy name.

15. **But the Lord said** unto him, Go thy way: for **he is a chosen vessel** unto me, **to bear my name before the Gentiles, and kings, and** the children of **Israel:**

16. For I will shew him how great things he must suffer for my name's sake.

17. **And Ananias**

went his way, and **entered** into **the house; and** putting his hands on him **said, Brother Saul, the Lord,** *even* **Jesus, that appeared unto thee** in the way as thou camest, **hath sent me, that thou mightest receive thy sight, and be filled with the Holy Ghost.**

18. **And immediately** there fell from his eyes as it had been scales: and **he received sight** forthwith, and arose, **and was baptized.**

19. And when he had received meat, he was strengthened. **Then was Saul certain days with the disciples** which were at Damascus.

20. **And** straightway **he preached Christ in the synagogues,** that he is the Son of God.

21. **But all** that heard *him* **were amazed, and said; Is not this he that destroyed them which called on this name** in Jerusalem, and came hither for that intent, that he might bring them bound unto the chief priests?

22. **But Saul increased** the more **in strength, and confounded the Jews** which dwelt at Damascus, **proving that this is very Christ.**

23. **And** after that many days were fulfilled, **the Jews took counsel to kill him:**

24. But their laying await was known of Saul. And they watched the gates day and night to kill him.

25. **Then the disciples took him by night, and let** *him* **down** by **the wall in a basket.**

26. **And when Saul was come to Jerusalem,** he assayed to join himself to **the disciples:** but they **were all afraid** of him, **and believed not that he was a disciple.**

27. **But Barnabas** took him, and **brought** *him* **to the apostles, and declared** unto them **how he had seen the Lord** in the way, and that he had spoken to him, **and how he had preached** boldly at Damascus **in the name of Jesus.**

28. And he was with them coming in and going out at Jerusalem.

29. **And he spake boldly in the name of** the Lord **Jesus, and disputed** against **the Grecians: but they went** about **to slay him.**

30. *Which* **when the brethren knew, they** brought him down to Caesarea, and **sent him forth to Tarsus.**

31. **Then had the churches rest** throughout all Judaea and Galilee and Samaria, and were edified; and walking in the fear of the Lord, **and** in the comfort of the Holy Ghost, **were multiplied.**

32. **And** it came to pass, as **Peter** passed throughout all *quarters*, he **came** down also **to** the saints which dwelt at **Lydda.**

33. **And there he found** a certain man named **Aeneas, which** had kept his bed eight years, and **was sick of the palsy.**

34. 34. **And Peter said** unto him, Aeneas, **Jesus Christ maketh thee whole: arise,** and make thy bed. **And he arose** immediately.

35. **And all** that dwelt **at Lydda** and Saron saw him, and **turned to the Lord.**

36. **Now there was at Joppa a** certain **disciple named Tabitha,** which by interpretation is called Dorcas: **this woman was full of good works** and almsdeeds which she did.

37. **And** it came to pass in those days, that **she** was sick, and **died:** whom when they had washed, they laid *her* in an upper chamber.

38. **And forasmuch as Lydda was nigh to Joppa, and the disciples had heard that Peter was there, they sent unto him** two men, desiring *him* that he would not delay to come to them.

39. **Then Peter** arose and **went with them.** When he was come, **they brought him into the upper chamber: and all the widows stood** by him **weeping,** and shewing the coats and garments which Dorcas made, while she was with them.

40. **But Peter** put them all forth, and **kneeled** down, **and prayed; and** turning *him* to the body **said, Tabitha, arise. And she opened her eyes:** and when she saw Peter, she sat up.

41. **And he** gave her *his* hand, and **lifted her up,** and when he had called the saints and widows, presented her alive.

42. And it was known throughout all Joppa; **and many believed in the Lord.**

43. **And** it came to pass, that **he tarried many days** in Joppa **with** one **Simon a tanner.**

CHAPTER 10

1. **There was** a certain man **in Caesarea** called **Cornelius, a centurion** of the band called the Italian *band*,

2. **A devout** *man*, **and one that feared God** with all his house, which gave much alms to the people, and prayed to God alway.

3. **He saw in a vision** evidently about the ninth hour of the day **an angel** of God coming in to him, and **saying** unto him, **Cornelius.**

4. And when he looked on him, he was afraid, and said, What is it, Lord? And he said unto him, **Thy prayers** and thine alms **are come up for a memorial before God.**

5. **And now** send men to Joppa, and **call for** *one* **Simon, whose surname is Peter:**

6. He lodgeth with one Simon a tanner, whose house is by the sea side: **he shall tell thee what thou oughtest to do.**

7. **And** when the angel which spake unto Cornelius was departed, **he called two** of his household **servants, and a devout soldier** of them that waited on him continually;

8. **And** when he had declared all *these* things unto them, **he sent them to Joppa.**

9. On the morrow, **as they** went on their journey, and **drew** nigh **unto the city, Peter went up upon the housetop to pray** about the sixth hour:

10. **And** he became very hungry, and would have eaten: but while they made ready, **he fell into a trance,**

11. **And saw heaven opened, and a** certain **vessel descending** unto him, **as** it had been **a great sheet knit at the four corners,** and let down to the earth:

12. **Wherein were all manner of** fourfooted **beasts** of the earth, and wild beasts, **and creeping things, and fowls** of the air.

13. **And there came a voice to him, Rise, Peter; kill, and eat.**

14. **But Peter said, Not so, Lord; for I have never eaten any thing** that is **common or unclean.**

15. **And the voice** *spake* unto him again the second time, **What God hath cleansed,** *that* **call not** thou **common.**

16. This was done thrice: and the vessel was received up again into heaven.

17. **Now while Peter doubted** in himself **what this vision** which he had seen **should mean,** behold, **the men** which were **sent from Cornelius** had made inquiry for Simon's house, and stood before the gate,

18. And called, and **asked whether** Simon, which was surnamed **Peter, were lodged there.**

19. **While Peter thought on the vision, the Spirit said** unto him, Behold, **three men seek thee.**

20. **Arise** therefore, and get thee down, **and go with them,** doubting nothing: **for I have sent them.**

21. **Then Peter** went down to the men which were sent unto him from Cornelius; and **said, Behold, I am he whom ye seek:** what *is* the cause wherefore ye are come?

22. **And they said, Cornelius the centurion,** a just man, and one that feareth God, and of good

report among all the nation of the Jews,

■ **was warned from God** by an holy angel

■ **to send for thee** into his house,

■ **and to hear** words of

■ **thee.**

23. Then called he them in, and lodged *them*. And on the morrow Peter went away with them, and certain brethren from Joppa accompanied him.

■ 24. **And the morrow after**

■ **they entered** into

■ **Caesarea.** And Cornelius waited for them, and he had called together his kinsmen and near friends.

■ 25. **And as Peter was**

■ **coming** in,

■ **Cornelius met him,** and fell down at his feet,

■ **and worshipped** *him.*

■ 26. **But Peter took him up,**

■ **saying, Stand up; I myself**

■ **also am a man.**

■ 27. **And as he talked** with him,

■ **he** went in, and

■ **found many that were**

■ **come together.**

■ 28. **And he said** unto them,

■ **Ye know how that it is** an

■ **unlawful** thing

■ **for** a man that is

■ **a Jew to keep company, or**

■ **come unto one of another**

■ **nation; but God hath**

■ **shewed me that I should**

■ **not call any man common**

■ **or unclean.**

■ 29 **Therefore came I** *unto*

■ *you* without gainsaying, as soon as I was sent for: I ask therefore for what intent ye have sent for me?

■ 30. **And Cornelius said,**

■ **Four days ago I was**

■ **fasting** until this hour; and at the ninth hour I prayed in my house,

■ **and, behold, a man stood**

■ **before me** in bright clothing,

■ 31. **And said, Cornelius, thy**

■ **prayer is heard,** and thine alms are had in remembrance in the sight of God.

■ 32. **Send therefore to**

■ **Joppa, and call** hither Simon, whose surname is

■ **Peter;** he is lodged in the house of *one* Simon a tanner by the sea side:

■ **who,** when he cometh,

■ **shall speak unto thee.**

33. Immediately therefore I sent to thee; and thou hast well done that thou art come.

■ **Now therefore are we all**

■ **here** present before God,

■ **to hear all things that are**

■ **commanded thee of God.**

■ 34. **Then Peter** opened *his* mouth, and

■ **said, Of a truth I perceive**

■ **that God is no respecter**

■ **of persons:**

■ 35. **But in every nation he**

■ **that feareth him, and**

■ **worketh righteousness,**

■ **is accepted** with him.

■ 36. **The word which** *God*

■ **sent unto the children of**

■ **Israel,** preaching peace by Jesus Christ: (he is Lord of all:)

37. That word, *I say*, ye know, which was published throughout all Judaea, and began from Galilee, after the baptism which John preached;

■ 38. **How God anointed**

■ **Jesus** of Nazareth with the Holy Ghost and with power: who went about doing good, and healing all that were oppressed of the devil; for God was with him.

■ 39. **And we are witnesses of**

■ **all things which he did** both in the land of the Jews, and in Jerusalem; whom they slew and hanged on a tree:

■ 40. **Him God raised up the**

■ **third day,** and shewed him openly;

41. Not to all the people, but unto witnesses chosen before God, *even* to us, who did eat and drink with him after he rose from the dead.

■ 42. **And he commanded us**

■ **to preach unto the people,**

■ **and to testify that it is he**

■ **which was ordained of**

■ **God** *to be* **the Judge of**

■ **quick and dead.**

43. To him give all the prophets witness,
that through his name whosoever believeth in him **shall receive remission of sins.**
44. **While Peter yet spake** these words, **the Holy Ghost fell on all** them which heard the word.
45. **And they of the circumcision** which believed **were astonished,** as many as came with Peter,
because that on the Gentiles also was poured out the gift of the Holy Ghost.
46. **For they heard them speak with tongues,** and magnify God.
Then answered Peter,
47. **Can any man forbid water, that these should not be baptized, which have received the Holy Ghost** as well as we?
48. **And he commanded them to be baptized** in the name of the Lord. Then prayed they him to tarry certain days

CHAPTER 11

1. And the apostles and brethren that were in Judaea heard that the Gentiles had also received the word of God.
2. **And when Peter was come up to Jerusalem, they that were of the circumcision contended with him,**
3. **Saying, Thou wentest in to men uncircumcised, and didst eat with them.**
4. **But Peter rehearsed** *the matter* **from the beginning, and expounded** *it* **by order unto them, saying,**
5. I was in the city of Joppa praying: and in a trance I saw a vision, A certain vessel descend, as it had been a great sheet, let down from heaven by four corners; and it came even to me:
6. Upon the which when I had fastened mine eyes, I considered, and saw fourfooted beasts of the earth, and wild beasts, and creeping things, and fowls of the air.
7. And I heard a voice saying unto me, Arise, Peter; slay and eat.
8. But I said, Not so, Lord: for nothing common or unclean hath at any time entered into my mouth.
9. But the voice answered me again from heaven, What God hath cleansed, *that* call not thou common.
10. And this was done three times: and all were drawn up again into heaven.
11. And, behold, immediately there were three men already come unto the house where I was, sent from Caesarea unto me.
12. And the Spirit bade me go with them, nothing doubting. Moreover these six brethren accompanied me, and we entered into the man's house:
13. And he shewed us how he had seen an angel in his house, which stood and said unto him, Send men to Joppa, and call for Simon, whose surname is Peter;
14. Who shall tell thee words, whereby thou and all thy house shall be saved.
15. And as I began to speak, the Holy Ghost fell on them, as on us at the beginning.
16. Then remembered I the word of the Lord, how that he said, John indeed baptized with water; but ye shall be baptized with the Holy Ghost.
17. **Forasmuch then as God gave them the like gift as** *he* **did unto us, who believed on the Lord Jesus Christ; what was I, that I could withstand God?**
18. **When they heard these things, they held their peace,** and glorified God, **saying, Then hath God also to the Gentiles granted repentance unto life.**
19. **Now they which were**

- **scattered abroad** upon the persecution that arose about Stephen travelled as far as Phenice, and Cyprus, and Antioch,
- **preaching the word to none**
- **but unto the Jews** only.
- 20. **And some of them** were men of Cyprus and Cyrene, which, when they were come to Antioch,
- **spake unto the Grecians,**
- **preaching the LORD Jesus.**
- 21. And the hand of the Lord was with them:
- **and a great number**
- **believed,** and turned unto the Lord.
- 22. **Then tidings** of these things
- **came unto** the ears of
- **the church** which was
- **in Jerusalem: and they sent** forth
- **Barnabas,** that he should go as far as Antioch.
- 23. **Who,** when he came, and had seen the grace of God, was glad, and
- **exhorted them all, that with**
- **purpose of heart they**
- **would cleave**
- **unto the Lord.**
- 24. **For he was a good man,**
- **and full of the Holy Ghost**
- **and of faith:** and much people was added unto the Lord.
- 25. **Then departed**
- **Barnabas to Tarsus,** for to seek Saul:
- 26. **And** when he had found him,
- **he brought him unto**
- **Antioch. And** it came to pass, that
- **a whole year they**
- **assembled themselves**
- **with the church, and**
- **taught much people. And**
- **the disciples were called**
- **Christians first in Antioch.**
- 27. **And** in these days
- **came prophets from**
- **Jerusalem** unto Antioch.
- 28. **And there stood up one** of them
- **named Agabus, and**
- **signified** by the Spirit

- **that there should be great**
- **dearth throughout all the**
- **world:** which came to pass in the days of Claudius Caesar.
- 29. **Then the disciples,** every man according to his ability,
- **determined to send relief**
- **unto the brethren** which dwelt
- **in Judaea:**
- 30. Which also they did, and sent it to the elders
- **by the hands of**
- **Barnabas and Saul.**

CHAPTER 12

- 1. **Now about that time**
- **Herod the king stretched**
- **forth** *his* hands
- **to vex certain of the church.**
- 2. **And he killed James** the brother of John with the sword.
- 3. **And because** he saw
- **it pleased the Jews, he**
- **proceeded** further
- **to take Peter** also. (Then were the days of unleavened bread.)
- 4. **And** when he had apprehended him,
- **he put** *him* **in prison,** and delivered *him* to four quaternions of soldiers to keep him; intending after Easter to bring him forth to the people.
- 5. **Peter therefore was kept**
- **in prison: but prayer was**
- **made without ceasing of**
- **the church** unto God
- **for him.**
- 6. **And when Herod would**
- **have brought him forth, the**
- **same night Peter was**
- **sleeping between two**
- **soldiers, bound with two**
- **chains:** and the keepers before the door kept the prison.
- 7. **And, behold, the angel of**
- **the Lord came** upon *him,* and a light shined in the prison:
- **and he smote Peter** on the side,
- **and raised him up, saying,**
- **Arise** up quickly.
- **And his chains fell off** from *his* hands.

■ 8. **And the angel** said unto him, Gird thyself, and bind on thy sandals. And so he did. And he

■ **saith unto him,** Cast thy garment about thee, and

■ **follow me.**

■ 9. **And he went out,** and followed him; and wist not that it was true which was done by the angel;

■ **but thought he**

■ **saw a vision.**

10. When they were past the first and the second ward, they came unto the iron gate that leadeth unto the city; which opened to them of his own accord:

■ **and they went out, and**

■ **passed on through one**

■ **street; and** forthwith

■ **the angel departed** from him.

■ 11. **And when Peter was**

■ **come to himself, he said,**

■ **Now I know** of a surety,

■ **that the LORD hath** sent his angel, and hath

■ **delivered me out of the**

■ **hand of Herod,** and *from* all the expectation of the people of the Jews.

■ 12. **And** when he had considered *the thing*,

■ **he came to the house of**

■ **Mary the mother of** John, whose surname was

■ **Mark;** where many were gathered together praying.

■ 13. **And as Peter knocked** at the door of the gate,

■ **a damsel came** to hearken,

■ **named Rhoda.**

■ 14. **And when she knew**

■ **Peter's voice, she** opened not the gate for gladness, but ran in, and

■ **told how Peter stood**

■ **before the gate.**

■ 15. **And they said unto her,**

■ **Thou art mad.** But she constantly affirmed that it was even so. Then said they, It is his angel.

■ 16. **But Peter continued**

■ **knocking: and when they** had

■ **opened** *the door,*

and saw him,

■ **they were astonished.**

■ 17. **But he,** beckoning unto them with the hand to hold their peace,

■ **declared** unto them

■ **how the Lord had brought**

■ **him out of the prison. And**

■ **he said, Go shew these**

■ **things unto James,** and to the brethren.

■ **And he departed,** and went into another place.

18. Now as soon as it was day, there was no small stir among the soldiers, what was become of Peter.

■ 19. **And when Herod had**

■ **sought for him, and found**

■ **him not, he examined**

■ **the keepers, and**

■ **commanded that** *they* should

■ **be put to death. And he**

■ **went down from Judaea to**

■ **Caesarea,** and *there* abode.

20. And Herod was highly displeased with them of Tyre and Sidon: but they came with one accord to him, and, having made Blastus the king's chamberlain their friend, desired peace; because their country was nourished by the king's *country*.

■ 21. **And** upon a set day

■ **Herod, arrayed in**

■ **royal apparel,** sat upon his throne, and

■ **made an oration**

■ **unto them.**

■ 22. **And the people gave a**

■ **shout,** *saying, It is* **the**

■ **voice of a god,** and not of a man.

■ 23. **And immediately the**

■ **angel of the Lord smote**

■ **him, because he gave not**

■ **God the glory: and he was**

■ **eaten of worms, and gave**

■ **up the ghost.**

24. But the word of God grew and multiplied.

■ 25. **And Barnabas and Saul**

■ **returned from Jerusalem,** when they had fulfilled *their* ministry,

■ **and took with them** John, whose surname was

■ Mark.

CHAPTER 13

■ 1. **Now there were in the**
■ **church** that was
■ **at Antioch certain prophets**
■ **and teachers; as**
■ **Barnabas, and Simeon**
that was called Niger,
■ **and Lucius** of Cyrene,
■ **and Manaen,** which had been
brought up with Herod the tetrarch,
■ **and Saul.**
■ 2. **As they ministered**
to the Lord, and fasted,
■ **the Holy Ghost said,**
■ **Separate me Barnabas**
■ **and Saul for the work**
whereunto
■ **I have called them.**
■ 3. **And when they had fasted**
■ **and prayed,**
and laid *their* hands on them,
■ **they sent** *them* **away.**
■ 4. **So they, being sent** forth
■ **by the Holy Ghost,** departed
unto Seleucia; and from thence they
■ **sailed to Cyprus.**
■ 5. **And** when they were at Salamis,
■ **they preached the word**
of God
■ **in the synagogues of the**
■ **Jews:** and they had also John to
their minister.
■ 6. **And** when they had gone through
the isle unto Paphos,
■ **they found a** certain
■ **sorcerer, a false prophet,**
■ **a Jew, whose name**
■ *was* **Barjesus:**
■ 7. **Which was with the**
■ **deputy of the country,**
■ **Sergius Paulus,**
a prudent man;
■ **who called** for
■ **Barnabas and Saul, and**
■ **desired to hear the word**
of God.
■ 8. **But Elymas** the sorcerer
■ **(for so is his name by**
■ **interpretation) withstood**
■ **them, seeking to turn away**
■ **the deputy from the faith.**

■ 9. **Then Saul,** (who also *is called*
Paul,) filled with the Holy Ghost,
■ **set his eyes on him.**
■ 10. **And said,**
O full of all subtilty and all mischief,
■ *thou* **child of the devil,**
thou enemy of all righteousness, wilt
thou not cease to pervert the right
ways of the Lord?
11. And now, behold, the hand of the
Lord *is* upon thee, and
■ **thou shalt be blind,**
not seeing the sun
■ **for a season. And**
■ **immediately there fell on**
■ **him** a mist and a
■ **darkness;**
and he went about seeking some to
lead him by the hand.
■ 12. **Then the deputy,**
when he saw what was done,
■ **believed,** being astonished at the
doctrine of the Lord.
■ 13. **Now when Paul and his**
■ **company loosed from**
■ **Paphos,** they came to Perga in
Pamphylia: and
■ **John** departing from them
■ **returned to Jerusalem.**
■ 14. **But** when they
departed from Perga,
■ **they came to Antioch in**
■ **Pisidia, and went**
■ **into the synagogue**
on the sabbath day, and sat down.
15. And after the reading of the law
■ **and** the prophets
■ **the rulers of the synagogue**
■ **sent unto them, saying,**
Ye men *and* brethren,
■ **if ye have any word**
of exhortation
■ **for the people, say on.**
■ 16. **Then Paul stood up, and**
beckoning with *his* hand
■ **said,** Men of Israel, and ye that fear
God, give audience.
■ 17. **The God** of this people
■ **of Israel chose our fathers,**
and exalted the people when they
dwelt as strangers in the land of
Egypt, and with an high arm brought
he them out of it.

18. **And about** the time of **forty years suffered he their manners in the wilderness.** 19. **And** when he had destroyed seven nations in the land of Chanaan, **he divided their land to them by lot.** 20. **And after that he gave** *unto* **them judges** about the space of four hundred and fifty years, **until Samuel the prophet.** 21. **And afterward they desired a king: and God gave unto them Saul** the son of Cis, a man of the tribe of Benjamin, by the space of forty years. 22. **And when he had removed him, he raised up** unto them **David to be their king;** to whom also he gave their testimony, and said, I have found David the *son* of Jesse, a man after mine own heart, which shall fulfil all my will. 23. **Of this man's seed hath God** according to *his* promise **raised unto Israel a Saviour, Jesus:** 24. When John had first preached before his coming the baptism of repentance to all the people of Israel. 25. **And as John fulfilled his course, he said, Whom think ye that I am? I am not he. But,** behold, **there cometh one after me,** whose shoes of *his* feet I am not worthy to loose. 26. **Men** *and* **brethren,** children of the stock of Abraham, and whosoever among you feareth God, **to you is the word of this salvation sent.** 27. **For they that dwell at Jerusalem,** and their rulers, **because they knew him not, nor yet the voices of the prophets** which are read every sabbath day, **they have fulfilled** *them* **in condemning** *him.*

28. **And though they found no cause of death** *in him,* **yet desired they Pilate that he should be slain.** 29. **And when they had fulfilled all that was written of him, they** took *him* down from the tree, and **laid** *him* **in a sepulchre.** 30. **But God raised him from the dead:** 31. And he was seen many days of them which came up with him from Galilee to Jerusalem, who are his witnesses unto the people. 32. **And we declare** unto you glad tidings, how **that the promise** which was **made unto the fathers,** 33. **God hath fulfilled** the same unto us their children, **in** that he hath raised up **Jesus** again; as it is also written in the second psalm, Thou art my Son, this day have I begotten thee. 34. **And as concerning that he raised him up** from the dead, **now no more to return to corruption,** he said on this wise, I will give you the sure mercies of David. 35. **Wherefore he saith** also **in another** *psalm,* **Thou shalt not suffer thine Holy One to see corruption.** 36. **For David,** after he had served his own generation by the will of God, fell on sleep, and was laid unto his fathers, and **saw corruption:** 37. **But he, whom God raised again, saw no corruption.** 38. **Be it known** unto you therefore, men *and* brethren, **that through this man is preached unto you the forgiveness of sins:** 39. And by him all that believe are justified from all things, from which ye could not be justified by the law of Moses. 40. **Beware** therefore,

lest that come upon you, which is spoken of in the prophets; 41. **Behold, ye despisers,** and wonder, and perish: **for I work a work in your days,** a work **which ye shall in no wise believe,** though a man declare it unto you. 42. **And** when the Jews were gone out of the synagogue, **the Gentiles besought that these words might be preached to them** the next sabbath. 43. **Now** when the congregation was broken up, **many of the Jews** and religious proselytes **followed Paul and Barnabas:** who, speaking to them, persuaded them to continue in the grace of God. 44. **And the next sabbath day came almost the whole city together to hear the word of God.** 45. **But when the Jews saw** the multitudes, **they were filled with envy, and spake against** those things which were spoken by **Paul,** contradicting and blaspheming. 46. **Then Paul and Barnabas waxed bold, and said, It was necessary that the word** of God **should first have been spoken to you: but seeing ye put it from you,** and judge yourselves unworthy of everlasting life, lo, **we turn to the Gentiles.** 47. **For so hath the Lord commanded us,** *saying,* **I have set thee to be a light of the Gentiles,** that thou shouldest be for salvation unto the ends of the earth. 48. **And when the Gentiles heard** this,

they were glad, and glorified the word of the Lord: **and as many as were ordained to eternal life believed.** 49. And the word of the Lord was published throughout all the region. 50. **But the Jews stirred up** the devout and honourable women, and the chief men of the city, and raised **persecution against Paul and Barnabas, and expelled them** out of their coasts. 51. But they shook off the dust of their feet against them, and came unto Iconium. 52. And the disciples were filled with joy, and with the Holy Ghost.

CHAPTER 14

1. And it came to pass **in Iconium, that they went** both together **into the synagogue** of the Jews, **and so spake, that a great multitude both of** the **Jews and** also of the **Greeks believed.** 2. **But the unbelieving Jews stirred up the Gentiles,** and made their minds evil affected against the brethren. 3. **Long time therefore abode they speaking boldly in the Lord,** which gave testimony unto the word of his grace, and granted signs and wonders to be done by their hands. 4. **But the** multitude of the **city was divided:** and part held with the Jews, and part with the apostles. 5. **And when there was an assault made both of the Gentiles, and** also of the **Jews** with their rulers, to use *them* despitefully, and **to stone them,** 6. **They were ware of** *it,* **and fled unto Lystra** and Derbe,

cities of Lycaonia, and unto the region that lieth round about:

7. And there they preached the gospel.

8. **And there sat a certain man at Lystra,** impotent in his feet, **being a cripple from his mother's womb,** who never had walked:

9. **The same heard Paul speak: who** stedfastly beholding him, and **perceiving that he had faith** to be healed,

10. **Said with a loud voice, Stand upright on thy feet. And he leaped and walked.**

11. **And when the people saw what Paul had done, they lifted** up their **voices, saying** in the speech of Lycaonia, **The gods are come down to us in the likeness of men.**

12. **And they called Barnabas, Jupiter; and Paul, Mercurius,** because he was the chief speaker.

13. Then the priest of Jupiter, which was before their city, brought oxen and garlands unto the gates, and would have done sacrifice with the people.

14. **Which when the apostles, Barnabas and Paul, heard of, they rent their clothes, and ran in among the people, crying out,**

15. And saying, **Sirs,** why do ye these things? **We also are men** of like passions with you, **and preach** unto you **that ye should turn** from these vanities **unto the living God,** which made heaven, and earth, and the sea, and all things that are therein:

16. **Who in times past suffered all nations to walk in their own ways.**

17. **Nevertheless he left not himself without witness,** in that he did good, **and gave us rain** from heaven, **and fruitful seasons,** filling our hearts with food and gladness.

18. And with these sayings scarce restrained they the people, that they had not done sacrifice unto them.

19. **And there came** thither **certain Jews from Antioch and Iconium,** who persuaded the people, **and having stoned Paul, drew** *him* **out of the city, supposing he had been dead.**

20. **Howbeit,** as the disciples stood round about him, **he rose up, and came into the city: and the next day he departed with Barnabas to Derbe.**

21. **And when they** had **preached the gospel** to that city, **and** had taught many, **they returned again to Lystra, and** *to* **Iconium, and Antioch,**

22. **Confirming** the souls of the disciples, **and exhorting them to continue in the faith, and that we must through much tribulation enter into the kingdom** of God.

23. **And when they had ordained them elders** in every church, and had prayed with fasting, **they commended them to the Lord,** on whom they believed.

24. And after they had passed throughout Pisidia, they came to Pamphylia.

25. And when they had preached the word in Perga, they went down into Attalia:

26. And thence sailed to Antioch, from whence they had been recommended to the grace of God for the work which

they fulfilled.

27. And when they were come, and had gathered the church together, they rehearsed all that God had done with them, and how he had opened the door of faith unto the Gentiles.

28. And there they abode long time with the disciples.

CHAPTER 15

1. **And certain men** which came down **from Judaea taught the brethren,** *and said*, **Except ye be circumcised** after the manner of Moses, **ye cannot be saved.**

2. **When therefore Paul and Barnabas had** no small dissension and **disputation with them, they determined that Paul and Barnabas,** and certain other of them, **should go** up to Jerusalem **unto the apostles** and elders **about this question.**

3. And being brought on their way by the church, they passed through Phenice and Samaria, declaring the conversion of the Gentiles: and they caused great joy unto all the brethren.

4. **And when they were come to Jerusalem, they were received of the church,** and *of* the apostles and elders, **and they declared all things that God had done** with them.

5. But there rose up certain of the sect of the **Pharisees which believed, saying, That it was needful to circumcise them,** and to command *them* to keep the law of Moses.

6. And the apostles and elders came together for to consider of this matter.

7. **And** when there had been much disputing, **Peter rose up, and said** unto them, Men *and* brethren, **ye know how**

that a good while ago **God made choice** among us, **that the Gentiles by my mouth should hear the word** of the gospel, **and believe.**

8. **And God,** which knoweth the hearts, **bare them witness, giving them the Holy Ghost,** even as *he did* unto us;

9. **And put no difference between us and them,** purifying their hearts by faith.

10. **Now therefore why tempt ye God, to put a yoke upon the neck of the disciples,** which neither our fathers nor we were able to bear?

11. But we believe that through the grace of the LORD Jesus Christ we shall be saved, even as they.

12. **Then all the multitude** kept silence, and **gave audience to Barnabas and Paul,** declaring what miracles and wonders God had wrought among the Gentiles by them.

13. **And after** they had held their peace, **James answered,** saying, Men *and* brethren, hearken unto me:

14. **Simeon hath declared how God** at the first **did visit the Gentiles, to take out of them a people for his name.**

15. **And to this agree the words of the prophets;** as it is written,

16. **After this I** will return, and **will build again the tabernacle of David,** which is fallen down; and I will build again the ruins thereof, and I will set it up:

17. **That the residue of men might seek after the Lord, and all the Gentiles, upon whom my name is called,** saith the Lord, who doeth all these things.

18. Known unto God are all his works

from the beginning of the world.

19. **Wherefore my sentence is, that we trouble not them, which from among the Gentiles are turned to God:**

20. **But that we write** unto them, **that they abstain from pollutions** of idols, **and *from* fornication,** and *from* things strangled, **and *from* blood.**

21. For Moses of old time hath in every city them that preach him, being read in the synagogues every sabbath day.

22. **Then pleased it the apostles** and elders with the whole church, **to send chosen men of their own company to Antioch with Paul and Barnabas;** *namely*, Judas surnamed Barsabas and Silas, chief men among the brethren:

23. **And they wrote *letters* by them after this manner;** The apostles and elders and brethren *send* greeting unto the brethren which are of the Gentiles in Antioch and Syria and Cilicia.

24. **Forasmuch as we have heard, that certain which went out from us have troubled you** with words, subverting your souls, **saying, *Ye must* be circumcised,** and keep the law: **to whom we gave no *such* commandment:**

25. **It seemed good unto us,** being assembled with one accord, **to send chosen men** unto you **with our beloved Barnabas and Paul,**

26. Men that have hazarded their lives for the name of our Lord Jesus Christ.

27. **We have sent therefore Judas and Silas,** who shall also tell *you* the same things by mouth.

28. **For it seemed good to the Holy Ghost,** and to us, **to lay upon you no greater burden than these necessary things;**

29. **That ye abstain from meats offered to idols,** and **from blood,** and **from things strangled, and** from **fornication:** from which if ye keep yourselves, ye shall do well. Fare ye well.

30. **So when they were dismissed, they came to Antioch: and** when they had gathered the multitude together, they **delivered the epistle:**

31. ***Which* when they had read, they rejoiced** for the consolation.

32. And Judas and Silas, being prophets also themselves, exhorted the brethren with many words, and confirmed *them*.

33. **And after** they had tarried *there* **a space, they were let go** in peace from the brethren unto the apostles.

34. **Notwithstanding it pleased Silas to abide there still.**

35. **Paul also and Barnabas continued in Antioch,** teaching and preaching the word of the Lord, with many others also.

36. **And** some days after **Paul said unto Barnabas, Let us** go again and **visit** our brethren in **every city where we have preached the word** of the LORD, **and see how they do.**

37. **And Barnabas determined to take** with them John, whose surname was **Mark.**

38. **But Paul thought not good to take him** with them, **who departed from them from Pamphylia,** and went not with them to the work.

39. **And the contention was so sharp** between them, **that they departed** asunder **one from the other: and so**

Barnabas took Mark, and sailed unto Cyprus; 40. **And Paul chose Silas, and departed,** being recommended by the brethren unto the grace of God. 41. **And he went through Syria and Cilicia,** confirming the churches.

CHAPTER 16

1. **Then came he to Derbe** and Lystra: **and,** behold, **a certain disciple was there, named Timotheus,** the son of a certain woman, which was a Jewess, and believed; but his father *was* a Greek: 2. **Which was well reported of by the brethren** that were at Lystra and Iconium. 3. **Him would Paul have to go forth with him; and took and circumcised him because of the Jews** which were **in those quarters:** for they knew all that his father was a Greek. 4. **And** as they went through the cities, **they delivered** them **the decrees** for to keep, **that were ordained of the apostles** and elders which were at Jerusalem. 5. **And so were the churches established in the faith,** and increased in number daily. 6. Now when they had gone throughout Phrygia and the region of Galatia, and were forbidden of the Holy Ghost to preach the word in Asia, 7. After they were come to Mysia, they assayed to go into Bithynia: but the Spirit suffered them not. 8. **And they** passing by Mysia **came down to Troas.** 9. **And a vision appeared to Paul** in the night; **There stood a man of**

Macedonia, and prayed him, **saying, Come over into Macedonia, and help us.** 10. **And** after he had seen the vision, **immediately we endeavoured to go** into Macedonia, assuredly gathering that the Lord had called us for to preach the gospel unto them. 11. **Therefore loosing from Troas, we came** with a straight course to Samothracia, and the next day to Neapolis; 12. And from thence **to Philippi, which is** the chief city of that **part of Macedonia,** *and* a colony: and we were in that city abiding certain days. 13. **And on the sabbath we went out of the city** by a river side, where prayer was wont to be made; and we sat down, and spake unto the women which resorted *thither.* 14. **And a certain woman named Lydia,** a seller of purple, of the city of Thyatira, **which worshipped God, heard us:** whose heart the Lord opened, that she attended unto the things which were spoken of Paul. 15. **And when she was baptized,** and her household, **she besought** *us,* **saying,** If ye have judged me to be faithful to the Lord, **come into my house, and abide** *there.* And she constrained us. 16. **And** it came to pass, as we went to prayer, **a certain damsel possessed with a spirit of divination met us, which brought her masters much gain by soothsaying:** 17. **The same followed Paul** and us, **and cried,** saying, **These men are the servants of** the most high

God, which shew unto us the way of salvation. 18. **And this did she many days. But Paul,** being grieved, **turned and said to the spirit, I command thee in the name of Jesus** Christ **to come out** of her. **And he came out** the same hour. 19. **And when her masters saw that the hope of their gains was gone, they caught Paul and Silas,** and drew *them* into the marketplace unto the rulers, 20. **And brought them to the magistrates,** saying, These men, being Jews, do exceedingly trouble our city, 21. And teach customs, which are not lawful for us to receive, neither to observe, being Romans. 22. **And the multitude rose** up together **against them: and the magistrates** rent off their clothes, and **commanded to beat** *them.* 23. **And** when they had laid many stripes upon them, **they cast** *them* **into prison, charging the jailor to keep them safely:** 24. Who, having received such a charge, thrust them into the inner prison, and made their feet fast in the stocks. 25. **And at midnight Paul and Silas prayed, and sang praises unto God:** and the prisoners heard them. 26. **And suddenly there was a great earthquake,** so that the foundations of the prison were shaken: **and immediately all the doors were opened,** and every one's bands were loosed. 27. **And the keeper** of the prison awaking out of his sleep, and **seeing the** prison **doors open,** he

drew out **his sword, and would have killed himself, supposing** that **the prisoners had** been **fled.** 28. **But Paul cried** with a loud voice, saying, **Do thyself no harm: for we are all here.** 29. **Then he** called for a light, and sprang in, and came trembling, and **fell down before Paul and Silas,** 30. **And** brought them out, and **said, Sirs, what must I do to be saved?** 31. **And they said, Believe on the Lord Jesus Christ, and thou shalt be saved, and thy house.** 32. And they spake unto him the word of the Lord, and to all that were in his house. 33. **And he took them** the same hour of the night, **and washed** *their* **stripes; and was baptized,** he and all his, straightway. 34. **And when he had brought them into his house, he** set meat before them, and **rejoiced, believing in God** with all his house. 35. **And** when it was day, **the magistrates sent** the **sergeants, saying, Let those men go.** 36. **And the keeper** of the prison **told** this saying to **Paul,** The magistrates have sent **to** let you go: now therefore **depart, and go in peace.** 37. **But Paul said** unto them, **They have beaten us openly** uncondemned, **being Romans, and** have **cast** *us* **into prison; and now** do **they thrust us out privily? nay** verily;

but let them come
themselves and fetch us out.
38. And the sergeants told
these words unto
the magistrates: and they
feared, when they heard that
they were Romans.
39. And they came
and besought them,
and brought *them* out, and
desired *them* to depart
out of the city.
40. And they
went out of the prison, and
entered into *the house* of
Lydia: and
when they had seen the brethren,
they comforted them,
and departed.

CHAPTER 17
1. Now when they had passed
through Amphipolis and Apollonia,
they came to
Thessalonica, where was a
synagogue of the Jews:
2. And Paul, as his manner was,
went in unto them,
and three sabbath days
reasoned with them out of
the scriptures,
3. Opening and
alleging, that Christ must
needs
have suffered, and risen
again from the dead;
and that this
Jesus, whom I preach unto you,
is Christ.
4. And some of them
believed, and consorted with
Paul and Silas;
and of the devout Greeks a
great multitude, and of the
chief women not a few.
5. But the Jews which
believed not, moved with envy,
took unto them certain lewd fellows of
the baser sort, and gathered a
company, and
set all the city on an
uproar, and assaulted the
house of Jason, and sought to

bring them out to the people.
6. And when they found them not,
they drew Jason
and certain brethren
unto the rulers of the city,
crying, These that have turned
the world upside down are come
hither also;
7. Whom Jason hath
received: and these all
do contrary to the decrees
of Caesar, saying that
there is another king,
one Jesus.
8. And they troubled the people and
the rulers of the city, when they
heard these things.
9. And when they had taken security
of Jason, and of the other,
they let them go.
10. And the brethren
immediately sent away
Paul and Silas
by night unto Berea:
who coming *thither*
went into the synagogue
of the Jews.
11. These were more noble than those
in Thessalonica, in that they
received the word with all readiness
of mind, and searched the scriptures
daily, whether those things were so.
12. Therefore many of them
believed; also of honourable
women which were Greeks,
and of men, not a few.
13. But when the Jews of
Thessalonica had
knowledge that the word of
God was preached of Paul
at Berea,
they came thither
also, and stirred up the people.
14. And then immediately
the brethren sent away
Paul to go as it were to the sea:
but Silas and Timotheus
abode there still.
15. And they that conducted Paul
brought him unto
Athens: and
receiving a commandment
unto Silas and Timotheus

■ **for to come to him**
with all speed, they departed.

■ 16. **Now while Paul waited**
for them at Athens, his spirit was
stirred in him, when

■ **he saw the city wholly**
■ **given to idolatry.**

■ 17. **Therefore disputed he**
in the synagogue

■ **with the Jews, and with** the
■ **devout persons, and in the**
■ **market** daily with them
that met with him.

■ 18. **Then certain**
■ **philosophers of the**
■ **Epicureans, and** of the
■ **Stoics, encountered him.**
■ **And** some
■ **said, What will this babbler**
■ **say?** other some, He seemeth to be
a setter forth of strange gods:
because he preached unto them
Jesus, and the resurrection.

■ 19. **And they took him,**
and brought him

■ **unto Areopagus, saying,**
■ **May we know what this new**
■ **doctrine,** whereof thou speakest,
■ **is?**
20. For thou bringest certain strange
things to our ears: we would know
therefore what these things mean.

■ 21. **(For all the Athenians**
and strangers which were there

■ **spent their time in nothing**
else,

■ **but either to tell, or to hear**
■ **some new thing.)**

■ 22. **Then Paul stood in the**
■ **midst of Mars' hill, and**
■ **said,** Ye men of Athens, I perceive
that in all things

■ **ye are too superstitious.**

■ 23. **For** as I passed by, and beheld
your devotions,

■ **I found an altar with this**
■ **inscription, TO THE**
■ **UNKNOWN GOD.** Whom
therefore ye ignorantly worship,

■ **him declare I unto you.**

■ 24. **God that made the world**
■ **and all things therein,**
seeing that

■ **he** is Lord of heaven and earth,
■ **dwelleth not in temples**
made with hands;

■ 25. **Neither is worshipped**
■ **with** men's

■ **hands, as though he**
■ **needed any thing, seeing**
■ **he giveth to all life,**
and breath, and all things;

■ 26. **And hath made**
of one blood all nations of

■ **men** for to dwell on all the face of the
earth, and hath determined the times
before appointed, and the bounds of
their habitation;

■ 27. **That they should seek**
■ **the Lord,** if haply they might feel
after him, and find him,

■ **though he be not far from**
■ **every one of us:**

■ 28. **For in him we live, and**
■ **move, and have our being;**
as certain also of your own poets
have said, For we are also
his offspring.
29. Forasmuch then as we are the
offspring of God,

■ **we ought not to think that**
■ **the Godhead is like** unto
■ **gold, or silver, or stone,**
graven by art and man's device.

■ 30. **And the times of this**
■ **ignorance God winked at;**
■ **but now commandeth**
■ **all men** everywhere
■ **to repent:**

31. **Because** he hath appointed a
day, in the which

■ **he will judge the world in**
■ **righteousness by** *that* **man**
■ **whom he hath ordained;**
whereof he hath given assurance unto
all *men,*

■ **in that he hath raised him**
■ **from the dead.**

■ 32. **And when they heard of**
■ **the resurrection** of the dead,
■ **some mocked: and others**
■ **said, We will hear thee**
■ **again** of this *matter.*

■ 33. **So Paul departed from**
■ **among them.**

34. Howbeit certain men clave unto

him, and believed: among the which *was* Dionysius the Areopagite, and a woman named Damaris, and others with them

CHAPTER 18

1. **After these things Paul** departed from Athens, and **came to Corinth;** 2. **And found a** certain **Jew named Aquila,** born in Pontus, lately come from Italy, **with his wife Priscilla;** (because that Claudius had commanded all Jews to depart from Rome:) and came unto them. 3. **And** because he was of the same craft, **he abode with them,** and wrought: **for by their occupation they were tentmakers.** 4. **And he reasoned in the synagogue** every sabbath, **and persuaded the Jews and the Greeks.** 5. **And when Silas and Timotheus were come** from Macedonia, **Paul** was pressed in the spirit, and **testified to the Jews** *that* **Jesus** *was* **Christ.** 6. **And when they opposed** themselves, **and blasphemed, he shook** *his* **raiment, and said** unto them, **Your blood** *be* **upon your own heads; I** *am* **clean; from henceforth I will go unto the Gentiles.** 7. **And he departed** thence, **and entered into a** certain **man's house, named Justus,** *one* that worshipped God, whose house joined hard to the synagogue. 8. **And Crispus, the chief ruler of the synagogue, believed on the Lord** with all his house; **and many of the Corinthians** hearing

believed, and were baptized. 9. **Then spake the Lord to Paul** in the night **by a vision, Be not afraid, but speak,** and hold not thy peace: 10. **For I am with thee, and no man shall** set on thee to **hurt thee:** for I have much people in this city. 11. **And he continued** *there* **a year and six months, teaching the word** of God among them. 12. **And when Gallio was the deputy** of Achaia, **the Jews made insurrection** with one accord **against Paul, and brought him to the judgment seat,** 13. Saying, This *fellow* **persuadeth men to worship God contrary to the law.** 14. **And** when Paul was now about to open *his* mouth, **Gallio said** unto the Jews, **If it were a matter of wrong** or wicked lewdness, O *ye* Jews, reason would that **I should bear with you:** 15. **But if it be** a question of words and names, and *of* **your law,** look ye *to it*; for **I will be no judge** of such *matters*. 16. **And he drave them from the judgment seat.** 17. **Then all the Greeks took** Sosthenes, **the chief ruler of the synagogue, and beat** *him* before the judgment seat. And Gallio cared for none of those things. 18. **And Paul** *after this* tarried *there* yet a good while, and then took his leave of the brethren, and **sailed thence into Syria,** and with him Priscilla and Aquila; having shorn *his* head in Cenchrea: for he had a vow 19. **And he came to**

■ **Ephesus, and** left them there: but he himself
■ **entered into the**
■ **synagogue,** and reasoned with the Jews.
■ 20. **When they desired** *him*
■ **to tarry** longer time with them,
■ **he consented not;**
21. But bade them farewell, saying, I must by all means keep this feast that cometh in Jerusalem: but I will return again unto you, if God will.
■ **And he sailed from**
■ **Ephesus.**
■ 22. **And** when he had
■ **landed at Caesarea,** and gone up,
■ **and** saluted the church, he
■ **went** down
■ **to Antioch.**
■ 23. **And after** he had spent some
■ **time** *there,* **he departed,**
■ **and went over** *all* **the**
■ **country of Galatia and**
■ **Phrygia** in order,
■ **strengthening** all
■ **the disciples.**
■ 24. **And a** certain
■ **Jew named Apollos,** born at Alexandria,
■ **an eloquent man,** *and*
■ **mighty in** the
■ **scriptures, came**
■ **to Ephesus.**
25. **This man** was instructed in the way of the Lord; and
■ **being fervent in the spirit,** he spake and
■ **taught diligently the things**
■ **of the Lord, knowing only**
■ **the baptism of John.**
26. And he began to speak boldly in the synagogue: whom
■ **when Aquila and Priscilla** had
■ **heard, they** took him unto *them,* and
■ **expounded unto him the**
■ **way of God more perfectly.**
■ 27. **And** when he was disposed to pass into Achaia,
■ **the brethren wrote,** exhorting
■ **the disciples to receive**

■ **him: who, when he was**
■ **come, helped them** much
■ **which had believed**
■ **through grace:**
■ 28. **For he mightily**
■ **convinced the Jews,** *and that* publicly,
■ **shewing by the scriptures**
■ **that Jesus was Christ.**

CHAPTER 19
1. And it came to pass, that, while Apollos was at Corinth,
■ **Paul** having passed through the upper coasts
■ **came to Ephesus: and**
■ **finding** certain
■ **disciples,**
■ 2. **He said** unto them,
■ **Have ye received the Holy**
■ **Ghost since ye believed?**
■ **And they said** unto him,
■ **We have not** so much as
■ **heard whether there be**
■ **any Holy Ghost.**
3. And he said unto them, Unto what then were ye baptized? And they said, Unto John's baptism.
■ 4. **Then said Paul, John** verily
■ **baptized** with the baptism
■ **of repentance, saying** unto the people,
■ **that they should believe** on him which should come after him, that is,
■ **on Christ Jesus.**
■ 5. **When they heard** *this,*
■ **they were baptized in the**
■ **name of the Lord Jesus.**
■ 6. **And when Paul** had
■ **laid** *his* **hands upon them,**
■ **the Holy Ghost came** on them;
■ **and they spake with**
■ **tongues, and prophesied.**
7. And all the men were about twelve.
■ 8. **And he** went into the synagogue, and
■ **spake boldly for** the space of
■ **three months, disputing**
■ **and persuading** the things
■ **concerning the kingdom** of God.
■ 9. **But when divers were**

■ **hardened,** and believed not, but spake evil of that way before the multitude,

■ **he departed** from them, and separated the disciples,

■ **disputing daily** in the school of one Tyrannus.

■ 10. **And this continued** by the space of

■ **two years; so that all** they which dwelt

■ **in Asia heard the word** of the Lord Jesus, both Jews and Greeks.

■ 11. **And God wrought** special

■ **miracles by** the hands of

■ **Paul:**

■ 12. **So that from his body**

■ **were brought unto the sick**

■ **handkerchiefs** or aprons,

■ **and the diseases departed** from them,

■ **and the evil spirits went**

■ **out** of them.

■ 13. **Then** certain of the

■ **vagabond Jews,** exorcists,

■ **took upon them to call**

■ **over them which had evil**

■ **spirits the name of** the LORD

■ **Jesus, saying, We adjure**

■ **you by Jesus whom**

■ **Paul preacheth.**

■ 14. And there were seven sons of *one* Sceva, a Jew, *and* chief of the priests, which did so.

■ 15. **And the evil spirit**

■ **answered** and said,

■ **Jesus I know, and Paul I**

■ **know; but who are ye?**

■ 16. **And the man in whom the**

■ **evil spirit was leaped on**

■ **them,** and overcame them,

■ **and prevailed against**

■ **them, so that they fled out**

■ **of that house naked**

■ **and wounded.**

■ 17. **And this was known to**

■ **all** the

■ **Jews and Greeks** also dwelling

■ **at Ephesus;**

and fear fell on them all,

■ **and the name of the Lord**

■ **Jesus was magnified.**

■ 18. **And many that believed**

■ **came, and confessed,** and shewed their deeds.

■ 19. **Many** of them also

■ **which used curious arts**

■ **brought their books** together,

■ **and burned them** before all *men*: and they counted the price of them, and found *it* fifty thousand *pieces* of silver.

■ 20. **So mightily grew the**

■ **word** of God and prevailed.

■ 21. **After these things were**

■ **ended, Paul** purposed in the spirit, when he had passed through Macedonia and Achaia, to go to Jerusalem, saying, After I have been there, I must also see Rome.

22. So he sent into Macedonia two of them that ministered unto him, Timotheus and Erastus; but he himself

■ **stayed in Asia for**

■ **a season.**

23. And the same time there arose no small stir about that way.

24. For a certain *man* named Demetrius,

■ **a silversmith, which made**

■ **silver shrines for Diana,**

■ **brought** no small

■ **gain unto the craftsmen;**

■ 25. **Whom he called together** with the workmen of like occupation,

■ **and said, Sirs,** ye know that

■ **by this craft we have**

■ **our wealth.**

■ 26. **Moreover** ye see and hear, that not alone at Ephesus, but almost throughout all Asia, this

■ **Paul hath persuaded** and turned away

■ **much people, saying that**

■ **they be no gods,** which are

■ **made with hands:**

■ 27. **So that not only this our**

■ **craft is in danger** to be set at nought;

■ **but also** that

■ **the temple of** the great goddess

■ **Diana should be** despised, and her magnificence should be

■ **destroyed,** whom all Asia and the world worshippeth.

28. **And** when they heard *these sayings,* **they were full of wrath, and cried out,** saying, **Great** *is* **Diana** of the Ephesians.
29. And the whole city was filled with confusion: **and having caught Gaius and Aristarchus,** men of Macedonia, **Paul's companions** in travel, **they rushed** with one accord **into the theatre.**
30. **And when Paul would have entered** in unto the people, **the disciples suffered him not.**
31. **And certain of the chief of Asia,** which were his friends, **sent unto him, desiring** *him* **that he would not adventure** himself **into the theatre.**
32. Some therefore cried one thing, and some another: for the assembly was confused: and the more part knew not wherefore they were come together.
33. **And they drew Alexander out of the multitude,** the Jews putting him forward. **And Alexander** beckoned with the hand, and **would have made his defence** unto the people.
34. **But when they knew** that **he was a Jew, all with one voice about** the space of **two hours cried out, Great** *is* **Diana** of the Ephesians.
35. **And** when **the townclerk** had appeased the people, he **said,** Ye **men of Ephesus, what man** is there that **knoweth not** how **that the city** of the Ephesians **is a worshipper of** the great goddess **Diana,** and of the *image* which fell down from Jupiter?
36. **Seeing** then **that** these things **cannot be spoken against, ye ought to be quiet,** and to do nothing rashly.
37. **For** ye have brought hither **these men,** which **are neither robbers of churches, nor yet blasphemers** of your goddess.
38. **Wherefore if** Demetrius, and **the craftsmen** which are with him, **have a matter against any** man, **the law is open,** and there are deputies: **let them implead one another.**
39. But if ye inquire any thing concerning other matters, it shall be determined in a lawful assembly.
40. **For we are in danger to be called in question for this day's uproar,** there being no cause whereby we may give an account of this concourse.
41. **And** when he had thus spoken, **he dismissed the assembly.**

CHAPTER 20

1. **And after the uproar** was ceased, **Paul called** unto *him* **the disciples, and embraced** *them,* **and departed** for to go into Macedonia.
2. **And** when he had gone over those parts, and had given them much exhortation, **he came into Greece,**
3. **And** *there* **abode three months. And when the Jews laid wait for him,** as he was about to sail into Syria, **he purposed to return through Macedonia.**
4. And there accompanied him into Asia Sopater of Berea; and of the Thessalonians, Aristarchus and Secundus; and Gaius of Derbe, and

Timotheus; and of Asia, Tychicus and Trophimus.

5. These going before tarried for us at Troas.

6. **And we sailed away from Philippi** after the days of unleavened bread, **and came** unto them **to Troas** in five days; **where we abode seven days.**

7. **And upon the first** *day* **of the week,** when the disciples came together to break bread, **Paul preached unto them,** ready to depart on the morrow; **and continued his speech until midnight.**

8. And there were many lights in the upper chamber, where they were gathered together.

9. **And there sat in a window** **a** certain **young man named Eutychus, being fallen into a deep sleep:** and **as Paul was long preaching, he sunk down** with sleep, **and fell** down **from the third loft, and was taken up dead.**

10. **And Paul** went down, and fell on him, and **embracing** *him* **said, Trouble not yourselves; for his life is in him.**

11. When he therefore was come up again, and had broken bread, and eaten, and talked a long while, even till break of day, so he departed.

12. **And they brought the young man alive,** and were not a little comforted.

13. **And we went** before to ship, and sailed **unto Assos, there intending to take** in **Paul: for so had he appointed,** minding himself to go afoot.

14. **And** when he met with us at Assos,

we took him in, and came to Mitylene.

15. **And we sailed** thence, **and** came the next *day* over against Chios; and the next *day* we arrived at Samos, and tarried at Trogyllium; and the next *day* we came to Miletus.

16. **For Paul had determined** to sail by Ephesus, because he would not spend the time in Asia: for he hasted, if it were possible for him, **to be at Jerusalem the day of Pentecost.**

17. **And from Miletus he sent to Ephesus, and called the elders** of the church.

18. **And when they were come** to him, **he said** unto them, **Ye know,** from the first day that I came into Asia, after what manner **I have been with you at all seasons,**

19. **Serving the LORD** with all humility of mind, and **with many tears, and temptations,** which befell me **by** the lying in wait of **the Jews:**

20. *And* **how I** kept back nothing that was profitable *unto you*, but have shewed you, and **have taught** you publicly, and from house to house,

21. **Testifying both to the Jews, and** also to the **Greeks, repentance** toward God, **and faith toward our Lord Jesus Christ.**

22. **And now, behold, I go bound in the spirit unto Jerusalem, not knowing the things that shall befall me** there:

23. Save that the Holy Ghost witnesseth in every city, saying that bonds and afflictions abide me.

24. **But none of these things move me, neither count I my life dear** unto myself, **so that I might finish my course with joy,**

and the ministry, which I have received of the Lord Jesus, to testify the gospel of the grace of God.

25. **And now,** behold, **I know that ye** all, among whom I have gone preaching the kingdom of God, **shall see my face no more.**

26. **Wherefore I take you to record** this day, **that I** *am* **pure from the blood of all** *men.*

27. **For I have not shunned to declare** unto you **all the counsel of God.**

28. **Take heed therefore** unto yourselves, and to all the flock, over the which the Holy Ghost hath made you overseers, **to feed the church of God,** which he hath **purchased with his own blood.**

29. **For I know** this, that **after my departing shall** grievous **wolves enter in among you,** not sparing the flock.

30. **Also of your own selves shall men arise, speaking perverse things,** to draw away disciples after them.

31. **Therefore** watch, and **remember, that** by the space of three years **I ceased not to warn every one** night and day **with tears.**

32. **And now, brethren, I commend you to God, and to the word** of his grace, **which is able to build you** up, and to give you an inheritance among all them which are sanctified.

33. **I have coveted no man's** silver, or **gold,** or apparel.

34. Yea, ye yourselves know, that these hands have ministered unto my necessities, and to them that were with me.

35. I have shewed you all things, how that so labouring **ye ought to support the weak, and to remember** the words of the Lord **Jesus, how he said, It is more blessed to give** than to receive.

36. **And** when he had thus spoken, **he kneeled** down, **and prayed with them** all.

37. **And they all wept** sore, **and fell on Paul's neck, and kissed him,**

38. Sorrowing most of all for the words which he spake, that they should see his face no more. And they accompanied him unto the ship.

CHAPTER 21

1. **And** it came to pass, that **after we were gotten from them,** and had launched, we came with a straight course unto Coos, and the *day* following unto Rhodes, and from thence unto Patara:

2. And finding a ship sailing over unto Phenicia, **we went aboard,** and set forth.

3. Now when we had discovered Cyprus, we left it on the left hand, **and sailed into Syria, and landed at Tyre:** for there the ship was to unlade her burden.

4. **And finding disciples, we tarried there seven days: who said to Paul through the Spirit, that he should not go up to Jerusalem.**

5. And when we had accomplished those days, we departed and went our way; and they all brought us on our way, with wives and children, till *we were* out of the city: and we kneeled down on the shore, and prayed.

6. And when we had taken our leave one of another, we took ship; and they returned home again.

7. **And** when we had finished *our* course from Tyre, **we came to Ptolemais, and saluted the brethren,** and abode with them one day.

8. **And the next** *day* **we** that were of Paul's company

departed, and came
unto Caesarea: and we
entered into the house of
Philip the evangelist, which
was *one* of the seven; and
abode with him.
9. And the same man had four
daughters, virgins, which
did prophesy.
10. **And** as we tarried
there many days,
there came down from Judaea
a certain prophet,
named Agabus.
11. **And** when he was come unto us,
he took Paul's girdle, and
bound his own hands and
feet, and said, Thus saith
the Holy Ghost, So shall the
Jews at Jerusalem bind the
man that owneth this girdle,
and shall deliver *him* **into**
the hands of
the Gentiles.
12. **And when we heard**
these things, both
we, and they of that place,
besought him not to go
up to Jerusalem.
13. **Then Paul answered,**
What mean ye to weep
and to break mine heart?
for I am ready not to be
bound only, but also to die
at Jerusalem
for the name of
the Lord Jesus.
14. And when he would not be
persuaded, we ceased, saying, The
will of the Lord be done.
15. **And** after those days
we took up our carriages, and
went up to Jerusalem.
16. There went with us also *certain* of
the disciples of Caesarea, and
brought with them one Mnason of
Cyprus, an old disciple, with whom we
should lodge.
17. **And** when we were
come to Jerusalem,
the brethren received
us gladly.
18. **And** the *day* following

Paul went in with us
unto James; and all the
elders were present.
19. **And** when he had saluted them,
he declared particularly
what things God had
wrought among the
Gentiles by his ministry.
20. **And when they heard** *it,*
they glorified the Lord, and
said unto him,
Thou seest, brother,
how many thousands of
Jews there are which
believe; and
they are all zealous of the law:
21. **And they are informed of**
thee, that thou teachest all
the Jews which are among
the Gentiles
to forsake Moses, saying
that
they ought not to
circumcise *their* children, neither
to walk after the customs.
22. What is it therefore?
the multitude must needs
come together: for they will
hear that thou art come.
23. Do therefore this
that we say to thee:
We have four men which
have a vow on them;
24. Them take, and
purify thyself with them,
and be at charges with
them, that they may
shave *their* heads:
and all may know that those
things, whereof they were informed
concerning thee, are nothing; but
that **thou thyself**
also walkest orderly, and
keepest the law
25. As touching the Gentiles which
believe, we have written *and*
concluded that they observe no such
thing, save only that they keep
themselves from *things* offered to
idols, and from blood, and from
strangled, and from fornication.
26. **Then Paul**
took the men, and the next day

purifying himself with them
entered into the temple, to
signify the accomplish-
ment of the days of purification, until
that an offering should be offered for
every one of them.
27. And when the seven days were
almost ended,
the Jews which were
of Asia, when they saw him
in the temple,
stirred up all the people,
and laid hands on him,
28. Crying out, Men of Israel,
help: This is the man, that
teacheth all *men* every where
against the people, and
the law, and this place:
and further brought Greeks
also
into the temple, and hath
polluted this holy place.
29. (For they had seen before with
him in the city Trophimus an
Ephesian, whom they supposed that
Paul had brought into the temple.)
30. And all the city
was moved,
and the people ran together:
and they took Paul, and
drew him out of the temple:
and forthwith the doors were shut.
31. And as they went about
to kill him, tidings came
unto the chief captain
of the band,
that all Jerusalem was in
an uproar.
32. Who immediately took
soldiers and centurions,
and ran down
unto them: and when they
saw the chief captain and
the soldiers, they left
beating of Paul.
33. Then the chief captain
came near, and took him, and
commanded *him* to be
bound with two chains;
and demanded who he
was, and what he
had done.
34. And some cried one thing, some

another, among the multitude:
and when he could not
know the certainty for the
tumult, he commanded him
to be carried into
the castle.
35. And when he came upon the
stairs, so it was, that he was borne
of the soldiers for the violence
of the people.
36. For the multitude
of the people
followed after, crying,
Away with him.
37. And as Paul was to be
led into the castle,
he said unto the chief captain,
May I speak unto thee? Who said,
Canst thou speak Greek?
38. Art not thou that Egyptian, which
before these days madest an
uproar, and leddest out into the
wilderness four thousand men that
were murderers?
39. But Paul said,
I am a man *which am*
a Jew of Tarsus, *a city* in
Cilicia, a citizen of no mean city: and,
I beseech thee, suffer me to
speak unto the people.
40. And when he had
given him licence,
Paul stood on the stairs,
and beckoned with the hand unto
the people.
And when there was
made a great
silence, he spake unto *them*
in the Hebrew tongue,
saying,

CHAPTER 22
1. Men, brethren, and fathers,
hear ye my defence
which I *make* now unto you.
2. (And when they heard
that he spake in
the Hebrew tongue to them,
they kept the more silence:
and he saith,)
3. I am verily a man *which am*
a Jew, born in Tarsus,
a city in Cilicia,

yet brought up in this city at
the feet of Gamaliel, *and*
taught according to
the perfect manner of the
law of the fathers, and was
zealous toward God,
as ye all are this day.
4. And I persecuted this way
unto the death,
binding and delivering into prisons
both men and women.
5. As also the high priest
doth bear me witness,
and all the estate of the elders:
from whom also
I received letters
unto the brethren,
and went to Damascus, to
bring them which were there
bound unto Jerusalem, for
to be punished.
6. And it came to pass, that,
as I made my journey,
and was come nigh unto
Damascus about noon,
suddenly there shone
from heaven
a great light round about me.
7. And I fell unto the ground,
and heard a voice saying
unto me,
Saul, Saul, why persecutest
thou me?
8. And I answered, Who art
thou, Lord? And he said
unto me,
I am Jesus of Nazareth,
whom thou persecutest.
9. And they that were with me saw
indeed the light, and were afraid; but
they heard not the voice of him that
spake to me.
10. And I said, What shall I
do, LORD? And the Lord
said unto me, Arise, and
go into Damascus; and there it
shall be told thee of all things
which are appointed for thee to do.
11. And when I could not see for the
glory of that light,
being led by the hand
of them that were with me,
I came into Damascus.

12. And one Ananias,
a devout man according to the law,
having a good report of all the Jews
which dwelt there,
13. Came unto me, and stood,
and said unto me,
Brother Saul, receive thy
sight. And the same hour I looked
up upon him.
14. And he said, The God of
our fathers hath chosen
thee, that thou shouldest
know his will, and see that
Just One, and shouldest
hear the voice of
his mouth.
15. For thou shalt be his
witness unto all men of what thou
hast seen and heard.
16. And now
why tarriest thou? arise, and
be baptized,
and wash away thy sins,
calling on the name
of the Lord.
17. And it came to pass, that, when I
was come again to Jerusalem, even
while I prayed in the temple,
I was in a trance;
18. And saw him saying
unto me, Make haste, and
get thee quickly
out of Jerusalem:
for they will not receive thy
testimony concerning me.
19. And I said, Lord, they
know that I imprisoned
and beat in every synagogue
them that believed on thee:
20. And when the blood of
thy martyr Stephen was
shed, I also
was standing by, and
consenting unto his death,
and kept the raiment of them that
slew him.
21. And he said unto me,
Depart: for I will send thee
far hence
unto the Gentiles.
22. And they gave him
audience unto this word,
and *then*

lifted up their voices, and

■ **said, Away with such a**
■ *fellow* from the earth: for
■ **it is not fit that he**
■ **should live.**

23. And as they cried out, and cast off
their clothes, and threw dust
into the air,

■ 24. **The chief captain**
■ **commanded him** to be brought
■ **into the castle,** and bade that he
should be examined by scourging;
that he might know wherefore
they cried so against him.

■ 25. **And as they bound him**
with thongs,

■ **Paul said** unto the centurion
that stood by,

■ **Is it lawful for you to**
■ **scourge** a man that is
■ **a Roman,** and uncondemned?

■ 26. **When the centurion**
■ **heard** *that,*
■ **he went and told the chief**
captain,

■ **saying, Take heed**
what thou doest:

■ **for this man is a Roman.**

■ 27. **Then the chief captain**
came, and

■ **said unto him,** Tell me,
■ **art thou a Roman?**
■ **He said, Yea.**

■ 28. **And the chief captain**
■ **answered, With a great**
■ **sum obtained I this**
■ **freedom. And Paul said,** But
■ **I was** *free* **born.**

■ 29. **Then** straightway they departed
from him which should have examined
him: and

■ **the chief captain also was**
■ **afraid,** after he knew that he was a
Roman, and

■ **because he had**
■ **bound him.**

■ 30. **On the morrow,**
because he would have known the
certainty wherefore he was accused
of the Jews,

■ **he loosed him** from *his* bands,
■ **and commanded the** chief
■ **priests and** all

■ **their council to appear,**
■ **and brought Paul**
down, and set him

■ **before them.**

CHAPTER 23

■ 1. **And Paul,**
earnestly beholding the council,

■ **said,** Men *and* brethren,
■ **I have lived in all good**
■ **conscience before God**
until this day.

■ 2. **And the high priest**
■ **Ananias commanded them**
that stood by him

■ **to smite him on the mouth.**

■ 3. **Then said Paul unto him,**
■ **God shall smite thee,**
thou whited wall:

■ **for sittest thou** to judge me
■ **after the law, and**
■ **commandest me to be**
■ **smitten contrary to**
■ **the law?**

■ 4. **And they** that stood by
■ **said, Revilest thou God's**
■ **high priest?**

■ 5. **Then said Paul, I wist not,**
■ **brethren, that he was**
■ **the high priest:**
for it is written, Thou shalt not speak
evil of the ruler of thy people.

■ 6. **But when Paul perceived**
■ **that the one part were**
■ **Sadducees, and the**
■ **other Pharisees, he cried**
■ **out** in the council, Men *and* brethren,

■ **I am a Pharisee,**
the son of a Pharisee:

■ **of the hope and**
■ **resurrection of the dead**
■ **am called in question.**

■ 7. **And** when he had so said,
■ **there arose a dissension**
■ **between the Pharisees and**
the

■ **Sadducees:** and the multitude
was divided.

■ 8. **For the Sadducees say**
that

■ **there is no resurrection,**
neither angel, nor spirit:

■ **but the Pharisees**

confess both.
9. **And** there arose a great cry: and
the scribes *that were* of
the Pharisees' part arose,
and strove,
**saying, We find no evil in
this man:** but if a spirit or an angel
hath spoken to him, let us not fight
against God.
10. **And** when there arose
a great dissension,
**the chief captain, fearing
lest Paul should have been
pulled in pieces** of them,
**commanded the soldiers
to** go down, and to
take him by force
from among them,
and to
bring *him* **into the castle.**
11. **And the night following
the Lord stood by him, and
said, Be of good cheer,
Paul: for as thou hast
testified of me in
Jerusalem, so must thou
bear witness** also
at Rome.
12. **And** when it was day,
certain of the
Jews banded together, and
bound themselves under a curse,
saying that they would neither eat nor
drink till they had killed Paul.
13. And they were more than forty
which had made this conspiracy.
14. **And they came to the
chief priests** and elders,
**and said, We have bound
ourselves** under a great curse,
**that we will eat nothing until
we have slain Paul.**
15. **Now therefore**
ye with the council
**signify to the chief captain
that he bring him down** unto
you to-morrow, as though ye would
inquire something more perfectly
concerning him:
and we, or ever he come near,
are ready to kill him.
16. **And when Paul's sister's
son heard** of their lying in wait,

he went
and entered into the castle,
and told Paul.
17. **Then Paul called one of
the centurions** unto *him,*
**and said, Bring this young
man unto the chief captain:**
for he hath a certain thing to tell him.
18. So he took him, and brought *him* to
the chief captain, and said, Paul
the prisoner called me unto *him,* and
prayed me to bring this young man
unto thee, who hath something to say
unto thee.
19. **Then the chief captain
took him** by the hand, and went
with him aside privately,
and asked *him,*
**What is that thou hast
to tell** me?
20. **And he said, The Jews**
have agreed to
desire thee
that thou wouldest bring
down
Paul to-morrow
into the council,
as though they would inquire
somewhat of him more perfectly.
21. **But do not** thou
**yield unto them: for there lie
in wait** for him of them more than
forty men, which have
bound themselves
**with an oath, that they will
neither eat nor drink till
they have killed him:**
and now are they ready, looking for a
promise from thee.
22. **So the chief captain** then
let the young man depart,
and charged *him, See thou* tell no man
that thou hast shewed these
things to me.
23. **And he called** unto *him*
**two centurions, saying,
Make ready two hundred
soldiers to go to
Caesarea,** and horsemen
threescore and ten, and spearmen
two hundred, at the third hour
of the night;
24. And provide *them* beasts,

that they may set Paul on, and bring *him* safe unto Felix the governor. 25. **And he wrote a letter** after this manner: 26. Claudius Lysias **unto** the most excellent governor **Felix** *sendeth* greeting. 27. This man was taken of the Jews, and should have been killed of them: then came I with an army, and rescued him, having understood that he was a Roman. 28. And when I would have known the cause wherefore they accused him, I brought him forth into their council: 29. Whom I perceived to be accused of questions of their law, but to have nothing laid to his charge worthy of death or of bonds. 30. And when it was told me how that the Jews laid wait for the man, I sent straightway to thee, and gave commandment to his accusers also to say before thee what *they had* against him. Farewell. 31. **Then the soldiers,** as it was commanded them, **took Paul,** and brought *him* by night to Antipatris. 32. On the morrow they left the horsemen to go with him, and returned to the castle: 33. Who, when they came **to Caesarea** and delivered the epistle **to the governor,** presented Paul also before him. 34. **And when the governor had read** *the letter,* **he asked of what province he was.** And when he understood that *he was* of Cilicia; 35. **I will hear thee, said he, when thine accusers** are also **come.** And he commanded him to be kept in Herod's judgment hall.

CHAPTER 24

1. **And after five days Ananias** the high priest **descended** with the elders, and **with** a certain **orator** *named* **Tertullus, who** informed the governor against Paul. 2. **And** when he was called forth, **Tertullus began to accuse him, saying,** Seeing that by thee we enjoy great quietness, and that **very worthy deeds are done unto this nation by thy providence,** 3. **We accept** *it* **always,** and in all places, **most noble Felix, with all thankfulness.** 4. Notwithstanding, that I be not further tedious unto thee, **I pray** thee **that thou wouldest hear us** of thy clemency a few words. 5. **For we have found this man** *a* pestilent *fellow,* and **a mover of sedition among** all the **Jews throughout the world, and a ringleader** of the sect **of the Nazarenes:** 6. Who also hath gone about to profane the temple: **whom we** took, and **would have judged** according to our law. 7. **But the chief captain Lysias** came *upon us,* and with great violence **took** *him* **away** out of our hands, 8. **Commanding his accusers to come unto thee:** by examining of whom thyself mayest take knowledge of all these things, whereof we accuse him. 9. And the Jews also assented, saying that these things were so. 10. **Then Paul,** after that the governor had beckoned unto him to speak, **answered, Forasmuch as I know that thou hast been of many years a judge unto this nation, I do** the more cheerfully **answer for myself:** 11. **Because that thou**

■ mayest understand, that
■ there are yet
■ but twelve days
since I went up
■ to Jerusalem for to worship.
■ 12. And they neither found
■ me in the temple
■ disputing with any man,
neither raising up the people, neither
■ in the synagogues,
■ nor in the city:
13. Neither can they prove the things
whereof they now accuse me.
■ 14. But this I confess unto thee,
■ that after the way which
■ they call heresy, so
■ worship I the God of my
■ fathers, believing
all things which are written
■ in the law and in
■ the prophets:
15. And have hope toward God,
which they themselves also allow,
■ that there shall be a
■ resurrection of the dead,
■ both of the just and unjust.
16. And herein do I exercise myself,
to have always a conscience void to
offence toward God, and *toward* men.
■ 17. Now after many years
■ I came to bring alms to my
■ nation, and offerings.
■ 18. Whereupon certain Jews
■ from Asia found me
■ purified in the temple,
neither with multitude, nor with tumult.
■ 19. Who ought to have been
■ here before thee, and object,
■ if they had aught
■ against me.
■ 20. Or else
■ let these same *here*
■ say, if they have found any
■ evil doing in me,
while I stood before the council,
■ 21. Except it be for this one voice,
■ that I cried standing among them,
■ Touching the resurrection
■ of the dead I am called in
question by you this day.
■ 22. And when Felix heard
these things, having more perfect
knowledge of *that* way,

■ he deferred them, and
■ said, When Lysias
the chief captain
■ shall come down,
■ I will know the uttermost
■ of your matter.
■ 23. And he commanded a
■ centurion to keep Paul,
■ and to
■ let *him* have liberty, and
■ that he should forbid none
of his acquaintance
■ to minister or
■ come unto him.
■ 24. And after certain days,
■ when Felix came with his
■ wife Drusilla,
which was a Jewess,
■ he sent for Paul, and heard
■ him concerning the faith in
■ Christ.
■ 25. And as he reasoned of
■ righteousness,
■ temperance, and judgment
to come,
■ Felix trembled, and
■ answered, Go thy way
for this time;
■ when I have a
■ convenient season, I will
■ call for thee.
26. He hoped also that money should
have been given him of Paul, that he
might loose him: wherefore he sent for
him the oftener, and
communed with him.
■ 27. But after two years Porcius
■ Festus came into Felix'
■ room: and Felix, willing to
■ shew the Jews a pleasure,
■ left Paul bound.

CHAPTER 25
■ 1. Now when Festus was
■ come into the province, after three
days he ascended from Caesarea
■ to Jerusalem.
2. Then the high priest and the chief of
■ the Jews informed him
■ against Paul, and besought him,
■ 3. And desired
favour against him,
■ that he would send for him

to Jerusalem, laying wait
in the way
to kill him.
4. But Festus answered, that
Paul should be kept at
Caesarea, and that he himself
would depart shortly *thither.*
5. Let them therefore, said he,
which among you are able,
go down with *me,*
and accuse this man, if there
be any wickedness in him.
6. And when he had tarried among
them more than ten days,
he went down unto Caesarea;
and the next day sitting on
the judgment seat
commanded Paul
to be brought.
7. And when he was come,
the Jews which came down from
Jerusalem stood round about, and
laid many and grievous
complaints against Paul,
which they
could not prove.
8. While he answered
for himself,
Neither against the law
of the Jews, neither against
the temple, nor yet against
Caesar, have I offended
any thing at all.
9. But Festus, willing to do
the Jews a
pleasure, answered Paul, and
said, Wilt thou go up
to Jerusalem, and there be
judged of these things
before me?
10. Then said Paul, I stand
at Caesar's judgment seat,
where I ought to be judged:
to the Jews have I done no wrong,
as thou very well
knowest.
11. For if I be an offender,
or have committed any thing
worthy of death,
I refuse not to die: but if
there be none of these
things whereof these
accuse me, no man may

deliver me unto them.
I appeal unto Caesar.
12. Then Festus, when he had
conferred with the council,
answered, Hast thou appealed
unto Caesar?
unto Caesar shalt thou go.
13. And after certain days
king Agrippa and Bernice
came unto Caesarea
to salute Festus.
14. And when they had been there
many days,
Festus declared Paul's
cause unto the king,
saying, There is a certain man left
in bonds by Felix:
15. About whom,
when I was at Jerusalem,
the chief priests
and the elders of
the Jews informed *me,*
desiring *to have* judgment
against him.
16. To whom I answered, It is not the
manner of the Romans to deliver
any man to die, before that he which is
accused have the accusers face to
face, and have licence to answer for
himself concerning the crime
laid against him.
17. Therefore,
when they were come
hither, without any
delay on the morrow
I sat on the judgment seat, and
commanded the man to be
brought forth.
18. Against whom
when the accusers stood
up, they brought none
accusation of such things
as I supposed:
19. But had certain
questions against him
of their own superstition,
and of one Jesus, which
was dead, whom Paul
affirmed to be alive.
20. And because I doubted of such
manner of questions,
I asked *him* whether he
would go to Jerusalem,

■ **and** there
■ **be judged** of these matters.
■ 21. **But when Paul** had
■ **appealed to be reserved**
■ **unto** the hearing of
■ **Augustus, I commanded**
■ **him to be kept till I might**
■ **send him to Caesar.**
■ 22. **Then Agrippa said**
unto Festus,
■ **I would also hear the man**
■ **myself.** To-morrow, said he, thou
shalt hear him.
■ 23. **And on the morrow,**
■ **when Agrippa was come,**
■ **and Bernice,** with great pomp,
and was entered into the place of
hearing, with the chief captains, and
principal men of the city,
at Festus' commandment
■ **Paul was brought forth.**
■ 24. **And Festus said, King**
■ **Agrippa,** and all men which are
here present with us,
■ **ye see this man, about**
■ **whom all the multitude**
of the Jews
■ **have dealt with me,**
both at Jerusalem, and *also* here,
■ **crying that he ought not to**
■ **live** any longer.
25. But when I found that he had
committed nothing worthy of death,
and that he himself hath appealed to
Augustus, I have determined
to send him.
26. Of whom I have no certain thing to
write unto my lord.
■ **Wherefore I have brought**
■ **him forth before you,**
and specially before thee,
■ **O king Agrippa,**
that, after examination had, I might
have somewhat to write.
27. For it seemeth to me unreasonable
to send a prisoner, and not withal
to signify the crimes *laid* against him.

CHAPTER 26
■ 1. **Then Agrippa said unto**
■ **Paul, Thou art permitted to**
■ **speak** for thyself.
■ **Then Paul**

stretched forth the hand, and
■ **answered** for himself:
■ 2. **I think myself happy, king**
■ **Agrippa, because I shall**
■ **answer** for myself
this day before thee
touching all the things
■ **whereof I am accused**
■ **of the Jews:**
■ 3. **Especially** *because I*
■ *know* **thee to be expert in**
■ **all customs**
and questions which are
■ **among the Jews:** wherefore I
beseech thee to hear me patiently.
■ 4. **My manner of life from** my
■ **youth,** which was at the first among
mine own nation at Jerusalem,
■ **know all the Jews;**
5. Which knew me from the beginning,
if they would testify, that after the
most straitest sect
of our religion
■ **I lived a Pharisee.**
■ 6. **And now I** stand and
■ **am judged for the hope of**
the promise made of God, unto
■ **our fathers:**
7. Unto which *promise* our twelve
tribes, instantly serving *God* day and
night, hope to come. For which hope's
sake, king Agrippa, I am accused
of the Jews.
■ 8. **Why should it be thought**
a thing
■ **incredible** with you,
■ **that God should raise**
■ **the dead?**
■ 9. **I verily thought** with myself,
■ **that I ought to do** many things
■ **contrary to** the name of
■ **Jesus** of Nazareth.
■ 10. **Which thing I** also
■ **did** in Jerusalem:
■ **and many** of the
■ **saints did I shut up in**
■ **prison,** having received authority
from the chief priests;
■ **and when they were put to**
■ **death, I gave my voice**
■ **against** *them.*
11. And I punished them oft in every
synagogue, and compelled *them* to

blaspheme; and being exceedingly mad against them,

■ **I persecuted** *them* **even unto strange cities.**

■ 12. **Whereupon as I went to Damascus** with authority and commission from the chief priests,

13. At midday, O king,

■ **I saw** in the way

■ **a light from heaven,** above the brightness of the sun, shining round about me and them which journeyed with me.

■ 14. **And when we were all fallen** to the earth,

■ **I heard a voice** speaking unto me, and

■ **saying** in the Hebrew tongue, Saul,

■ **Saul, why persecutest thou me?** *it is* hard for thee to kick against the pricks.

■ 15. **And I said, Who art thou, Lord? And he said, I am Jesus whom thou persecutest**

16. But rise, and stand upon thy feet: for

■ **I have appeared unto thee** for this purpose,

■ **to make thee a minister** and a witness both of these things which thou hast seen, and of those things in the which I will appear unto thee;

17. Delivering thee from the people, and *from* the Gentiles, unto whom now I send thee,

18. To open their eyes, *and*

■ **to turn** *them* from darkness to light, and

■ **from the power of Satan**

■ **unto God,** that they may receive forgiveness of sins, and inheritance among them which are sanctified by faith that is in me.

■ 19. **Whereupon,** O king Agrippa,

■ **I was not disobedient unto**

■ **the** heavenly

■ **vision:**

■ 20. **But shewed first** unto

■ **them of Damascus, and** at

■ **Jerusalem, and**

■ **throughout all the coasts of**

■ **Judaea, and** *then* **to the**

■ **Gentiles,** that they should repent and turn to God, and do works meet for repentance.

■ 21. **For these causes the**

■ **Jews** caught me in the temple, and

■ **went about to kill** *me.*

■ 22. **Having therefore**

■ **obtained help of God, I**

■ **continue** unto this day,

■ **witnessing** both to small and great,

■ **saying none other things**

■ **than those which the**

■ **prophets and Moses did**

■ **say** should come

■ 23. **That Christ should suffer,** *and* that he should be the first that

■ **should rise from the dead,**

■ **and should shew light unto**

■ **the people, and** to

■ **the Gentiles.**

■ 24. **And** as he thus spake for himself,

■ **Festus said** with a loud voice,

■ **Paul,** thou art beside thyself;

■ **much learning doth**

■ **make thee mad.**

■ 25. **But he said, I am not**

■ **mad,** most noble

■ **Festus; but speak** forth the

■ **words of truth** and soberness.

□ 26. **For the king knoweth** of these things, before whom also I speak freely: for I am persuaded that none of these things are hidden from him; for

■ **this thing was not done**

■ **in a corner.**

■ 27. **King Agrippa, believest** thou

■ **the prophets? I know** that

■ **thou believest.**

■ 28. **Then Agrippa said** unto Paul,

■ **Almost thou persuadest**

■ **me to be a Christian**

■ 29. **And Paul said, I would** to God,

■ **that not only thou, but** also

■ **all** that hear me this day,

■ **were** both almost, and altogether such

■ **as I am,** except these bonds.

30. And when he had thus spoken, the king rose up, and the governor, and Bernice, and they that sat with them: 31. And when they were gone aside, they talked between themselves, saying, This man doeth nothing worthy of death or of bonds.

32. **Then said Agrippa unto Festus, This man might have been set at liberty, if he had not appealed unto Caesar.**

CHAPTER 27

1. **And when it was determined that we should sail into Italy, they delivered Paul** and certain other prisoners **unto** *one* named **Julius, a centurion** of Augustus' band.

2. And entering into a ship of Adramyttium, we launched, meaning to sail by the coasts of Asia; *one* Aristarchus, a Macedonian of Thessalonica, being with us.

3. And the next *day* we touched at Sidon. And Julius courteously entreated Paul, and gave *him* liberty to go unto his friends to refresh himself.

4. And when we had launched from thence, we sailed under Cyprus, because the winds were contrary.

5. **And when we had sailed over the sea of Cilicia** and Pamphylia, **we came to Myra,** *a city* of Lycia.

6. **And there the centurion found a ship** of Alexandria **sailing into Italy; and he put us therein.**

7. And when we had sailed slowly many days, and scarce were come over against Cnidus, the wind not suffering us, we sailed under Crete, over again Salmone;

8. And, hardly passing it, came unto a place which is called The fair havens; nigh whereunto was the city of Lasea.

9. Now when much time was spent, **and when sailing was now dangerous, because the fast was** now **already past, Paul admonished** *them,*

10. **And said** unto them, Sirs, **I perceive that this voyage will be with hurt and** much **damage, not only of the** lading and **ship, but also** of **our lives.**

11. **Nevertheless the centurion believed the master** and the owner **of the ship, more than** those things which were spoken by **Paul.**

12. **And because the haven was not commodious to winter in, the more part advised to depart** thence also, if by any means they might attain to Phenice, *and there* to winter; *which is* an haven of Crete, and lieth toward the south-west and north-west.

13. **And when the south wind blew softly,** supposing that they had obtained *their* purpose, loosing *thence,* **they sailed close by Crete.**

14. **But** not long after **there arose** against it **a tempestuous wind,** called Euroclydon.

15. **And when the ship was caught,** and could not bear up into the wind, **we let** *her* **drive.**

16. **And running under a** certain **island** which is **called Clauda, we had much work** to come by the boat:

17. Which when they had taken up, they used helps, undergirding the ship; and, fearing lest they should fall into the quicksands, strake sail, and so were driven.

18. **And we being** exceedingly **tossed with a tempest, the**

next *day* they
lightened the ship;
19. And the third *day* we
cast out with our own hands
the tackling of the ship.
20. And when neither sun
nor stars in many days
appeared, and no small
tempest lay on *us*,
all hope that we should be saved
was then taken away.
21. But after long abstinence
Paul stood forth in
the midst of them,
and said, Sirs, ye should have
hearkened unto me, and not have
loosed from Crete, and to have gained
this harm and loss.
22. And now I exhort you to
be of good cheer: for there
shall be no loss of *any man's*
life among you, but
of the ship.
23. For there stood by me
this night the angel of God,
whose I am, and whom I serve,
24. Saying, Fear not,
Paul; thou must be brought
before Caesar: and, lo,
God hath given thee all
them that sail with thee.
25. Wherefore, sirs,
be of good cheer: for
I believe God, that it shall
be even as it was told me
26. Howbeit we must be cast
upon a certain island.
27. But when the fourteenth
night was come, as we
were driven up and down in Adria,
about midnight
the shipmen deemed that
they drew near to
some country;
28. And sounded, and
found *it* twenty fathoms:
and when they had gone
a little further, they
sounded again, and found
it fifteen fathoms.
29. Then fearing lest we
should have fallen upon
rocks, they cast four

anchors out of the stern,
and wished for the day.
30. And as the shipmen
were about to flee out of the
ship, when they had let down the boat
into the sea, under colour as though
they would have cast anchors
out of the foreship,
31. Paul said to
the centurion and to
the soldiers, Except these
abide in the ship, ye
cannot be saved.
32. Then the soldiers cut off
the ropes of the
boat, and let her fall off.
33. And while the
day was coming on,
Paul besought *them*
all to take meat,
saying, This day
is the fourteenth day that ye
have tarried and
continued fasting,
having taken nothing.
34. Wherefore I pray you to
take *some* meat: for this is
for your health: for there
shall not an hair fall from
the head of
any of you.
35. And when he had thus spoken,
he took bread, and gave
thanks to God
in presence of them all:
and when he had broken *i t*, he
began to eat.
36. Then were they all of
good cheer, and they also
took *some* meat.
37. And we were in all in the ship two
hundred threescore and
sixteen souls.
38. And when they had
eaten enough,
they lightened the ship, and
cast out the wheat into the sea.
39. And when it was day,
they knew not the land: but
they discovered a certain
creek with a shore,
into the
which they were minded,

if it were possible,
to thrust in
the ship.
40. And when they had
taken up the anchors,
they committed *themselves*
unto the sea, and loosed the
rudder bands, and hoised up the
mainsail to the wind, and made
toward shore.
41. And falling into a place where
two seas met,
they ran the ship
aground; and the forepart
stuck fast,
and remained unmoveable,
but the hinder
part was broken
with the violence of the waves.
42. And the soldiers'
counsel was to kill the
prisoners, lest any of them
should swim out, and escape.
43. But the centurion,
willing to save Paul,
kept them from *their*
purpose; and commanded
that they which could swim
should cast *themselves* first *into*
the sea , and
get to land:
44. And the rest, some
on boards, and some on
broken pieces of the ship.
And so it came to pass, that they
escaped all safe
to land.

CHAPTER 28

1. And when they were escaped,
then they knew that
the island was
called Melita.
2. And the barbarous
people shewed us no little
kindness: for they
kindled a fire, and
received us every one,
because of the present
rain, and because of the
cold.
3. And when Paul had
gathered a bundle of

sticks, and laid *them* on the
fire, there came a viper
out of the heat,
and fastened on his hand.
4. And when the barbarians
saw the *venomous* beast
hang on his hand, they
said among themselves, No doubt
this man is a murderer,
whom, though he hath
escaped the sea, yet
vengeance suffereth
not to live.
5. And he shook off the
beast into the fire,
and felt no harm.
6. Howbeit they looked when
he should have swollen, or fallen down
dead suddenly: but after they had
looked a great while,
and saw no harm come to
him, they changed their minds,
and said that he was
a god.
7. In the same quarters were
possessions of
the chief man of the island,
whose name was Publius;
who received us, and
lodged us three days
courteously.
8. And it came to pass,
that the father of Publius
lay sick of a fever and of a
bloody flux: to whom Paul
entered in, and prayed,
and laid his
hands on him,
and healed him.
9. So when this was done,
others also,
which had diseases
in the island,
came, and were healed:
10. Who also honoured us with many
honours; and when we departed, they
laded *us* with such things as
were necessary.
11. And after three months
we departed in a ship of
Alexandria, which had wintered in the
isle, whose sign was
Castor and Pollux.

12. **And landing at Syracuse, we tarried** *there* three days. 13. **And from thence** we fetched a compass, and **came to Rhegium:** and after one day the south wind blew, **and** we came the **next** day **to Puteoli:** 14. **Where we found brethren, and** were **desired to tarry** with them **seven days: and so we went toward Rome.** 15. **And** from thence, **when the brethren heard of us, they came to meet us as far as Appii forum,** and The three taverns: whom when Paul saw, he thanked God, and took courage. 16. **And when we came to Rome, the centurion delivered** the prisoners to the captain of the guard: but **Paul** was suffered **to dwell by himself with a soldier** that kept him. 17. **And** it came to pass, that **after three days Paul called the chief of the Jews together: and** when they were come together, he **said unto them,** Men *and* brethren, **though I have committed nothing against the people,** or customs of our fathers, **yet was I delivered prisoner from Jerusalem into the hands of the Romans.** 18. **Who,** when they had examined me, **would have let** *me* **go,** because there was no cause of death in me. 19. **But** when **the Jews spake against** *it,* **I was constrained to appeal unto Caesar;** not that I had ought to accuse my nation of.

20. **For this cause** therefore have **I called for you,** to see *you* , and to speak with *you* : **because** that **for the hope of Israel I am bound** with this chain. 21. **And they said** unto him, **We neither received letters** out of Judaea concerning thee, **neither any of the brethren** that came shewed or **spake any harm of thee.** 22. **But we desire to hear** of thee **what thou thinkest:** for as concerning this sect, we know that every where it is spoken against. 23. **And** when they had appointed him a day, **there came many to** him into **his lodging; to whom he** expounded and **testified the kingdom of God, persuading them concerning Jesus, both out of the law of Moses, and** out of **the prophets,** from morning till evening. 24. **And some believed** the things which were spoken, **and some believed not.** 25. **And** when they agreed not among themselves, **they departed, after** that **Paul had spoken** one word, **Well spake the Holy Ghost by Esaias** the prophet unto our fathers, 26. **Saying, Go unto this people, and say, Hearing ye shall hear, and shall not understand;** and seeing ye shall see, and not perceive: 27. **For the heart of this people is waxed gross, and their ears are dull of hearing,** and their eyes have they closed; lest they should see with *their* eyes, and hear with *their* ears, and understand with *their* heart,

and should be converted,
and I should heal them.
28. Be it known therefore
unto you,
that the salvation of God is
sent unto the Gentiles,
and *that* they will hear it.
29. And when he had said
these words, the Jews
departed, and had great
reasoning among themselves.

30. And Paul dwelt two whole
years in his own hired
house, and received
all that came in unto him,
31. Preaching the kingdom
of God,
and teaching
those things which concern
the Lord Jesus Christ, with
all confidence,
no man forbidding him.

THE EPISTLE TO THE ROMANS

BACKGROUND INFORMATION

Author – Paul, an Apostle.
Date Written – probably
between 58 and **60** A.D.

Number of:
Verses -   433
Chapters -   16
Total Words - 9,447
Scan Words - 4,700
Scan Words represent 49 %
of Total Words.

**Theme – the righteousness
of God** revealed and
accomplished
in Jesus Christ and how
believers should live in light of
God's righteousness.

OUTLINE OF THE EPISTLE

Prologue
Chapter 1—1:15

I. The righteousness of God
    revealed in the
    judgment of sin.
    Chapters 1—3
II. The righteousness of God
    revealed in
    justification by faith.
    Chapters 3—4
III. The righteousness of God
    revealed in
    salvation.
    Chapters 5—8
IV. The righteousness of God
    revealed in
    history.
    Chapters 9—12
V. The righteousness of God
    revealed in
    Christian living.
    Chapters 12—16.

CHAPTER 1

■ 1. **Paul,** a servant of Jesus Christ,
■ **called** *to be* **an apostle,**
separated unto the gospel of God,
2. (Which he had promised afore by
his prophets in the holy scriptures,)
■ 3. **Concerning** his Son Jesus
■ **Christ** our Lord, which was made of
the seed of David
according to the flesh;
4. And declared *to be*
■ **the Son of God with power,**
according to the spirit of holiness,
■ **by the resurrection**
from the dead:
5. By whom we have received grace
and apostleship, for obedience to the
faith among all nations, for his name:
6. Among whom are ye also the called
of Jesus Christ:
■ 7. **To all that be in Rome,**
beloved of God,
■ **called** *to be* **saints: Grace**
to you and peace
■ **from God** our Father,
■ **and the Lord Jesus** Christ.
■ 8. **First, I thank my God**
through Jesus Christ for you all,
■ **that your faith is spoken**
■ **of throughout the**
■ **whole world.**
■ 9. **For God is my witness,**
whom I serve with my spirit in the
gospel of his Son, that
■ **without ceasing I make**
■ **mention of you** always
■ **in my prayers;**
10. Making request, if by any means
now at length I might have a
prosperous journey by the will of God
to come unto you.
■ 11. **For I long to see you, that**
■ **I may impart unto you**
■ **some spiritual gift,** to the end
ye may be established;
12. That is, that I may be comforted
together with you by the mutual faith
both of you and me.
13. Now I would not have you
ignorant, brethren, that oftentimes I
purposed to come unto you, (but was
let hitherto,) that I might have some
fruit among you also, even as among

other Gentiles.
■ 14. **I am debtor both to the**
■ **Greeks, and** to the
■ **Barbarians;** both to the wise,
and to the unwise.
■ 15. **So,** as much as in me is,
■ **I am ready to preach the**
■ **gospel to you**
that are at Rome also.
■ 16. **For I am not ashamed of**
■ **the gospel of Christ:**
■ **for it is the power of**
■ **God unto salvation to**
■ **every one that believeth;** to
the Jew first, and also to the Greek.
■ 17. **For therein is the**
■ **righteousness of God**
■ **revealed** from faith to faith:
■ **as it is written, The just**
■ **shall live by faith.**
■ 18. **For the wrath of God is**
revealed from heaven
■ **against all** ungodliness and
unrighteousness of men,
■ **who hold the truth in**
■ **unrighteousness;**
19. Because that which may be known
of God is manifest in them; for God
hath shewed *it* unto them.
■ 20. **For the invisible things**
■ **of him from the creation**
■ **of the world**
■ **are clearly seen,**
being understood
■ **by the things** that are
■ **made,** *even* his eternal
■ **power and Godhead; so**
■ **that they are**
■ **without excuse:**
■ 21. **Because that, when they**
■ **knew God, they glorified**
■ *him* **not**
as God, neither were thankful;
■ **but became vain** in their
imaginations, and their foolish heart
was darkened.
■ 22. **Professing themselves**
■ **to be wise, they**
■ **became fools,**
■ 23. **And changed the glory**
■ **of the uncorruptible God**
■ **into an image** made
like to corruptible man, and to birds,

and fourfooted beasts, and creeping things.

24. **Wherefore God also gave them up to** uncleanness through the **lusts** of their own hearts, **to dishonour their own bodies between themselves:**

25. **Who changed the truth of God into a lie, and worshipped** and served **the creature more than the Creator,** who is blessed for ever. Amen.

26. For this cause God gave them up unto vile affections: **for even their women did change the natural use into that which is against nature:**

27. **And likewise also the men,** leaving the natural use of the woman, **burned in** their **lust one toward another;** men with men working that which is unseemly, and **receiving in themselves that recompence of their error** which was meet.

28. **And** even as they did not like to retain God in *their* knowledge, **God gave them over to a reprobate mind,** to do those things which are not convenient;

29. **Being filled with all unrighteousness,** fornication, wickedness, covetousness, maliciousness; full of envy, murder, debate, deceit, malignity; whisperers,

30. Backbiters, haters of God, despiteful, proud, boasters, inventors of evil things, disobedient to parents,

31. Without understanding, covenant breakers, without natural affection, implacable, unmerciful:

32. **Who knowing the judgment of God, that they which commit such things are worthy of death, not only do the same, but have pleasure in them**

that do them.

CHAPTER 2

1. **Therefore thou art inexcusable, O man,** whosoever thou art that judgest: **for wherein thou judgest another, thou condemnest thyself;** for thou that judgest doest the same things.

2. **But** we are sure that **the judgment of God is according to truth** against them which commit such things.

3. **And thinkest thou** this, O man, **that judgest them which do such things, and doest the same, that thou shalt escape the judgment** of God?

4. **Or despisest thou** the riches of **his goodness** and forbearance and longsuffering; **not knowing that the goodness of God leadeth** thee **to repentance?**

5. **But after thy** hardness and **impenitent heart treasurest up** unto thyself **wrath against the day of** wrath and **revelation of the righteous judgment of God;**

6. **Who will render to every man according to his deeds:**

7. **To them who** by patient continuance in well-doing **seek for glory** and honour **and immortality, eternal life:**

8. **But unto them that** are contentious, and **do not obey the truth,** but obey unrighteousness, indignation and wrath,

9. **Tribulation and anguish,** upon every soul of man that doeth evil, of the Jew first, and also of the Gentile;

10. But glory, honour, and peace, to

every man that worketh good, to the Jew first, and also to the Gentile:

■ 11. **For there is no respect of persons with God.**

■ 12. **For as many as have sinned without law shall** also **perish without law: and as many as have sinned in the law shall be judged by the law;**

■ 13. **(For not the hearers** of the law *are* just before God,

■ **but the doers of the law shall be justified.**

■ 14. **For when the Gentiles, which have not the law, do by nature** the **things** contained **in the law, these,** having not the law,

■ **are a law unto themselves:**

■ 15. **Which shew the work of the law written in their hearts,** their conscience also bearing witness, and *their* thoughts the mean while accusing or else excusing one another;)

■ 16. **In the day when God shall judge the secrets of men by Jesus** Christ according to my gospel.

■ 17. **Behold, thou art called a Jew, and** restest in the law, and makest thy boast of God,

18. And knowest *his* will, and approvest the things that are more excellent, being instructed out of the law;

19. And art confident that thou thyself art a guide of the blind, a light of them which are in darkness,

■ 20. **An instructor** of the foolish, a teacher of babes, which hast the form of knowledge and of the truth **in the law.**

■ 21. **Thou therefore which teachest another, teachest thou not thyself?** thou that preachest a man should not steal, dost thou steal?

■ 22. **Thou that sayest a man should not commit adultery, dost thou commit**

■ **adultery?** thou that abhorrest idols, dost thou commit sacrilege?

23. Thou that makest thy boast of the law, through breaking the law dishonourest thou God?

24. For the name of God is blasphemed among the Gentiles through you, as it is written.

■ 25. **For circumcision** verily **profiteth, if thou keep the law: but if thou be a breaker** of the law, **thy circumcision is made uncircumcision.**

■ 26. **Therefore if the uncircumcision keep the** righteousness of the **law, shall not his uncircumcision be counted for circumcision?**

■ 27. **And shall not uncircumcision which** is by nature, if it **fulfil the law, judge thee, who** by the letter and circumcision **dost transgress the law?**

■ 28. **For he is not a Jew, which is one outwardly;** neither *is that* circumcision, which is outward in the flesh:

■ 29. **But he** *is* **a Jew, which is one inwardly; and circumcision** *is that* of the heart, **in the spirit,** *and* **not in the letter;** whose praise *is* not of men, but of God.

CHAPTER 3

■ 1. **What advantage then hath the Jew?** or what profit *is there* of circumcision?

■ 2. **Much** every way: chiefly, **because** that **unto them were committed the oracles of God.**

■ 3. **For what if some did not believe? shall their unbelief make the faith of God without effect?**

■ 4. **God forbid:** yea, **let God be true, but every man a liar;** as it is written, That thou mightest be justified in thy sayings, and mightest overcome when thou art judged.

5. **But if our unrighteousness commend the righteous- ness of God,** what shall we say? *Is* **God unrighteous who taketh vengeance?** (I speak as a man)

6. **God forbid: for then how shall God judge the world?**

7. **For if the truth** of God hath more **abounded through my lie unto his glory; why** yet **am I** also **judged** as **a sinner?**

8. And not *rather,* (as we be slander- ously reported, and as some affirm that we say,) Let us do evil, that good may come? whose damnation is just.

9. **What then? are we better** *than they***? No,** in no wise: for **we have** before **proved both Jews and Gentiles,** that they **are** all **under sin;**

10. **As it is written, There is none righteous,** no, not one:

11. **There is none** that understandeth, there is none **that seeketh after God.**

12. They are all gone out of the way, they are together become unprofitable;

there is none that doeth good, no, not one.

13. Their throat *is* an open sepulchre; with their tongues they have used deceit; the poison of asps *is* under their lips:

14. Whose mouth *is* full of cursing and bitterness:

15. Their feet *are* swift to shed blood:

16. Destruction and misery *are* in their ways:

17. And the way of peace have they not known:

18. There is no fear of God before their eyes.

19. **Now we know that** what things soever

the law saith, it saith **to them** who are **under the law: that every mouth** may **be stopped, and all** the world **may become guilty before God.**

20. **Therefore by the** deeds of the **law** there **shall no flesh be justified** in his sight: **for by the law** *is* **the knowledge of sin.**

21. **But now the righteous- ness of God without the law is manifested,** being witnessed by the law and the prophets;

22. Even the righteousness of God **which is by faith of Jesus Christ unto all** and upon all them **that believe: for there is no difference:**

23. **For all have sinned, and come short of the glory of God;**

24. **Being justified** freely **by his grace through** the **redemption** that is **in Christ Jesus:**

25. **Whom God hath set forth** *to be* **a propitiation through faith in his blood, to** declare his righteousness for **the remission of sins** that are past, through the forbearance of God;

26. To declare, *I say*, at this time his righteousness: that he might be just, and the justifier of him which believeth in Jesus.

27. **Where is boasting then? It is excluded.** By what law? of works? Nay: but by the law of faith.

28. **Therefore we conclude that a man is justified by faith without the deeds of the law.**

29. *Is he* the God of the Jews only? *is he* not also of the Gentiles? Yes, of the Gentiles also:

30. **Seeing** *it is* **one God, which shall justify the**

■ circumcision by faith,
■ and uncircumcision
■ through faith.
■ 31. Do we then make void
■ the law through faith? God
■ forbid: yea,
■ we establish the law.

CHAPTER 4
■ 1. What shall we say then
■ that Abraham our father, as
pertaining to the flesh,
■ hath found?
■ 2. For if Abraham were
■ justified by works, he hath
■ *whereof* to glory; but
not before God.
3. For what saith the scripture?
■ Abraham believed God,
■ and it was counted
unto him for
■ righteousness.
■ 4. Now to him that worketh
■ is the reward not reckoned
■ of grace, but of debt.
■ 5. But to him that worketh
■ not, but believeth on him
■ that justifieth the ungodly,
■ his faith is counted for
■ righteousness.
■ 6. Even as
■ David also
■ describeth the blessedness of
the man, unto whom God imputeth
righteousness without works,
■ 7. *Saying,* Blessed *are* they
■ whose iniquities are
■ forgiven, and whose sins
are covered.
8. Blessed *is* the man to whom the
Lord will not impute sin.
■ 9. *Cometh* this blessedness
■ then upon the circumcision
■ *only,* or upon the
■ uncircumcision also? for
we say that
■ faith was reckoned to
■ Abraham for
■ righteousness.
■ 10. How was it then
■ reckoned? when he was in
circumcision, or in uncircumcision?
■ Not in circumcision, but in

■ uncircumcision.
11. And he received the sign of
circumcision, a seal of the
righteousness of the faith which *he*
had yet being uncircumcised:
■ that he might be the
■ father of all them
■ that believe, though they be
■ not circumcised;
that righteousness might be imputed
unto them also:
■ 12. And the father of
circumcision to
■ them who are not of the
circumcision only, but who also
■ walk in the steps of that
■ faith of our father
Abraham, which *he had*
■ being *yet* uncircumcised.
■ 13. For the promise, that he
should be the heir of the world,
■ *was* not to Abraham,
or to his seed,
■ through the law, but
■ through the righteousness
■ of faith.
■ 14. For if they which are
■ of the law *be* heirs,
■ faith is made
■ void, and the promise
made of none effect:
15. Because the law worketh wrath:
for where no law is, *there is* no
transgression.
■ 16. Therefore *it is* of faith,
■ that *it might be* by grace; to
the end the promise might be sure to
all the seed; not to that only which is
of the law, but to that also which is of
the faith of
■ Abraham; who is the father
■ of us all,
17. (As it is written, I have made thee
a father of many nations,)
■ before him whom he believed, *even*
■ God, who quickeneth the
■ dead, and calleth those
■ things which be not as
■ though they were.
■ 18. Who against hope
■ believed in hope,
■ that he might become the
■ father of many nations,

according to that which was spoken, So shall thy seed be.

19. **And being not weak in faith,** he **considered not his own body** now dead, when he was about an hundred years old, **neither** yet **the deadness of Sarah's womb:**

20. **He staggered not at the promise of God** through unbelief; **but was strong in faith,** giving glory to God;

21. And being fully **persuaded that, what he had promised, he was able** also **to perform.**

22. **And therefore it was imputed to him for righteousness.**

23. **Now it was not written for his sake alone,** that it was imputed to him;

24. **But for us also, to whom it shall be imputed, if we believe on him that raised up Jesus** our Lord from the dead;

25. Who was delivered for our offences, and was raised again **for our justification.**

CHAPTER 5

1. **Therefore being justified by faith, we have peace with God through** our Lord Jesus **Christ:**

2. **By whom also we have access by faith** into this grace wherein we stand, and rejoice in hope of the glory of God.

3. And not only *so,* **but we glory in tribulations also: knowing that tribulation worketh patience;**

4. **And patience, experience; and experience, hope:**

5. **And hope maketh not ashamed; because the love of God is** shed abroad **in our hearts by the Holy Ghost** which is given unto us.

6. **For when we were** yet **without strength,** in due time **Christ died for the ungodly.**

7. **For scarcely for a righteous man will one die:** yet peradventure for a good man some would even dare to die.

8. **But God commendeth his love** toward us, **in that, while we were** yet **sinners, Christ died for us.**

9. Much more then, **being now justified by his blood, we shall be saved** from wrath through him.

10. **For if, when we were enemies, we were reconciled** to God **by the death of his Son, much more, being reconciled, we shall be saved by his life.**

11. And not only *so,* but **we also joy in God through** our Lord Jesus **Christ, by whom we** have now **received the atonement.**

12. **Wherefore, as by one man sin entered** into the world, **and death by sin; and so death passed upon all** men, for that all have sinned:

13. **(For until the law sin was in the world: but sin is not imputed when there is no law.)**

14. **Nevertheless death reigned from Adam to Moses,** even over them that had not sinned **after the similitude of Adam's transgression,** who is the figure of him that was to come.

15. But not as the offence, so also *is* the free gift. For if through the offence of one many be dead, much more the grace of God, and the gift by grace, *which is* by one man, Jesus Christ, hath abounded unto many.

16. And not as *it was* by one that sinned, *so is* the gift: for the judgment *was* by one to condemnation, but the free gift *is* of many offences unto justification.
17. For if by one man's offence death reigned by one; much more they which receive abundance of grace and of the gift of righteousness shall reign in life by one, Jesus Christ.)
18. **Therefore as by the offence of one *judgment came*** upon all men to condemnation;
even so by the righteousness of one *the free gift came* upon all men unto justification of life.
19. **For as by one man's disobedience many were made sinners, so by the obedience of one shall many be made righteous.**
20. **Moreover the law entered, that the offence might abound. But where sin abounded, grace did much more abound:**
21. That as sin hath reigned unto death, even so might grace reign through righteousness unto eternal life by Jesus Christ our Lord.

CHAPTER 6
1. What shall we say then? **Shall we continue in sin, that grace may abound?**
2. **God forbid.** How shall we, that are dead to sin, live any longer therein?
3. **Know ye not, that so many of us as were baptized into Jesus Christ were baptized into his death?**
4. **Therefore we are buried with him by baptism into death: that** like **as Christ was raised** up from the dead by the glory of the Father, even **so we also should walk in newness of life.**

5. For if we have been planted together in the likeness of his death, we shall be also *in the likeness* of *his* resurrection:
6. Knowing this, that **our old man is crucified with *him*, that the body of sin might be destroyed, that** henceforth **we should not serve sin.**
7. For he that is dead is freed from sin.
8. **Now if we be dead with Christ,** we believe that **we shall also live with him:**
9. **Knowing that Christ** being raised from the dead **dieth no more;** death hath no more dominion over him.
10. **For** in that he died, **he died unto sin once:** but in that he liveth, **he liveth unto God.**
11. **Likewise reckon** ye also **yourselves to be dead** indeed **unto sin, but alive unto God through Jesus** Christ our Lord.
12. **Let not sin** therefore **reign in your mortal body,** that ye should obey it in the lusts thereof.
13. Neither yield ye your members *as* instruments of unrighteousness unto sin: **but yield yourselves unto God,** as those that are alive from the dead, **and your members *as* instruments of righteousness** unto God.
14. **For sin shall not have dominion over you:** for ye are not under the law, but under grace.
15. **What then? shall we sin, because we are** not under the law, but **under grace? God forbid.**
16. **Know ye not, that** to whom ye yield yourselves servants to obey, **his servants ye are to whom ye obey;** whether of sin unto death, or of obedience unto righteousness?

17. But God be thanked, that ye were the servants of sin, but ye have obeyed from the heart that form of doctrine which was delivered you. 18. **Being then made free from sin, ye became** the **servants of righteousness.** 19. I speak after the manner of men because of the infirmity of your flesh: for **as ye have yielded** your members servants **to uncleanness** and to iniquity unto iniquity; **even so now yield** your members servants **to righteousness unto holiness.** 20. For when ye were the servants of sin, ye were free from righteousness. 21. What fruit had ye then in those things whereof ye are now ashamed? for the end of those things *is* death. 22. **But now** being made **free from sin, and** become **servants to God, ye have your fruit unto holiness, and** the end **everlasting life.** 23. **For the wages of sin** *is* **death; but the gift of God** *is* **eternal life through Jesus Christ** our Lord.

CHAPTER 7

1. **Know ye not,** brethren, (for I speak to them that know the law,) how **that the law hath dominion over a man as long as he liveth?** 2. **For the woman** which hath an husband **is bound by the law to** *her* **husband so long as he liveth; but if the husband be dead, she is loosed** from the law of *her* husband. 3. So then if, while *her* husband liveth, she be married to another man, she shall be called an adulteress: but if her husband be dead, she is free from that law; so that she is no adulteress, though she be married to another man. 4. Wherefore, my brethren, **ye also are become dead to the law by** the body of **Christ; that ye should be married** to another, *even* **to him who is raised** from the dead, **that we should bring forth fruit** unto God. 5. For when we were in the flesh, the motions of sins, which were by the law, did work in our members to bring forth fruit unto death. 6. **But now we are delivered from the law,** that being dead wherein we were held; **that we should serve in newness of spirit,** and not *in* the oldness of the letter. 7. What shall we say then? *Is* **the law sin?** God forbid. **Nay, I had not known sin, but by the law:** for I had not known lust, except the law had said, Thou shalt not covet. 8. **But sin,** taking occasion **by the commandment, wrought** in me all manner of **concupiscence.** For without the law sin *was* dead. 9. **But I was alive without the law once: but when the commandment came, sin revived, and I died.** 10. **And the commandment, which** *was* *ordained* **to life, I found** *to be* **unto death.** 11. **For sin,** taking occasion **by the commandment,** deceived me, and by it **slew** *me.* 12. **Wherefore the law is holy,** and the commandment holy, and just, **and good.** 13. Was then that which is good made death unto me? God forbid. But sin, that it might appear sin, working death in me by that which is good; that sin by the commandment might become exceeding sinful. 14. **For** we know that

the law is spiritual: but I am carnal, sold under sin. 15. For that which I do I allow not: for what I would, that do I not; but what I hate, that do I.

16. If then I do that which I would not, I consent unto the law that *it is* good.

17. Now then it is no more I that do it, but sin that dwelleth in me.

18. For I know that in me (that is, in my flesh,) dwelleth no good thing:

for to will is present with me; but how to perform that which is good I find not. 19. For the good that I would do not: but the evil

which I would not, that I do.

20. Now if I do that I would not, it is no more I that do it, but sin that dwelleth in me.

21. I find then a law, that, when I would do good, evil is present with me.

22. For I delight in the law of God after the inward man: 23. But I see another law

in my members, warring against the law of my mind, and bringing me into captivity to the law of sin which is in my members.

24. O wretched man that I am! who shall deliver me from the body of this death? 25. I thank God through Jesus Christ our Lord. So then with the mind I myself serve the law of God; but with the flesh the law of sin.

CHAPTER 8

1. *There is* therefore now no condemnation to them

which are

in Christ Jesus, who walk not after the flesh, but after the Spirit. 2. For the law of the Spirit

of life in Christ Jesus

hath made me free

from the law of sin and death. 3. For what the law could not do, in that it was weak through the flesh,

God sending his own Son in the likeness of sinful flesh, and for sin, condemned sin in the flesh: 4. That the righteousness of the law might be fulfilled in us, who walk not after the flesh, but after the Spirit.

5. For they that are after the flesh do mind the things of the flesh; but they that are after the Spirit the things of the Spirit.

6. For to be carnally minded *is* death; but to be spiritually minded *is* life and peace. 7. Because the carnal mind *is* enmity against God:

for it is not subject to the law of God, neither indeed can be.

8. So then they that are in the flesh cannot please God. 9. But ye are not in the flesh, but in the Spirit, if so be that the Spirit of God dwell in you. Now if any man have not the Spirit of Christ, he is none of his.

10. And if Christ *be* in you, the body *is* dead because of sin; but the Spirit *is* life because of righteousness. 11. But if the Spirit of him that raised up Jesus

from the dead

dwell in you, he that raised up Christ from the dead shall also quicken your mortal bodies by his Spirit

that dwelleth in you.

12. Therefore, brethren, we are debtors, not to the flesh, to live after the flesh.

13. For if ye live after the flesh, ye shall die: but if ye through the Spirit do mortify the deeds of the body, ye shall live.

14. For as many as are led by the Spirit of God, they are the sons of God.

15. **For ye** have not received the spirit of bondage again to fear; but ye **have received the Spirit of adoption, whereby we cry, Abba, Father.**

16. **The Spirit itself beareth witness with our spirit, that we are the children of God:**

17. **And if children,** then heirs; **heirs of God, and joint-heirs with Christ; if so be that we suffer with** *him*, **that we may be also glorified together.**

18. **For** I reckon that **the sufferings of this present time** *are* **not** worthy *to be compared* **with the glory which shall be revealed** in us.

19. **For** the earnest expectation of **the creature waiteth for the manifestation of the sons of God.**

20. For the creature was made subject to vanity, not willingly, but by reason of him who hath subjected *the same* in hope,

21. **Because the creature itself also shall be delivered from** the bondage of **corruption into** the **glorious liberty** of the children of God.

22. **For we know that the whole creation groaneth and travaileth in pain together until now.**

23. **And** not only *they*, but **ourselves also,** which have the first fruits of the Spirit, even we ourselves **groan within** ourselves, **waiting for** the adoption, *to wit*, **the redemption of our body.**

24. **For we are saved by hope:** but hope that is seen is not hope: for what a man seeth, why doth he yet hope for?

25. **But if we hope for that we see not,** *then* **do we with patience wait for** *it*.

26. **Likewise the Spirit** also **helpeth our infirmities: for we know not what we should pray** for as we ought: **but the Spirit itself maketh intercession for us** with groanings which cannot be uttered.

27. **And** he that searcheth the hearts knoweth what *is* the mind of **the Spirit,** because he **maketh intercession** for the saints **according to** *the will* **of God.**

28. **And we know that all things work together for good to them that love God, to them** who are the **called according to** *his* **purpose.**

29. **For whom he did foreknow, he** also **did predestinate** *to be* **conformed to the image of his Son,** that he might be the firstborn among many brethren.

30. Moreover whom he did predestinate, **them he also called:** and whom he called, **them he also justified:** and whom he justified, **them he also glorified.**

31. What shall we then say to these things? **If God** *be* **for us, who** *can* **be against us?**

32. **He that spared not his own Son,** but delivered him up for us all, how **shall he not with him** also **freely give us all things?**

33. **Who shall lay any thing to the charge of God's elect? It** *is* **God that justifieth.**

34. Who *is* he that condemneth? *It is* **Christ that died,** **yea** rather, **that is risen** again, who is even at the right hand of God, **who also maketh**

intercession for us.

35. Who shall separate us from the love of Christ? *shall* tribulation, or distress, or persecution, or famine, or nakedness, or peril,

or sword?

36. As it is written, For thy sake we are killed all the day long; we are accounted as sheep for the slaughter.

37. Nay, in all these things we are more than conquerors through him that loved us.

38. For I am persuaded, that neither death, nor life, nor angels, nor principalities, nor powers, nor things present, nor things to come,

39. Nor height, nor depth, nor any other creature, shall be able to separate us from the love of God, which is in Christ Jesus our Lord.

CHAPTER 9

1. I say the truth in Christ, I lie not, my conscience also bearing me witness in the Holy Ghost,

2. That I have great heaviness and continual sorrow in my heart.

3. For I could wish that myself were accursed from Christ for my brethren, my kinsmen according to the flesh:

4. Who are Israelites; to whom *pertaineth* the adoption, and the glory, and the covenants, and the giving of the law, and the service *of God*, and the promises;

5. Whose *are* the fathers, and of whom as concerning the flesh Christ *came*, who is over all, God blessed for ever. Amen.

6. Not as though the word of God hath taken none effect. For they *are* not all Israel, which are of

Israel:

7. Neither, because they are the seed of Abraham, *are they* all children: but, In Isaac shall thy seed be called.

8. That is, They which are the children of the flesh, these *are* not the children of God: but the children of the promise are counted for the seed.

9. For this *is* the word of promise, At this time will I come, and Sarah shall have a son.

10. And not only *this*; but when Rebecca also had conceived by one, *even* by our father Isaac;

11. (For *the children* being not yet born, neither having done any good or evil, that the purpose of God according to election might stand, not of works, but of him that calleth;)

12. It was said unto her, The elder shall serve the younger.

13. As it is written, Jacob have I loved, but Esau have I hated.

14. What shall we say then? *Is there* unrighteousness with God? God forbid.

15. For he saith to Moses, I will have mercy on whom I will have mercy, and I will have compassion on whom I will have compassion.

16. So then *it is* not of him that willeth, nor of him that runneth, but of God that sheweth mercy.

17. For the scripture saith unto Pharaoh, Even for this same purpose have I raised thee up, that I might shew my power in thee, and that my name might be declared throughout all

the earth.

■ 18. **Therefore hath he mercy**
■ **on whom he will** *have mercy,*
■ **and whom he will**
■ **he hardeneth.**
■ 19. **Thou wilt say then unto**
■ **me, Why doth he yet find**
■ **fault? For who hath**
■ **resisted his will?**

20. Nay but, O man,

■ **who art thou that repliest**
■ **against God? Shall the**
■ **thing formed say to him**
■ **that formed** *it,* **Why hast**
■ **thou made me thus?**
■ 21. **Hath not the potter**
■ **power over the clay,** of the

same lump to make one vessel unto
honour, and another unto dishonour?
22. *What* if God, willing to shew *his*
wrath, and to make his power known,
endured with much longsuffering the
vessels of wrath fitted to destruction:
23. And that he might make known the
riches of his glory on the vessels
of mercy, which he had afore prepared
unto glory,
24. Even us, whom he hath called, not
of the Jews only, but also
of the Gentiles?

■ 25. **As he saith also in Osee,**
■ **I will call them my people,**
■ **which were not**
■ **my people;** and her beloved,

which was not beloved.
26. And it shall come to pass, *that* in
the place where it was said unto
them, Ye *are* not my people; there
shall they be called the children of the
living God.
27. Esaias also crieth concerning
Israel, Though the number of the
children of Israel be as the sand of the
sea, a remnant shall be saved:
28. For he will finish the work, and cut
it short in righteousness:
because a short work will the Lord
make upon the earth.
29. And as Esaias said before,
Except the Lord of Sabaoth had left
us a seed, we had been as Sodoma,
and been made like unto Gomorrha.

■ 30. **What shall we say then?**

■ **That the Gentiles, which**
■ **followed not after**
■ **righteousness, have**
■ **attained** to righteousness, even
■ **the righteousness** which is
■ **of faith.**
■ 31. **But Israel, which**
■ **followed after the law of**
■ **righteousness, hath not**
■ **attained** to the law of
■ **righteousness.**
■ 32. **Wherefore? Because**
■ *they sought it* **not by faith,**
■ **but** as it were
■ **by the works of the law.**

For they stumbled at
that stumblingstone;
33. As it is written, Behold, I lay in
Sion a stumblingstone and rock of
offence: and whosoever believeth on
him shall not be ashamed.

CHAPTER 10

■ 1. **Brethren, my heart's**
■ **desire** and prayer to God
■ **for Israel is, that they might**
■ **be saved.**
■ 2. **For** I bear them record that
■ **they have a zeal of God,**
■ **but not according**
■ **to knowledge.**
■ 3. **For they being ignorant of**
■ **God's righteousness, and**
■ **going about to establish**
■ **their own righteousness,**
■ **have not submitted**
  themselves
■ **unto the righteousness**
■ **of God.**
■ 4. **For Christ** *is* **the end of the**
■ **law for righteousness to**
■ **every one that believeth.**
■ 5. **For Moses describeth the**
■ **righteousness** which is
■ **of the law,** That the man which
  doeth those things shall live by them.
■ 6. **But the righteousness**
  which is
■ **of faith speaketh on this**
■ **wise,** Say not in thine heart, Who
  shall ascend into heaven? (that is, to
  bring Christ down *from above:*)
7. Or, Who shall descend into the

deep? (that is, to bring up Christ again from the dead.)

8. But what saith it? The word is nigh thee, *even* in thy mouth, and in thy heart: that is, the word of faith, which we preach;

9. **That if thou shalt confess with thy mouth the Lord Jesus, and shalt believe in thine heart that God hath raised him from the dead, thou shalt be saved.**

10. **For with the heart man believeth unto righteousness; and with the mouth confession is made unto salvation.**

11. **For the scripture saith, Whosoever believeth on him shall not be ashamed.**

12. For there is no difference between the Jew and the Greek: for the same Lord over all is rich unto all that call upon him.

13. **For whosoever shall call upon the name of the Lord shall be saved.**

14. **How then shall they call on him** in **whom they have not believed? and how shall they believe in him of whom they have not heard? and how shall they hear without a preacher?**

15. **And how shall they preach, except they be sent? as it is written, How beautiful are the feet of them that preach the gospel** of peace, and bring glad tidings of good things!

16. But they have not all obeyed the gospel. For Esaias saith, Lord, who hath believed our report?

17. **So then faith *cometh* by hearing, and hearing by the word of God.**

18. But I say, Have they not heard? Yes verily, their sound went into all the earth, and their words unto the ends of the world.

19. **But I say, Did not Israel know? First Moses saith,** I will provoke you to jealousy by *them that are* no people, *and* **by a foolish nation I will anger you.**

20. **But Esaias** is very bold, and **saith, I was found of them that sought me not;** I was made manifest unto them that asked not after me.

21. **But to Israel he saith,** All day long **I have stretched** forth **my hands unto a disobedient** and gainsaying **people.**

CHAPTER 11

1. **I say then, Hath God cast away his people? God forbid. For I also am an Israelite,** of the seed of Abraham, *of* the tribe of Benjamin.

2. **God hath not cast away his people** which he foreknew. Wot ye not what **the scripture saith of Elias? how he maketh intercession** to God **against Israel saying,**

3. **Lord, they have killed thy prophets,** and digged down thine altars; and I am left alone, **and they seek my life.**

4. **But what saith** the answer of **God** unto him? **I have reserved** to myself **seven thousand men,** who have not bowed the knee to *the image* of Baal.

5. **Even so then at this present time also there is a remnant according to the election of grace.**

6. **And if by grace, then *is it* no more of works:** otherwise grace is no more grace. But if *it be* of works, then it is no more grace: otherwise work is no more work.

7. **What then? Israel hath not obtained that which he seeketh** for; **but the election hath**

■ obtained it, and the rest
■ were blinded.
8. (According as it is written, God hath given them the spirit of slumber, eyes that they should not see, and ears that they should not hear;) unto this day.
9. And David saith, Let their table be made a snare, and a trap, and a stumblingblock, and a recompence unto them:
10. Let their eyes be darkened, that they may not see, and bow down their back alway.
■ 11. **I say then, Have they**
■ **stumbled that they should**
■ **fall? God forbid: but** *rather*
■ **through their fall salvation**
■ *is come* **unto the Gentiles,**
for to provoke them to jealousy.
12. Now if the fall of them *be* the riches of the world, and the diminishing of them the riches of the Gentiles; how much more their fulness?
■ 13. **For** I speak to you Gentiles, inasmuch
■ **as I am the apostle of the**
■ **Gentiles, I magnify mine**
■ **office:**
■ 14. **If by any means I may**
■ **provoke to emulation** *them*
■ *which are* **my flesh, and**
■ **might save some of them.**
15. For if the casting away of them *be* the reconciling of the world, what *shall* the receiving *of them be*, but life from the dead?
■ 16. **For if the firstfruit** *be*
■ **holy, the lump** *is* also
■ *holy*: **and if the**
■ **root** *be* **holy, so** *are*
■ **the branches.**
■ 17. **And if some** of the
■ **branches be broken off,**
■ **and thou, being a wild**
■ **olive tree, wert grafted in**
■ **among them, and** with them
■ **partakest of the root**
and fatness of the olive tree;
■ 18. **Boast not against the**
■ **branches.** But if thou boast,
■ **thou bearest not the root,**

■ **but the root thee.**
■ 19. **Thou wilt say** then,
■ **The branches were**
■ **broken** off,
■ **that I might be**
■ **grafted** in.
■ 20. **Well; because of**
■ **unbelief they were**
■ **broken** off,
■ **and thou standest by**
■ **faith. Be not highminded**:
but fear:
■ 21. **For if God spared not the**
■ **natural branches,** *take*
■ *heed* **lest he also**
■ **spare not thee.**
22. **Behold therefore the**
goodness and severity of
God: on them which fell,
severity; but toward thee,
goodness, if thou continue in *his* goodness: otherwise thou also shalt be cut off.
■ 23. **And they also, if they**
■ **abide not** still
■ **in unbelief, shall be grafted**
■ **in:** for God is able to graft them in
■ **again.**
24. For if thou wert cut out of the olive tree which is wild by nature, and wert grafted contrary to nature into a good olive tree: how much more shall these, which be the natural *branches*, be grafted into their own olive tree?
■ 25. **For** I would not, brethren, that ye should be ignorant of this mystery, lest ye should be wise in your own conceits; that
■ **blindness in part is**
■ **happened to Israel, until**
■ **the fulness of the Gentiles**
be come in.
■ 26. **And so all Israel shall**
■ **be saved: as it is written,**
There shall come out of Sion the Deliverer, and shall turn away ungodliness from Jacob:
■ 27. **For this** *is* **my covenant**
unto them, when
■ **I shall take away their sins.**
■ 28. **As concerning the**
■ **gospel,** *they are* **enemies**

■ for your sakes: but as
■ touching the election, *they*
■ *are* beloved for the
■ father's sakes.

29. For the gifts and calling of God *are*
without repentance.

■ 30. **For as ye** in times past have
not believed God, yet have now

■ **obtained mercy through**
■ **their unbelief:**

■ 31. **Even so** have these also
now not believed, that

■ **through your mercy**
■ **they also may obtain**
■ **mercy.**

32. For God hath concluded them all in
unbelief, that he might have mercy
upon all.

■ 33. **O the depth** of the riches both
■ **of the wisdom and**
■ **knowledge of God!**
■ **how unsearchable** *are* his
■ **judgments,** and his ways past
finding out!

■ 34. **For who hath known the**
■ **mind of the Lord?** or who hath
been his counsellor?

35. Or who hath first given to him, and
it shall be recompensed unto him
again?

■ 36. **For of him, and through**
■ **him, and to him,** *are* all
■ **things:** to whom *be* glory for ever.
Amen.

CHAPTER 12
■ 1. **I beseech you**
therefore, brethren,

■ **by the mercies of God, that**
■ **ye present your bodies a**
■ **living sacrifice, holy,**
■ **acceptable unto God,**
which is your reasonable service.

■ 2. **And be not conformed to**
■ **this world: but be ye**
■ **transformed by the**
■ **renewing of your mind,** that
ye may prove what *is* that good, and
acceptable, and perfect, will of God.

■ 3. **For I say,** through the grace
given unto me,
■ **to every man**
that is among you,

■ not to think *of himself* more
■ highly than he ought to think;
■ but to think soberly,
according as God hath dealt to every
man the measure of faith.

■ 4. **For as we have many**
■ **members in one body,** and all
members have not the same office:

■ 5. So we, *being* many, are
■ one body in Christ, and every
one members one of another.

■ 6. **Having then gifts differing**
■ **according to the grace** that is
■ **given to us,** whether prophecy, *let*
us prophesy according to the
proportion of faith;

7. Or ministry, *let us wait* on *our*
ministering: or he that teacheth, on
teaching;

8. Or he that exhorteth, on
exhortation: he that giveth, *let him do*
it with simplicity; he that ruleth, with
diligence; he that sheweth mercy, with
cheerfulness.

■ 9. *Let* love be without
■ dissimulation. Abhor that
■ which is evil; cleave
■ to that which is good.

■ 10. *Be* kindly affectioned
■ one to another
with brotherly love; in honour
■ preferring one another;

■ 11. Not slothful in business;
■ fervent in spirit;
serving the Lord;

■ 12. Rejoicing in hope;
■ patient in tribulation;
■ continuing instant
■ in prayer;

■ 13. Distributing to the
■ necessity of saints;
given to hospitality.

■ 14. Bless them which
■ persecute you:
bless, and curse not.

■ 15. Rejoice with them that do
■ rejoice, and weep with
■ them that weep.

16. *Be* of the same mind
one toward another.

■ Mind not high things, but
■ condescend to men of low
■ estate. Be not wise in your

own conceits.

17. **Recompense to no man evil for evil.** Provide things honest in the sight of all men.

18. **If it be possible,** as much as lieth in you, **live peaceably with all men.**

19. **Dearly beloved, avenge not yourselves,** but *rather* give place unto wrath: **for it is written, Vengeance** *is* **mine;** I will repay, **saith the Lord.**

20. **Therefore if thine enemy hunger, feed him;** if he thirst, give him drink: for **in so doing thou shalt heap coals of fire on his head.**

21. **Be not overcome of evil, but overcome evil with good.**

CHAPTER 13

1. **Let every soul be subject unto the higher powers. For there is no power but** of God: the powers **that** be are **ordained of God.**

2. **Whosoever therefore resisteth the power, resisteth** the ordinance of **God: and** they that resist **shall receive** to themselves **damnation.**

3. **For rulers are not a terror to good works, but to the evil.** Wilt thou then not be afraid of the power? do that which is good, and thou shalt have praise of the same:

4. **For he is the minister of God to thee for good. But if thou do** that which is **evil, be afraid;** for he beareth not the sword in vain: **for he is** the minister of God, **a revenger to** *execute* **wrath upon him that doeth evil.**

5. **Wherefore** *ye* **must needs be subject,** not only for wrath, but also for conscience sake.

6. For for this cause **pay ye tribute also: for they are God's ministers,** attending continually upon this very thing.

7. **Render therefore to all their dues:** tribute to whom tribute *is due*; custom to whom custom; fear to whom fear; honour to whom honour.

8. **Owe no man any thing, but to love one another: for he that loveth** another hath **fulfilled the law.**

9. For this, Thou shalt not commit adultery, Thou shalt not kill, Thou shalt not steal, Thou shalt not bear false witness, Thou shalt not covet; and **if** *there be* **any other commandment, it is** briefly comprehended **in this saying,** namely, **Thou shalt love thy neighbour as thyself.**

10. Love worketh no ill to his neighbour: therefore love *is* the fulfilling of the law.

11. And that, knowing the time, that now *it is* high time to awake out of sleep: for now is our salvation nearer than when we believed.

12. The night is far spent, the day is at hand: **let us** therefore **cast off the works of darkness, and** let us **put on the armour of light.**

13. **Let us walk honestly,** as in the day; not in rioting and drunkenness, not in chambering and wantonness, not in strife and envying.

14. **But put ye on the Lord Jesus Christ, and make not provision for the flesh,** to *fulfil* the lusts *thereof.*

CHAPTER 14

1. **Him that is weak in the faith receive** ye, *but* **not to** doubtful **disputations.**

2. **For one believeth that he**

may eat all things: another, who is weak, eateth herbs.

3. Let not him that eateth despise him that eateth not; and let not him which eateth not judge him that eateth: for God hath received him.

4. Who art thou that judgest another man's servant? to his own master he standeth or falleth. Yea, he shall be holden up: for God is able to make him stand.

5. One man esteemeth one day above another: another esteemeth every day *alike*. Let every man be fully persuaded in his own mind.

6. He that regardeth the day, regardeth *it* unto the Lord; and he that regardeth not the day, to the Lord he doth not regard *it*.

He that eateth, eateth to the Lord, for he giveth God thanks; and he that eateth not, to the Lord he eateth not, and giveth God thanks.

7. For none of us liveth to himself, and no man dieth to himself.

8. For whether we live, we live unto the Lord; and whether we die, we die unto the Lord:

whether we live therefore, or die, we are the Lord's.

9. For to this end Christ both died, and rose, and revived, that he might be Lord both of the dead and living.

10. But why dost thou judge thy brother? or why dost thou set at nought thy brother? for we shall all stand before the judgment seat of Christ.

11. For it is written, *As* I live, saith the Lord, every knee shall bow to me, and every tongue shall confess to God.

12. So then every one of us shall give account of himself to God.

13. Let us not therefore judge one another any more: but judge this rather, that no man put a stumblingblock or an occasion to fall in *his* brother's way.

14. I know, and am persuaded by the Lord Jesus, that *there is* nothing unclean of itself: but to him that esteemeth any thing to be unclean, to him *it is* unclean.

15. But if thy brother be grieved with *thy* meat, now walkest thou not charitably. Destroy not him with thy meat, for whom Christ died.

16. Let not then your good be evil spoken of:

17. For the kingdom of God is not meat and drink; but righteousness, and peace, and joy in the Holy Ghost.

18. For he that in these things serveth Christ *is* acceptable to God, and approved of men.

19. Let us therefore follow after the things which make for peace, and things wherewith one may edify another.

20. For meat destroy not the work of God. All things indeed *are* pure; but *it is* evil for that man who eateth with offence.

21. *It is* good neither to eat flesh, nor to drink wine, nor *any thing* whereby thy brother stumbleth, or is offended, or is made weak.

22. Hast thou faith? have *it* to thyself before God. Happy *is* he that condemneth not himself in that thing which he alloweth.

23. And he that doubteth is

damned if he eat,
because *he eateth* not of faith:
for whatsoever *is* not of faith is sin.

CHAPTER 15
1. We then that are strong ought to bear the infirmities of **the weak, and not to please ourselves.**
2. Let every one of us please *his* neighbour for *his* good to edification.
3. For even Christ pleased not himself; but, as it is written, The reproaches of them that reproached thee fell on me.
4. For whatsoever things were written aforetime were written for our learning, that we through patience and comfort of **the scriptures might have hope.**
5. Now the God of patience and consolation grant you to be likeminded one toward another according to Christ Jesus:
6. That ye may with one mind *and* one mouth glorify God, even the Father of our Lord Jesus Christ.
7. Wherefore receive ye one another, as Christ also received us to the glory of God.
8. Now I say that Jesus Christ was a minister of the circumcision for the truth of God, **to confirm the promises *made* unto the fathers:**
9. **And that the Gentiles might glorify God for *his* mercy; as it is written,** For this cause **I will confess to thee among the Gentiles,** and sing unto thy name.
10. And again he saith, Rejoice, ye Gentiles, with his people.
11. **And again, Praise the Lord, all ye Gentiles;** and laud him, all ye people.
12. **And again, Esaias saith, There shall be a root of**

Jesse, and he that shall rise to reign over the Gentiles; **in him shall the Gentiles trust.**
13. **Now the God of hope fill you with all joy** and peace **in believing,** that ye may abound in hope, **through** the power of **the Holy Ghost.**
14. **And I myself** also **am persuaded** of you, my brethren, **that ye also are full of goodness,** filled with all knowledge, **able also to admonish one another.**
15. **Nevertheless, brethren, I have written the more boldly** unto you in some sort, as putting you in mind, **because of the grace that is given to me** of God,
16. **That I should be the minister of Jesus Christ to the Gentiles,** ministering the gospel of God, **that** the offering up of the Gentiles might be acceptable, being sanctified by the Holy Ghost.
17. **I have therefore whereof I may glory through Jesus** Christ in those things which pertain to God.
18. **For I will not dare to speak of** any of those **things which Christ hath not wrought by me, to make the Gentiles obedient,** by word and deed,
19. **Through mighty signs and wonders, by the power of the Spirit of God; so** that from Jerusalem, and round about unto Illyricum, **I have fully preached the gospel** of Christ.
20. Yea, so have I strived to preach the gospel, **not where Christ was named,** lest I should build upon another man's foundation:

■ 21. **But as it is written, To**
■ **whom he was not spoken**
■ **of, they shall see:** and they that
have not heard shall understand.
■ 22. **For which cause** also
■ **I have been much hindered**
■ **from coming to you.**
■ 23. **But** now having no more place in
these parts, and
■ **having a great desire**
these many years
■ **to come unto you;**
■ 24. **Whensoever I take my**
■ **journey into Spain, I will**
■ **come to you:** for I trust to see
you in my journey, and to be brought
on my way thitherward by you, if first I
be somewhat filled with your *company.*
■ 25. **But now I go**
■ **unto Jerusalem**
to minister unto the saints.
■ 26. **For it hath pleased them**
■ **of Macedonia and Achaia**
■ **to make a certain**
■ **contribution for the poor**
■ **saints** which are
■ **at Jerusalem.**
27. It hath pleased them verily; and
their debtors they are. For if the
Gentiles have been made partakers of
their spiritual things, their duty is
also to minister unto them in carnal
things.
28. When therefore I have performed
this, and have sealed to them this
fruit, I will come by you into Spain.
29. And I am sure that, when I come
unto you, I shall come in the fulness
of the blessing of the gospel of Christ.
■ 30. **Now I beseech you,**
■ **brethren, for** the Lord Jesus
■ **Christ's sake, and**
for the love of the Spirit,
■ **that ye strive together** with me
■ **in** *your* **prayers to**
■ **God for me;**
■ 31. **That I may be delivered**
■ **from them that do not**
■ **believe in Judaea; and**
■ **that my service** which *I have*
■ **for Jerusalem may be**
■ **accepted of the saints;**
32. That I may come unto you with joy

by the will of God, and may with you
be refreshed.
33. Now the God of peace *be* with you
all. Amen.

CHAPTER 16
1. I commend unto you Phoebe our
sister, which is a servant of the
church which is at Cenchrea:
2. That ye receive her in the Lord, as
becometh saints, and that ye
assist her in whatsoever business
she hath need of you: for she hath
been a succourer of many, and of
myself also.
3. Greet Priscilla and Aquila my
helpers in Christ Jesus:
4. Who have for my life laid down their
own necks: unto whom not only I
give thanks, but also all the churches
of the Gentiles.
5. Likewise *greet* the church that is in
their house. Salute my well-beloved
Epaenetus, who is the firstfruits of
Achaia unto Christ.
6. Greet Mary, who bestowed much
labour on us.
7. Salute Andronicus and Junia, my
kinsmen, and my fellow-prisoners,
who are of note among the apostles,
who also were in Christ before me.
8. Greet Amplias my beloved
in the Lord.
9. Salute Urbane, our helper in Christ,
and Stachys my beloved.
10. Salute Apelles approved in Christ.
Salute them which are of Aristobulus'
household.
11. Salute Herodion my kinsman.
Greet them that be of the *household* of
Narcissus, which are in the Lord.
12. Salute Tryphena and Tryphosa,
who labour in the Lord. Salute the
beloved Persis, which laboured much
in the Lord.
13. Salute Rufus chosen in the Lord,
and his mother and mine.
14. Salute Asyncritus, Phlegon,
Hermas, Patrobas, Hermes, and the
brethren which are with them.
15. Salute Philologus, and Julia,
Nereus, and his sister, and Olympas,
and all the saints which are with them.

16. **Salute one another with an holy kiss.** The churches of Christ salute you.

17. **Now I beseech you, brethren, mark them which cause divisions** and offences contrary to the doctrine which ye have learned; **and avoid them.**

18. **For they** that are such **serve not our Lord** Jesus Christ, **but their own belly; and** by good words and fair speeches **deceive the hearts of the simple.**

19. For your obedience is come abroad unto all *men*. I am glad therefore on your behalf: but yet **I would have you wise unto that which is good,** and simple concerning evil.

20. **And the God of peace shall bruise Satan under your feet shortly.** The grace of our Lord Jesus Christ *be* with you. Amen.

21. Timotheus my workfellow, and Lucius, and Jason, and Sosipater, my kinsmen, salute you.

22. I Tertius, who wrote *this* epistle, salute you in the Lord.

23. Gaius mine host, and of the whole church, saluteth you. Erastus the chamberlain of the city saluteth you, and Quartus a brother.

24. The grace of our Lord Jesus Christ *be* with you all. Amen.

25. **Now to him that is of power to stablish you according to** my gospel, and the preaching of Jesus **Christ, according to the revelation of the mystery, which was** kept **secret since the world began,**

26. **But now is made manifest,** and **by the scriptures** of the prophets, **according to the commandment of** the everlasting **God,** made known to all nations **for the obedience of faith:**

27. **To God only wise,** *be* **glory through Jesus Christ** for ever. **Amen.**

THE EPISTLE TO THE ROMANS
The bridge between the Gospels, the Acts, and the New Testament

Paul's Epistle to the
■ **Romans is** recognized as
■ **one of the great**
■ **masterpieces of literature,**
both sacred
■ **and** secular. Addressed to
Christians living in Rome – the city
which was the center of the ancient
world – Romans
■ **is the only book in the New**
■ **Testament,** with the possible
exception of Hebrews,
■ **which was written as a**
■ **Theological Treatise**
rather than an encouraging or
correcting letter.
■ **In Romans, Paul** forcefully
■ **presents the entire scope**
■ **of Christian doctrine and**
provides an authoritative theology as
well as expresses the universality of
the Gospel. Romans
■ **gives a comprehensive**
■ **interpretation of the**
■ **Incarnation and the**
■ **ministry of Christ, showing**
with convincing logic and supported
by Old Testament scriptures,
■ **that God has made a**
■ **radical breakthrough**

into human history
■ **in the life, death, and**
■ **resurrection of His Son.**
■ **The** dilemma of the
■ **human condition,**
■ **sinfulness, is met with**
a profound solution –
■ **the righteousness of God**
■ **made real** for the individual
■ **by faith.** Many of the great revivals
began with a study of Romans.
■ **Augustine, Luther and**
■ **Wesley, credit Romans as**
■ **the source from which they**
■ **gained an understanding**
■ **of the Gospel.**
■ **Christian theology has**
■ **never had a higher**
■ **expression** than presented by
Paul in Romans under the inspiration
of the Holy Spirit.
■ **The Epistle has another**
■ **significance** for the student of
the Bible.
■ **It interprets the**
■ **life of Jesus as seen in the**
■ **Gospels, and** finally, it
■ **forms a bridge between**
■ **the Acts and the rest of the**
■ **New Testament.**

THE FIRST EPISTLE TO THE CORINTHIANS

BACKGROUND INFORMATION

Author – Paul, an Apostle.
Date Written – probably
between 55 and **60** A.D.

Number of:
Verses -   437
Chapters -   16
Total Words - 9,489
Scan Words - 4,543
Scan Words represent 47 %
of Total Words.

Theme – written to reveal the
new life believers have in
Christ and
**how believers should
conduct themselves
individually and as
members of the Church.**

OUTLINE OF THE EPISTLE

I.   Paul denounces factions
and stresses
**the need for Church
discipline.**
Chapters 1—6

II. Paul answers questions
**concerning marriage
and** the Christian's
influence upon others.
Chapters 6—10

III. Paul contrasts
disorderly worship with
the way of love and
explains
the meaning of the
resurrection.
Chapter 11—16

CHAPTER 1

1. **Paul** called *to be* an apostle of Jesus Christ through the will of God,

and Sosthenes our brother,

2. **Unto the church of God** which is **at Corinth,** to them that are sanctified in Christ Jesus, called *to be* saints, with all that in every place call upon the name of Jesus Christ our Lord, both theirs and ours:

3. **Grace** *be* **unto you,** and peace, from God our Father, and *from* the Lord Jesus Christ.

4. **I thank** my **God** always on your behalf, **for the grace** of God which is **given you by Jesus Christ;**

5. **That in every thing ye are enriched by him,** in all utterance, and *in* all knowledge;

6. Even as the testimony of Christ was confirmed in you:

7. **So that ye come behind in no gift; waiting for the coming of** our Lord Jesus **Christ:**

8. **Who shall also confirm you** unto the end, *that ye may be* **blameless** in the day of our Lord Jesus Christ.

9. God *is* faithful, by whom ye were called unto the fellowship of his Son Jesus Christ our Lord.

10. **Now I beseech you,** brethren, **by** the name of **our Lord** Jesus Christ, that ye all speak the same thing, and *that* **there be no divisions among you;** but *that* ye be perfectly joined together in the same mind and in the same judgment.

11. **For it hath been declared** unto me of you, my brethren, by them *which are of the house* of Chloe, **that there are contentions among you.**

12. Now this I say, that **every one of you saith, I am of Paul;** and **I of Apollos;** and **I of Cephas; and I of Christ.**

13. **Is Christ divided? was Paul crucified for you? or were ye baptized in the name of Paul?**

14. **I thank God that I baptized none of you, but Crispus and Gaius;**

15. **Lest any should say that I** had **baptized in mine own name.**

16. And I baptized also the household of Stephanas: besides, I know not whether I baptized any other.

17. **For Christ sent me not to baptize, but to preach** the gospel: **not with wisdom of words, lest the cross** of Christ should **be made of none effect.**

18. **For** the preaching of **the cross is to them that perish foolishness; but unto us which are saved it is the power of God.**

19. **For it is written, I will destroy the wisdom of the wise,** and will bring to nothing the understanding of the prudent.

20. Where *is* the wise? where *is* the scribe? where *is* the disputer of this world? **hath not God made foolish the wisdom of this world?**

21. **For after** that in the wisdom of God **the world by wisdom knew not God, it pleased God by the foolishness of preaching to save them that believe.**

22. **For the Jews require a sign, and the Greeks** seek after **wisdom:**

23. **But we preach Christ crucified,** unto the Jews a stumblingblock, and unto the Greeks foolishness;

24. But unto them which are called, both Jews and Greeks, Christ

the power of God, and the wisdom of God.

25. Because the foolishness of God is wiser than men; and the weakness of God is stronger than men.

26. For ye see your calling, brethren, how that not many wise men after the flesh, not many mighty, not many noble, *are called:*

27. But God hath chosen the foolish things of the world to confound the wise; and God hath chosen the weak things of the world to confound the things which are mighty;

28. And base things of the world, and things which are despised, hath God chosen, *yea*, and things which are not, to bring to nought things that are:

29. That no flesh should glory in his presence.

30. But of him are ye in Christ Jesus, who of God is made unto us wisdom, and righteousness, and sanctification, and redemption:

31. That, according as it is written, He that glorieth, let him glory in the Lord.

CHAPTER 2

1. And I, brethren, when I came to you, came not with excellency of speech or of wisdom, declaring unto you the testimony of God.

2. For I determined not to know any thing among you, save Jesus Christ, and him crucified.

3. And I was with you in weakness, and in fear, and in much trembling.

4. And my speech and my preaching *was* not with enticing words of man's wisdom, but in demonstration of the Spirit and of power:

5. That your faith should not stand in the wisdom of men, but in the power of God.

6. Howbeit we speak wisdom among them that are perfect: yet not the wisdom of this world, nor of the princes of this world, that come to nought:

7. But we speak the wisdom of God in a mystery, *even* the hidden *wisdom*, which God ordained before the world unto our glory:

8. Which none of the princes of this world knew: for had they known *it*, they would not have crucified the Lord of glory.

9. But as it is written, Eye hath not seen, nor ear heard, neither have entered into the heart of man, the things which God hath prepared for them that love him.

10. But God hath revealed *them* unto us by his Spirit: for the Spirit searcheth all things, yea, the deep things of God.

11. For what man knoweth the things of a man, save the spirit of man which is in him? even so the things of God knoweth no man, but the Spirit of God.

12. Now we have received, not the spirit of the world, but the spirit which is of God; that we might know the things that are freely given to us of God.

13. Which things also we speak, not in the words which man's wisdom teacheth, but which the Holy Ghost teacheth; comparing spiritual things with spiritual.

14. But the natural man receiveth not the things of the Spirit of God: for they are foolishness unto him: neither can he know *them*, because they are

spiritually discerned.

15. But he that is spiritual judgeth all things, yet he himself is judged of no man.

16. For who hath known the mind of the Lord, that he may instruct him? But we have the mind of Christ.

CHAPTER 3

1. And I, brethren, could not speak unto you as unto spiritual, but as unto carnal, *even* as unto babes in Christ.

2. I have fed you with milk, and not with meat: for hitherto ye were not able *to bear it*, neither yet now are ye able.

3. For ye are yet carnal: for whereas *there is* among you envying, and strife, and divisions, are ye not carnal, and walk as men?

4. For while one saith, I am of Paul; and another, I *am* of Apollos; are ye not carnal?

5. Who then is Paul, and who *is* Apollos, but ministers by whom ye believed, even as the Lord gave to every man?

6. I have planted, Apollos watered; but God gave the increase.

7. So then neither is he that planteth any thing, neither he that watereth; but God that giveth the increase.

8. Now he that planteth and he that watereth are one: and every man shall receive his own reward according to his own labour.

9. For we are labourers together with God: ye are God's husbandry, *ye are* God's building.

10. According to the grace of God which is given unto me, as a wise masterbuilder,

I have laid the foundation, and another buildeth thereon.

But let every man take heed how he buildeth thereupon.

11. For other foundation can no man lay than that is laid, which is Jesus Christ.

12. Now if any man build upon this foundation gold, silver, precious stones, wood, hay, stubble;

13. Every man's work shall be made manifest: for the day shall declare it, because it shall be revealed by fire; and the fire shall try every man's work of what sort it is.

14. If any man's work abide which he hath built thereupon, he shall receive a reward.

15. If any man's work shall be burned, he shall suffer loss: but he himself shall be saved; yet so as by fire.

16. Know ye not that ye are the temple of God, and *that* the Spirit of God dwelleth in you?

17. If any man defile the temple of God, him shall God destroy: for the temple of God is holy, which *temple* ye are.

18. Let no man deceive himself. If any man among you seemeth to be wise in this world, let him become a fool, that he may be wise

19. For the wisdom of this world is foolishness with God. For it is written, He taketh the wise in their own craftiness.

20. And again, The Lord knoweth the thoughts of the wise, that they are vain.

21. Therefore let no man glory in men. For all things are yours;

22. Whether Paul, or Apollos, or Cephas, or the world, or life, or death, or things present, or things to come;

all are yours;

■ 23. **And ye are Christ's; and**
■ **Christ** *is* **God's.**

CHAPTER 4
■ 1. **Let a man so account** of
■ **us, as** of the
■ **ministers** of Christ,
■ **and stewards** of the mysteries
■ **of God.**
■ 2. **Moreover it is required in**
■ **stewards, that a**
■ **man be** found
■ **faithful.**
3. But with me
■ **it is a very small thing**
■ **that I** should
■ **be judged** of you, or
■ **of man's judgment:**
yea, I judge not mine own self.
■ 4. **For** I know nothing by myself; yet
am I not hereby justified: but
■ **he that judgeth me**
■ **is the Lord.**
■ 5. **Therefore judge nothing**
before the time,
■ **until the Lord come,** who both
will bring to light the hidden things of
darkness, and will make manifest the
counsels of the hearts: and then shall
every man have praise of God.
■ 6. **And these things,**
■ **brethren, I have in a figure**
■ **transferred to myself and** *to*
■ **Apollos** for your sakes;
■ **that ye might learn** in us
■ **not to think** *of men*
above that which is written, that no
one of you be puffed up for one
against another.
7. For who maketh thee to differ *from
another*? and
what hast thou that thou didst not
receive? now if thou didst receive *it*,
why dost thou glory, as if thou hadst
not received *it*?
8. Now ye are full, now ye are rich,
■ **ye have reigned as kings**
■ **without us: and I would to**
■ **God ye did reign,**
that we also might reign with you.
■ 9. **For I think that God hath**
■ **set forth** us

■ **the apostles last,**
as it were appointed to death: for we
are made a spectacle unto the world,
and to angels, and to men.
■ 10. **We** *are* **fools for Christ's**
■ **sake,** but ye *are* wise in Christ; we
are weak, but ye *are* strong; ye *are*
honourable, but we *are* despised.
■ 11. **Even unto this** present
■ **hour we** both
■ **hunger,** and
■ **thirst,** and are naked,
and are buffeted,
■ **and have no certain**
■ **dwellingplace;**
■ 12. **And labour,** working
■ **with our own hands:**
being reviled, we bless; being
persecuted, we suffer it:
13. Being defamed, we entreat:
■ **we are made as the filth of**
■ **the world,** *and are* the offscouring
of all things unto this day.
■ 14. **I write not these things to**
■ **shame you, but** as my
beloved sons
■ **I warn** *you.*
■ 15. **For though ye have ten**
■ **thousand instructors in**
■ **Christ, yet** *h ave ye* **not**
■ **many fathers:**
for in Christ Jesus I have begotten
you through the gospel.
■ 16. **Wherefore** I beseech you,
■ **be** ye
■ **followers of me.**
■ 17. **For this cause have I**
■ **sent** unto you
■ **Timotheus,** who is my beloved
son, and faithful in the Lord,
■ **who shall bring you into**
■ **remembrance of my ways**
which be
■ **in Christ,** as I teach every where in
every church.
■ 18. **Now some are puffed**
■ **up, as though I would not**
■ **come** to you.
■ 19. **But I will come** to you shortly,
■ **if the Lord will,** and will know, not
the speech of them which are puffed
up, but the power.
20. For the kingdom of God *is* not in

word, but in power.

21. **What will ye? shall I come** unto you **with a rod, or in love,** and *in* the spirit of meekness?

CHAPTER 5

1. **It is reported** commonly *that there is* **fornication among you, and** such fornication as is not so much as named among the Gentiles, **that one should have his father's wife.**

2. **And ye** are puffed up, and **have not** rather **mourned, that he that hath done this deed might be taken away** from among you.

3. **For I** verily, as absent in body, but present in spirit, **have judged already,** as though I were present, *concerning* **him that hath so done this deed,**

4. In the name of our Lord Jesus Christ, when ye are gathered together, and my spirit, with the power of our Lord Jesus Christ,

5. **To deliver such an one unto Satan for the destruction of the flesh, that the spirit may be saved** in the day of the Lord Jesus.

6. Your glorying *is* not good. **Know ye not that a little leaven leaveneth the whole lump?**

7. **Purge out therefore the old leaven,** that ye may be a new lump, as ye are unleavened. For even Christ our passover is sacrificed for us:

8. **Therefore let us keep the feast, not with old leaven,** neither with the leaven of malice and wickedness; **but with** the unleavened *bread* of **sincerity and truth.**

9. **I wrote unto you** in an epistle **not to company with fornicators:**

10. **Yet not altogether with the fornicators of this world,** or with the covetous, or extortioners, or with idolaters; **for then must ye needs go out of the world.**

11. **But now I have written** unto you **not to keep company, if any man that is called a brother be a fornicator,** or covetous, or an idolater, or a railer, or a drunkard, or an extortioner; **with such an one no not to eat.**

12. For what have I to do to judge them also that are without? do not ye judge them that are within?

13. But them that are without God judgeth. **Therefore put away from among yourselves that wicked person.**

CHAPTER 6

1. **Dare any** of you, having a matter against another, **go to law before the unjust, and not before the saints?**

2. **Do ye not know that the saints shall judge the world? and** if the world shall be judged by you, **are ye unworthy to judge the smallest matters?**

3. **Know ye not that we shall judge angels?** how much more things that pertain to this life?

4. **If then ye have judgments** of things pertaining to this life, **set them to judge who are least esteemed in the church.**

5. I speak to your shame. Is it so, that there **is not a wise man among you?** no, not one that shall be **able to judge between** his **brethren?**

6. **But brother goeth to law with brother,** and that **before the unbelievers.**

7. Now therefore there is utterly a fault

among you, because ye go to law one with another.

■ **Why** do ye
■ **not rather take wrong? why** do ye
■ **not rather** *suffer yourselves to* **be defrauded?**

8. Nay, ye do wrong, and defraud, and that *your* brethren.

9. ■ **Know ye not that the** ■ **unrighteous shall not** ■ **inherit the kingdom** of God? ■ **Be not deceived: neither** ■ **fornicators,** nor ■ **idolaters,** nor ■ **adulterers,** nor ■ **effeminate,** nor ■ **abusers of themselves** ■ **with mankind,**

10. ■ **Nor thieves,** nor ■ **covetous,** nor ■ **drunkards,** nor ■ **revilers, nor extortioners,** ■ **shall inherit the kingdom** of God

11. ■ **And such were some of** ■ **you:** but ye are washed, but ye are sanctified, ■ **but ye are justified in the** ■ **name of** the Lord ■ **Jesus, and by the Spirit** of our God.

12. ■ **All things are lawful** unto me, ■ **but all things are not** ■ **expedient:** all things are lawful for me, but I will not be brought under the power of any.

13. Meats for the belly, and the belly for meats: but God shall destroy both it and them. Now ■ **the body** *is* **not for** ■ **fornication, but for the** ■ **Lord;** and the Lord for the body.

14. ■ **And God** hath both ■ **raised up the Lord, and will** ■ **also raise up us** by his own power.

15. ■ **Know ye not that your** ■ **bodies are the members of** ■ **Christ?** shall I then take the members of Christ, and ■ **make** *them* **the members of**

■ **an harlot?** God forbid.

16. What? know ye not that he which is joined to an harlot is one body? for two, saith he, shall be one flesh.

17. But he that is joined unto the Lord is one spirit.

18. ■ **Flee fornication.** Every sin that a man doeth is without the body; but he that committeth fornication sinneth against his own body.

19. ■ **What? know ye not that** ■ **your body is the temple of** ■ **the Holy Ghost** *which is* in you, which ye have of God, ■ **and ye are not your own?**

20. ■ **For ye are bought with a** ■ **price: therefore glorify God** ■ **in your body,** and in your spirit, which are God's.

CHAPTER 7

1. Now concerning the things whereof ye wrote unto me: ■ *It is* **good for a man not to** ■ **touch a woman.**

2. ■ **Nevertheless,** *to avoid* ■ **fornication, let every man** ■ **have his own wife, and let** ■ **every woman have** ■ **her own husband.**

3. ■ **Let the husband render** unto the wife ■ **due benevolence: and** ■ **likewise** also ■ **the wife** unto the husband.

4. ■ **The wife hath not power of** ■ **her own body,** but the husband: and ■ **likewise also the husband** ■ **hath not power of his own** ■ **body,** but the wife.

5. ■ **Defraud ye not one the** ■ **other, except** *it be* with consent for a time, ■ **that ye may give** ■ **yourselves to fasting and** ■ **prayer;** and come together again, that Satan tempt you not for your incontinency.

6. ■ **But I speak this by** ■ **permission,** *and* **not of** ■ **commandment.**

7. ■ **For I would that all men**

were even
as I myself. But every man
hath his proper gift of God,
one after this manner,
and another after that.
8. I say therefore to the
unmarried and widows, It
is good for them
if they abide even
as I.
9. But if they cannot contain,
let them marry:
for it is better to marry than to burn.
10. And unto the married I
command, *yet* not I, but the
Lord, Let not the wife depart
from *her* husband:
11. But and if she depart, let
her remain unmarried or be
reconciled to *her* husband: and
let not the husband put
away *his* wife.
12. But to the rest speak I,
not the Lord:
If any brother hath a wife
that believeth not, and she
be pleased to dwell with
him, let him not put
her away.
13. And the woman which hath an
husband that believeth not, and if he
be pleased to dwell with her, let her
not leave him.
14. For the unbelieving
husband is sanctified by
the wife, and the
unbelieving wife is sanctified
by the husband:
else were your children unclean;
but now are they holy.
15. But if the unbelieving
depart, let him depart. A
brother or a sister is not
under bondage in such
cases: but God hath
called us to peace.
16. For what
knowest thou, O wife,
whether thou shalt save *thy*
husband? or how knowest thou,
O man, whether thou shalt save
thy wife?
17. But as God hath distributed to
every man,
as the Lord hath called
every one, so let him walk.
And so ordain I in all churches.
18. Is any man called being
circumcised? let him not
become uncircumcised. Is
any called in
uncircumcision? let him not
be circumcised.
19. Circumcision is nothing,
and uncircumcision is
nothing, but the keeping of
the commandments
of God.
20. Let every man abide in the same
calling wherein he was called.
21. Art thou called *being* a servant?
care not for it: but if thou mayest be
made free, use *it* rather.
22. For he that is called
in the Lord,
being a servant, is the
Lord's freeman: likewise
also
he that is called, *being*
free, is Christ's servant.
23. Ye are bought with a
price; be not ye the
servants of men.
24. Brethren, let every man, wherein
he is called, therein abide with God.
25. Now concerning virgins I
have no commandment of
the Lord: yet I give my
judgment, as one that hath
obtained mercy of the Lord
to be faithful.
26. I suppose therefore that this
is good for the present distress,
I say,
that *it is* good for a man so
to be.
27. Art thou bound unto a wife? seek
not to be loosed. Art thou loosed
from a wife? seek not a wife.
28. But and if thou marry,
thou hast not sinned; and if a
virgin marry, she hath not sinned.
Nevertheless such shall have trouble
in the flesh: but I spare you.
29. But this I say,
brethren, the time *is* short: it

■ **remaineth, that** both
■ **they that have wives be as**
■ **though they had none;**
30. And they that weep, as though they wept not; and they that rejoice, as though they rejoiced not; and they that buy, as though they possessed not;
31. And they that use this world, as not abusing *it*: for the fashion of this world passeth away.
32. But I would have you without carefulness.
■ **He that is unmarried careth**
■ **for the things that belong**
■ **to the Lord,**
how he may please the Lord:
■ 33. **But he that is married**
■ **careth for the things that**
■ **are of the world,**
how he may please *his* wife.
■ 34. **There is difference** *also*
■ **between a wife and a**
■ **virgin. The unmarried**
■ **woman careth for the**
■ **things of the Lord,** that she may be holy both in body and in spirit:
■ **but she that is married**
■ **careth for the things**
■ **of the world,**
how she may please *her* husband.
35. And this I speak for your own profit; not that I may cast a snare upon you, but for that which is comely, and that ye may attend upon the Lord without distraction.
■ 36. **But if any man** think that he
■ **behaveth himself**
■ **uncomely toward his**
■ **virgin, if she pass the**
■ **flower of** *her* **age,**
and need so require,
■ **let him do what he will, he**
■ **sinneth not: let them marry.**
37. Nevertheless he that standeth stedfast in his heart, having no necessity, but hath power over his own will, and hath so decreed in his heart that he will keep his virgin, doeth well.
■ 38. **So then he that giveth** *her*
■ **in marriage doeth well; but**
■ **he that giveth** *her* **not**

in marriage
■ **doeth better.**
■ 39. **The wife** is bound by the law as long as her husband liveth; but
■ **if her husband be dead,** she
■ **is at liberty to be married**
to whom she will; only
■ **in the Lord.**
■ 40. **But she is happier if**
■ **she so abide,**
after my judgment: and I think also that I have the Spirit of God.

CHAPTER 8

1. Now as touching things offered unto idols, we know that we all have knowledge. Knowledge puffeth up, but charity edifieth.
2. And if any man think that he knoweth any thing, he knoweth nothing yet as he ought to know.
3. But if any man love God, the same is known of him.
■ 4. **As concerning** therefore the
■ **eating** of those
■ **things** that are
■ **offered** in sacrifice
■ **unto idols, we know** that
■ **an idol** *is* **nothing** in the world,
■ **and** that
■ *there is* **none other**
■ **God but one.**
5. For though there be that are called gods, whether in heaven or in earth, (as there be gods many, and lords many,)
6. But to us *there is but* one God, the Father, of whom *are* all things, and we in him;
■ **and one Lord Jesus Christ,**
by whom *are* all things, and we by him.
■ 7. **Howbeit** *there* **is not in**
■ **every man that knowledge:**
■ **for some** with conscience of the idol unto this hour
■ **eat** *it* **as a thing offered**
■ **unto an idol; and their**
■ **conscience** being weak
■ **is defiled.**
8. But meat commendeth us not to God:
■ **for neither, if we eat, are we**
■ **the better; neither, if we eat**

■ **not, are we the worse.**
■ **9. But take heed lest**
by any means
■ **this liberty** of yours
■ **become a stumblingblock**
■ **to them that are weak.**
10. For if any man see thee which hast knowledge sit at meat in the idol's temple, shall not the conscience of him which is weak be emboldened to eat those things which are offered to idols;
11. And through thy knowledge shall the weak brother perish, for whom Christ died?
12. But when ye sin so against the brethren, and wound their weak conscience, ye sin against Christ.
■ **13. Wherefore, if meat make**
■ **my brother to offend, I will**
■ **eat no flesh**
while the world standeth, lest I make my brother to offend.

CHAPTER 9
■ **1. Am I not an apostle? am I**
■ **not free? have I not seen**
■ **Jesus Christ** our Lord?
are not ye my work in the Lord?
2. If I be not an apostle unto others, yet doubtless I am to you: for the seal of mine apostleship are ye in the Lord.
■ **3. Mine answer to them that**
■ **do examine me is this,**
■ **4. Have we not power to eat**
■ **and to drink?**
■ **5. Have we not power to**
■ **lead** about a sister,
■ **a wife, as well as other**
■ **apostles,** and *as* the brethren of the Lord, and Cephas?
6. Or I only and Barnabas,
■ **have not we power to**
■ **forbear working?**
7. Who goeth a warfare any time at his own charges? who planteth a vineyard, and eateth not of the fruit thereof? or
■ **who feedeth a flock, and**
■ **eateth not of the milk**
■ **of the flock?**
8. Say I these things as a man? or

saith not the law the same also?
9. For it is written in the law of Moses, Thou shalt not muzzle the mouth of the ox that treadeth out the corn. Doth God take care for oxen?
10. Or saith he *it* altogether for our sakes?
■ **For our sakes, no doubt,**
■ *this* **is written: that he that**
■ **ploweth should plow in**
■ **hope; and**
that he that thresheth in hope
■ **should be partaker**
■ **of his hope.**
■ **11. If we have sown** unto you
■ **spiritual things,** *is it* **a great**
■ **thing if we shall reap your**
■ **carnal things?**
12. If others be partakers of *this* power over you, *are* not we rather?
■ **Nevertheless we have not**
■ **used this power; but suffer**
■ **all things, lest we should**
■ **hinder the gospel** of Christ.
■ **13. Do ye not know that they**
■ **which minister** about holy things
■ **live** *of the things* **of the**
■ **temple?** and they which wait at the altar are partakers with the altar?
■ **14. Even so hath the Lord**
■ **ordained that they which**
■ **preach** the gospel
■ **should live of the gospel.**
■ **15. But I have used none of**
■ **these things:**
neither have I written these things, that it should be so done unto me:
■ **for** *it were* **better for me to**
■ **die, than that any man** should
■ **make my glorying void.**
16. **For though I preach**
the gospel,
■ **I have nothing to glory of:**
for necessity is laid upon me; yea,
■ **woe is unto me, if I preach**
■ **not the gospel!**
17. For if I do this thing willingly, I have a reward: but if against my will, a dispensation of *the gospel* is committed unto me.
■ 18. **What is my reward then?**
■ *Verily* **that, when I preach**
the gospel, I may make the gospel of

Christ without charge,

that I abuse not my power in the gospel.

19. For though I be free from all *men*,

yet have I made myself servant unto all, that I might gain the more.

20. And unto the Jews I became as a Jew, that I might gain the Jews; to them that are under the law, as under the law, that I might gain them that are under the law;

21. To them that are without law, as without law, (being not without law to God, but under the law to Christ,)

that I might gain them that are without law.

22. To the weak became I as weak, that I might gain the weak:

I am made all things to all men, that I might by all means save some.

23. And this I do for the gospel's sake, that I might be partaker thereof with *you*.

24. Know ye not that they which run in a race run all, but one receiveth the prize? So run, that ye may obtain.

25. And every man that striveth for the mastery is temperate in all things. Now they *do it* to obtain a corruptible crown; but we an incorruptible.

26. I therefore so run, not as uncertainly; so fight I, not as one that beateth the air:

27. But I keep under my body, and bring *it* into subjection: lest that by any means,

when I have preached to others,

I myself should be a castaway.

CHAPTER 10

1. Moreover, brethren, I would not that ye should be ignorant, how that all our fathers were under the cloud, and all passed through the sea;

2. And were all baptized unto Moses in the cloud and in the sea;

3. And did all eat the same spiritual meat;

4. And did all drink the same spiritual drink: for they drank of that spiritual Rock that followed them: and that Rock was Christ.

5. But with many of them God was not well pleased: for they were overthrown in the wilderness.

6. Now these things were our examples, to the intent

we should not lust after evil things, as they also lusted.

7. Neither be ye idolaters, as *were* some of them; as it is written, The people sat down to eat and drink, and rose up to play.

8. Neither let us commit fornication, as some of them committed, and fell in one day three and twenty thousand.

9. Neither let us tempt Christ, as some of them also tempted, and were destroyed of serpents.

10. Neither murmur ye, as some of them also murmured, and were destroyed of the destroyer.

11. Now all these things happened unto them for ensamples: and they are written for our admonition, upon whom the ends of the world are come.

12. Wherefore let him that thinketh he standeth take heed lest he fall.

13. There hath no temptation taken you but such as is common to man: but God *is* faithful, who will not suffer you to be tempted above that ye are able; but will with the temptation also make a way to escape, that ye may be able to bear *it*.

14. Wherefore, my dearly beloved, flee from idolatry.

15. I speak as to wise men; judge ye what I say.

16. **The cup of blessing which we bless, is it not the communion of the blood of Christ? The bread** which we break, **is it not the communion of the body of Christ?** 17. **For we** *being* **many are** one bread, *and* **one body: for we are all partakers of that one bread.**

18. Behold Israel after the flesh: are not they which eat of the sacrifices partakers of the altar?

19. **What** say I then? that the idol is any thing, or that which is offered in sacrifice to idols is any thing?

20. But *I say*, that **the things which the Gentiles sacrifice, they sacrifice to devils,** and not to God: **and I would not that ye should have fellowship with devils.**

21. **Ye cannot drink the cup of the Lord, and** the cup **of devils:** ye cannot be partakers of the Lord's table, and of the table of devils.

22. Do we provoke the Lord to jealousy? are we stronger than he?

23. **All things are lawful for me, but all things are not expedient:** all things are lawful for me, but all things edify not.

24. **Let no man seek his own, but every man another's** *wealth.*

25. **Whatsoever is sold** in the shambles, **that eat, asking no question for conscience sake:**

26. **For the earth** *is* **the Lord's, and the fulness thereof.**

27. **If any** of them **that believe not bid you** *to* **a feast,** and ye be disposed to go; **whatsoever is set before you, eat, asking no question** for conscience sake.

28. **But if any man say** unto you, **This is offered** in sacrifice **unto idols, eat not for his sake** that shewed it, **and for conscience sake:** for the earth *is* the Lord's, and the fulness thereof:

29. Conscience, I say, not thine own, but of the other: for why is my liberty judged of another *man's* conscience?

30. For if I by grace be a partaker, why am I evil spoken of for that for which I give thanks?

31. **Whether therefore ye eat, or drink, or whatsoever ye do, do all to the glory of God.**

32. **Give none offence,** neither to the Jews, nor to the Gentiles, nor to the church of God:

33. **Even as I please all** *men* in all *things,* **not seeking mine own profit, but the** *profit* **of many, that they may be saved.**

CHAPTER 11

1. Be ye followers of me, even as I also *am* of Christ.

2. Now I praise you, brethren, that ye remember me in all things, and keep the ordinances, as I delivered *them* to you.

3. **But I would have you know, that the head of every man is Christ; and the head of the woman** *is* **the man; and the head of Christ** *is* **God.**

4. **Every man** praying or prophesying, **having** *his* **head covered, dishonoureth his head.**

5. **But every woman that prayeth** or prophesieth **with** *her* **head uncovered dishonoureth her head:** for that is even all one

as if she were shaven.
6. **For if the woman be not covered, let her also be shorn:** but if it be a shame for a woman to be shorn or shaven, let her be covered.
7. **For a man indeed ought not to cover** *his* **head,** forasmuch **as he is the image** and glory **of God: but the woman is the glory of the man.**
8. **For** the **man is not of** the **woman: but** the **woman of** the **man.**
9. Neither was the man created for the woman; but the woman for the man.
10. For this cause ought the woman to have power on *her* head because of the angels.
11. Nevertheless neither is the man without the woman, neither the woman without the man, in the Lord.
12. **For as the woman** *is* **of the man, even so** *is* **the man also by** the **woman; but all things of God.**
13. Judge in yourselves: is it comely that a woman pray unto God uncovered?
14. **Doth not even nature** itself **teach you, that, if a man have long hair, it is a shame** unto him?
15. **But if a woman have long hair, it is a glory to her:** for *her* hair is given her for a covering.
16. But if any man seem to be contentious, we have no such custom, neither the churches of God.
17. **Now in this** that I declare *unto you* **I praise** *you* **not, that ye come together not for the better, but** for **the worse.**
18. For first of all, **when ye come together in the church, I hear that there be divisions among**

you; and I partly believe it.
19. **For there must be also heresies among you,** that they which are approved may be made manifest among you.
20. **When ye come together** therefore into one place, *this* **is not to eat the Lord's supper.**
21. **For in eating every one taketh** before *other* his own supper: **and one is hungry, and another is drunken.**
22. **What? have ye not houses to eat** and to drink **in? or despise ye the church** of God, and shame them that have not? What shall I say to you? shall I praise you in this? I praise *you* not.
23. **For** I have received of the Lord that which also **I delivered unto you, That the Lord Jesus** the *same* night in which he was betrayed **took bread:**
24. **And when he had given thanks, he brake** *it,* **and said, Take, eat: this is my body,** which is **broken for you: this do in remembrance of me.**
25. After the same manner **also** *he took* **the cup,** when he had supped, **saying, This cup is the new testament in my blood: this do ye,** as oft as ye drink *it,* **in remembrance of me.**
26. **For as** often as **ye eat this bread, and drink this cup, ye do shew the Lord's death till he come.**
27. Wherefore whosoever shall eat this bread, and drink *this* cup of the Lord, unworthily, shall be guilty of the body and blood of the Lord.
28. **But let a man examine himself,** and so let him eat of *that* bread, and drink of *that* cup.
29. **For he that eateth and drinketh unworthily, eateth**

and drinketh damnation to himself, not discerning the Lord's body.

30. For this cause many *are* weak and sickly among you, and many sleep.

31. For if we would judge ourselves, we should not be judged.

32. But when we are judged, we are chastened of the Lord, that we should not be condemned with the world.

33. Wherefore, my brethren, when ye come together to eat, tarry one for another.

34. And if any man hunger, let him eat at home; that ye come not together unto condemnation. And the rest will I set in order when I come.

CHAPTER 12

1. Now concerning spiritual gifts, brethren, I would not have you ignorant.

2. Ye know that ye were Gentiles, carried away unto these dumb idols, even as ye were led.

3. Wherefore I give you to understand, that no man speaking by the Spirit of God calleth Jesus accursed: and *that* no man can say that Jesus is the Lord, but by the Holy Ghost.

4. Now there are diversities of gifts, but the same Spirit.

5. And there are differences of administrations, but the same Lord.

6. And there are diversities of operations, but it is the same God which worketh all in all.

7. But the manifestation of the Spirit is given to every man to profit withal.

8. For to one is given by the Spirit the word of wisdom; to another the word of knowledge by the same Spirit;

9. To another faith by the same Spirit; to another the gifts of healing by the same Spirit;

10. To another the working of miracles; to another prophecy; to another discerning of spirits; to another *divers* kinds of tongues; to another the interpretation of tongues:

11. But all these worketh that one and the selfsame Spirit, dividing to every man severally as he will.

12. For as the body is one, and hath many members, and all the members of that one body, being many, are one body: so also *is* Christ.

13. For by one Spirit are we all baptized into one body, whether *we be* Jews or Gentiles, whether *we be* bond or free; and have been all made to drink into one Spirit.

14. For the body is not one member, but many.

15. If the foot shall say, Because I am not the hand, I am not of the body; is it therefore not of the body?

16. And if the ear shall say, Because I am not the eye, I am not of the body; is it therefore not of the body?

17. If the whole body *were* an eye, where *were* the hearing? If the whole *were* hearing, where *were* the smelling?

18. But now hath God set the members every one of them in the body, as it hath pleased him.

19. And if they were all one member, where *were* the body?

20. But now *are they* many members, yet but one body.

21. And the eye cannot say unto the hand, I have no need of thee: nor again the head to the feet, I have no need of you.

22. Nay, much more those members of the body, which seem to be more feeble, are necessary:

23. And those *members* of the body, which we think to be

less honourable,
upon these we
bestow more abundant
honour; and our uncomely *parts*
have more abundant comeliness.
24. For our comely *parts* have
no need:
but God hath tempered the
body together, having
given more
abundant honour to that
part which lacked.
25. That there should be no
schism in the body; but *that* the
members should have the same care
one for another.
26. And whether one
member suffer, all the
members suffer with it; or
one member be honoured, all the
members rejoice with it.
27. Now ye are the body of
Christ, and members
in particular.
28. And God hath set some
in the church, first
apostles, secondarily
prophets, thirdly teachers,
after that miracles, then
gifts of healings,
helps, governments,
diversities of tongues.
29. *Are* all apostles? *are* all
prophets? *are* all teachers? *are* all
workers of miracles?
30. Have all the gifts of healing? do all
speak with tongues? do all interpret?
31. But covet earnestly
the best
gifts: and yet shew I unto you
a more excellent way.

CHAPTER 13
1. Though I speak with the
tongues of men and of
angels, and have not
charity, I am become *as*
sounding brass, or
a tinkling cymbal.
2. And though I have *the gift*
of prophecy, and
understand all mysteries,
and all knowledge; and

though I
have all faith, so
that I could remove
mountains, and have not
charity, I am nothing.
3. And though I
bestow all my goods to
feed *the poor*, and though I
give my body to be burned,
and have not charity, it
profiteth me nothing.
4. Charity suffereth long,
and is kind; charity envieth
not; charity vaunteth not itself,
is not puffed up,
5. Doth not behave itself
unseemly, seeketh not her
own, is not easily
provoked, thinketh no evil;
6. Rejoiceth not in iniquity, but
rejoiceth in the truth;
7. Beareth all things, believeth all things, hopeth all
things, endureth all things.
8. Charity never faileth: but
whether *there be*
prophecies, they
shall fail; whether *there be*
tongues, they
shall cease; whether *there be*
knowledge, it
shall vanish away.
9. For we know in part,
and we prophesy in part.
10. But when that which is
perfect is come, then
that which is
in part shall be
done away.
11. When I was a child, I
spake as a child,
I understood as a child,
I thought as a child: but
when I became a man, I put
away childish things.
12. For now we see through
a glass, darkly; but then
face to face: now I know in
part; but then shall I know
even as also
I am known.
13. And now abideth faith,
hope, charity, these three;

■ **but the greatest of**
■ **these** *is* **charity.**

CHAPTER 14
■ 1. **Follow after charity,**
and desire spiritual *gifts,* but rather
that ye may prophesy.
■ 2. **For he that speaketh** in
■ **an** *unknown* **tongue**
■ **speaketh** not unto men, but
■ **unto God: for no man**
■ **understandeth** *him* **;**
■ **howbeit** in the spirit
■ **he speaketh mysteries.**
■ 3. **But he that prophesieth**
■ **speaketh unto men**
■ *to* **edification,**
and exhortation, and comfort.
■ 4. **He that speaketh in an**
■ *unknown* **tongue edifieth**
■ **himself;** but he that
prophesieth edifieth the church.
■ 5. **I would that ye all spake**
■ **with tongues but rather that**
■ **ye prophesied:** for greater *is* he
that prophesieth than he that
speaketh with tongues, except he
interpret, that the church may
receive edifying.
■ 6. **Now, brethren, if I come**
unto you
■ **speaking with tongues,**
■ **what shall I profit you,**
■ **except I** shall
■ **speak** to you either
■ **by revelation, or by know-**
■ **ledge, or by prophesying,**
■ **or by doctrine?**
7. And even things without life giving
sound, whether pipe or harp,
except they give a distinction in the
sounds, how shall it be known what is
piped or harped?
8. For if the trumpet give an uncertain
sound, who shall prepare himself
to the battle?
9. So likewise ye,
■ **except ye utter by the**
■ **tongue words easy to be**
■ **understood, how shall it be**
■ **known what is spoken?**
for ye shall speak into the air.
10. There are, it may be, so many

kinds of voices in the world, and none
of them *is* without signification.
11. Therefore if I know not the
meaning of the voice, I shall be unto
him that speaketh a barbarian, and he
that speaketh *shall be* a barbarian
unto me.
12. Even so ye,
■ **forasmuch as ye are**
■ **zealous of spiritual** *gifts,*
■ **seek that ye may excel to**
■ **the edifying of the church.**
■ 13. **Wherefore let him that**
■ **speaketh in an** *unknown*
■ **tongue pray that he**
■ **may interpret.**
■ 14. **For if I pray in an**
■ *unknown* **tongue, my spirit**
■ **prayeth, but my**
■ **understanding is unfruitful.**
15. What is it then?
■ **I will pray with the spirit,**
■ **and** I will pray
■ **with the understanding** also: I
will sing with the spirit, and I will sing
with the understanding also.
16. Else when thou shalt bless with
the spirit, how shall he that occupieth
the room of the unlearned say Amen
at thy giving of thanks, seeing
he understandeth not what
thou sayest?
17. For thou verily givest thanks well,
but the other is not edified.
■ 18. **I thank my God, I speak**
■ **with tongues more than**
■ **ye all:**
■ 19. **Yet in the church I had**
■ **rather speak five words**
■ **with** my
■ **understanding, that**
by my voice
■ **I might teach others** also,
■ **than ten thousand words in**
■ **an** *unknown* **tongue.**
■ 20. **Brethren, be not children**
in understanding: howbeit in malice be
ye children,
■ **but** in understanding
■ **be men.**
21. In the law it is written, With *men of*
other tongues and other lips
will I speak unto this people; and yet

for all that will they not hear me, saith the LORD.

22. **Wherefore tongues are for a sign,** not to them that believe, but **to them that believe not: but prophesying** *serveth* not for **them that believe** not, but for them which believe.

23. **If therefore the** whole **church be come together** into one place, **and all speak with tongues, and there come** in **those that are** unlearned, **or unbelievers, will they not say** that **ye are mad?**

24. **But if all prophesy, and there come in one that believeth not,** or *one* unlearned, he is convinced of all, he is judged of all:

25. **And thus are the secrets of his heart made manifest;** and so falling down on *his* face **he will worship God,** and report that God is in you of a truth.

26. **How is it then,** brethren? **when ye come together, every one of you hath a psalm,** hath **a doctrine,** hath **a tongue,** hath **a revelation,** hath **an interpretation.** Let all things be done unto edifying.

27. **If any man speak in an** *unknown* **tongue,** *let it be* by two, or at the most *by* three, and *that* by course; and **let one interpret.**

28. **But if there be no interpreter, let him keep silence** in the church; and let him speak to himself, and to God.

29. **Let the prophets speak** two or three, **and let the other judge.**

30. **If** *any thing* **be revealed to another** that sitteth by, **let the first hold his peace.**

31. For ye may all prophesy one by

one, that all may learn, and all may be comforted.

32. And the spirits of the prophets are subject to the prophets.

33. **For God is not** *the author* **of confusion, but of peace,** as in all churches of the saints.

34. **Let your women keep silence in the churches:** for it is not permitted unto them to speak; but *they are commanded* to be under obedience as also saith the law.

35. **And if they will learn any thing, let them ask their husbands at home:** for it is a shame for women to speak in the church.

36. What? came the word of God out from you? or came it unto you only?

37. **If any man think himself to be a prophet, or spiritual, let him acknowledge that the things that I write** unto you **are the commandments of the Lord.**

38. But if any man be ignorant, let him be ignorant.

39. Wherefore, brethren, **covet to prophesy, and forbid not to speak with tongues.**

40. **Let all things be done** decently and **in order.**

CHAPTER 15

1. Moreover, brethren, **I declare** unto you **the gospel** which I preached unto you, which also ye have received, and wherein ye stand;

2. **By which also ye are saved,** if ye keep in memory what I preached unto you, **unless ye have believed in vain.**

3. **For I delivered** unto you **first** of all that which I also received, how **that Christ died for our sins according to the scriptures;**

4. And that he was buried, and **that he rose again the third day** according to the scriptures: **5. And that he was seen of Cephas, then of the twelve: 6. After that, he was seen of above five hundred** brethren at once; of whom the greater part remain unto this present, but some are fallen asleep. **7. After that, he was seen of James; then of all the apostles. 8. And last** of all **he was seen of me** also, as of one born out of due time. **9. For I am the least of the apostles,** that am not meet to be called an apostle, **because I persecuted the church** of God. **10. But by the grace of God I am what I am: and his grace** which *was bestowed* upon me **was not in vain; but I laboured more abundantly than they all: yet not I, but the grace of God** which was **with me.** 11. Therefore whether *it were* I or they, so we preach, and so ye believed. **12. Now if Christ** be preached that he **rose from the dead, how say some** among you that **there is no resurrection** of the dead? 13. But if there be no resurrection of the dead, then is Christ not risen: **14. And if Christ be not risen, then *is* our preaching vain,** and your faith *is* also vain. **15. Yea, and we are** found **false witnesses of God; because we** have **testified of God that he raised** up **Christ:** whom he raised not up, if so be that the dead rise not. 16. For if the dead rise not, then is not Christ raised **17. And if Christ be not raised, your faith *is* vain;**

ye are yet in your sins. 18. Then they also which are fallen asleep in Christ are perished. **19. If in this life only we have hope in Christ, we are of all men most miserable. 20. But now is Christ risen** from the dead, *and* become the firstfruits of them that slept. **21. For since by man *came* death, by man *came* also the resurrection** of the dead. **22. For as in Adam all die, even so in Christ shall all be made alive.** 23. But every man in his own order: Christ the firstfruits; afterward they that are Christ's at his coming. **24. Then *cometh* the end,** when he shall have delivered up the kingdom to God, even the Father; **when he shall have put down all** rule and all **authority and power. 25. For he must reign, till he hath put all enemies under his feet. 26. The last enemy *that* shall be destroyed *is* death.** 27. For he hath put all things under his feet. But when he saith all things are put under *him, it is* manifest that he is excepted, which did put all things under him. **28. And when all things shall be subdued unto him, then shall the Son also** himself **be subject unto him** that put all things under him, **that God may be all in all. 29. Else what shall they do which are baptized for the dead, if the dead rise not** at all? why are they then baptized for the dead? **30. And why stand** we **in jeopardy every hour?** 31. I protest by your rejoicing which I have in Christ Jesus our LORD, I die daily. **32. If after the manner of men I have fought with beasts** at Ephesus,

what advantageth it me, if
the dead rise not? let us eat
and drink; for to-morrow
we die.
33. Be not deceived: evil
communications corrupt
good manners.
34. Awake to righteousness,
and sin not; for some have not
the knowledge of God: I speak *this* to
your shame.
35. But some *man* will say,
How are the dead raised
up? and with what body do
they come?
36. *Thou* fool, that which
thou sowest is not
quickened, except it die:
37. And that which thou sowest, thou
sowest not that body that shall be,
but bare grain, it may chance of
wheat, or of some other *grain*:
38. But God giveth it a body as it hath
pleased him, and to every seed
his own body.
39. All flesh *is* not the same flesh: but
there is one *kind of* flesh of men,
another flesh of beasts, another of
fishes, *and* another of birds.
40. *There are* also celestial bodies,
and bodies terrestrial: but the
glory of the celestial *is* one, and the
glory of the terrestrial *is* another.
41. *There is* one glory of the sun, and
another glory of the moon, and
another glory of the stars: for *one* star
differeth from *another* star in glory.
42. So also *is* the
resurrection of the dead.
It is sown in corruption;
it is raised in incorruption:
43. It is sown in dishonour; it is raised
in glory: it is sown in weakness; it is
raised in power:
44. It is sown a natural
body; it is raised a
spiritual body.
There is a natural body,
and there is a spiritual body.
45. And so it is written,
The first man Adam was
made a living soul; the
last Adam *was made* a

quickening spirit.
46. Howbeit that *was* not first which is
spiritual, but that which is natural; and
afterward that which is spiritual.
47. The first man *is* of the
earth, earthy;
the second man *is* the Lord
from heaven.
48. As *is* the earthy, such *are* they
also that are earthy: and as *is* the
heavenly, such *are* they also that
are heavenly.
49. And as we have borne the image
of the earthy, we shall also bear the
image of the heavenly.
50. Now this I say, brethren, that
flesh and blood cannot
inherit the kingdom of God;
neither doth corruption
inherit incorruption.
51. Behold, I shew you a
mystery; We shall not all
sleep, but we shall
all be changed,
52. In a moment,
in the twinkling of an eye,
at the last trump:
for the trumpet shall sound, and
the dead shall be raised
incorruptible, and we shall
be changed.
53. For this corruptible must put on
incorruption, and
this mortal *must* put
on immortality.
54. So when this corruptible
shall have put on
incorruption, and this
mortal shall have put on
immortality, then shall be
brought to pass the saying
that is written,
Death is swallowed up
in victory.
55. O death, where *is* thy
sting? O grave, where *is*
thy victory?
56. The sting of death *is* sin;
and the strength of sin *is*
the law.
57. But thanks *be* to God,
which giveth us the
victory through our Lord Jesus

Christ.
58. **Therefore,**
my beloved brethren,
be ye stedfast, unmoveable,
always abounding in the work of
the Lord,
forasmuch as ye know that
**your labour is not in vain in
the Lord.**

CHAPTER 16
1. **Now concerning the
collection for the saints,**
as I have given order to the churches
of Galatia, even so do ye.
2. **Upon the first** *day* **of the
week let every one** of you
lay by him in store, as *God*
hath prospered him, that
there be no gatherings when I come.
3. And when I come,
whomsoever ye shall
approve by *your* letters,
**them will I send to bring
your liberality
unto Jerusalem.**
4. And if it be meet that I go also, they
shall go with me.
5. **Now I will come unto you,**
when I shall pass through Macedonia:
for I do pass through Macedonia.
6. **And it may be that I will
abide,** yea,
and winter with you,
that ye may bring me on my journey
whithersoever I go.
7. For I will not see you now
by the way; but
**I trust to tarry a while with
you,** if the Lord permit.
8. **But I will tarry at Ephesus
until Pentecost.**
9. **For a great door**
and effectual
**is opened unto me,
and** *there are*
many adversaries.
10. **Now if Timotheus come,
see that he may be with you
without fear:** for he worketh the
work of the Lord, as I also *do*.

11. Let no man therefore despise him:
but conduct him forth in peace, that
he may come unto me: for I look for
him with the brethren.
12. **As touching** *our* brother
Apollos, I greatly
**desired him to come unto
you** with the brethren:
but his will was not at all
to come at this time;
but he will come when he shall have
convenient time.
13. **Watch ye, stand fast
in the faith,**
quit you like men,
be strong.
14. **Let all your things be
done with charity.**
15. I beseech you, brethren, (ye know
the house of Stephanas, that it is
the firstfruits of Achaia, and *that* they
have addicted themselves to the
ministry of the saints,)
16. That ye submit yourselves unto
such, and to every one that helpeth
with *us*, and laboureth.
17. I am glad of the coming of
Stephanas and Fortunatus and
Achaicus: for that which was lacking
on your part they have supplied.
18. For they have refreshed my spirit
and yours: therefore acknowledge
ye them that are such.
19. The churches of Asia salute you.
Aquila and Priscilla salute you much in
the Lord, with the church that is in
their house.
20. **All the brethren greet
you.** Greet ye one another with an
holy kiss.
21. The salutation of *me* Paul with
mine own hand.
22. **If any man love not the
Lord Jesus** Christ,
**let him be Anathema
Maranatha.**
23. The grace of our Lord Jesus Christ
be with you.
24. My love *be* with you all in Christ
Jesus.
Amen.

THE SECOND EPISTLE TO THE CORINTHIANS

BACKGROUND INFORMATION

Author – Paul, an Apostle of Jesus Christ.
Date Written – probably **between 55** and **60** A.D.

Number of:
Verses -   257
Chapters -   13
Total Words - 6,092
Scan Words -2,646
Scan Words represent 47 % of Total Words.

Theme – written by Paul to recount his perils in the service of Christ **and to lay claim on the Corinthians as his children in Christ.**

OUTLINE OF THE EPISTLE

I. **Paul's personal Testimony.**
Chapters 1:1—2:13

II. **Paul's account of his ministry.**
Chapters 2:14—6:10

III. **Paul's plea** for reconciliation.
Chapters 6:11—7:16

IV. **Paul's appeal for an** offering for **the poor.**
Chapters 8—9

V. **Paul's defense of his Apostleship.**
Chapters 10:1—13:10

VI. **Paul's closing words** to the Corinthian Church.
Chapters 13:11—14

CHAPTER 1

1. **Paul,** an apostle of Jesus Christ by the will of God, **and Timothy** *our* brother, **unto the church** of God which is **at Corinth,** with all the saints which are in all Achaia:

2. **Grace** *be* **to you and peace from God** our Father, **and** *from* **the Lord Jesus** Christ.

3. **Blessed** *be* **God, even the Father of our Lord Jesus Christ,** the Father of mercies, and the God of all comfort;

4. **Who comforteth us** in all our tribulation, **that we may** be able to **comfort them** which are **in** any **trouble,** by the comfort wherewith we ourselves are comforted of God.

5. For as the sufferings of Christ abound in us, so our consolation also aboundeth by Christ.

6. **And whether we be afflicted,** *it is* **for your consolation and salvation,** which is effectual in the enduring of the same sufferings which we also suffer: or whether we be comforted, *it is* for your consolation and salvation.

7. And our hope of you *is* stedfast, **knowing, that as ye are partakers of the sufferings, so** *shall ye be* also **of the consolation.**

8. **For** we would not, brethren, have you ignorant of our trouble which came to us in Asia, that **we were pressed out of measure,** above strength, **insomuch that we despaired** even of life:

9. **But we had the sentence of death** in ourselves, **that we should not trust in ourselves, but in God which raiseth the dead:**

10. **Who delivered us** from so great a death, **and** doth deliver:

in whom we trust that he will yet deliver *us*;

11. Ye also helping together by prayer for us, that for the gift *bestowed* upon us by the means of many persons thanks may be given by many on our behalf.

12. **For our rejoicing is** this, the testimony of our conscience, *that* **in** simplicity and **godly sincerity,** not with fleshly wisdom, but by the grace of God, we have had our conversation in the world, and more abundantly to you-ward.

13. For we write none other things unto you, than what ye read or acknowledge; and I trust ye shall acknowledge even to the end;

14. **As** also **ye have acknowledged** us in part, **that we are your rejoicing, even as ye** also *are* **our's in the day of the Lord** Jesus.

15. And in this confidence **I was minded to come unto you** before, that ye might have a second benefit;

16. **And to pass by you into Macedonia,** and to come again out of Macedonia unto you, and of you to be brought on my way toward Judaea.

17. When I therefore was thus minded, did I use lightness? or the things that I purpose, do I purpose according to the flesh, that with me there should be yea yea, and nay nay?

18. But *as* God *is* true, **our word toward you was not yea and nay.**

19. **For the Son of God,** Jesus Christ, **who was preached among you** by us, *even* by me and Silvanus and Timotheus, **was not yea and nay, but** in him was **yea.**

20. **For all the promises**

of God

■ **in him** *are* **yea,** and in him Amen, unto the glory of God by us.

■ 21. **Now he which**
■ **stablisheth us with you in**
■ **Christ,** and hath anointed us,
■ *is* **God;**

22. Who hath also sealed us, and given the earnest of the Spirit in our hearts.

23. Moreover I call God for a record upon my soul, that to spare you I came not as yet unto Corinth.

■ 24. **Not** for
■ **that we have dominion**
■ **over your faith,**
but are helpers of your joy:

■ **for by faith ye stand.**

CHAPTER 2

■ 1. **But** I determined
this with myself, that

■ **I would not come again to**
■ **you in heaviness.**

2. For if I make you sorry, who is he then that maketh me glad, but the same which is made sorry by me?

3. And I wrote this same unto you, lest, when I came, I should have sorrow from them of whom I ought to rejoice; having confidence in you all, that my joy is *the joy* of you all.

4. For out of much affliction and anguish of heart I wrote unto you with many tears; not that ye should be grieved, but that ye might know the love which I have more abundantly unto you.

■ 5. **But if any have caused**
■ **grief, he hath not grieved**
■ **me,** but in part: that I may not overcharge you all.

■ 6. **Sufficient to such a man** *is*
■ **this punishment,** which *was* *inflicted* of many.

7. So that contrariwise
■ **ye** *ought* rather
■ **to forgive** *him*, and comfort *him*,
■ **lest** perhaps
■ **such a one** should
■ **be swallowed** up
■ **with** overmuch
■ **sorrow.**

8. Wherefore I beseech you that ye would

■ **confirm** *your* **love**
■ **toward him.**

9. For to this end also did I write, that I might know the proof of you, whether ye be obedient in all things.

■ 10. **To whom ye forgive**
any thing,

■ I *forgive* also: for if I forgave any thing, to whom I forgave *it*, for your sakes *forgave I it* in the person of Christ;

■ 11. **Lest Satan should get an**
■ **advantage** of us:
■ **for we are not ignorant of**
■ **his devices.**

■ 12. **Furthermore, when I**
■ **came to Troas**
to *preach* Christ's gospel, and

■ **a door was opened** unto me
■ **of the Lord,**

■ 13. **I had no rest** in my spirit,
■ **because I found not Titus**
my brother: but taking my leave of them, I went from thence into Macedonia.

■ 14. **Now thanks** *be* **unto**
■ **God, which** always
■ **causeth us to triumph in**
■ **Christ,** and maketh manifest the savour of his knowledge by us in every place.

■ 15. **For we are unto God a**
■ **sweet savour of Christ,**
in them that are saved, and in them that perish:

■ 16. **To the one** *we are* **the**
■ **savour of death** unto death;
■ **and to the other the savour**
■ **of life** unto life. And who *is* sufficient for these things?

■ 17. **For we are not as many,**
■ **which corrupt the word**
of God: but as of sincerity, but as of God, in the sight of God speak we in Christ.

CHAPTER 3

1. Do we begin again to commend ourselves? or need we, as some *others*, epistles of commendation to you, or *letters* of commendation

from you?

■ **2. Ye are our epistle** written in our hearts,

■ **known and read of all** men:

3. Forasmuch as ye are manifestly declared to be the epistle of Christ ministered by us,

■ **written not with ink, but with**
■ **the Spirit** of the living God; not in tables of stone, but in fleshy tables of the heart.

■ **4. And such trust have we**
■ **through Christ** to God-ward:
■ **5. Not that we are sufficient** of ourselves to think any thing as of ourselves;

■ **but our sufficiency**
■ *is* **of God;**
■ **6. Who also hath made us**
■ **able ministers** of the new testament; not of the letter, but

■ **of the spirit: for the letter**
■ **killeth, but the spirit**
■ **giveth life.**
■ **7. But if the ministration** of death,

■ **written** *and* engraven
■ **in stones, was glorious,** so that the children of Israel could not stedfastly behold the face of Moses for the glory of his countenance; which *glory* was to be done away:

■ **8. How shall not the**
■ **ministration of the spirit be**
■ **rather glorious?**

9. For if the ministration of condemnation *be* glory, much more doth the ministration of righteousness exceed in glory.

10. For even that which was made glorious had no glory in this respect, by reason of the glory that excelleth.

■ **11. For if that which is done**
■ **away** *was* **glorious, much**
■ **more that which remaineth**
■ *is* **glorious.**
■ **12. Seeing then that we have**
■ **such hope, we use** great
■ **plainness of speech:**
■ **13. And not as Moses,**
■ **which put a vail over his**
■ **face,** that the children of Israel could not stedfastly look to the end of

that which is abolished:

14. But their minds were blinded:
■ **for until this day remaineth**
■ **the same vail** untaken away in the reading of the old testament;

■ **which** *vail* **is done**
■ **away in Christ.**
■ **15. But even unto this day,**
■ **when Moses is read, the**
■ **vail is upon their heart.**

16. Nevertheless when it shall turn to the Lord, the vail shall be taken away.

■ **17. Now the Lord is that**
■ **Spirit: and where the Spirit** of the Lord

■ *is,* **there** *is* **liberty.**
■ **18. But we all, with open**
■ **face beholding** as in a glass
■ **the glory of the Lord, are**
■ **changed into the same**
■ **image** from glory to glory, *even* as
■ **by the Spirit** of the LORD.

CHAPTER 4

■ **1. Therefore** seeing we have this ministry, as we have received mercy,

■ **we faint not;**
■ **2. But have renounced the**
■ **hidden things of**
■ **dishonesty, not walking in**
■ **craftiness, nor handling the**
■ **word** of God

■ **deceitfully; but by**
■ **manifestation of the truth** commending ourselves to every man's conscience

■ **in the sight of God.**
■ **3. But if our gospel be hid, it**
■ **is hid to them that are lost:**
■ **4. In whom the god of this**
■ **world hath blinded the**
■ **minds of them which**
■ **believe not,** lest the light of the glorious gospel of Christ, who is the image of God, should shine unto them.

5. For we preach not ourselves, but Christ Jesus the Lord; and ourselves your servants for Jesus' sake.

■ **6. For God,** who commanded the light to shine out of darkness,

■ **hath shined in our hearts,**
■ **to** *give* **the light**

of the knowledge
■ **of the glory of God in the**
■ **face of Jesus** Christ.
■ 7. **But we have this treasure**
■ **in earthen vessels, that**
the excellency of
■ **the power** may
■ **be of God, and not of us.**
■ 8. **We** *are* **troubled**
on every side,
■ **yet not distressed;** *we are*
perplexed, but not in despair;
9. Persecuted, but not forsaken;
■ **cast down,**
■ **but not destroyed;**
■ 10. **Always bearing about in**
■ **the body the dying of** the Lord
■ **Jesus, that the life** also
■ **of Jesus might be** made
■ **manifest in our body.**
11. For we which live are alway
delivered unto death for Jesus' sake,
that the life also of Jesus might be
made manifest in our mortal flesh.
12. So then death worketh in us,
but life in you.
■ 13. **We having the same**
■ **spirit of faith, according as**
■ **it is written,** I believed, and
therefore have I spoken;
■ **we** also
■ **believe, and**
■ **therefore speak;**
■ 14. **Knowing that he which**
■ **raised up** the Lord
■ **Jesus shall raise** up
■ **us** also
■ **by Jesus,**
and shall present *us* with you.
15. For all things *are* for your sakes,
that the abundant grace might
through the thanksgiving of many
redound to the glory of God.
16. For which cause
■ **we faint not; but though our**
■ **outward man perish, yet**
■ **the inward** *man*
■ **is renewed** day by day.
17. For our light affliction, which is but
for a moment, worketh for us a
far more exceeding *and* eternal
weight of glory;
■ 18. **While we look not at** the

■ **things** which are
■ **seen, but at** the
■ **things** which are
■ **not seen: for** the
■ **things** which are
■ **seen** *are* **temporal; but** the
■ **things** which are
■ **not seen** *are* **eternal.**

CHAPTER 5
■ 1. **For we know that if our**
■ **earthly** house of *this*
■ **tabernacle were**
■ **dissolved, we have a**
■ **building of God,** an house not
made with hands, eternal
■ **in the heavens.**
■ 2. **For** in this
■ **we groan, earnestly**
■ **desiring** to be clothed upon with
■ **our house** which is
■ **from heaven:**
3. If so be that being clothed we shall
not be found naked.
4. For we that are in *this* tabernacle do
groan, being burdened: not for that we
would be unclothed, but clothed upon,
that mortality might be
swallowed up of life.
■ 5. **Now he that hath wrought**
■ **us** for the selfsame thing
■ *is* **God, who** also
■ **hath given unto us**
the earnest of
■ **the Spirit.**
■ 6. **Therefore**
we are always confident,
■ **knowing that, whilst** we are
■ **at home in the body, we are**
■ **absent from the Lord:**
7. (For we walk by faith, not by sight:)
■ 8. **We are** confident, *I say*, and
■ **willing rather to be absent**
■ **from the body, and to be**
■ **present with the Lord.**
9. **Wherefore we labour,**
■ **that,** whether present or absent,
■ **we may be accepted** of him.
■ 10. **For we must all appear**
■ **before the judgment seat of**
■ **Christ;** that every one may receive
the things *done* in *his* body, according
to that he hath done, whether *it be*

good or bad.

■ 11. **Knowing therefore the**
■ **terror of the Lord, we**
■ **persuade men;** but we are
made manifest unto God; and I trust
also are made manifest in
your consciences.
12. For we commend not ourselves
again unto you, but give you occasion
to glory on our behalf, that ye may
have somewhat to *answer* them which
glory in appearance, and not in heart.
13. For whether we be beside
ourselves, *it is* to God: or whether we
be sober, *it is* for your cause.
■ 14. **For the love of Christ**
constraineth us; because we thus
judge, that if one died for all, then
were all dead:
15. And *that* he died for all, that
■ **they which live should not**
henceforth
■ **live unto themselves, but**
■ **unto him which died** for them,
■ **and rose** again.
16. Wherefore henceforth know we no
man after the flesh: yea,
though we have known Christ after the
flesh, yet now henceforth
know we *him* no more.
■ 17. **Therefore if any man** *be*
■ **in Christ,** *he is* **a new**
■ **creature: old things are**
■ **passed away; behold, all**
■ **things are become new.**
■ 18. **And** all things *are* of
■ **God,** who
■ **hath reconciled us** to himself
■ **by Jesus** Christ,
■ **and** hath
■ **given** to
■ **us the ministry of**
■ **reconciliation;**
■ 19. **To wit, that God was in**
■ **Christ, reconciling the**
■ **world** unto himself, not imputing
their trespasses unto them;
■ **and hath committed unto**
■ **us the word of**
■ **reconciliation.**
■ 20. **Now then we are**
■ **ambassadors** for Christ, as
though God did beseech *you* by us:

we pray *you*
■ **in Christ's stead,**
be ye reconciled to God.
■ 21. **For he hath made him**
to be
■ **sin** for us,
■ **who knew no sin; that we**
■ **might be made the**
■ **righteousness of**
■ **God in him.**

CHAPTER 6
■ 1. **We** then, *as* workers
together *with him,*
■ **beseech** *you* **also**
■ **that ye receive not the**
■ **grace of God in vain.**
■ 2. **(For he saith,** I have heard thee
in a time accepted, and in the day of
salvation have I succoured thee:
■ **behold, now** *is* **the**
■ **accepted time;** behold,
■ **now** *is* **the day**
■ **of salvation.)**
■ 3. **Giving no offence**
in any thing,
■ **that the ministry be**
■ **not blamed:**
■ 4. **But** in all *things*
■ **approving ourselves as** the
■ **ministers** of God,
■ **in much patience,** in afflictions,
in necessities, in distresses,
■ 5. **In stripes, in**
■ **imprisonments,** in tumults, in
labours, in watchings,
■ **in fastings;**
■ 6. **By pureness, by**
■ **knowledge,** by longsuffering,
by kindness,
■ **by the Holy Ghost,**
by love unfeigned,
■ 7. **By the word** of truth,
■ **by the power of God,**
by the armour of righteousness on the
right hand and on the left,
8. By honour and dishonour, by evil
report and good report: as deceivers,
and *yet* true;
9. As unknown, and *yet* well known;
■ **as dying, and, behold, we**
■ **live;** as chastened, and not killed;
■ 10. **As sorrowful, yet alway**

rejoicing; as poor, yet making many rich; as **having nothing, and** *yet* **possessing all** things.

11. O ye Corinthians, our mouth is open unto you, our heart is enlarged.

12. Ye are not straitened in us, but ye are straitened in your own bowels.

13. Now for a recompence in the same, (I speak as unto my children,) be ye also enlarged.

14. Be ye not unequally yoked together **with unbelievers:** for what fellowship hath righteousness with unrighteousness? and **what communion hath light with darkness?**

15. And what concord hath Christ with Belial? **or what part hath he that believeth with an infidel?**

16. And what agreement hath the temple of God with idols? for ye are the temple of the living **God; as God hath said, I will dwell in them,** and walk in *them*; and I will be their God, and they shall be my people.

17. Wherefore come out from among them, **and be** ye **separate,** saith the Lord, and touch not the unclean *thing*; **and I will receive you.**

18. And will be a Father unto you, and ye shall be my sons and daughters, saith the Lord Almighty.

CHAPTER 7

1. Having therefore these promises, dearly beloved, **let us cleanse ourselves from** all **filthiness** of the flesh and spirit, **perfecting holiness in the fear of God.**

2. Receive us; we have wronged no man, we have corrupted no man, we have defrauded no man.

3. I speak not *this* **to condemn** *you:* **for** I have said before, that **ye are in our hearts** to die and live with *you.*

4. Great *is* **my boldness of speech toward you,** great *is* my glorying of you: I am filled with comfort, I am exceeding joyful in all our tribulation.

5. For, when we were come into Macedonia, our flesh had no rest, but **we were troubled on every side;** without *were* fightings, within *were* fears.

6. Nevertheless God, that comforteth those that are cast down, **comforted us by the coming of Titus;**

7. And not by his coming only, but **by the consolation** wherewith he was comforted in you, **when he told us** your earnest desire, your mourning, **your fervent mind toward me;** so that I rejoiced the more.

8. For though I made you sorry with a letter, I do not repent, though I did repent: for I perceive that the same epistle hath made you sorry, though *it were* but for a season.

9. Now I rejoice, not that ye were made sorry, but **that ye sorrowed to repentance:** for ye were made sorry after a godly manner, that ye might receive damage by us in nothing.

10. For godly sorrow worketh repentance to salvation not to be repented of: **but the sorrow of the world worketh death.**

11. For behold this self same thing, that **ye sorrowed after a godly sort,** what carefulness it wrought in you, yea, *what* clearing of yourselves, yea, *what* indignation, yea, *what* fear, yea, *what* vehement desire, yea, *what* zeal, yea, *what* revenge! **In all** *things* **ye have**

■ approved yourselves to be
■ clear in this matter.
■ 12. **Wherefore,** though
■ I wrote unto you,
I did it not for his cause that had done
the wrong, nor for his cause that
suffered wrong, but
■ that our care for you
in the sight of God
■ might appear unto you.
■ 13. **Therefore we were**
■ comforted in your comfort:
yea, and exceedingly the more joyed
we for the joy of Titus, because his
spirit was refreshed by you all.
■ 14. **For** if I have boasted any thing to
him of you, I am not ashamed;
but as
■ we spake all things to you
■ in truth, even so
■ our boasting, which *I made*
■ before Titus, is found a truth.
■ 15. **And his inward affection**
■ is more abundant toward
■ you, whilst he remembereth
■ the obedience of you all,
■ how with fear and trembling
■ ye received him.
16. I rejoice therefore that I have
confidence in you in all *things*.

CHAPTER 8
■ 1. **Moreover,** brethren,
we do you to wit of the grace
of God bestowed on
■ the churches
■ of Macedonia;
2. How that
■ in a great trial of affliction
■ the abundance of their joy
■ and their deep
■ poverty abounded unto
the riches of their
■ liberality.
■ 3. **For** to *their* power, I bear record,
yea, and beyond *their* power
■ *they were* willing
■ of themselves;
■ 4. **Praying** us with much entreaty
■ that we would receive the
■ gift, and *take upon us* the fellowship
of the ministering to the saints.
5. And *this they did*, not as we hoped,

■ but first gave their own
■ selves to the Lord,
and unto us by the will of God.
■ 6. **Insomuch that we desired**
■ Titus, that as he had begun, so
■ he would also finish in you
■ the same grace also.
■ 7. **Therefore, as ye abound**
■ in every *thing,* in faith, and
utterance, and knowledge, and *in* all
diligence, and *in* your love to us,
■ see that ye abound in this
■ grace also.
8. I speak not by commandment, but
by occasion of the forwardness of
others, and to prove the sincerity of
your love.
■ 9. **For ye know the grace of**
■ our Lord Jesus Christ,
■ that, though he was rich,
■ yet for your sakes he
■ became poor, that ye
■ through his poverty
■ might be rich.
10. And herein I give *my* advice: for
this is expedient for you, who have
begun before, not only to do, but also
to be forward a year ago.
■ 11. **Now therefore perform**
■ the doing *of it* ; that as *there was*
a readiness to will, so *there may be* a
performance also out of that
which ye have.
12. For if there be first a willing mind,
■ *it is* accepted according to
■ that a man hath, *and* not
■ according to that
■ he hath not.
■ 13. **For** *I mean* not that other
■ men be eased,
■ and ye burdened:
■ 14. **But by an equality,** *that*
now at this time
■ your abundance *may be a*
■ supply for their want, that
■ their abundance also
■ may be *a supply* for your
■ want: that there may be equality:
■ 15. **As it is written, He that** *had*
■ *gathered* much had
■ nothing over; and he
■ that *had*
■ *gathered* little had no lack.

■ 16. **But thanks** *be* **to God,**
■ **which put the same earnest**
■ **care into the heart of Titus**
■ **for you.**
17. For indeed he accepted the
exhortation; but being more forward,
of his own accord he went unto you.
■ 18. **And we have sent with**
■ **him the brother, whose**
■ **praise** *is* **in the gospel**
throughout all the churches;
■ 19. **And** not *that* only, but
■ **who was** also
■ **chosen of the churches to**
■ **travel with us** with this grace,
which is administered by us to the
glory of the same Lord, and
declaration of your ready mind:
20. Avoiding this, that no man should
blame us in this abundance which is
administered by us:
21. Providing for honest things, not
only in the sight of the Lord, but
also in the sight of men.
■ 22. **And we have sent**
with them
■ **our brother, whom we have**
■ **oftentimes proved diligent**
in many things, but now much more
diligent, upon the great confidence
which *I* have in you.
■ 23. **Whether** *any do inquire*
■ **of Titus,** *he is* **my partner**
■ **and fellow-helper**
■ **concerning you: or our**
■ **brethren** be inquired of,
■ **they are the messengers**
■ **of the churches,**
and the glory of Christ.
■ 24. **Wherefore shew ye to**
■ **them** and before the churches,
■ **the proof of your love,**
and of our boasting on your behalf.

CHAPTER 9
■ 1. **For as touching the**
■ **ministering to the saints, it**
■ **is superfluous** for me
■ **to write** to you:
■ 2. **For I know the**
■ **forwardness of your mind,**
■ **for which I boast** of you to them
of Macedonia, that Achaia was ready

a year ago;
■ **and your zeal hath**
■ **provoked** very
■ **many.**
■ 3. **Yet have I sent the**
■ **brethren, lest our boasting**
of you should
■ **be in vain** in this behalf; that, as I
said, ye may be ready:
4. Lest haply if they of Macedonia
come with me, and find you
unprepared, we (that we say not, ye)
should be ashamed in this same
confident boasting.
■ 5. **Therefore I thought it**
■ **necessary to exhort the**
■ **brethren, that they would**
■ **go** before unto you,
■ **and make up** beforehand
■ **your bounty,** whereof ye had
notice before, that the same might be
ready, as *a matter of* bounty, and not
as *of* covetousness.
■ 6. **But this** *I say,* **He which**
■ **soweth sparingly shall**
■ **reap** also
■ **sparingly; and he which**
■ **soweth bountifully shall**
■ **reap** also
■ **bountifully.**
■ 7. **Every man according as**
■ **he purposeth in his heart,**
■ *so let him give***; not**
■ **grudgingly,** or of necessity:
■ **for God loveth a**
■ **cheerful giver.**
■ 8. **And God** *is* **able to make**
■ **all grace abound toward**
■ **you;** that ye, always having all
sufficiency in all *things*, may abound
to every good work:
■ 9. **(As it is written,**
He hath dispersed abroad;
■ **he hath given to the poor:**
■ **his righteousness**
■ **remaineth** for ever.
■ 10. **Now he that ministereth**
■ **seed to the sower both**
■ **minister bread for** *your*
■ **food, and multiply your**
■ **seed sown,** and increase the
fruits of your righteousness;)
11. Being enriched in every thing to all

bountifulness, which causeth
through us thanksgiving to God.

12. **For** the administration of
this service not only
supplieth the want of
the saints, but is abundant
also by many
thanksgivings unto God;

13. **Whiles** by the experiment
of this ministration
they glorify God for your
professed
subjection unto the gospel
of Christ,
and for *your* **liberal**
distribution unto them, and
unto all *men* **;**

14. **And by their prayer**
for you, which long after you
for the exceeding
grace of God in you.

15. **Thanks** *be* **unto God for**
his unspeakable gift.

CHAPTER 10

1. Now I Paul myself beseech you by
the meekness and gentleness of
Christ, who in presence *am* base
among you, but being absent am bold
toward you:

2. **But I beseech** *you,* **that I**
may not be bold when I am
present with that confidence,
wherewith I think to be bold
against some, which think
of us as if we walked
according to the flesh.

3. For though we walk in the flesh,
we do not war
after the flesh:

4. **(For the weapons of our**
warfare *are* **not carnal, but**
mighty through God to the
pulling down of
strong holds;)

5. **Casting down**
imaginations, and every
high thing that exalteth itself
against the knowledge of
God, and bringing into
captivity every thought
to the obedience of Christ;

6. **And having in a**

readiness to revenge all
disobedience,
when your obedience is fulfilled.

7. Do ye look on things after the
outward appearance?
If any man trust
to himself
that he is Christ's,
let him of himself think this again,
that, as he *is* Christ's,
even so *are* **we Christ's.**

8. **For though I should boast**
somewhat more
of our
authority, which the Lord
hath given us
for edification, and not
for your
destruction,
I should not be ashamed:

9. **That I may not seem as if I**
would
terrify you by letters.

10. **For** *his* **letters, say they,**
are **weighty** and powerful;
but *his* bodily
presence *is* **weak, and** *his*
speech contemptible.

11. Let such an one
think this, that, such
as we are in word
by letters when we are
absent, such *will we be* also
in deed when we are
present.

12. **For we dare not**
make ourselves of the number, or
compare ourselves
with some that commend
themselves: but they measuring
themselves by themselves, and
comparing themselves
among themselves,
are not wise.

13. **But we will not boast of**
things without
our **measure, but**
according to the measure
of the rule which
God hath distributed to us,
a measure to reach even unto
you.

14. For we stretch not ourselves

beyond *our measure*, as though we reached not unto you: for we are come as far as to you also in *preaching* the gospel of Christ:

15. **Not boasting of** things without *our* measure, *that is*, of **other men's labours; but having hope,** when your faith is increased, **that we shall be enlarged by you** according to our rule abundantly,

16. To preach the gospel in the *regions* beyond you, **and not to boast in another man's line of things** made ready to our hand.

17. But he that glorieth, let him glory in the Lord.

18. **For not he that commendeth himself is approved, but whom the Lord commendeth.**

CHAPTER 11

1. Would to God ye could bear with me a little in *my* folly: and indeed bear with me.

2. **For I am jealous over you with godly jealousy: for I have espoused you** to one husband, that I may present *you* **as a** chaste **virgin to Christ.**

3. **But I fear,** lest by any means, **as the serpent beguiled Eve** through his subtilty, **so your minds should be corrupted from the simplicity** that is **in Christ.**

4. **For if he that cometh preacheth another Jesus,** whom we have not preached, or *if* ye receive another spirit, which ye have not received, **or another gospel,** which ye have not accepted, **ye might** well **bear with** *him.*

5. For I suppose **I was not** a whit **behind the** very **chiefest apostles.**

6. **But though** *I be* **rude in speech,** yet not in knowledge; but we have been throughly made manifest among you in all things.

7. Have I committed an offence in abasing myself that ye might be exalted, because **I have preached** to you **the gospel** of God **freely?**

8. **I robbed other churches,** taking wages *of them*, **to do you service.**

9. **And when I was present with you,** and wanted, I was chargeable to no man: for that which was lacking to me the brethren which came from Macedonia supplied: and in all *things* **I have kept myself from being burdensome** unto you, and *so* will I keep *myself.*

10. **As the truth of Christ is in me, no man shall stop** me of **this boasting** in the regions of Achaia.

11. Wherefore? because I love you not? God knoweth.

12. But what I do, that I will do, **that I may cut off occasion from them which desire occasion;** that wherein they glory, they may be found even as we.

13. **For such** *are* **false apostles,** deceitful workers, **transforming themselves into the apostles of Christ.**

14. **And no marvel; for Satan** himself **is transformed into an angel of light.**

15. **Therefore** *it is* **no great thing if his ministers** also **be transformed** as the ministers of righteousness; whose end shall be according to their works.

16. **I say again, Let no man think me a fool;** if otherwise, yet as a fool receive me, that I may boast myself a little.

17. That which I speak, I speak *it* not

after the Lord, but as it were foolishly, in this confidence of boasting.

18. Seeing that many glory after the flesh, I will glory also.

19. For ye suffer fools gladly, seeing ye *yourselves* are wise.

20. For ye suffer, if a man bring you into bondage, if a man devour *you*, if a man take *of you*, if a man exalt himself, if a man smite you on the face.

21. I speak as concerning reproach, as though we had been weak. **Howbeit whereinsoever any is bold, (I speak foolishly,) I am bold also.**

22. **Are they Hebrews? so am I.** Are they Israelites? so am I. **Are they the seed of Abraham? so am I.**

23. **Are they ministers of Christ?** (I speak as a fool) **I am more;** in labours more abundant, in stripes above measure, **in prisons more frequent, in deaths oft.**

24. **Of the Jews five times received I forty *stripes* save one.**

25. **Thrice was I beaten with rods, once was I stoned, thrice I suffered shipwreck,** a night and a day **I have been in the deep;**

26. *In* journeyings often, *in* perils of waters, *in* **perils of robbers,** *in* perils by *mine own* countrymen, *in* perils by the heathen, *in* perils in the city, *in* perils in the wilderness, *in* perils in the sea, *in* perils among false brethren;

27. **In weariness and painfulness,** in watchings often, **in hunger** and thirst, **in fastings** often, **in cold and nakedness.**

28. Beside those things that are without, that which cometh upon me daily, the care of all the churches.

29. Who is weak, and I am not weak? who is offended, and I burn not?

30. **If I must needs glory, I will glory** of the things which concern

mine infirmities.

31. **The God and Father of our Lord** Jesus Christ, which is blessed for evermore, **knoweth that I lie not.**

32. **In Damascus the governor** under Aretas the king kept the city of the Damascenes with a garrison, **desirous to apprehend me:**

33. **And through a window** in a basket was **I** let down by the wall, and **escaped his hands.**

CHAPTER 12

1. It is not expedient for me doubtless to glory. **I will come to visions and revelations of the Lord.**

2. **I knew a man in Christ** above fourteen years ago, **(whether in the body, I cannot tell;** or whether out of the body, I cannot tell: **God knoweth;) such an one caught up to the third heaven.**

3. And I knew such a man, (whether in the body, or out of the body, I cannot tell: God knoweth;)

4. **How that he was caught up into paradise, and heard unspeakable words,** which it is **not lawful** for a man **to utter.**

5. **Of such an one will I glory:** yet of myself I will not glory, but in mine infirmities.

6. For though I would desire to glory, I shall not be a fool; for I will say the truth: but *now* I forbear, lest any man should think of me above that which he seeth me *to be*, or *that* he heareth of me.

7. **And lest I should be exalted** above measure **through** the abundance of **the revelations, there was given to me a thorn** in the flesh, **the messenger of Satan to**

buffet me, lest I should be exalted above measure.

8. For this thing **I besought the Lord thrice, that it might depart** from me. 9. **And he said** unto me, **My grace is sufficient** for thee: for my strength is made perfect in weakness. **Most gladly therefore will I** rather **glory in my infirmities, that the power of Christ may rest upon me.** 10. **Therefore I take pleasure in** infirmities, in reproaches, in necessities, in persecutions, in **distresses for Christ's sake: for when I am weak, then am I strong.** 11. I am become a fool in glorying; ye have compelled me: for I ought to have been commended of you: for **in nothing am I behind the** very **chiefest apostles,** though I be nothing. 12. **Truly the signs of an apostle were wrought among you** in all patience, in signs, and wonders, and mighty deeds. 13. For what is it wherein ye were inferior to other churches, except *it be* that I myself was not burdensome to you? forgive me this wrong. 14. **Behold, the third time I am ready to come to you; and I will not be burdensome** to you: for I seek not your's but you: for the children ought not to lay up for the parents, but the parents for the children. 15. **And I will very gladly spend and be spent for you;** though the more abundantly I love you, the less I be loved. 16. But be it so, I did not burden you: nevertheless, being crafty, I caught you with guile. 17. Did I make a gain of you by any of them whom I sent unto you?

18. I desired Titus, and with *him* I sent a brother. Did Titus make a gain of you? walked we not in the same spirit? *walked we* not in the same steps? 19. Again, think ye that we excuse ourselves unto you? we speak before God in Christ: but **we do all things,** dearly beloved, **for your edifying.** 20. **For I fear, lest, when I come,** I shall not find you such as I would, and *that* I shall be found unto you such as ye would not: lest **there be debates,** envyings, wraths, strifes, **backbitings, whisperings** swellings, tumults: 21. *And* lest, when I come **again,** my God will humble me among you, and *that* **I shall bewail many which have sinned** already, **and have not repented of the uncleanness** and fornication and lasciviousness **which they have committed.**

CHAPTER 13

1. This *is* the third *time* I am coming to you. In the mouth of two or three witnesses shall every word be established. 2. I told you before, and foretell you, as if I were present, the second time; and being absent now **I write to them which** heretofore **have sinned,** and to all other, **that, if I come again, I will not spare:** 3. **Since ye seek a proof of Christ speaking in me, which to you-ward is not weak, but is mighty in you.** 4. **For though he was crucified through weakness, yet he liveth by the power of God. For we** also **are weak in him, but we shall live with him by the power of God** toward you.

5. **Examine yourselves, whether ye be in the faith;** prove your own selves. Know ye not your own selves, how that Jesus Christ is in you, except ye be reprobates? 6. But I trust that ye shall know that we are not reprobates. 7. **Now I pray to God that ye do no evil;** not that we should appear approved, **but that ye should do that which is honest,** though we be as reprobates. 8. For we can do nothing against the truth, but for the truth. 9. For we are glad, when we are weak, and ye are strong: and this also we wish, *even* your perfection. 10. **Therefore I write** these things **being absent, lest being present I should use sharpness, according to the power which the Lord hath given me to edification,** and not to destruction. 11. **Finally,** brethren, farewell. **Be perfect,** be of good comfort, be of one mind, **live in peace; and** the **God** of love and peace **shall be with you.** 12. Greet one another with an holy kiss. 13. All the saints salute you. 14. **The grace of the Lord Jesus** Christ, **and the love of God, and the communion of the Holy Ghost, be with you all. Amen.**

THE EPISTLE TO THE GALATIANS

BACKGROUND INFORMATION

Author – Paul, an Apostle.
Date Written – probably
between 45 and **56** A.D.

Number of:
Verses -   149
Chapters -   6
Total Words - 3,098
Scan Words - 1,496
Scan Words represent 48 %
of Total Words.

Theme – written to show that
we are
justified by God
through faith and not
through keeping laws.

OUTLINE OF THE EPISTLE

I.   **Paul's vindication of his Apostleship** and of our redemption through Christ.
     Chapter 1
II. Paul's rebuke of Peter, and **a defense of justification by faith.**
     Chapters 2—3:9
III. Paul's explanation of **the curse of the law,** and Christ's power to redeem.
     Chapters 3:9—4
IV. Paul's exposition of our **freedom and benefits as sons of God.**
     Chapters 4—5:13
V.   Paul's teaching on **subjecting the flesh to the Holy Spirit.**
     Chapters 5:15—6

CHAPTER 1

1. **Paul,** an apostle, (not of men, neither by man, but by Jesus Christ, and God the Father, who raised him from the dead;)

2. And all the brethren which are with me,

unto the churches of Galatia:

3. **Grace** *be* **to you and peace from God the Father, and** *from* **our Lord Jesus Christ,**

4. **Who gave himself for our sins, that he might deliver us from this present evil world, according to the will of God** and our Father:

5. To whom *be* glory for ever and ever. Amen.

6. **I marvel that ye are so soon removed** from him that called you into the grace of Christ **unto another gospel:**

7. **Which is not another; but there be some that** trouble you, and would **pervert the gospel of Christ.**

8. **But though we, or an angel** from heaven, **preach any other gospel** unto you than that which we have preached unto you, **let him be accursed.**

9. As we said before, **so say I now again, if any man preach any other gospel** unto you than that ye have received, **let him be accursed.**

10. For do I now persuade men, or God? or do I seek to please men? for if I yet pleased men, I should not be the servant of Christ.

11. But I certify you, brethren, that **the gospel which was preached of me is not after man.**

12. For I neither received it of man, neither was I taught *it*, **but by the revelation of Jesus Christ.**

13. **For ye have heard** of my conversation in time past in the Jews' religion, **how that** beyond measure **I persecuted the church** of God, **and wasted it:**

14. **And profited in the Jews' religion** above many my equals in mine own nation, **being more** exceedingly **zealous of the traditions** of my fathers.

15. **But when it pleased God,** who separated me from my mother's womb, and called *me* by his grace,

16. **To reveal his Son in me,** that I might preach him among the heathen; **immediately I conferred not with flesh and blood:**

17. Neither went I up to Jerusalem to them which were apostles before me; **but I went into Arabia, and returned** again **unto Damascus.**

18. **Then after three years I went** up to Jerusalem **to see Peter,** and abode with him fifteen days.

19. **But other of the apostles saw I none, save James** the Lord's brother.

20. Now the things which I write unto you, behold, before God, I lie not.

21. **Afterwards I came into** the regions of **Syria and Cilicia;**

22. **And was unknown by face** unto the churches of Judaea which were in Christ:

23. **But they had heard only, That he which persecuted us** in times past **now preacheth the faith** which once he destroyed.

24. And they glorified God in me.

CHAPTER 2

1. **Then fourteen years after I went up again to Jerusalem** with Barnabas, and took Titus with *me* also.

2. And I went up **by revelation, and communicated** unto them **that gospel which I preach among the Gentiles,** but privately to them which were of reputation, lest by any means I should run, or had run, in vain. 3. **But neither Titus,** who was with me, **being a Greek, was compelled to be circumcised:** 4. **And** that because of **false brethren** unawares brought in, who **came in privily to spy out our liberty** which we have **in Christ Jesus, that they might bring us into bondage:** 5. **To whom we gave place** by subjection, no, **not for an hour; that the truth** of the gospel **might continue** with you. 6. But of these who seemed to be somewhat, (whatsoever they were, it maketh no matter to me: God accepteth no man's person:) for they who seemed *to be somewhat* in conference added nothing to me: 7. **But** contrariwise, when **they saw that the gospel of the uncircumcision was committed unto me, as** *the gospel* of **the circumcision** *was* **unto Peter;** 8. (For he that wrought effectually in Peter to the apostleship of the circumcision, the same was mighty in me toward the Gentiles:) 9. **And when James, Cephas, and John,** who seemed to be pillars, **perceived the grace** that was **given** unto **me, they gave to me and Barnabas the right hands of fellowship; that we** *should go* **unto the heathen,** and they unto the circumcision.

10. Only *they would* that we should remember the poor; the same which I also was forward to do. 11. **But when Peter was come to Antioch, I withstood him to the face, because he was to be blamed.** 12. **For before** that certain came from James, **he did eat with the Gentiles: but** when they were come, **he** withdrew and **separated himself, fearing them** which were **of the circumcision.** 13. **And the other Jews dissembled likewise** with him; insomuch that **Barnabas also was carried away** with their dissimulation. 14. **But when I saw that they walked not** uprightly **according to** the truth of **the gospel, I said unto Peter** before *them* all, **If thou, being a Jew, livest after the manner of Gentiles, and not as** do the **Jews, why compellest** thou the **Gentiles to live as** do the **Jews?** 15. We *who are* Jews by nature, and not sinners of the Gentiles, 16. Knowing that a **man is not justified by the works of the law, but by the faith of Jesus Christ,** even we have believed in Jesus Christ, that we might be justified by the faith of Christ, and not by the works of the law: **for by the works of the law shall no flesh be justified.** 17. But if, while we seek to be justified by Christ, we ourselves also are found sinners, *is* therefore Christ the minister of sin? God forbid. 18. For if I build again the things which

I destroyed, I make myself a transgressor.

19. **For I through the law am dead** to the law, **that I might live unto God.** 20. **I am crucified with Christ: neverthless I live; yet not I, but Christ liveth in me: and the life which I now live in the flesh I live by the faith of the Son of God, who loved me, and gave himself for me.** 21. I do not frustrate the grace of God: for **if righteousness** *come* **by the law, then Christ is dead in vain.**

CHAPTER 3

1. **O foolish Galatians, who hath bewitched you,** that ye should not obey the truth, before whose eyes Jesus Christ hath been evidently set forth, crucified among you? 2. This only would I learn of you, Received ye the Spirit by the works of the law, or by the hearing of faith? 3. **Are ye so foolish? having begun in the Spirit, are ye now made perfect by the flesh?** 4. Have ye suffered so many things in vain? if *it be* yet in vain. 5. **He therefore that ministereth** to you **the Spirit, and worketh miracles** among you, *doeth he it* **by** the works of **the law, or by** the hearing of **faith?** 6. **Even as Abraham believed God, and it was accounted** to him for **righteousness.** 7. Know ye therefore that **they** which are **of faith, the same are the children of Abraham.** 8. **And the scripture, foreseeing that God would**

justify the heathen through faith, preached before the gospel **unto Abraham,** *saying,* **In thee shall all nations be blessed.** 9. So then they which be of faith are blessed with faithful Abraham. 10. **For as many as are of the** works of the **law are under the curse:** for it is written, Cursed *is* every one that continueth not in all things which are written in the book of the law to do them. 11. **But that no man is justified by the law** in the sight of God, *it* **is evident: for, The just shall live by faith.** 12. And the law is not of faith: but, The man that doeth them shall live in them. 13. **Christ hath redeemed us from the curse of the law, being made a curse for us:** for it is written, Cursed *is* every one that hangeth on a tree: 14. **That the blessing of Abraham might come on the Gentiles through Jesus Christ;** that we might receive the promise of the Spirit through faith. 15. Brethren, I speak after the manner of men; Though *it be* but a man's covenant, yet *if it be* confirmed, no man disannulleth, or addeth thereto. 16. **Now to Abraham and his seed were the promises made. He saith not, And to seeds,** as of many; **but as of one, And to thy seed, which is Christ.** 17. And this I say, *that* the covenant, that was confirmed before of God in Christ, the law, which was four hundred and thirty years after, cannot disannul, that it should make the promise of none effect. 18. For if the inheritance *be* of the law, *it is* no more of promise: but **God gave** *it* **to Abraham by promise.** 19. **Wherefore then** *serveth*

the law? It was added because of transgressions, till the seed should come to whom the promise was made; and it was ordained by angels in the hand of a mediator. 20. Now a mediator is not a *mediator* of one, but God is one. 21. *Is* **the law then against the promises of God? God forbid: for if** there had been **a law** given which **could have given life,** verily **righteousness should have been by the law.** 22. **But the scripture hath concluded all under sin, that the** promise by **faith of Jesus Christ might be given** to them that believe. 23. But before faith came, we were kept under the law, shut up unto the faith which should afterwards be revealed. 24. **Wherefore the law was our schoolmaster** *to bring us* **unto Christ,** that we might be justified by faith. 25. **But after** that **faith is come, we are no longer under a schoolmaster.** 26. **For ye are all the children of God by faith in Christ Jesus.** 27. **For** as many of **you** as have been **baptized into Christ have put on Christ.** 28. **There is neither Jew nor Greek,** there is neither **bond nor free,** there is **neither male nor female: for ye are all one in Christ Jesus.** 29. And if ye *be* Christ's, then are ye Abraham's seed, **and heirs according to the promise.**

CHAPTER 4

1. Now I say, *That*

the heir, as long as he is **a child,** differeth nothing from a servant, **though he be lord of all;** 2. **But is under tutors** and governors **until the time appointed of the father.** 3. **Even so we, when we were children, were in bondage under the elements** of the world: 4. **But** when the fulness of the time was come, **God sent** forth **his Son,** made of a woman, **made under the law,** 5. **To redeem them** that were **under the law,** that we might receive the adoption of sons. 6. **And because ye are sons, God** hath **sent** forth **the Spirit of his Son into your hearts, crying, Abba, Father.** 7. **Wherefore thou art no more a servant, but a son;** and if a son, then **an heir of God through Christ.** 8. Howbeit then, when ye knew not God, ye did service unto them which by nature are no gods. 9. **But now, after that ye have known God,** or rather are known of God, **how turn ye again** to the weak and beggarly elements, whereunto ye desire again **to be in bondage?** 10. Ye observe days, and months, and times, and years. 11. **I am afraid of you, lest I have bestowed upon you labour in vain.** 12. Brethren, I beseech you, be as I am; for I am as ye are: ye have not injured me at all. 13. Ye know how **through infirmity of the flesh I preached the gospel** unto you at the first.

14. **And** my temptation which was in my flesh **ye despised not, nor rejected; but received me** as an angel of God, *even* **as Christ Jesus.**

15. Where is then the blessedness ye spake of? for I bear you record, that, if *it had been* possible, **ye would have plucked out your own eyes, and have given them to me.**

16. **Am I therefore** become **your enemy, because I tell you the truth?**

17. They zealously affect you, *but* not well; yea, they would exclude you, that ye might affect them.

18. But *it is* good to be zealously affected always in *a* good *thing*, and not only when I am present with you.

19. **My little children, of whom I travail in birth** again **until Christ be formed in you,**

20. I desire to be present with you now, and to change my voice; for I stand in doubt of you.

21. Tell me, ye that desire to be under the law, **do ye not hear the law**

22. For it is written, that **Abraham had two sons, the one by a bondmaid, the other by a freewoman.**

23. **But he** *who was* **of the bondwoman was born after the flesh; but he of the freewoman** *was* **by promise.**

24. **Which things are an allegory: for** these are the **two covenants;** the **one** from the mount Sinai, which **gendereth to bondage, which is Agar.**

25. For this Agar is mount Sinai in Arabia, and answereth to Jerusalem which now is, and is in bondage with her children.

26. **But Jerusalem** which is above **is free, which is the mother**

of us all.

27. For it is written, Rejoice, *thou* barren that bearest not; break forth and cry, thou that travailest not: for the desolate hath many more children than she which hath an husband.

28. **Now we,** brethren, **as Isaac** was, **are the children of promise.**

29. **But** as then **he that was born after the flesh persecuted him** *that was* **born after the Spirit,** even so *it is* now.

30. **Nevertheless what saith the scripture? Cast out the bondwoman and her son: for the son of the bondwoman shall not be heir** with the son of the freewoman.

31. So then, brethren, **we are** not **children** of the bondwoman, but **of the free.**

CHAPTER 5

1. **Stand fast** therefore in the liberty wherewith **Christ hath made us free, and be not entangled again with the yoke of bondage.**

2. Behold, I Paul say unto you, that **if ye be circumcised, Christ shall profit you nothing.**

3. For I testify again to **every man that is circumcised,** that he **is a debtor to do the whole law.**

4. Christ is become of no effect unto you, **whosoever of you are justified by the law; ye are fallen from grace.**

5. For we through the Spirit wait for the hope of righteousness by faith.

6. **For in Jesus Christ neither circumcision availeth any thing, nor uncircumcision; but faith which worketh by love.**

7. Ye did run well;
■ who did hinder you that ye
■ should not obey the truth?
■ 8. This persuasion *cometh*
■ not of him that calleth you.
9. A little leaven leaveneth
the whole lump.
■ 10. I have confidence
in you through the Lord,
■ that ye will be none
■ otherwise minded: but he
■ that troubleth you shall
■ bear his judgment,
whosoever he be.
11. And I, brethren, if I yet preach
circumcision, why do I yet suffer
persecution? then is the offence of
the cross ceased.
12. I would they were even cut off
which trouble you.
13. For, brethren,
■ ye have been called unto
■ liberty; only *use* not liberty
for an occasion
■ to the flesh,
but by love serve one another.
■ 14. For all the law is fulfilled
■ in one word, *even* in this;
■ Thou shalt love thy
■ neighbour as thyself.
15. But if ye bite and devour one
another, take heed that ye be not
consumed one of another.
16. *This* I say then,
■ Walk in the Spirit, and ye
■ shall not fulfil the lust of
■ the flesh.
■ 17. For the flesh
lusteth against the Spirit,
■ and the Spirit
against the flesh: and these
■ are contrary the one to the
■ other: so that ye cannot do the
things that ye would.
18. But if ye be led of the Spirit,
ye are not under the law.
■ 19. Now the works of the
■ flesh are manifest, which
■ are *these*; Adultery,
■ fornication, uncleanness,
■ lasciviousness,
■ 20. Idolatry, witchcraft,
■ hatred, variance,

■ emulations, wrath, strife,
■ seditions, heresies,
■ 21. Envyings, murders,
■ drunkenness, revellings,
and such like: of the which I tell you
before, as I have also told *you* in time
past, that
■ they which do such things
■ shall not inherit the
■ kingdom of God.
22. But the fruit of the Spirit is
■ love, joy, peace, long-
■ suffering, gentleness,
■ goodness, faith,
23. Meekness, temperance:
■ against such there
■ is no law.
24. And they that are Christ's have
crucified the flesh with the
affections and lusts.
■ 25. If we live in the Spirit, let
■ us also walk in the Spirit.
26. Let us not be desirous of vain
glory, provoking one another, envying
one another.

CHAPTER 6
■ 1. Brethren, if a man be
■ overtaken in a fault,
ye which are spiritual,
■ restore such an one in the
■ spirit of meekness;
considering thyself, lest thou also
be tempted.
■ 2. Bear one another's
■ burdens, and so fulfil the law
of Christ.
■ 3. For if a man think himself
■ to be something, when
■ he is nothing, he
■ deceiveth himself.
4. But let every man prove his own
work, and then shall he have rejoicing
in himself alone, and not in another.
5. For every man shall bear his
own burden.
6. Let him that is taught in the word
communicate unto him that teacheth
in all good things.
■ 7. Be not deceived; God is
■ not mocked: for what-
■ soever a man soweth, that
■ shall he also reap.

■ 8. **For he that soweth to his**
■ **flesh shall** of the flesh
■ **reap corruption;**
■ **but he that soweth to the**
■ **Spirit shall** of the Spirit
■ **reap life everlasting.**

9. And let us not be weary in well-doing: for in due season we shall reap, if we faint not.

■ 10. **As we have** therefore
■ **opportunity, let us do good**
■ **unto all** *men,*

especially unto them who are of the household of faith.

11. Ye see how large a letter I have written unto you with mine own hand.

12. As many as desire to make a fair shew in the flesh, they constrain you to be circumcised; only lest they should suffer persecution for the cross of Christ.

■ 13. **For neither they**
■ **themselves who are**
■ **circumcised keep the law;**
■ **but desire to have you**
■ **circumcised, that they may**
■ **glory in your flesh.**
■ 14. **But God forbid that I**
■ **should glory, save in the**
■ **cross of our Lord**
■ **Jesus Christ,**

by whom the world is crucified unto me, and I unto the world.

■ 15. **For in Christ Jesus**
■ **neither circumcision**
■ **availeth** any thing,
■ **nor uncircumcision, but a**
■ **new creature.**

16. And as many as walk according to this rule, peace *be* on them, and mercy, and upon the Israel of God.

17. From henceforth let no man trouble me: for I bear in my body the marks of the Lord Jesus.

18. Brethren, the grace of our Lord Jesus Christ *be* with your spirit.

■ **Amen.**

THE EPISTLE TO THE EPHESIANS

BACKGROUND INFORMATION

Author – Paul, an Apostle.
Date Written – probably
between 60 and **65** A.D.

Number of:
Verses -   155
Chapters -   6
Total Words - 3,039
Scan Words - 1,486
Scan Words represent 48 %
of Total Words.

Theme – written to show that
**the Church is the Body of
Christ, and** the quality of
Christian conduct which
should follow.

OUTLINE OF THE EPISTLE

I.   **The supremacy
of Christ,**
God's gift of salvation to
both Jew and Gentile and
Paul's mission to
the Gentiles.
Chapters 1—3

II. **The ministry of
the Church** in God's plan
of reconciliation through
Christ, the unity of the
Church despite its
variety of gifts and his
instructions to the family.
Chapters 4—6

III. A discourse to
Christians on
the full armor of Christ
and the responsibility of
the believer to the
Church.
Chapter 6

CHAPTER 1

1. **Paul,** an apostle of Jesus Christ by the will of God,
to the saints which are **at Ephesus, and to the faithful in Christ Jesus:**

2. Grace *be* to you, and peace, from God our Father, and *from* the Lord Jesus Christ.

3. **Blessed** *be* **the God** and Father **of** our Lord **Jesus** Christ, **who hath blessed us with** all **spiritual blessings in heavenly** *places* **in Christ:**

4. **According as he hath chosen us in him before the foundation of the world,** that we should be holy and without blame before him in love:

5. **Having predestinated us unto the adoption of children by Jesus** Christ to himself, according to the good pleasure of his will,

6. To the praise of the glory of his grace, wherein he hath made us accepted in the beloved.

7. **In whom we have redemption through his blood, the forgiveness of sins, according to** the riches of **his grace;**

8. **Wherein he hath abounded toward us in all wisdom** and prudence;

9. **Having made known unto us the mystery of his will,** according to his good pleasure which he hath purposed in himself:

10. **That in** the dispensation of **the fulness of times he might gather together** in one **all things in Christ, both** which are **in heaven, and** which are on **earth;** *even* in him:

11. **In whom also we have** obtained **an inheritance, being predestinated according to the purpose of him who worketh all things** after the counsel **of his own will:**

12. **That we should be to the praise of his glory, who first trusted in Christ.**

13. **In whom** ye also *trusted*, after that ye heard the word of truth, the gospel of your salvation: in whom also after that ye believed, **ye were sealed with that holy Spirit of promise,**

14. **Which is the earnest of our inheritance until the redemption of the purchased possession,** unto the praise of his glory.

15. **Wherefore I** also, after I heard of your faith in the Lord Jesus, and love unto all the saints,

16. **Cease not to give thanks for you, making mention of you in my prayers;**

17. **That the God of our Lord** Jesus Christ, the Father of glory, **may give** unto **you** the spirit of **wisdom and revelation in the knowledge of him:**

18. The eyes of your understanding being enlightened; **that ye may know what is the hope of his calling, and** what the riches of **the glory of his inheritance in the saints,**

19. **And what** *is* **the** exceeding **greatness of his power to us-ward who believe, according to** the working of **his** mighty **power,**

20. Which he wrought **in Christ, when he raised him** from the dead, **and set** *him* **at his** own **right hand** in the heavenly *places*,

21. **Far above all principality, and power,** and might, and dominion, and every name that is named, not only in this world,

but also in that which is to come:

■ 22. **And hath put all *things***
■ **under his feet, and gave**
■ **him *to be* the head over all**
■ ***things* to the church,**
■ 23. **Which is his body,** the
fulness of him that filleth all in all.

CHAPTER 2

■ 1. **And you *hath he***
■ ***quickened*, who were dead**
■ **in** trespasses and
■ **sins;**
■ 2. **Wherein in time past ye**
■ **walked according to**
the course of
■ **this world, according to the**
■ **prince of** the power of
■ **the air,** the spirit that now worketh
in the children of disobedience:
■ 3. **Among whom also we all**
■ **had our conversation**
in times past
■ **in the lusts of our flesh,**
fulfilling the desires of the flesh and of
the mind; and were by nature the
children of wrath, even as others.
■ 4. **But God, who is rich in**
■ **mercy,** for his great love
wherewith he loved us,
■ 5. **Even when we were dead**
■ **in sins, hath quickened us**
■ **together with Christ,**
(by grace ye are saved;)
■ 6. **And hath raised *us* up**
■ **together,** and made *us* sit together
in heavenly *places* in Christ Jesus:
■ 7. **That in the ages to come**
■ **he might shew the**
■ **exceeding riches of his**
■ **grace** in *his* kindness
toward us through Christ Jesus.
■ 8. **For by grace are ye**
■ **saved through faith; and**
that
■ **not of yourselves:**
■ ***it is* the gift of God:**
■ 9. **Not of works, lest any**
■ **man should boast.**
■ 10. **For we are his**
■ **workmanship, created in**
■ **Christ Jesus unto good**
■ **works,** which God hath before

ordained that we should walk in them.
■ 11. **Wherefore remember,**
■ **that ye *being*** in time past
■ **Gentiles in the flesh,**
who are called Uncircumcision by that
which is called the Circumcision in the
flesh made by hands;
■ 12. **That at that time ye were**
■ **without Christ, being** aliens
from the commonwealth of Israel, and
■ **strangers from the**
■ **covenants of promise,**
having no hope,
■ **and without God** in the world:
■ 13. **But now in Christ Jesus**
■ **ye** who sometimes were far off
■ **are made nigh by the**
■ **blood** of Christ.
■ 14. **For he is our peace,** who
hath made both one,
■ **and hath broken down the**
■ **middle wall of partition**
between us;
15. Having abolished in his flesh the
enmity, *even* the law of
commandments *contained* in
ordinances; for to make in himself of
twain one new man, *so* making peace;
■ 16. **And that he might**
■ **reconcile both unto God in**
■ **one body by the cross,**
having slain the enmity thereby:
17. And came and preached peace to
you which were afar off, and to them
that were nigh.
■ 18. **For through him we both**
■ **have access by one Spirit**
■ **unto the Father.**
■ 19. **Now therefore ye are** no
more strangers and foreigners, but
■ **fellow-citizens with the**
■ **saints,** and of the household
of God;
■ 20. **And are built upon the**
■ **foundation of the apostles**
■ **and prophets, Jesus**
■ **Christ himself being the**
■ **chief corner *stone*;**
21. In whom all the building fitly
framed together groweth unto an holy
temple in the Lord:
■ 22. **In whom ye also are**
■ **builded** together

■ **for an habitation of God**
through the Spirit.

CHAPTER 3

1. For this cause I Paul, the prisoner of Jesus Christ for you Gentiles,
■ **2. If ye have heard of the**
■ **dispensation of the grace**
■ **of God which is given me to**
■ **you-ward:**
■ **3. How that by revelation he**
■ **made known** unto me
■ **the mystery;**
(as I wrote afore in few words,
4. Whereby, when ye read, ye may understand my knowledge in the mystery of Christ)
5. Which in other ages was not made known unto the sons of men, as it is now revealed unto his holy apostles and prophets by the Spirit;
■ **6. That the Gentiles should**
■ **be fellow heirs, and**
of the same body, and
■ **partakers of his promise in**
■ **Christ** by the gospel:
■ **7. Whereof I was made a**
■ **minister,** according to the gift of the grace of God given unto me by the effectual working of his power.
8. Unto me, who am less than the least of all saints, is this grace given,
■ **that I should preach**
■ **among the Gentiles**
the unsearchable riches of Christ;
■ **9. And to make all** *men* **see**
■ **what** *is* **the fellowship of the**
■ **mystery, which**
from the beginning of the world
■ **hath been hid in God, who**
■ **created all things by**
■ **Jesus Christ:**
10. To the intent that now unto the principalities and powers in heavenly *places* might be known by the church the manifold wisdom of God,
11. According to the eternal purpose which he purposed in Christ Jesus our Lord:
■ **12. In whom we have**
■ **boldness and access**
with confidence

■ **by the faith of him.**
■ **13. Wherefore I desire that**
■ **ye faint not at my**
■ **tribulations for you,**
which is your glory
■ **14. For this cause I bow**
my knees
■ **unto** the Father of
■ **our Lord Jesus Christ,**
15. Of whom the whole family in heaven and earth is named,
■ **16. That he would grant you,**
according to the riches of his glory,
■ **to be strengthened with**
■ **might by his Spirit**
in the inner man;
■ **17. That Christ may dwell in**
■ **your hearts by faith;** that ye, being rooted and grounded in love,
18. May be able to comprehend with all saints what *is* the breadth, and length, and depth, and height;
■ **19. And to know the love of**
■ **Christ,** which passeth knowledge, that ye might be filled with all the fulness of God.
■ **20. Now unto him that is**
■ **able to do** exceeding abundantly
■ **above all that we ask or**
■ **think,** according to the power that worketh in us,
■ **21. Unto him** *be* **glory**
in the church by Christ Jesus
■ **throughout all ages,**
world without end. Amen.

CHAPTER 4

■ 1. I therefore,
the prisoner of the Lord,
■ **beseech you that ye walk**
■ **worthy of the vocation**
■ **wherewith ye are called,**
■ 2. With all lowliness and
meekness, with longsuffering,
■ **forbearing one another**
■ **in love;**
■ **3. Endeavouring to keep the**
■ **unity of the Spirit**
in the bond of peace.
■ **4.** *There is* **one body,**
and one Spirit, even as ye are called in one hope of your calling;
■ **5. One Lord, one faith,**

one baptism,

6. **One God and Father of all,** who *is* above all, and through all, and in you all.

7. **But unto every one of us is given grace** according to the measure of the gift of Christ.

8. Wherefore he saith, When he ascended up on high, he led captivity captive, and gave gifts unto men.

9. (Now that he ascended, what is it but that he also descended first into the lower parts of the earth?

10. He that descended is the same also that ascended up far above all heavens, that he might fill all things.)

11. **And he gave some, apostles;** and **some, prophets;** and **some, evangelists; and some, pastors and teachers;**

12. **For the perfecting of the saints,** for the work of the ministry, **for the edifying of the body of Christ:**

13. **Till we all come** in the unity of the faith, and of the knowledge of the Son of God, unto a perfect man, **unto the measure of the** stature of the **fulness of Christ:**

14. **That we** *henceforth* **be no more children,** tossed to and fro, and **carried about with every wind of doctrine,** by the sleight of men, *and* cunning craftiness, whereby they lie in wait to deceive;

15. **But speaking the truth in love,** may grow up into him in all things, which is the head, *even* Christ:

16. From whom the whole body fitly joined together and compacted by that which every joint supplieth, according to the effectual working in the measure of every part, maketh increase of the body unto the edifying of itself in love.

17. **This I say therefore,** and testify in the Lord, that ye henceforth **walk not as other Gentiles**

walk, **in the vanity of their mind,**

18. **Having the understanding darkened,** being alienated from the life of God through the ignorance that is in them, **because of the blindness of their heart:**

19. **Who being past feeling have given themselves over unto lasciviousness,** to work all uncleanness with greediness.

20. **But ye have not so learned Christ;**

21. If so be that **ye** have heard him, and **have been taught** by him, as **the truth is in Jesus:**

22. **That ye put off concerning the former conversation the old man,** which is corrupt according to the deceitful lusts;

23. **And be renewed in the spirit of your mind;**

24. **And that ye put on the new man,** which after God is created in righteousness and true holiness.

25. **Wherefore putting away lying, speak** every man **truth** with his neighbour: for we are members one of another.

26. Be ye angry, and sin not: **let not the sun go down upon your wrath:**

27. **Neither give place to the devil.**

28. **Let him that stole steal no more: but rather let him labour,** working with *his* hands the thing which is good, that he may have to give to him that needeth.

29. **Let no corrupt communication proceed out of your mouth,** but that which is good to the use of edifying, that it may minister grace unto the hearers.

30. **And grieve not the holy**

Spirit of God, whereby ye are sealed unto the day of redemption.

31. **Let all bitterness, and wrath, and anger,** and clamour, **and evil speaking, be put away from you,** with all malice:

32. **And be ye kind** one to another, **tenderhearted, forgiving one another,** even as God for Christ's sake hath forgiven you.

CHAPTER 5

1. **Be ye therefore followers of God,** as dear children;

2. **And walk in love, as Christ also hath loved us, and hath given himself for us an offering and a sacrifice to God** for a sweet smelling savour.

3. But fornication, and all uncleanness, or covetousness, let it not be once named among you, as becometh saints;

4. Neither filthiness, nor foolish talking, nor jesting, which are not convenient: but rather giving of thanks.

5. **For this ye know, that no** whoremonger, nor **unclean person,** nor covetous man, who is an idolater, **hath any inheritance in the kingdom** of Christ and of God.

6. **Let no man deceive you with vain words:** for because of these things cometh the wrath of God upon the children of disobedience.

7. **Be not ye therefore partakers with them.**

8. **For ye were sometimes darkness, but now** *are ye* light in the Lord: **walk as children of light:**

9. (For the fruit of the Spirit *is* in all goodness and righteousness and truth;)

10. Proving what is acceptable unto the Lord.

11. **And have no fellowship with the unfruitful works of darkness, but rather reprove** *them.*

12. For it is a shame even to speak of those things which are done of them in secret.

13. **But all things that are reproved are made manifest by the light:** for whatsoever doth make manifest is light.

14. **Wherefore he saith,** Awake thou that sleepest, and **arise from the dead, and Christ shall give thee light.**

15. See then that ye walk circumspectly, not as fools, but as wise,

16. Redeeming the time, because the days are evil.

17. **Wherefore be ye not unwise, but understanding what the will of the Lord** *is.*

18. **And be not drunk with wine,** wherein is excess; **but be filled with the Spirit;**

19. **Speaking to yourselves in psalms and hymns and spiritual songs, singing** and making melody **in your heart to the Lord;**

20. **Giving thanks always for all things unto God** and the Father in the name of our Lord Jesus Christ;

21. **Submitting yourselves one to another in the fear of God.**

22. **Wives, submit** yourselves **unto your** own **husbands,** as unto the Lord.

23. **For the husband is the head of the wife, even as Christ is the head of the church:** and he is the saviour of the body.

24. **Therefore as the church is subject unto Christ, so** *let* **the wives** *be* **to their own husbands** in every thing.

25. **Husbands, love your wives, even as Christ also loved the church, and gave himself for it;**

26. That he might sanctify and

cleanse it with the washing of water by the word,

27. That he might present it to himself a glorious church, not having spot, or wrinkle, or any such thing; but that it should be holy and without blemish.

28. **So ought men to love their wives as their own bodies.** He that loveth his wife loveth himself.

29. **For no man ever yet hated his own flesh; but** nourisheth and **cherisheth it,** even as the Lord the church:

30. For we are members of his body, of his flesh, and of his bones.

31. **For this cause shall a man leave his father and mother, and shall be joined unto his wife, and they two shall be one flesh.**

32. **This is a great mystery: but I speak concerning Christ and the church.**

33. Nevertheless let every one of you in particular so love his wife even as himself; and the wife see that she reverence her husband.

CHAPTER 6

1. **Children, obey your parents** in the Lord: for this is right.

2. **Honour thy father and mother;** which is the first commandment with promise;

3. **That it may be well with thee, and thou mayest live long** on the earth.

4. **And, ye fathers, provoke not your children to wrath: but bring them up in the nurture and admonition of the Lord.**

5. **Servants, be obedient to** them that are **your masters** according to the flesh, with fear and trembling, in singleness of your heart, as unto Christ;

6. Not with eye service, as men pleasers; but as the servants of

Christ, doing the will of God from the heart;

7. **With good will doing service, as to the Lord, and not to men:**

8. **Knowing that whatsoever good thing any man doeth, the same shall he receive of the Lord, whether** he be **bond or free.**

9. **And, ye masters, do the same** things unto them, forbearing threatening: knowing that your Master also is in heaven; neither is there respect of persons with him.

10. **Finally,** my brethren, **be strong in the Lord,** and in the power of his might.

11. **Put on the whole armour of God,** that ye may be able **to stand against the wiles of the devil.**

12. **For we wrestle not against flesh** and blood, **but against** principalities, against powers, against **the rulers of the darkness of this world, against spiritual wickedness in high** places.

13. Wherefore take unto you the whole armour of God, that ye may be able to withstand in the evil day, and having done all, to stand.

14. **Stand therefore, having your loins girt about with truth, and having on the breastplate of righteousness;**

15. **And your feet shod with the** preparation of the **gospel of peace;**

16. **Above all, taking the shield of faith,** wherewith ye shall be able **to quench all the fiery darts of the wicked.**

17. **And take the helmet of salvation, and the sword of the Spirit, which is the word of God:**

18. **Praying always with all prayer and supplication in**

■ **the Spirit,** and watching thereunto with all perseverance and supplication for all saints;

■ 19. **And for me,** that utterance may be given unto me,

■ **that I may open my mouth**
■ **boldly, to make known** the mystery of

■ **the gospel,**
■ 20. **For which I am an**
■ **ambassador in bonds:** that therein I may speak boldly, as I ought to speak.

21. But that ye also may know my affairs, *and* how I do, Tychicus, a beloved brother and faithful minister in the Lord, shall make known to you all things:

22. Whom I have sent unto you for the same purpose, that ye might know our affairs, and *that* he might comfort your hearts.

■ 23. **Peace** *be* to the brethren,
■ **and love with faith, from**
■ **God** the Father
■ **and the Lord Jesus** Christ.
■ 24. **Grace** *be* with all them
■ **that love our Lord** Jesus Christ
■ **in sincerity.**
■ **Amen.**

THE EPISTLE TO THE PHILIPPIANS

BACKGROUND INFORMATION

Author – Paul, an Apostle.
Date Written – probably
between 60 and **65** A.D.

Number of:
Verses -   104
Chapters -   4
Total Words - 2,002
Scan Words - 1,055
Scan Words represent 52 %
of Total Words.

Theme – written to show the
radiant joy which the
believer possesses even
in the stresses and
storms of life.

OUTLINE OF THE EPISTLE

I. **Paul's call to live
   worthy of the gospel**
   and to follow Christ's
   example of humility.
   Chapters 1—3:2

II. **Paul's warning against
   the Judaizers** and his
   appeal for harmony and
   joy.
   Chapter 3—4:17

III. **Paul's caution about
   worldliness** and his
   appeal for steadfastness.
   Chapters 3:18—4

CHAPTER 1

1. **Paul and Timotheus,** the servants of Jesus Christ, **to all the saints** in Christ Jesus which are **at Philippi,** with the bishops and deacons:
2. Grace *be* unto you, and peace, from God our Father, and *from* the Lord Jesus Christ.
3. **I thank** my **God upon** every **remembrance of you,**
4. **Always in** every **prayer** of mine for you all **making request** with joy,
5. **For your fellowship in the gospel** from the first day until now;
6. **Being confident** of this very thing, **that he which hath begun a good work in you will perform** *it* until the day of Jesus Christ:
7. Even as it is meet for me to think this of you all, because **I have you in my heart;** inasmuch as both **in my bonds, and in the defence** and confirmation **of the gospel, ye all are partakers of my grace.**
8. For God is my record, how greatly **I long** after you all in the bowels of Jesus Christ.
9. And this I pray, **that your love may abound** yet more and more **in knowledge and** *in* all **judgment;**
10. **That ye** may **approve things** that are **excellent; that ye** may **be sincere and without offence** till the day of Christ;
11. **Being filled with** the fruits of **righteousness,** which are **by Jesus Christ,** unto the glory and praise of God.
12. **But** I would ye should **understand,** brethren, **that the things** *which* **happened** unto me have **fallen** out rather **unto the furtherance of the gospel;**
13. **So that my bonds in Christ are manifest** in all the palace, and in all other *places;*
14. **And** many of **the brethren** in the Lord, **waxing confident by my bonds, are** much more **bold to speak the word** without fear.
15. **Some** indeed **preach Christ** even **of** envy and **strife; and some** also **of good will:**
16. **The one preach Christ** of contention, **not sincerely,** supposing to add affliction to my bonds:
17. **But the other of love,** knowing that I am set for the defence of the gospel.
18. **What then?** notwithstanding, every way, whether **in pretence, or in truth, Christ is preached; and I** therein do rejoice, yea, and will **rejoice.**
19. For I know that **this shall turn to my salvation through your prayer, and the supply of the Spirit** of Jesus Christ,
20. According to my earnest expectation and **my hope, that in nothing I shall be ashamed, but** *that* **with all boldness,** as always, *so* now also **Christ shall be magnified** in my body, whether *it be* **by life, or by death.**
21. **For to me to live** *is* **Christ, and to die** *is* **gain.**
22. But if I live in the flesh, this *is* the fruit of my labour: yet what I shall choose I wot not.
23. **For I am** in a strait **betwixt two, having a desire to depart, and to be with Christ;** which is far better:

■ **24. Nevertheless to abide** in the flesh

■ ***is*** more

■ **needful for you.** 25. And having this confidence,

■ **I know** that

■ **I shall abide** and continue

■ **with you** all

■ **for your furtherance** and joy

■ **of faith;** 26. That your rejoicing may be more abundant in Jesus Christ for me by my coming to you again.

■ **27. Only let your**

■ **conversation be** as it becometh the gospel

■ **of Christ: that** whether I come and see you, or else be absent,

■ **I may hear** of your affairs,

■ **that ye stand** fast

■ **in one spirit, with one mind** striving together

■ **for the** faith of the

■ **gospel;** 28. **And in nothing terrified**

■ **by your adversaries:** which is to them an evident token of perdition, but to you of salvation, and that of God. 29. For unto you

■ **it is given in the behalf of**

■ **Christ, not only to believe**

■ **on him, but also to suffer**

■ **for his sake;** 30. Having the same conflict which ye saw in me, and now hear *to be* in me.

CHAPTER 2

■ 1. **If *there be*** therefore

■ **any consolation in Christ,** if any comfort of love, if any fellowship of the Spirit, if any bowels and mercies,

■ 2. **Fulfil ye my joy,** that ye be like-minded,

■ **having the same love,**

■ ***being*** of one accord,

■ **of one mind.** 3. *Let* nothing *be done*

■ **through strife or vainglory;** but in lowliness of mind let each esteem other better than themselves.

■ 4. **Look not every man on**

■ **his own things, but** every man also

■ **on the things of others.**

■ **5. Let this mind be in you,**

■ **which was** also

■ **in Christ Jesus:**

■ **6. Who, being in the form of**

■ **God, thought it not robbery**

■ **to be equal with God:**

■ **7. But** made himself of no reputation, and took upon him the form of a servant, and

■ **was made in the likeness**

■ **of men:**

■ **8. And** being found in fashion

■ **as a man, he humbled**

■ **himself, and became**

■ **obedient unto death,** even the death of the cross.

■ **9. Wherefore God** also

■ **hath** highly

■ **exalted him, and given him**

■ **a name** which is

■ **above every name:**

■ **10. That at the name of**

■ **Jesus every knee should**

■ **bow,** of *things* in heaven, and *things* in earth, and *things* under the earth;

■ **11. And** *that*

■ **every tongue** should

■ **confess that Jesus Christ**

■ ***is* Lord,** to the glory of God the Father.

■ **12. Wherefore,** my beloved, as ye have always obeyed, not as in my presence only, but now much more in my absence,

■ **work out your own**

■ **salvation with fear**

■ **and trembling.**

■ **13. For it is God which**

■ **worketh in you both to will**

■ **and to do** of

■ ***his*** **good pleasure.**

■ 14. **Do all things without** murmurings and

■ **disputings:**

■ 15. **That ye may be**

■ **blameless** and harmless, the sons of God, without rebuke,

■ **in** the midst of

■ **a** crooked and

■ **perverse nation, among**

■ **whom ye shine as lights**
in the world;
■ 16. **Holding forth the word**
of life;
■ **that I may rejoice in the day**
■ **of Christ,** that I have not run in
vain, neither laboured in vain.
17. Yea, and if I be offered upon the
sacrifice and service of your faith, I
joy, and rejoice with you all.
18. For the same cause also do ye
joy, and rejoice with me.
■ 19. **But I trust in the Lord**
■ **Jesus to send Timotheus**
shortly unto you, that I also may be of
good comfort, when I know
your state.
20. For I have no man like minded,
who will naturally care for your state.
■ 21. **For all seek their own,**
■ **not the things which are**
■ **Jesus Christ's.**
■ 22. **But ye know the proof of**
■ **him, that, as a son**
with the father,
■ **he hath served with me**
in the gospel.
23. Him therefore I hope to send
presently, so soon as I shall see how
it will go with me.
24. But I trust in the Lord that
■ **I also myself shall come**
shortly.
■ 25. **Yet I** supposed it necessary to
■ **send** to you
■ **Epaphroditus, my brother,**
and companion in labour,
■ **and fellow-soldier, but**
■ **your messenger,** and he that
ministered to my wants.
■ 26. **For he longed after you**
all, and was full of heaviness,
■ **because** that
■ **ye had heard** that
■ **he had been sick.**
■ 27. **For indeed he was sick**
nigh
■ **unto death: but God had**
■ **mercy on him; and**
not on him only, but
■ **on me also, lest I should**
■ **have sorrow** upon sorrow.
■ 28. **I sent him therefore**

the more carefully,
■ **that,** when ye see him again,
■ **ye may rejoice, and** that
■ **I** may
■ **be** the
■ **less sorrowful.**
■ 29. **Receive him**
therefore in the Lord
■ **with** all
■ **gladness;** and hold
such in reputation:
■ 30. **Because for** the work of
■ **Christ he was** nigh
■ **unto death, not regarding**
■ **his life,** to supply your lack of
service toward me.

CHAPTER 3
■ 1. **Finally,** my brethren,
rejoice in the Lord.
■ **To write the same things**
to you, to me indeed
■ *is* **not grievous,** but for you
■ *it is* **safe.**
2. Beware of dogs,
■ **beware of evil workers,**
beware of the concision.
■ 3. **For we are the**
■ **circumcision, which**
■ **worship God in the spirit,**
■ **and rejoice in Christ** Jesus,
■ **and have no confidence in**
■ **the flesh.**
4. Though I might also have
confidence in the flesh.
■ **If any** other
■ **man thinketh** that
■ **he hath whereof he might**
■ **trust in the flesh, I more:**
5. Circumcised the eighth day,
of the stock of Israel, *of* the
tribe of Benjamin,
■ **an Hebrew of the Hebrews;**
as touching the law,
■ **a Pharisee;**
■ 6. **Concerning** zeal, persecuting
the church; touching the
righteousness which is in
■ **the law, blameless.**
■ 7. **But what things were gain**
■ **to me, those I counted loss**
■ **for Christ**
8. Yea doubtless, and

I count all things *but* loss
for the excellency of
the knowledge of Christ
Jesus my Lord:
for whom I have
suffered the loss of all
things, and do
count them *but* dung, that I
may win Christ,
9. And be found in him,
not having mine own
righteousness, which is
of the law, but that which is
through the faith of Christ,
the righteousness which is
of God by faith:
10. That I may know him,
and the power of his
resurrection, and
the fellowship of
his sufferings, being made
conformable unto
his death;
11. If by any means I might attain unto
the resurrection of the dead.
12. Not as though I
had already attained, either
were already
perfect: but I follow after, if
that I may apprehend that
for which also
I am apprehended of
Christ Jesus.
13. Brethren, I count not myself to
have apprehended: but
this one thing *I do,*
forgetting those things
which are
behind, and reaching forth
unto those things which are before,
14. I press toward
the mark for the prize of
the high calling of God in
Christ Jesus.
15. Let us therefore,
as many as be perfect,
be thus minded: and if
in any thing
ye be otherwise minded,
God shall reveal even
this unto you.
16. Nevertheless, whereto
we have already

attained, let us walk by the
same rule,
let us mind the same thing.
17. Brethren, be followers together of
me, and mark them which walk so as
ye have us for an ensample.
18. (For many walk,
of whom I have told you often, and
now tell you even weeping,
that they
are the
enemies of the cross
of Christ:
19. Whose end
is destruction,
whose God *is their* belly, and *whose*
glory *is* in their shame,
who mind earthly things.)
20. For our conversation is
in heaven; from whence
also we look for the
Saviour, the Lord Jesus Christ:
21. Who shall change our
vile body, that it may be
fashioned
like unto
his glorious body,
according to the working whereby he
is able even to subdue all things
unto himself.

CHAPTER 4
1. Therefore, my brethren dearly
beloved and longed for, my joy and
crown, so stand fast in the Lord, *my*
dearly beloved.
2. I beseech Euodias, and beseech
Syntyche, that they be of the same
mind in the Lord.
3. And I entreat thee also, true yoke-
fellow, help those women which
laboured with me in the gospel, with
Clement also, and *with* other my
fellow-labourers, whose names *are* in
the book of life.
4. Rejoice in the Lord alway:
and again I say, Rejoice.
5. Let your moderation be
known unto all men.
The Lord *is* at hand.
6. Be careful for nothing; but
in every thing by prayer
and supplication with

thanksgiving let your requests be made known unto God.

7. And the peace of God, which passeth all understanding, shall keep your hearts and minds through Christ Jesus.

8. Finally, brethren, whatsoever things are true, whatsoever things *are* honest, whatsoever things *are* just, whatsoever things *are* pure, whatsoever things *are* lovely, whatsoever things *are* of good report; if *there be* any virtue, and if *there be* any praise, think on these things.

9. Those things, which ye have both learned, and received, and heard, and seen in me, do: and the God of peace shall be with you.

10. But I rejoiced in the Lord greatly, that now at the last your care of me hath flourished again; wherein ye were also careful, but ye lacked opportunity.

11. Not that I speak in respect of want: for I have learned, in whatsoever state I am, *therewith* to be content.

12. I know both how to be abased, and I know how to abound: every where and in all things I am instructed both to be full and to be hungry,

both to abound and to suffer need.

13. I can do all things through Christ which strengtheneth me.

14. Notwithstanding ye have well done, that ye did communicate with my affliction.

15. Now ye Philippians know also, that in the beginning of the gospel, when I departed from Macedonia, no church communicated with me as concerning giving and receiving, but ye only.

16. For even in Thessalonica ye sent once and again unto my necessity.

17. Not because I desire a gift: but I desire fruit that may abound to your account.

18. But I have all, and abound: I am full, having received of Epaphroditus the things *which were* sent from you, an odour of a sweet smell, a sacrifice acceptable, well-pleasing to God.

19. But my God shall supply all your need according to his riches in glory by Christ Jesus.

20. Now unto God and our Father *be* glory for ever and ever. Amen.

21. Salute every saint in Christ Jesus. The brethren which are with me greet you.

22. All the saints salute you, chiefly they that are of Caesar's household.

23. The grace of our Lord Jesus Christ *be* with you all. Amen.

THE EPISTLE TO THE COLOSSIANS

BACKGROUND INFORMATION

Author – Paul, an Apostle.
Date Written – probably
between 60 and **65** A.D.

Number of:
Verses -   95
Chapters -   4
Total Words - 1,998
Scan Words -844
Scan words represent 42 %
of total words.

Theme – written to show
the pre-eminence of Christ
over all competing systems,
and how believers should
conduct their lives.

OUTLINE OF THE EPISTLE

I.   Paul describes
     **the pre-eminence of
     Christ,** our reconciliation
     in Christ and his own
     service for Christ.
     Chapters 1—2:3

II. Paul warns against false
     teaching, explains
     the new life in Christ,
     Christian virtues and gives
     advice for domestic life.
     Chapters 2:4—4

CHAPTER 1

1. **Paul,** an apostle of Jesus Christ by the will of God,
and Timotheus *our* brother,
2. **To the saints** and faithful brethren in Christ which are
at Colosse: Grace *be* unto you, and peace, from God our Father and the Lord Jesus Christ.
3. **We give thanks to God** and the Father of our Lord Jesus Christ, praying always for you,
4. **Since we heard of your faith in Christ Jesus, and of the love** *which ye have* **to all the saints,**
5. For the hope which is laid up for you in heaven, whereof ye heard before in the word of the truth of the gospel;
6. Which is come unto you, as *it is* in all the world; and bringeth forth fruit, as *it doth* also in you, since the day ye heard *of it,* and knew the grace of God in truth:
7. As ye also learned of Epaphras our dear fellow-servant, who is for you a faithful minister of Christ;
8. Who also declared unto us your love in the Spirit.
9. **For this cause we** also, since the day we heard *it,*
do not cease to pray for you, and to desire
that ye might be filled with the knowledge of his
will in all wisdom
and spiritual understanding;
10. **That ye might walk worthy of the Lord**
unto all pleasing,
being fruitful in every good work, and increasing in the knowledge of God;
11. **Strengthened** with all might,
according to his glorious
power, unto all
patience and longsuffering
with joyfulness;
12. **Giving thanks unto the**
Father, which hath made us meet to be partakers of the inheritance of the saints in light:

13. **Who hath delivered us**
from the power of
darkness, and hath
translated *us* **into the**
kingdom of his dear Son:
14. **In whom we have**
redemption through
his blood,
even the forgiveness of sins:
15. **Who is the image of the**
invisible God,
the firstborn of every creature:
16. **For by him were all**
things created, that are in heaven, and that are in earth,
visible and invisible, whether *they be* thrones, or dominions, or principalities, or powers: all things were created by him, and for him:
17. **And he is before all**
things, and by him all
things consist.
18. **And he is the**
head of the body,
the church:
who is the beginning, the firstborn from the dead;
that in all *things* **he might**
have the preeminence.
19. **For it pleased** *the Father*
that in him should all
fulness dwell;
20. **And, having made**
peace through the blood of
his cross, by him to
reconcile all things unto
himself; by him, *I say,* whether *they be* things in earth, or things in heaven.
21. **And you,** that were sometime alienated and enemies in *your* mind by wicked works, yet now
hath he reconciled
22. **In** the body of
his flesh through death, to
present you holy and
unblameable and unreproveable
in his sight:
23. **If ye continue in the faith** grounded and settled,
and *be* **not moved away**
from the hope of
the gospel, which ye have heard, *and* which was preached to every

creature which is under heaven; whereof **I Paul** am made a minister; **24. Who now rejoice in my sufferings for you,** and fill up that which is behind of the afflictions of Christ in my flesh for his body's sake, which is the church: **25. Whereof I am made a minister,** according to the dispensation of God which is given to me for you, **to fulfil the word of God; 26.** *Even* **the mystery which hath been hid** from ages and **from generations,** but now **is made manifest to his saints:** 27. To whom God would make known what *is* the riches of the glory of this mystery among the Gentiles; which is **Christ** in you, the hope of glory: **28. Whom we preach, warning** every man, **and teaching every man** in all wisdom; **that we may present every man perfect in Christ** Jesus: 29. Whereunto I also labour, striving according to his working, which worketh in me mightily.

CHAPTER 2

1. For I would that ye knew what great conflict I have for you, and *for* them at Laodicea, and *for* as many as have not seen my face in the flesh; 2. That their hearts might be comforted, being knit together in love, and unto all riches of the full assurance of understanding, to the acknowledgement of the mystery of God, and of the Father, and of Christ; 3. In whom are hid all the treasures of wisdom and knowledge. **4. And this I say, lest any** man should **beguile you** with enticing words. **5. For though I be absent in the flesh, yet am I with you in the spirit,** joying and beholding your order, and the stedfastness of your faith in Christ.

6. As ye have therefore **received Christ** Jesus the Lord, *so* **walk ye in him: 7. Rooted and built up in him, and stablished in the faith,** as ye have been taught, abounding therein with thanksgiving. **8. Beware lest any man spoil you through philosophy** and vain deceit, **after the tradition of men,** after the rudiments of the world, **and not after Christ.** 9. **For in him dwelleth all the fulness of the Godhead bodily.** 10. **And ye are complete in him,** which is the head of all principality and power: **11. In whom also ye are circumcised** with the circumcision made without hands, **in putting off the body of** the **sins** of the flesh **by the circumcision of Christ:** 12. **Buried with him in baptism, wherein also ye are risen** with *him* **through** the **faith** of the operation of God, who hath raised him from the dead. 13. **And you, being dead in** your **sins** and the uncircumcision of your flesh, **hath he quickened** together with him, **having forgiven you** all trespasses; **14. Blotting out** the handwriting of **ordinances** that was **against us,** which was contrary to us, **and** took it out of the way, **nailing it to his cross; 15.** *And* **having spoiled principalities and powers,** he made a shew of them openly, **triumphing over them** in it. 16. **Let no man therefore judge you in meat, or in drink, or in respect of an**

holyday, or of the new moon, or of the sabbath *days*: 17. Which are a shadow of things to come; but the body *is* of Christ. 18. **Let no man beguile you** of your reward **in a voluntary humility and worshipping of angels,** intruding into those things which he hath not seen, **vainly puffed up by his fleshly mind,** 19. **And not holding the Head, from which all the body by joints** and bands **having nourishment** ministered, **and knit together, increaseth** with the increase of God. 20. **Wherefore if ye be dead with Christ** from the rudiments of the world, **why, as though living in the world, are ye subject to** ordinances, 21. (Touch not; taste not; handle not; 22. Which all are to perish with the using;) after **the** commandments and **doctrines of men?** 23. **Which things have indeed a shew of wisdom in** will-worship, and humility, and **neglecting** of **the body; not in any honour to the satisfying of the flesh.**

CHAPTER 3
1. **If ye then be risen with Christ, seek** those **things** which are **above,** where Christ sitteth on the right hand of God. 2. Set your affection on things above, **not** on **things on the earth.** 3. For ye are dead, and your life is hid with Christ in God. 4. When Christ, *who is* our life, shall appear, then shall ye also appear with

him in glory. **5. Mortify therefore your members** which are **upon the earth;** fornication, uncleanness, inordinate affection, evil concupiscence, and covetousness, which is idolatry: 6. For which things' sake the wrath of God cometh on the children of disobedience: 7. In the which ye also walked some time, when ye lived in them. 8. But now ye also put off all these; anger, wrath, malice, blasphemy, filthy communication out of your mouth. **9. Lie not one to another, seeing that ye have put off the old man with his deeds;** 10. **And have put on the new *man,*** which is renewed in knowledge **after the image of him that created him:** 11. **Where there is neither Greek nor Jew, circumcision nor uncircumcision,** Barbarian, Scythian, **bond *nor* free: but Christ *is* all, and in all.** 12. **Put on therefore, as the elect of God,** holy and beloved, bowels of mercies, **kindness, humbleness of mind,** meekness, **longsuffering;** 13. **Forbearing** one another, **and forgiving one another,** if any man have a quarrel against any: even as Christ forgave you, so also *do* ye. 14. **And above all** these things **put on charity, which is the bond of perfectness.** 15. **And let the peace of God rule in your hearts,** to the which also ye are called in one body; **and be ye thankful.** 16. **Let the word of Christ dwell in you** richly in all wisdom; **teaching and admonishing one another in psalms** and hymns and spiritual songs, singing with grace in your hearts to the Lord.

17. And whatsoever ye do in word or deed, *do* all in the name of the Lord Jesus, giving thanks to God and the Father by him.

18. Wives, submit yourselves unto your own husbands, as it is fit in the Lord.

19. Husbands, love *your* wives, and be not bitter against them.

20. Children, obey *your* parents in all things: for this is well pleasing unto the Lord.

21. Fathers, provoke not your children *to anger,* lest they be discouraged.

22. Servants, obey in all things your masters according to the flesh; not with eye-service, as men pleasers; but in singleness of heart, fearing God:

23. And whatsoever ye do, do *it* heartily, as to the Lord, and not unto men;

24. Knowing that of the Lord ye shall receive the reward of the inheritance: for ye serve the Lord Christ.

25. But he that doeth wrong shall receive for the wrong which he hath done: and there is no respect of persons.

CHAPTER 4

1. Masters, give unto your servants that which is just and equal; knowing that ye also have a Master in heaven.

2. Continue in prayer, and watch in the same with thanksgiving;

3. Withal praying also for us, that God would open unto us a door of utterance, to speak the mystery of Christ, for which I am also in bonds:

4. That I may make it manifest, as I ought to speak.

5. Walk in wisdom toward them that are without, redeeming the time.

6. Let your speech *be* alway with grace, seasoned with salt, that ye may know how ye ought to answer every man.

7. All my state shall Tychicus declare unto you, *who is* a beloved brother, and a faithful minister and fellow-servant in the Lord:

8. Whom I have sent unto you for the same purpose, that he might know your estate, and comfort your hearts;

9. With Onesimus, a faithful and beloved brother, who is *one* of you. They shall make known unto you all things which *are done* here.

10. Aristarchus my fellow prisoner saluteth you, and Marcus, sister's son to Barnabas, (touching whom ye received commandments: if he come unto you, receive him;)

11. And Jesus, which is called Justus, who are of the circumcision. These only *are my* fellow-workers unto the kingdom of God, which have been a comfort unto me.

12. Epaphras, who is *one* of you, a servant of Christ, saluteth you, always labouring fervently for you in prayers, that ye may stand perfect and complete in all the will of God.

13. For I bear him record, that he hath a great zeal for you, and them *that are* in Laodicea, and them in Hierapolis.

14. Luke, the beloved physician, and Demas, greet you.

15. Salute the brethren which are in Laodicea, and Nymphas, and the church which is in his house.

16. And when this epistle is read among you, cause that it be read also

■ | **in the church** of the Laodiceans;
and that ye likewise read the *epistle*
from Laodicea.

17. And say to Archippus, Take heed
to the ministry which thou hast
received in the Lord, that thou fulfil it.

■ | 18. **The salutation by the**
■ | **hand of me Paul.**
■ | **Remember my bonds.**
Grace *be* with you.

■ | **Amen.**

THE FIRST EPISTLE TO THE THESSALONIANS

BACKGROUND INFORMATION

Author – Paul, an Apostle.
Date Written – probably
between 50 and **52** A.D.

Number of:
Verses -   89
Chapters -   5
Total Words - 1,857
Scan Words -878
Scan Words represent 48 %
of Total Words.

Theme – written to instruct
the church in practical
Christian living and
**how Christians should
respond to the Second
Coming.**

OUTLINE OF THE EPISTLE

I. **Paul** gives thanks for the
Thessalonian's spiritual
progress and
defends his message.
Chapters 1—2

II. Paul sends Timothy to the
Thessalonians and
Paul's prayer for them.
Chapter 3

III. Paul outlines Christian
doctrine concerning
morality,
**the Second Coming
and church life.**
Chapters 4—5

CHAPTER 1

1. **Paul,** and **Silvanus, and Timotheus, unto the church of the Thessalonians** which is in God the Father and in the Lord Jesus Christ: Grace be unto you, and peace, from God our Father, and the Lord Jesus Christ.

2. **We give thanks** to God always **for you** all, making mention of you **in our prayers;**

3. **Remembering** without ceasing **your** work of **faith,** and labour of **love, and patience** of hope **in our Lord** Jesus Christ, in the sight of God and our Father;

4. **Knowing,** brethren beloved, **your election** of God.

5. **For our gospel came not** unto you **in word only, but** also **in power,** and **in the Holy Ghost,** **and in** much **assurance;** as ye know what manner of men we were among you for your sake.

6. **And ye became followers of us, and** of **the Lord, having received the word in** much **affliction, with joy of the Holy Ghost:**

7. **So that ye were ensamples** to all that believe in Macedonia and Achaia.

8. **For from you sounded out the word** of the Lord **not only in Macedonia and Achaia, but also in every place your faith** to God-ward **is spread** abroad; so that we need not to speak any thing.

9. **For they themselves shew** of us what manner of entering in we had unto you, and **how ye turned** to God **from idols to serve the** living and **true God;**

10. **And to wait for his Son** from heaven, **whom he raised** from the dead, **even Jesus, which delivered us from the wrath to come.**

CHAPTER 2

1. For yourselves, brethren, know our entrance in unto you, that it was not in vain:

2. **But even after that we had suffered** before, and were shamefully entreated, as ye know, **at Philippi, we were bold** in our God **to speak** unto you **the gospel** of God with much contention.

3. For our exhortation was not of deceit, nor of uncleanness, nor in guile:

4. **But as we were** allowed of God to be **put in trust with the gospel,** even so **we speak; not as pleasing men, but God,** which trieth our hearts.

5. **For neither** at any time **used we flattering words,** as ye know, nor a cloak of covetousness; God is witness:

6. **Nor** of men **sought we glory,** neither of you, nor yet of others, when we might have been burdensome, as the apostles of Christ.

7. **But we were gentle among you,** even as a nurse cherisheth her children:

8. So being affectionately desirous of you, **we were willing to have imparted** unto you, **not the gospel** of God **only, but also our own souls,** because ye were dear unto us.

9. **For ye remember, brethren, our labour and travail:** for labouring night and day,

- because we would not be
- chargeable unto any of
- you, we preached unto you
- the gospel of God.
- 10. Ye *are* witnesses, and
- God *also*, how
holily and justly and
- unblameably we behaved
ourselves
- among you that believe:
- 11. As ye know how we
- exhorted and comforted
and charged every one of
- you, as a father *doth* his children,
- 12. That ye would walk
- worthy of God, who hath called
you unto his kingdom and glory
- 13. For this cause also
- thank we God without ceasing,
- because, when ye
- received the word of God
which ye heard of us,
- ye received *it* not *as* the word
- of men, but as it is
- in truth, the word of God, which
effectually worketh also in
you that believe.
- 14. For ye, brethren,
- became followers of the
- churches of God which
- in Judaea are in Christ Jesus:
- for ye also have suffered
like things
- of your own countrymen,
even as they *have* of the Jews:
- 15. Who both killed the Lord
- Jesus, and their own
- prophets, and have
- persecuted us; and they please
not God, and are contrary to all men:
- 16. Forbidding us to speak
- to the Gentiles that they might be
saved, to fill up their sins alway: for
the wrath is come upon them
to the uttermost.
- 17. But we, brethren, being
- taken from you for a short time
- in presence, not in heart,
- endeavoured
the more abundantly
- to see your face
with great desire.
- 18. Wherefore we would

- have come unto you,
even I Paul, once and again;
- but Satan hindered us.
19. For what *is* our hope, or joy, or
crown of rejoicing? *Are* not even ye
in the presence of our Lord Jesus
Christ at his coming?
20. For ye are our glory and joy.

CHAPTER 3

1. Wherefore when we could
no longer forbear,
- we thought it good to be
- left at Athens alone;
- 2. And sent Timotheus, our
brother, and minister of God, and our
fellow-labourer in the gospel of Christ,
- to establish you,
and to comfort you
- concerning your faith:
- 3. That no man should be
- moved by these
- afflictions: for yourselves know
that we are appointed thereunto.
4. For verily, when we were with you,
- we told you before that we
- should suffer tribulation;
even as it came to pass, and ye know.
- 5. For this cause, when I could
no longer forbear,
- I sent to know your faith,
- lest by some means the
- tempter have tempted you,
- and our labour be in vain.
- 6. But now when
- Timotheus came from
you unto us, and
- brought us good tidings
of your faith and charity, and that ye
have good remembrance of us
always, desiring greatly to see us, as
we also *to see* you:
- 7. Therefore, brethren, we
- were comforted over you in all
our affliction and distress
- by your faith:
8. For now we live, if ye stand
fast in the Lord.
9. For what thanks can we
render to God again for you, for
all the joy wherewith
- we joy for your sakes
before our God;

10. **Night and day praying exceedingly that we might see your face,** and might perfect that which is lacking in your faith?

11. **Now God himself** and our Father, and our Lord Jesus Christ, **direct our way unto you.**

12. **And the Lord make you to increase and abound in love** one toward another, and toward all *men*, even as we *do* toward you:

13. **To the end he may stablish your hearts unblameable** in holiness before God, even our Father, **at the coming of** our Lord Jesus **Christ** with all his saints.

CHAPTER 4

1. **Furthermore then we beseech you,** brethren, and exhort *you* by the Lord Jesus, **that as ye have received of us** how **ye ought to** walk and to **please God,** *so* ye would abound **more** and more.

2. For ye know what commandments we gave you by the Lord Jesus.

3. **For this is the will of God,** *even* **your sanctification, that ye** should **abstain from fornication:**

4. **That every one of you** should **know how to possess his vessel in sanctification and honour;**

5. Not in the lust of concupiscence, even as the Gentiles which know not God:

6. **That no *man*** go beyond and **defraud his brother in** *any* **matter:** because that the Lord *is* the avenger of all such, as we also have forewarned you and testified.

7. **For God hath not called us unto uncleanness,** but unto holiness.

8. **He therefore that despiseth, despiseth not man, but God,** who hath also given unto us his holy Spirit

9. **But as touching brotherly love** ye need not that I write unto you: for **ye yourselves are taught of God to love one another.**

10. **And indeed ye do** it toward all the brethren which are in all Macedonia: **but we beseech you,** brethren, **that ye increase more** and more;

11. **And that ye study to be quiet, and to do your own business, and to work with your own hands,** as we commanded you;

12. **That ye may walk honestly** toward them that are without, **and** *that* ye may **have lack of nothing.**

13. **But I would not have you to be ignorant, brethren, concerning them which are asleep, that ye sorrow not,** even as others which have no hope.

14. **For** if we believe that Jesus died and rose again, even so **them** also **which sleep in Jesus will God bring with him.**

15. **For** this we say unto you by the word of the Lord, that **we which are alive** *and* remain **unto the coming of the Lord shall not prevent them** which are **asleep.**

16. **For the Lord himself shall descend from heaven with a shout, with the voice of the archangel, and with the trump of God: and the dead in Christ shall rise first:**

17. **Then we which** are alive *and* **remain shall be caught up** together **with them in the clouds, to meet the Lord** in the air: **and so shall we ever be with the Lord.**

18. **Wherefore comfort one**

another with these words.

CHAPTER 5

1. **But of the times** and the seasons, brethren, **ye have no need that I write** unto you.

2. **For** yourselves know perfectly that **the day of the Lord so cometh as a thief in the night.**

3. **For when they shall say, Peace and safety; then sudden destruction cometh** upon them, as travail upon a woman with child; and they shall not escape.

4. **But ye, brethren, are not in darkness, that that day should overtake you** as a thief.

5. **Ye are all the children of light,** and the children of the day: we are not of the night, nor of darkness.

6. **Therefore** let us not sleep, as *do* others; but **let us watch and be sober.**

7. For they that sleep sleep in the night; and they that be drunken are drunken in the night.

8. But let us, who are of the day, be sober, **putting on the breastplate of faith and love; and for an helmet, the hope of salvation.**

9. **For God hath not appointed us to wrath, but to obtain salvation by** our Lord Jesus **Christ,**

10. **Who died for us, that, whether we wake or sleep, we should live** together **with him.**

11. Wherefore comfort yourselves together, and edify one another, even as also ye do.

12. And we beseech you, brethren, to know **them which labour among you, and are over you in the Lord,** and admonish you;

13. And to **esteem them** very highly **in love** for their work's sake. *And* be at peace among yourselves.

14. Now we exhort you, brethren, **warn them that are unruly,** comfort the feebleminded, **support the weak, be patient** toward all *men.*

15 . **Seeing that none render evil for evil** unto any *man*; but ever follow that which is good, both among yourselves, and to all *men.*

16. Rejoice evermore.

17. **Pray without ceasing.**

18. **In every thing give thanks: for this is the will of God** in Christ Jesus concerning you.

19. **Quench not the Spirit.**

20. **Despise not prophesyings.**

21. Prove all things; hold fast that which is good.

22. **Abstain from all appearance of evil.**

23. And the very God of peace sanctify you wholly; **and *I pray God* your whole spirit and soul and body be preserved blameless unto the coming of our Lord** Jesus Christ.

24. Faithful *is* he that calleth you, who also will do *it.*

25. Brethren, pray for us.

26. Greet all the brethren with an holy kiss.

27. I charge you by the Lord that this epistle be read unto all the holy brethren.

28. The grace of our Lord Jesus Christ *be* with you. **Amen.**

THE SECOND EPISTLE TO THE THESSALONIANS

BACKGROUND INFORMATION

Author – Paul, an apostle.
**Date Written – probably
between 50** and **52** A.D.

Number of:
Verses -   47
Chapters -   3
Total Words - 1,042
Scan Words - 487
Scan Words represent 46 %
of Total Words.

Theme – written to instruct
Christians in
practical conduct and the
continued
**need for industry in light of
the Second Coming.**

OUTLINE OF THE EPISTLE

I.   Paul offers
     **encouragement
     in persecution and
     instruction** concerning
     the day of the Lord.
     Chapters 1—2.

II. Paul gives confession of
     confidence and
     **commandments to
     work.**
     Chapter 3

CHAPTER 1

■ 1. **Paul, and Silvanus, and**
■ **Timotheus, unto the church**
■ **of the Thessalonians** in God
our Father and the Lord Jesus Christ:
2. Grace unto you, and peace,
from God our Father and the
Lord Jesus Christ.
■ 3. **We** are bound to
■ **thank God** always for you,
brethren, as it is meet,
■ **because** that
■ **your faith groweth**
exceedingly, and the charity of every
one of you all toward each
other aboundeth;
■ 4. **So that we** ourselves
■ **glory in you**
in the churches of God
■ **for your patience** and faith
■ **in** all your
■ **persecutions** and
tribulations that ye endure:
■ 5. **Which is a manifest token**
■ **of the righteous judgment**
■ **of God, that ye may be**
■ **counted worthy of the**
■ **kingdom** of God, for
which ye also suffer:
■ 6. **Seeing** *it is* **a righteous**
■ **thing with God to**
■ **recompense tribulation**
■ **to them that trouble you;**
7. And to you who are
troubled rest with us,
■ **when** the Lord
■ **Jesus shall be revealed**
■ **from heaven with his**
■ **mighty angels,**
■ 8. **In flaming fire taking**
■ **vengeance on them that**
■ **know not God, and that**
■ **obey not the gospel**
of our Lord Jesus Christ:
■ 9. **Who shall be punished**
■ **with everlasting**
■ **destruction** from the presence
of the Lord, and from the
glory of his power;
■ 10. **When he shall come to**
■ **be glorified in his saints,**
and to be admired in all them that
believe (because our testimony

among you was believed) in that day.
■ 11. **Wherefore also we pray**
always for you,
■ **that** our
■ **God** would
■ **count you worthy of** *this*
■ **calling,** and fulfil all the good
pleasure of *his* goodness, and
the work of faith with power:
■ 12. **That** the name of our Lord
■ **Jesus Christ may be**
■ **glorified in you, and ye in**
■ **him,** according to the grace of our
God and the Lord Jesus Christ.

CHAPTER 2

■ 1. **Now we beseech you,**
brethren, by the coming of our Lord
Jesus Christ, and *by* our gathering
together unto him,
■ 2. **That ye be not soon**
■ **shaken in mind,** or be troubled,
neither by spirit, nor by word, nor by
letter as from us, as that the day of
Christ is at hand.
■ 3. **Let no man deceive you**
by any means:
■ **for** *that day shall not come,*
■ **except there come a falling**
■ **away first, and that man of**
■ **sin be revealed,**
the son of perdition;
■ 4. **Who opposeth and**
■ **exalteth himself above all**
■ **that is called God,**
or that is worshipped; so that he as
God sitteth in the temple of God,
■ **shewing himself that**
■ **he is God.**
5. Remember ye not, that, when I was
yet with you, I told you these things?
6. And now ye know what withholdeth
that he might be revealed in his time.
■ 7. **For the mystery of iniquity**
■ **doth already work: only he**
■ **who now letteth** *will let,*
■ **until he be taken out**
■ **of the way.**
■ 8. **And then shall that**
■ **Wicked be revealed, whom**
■ **the Lord shall consume**
■ **with the spirit of his mouth,**
■ **and** shall destroy with the

brightness of
his coming:
9. *Even him*, **whose coming**
is after the working
of Satan with all power and
signs and lying wonders,
10. **And with all**
deceivableness
of unrighteousness
in them that perish;
because they received not
the love of
the truth, that they might be saved.
11. **And for this cause God**
shall send them strong
delusion, that they
should believe a lie:
12. **That they** all might
be damned who believed
not the truth, but had pleasure
in unrighteousness.
13. **But** we are bound to give thanks
alway to God for you, brethren
beloved of the Lord, because
God hath from the beginning
chosen you to salvation
through sanctification of
the Spirit and belief of the truth:
14. Whereunto he called you by our
gospel, to the obtaining of the glory
of our Lord Jesus Christ.
15. **Therefore, brethren,**
stand fast, and hold the traditions
which ye have been taught, whether
by word, or our epistle.
16. **Now our Lord** Jesus Christ
himself, and God, even our Father,
which hath loved us, and hath given
us everlasting consolation and good
hope through grace,
17. **Comfort your hearts,**
and stablish you in every
good word and work.

CHAPTER 3
1. **Finally, brethren, pray for**
us, that the word of the Lord
may have *free* **course,** and
be glorified, even as *it is* with you:
2. **And that we may be**
delivered from
unreasonable and wicked
men: for all *men* have not faith.

3. **But the Lord is faithful,**
who shall stablish you, and
keep *you* **from evil.**
4. **And we have confidence**
in the Lord touching you, that ye
both do and will do the things which we
command you.
5. **And the Lord direct your**
hearts into the love of God,
and into the patient waiting
for Christ.
6. Now we command you, brethren,
in the name of our Lord
Jesus Christ, that ye
withdraw yourselves from
every brother that walketh
disorderly, and not after the
tradition which he received of us.
7. **For yourselves know how**
ye ought to follow us: for
we behaved not ourselves disorderly
among you;
8. **Neither did we eat any**
man's bread for nought;
but wrought with labour
and travail night and day,
that we might not be
chargeable to any of you:
9. Not because we have
not power, but
to make ourselves an
ensample unto you to follow us.
10. **For** even when
we were with you, this
we commanded you, that if
any would not work,
neither should he eat.
11. **For we hear that** there are
some which
walk among you
disorderly, working not at
all, but are busybodies.
12. Now them that are such we
command and exhort by our Lord
Jesus Christ, that with quietness they
work, and eat their own bread.
13. **But ye, brethren, be not**
weary in well-doing.
14. **And if any** man
obey not our word
by this epistle, note that man, and
have no company with him,
that he may be ashamed.

■ **15. Yet count *him* not as an**
■ **enemy, but admonish *him***
■ **as a brother.**
16. Now the Lord of peace himself
give you peace always by all means.
The Lord *be* with you all.
17. The salutation of Paul with mine
own hand, which is the token in
every epistle: so I write.
18. The grace of our Lord Jesus
Christ *be* with you all.
■ **Amen.**

THE FIRST EPISTLE TO TIMOTHY

BACKGROUND INFORMATION

Author – Paul, an Apostle.
Date Written – probably
between 60 and **65** A.D.

Number of:
Verses -   113
Chapters -   6
Total Words - 2,269
Scan Words - 1,059
Scan Words represent 46 %
of Total Words.

**Theme – written to
encourage a young
minister and instruct him**
in the proper conduct of
his ministry.

OUTLINE OF THE EPISTLE

I. **Paul** greets Timothy and
    **warns about false
    teachers.**
    Chapter 1:1—11

II. **Paul declares the
    apostolic commission.**
    Chapter 1:12—20

III. **Paul outlines
    rules for public
    worship and
    qualifications for
    church leaders.**
    Chapters 2—3

IV. **Paul gives Timothy
    personal advice.**
    Chapters 4—6.

CHAPTER 1

1. **Paul,** an apostle of Jesus Christ by the commandment of God our Saviour, and Lord Jesus Christ, *which is* our hope;

2. **Unto Timothy,** *my* own son in the faith: Grace, mercy, *and* peace, from God our Father and Jesus Christ our Lord.

3. **As I besought thee to abide still at Ephesus,** when I went into Macedonia, **that thou mightest charge some that they teach no other doctrine,**

4. **Neither give heed to fables and** endless **genealogies,** which minister questions, **rather than godly edifying** which is in faith: *so do.*

5. **Now the end of the commandment is charity out of a pure heart, and** *of* a good conscience, and *of* **faith unfeigned:**

6. **From which some** having swerved **have turned aside** unto vain jangling;

7. **Desiring to be teachers of the law;** understanding neither what they say, nor whereof they affirm.

8. But we know that **the law** *is* **good, if a man use it lawfully;**

9. **Knowing this, that the law is not made for a righteous man, but for the lawless and** disobedient, for the ungodly and for sinners, for unholy and profane, for murderers of fathers and murderers of mothers, for manslayers,

10. For whoremongers, for them that defile themselves with mankind, for menstealers, for liars, for perjured persons, and if there be any other thing that is contrary to sound doctrine;

11. According to the glorious gospel of the blessed God, which was committed to my trust.

12. **And I thank Christ** Jesus our Lord, who hath enabled me, **for** that he counted me faithful, **putting me into the ministry;**

13. **Who was before a blasphemer, and** a **persecutor, and injurious: but I obtained mercy, because I did** *it* **ignorantly in unbelief.**

14. And the grace of our Lord was exceeding abundant with faith and love which is in Christ Jesus.

15. **This** *is* **a faithful saying,** and worthy of all acceptation, **that Christ Jesus came into the world to save sinners; of whom I am chief.**

16. Howbeit for this cause **I obtained mercy, that in me** first Jesus **Christ might shew** forth all **longsuffering, for a pattern to them which should** hereafter **believe** on him to life everlasting.

17. Now unto the King eternal, immortal, invisible, the only wise God, *be* honour and glory for ever and ever. Amen.

18. **This charge I commit unto thee, son** Timothy, **according to the prophecies** which went before **on thee, that thou** by them **mightest war a good warfare;**

19. **Holding faith, and a good conscience;** which some having put away concerning faith have made shipwreck:

20. Of whom is Hymenaeus and Alexander; whom I have delivered unto Satan, that they may learn not to blaspheme.

CHAPTER 2

1. **I exhort therefore, that,** first of all, **supplications, prayers, intercessions,** *and* **giving of thanks, be made for all men;**

2. **For kings, and** *for* **all** that are **in authority; that we may lead a** quiet and **peaceable life** in all godliness and honesty.

3. **For this** *is* **good** and acceptable **in the sight of God our Saviour;**

4. **Who will have all men to be saved,** and to come unto the knowledge of the truth.

5. **For** *there is* **one God, and one mediator between God and men, the man Christ Jesus;**

6. **Who gave himself a ransom for all,** to be testified in due time.

7. **Whereunto I am** ordained a preacher, and **an apostle,** (I speak the truth in Christ, *and* lie not;) **a teacher of the Gentiles** in faith and verity.

8. **I will therefore that men pray** every where, **lifting up holy hands,** without wrath and doubting.

9. **In like manner also, that women adorn themselves in modest apparel, with** shamefacedness and **sobriety; not with** broided hair, or gold, or pearls, or **costly array;**

10. **But** (which becometh women professing godliness) **with good works.**

11. **Let the woman learn in silence** with all subjection.

12. **But I suffer not a woman** to teach, nor **to usurp authority over the man,** but to be in silence.

13. **For Adam was first formed,** then Eve.

14. **And Adam was not deceived, but the woman** being deceived was in the transgression.

15. Notwithstanding she shall be saved in childbearing, if they continue in faith and charity and holiness with sobriety.

CHAPTER 3

1. This *is* a true saying, **If a man desire the office of a bishop, he desireth a good work.**

2. **A bishop then must be blameless,** the husband of one wife, vigilant, sober, of good behaviour, given to hospitality, apt to teach;

3. Not given to wine, no striker, not greedy of filthy lucre; but patient, not a brawler, not covetous;

4. One that ruleth well his own house, having his children in subjection with all gravity;

5. (For if a man know not how to rule his own house, how shall he take care of the church of God?)

6. Not a novice, lest being lifted up with pride he fall into the condemnation of the devil.

7. **Moreover he must have a good report of them which are without;** lest he fall into reproach and the snare of the devil.

8. **Likewise** *must* **the deacons** *be* **grave, not double-tongued,** not given to much wine, not greedy of filthy lucre;

9. Holding the mystery of the faith in a pure conscience.

10. **And let these also first be proved;** then let them use the office of a deacon, being *found* blameless.

11. **Even so** *must their* **wives** *be* **grave, not slanderers,** sober, faithful in all things.

12. **Let the deacons be the husbands of one wife,** ruling their children and their own houses well.

13. **For they that have used the office of a deacon well purchase** to themselves **a good degree,** and great boldness in the faith which is in Christ Jesus.

14. These things write I unto thee, hoping to come unto thee shortly:

15. **But if I tarry** long, that **thou mayest know how thou oughtest to behave** thyself **in the house of God,** which is the church of the living God, the pillar and ground of the truth.

16. And without controversy **great is the mystery of godliness: God was manifest in the flesh, justified in the Spirit, seen** of angels, preached unto **the Gentiles, believed on in the world, received up into glory.**

CHAPTER 4

1. **Now the Spirit speaketh** expressly, **that in the latter times some shall depart** from the faith, **giving heed to seducing spirits,** and doctrines of devils;

2. **Speaking lies in hypocrisy;** having their conscience seared with a hot iron;

3. **Forbidding to marry,** *and commanding* **to abstain from meats, which God hath created to be received with thanksgiving** of them which believe and know the truth.

4. **For every creature of God** *is* **good, and nothing to be refused,** if it be received with thanksgiving:

5. **For it is sanctified by the word of God and prayer.**

6. **If thou put the brethren in remembrance of these things, thou shalt be a good minister** of Jesus Christ, nourished up in the words of faith and of good doctrine, whereunto thou hast attained.

7. **But refuse** profane and **old wives' fables, and exercise thyself** *rather* **unto godliness.**

8. **For bodily exercise profiteth little: but godliness is profitable unto all things, having promise of the life that now is, and of that** which is **to come.**

9. This *is* a faithful saying and worthy of all acceptation.

10. For therefore **we** both **labour and suffer** reproach, **because we trust** in the living **God, who is the Saviour** of all men, specially of those that believe.

11. **These things command and teach.**

12. **Let no man despise thy youth; but be thou an example** of the believers, in word, in conversation, in charity, in spirit, in faith, in purity.

13. **Till I come, give attendance to reading, to exhortation, to doctrine.**

14. **Neglect not the gift** that is in thee, which was **given thee by prophecy, with the laying on of the hands** of the presbytery.

15. **Meditate upon these things; give thyself wholly to them;** that thy profiting may appear to all.

16. **Take heed unto thyself, and** unto **the doctrine;** continue in them: for in doing this thou shalt both save thyself, and them that hear thee.

CHAPTER 5

1. **Rebuke not an elder,** but **entreat** *him* as a father; *and* **the younger men as brethren;**

2. **The elder women as mothers; the younger as sisters,** with all purity.

3. **Honour widows** that are widows indeed.

4. **But if any widow have children** or nephews, **let them learn**

first to shew piety at home, and
■ **to requite their parents:**
for that is good and acceptable
before God.
■ 5. **Now she that is a widow**
indeed,
■ **and desolate, trusteth in**
■ **God, and continueth in**
■ **supplications and prayers**
night and day.
■ 6. **But she that liveth in**
■ **pleasure is dead**
while she liveth.
7. And these things give in charge,
that they may be blameless.
■ 8. **But if any provide not for**
■ **his own,** and specially for those of
his own house,
■ **he** hath denied the faith, and
■ **is worse than an infidel.**
■ 9. **Let not a widow be taken**
■ **into the number under**
■ **threescore** years old, having
been the wife of one man,
10. Well reported of for good works; if
she have brought up children, if
she have lodged strangers, if she
have washed the saints' feet, if she
have relieved the afflicted, if she have
diligently followed every good work.
■ 11. **But the younger widows**
■ **refuse: for** when they have begun
to wax wanton against Christ,
■ **they will marry;**
12. Having damnation, because they
have cast off their first faith.
■ 13. **And withal they learn** *to*
■ *be* **idle,** wandering about from
house to house;
■ **and** not only idle, but
■ **tattlers also and**
■ **busybodies,** speaking things
which they ought not.
■ 14. **I will therefore that the**
■ **younger women marry,**
bear children, guide the house, give
none occasion to the adversary to
speak reproachfully.
15. For some are already turned aside
after Satan.
■ 16. **If any man**
or woman that believeth
■ **have widows, let them**

■ **relieve them, and let not the**
■ **church be charged;** that it may
relieve them that are widows indeed.
■ 17. **Let the elders that rule**
■ **well be counted worthy of**
■ **double honour,** especially they
who labour in the word and doctrine.
18. For the scripture saith, Thou shalt
not muzzle the ox that treadeth out
the corn. And, The labourer *is* worthy
of his reward.
■ 19. **Against an elder receive**
■ **not an accusation,**
■ **but before two or**
■ **three witnesses.**
■ 20. **Them that sin rebuke**
■ **before all,**
that others also may fear.
■ 21. **I charge** *thee* before God,
and the Lord Jesus Christ,
and the elect angels,
■ **that thou observe these**
■ **things without preferring**
▣ **one before another,**
doing nothing by partiality.
■ 22. **Lay hands suddenly on**
■ **no man,** neither be partaker of
other men's sins:
▣ **keep thyself pure.**
■ 23. **Drink no longer water,**
■ **but** use a little
■ **wine for thy stomach's**
■ **sake** and thine often infirmities.
■ 24. **Some men's sins are**
■ **open** beforehand, going
■ **before to judgment; and**
■ **some** *men* they
■ **follow** after.
■ 25. **Likewise also the good**
■ **works** *of some* are manifest
beforehand; and they that are
otherwise cannot be hid.

CHAPTER 6

■ 1. **Let** as many
■ **servants** as are under the yoke
■ **count their own masters**
■ **worthy of all honour,**
that the name of God and *his* doctrine
be not blasphemed.
■ 2. **And** they that have
believing masters,
■ **let them not despise** *them,*

because they are brethren; but rather do *them* service, because they are faithful and beloved, partakers of the benefit. These things teach and exhort.

3. **If any man teach otherwise,** and consent not to wholesome words, *even* the words of our Lord Jesus Christ, and to the doctrine which is according to godliness;

4. **He is proud, knowing nothing,** but doting about questions and strifes of words, whereof cometh envy, strife, railings, evil surmisings,

5. Perverse disputings of men of corrupt minds, and destitute of the truth, supposing that gain is godliness: **from such withdraw** thyself.

6. **But godliness with contentment is great gain.**

7. **For we brought nothing into** *this* **world, *and it is* certain we can carry nothing out.**

8. **And having food and raiment let us be** therewith **content.**

9. **But they that will be rich fall into temptation** and a snare, **and** *into* **many** foolish and hurtful **lusts,** which drown men in destruction and perdition.

10. **For the love of money is the root of all evil:** which while some coveted after, they have erred from the faith, and pierced themselves through with many sorrows.

11. **But thou, O man of God, flee these things; and follow after righteousness,** godliness, faith, love, patience, meekness.

12. **Fight the good fight of faith, lay hold on eternal life,** whereunto thou art also called, and hast professed a good profession before many witnesses.

13. **I give thee charge** in the sight of God, who quickeneth all things, and *before* Christ Jesus, who before Pontius Pilate witnessed a good confession;

14. **That thou keep** *this* **commandment** without spot, unrebukable, **until the appearing of our Lord** Jesus Christ:

15. Which in his times he shall shew, *who is* **the blessed and only Potentate,** the King of kings, and Lord of lords;

16. **Who only hath immortality, dwelling in the light which no man can approach** unto; **whom no man hath seen,** nor can see: to whom *be* honour and power everlasting. Amen.

17. **Charge them that are rich** in this world, **that they be not highminded, nor trust in** uncertain **riches, but in the living God,** who giveth us richly all things to enjoy;

18. **That they** do good, that they **be rich in good works, ready to distribute,** willing to communicate;

19. **Laying up** in store **for themselves a good foundation** against the time to come, **that they may lay hold on eternal life.**

20. **O Timothy, keep that** which is **committed to thy trust, avoiding profane** *and* vain **babblings, and oppositions of science falsely so called:**

21. Which some professing have erred concerning the faith. Grace *be* with thee. **Amen.**

THE SECOND EPISTLE TO TIMOTHY

BACKGROUND INFORMATION

Author – Paul, an Apostle.
Date Written – probably
between 64 and **65** A.D.

Number of:
Verses -   83
Chapters -   4
Total Words - 1,703
Scan Words - 782
Scan Words represent 45 %
of Total Words.

Theme – written to challenge
a young minister to
**hold fast to the truths of
the Gospel.**

OUTLINE OF THE EPISTLE

I.   **Paul gives thanks** for
Timothy, exhorts him to
endurance, and offers
advice on personal
conduct and
relationships.
Chapters 1—2

II. **Paul speaks of the
coming apostasy**
and the reliability of the
scriptures.
Chapter 3

III. **Paul charges Timothy
to preach**
and Paul presents
his own Last Testament.
Chapter 4

CHAPTER 1

1. **Paul,** an apostle of Jesus Christ by the will of God, according to the promise of life which is in Christ Jesus,

2. **To Timothy,** *my* dearly beloved son: Grace, mercy, *and* peace, from God the Father and Christ Jesus our Lord.

3. I thank God, whom I serve from *my* forefathers with pure conscience, that without ceasing I have remembrance of thee in my prayers night and day;

4. Greatly desiring to see thee, being mindful of thy tears, that I may be filled with joy;

5. When I call to remembrance the unfeigned faith that is in thee, which dwelt first in thy grandmother Lois, and thy mother Eunice; and I am persuaded that in thee also.

6. Wherefore I put thee in remembrance that thou **stir up the gift of God,** which is **in thee by the putting on of my hands.**

7. **For God hath not given us the spirit of fear; but of power,** and of **love, and of a sound mind.**

8. **Be not** thou therefore **ashamed** of the testimony **of our Lord, nor of me** his prisoner: **but be thou partaker of the afflictions of the gospel according to the power of God;**

9. **Who hath saved us, and called** *us* with an holy calling, **not according to** our **works, but according to his own purpose and grace,** which was **given us in Christ** Jesus **before the world began,**

10. **But is now made manifest by** the appearing of our Saviour Jesus **Christ, who** hath **abolished death, and** hath **brought life** and immortality to light through the gospel:

11. Whereunto **I am appointed a preacher,** and an **apostle, and** a **teacher of the Gentiles.**

12. **For** the **which cause I** also **suffer** these things: **nevertheless I am not ashamed: for I know whom I have believed, and am persuaded that he is able to keep that which I have committed unto him against that day.**

13. **Hold fast the form of sound words,** which thou hast heard of me, in faith and love which is in Christ Jesus.

14. **That good thing which was committed unto thee keep by the Holy Ghost** which dwelleth in us.

15. **This thou knowest,** that **all** they which are **in Asia be turned away from me;** of whom are Phygellus and Hermogenes.

16. **The Lord give mercy unto the house of Onesiphorus; for he oft refreshed me,** and was not ashamed of my chain:

17. But, when he was in Rome, he sought me out very diligently, and found *me.*

18. The Lord grant unto him that he may find mercy of the Lord in that day: and in how many things he ministered unto me at Ephesus, thou knowest very well.

CHAPTER 2

1. **Thou therefore,** my son, **be strong in** the **grace** that is in Christ Jesus.

2. **And the things** that thou hast **heard of me among many witnesses, the same commit thou to faithful men,** who shall be able to teach others also.

3. Thou therefore

■ endure hardness, as a
■ good soldier of Jesus Christ.
■ 4. No man that warreth
■ entangleth himself with the
■ affairs of *this* life;
that he may please him who hath
chosen him to be a soldier.
■ 5. And if a man also strive
■ for masteries, *yet* is he not
■ crowned, except he
■ strive lawfully.
6. The husbandman that laboureth
must be first partaker of the fruits.
■ 7. Consider what I say; and
■ the Lord give thee
■ understanding in all things.
■ 8. Remember that Jesus
■ Christ of the seed of David
■ was raised from the dead
according to my gospel:
■ 9. Wherein I suffer
trouble, as an evildoer,
■ *even* unto bonds; but the
■ word of God
■ is not bound.
■ 10. Therefore I endure all
things
■ for the elect's sakes, that they
may also obtain the salvation which is
in Christ Jesus with eternal glory.
11. *It is* a faithful saying:
■ For if we be dead with *him,*
■ we shall also live with *him:*
■ 12. If we suffer, we shall
■ also reign with *him:* if we
■ deny *him,* he also
■ will deny us:
13. If we believe not, *yet* he abideth
faithful: he cannot deny himself.
14. Of these things put *them* in
remembrance, charging *them* before
the Lord that they strive not about
words to no profit, *but* to the
subverting of the hearers.
■ 15. Study to shew thyself
■ approved unto God,
a workman that needeth not
to be ashamed,
■ rightly dividing the word
of truth.
■ 16. But shun profane *and*
■ vain babblings: for they will
increase unto more ungodliness.

■ 17. And their word will eat
■ as doth a
■ canker: of whom is
■ Hymenaeus and Philetus;
■ 18. Who concerning the truth have
■ erred, saying that the
■ resurrection is past
■ already; and overthrow the faith
of some.
■ 19. Nevertheless the
■ foundation of God
■ standeth sure, having this
■ seal, The Lord knoweth
■ them that are his. And, Let
every one that nameth the name
of Christ depart from iniquity.
■ 20. But in a great house
■ there are not only vessels
■ of gold and of
■ silver, but also
■ of wood and of
■ earth; and some to honour,
■ and some to dishonour.
21. If a man therefore purge himself
from these, he shall be a vessel
unto honour, sanctified, and meet for
the master's use, *and* prepared unto
every good work.
■ 22. Flee also youthful lusts:
■ but follow righteousness,
faith, charity, peace, with them that
call on the Lord out of a pure heart.
■ 23. But foolish and
■ unlearned questions
■ avoid, knowing that they do
gender strifes.
■ 24. And the servant of the
■ Lord must not strive; but
be gentle unto all *men,* apt to
teach, patient,
■ 25. In meekness instructing
■ those that oppose
■ themselves; if God
peradventure
■ will give them repentance
to the acknowledging of the truth;
26. And *that* they may recover
themselves out of the snare of the
devil, who are taken captive by him at
his will.

CHAPTER 3
■ 1. This know also, that in the

last days perilous times shall come. 2. For men shall be lovers of their own selves, covetous, boasters, proud, blasphemers, disobedient to parents, unthankful, unholy, 3. Without natural affection, trucebreakers, false accusers, incontinent, fierce, despisers of those that are good, 4. Traitors, heady, highminded, lovers of pleasures more than lovers of God; 5. Having a form of godliness, but denying the power thereof: from such turn away. 6. For of this sort are they which creep into houses, and lead captive silly women laden with sins, led away with divers lusts, 7. Ever learning, and never able to come to the knowledge of the truth. 8. Now as Jannes and Jambres withstood Moses, so do these also resist the truth: men of corrupt minds, reprobate concerning the faith. 9. But they shall proceed no further: for their folly shall be manifest unto all men, as theirs also was. 10. But thou hast fully known my doctrine, manner of life, purpose, faith, longsuffering, charity, patience, 11. Persecutions, afflictions, which came unto me at Antioch, at Iconium, at Lystra; what persecutions I endured: but out of them all the Lord delivered me. 12. Yea, and all that will live godly in Christ Jesus shall suffer persecution. 13. But evil men and seducers shall wax worse and worse,

deceiving, and being deceived. 14. But continue thou in the things which thou hast learned and hast been assured of, knowing of whom thou hast learned them; 15. And that from a child thou hast known the holy scriptures, which are able to make thee wise unto salvation through faith which is in Christ Jesus. 16. All scripture *is* given by inspiration of God, and *is* profitable for doctrine, for reproof, for correction, for instruction in righteousness: 17. That the man of God may be perfect, throughly furnished unto all good works.

CHAPTER 4

1. I charge *thee* therefore before God, and the Lord Jesus Christ, who shall judge the quick and the dead at his appearing and his kingdom; 2. Preach the word; be instant in season, out of season; reprove, rebuke, exhort with all longsuffering and doctrine. 3. For the time will come when they will not endure sound doctrine; but after their own lusts shall they heap to themselves teachers, having itching ears; 4. And they shall turn away *their* ears from the truth, and shall be turned unto fables. 5. But watch thou in all things, endure afflictions, do the work of an evangelist, make full proof of thy ministry. 6. For I am now ready to be offered, and the time of my departure is at hand. 7. I have fought a good fight, I have finished *my* course, I have kept the faith: 8. Henceforth there is laid

■ up for me a crown of
■ righteousness, which the
■ Lord, the righteous judge,
■ shall give me at that day:
■ and not to me only, but
■ unto all them also
■ that love his appearing.
9. Do thy diligence to
■ come shortly unto me:
■ 10. For Demas hath
■ forsaken me, having loved this
present world, and is departed unto
Thessalonica; Crescens to Galatia,
Titus unto Dalmatia.
■ 11. Only Luke is with me.
■ Take Mark, and bring him
■ with thee: for he is profitable to me
for the ministry.
12. And Tychicus have I sent
to Ephesus.
13. The cloak that I left at Troas with
Carpus, when thou comest, bring
with thee, and the books, *but*
especially the parchments.
14. Alexander the coppersmith
did me much evil: the Lord
reward him according
to his works:
15. Of whom be thou ware also; for he
hath greatly withstood our words.
■ 16. At my first answer no
■ man stood with me, but all *men*
forsook me: *I pray God* that it may not
be laid to their charge.
■ 17. Notwithstanding the
■ Lord stood with me,
and strengthened me;
■ that by me the preaching might be
fully known, and *that* all
■ the Gentiles might hear:
and I was delivered out of the mouth
of the lion.
■ 18. And the Lord shall
■ deliver me from every evil
■ work, and will preserve *me* unto his
heavenly kingdom: to whom *be* glory
for ever and ever. Amen.
19. Salute Prisca and Aquila, and the
household of Onesiphorus.
20. Erastus abode at Corinth: but
Trophimus have I left at Miletum sick.
21. Do thy diligence to come before
winter. Eubulus greeteth thee, and
Pudens, and Linus, and Claudia, and
all the brethren.
22. The Lord Jesus Christ *be* with thy
spirit. Grace *be* with you.
■ Amen.

THE EPISTLE TO TITUS

BACKGROUND INFORMATION

Author – Paul, an Apostle.
Date Written – probably
between **62** and **65** A.D.

Number of:
Verses -   46
Chapters -   3
Total Words - 921
Scan Words - 466
Scan Words represent 50 %
of Total Words.

Theme – written
to instruct a young
minister in the proper
**conduct and role of
believers in the Church.**

OUTLINE OF THE EPISTLE

I.   Paul presents
**the qualifications of
elders and bishops**
and warns against
false teachers.
Chapter 1

II. Paul describes
domestic regulations
and the Christian life.
Chapter 2

III. Paul tells Timothy the
bases of
Christian ethics and
advises him on how to
discipline factious men.
Chapter 3

CHAPTER 1

1. **Paul,** a servant of God, and **an apostle** of Jesus Christ, according to the faith of God's elect, and the acknowledging of the truth which is after godliness;

2. **In hope of eternal life, which God,** that cannot lie, **promised before the world began;**

3. But hath in due times manifested his word through preaching, which is committed unto me according to the commandment of God our Saviour;

4. **To Titus, *mine* own son after the** common **faith:** Grace, mercy, *and* peace, from God the Father and the Lord Jesus Christ our Saviour.

5. **For this cause left I thee in Crete, that thou shouldest set in order the things that are wanting, and ordain elders** in every city, as I had appointed thee:

6. If any be blameless, the husband of one wife, having faithful children not accused of riot or unruly.

7. **For a bishop must be blameless,** as the steward of God; **not selfwilled, not soon angry, not given to wine,** no striker, not given to filthy lucre;

8. **But a lover of hospitality,** a lover **of good men, sober, just, holy, temperate;**

9. **Holding fast the faithful word** as he hath been taught, **that he may be able by sound doctrine both to exhort and to convince the gainsayers.**

10. **For there are many** unruly and **vain talkers and deceivers,** specially they of the circumcision:

11. **Whose mouths must be stopped, who subvert whole houses,** teaching things which they ought not, for filthy lucre's sake

12. **One of** themselves, *even* a prophet of **their own, said, The Cretians *are* alway liars, evil beasts,** slow bellies.

13. **This witness is true. Wherefore rebuke them sharply, that they may be sound in the faith;**

14. **Not giving heed to Jewish fables, and** commandments of men, that turn from the truth.

15. **Unto the pure all things *are* pure: but unto them that are defiled** and unbelieving *is* **nothing pure;** but even their mind and conscience is defiled.

16. **They profess that they know God; but in works they deny *him*,** being abominable, and disobedient, and unto every good work reprobate.

CHAPTER 2

1. **But speak thou the things which become sound doctrine:**

2. That the aged men be **sober, grave, temperate, sound in faith, in charity, in patience.**

3. **The aged women likewise,** that *they be* in behaviour as becometh holiness, not false accusers, not given to much wine, teachers of good things;

4. **That they may teach the young women to be sober, to love their husbands, to love their children,**

5. *To be* **discreet, chaste, keepers at home, good, obedient to their** own **husbands,** that the word of God be not blasphemed.

6. **Young men likewise** exhort to be **sober minded.**

7. **In all things shewing** thyself a pattern of **good works: in doctrine**

shewing uncorruptness, gravity, sincerity,

8. Sound speech, that cannot be condemned; that he that is of the contrary part may be ashamed, having no evil thing to say of you.

9. *Exhort* servants to be obedient unto their own masters, *and* to please *them* well in all *things;* not answering again;

10. Not purloining, but shewing all good fidelity; that they may adorn the doctrine of God our Saviour in all things.

11. For the grace of God that bringeth salvation hath appeared to all men,

12. Teaching us that, denying ungodliness and worldly lusts, we should live soberly, righteously, and godly, in this present world;

13. Looking for that blessed hope, and the glorious appearing of the great God and our Saviour Jesus Christ;

14. Who gave himself for us, that he might redeem us from all iniquity, and purify unto himself a peculiar people, zealous of good works.

15. These things speak, and exhort, and rebuke with all authority. Let no man despise thee.

CHAPTER 3

1. Put them in mind to be subject to principalities and powers, to obey magistrates, to be ready to every good work,

2. To speak evil of no man, to be no brawlers, *but* gentle, shewing all meekness unto all men.

3. For we ourselves also were sometimes foolish, disobedient, deceived, serving divers lusts and pleasures, living in malice and envy, hateful, *and* hating one another.

4. But after that the kindness and love of God our Saviour toward man appeared,

5. Not by works of righteousness which we have done, but according to his mercy he saved us, by the washing of regeneration, and renewing of the Holy Ghost;

6. Which he shed on us abundantly through Jesus Christ our Saviour;

7. That being justified by his grace, we should be made heirs according to the hope of eternal life.

8. *This is* a faithful saying, and these things I will that thou affirm constantly, that they which have believed in God might be careful to maintain good works. These things are good and profitable unto men.

9. But avoid foolish questions, and genealogies, and contentions, and strivings about the law; for they are unprofitable and vain.

10. A man that is an heretic after the first and second admonition reject;

11. Knowing that he that is such is subverted, and sinneth, being condemned of himself.

12. When I shall send Artemas unto thee, or Tychicus, be diligent to come unto me to Nicopolis: for I have determined there to winter.

13. Bring Zenas the lawyer and Apollos on their journey diligently, that nothing be wanting unto them.

14. And let ours also learn to maintain good works for necessary uses, that they be not unfruitful.

15. All that are with me salute thee. Greet them that love us in the faith. Grace *be* with you all. **Amen.**

THE EPISTLE
TO PHILEMON

BACKGROUND INFORMATION

Author – Paul, an Apostle.
Date Written – probably
between 60 and **65** A.D.

Number of:
Verses -   25
Chapters -   1
Total Words - 445
Scan Words - 214
Scan Words represent 48 %
of Total Words.

Theme – written to show that
relationships
between people
**take on a new dimension
when** they become
Christians.

OUTLINE OF THE EPISTLE

I.   **Paul's greeting** to
     Philemon.
     Verses 1—3
II. **Paul's** offer of
     thanksgiving.
     Verses 4—7
III. **Paul's appeal for
     Onesimus,** a slave.
     Verses 8—21
IV. **Paul's conclusion.**
     Verses 22—25

CHAPTER 1

1. **Paul, a prisoner of** Jesus **Christ,** and Timothy *our* brother, **unto Philemon** our dearly beloved, and fellow-labourer,

2. And to *our* beloved Apphia, and Archippus our fellow-soldier, and to the church in thy house:

3. Grace to you, and peace, from God our Father and the Lord Jesus Christ.

4. **I thank my God,** making mention of thee always in my prayers,

5. **Hearing of thy love and faith, which thou hast toward the Lord Jesus, and toward all saints;**

6. That the communication of thy faith may become effectual by the acknowledging of every good thing which is in you in Christ Jesus.

7. **For we have great joy** and consolation in thy love, **because** the bowels of **the saints are refreshed by thee,** brother.

8. **Wherefore, though I might be** much **bold in Christ** to enjoin thee that which is convenient,

9. **Yet for love's sake I rather beseech** *thee*, **being** such an one as **Paul the aged, and** now also **a prisoner of Jesus Christ.**

10. **I beseech thee for my son Onesimus, whom I have begotten in my bonds:**

11. **Which in time past was to thee unprofitable, but now profitable to thee and to me:**

12. **Whom I have sent again: thou therefore receive him,** that is, mine own bowels:

13. **Whom I would have** retained **with me,** that in thy stead he might have ministered unto me in the bonds of the gospel:

14. **But without thy mind would I do nothing;** that thy benefit should not be as it were of necessity, but willingly.

15. **For perhaps he** therefore **departed** for a season, **that thou shouldest receive him for ever;**

16. **Not now as a servant, but** above a servant, **a brother beloved,** specially to me, but how much more unto thee, both in the flesh, and in the Lord?

17. **If thou count me** therefore **a partner, receive him as myself.**

18. **If he hath wronged thee,** or oweth *thee* aught, **put that on mine account;**

19. **I Paul have written** *it* with mine own hand, **I will repay** *it:* albeit I do not say to thee how thou owest unto me even thine own self besides.

20. **Yea, brother, let me have joy of thee in the Lord:** refresh my bowels in the Lord.

21. **Having confidence in thy obedience I wrote** unto thee, **knowing that thou wilt** also **do more than I say.**

22. But withal **prepare me also a lodging: for I trust that through your prayers I shall be given unto you.**

23. There salute thee Epaphras, my fellow-prisoner in Christ Jesus;

24. Marcus, Aristarchus, Demas, Lucas, my fellow-labourers.

25. The grace of our Lord Jesus Christ *be* with your spirit. **Amen.**

THE EPISTLE
TO THE HEBREWS

BACKGROUND INFORMATION

Author – Unknown
Date Written – probably
between 65 and **85** A.D.

Number of:
Versus -   303
Chapters -   13
Total Words - 6,913
Scan Words - 3,493
Scan Words represent 50 %
of Total Words.

Theme – written to
encourage believers,
especially Jewish believers, to
endure persecution and
remain faithful to the Lord,
showing the superiority of
Jesus Christ.

OUTLINE OF THE EPISTLE

I. **Christ as superior**
    to angels.
    Chapters 1—2
II. **Christ as superior to**
    Moses and Joshua.
    Chapters 3—4
III. **Christ's superiority as**
    the High Priest.
    Chapters 5—10
IV. **Christ and**
    the superiority of the
    new covenant
    Chapters 10:19—13

CHAPTER 1

■ 1. **God,** who at sundry times and in divers manners spake in time past unto the fathers by the prophets,

■ 2. **Hath in these last days**
■ **spoken** unto us
■ **by** *his* **Son, whom he hath**
■ **appointed heir of all**
■ **things, by whom also he**
■ **made the worlds;**
■ 3. **Who being**
the brightness of *his* glory, and
■ **the** express
■ **image of his person,**
■ **and upholding all things**
■ **by the word of his power,**
■ **when he had** by himself
■ **purged our sins, sat down**
■ **on the right hand of the**
■ **Majesty** on high;
■ 4. **Being made** so much
■ **better than** the
■ **angels,** as
■ **he hath** by inheritance
■ **obtained a more**
■ **excellent name** than they.
■ 5. **For unto which of the**
■ **angels said he** at any time,
■ **Thou art my Son, this day**
■ **have I begotten thee?**
And again, I will be to him a Father, and he shall be to me a Son?
■ 6. **And again,** when he bringeth in the first begotten into the world,
■ **he saith,** And
■ **let all the angels** of God
■ **worship him.**
■ 7. **And of the angels he**
■ **saith, Who maketh his**
■ **angels spirits,**
and his ministers a flame of fire.
■ 8. **But unto the Son** *he saith,*
■ **Thy throne, O God,**
■ *is* **for ever**
and ever: a sceptre of righteousness *is* the sceptre of thy kingdom.
9. Thou hast loved righteousness, and hated iniquity; therefore God, *even* thy God, hath anointed thee with the oil of gladness above thy fellows.
■ 10. **And, Thou,**
Lord, in the beginning

■ **hast laid the foundation of**
■ **the earth; and the heavens**
■ **are** the works
■ **of thine hands:**
■ 11. **They shall perish;**
but thou remainest; and they all shall wax old as doth a garment;
12. And as a vesture shalt thou fold them up, and they shall be changed:
■ **but thou art the same, and**
■ **thy years shall not fail.**
■ 13. **But to which of the**
■ **angels said he** at any time,
■ **Sit on my right hand,**
■ **until I make thine enemies**
■ **thy footstool?**
14. Are they not all ministering spirits, sent forth to minister for them who shall be heirs of salvation?

CHAPTER 2

■ 1. **Therefore** we ought to
■ **give** the more
■ **earnest heed to the things**
which we have
■ **heard, lest** at any time
■ **we should let** *them* **slip.**
■ 2. **For if the word spoken by**
■ **angels was stedfast, and**
■ **every transgression**
and disobedience
■ **received a just**
■ **recompence** of reward;
■ 3. **How shall we escape, if**
■ **we neglect** so great
■ **salvation;** which
at the first began to be
■ **spoken by the Lord, and**
was confirmed unto us by
■ **them that heard** *him;*
■ 4. **God also bearing** *them*
■ **witness,** both
■ **with signs** and
■ **wonders,** and with divers
■ **miracles, and gifts of the**
■ **Holy Ghost,**
according to his own will?
5. For unto the angels hath he not put in subjection the world to come, whereof we speak.
■ 6. **But one** in a certain place
■ **testified, saying,**
■ **What is man,**

**that thou art mindful
of him?**
or the son of man,
that thou visitest him?
7. **Thou madest him a little
lower than the angels;** thou
crownedst him with glory and honour,
and didst
**set him over the works
of thy hands:**
8. **Thou hast put all things**
in subjection
under his feet.
For in that he put all
in subjection under him, he left
nothing *that is* not put under him.
But now
we see not yet all things
put under him.
9. **But we see Jesus, who
was made a little lower
than** the
**angels for the suffering
of death,**
crowned with glory and honour;
that he by the
grace of God
**should taste death for
every man.**
10. **For it became him,**
for whom *are* all things, and by whom
are all things, in bringing many sons
unto glory,
to make the captain of their
**salvation perfect
through sufferings.**
11. **For both he
that sanctifieth
and they** who are
sanctified *are* all of
**one: for which cause
he is not ashamed to
call them brethren,**
12. Saying, I will declare thy
name unto my brethren,
in the midst of the church will
I sing praise unto thee.
13. And again, I will put my trust in
him. And again, Behold I and the
children which God hath given me.
14. **Forasmuch then as the
children are** partakers of
flesh and blood, he also

himself likewise
**took part of the same;
that through death he might
destroy** him that had
the power of death, that is,
the devil;
15. **And deliver them who**
through fear of death
were all their lifetime
subject to bondage.
16. For verily he took not on *him*
the nature of angels; but he took on
him the seed of Abraham.
17. Wherefore in all things
**it behoved him to be made
like unto** *his* **brethren, that
he might be a**
merciful and faithful
high priest
in things *pertaining* to God,
**to make reconciliation for
the sins of the people.**
18. For in that he himself
hath suffered being tempted, he is
able to succour them that
are tempted.

CHAPTER 3

1. **Wherefore,** holy brethren,
partakers of the heavenly calling,
consider the Apostle and High
Priest of our profession,
Christ Jesus;
2. Who was faithful to him that
appointed him, as also
Moses *was faithful* in all his house.
3. **For this** *man* **was** counted
**worthy of more glory than
Moses, inasmuch as
he who hath builded the
house hath more honour
than the house.**
4. For every house is builded
by some *man;* but
**he that built all things
is God.**
5. **And Moses verily
was faithful** in all his house,
as a servant,
for a testimony of those things which
were to be spoken after;
6. **But Christ as a son**
over his own house;

■ whose house are we, if we
■ hold fast the confidence and the
rejoicing of the hope firm
■ unto the end.
■ 7. Wherefore (as the Holy
■ Ghost saith, To-day if ye
■ will hear his voice,
■ 8. Harden not your hearts,
as in the provocation, in the day of
temptation in the wilderness:
9. When your fathers tempted me,
proved me, and saw
my works forty years.
10. Wherefore I was grieved with that
generation, and said, They do alway
err in *their* heart; and they
have not known my ways.
11. So I sware in my wrath, They shall
not enter into my rest.)
■ 12. Take heed, brethren,
■ lest there be
in any of you an evil heart of
■ unbelief, in departing
from the living God.
■ 13. But exhort one another
daily, while it is called To-day;
■ lest any of you
■ be hardened through the
■ deceitfulness of sin.
■ 14. For we are made
■ partakers of Christ, if we
■ hold the beginning of
our confidence
■ stedfast unto the end;
15. While it is said,
■ To-day if ye will
■ hear his voice, harden not
■ your hearts,
as in the provocation.
■ 16. For some, when they had
■ heard, did provoke:
■ howbeit not all that
■ came out of Egypt by Moses.
17. But with whom was he grieved
forty years? *was it* not
with them that had sinned,
■ whose carcases fell
■ in the wilderness?
18. And to whom sware he that they
should not enter into his rest, but
to them that believed not?
19. So we see that
■ they could not enter in

■ because of unbelief.

CHAPTER 4

■ 1. Let us therefore fear, lest,
a promise being left *us* of
■ entering into his rest, any
of you should seem to
■ come short of it.
■ 2. For unto us was the gospel
preached, as well as unto them: but
■ the word preached
■ did not profit them, not
■ being mixed with faith
in them that heard *it.*
■ 3. For we which have
■ believed do enter into rest,
as he said, As I have sworn in my
wrath, if they shall enter into my rest:
■ although the works were
■ finished from the
■ foundation of the world.
■ 4. For he spake in a certain place of
the seventh *day* on this wise, And
■ God did rest the seventh
■ day from all his works.
5. And in this *place* again, If
they shall enter into my rest.
■ 6. Seeing therefore it remaineth
■ that some
must enter therein, and they
■ to whom it was first
■ preached entered not in
■ because of unbelief:
■ 7. Again, he limiteth a certain day,
■ saying in David, To-day, after
so long a time; as it is said,
■ To-day if ye will hear
■ his voice, harden
■ not your hearts.
■ 8. For if Jesus had given
■ them rest, then would he
■ not afterward have spoken
■ of another day.
■ 9. There remaineth therefore
■ a rest to the people of God.
10. For he that is entered into his rest,
he also hath ceased from his own
works, as God *did* from his.
■ 11. Let us labour therefore
■ to enter into that rest,
lest any man fall after the same
example of unbelief.
■ 12. For the word of God *is*

quick, and powerful, and sharper than any two edged sword, piercing even to the dividing asunder of soul and spirit, and of the joints and marrow, and *is* a discerner of the thoughts and intents of the heart. 13. Neither is there any creature that is not manifest in his sight: but all things *are* naked and opened unto the eyes of him with whom we have to do. 14. Seeing then that we have a great high priest, that is passed into the heavens, Jesus the Son of God, let us hold fast our profession. 15. For we have not an high priest which cannot be touched with the feeling of our infirmities; but was in all points tempted like as *we are, yet* without sin. 16. Let us therefore come boldly unto the throne of grace, that we may obtain mercy, and find grace to help in time of need.

CHAPTER 5

1. For every high priest taken from among men is ordained for men in things *pertaining* to God, that he may offer both gifts and sacrifices for sins: 2. Who can have compassion on the ignorant, and on them that are out of the way; for that he himself also is compassed with infirmity. 3. And by reason hereof he ought, as for the people, so also for himself, to offer for sins.

4. And no man taketh this honour unto himself, but he that is called of God, as *was* Aaron. 5. So also Christ glorified not himself to be made an high priest; but he that said unto him, Thou art my Son, to-day have I begotten thee. 6. As he saith also in another *place*, Thou *art* a priest for ever after the order of Melchisedec. 7. Who in the days of his flesh, when he had offered up prayers and supplications with strong crying and tears unto him that was able to save him from death, and was heard in that he feared; 8. Though he were a Son, yet learned he obedience by the things which he suffered; 9. And being made perfect, he became the author of eternal salvation unto all them that obey him; 10. Called of God an high priest after the order of Melchisedec. 11. Of whom we have many things to say, and hard to be uttered, seeing ye are dull of hearing. 12. For when for the time ye ought to be teachers, ye have need that one teach you again which *be* the first principles of the oracles of God; and are become such as have need of milk, and not of strong meat. 13. For every one that useth milk *is* unskilful in the word of righteousness: for he is a babe. 14. But strong meat belongeth to them that are of full age, *even* those who

by reason of use have their senses exercised to ■ **discern both good** ■ **and evil.**

CHAPTER 6

■ 1. **Therefore** leaving the principles of the doctrine of Christ, ■ **let us go on unto** ■ **perfection; not laying** ■ **again the foundation of** ■ **repentance** from dead works, ■ **and of faith** toward God, ■ 2. **Of** the doctrine of ■ **baptisms, and of laying on** ■ **of hands, and of** ■ **resurrection** of the dead, ■ **and of** eternal ■ **judgment** 3. And this will we do, if God permit. ■ 4. **For** *it is* **impossible for** ■ **those who were once** ■ **enlightened, and have** ■ **tasted of the heavenly gift,** ■ **and were made partakers** ■ **of the Holy Ghost,** ■ 5. **And have tasted the** ■ **good word** of God, ■ **and the powers** of the world ■ **to come,** ■ 6. **If they shall fall away, to** ■ **renew them** again ■ **unto repentance; seeing** ■ **they crucify** to themselves ■ **the Son of God afresh,** and put *him* to an open shame. 7. For the earth which drinketh in the rain that cometh oft upon it, and bringeth forth herbs meet for them by whom it is dressed, receiveth blessing from God: 8. But that which beareth thorns and briers *is* rejected, and *is* nigh unto cursing; whose end *is* to be burned. ■ 9. **But, beloved, we are** ■ **persuaded better things** ■ **of you,** and things that accompany salvation, though we thus speak. ■ 10. **For God** *is* **not** ■ **unrighteous to forget** ■ **your** work and ■ **labour of love, which ye**

■ **have shewed** toward his name, ■ **in that ye have ministered** ■ **to the saints,** and do minister. ■ 11. **And** we desire that every one of you do ■ **shew the same diligence** to the full assurance of hope ■ **unto the end:** 12. That ye ■ **be not slothful, but** followers of them who ■ **through faith and patience** ■ **inherit the promises.** ■ 13. **For when God made** ■ **promise to Abraham,** because he could swear by no greater, ■ **he sware by himself,** ■ 14. **Saying,** Surely blessing ■ **I will bless thee,** and multiplying I will multiply thee. ■ 15. **And so, after he had** ■ **patiently endured,** ■ **he obtained** the promise. 16. For men verily swear by the greater: and an oath for confirmation *is* to them an end of all strife. ■ 17. **Wherein God,** willing more abundantly ■ **to shew** unto the heirs of promise ■ **the immutability of his** ■ **counsel, confirmed** *it* ■ **by an oath:** 18. That by two immutable things, ■ **in which** *it was* **impossible** ■ **for God to lie,** we might have a strong consolation, who have fled for refuge to lay hold upon the hope set before us: ■ 19. **Which** *hope* **we have** ■ **as an anchor** of the soul, both sure and stedfast, and ■ **which entereth into** that within ■ **the veil;** ■ 20. **Whither the forerunner is** for us entered, *even* ■ **Jesus, made an high** ■ **priest for ever after the** ■ **order of Melchisedec.**

CHAPTER 7

■ 1. **For this Melchisedec,** king of Salem, priest of the

most high God, who

■ **met Abraham** returning

from the slaughter of the kings,

■ **and blessed him;**

■ 2. **To whom also Abraham**

■ **gave a tenth part of all; first**

■ **being by interpretation**

■ **King of righteousness,**

and after that also King of Salem,

which is, King of peace;

■ 3. **Without father,**

without mother, without descent,

■ **having neither beginning**

of days,

■ **nor end of life; but made**

■ **like unto the Son** of God;

■ **abideth a**

■ **priest continually.**

■ 4. **Now consider how great**

■ **this man** *was,* **unto whom**

even the patriarch

■ **Abraham gave the tenth**

of the spoils.

5. And verily they that are of

■ **the sons of Levi,** who receive

the office of the priesthood,

■ **have a commandment to**

■ **take tithes** of the people

according to the law, that is,

■ **of their brethren,** though they

come out of the loins of Abraham:

■ 6. **But he whose descent is**

■ **not counted from them**

■ **received tithes of**

■ **Abraham,** and blessed

him that had the promises.

■ 7. **And** without all contradiction

■ **the less is blessed**

■ **of the better.**

8. And here men that die receive

tithes; but there he *receiveth them,* of

whom it is witnessed that he liveth.

9. And as I may so say,

■ **Levi also, who receiveth**

■ **tithes, payed tithes**

■ **in Abraham.**

10. For he was yet in the loins of his

father, when Melchisedec met him.

■ 11. **If therefore**

■ **perfection were by the**

■ **Levitical priesthood,** (for

under it the people received the law,)

■ **what** further

■ **need** *was there* **that**

■ **another priest should rise**

■ **after the order of**

■ **Melchisedec,** and not be called

after the order of Aaron?

12. For the priesthood being changed,

there is made of necessity a change

also of the law.

■ 13. **For he of whom these**

■ **things are spoken**

■ **pertaineth to another tribe,**

of which no man gave

attendance at the altar.

■ 14. **For** *it is* evident that

■ **our Lord sprang out of**

■ **Juda; of which** tribe

■ **Moses spake nothing**

■ **concerning priesthood.**

■ 15. **And** it is yet

far more evident: for that

■ **after the similitude of**

■ **Melchisedec** there

■ **ariseth another priest,**

■ 16. **Who is made, not**

after the law

■ **of a carnal commandment,**

■ **but after the power of an**

■ **endless life.**

■ 17. **For he testifieth, Thou** *art*

■ **a priest for ever after the**

■ **order of Melchisedec.**

18. For there is verily a disannulling of

the commandment going before

for the weakness and

unprofitableness thereof.

■ 19. **For the law made**

■ **nothing perfect, but**

the bringing in of

■ **a better hope** *did;* **by the**

■ **which we draw nigh**

■ **unto God.**

20. **And** inasmuch as

■ **not without an oath**

■ *he was made priest:*

21. (For those priests were made

without an oath; but this with an oath

by him that said unto him,

■ **The Lord sware**

and will not repent,

■ **Thou** *art* **a priest for**

■ **ever after the order**

■ **of Melchisedec:)**

22. By so much was

- **Jesus made a surety of a**
- **better testament.**
23. And they truly
were many priests, because they
were not suffered to continue
by reason of death:
24. But this *man,*
- **because he** continueth ever,
- **hath an unchangeable**
- **priesthood.**
- 25. **Wherefore he is able**
- **also to save them**
to the uttermost
- **that come unto God by him,**
- **seeing he ever liveth to**
- **make intercession** for them.
- 26. **For such an high priest**
- **became us, who is** holy,
harmless, undefiled,
- **separate from sinners,**
- **and** made
- **higher than the heavens;**
- 27. **Who needeth not daily,**
as those high priests,
- **to offer up sacrifice,** first
- **for his own sins, and** then for
- **the people's: for this he did**
- **once, when he offered**
- **up himself.**
28. For the law maketh men high
priests which have infirmity; but the
word of the oath, which was since the
law, *maketh* the Son, who is
consecrated for evermore.

CHAPTER 8
- 1. **Now** of the things which we have
spoken *this is* the sum:
- **We have** such
- **an high priest,** who is
- **set on the right hand of the**
- **throne of the Majesty**
in the heavens;
- 2. **A minister of**
the sanctuary, and of
- **the true tabernacle,** which
- **the Lord pitched,**
- **and not man.**
3. For every high priest is ordained to
offer gifts and sacrifices: wherefore *it
is* of necessity that this man have
somewhat also to offer.
- 4. **For if he were on earth, he**

- **should not be a priest,**
- **seeing that there are**
- **priests** that offer gifts
- **according to the law:**
- 5. **Who serve unto the**
- **example** and shadow
- **of heavenly things, as**
- **Moses was admonished of**
- **God** when he was
about to make the tabernacle:
- **for, See, saith he,** *that* thou
- **make all things**
- **according to the pattern**
- **shewed** to thee
- **in the mount.**
- 6. **But now hath he obtained**
- **a more excellent ministry,**
by how much
- **also he is the mediator of a**
- **better covenant,** which was
established upon better promises.
- 7. **For if that first** *covenant*
- **had been faultless, then**
- **should no place have been**
- **sought for the second.**
- 8. **For** finding fault with them,
- **he saith,** Behold,
- **the days** come, saith the Lord,
- **when I will make a new**
- **covenant with** the house of
- **Israel and** with the house of
- **Judah:**
9. Not according to the covenant that
I made with their fathers in the day
when I took them by the hand to lead
them out of the land of Egypt;
because they continued not in my
covenant, and I regarded them not,
saith the Lord.
- 10. **For this** *is* **the covenant**
- **that I will make**
with the house of Israel after those
days, saith the Lord;
- **I will put my laws into their**
- **mind, and write them in**
- **their hearts: and I will be to**
- **them a God, and they shall**
- **be to me a people:**
11. And they shall not teach every
man his neighbour, and every man his
brother, saying, Know the Lord: for all
shall know me, from the
least to the greatest.

12. **For I will be merciful** to their unrighteousness, **and their sins and** their **iniquities will I remember no more.**

13. In that he saith, A new *covenant*, he hath made the first old. Now that which decayeth and waxeth old *is* ready to vanish away.

CHAPTER 9

1. **Then verily the first** *covenant* had **also ordinances** of divine service, **and a worldly sanctuary.**

2. **For there was a tabernacle made;** the first, wherein *was* the candlestick, and the table, and the shewbread; **which is called the sanctuary.**

3. **And after the second veil, the** tabernacle which is called the **Holiest of all;**

4. **Which had** the golden censer, and **the ark of the covenant** overlaid round about with gold, wherein *was* the golden pot that had manna, **and Aaron's rod** that budded, **and** the **tables of the covenant;**

5. **And over it the cherubims** of glory **shadowing the mercyseat;** of which we cannot now speak particularly.

6. **Now** when these things were thus ordained, **the priests went** always **into the first tabernacle, accomplishing the service of God.**

7. **But into the second** *went* **the high priest alone once every year, not without blood,** which he **offered for himself, and** *for* **the errors of the people:**

8. **The Holy Ghost this signifying, that the way into the holiest** of all **was not yet** made **manifest, while** as **the first tabernacle was** yet **standing:**

9. Which *was* a figure for the time then present, in which were offered both gifts and sacrifices, that could not make him that did the service perfect, as pertaining to the conscience;

10. *Which stood* only in meats and drinks, and divers washings, and carnal ordinances, imposed *on them* until the time of reformation.

11. **But Christ being come an high priest** of good things to come, **by a** greater and more **perfect tabernacle, not made with hands,** that is to say, not of this building;

12. **Neither by the blood of goats and calves, but by his own blood he entered** in **once** into **the holy place, having obtained eternal redemption** *for us.*

13. **For if the blood of bulls and of goats,** and the ashes of an heifer sprinkling the unclean, **sanctifieth** to the purifying of **the flesh:**

14. **How much more shall the blood of Christ, who** through the eternal Spirit **offered himself without spot to God, purge your conscience** from dead works **to serve** the living **God?**

15. **And** for this cause **he is the mediator of the new testament,** that by means of death, for the redemption of the transgressions *that were* under the first testament, they which are called might receive the promise of eternal inheritance.

16. **For where a testament *is*,**

there must also of necessity
be the death of the testator.
17. For a testament *is* of
force after men are dead:
otherwise it is of no strength at all
while the testator liveth.
18. Whereupon neither the
first *testament* was
dedicated without blood.
19. For when Moses had
spoken every precept to all the
people according to the law,
he took the blood of calves
and of goats, with water, and
scarlet wool, and hyssop, and
sprinkled both the book,
and all the people,
20. Saying, This *is* the blood
of the testament which God
hath enjoined unto you.
21. Moreover he sprinkled
with blood
both the tabernacle, and
all the vessels
of the ministry.
22. And almost
all things are by the law
purged with blood;
and without shedding of
blood is no remission.
23. *It was* therefore necessary that
the patterns of things in the heavens
should be purified with these; but the
heavenly things themselves with
better sacrifices than these.
24. For Christ is not
entered into the holy places
made with hands, *which are* the figures
of the true; but into heaven itself,
now to appear in
the presence of God for us:
25. Nor yet that he should offer
himself often,
as the high priest entereth
into the holy place every
year with blood of others;
26. For then must he often have
suffered since the foundation
of the world:
but now
once in the end of the world hath
he appeared to put away
sin by the sacrifice

of himself.
27. And as it is appointed
unto men once to die, but
after this the judgment:
28. So Christ was once
offered to bear the sins of
many; and unto them
that look for him shall he
appear the second time
without sin unto salvation.

CHAPTER 10

1. For the law having a shadow of
good things to come, *and* not the very
image of the things,
can never with those
sacrifices which they
offered year by year
continually
make the comers
thereunto perfect.
2. For then would they not
have ceased to be offered?
because that
the worshippers once
purged should have had
no more conscience
of sins.
3. But in those *sacrifices*
there is a remembrance
again *made*
of sins every year.
4. For *it is* not possible that
the blood of bulls and of
goats should take
away sins.
5. Wherefore when he
cometh into the world,
he saith, Sacrifice and
offering thou wouldest not,
but a body hast thou
prepared me:
6. In burnt offerings and *sacrifices* for
sin thou hast had no pleasure.
7. Then said I, Lo, I come (in the
volume of the book it is written of
me,) to do thy will, O God.
8. Above when he said, Sacrifice and
offering and burnt offerings and
offering for sin thou wouldest not,
neither hadst pleasure *therein;* which
are offered by the law;
9. Then said he, Lo, I come

to do thy will, O God.
He taketh away the first, that he may establish the second.
10. **By the which will we are sanctified through the offering of the body of Jesus Christ once *for all.***
11. And every priest standeth daily ministering and offering oftentimes the same sacrifices, which can never take away sins:
12. **But this man, after he had offered one sacrifice for sins** for ever, **sat down on the right hand of God;**
13. From henceforth expecting **till his enemies be made his footstool.**
14. **For by one offering he hath perfected** for ever **them that are sanctified.**
15. *Whereof* the **Holy Ghost** also **is a witness** to us: **for** after that **he had said before,**
16. This *is* the covenant that I **will make** with them after those days, saith the Lord, **I will put my laws into their hearts,** and in their minds will I write them;
17. **And their sins** and iniquities **will I remember no more.**
18. **Now where remission** of these **is, there is no more offering for sin.**
19. **Having therefore,** brethren, **boldness to enter into the holiest by the blood of Jesus,**
20. **By a new and living way,** which he hath consecrated for us, **through the veil, that is** to say, **his flesh;**
21. **And** *having* **an high priest** over the house of God;
22. **Let us draw near with a true heart** in full assurance **of faith,** having our hearts sprinkled from an evil conscience, and our bodies washed with pure water.
23. **Let us hold fast the profession of** *our* **faith** without wavering; (for he *is* faithful that promised;)
24. **And let us consider one another** to provoke unto love and to good works:
25. **Not forsaking the assembling of ourselves together, as the manner of some** *is;* but exhorting *one another:* and so much the more, as ye see the day approaching.
26. **For if we sin wilfully after** that **we have received the knowledge of the truth, there remaineth no more sacrifice for sins,**
27. **But a certain** fearful looking for of **judgment and fiery indignation,** which shall devour the adversaries.
28. **He that despised Moses' law died** without mercy **under two or three witnesses:**
29. **Of how much sorer punishment,** suppose ye, **shall he be** thought **worthy, who hath trodden under foot the Son** of God, **and hath counted the blood** of the covenant, wherewith he was sanctified, **an unholy thing, and hath done despite unto the Spirit of grace?**
30. **For we know him that** hath **said,** Vengeance *belongeth* unto me, **I will recompense,** saith the Lord. And again, The Lord shall judge his people.
31. *It is* **a fearful thing to fall into the hands of the living God.**
32. But call to remembrance the former days, in which, after ye were

illuminated, ye endured a great fight of afflictions;

33. Partly, whilst ye were made a gazingstock both by reproaches and afflictions; and partly, whilst ye became companions of them that were so used.

34. For ye had compassion of me in my bonds, and took joyfully the spoiling of your goods, knowing in yourselves that ye have in heaven a better and an enduring substance.

35. **Cast not away therefore your confidence,** which hath great recompence of reward.

36. **For** ye have need of patience, that, **after ye have done the will of God, ye might receive the promise.**

37. For yet a little while, and he that shall come will come, and will not tarry.

38. **Now the just shall live by faith: but if** *any man* **draw back, my soul shall have no pleasure** in him.

39. **But we are not of them** who draw back unto perdition; **but of them that believe to the saving of the soul.**

CHAPTER 11

1. **Now faith is the substance of things hoped for, the evidence of things not seen.**

2. For by it the elders obtained a good report.

3. **Through faith** we understand that **the worlds were framed by the word of God, so that things** which are **seen were not made of things which do appear.**

4. **By faith Abel offered** unto God **a more excellent sacrifice** than Cain, by which he obtained witness that he was righteous, God testifying of his gifts: and by it he being dead yet speaketh.

5. **By faith Enoch was translated** that he should not see death; and was not found, because God had translated him: **for before his translation** he had this testimony, that **he pleased God.**

6. **But without faith** *it is* **impossible to please** *him:* for he that cometh to **God** must believe that he is, and *that* he is a rewarder of them that diligently seek him.

7. **By faith Noah,** being warned of God of things not seen as yet, moved with fear, **prepared an ark to the saving of his house;** by the which he condemned the world, **and became heir of the righteousness** which is **by faith.**

8. **By faith Abraham,** when he was called to go out into a place which he should after receive for an inheritance, obeyed; and he **went out, not knowing whither he went.**

9. **By faith he sojourned in the land of promise,** as *in* a strange country, dwelling in tabernacles **with Isaac and Jacob, the heirs with him** of the same promise:

10. **For he looked for a city which hath foundations, whose builder** and maker *is* **God.**

11. **Through faith also Sara** herself **received strength to conceive** seed, and was delivered of a child **when she was past age,** because she judged him faithful who had promised.

12. **Therefore sprang** there even **of one,** and him **as good as dead, so many** as the stars of the sky in multitude,

- **and** as
- **the sand** which is
- **by the sea** shore innumerable.
- 13. **These all died in faith,**
- **not having received the**
- **promises, but having seen**
- **them afar off,** and were
  persuaded of *them,*
  and embraced *them,*
- **and confessed that they**
- **were strangers**
  and pilgrims on the earth.
- 14. **For** they that say such things
  declare plainly that
- **they seek a country.**
  15. And truly, if they had been mindful
  of that *country* from whence they
  came out, they might have had
  opportunity to have returned.
  16. But now they desire
  a better *country,*
- **that is,** an
- **heavenly: wherefore God**
- **is not ashamed to be**
  called
- **their God: for he hath**
- **prepared for them a city.**
- 17. **By faith Abraham,**
  when he was tried,
- **offered up Isaac;** and he that
  had received the promises offered up
  his only begotten *son,*
- 18.**Of whom it was said,**
- **That in Isaac shall thy**
- **seed be called:**
- 19. **Accounting that God**
- *was* **able to raise** *him*
  up, even
- **from the dead;** from whence
  also he received him in a figure.
- 20. **By faith Isaac blessed**
- **Jacob** and Esau
  concerning things to come.
- 21. **By faith Jacob,**
  when he was a-dying,
- **blessed** both
- **the sons of Joseph;**
  and worshipped, *leaning* upon
  the top of his staff.
- 22. **By faith Joseph,**
  when he died,
- **made mention of**
  the departing of the children of

- **Israel;** and gave commandment
  concerning his bones.
- 23. **By faith Moses,**
  when he was born,
- **was hid three months of his**
- **parents,** because they saw *he was*
  a proper child; and they were not
  afraid of the king's commandment.
- 24. **By faith Moses,**
  when he was come to years,
- **refused to be called the**
- **son of Pharaoh's daughter;**
- 25. **Choosing rather to**
- **suffer affliction with the**
- **people of God, than to**
- **enjoy the pleasures of sin**
  for a season;
- 26. **Esteeming the reproach**
- **of Christ greater** riches
- **than the treasures in Egypt:**
  for he had respect unto the
  recompence of the reward.
- 27. **By faith he forsook**
- **Egypt,** not fearing the wrath of the
  king: for he endured, as
- **seeing him who**
- **is invisible.**
- 28. **Through faith he kept the**
- **passover,** and the sprinkling of
  blood, lest he that destroyed the
  firstborn should touch them.
- 29. **By faith they passed**
- **through the Red sea** as by dry
  land: which the Egyptians assaying to
  do were drowned.
- 30. **By faith the walls of**
- **Jericho fell** down, after they were
  compassed about seven days.
- 31. **By faith the harlot**
- **Rahab perished not**
  with them that believed not,when she
  had received the spies with peace.
- 32. **And what shall I more**
- **say?** for the
- **time would fail me to tell of**
- **Gedeon,** and *of*
- **Barak,** and *of*
- **Samson,** and *of*
- **Jephthae;** *of*
- **David** also, and
- **Samuel, and** *of*
- **the prophets:**
- 33. **Who through faith**

- subdued kingdoms,
- wrought righteousness,
- obtained promises,
- stopped the mouths
- of lions.
- 34. Quenched the violence of
- fire, escaped the edge of the
- sword, out of weakness were made strong, waxed valiant in fight,
- turned to flight the
- armies of the aliens.
- 35. Women received their
- dead raised to life again:
- and others were tortured, not accepting deliverance;
- that they might obtain a
- better resurrection:
- 36. And others had
- trial of *cruel*
- mockings and scourgings, yea, moreover of bonds
- and imprisonment:
- 37. They were stoned,
- they were sawn asunder, were tempted, were
- slain with the sword: they wandered about in sheepskins and goatskins; being
- destitute, afflicted,
- tormented;
- 38. (Of whom the world was
- not worthy:) they wandered in deserts, and *in* mountains, and *in* dens and caves of the earth.
- 39. And these all, having
- obtained a good report
- through faith, received not
- the promise:
- 40. God having provided
- some better thing for us,
- that they without us should
- not be made perfect.

CHAPTER 12
- 1. Wherefore seeing we also
- are compassed about with
- so great a cloud of
- witnesses, let us lay aside
- every weight, and the
- sin which doth so easily beset *us*,
- and let us
- run with patience
- the race that is set

- before us,
- 2. Looking unto Jesus the
- author and finisher of *our*
- faith; who for the joy that was set before him
- endured the cross, despising the shame,
- and is set down at the right
- hand of the throne of
- God.
- 3. For consider him that
- endured such contradiction of sinners against himself,
- lest ye be wearied and
- faint in your minds.
- 4. Ye have not yet resisted
- unto blood, striving against sin.
- 5. And ye have forgotten
- the exhortation which speaketh unto you as unto children,
- My son, despise not thou
- the chastening of the Lord, nor faint when thou art rebuked of him:
- 6. For whom the Lord loveth
- he chasteneth, and scourgeth every son whom he receiveth.
- 7. If ye endure chastening,
- God dealeth with you as
- with sons; for what son is he whom the father chasteneth not?
- 8. But if ye be without
- chastisement, whereof all are partakers,
- then are ye bastards, and not sons.
- 9. Furthermore we have had
- fathers of our flesh
- which corrected *us*, and we gave *them* reverence:
- shall we not much rather be
- in subjection unto the
- Father of spirits, and live?
- 10. For they verily for a few days
- chastened *us* after their own
- pleasure; but he for *our* profit,
- that *we* might be partakers
- of his holiness.
- 11. Now no chastening for the present seemeth to be joyous, but grievous: nevertheless afterward it yieldeth the peaceable fruit of righteousness unto them which are exercised thereby.

12. Wherefore lift up the hands which hang down, and the feeble knees;

13. And make straight paths for your feet, lest that which is lame be turned out of the way; but let it rather be healed.

14. Follow peace with all *men*, and holiness, without which no man shall see the Lord:

15. Looking diligently lest any man fail of the grace of God; lest any root of bitterness springing up trouble *you*, and thereby many be defiled;

16. Lest there *be* any fornicator, or profane person, as Esau, who for one morsel of meat **sold his birthright.**

17. For ye know how that **afterward,** when he would have inherited the blessing, **he was rejected: for he found no place of repentance,** though he sought it carefully with tears.

18. For ye are not come unto the mount that might be touched, and that burned with fire, nor unto blackness, and darkness, and tempest,

19. And the sound of a trumpet, and the voice of words; which *voice* they that heard entreated that the word should not be spoken to them any more:

20. (For they could not endure that which was commanded, And if so much as a beast touch the mountain, it shall be stoned, or thrust through with a dart:

21. And so terrible was the sight, *that* Moses said, I exceedingly fear and quake:)

22. But ye are come unto mount Sion, and unto **the city of** the living **God, the heavenly Jerusalem, and to** an innumerable company of **angels,**

23. To the general assembly and **church of the firstborn, which are written in heaven, and to God the Judge** of all, **and to the spirits of just men** made perfect,

24. And to Jesus the mediator of the new covenant, and to the blood of sprinkling, **that speaketh better things** than *that of* Abel.

25. See that ye refuse not him that speaketh. **For if they escaped not who refused him that spake on earth, much more *shall not* we *escape*, if we turn** away **from him that *speaketh* from heaven:**

26. Whose voice then shook the earth: but now he hath promised, saying, Yet once more I shake not the earth only, but also heaven.

27. And this *word*, Yet once more, signifieth the removing of those things that are shaken, as of things that are made, that those things which cannot be shaken may remain.

28. Wherefore we receiving a kingdom which cannot be moved, let us have grace, whereby we may **serve God** acceptably **with** reverence and godly **fear:**

29. For our God *is* a consuming fire.

CHAPTER 13

1. Let brotherly love continue.

2. Be not forgetful to **entertain strangers: for thereby some have entertained angels unawares.**

3. Remember them that are **in bonds,** as bound with them; *and* them which suffer adversity,

■ **as being yourselves**
also in the body.

■ 4. **Marriage** *is* **honourable**
in all,

■ **and the bed undefiled:**

■ **but** whoremongers and

■ **adulterers God will judge.**

5. *Let your* conversation
be without covetousness;

■ **and be content with such**

■ **things as ye have:**

■ **for he** hath

■ **said, I will never** leave thee, nor

■ **forsake thee.**

■ 6. **So that we may boldly**

■ **say, The Lord** *is* **my helper,**
and I will not fear what
man shall do unto me.

■ 7. **Remember them which**

■ **have the rule over you,** who
have spoken unto you the word of
God: whose faith follow, considering
the end of *their* conversation.

■ 8. **Jesus Christ the same**

■ **yesterday, and**

■ **to-day, and for ever.**

■ 9. **Be not carried about with**
divers and

■ **strange doctrines. For** *it is* **a**

■ **good thing that the heart be**

■ **established with grace; not**

■ **with meats, which have not**

■ **profited** them that have been
occupied therein.

10. We have an altar,
whereof they have no right to eat
which serve the tabernacle.

■ 11. **For the bodies of**

■ **those beasts, whose**

■ **blood is brought**
into the sanctuary

■ **by the high priest**

■ **for sin, are burned**

■ **without the camp.**

■ 12. **Wherefore Jesus also,**
that he might sanctify the
people with his own blood,

■ **suffered without the gate.**

■ 13. **Let us go** forth therefore

■ **unto him without the camp,**

■ **bearing his reproach.**

■ 14. **For here have we no**

■ **continuing city, but we seek**

■ **one to come.**

■ 15. **By him**
therefore let us

■ **offer the sacrifice of praise**

■ **to God continually,**
that is, the fruit of *our* lips
giving thanks to his name.

16. But to do good and to
communicate forget not:

■ **for with such sacrifices**

■ **God is well pleased.**

17. Obey them that have the rule over
you, and submit yourselves: for they
watch for your souls, as they that
must give account, that they may do
it with joy, and not with grief: for that *is*
unprofitable for you.

■ 18. **Pray for us:** for we trust we
have a good conscience, in all things
willing to live honestly.

19. But I beseech *you* the rather to do
this, that I may be restored
to you the sooner.

■ 20. **Now the God of peace,**

■ **that brought** again

■ **from the dead our Lord**

■ **Jesus, that great shepherd**
of the sheep,

■ **through the blood of the**

■ **everlasting covenant,**

■ 21. **Make you perfect**
in every good work to do his will,

■ **working in you that which is**

■ **well-pleasing** in his sight,

■ **through Jesus** Christ; to whom
be glory for ever and ever. Amen.

22. And I beseech you, brethren,
suffer the word of exhortation:
for I have written a letter
unto you in few words.

23. Know ye that *our* brother Timothy
is set at liberty; with whom, if he come
shortly, I will see you.

24. Salute all them that have the rule
over you, and all the saints.
They of Italy salute you.

25. Grace *be* with you all.

■ **Amen.**

THE EPISTLE OF JAMES

BACKGROUND INFORMATION

Author – James, a pastor in Jerusalem.
Date Written – probably between **45** and **60** A.D.

Number of:
Verses -   108
Chapters -   5
Total Words - 2,309
Scan Words - 1,129
Scan Words represent 48 % of Total Words.

Theme – written to instruct believers of the necessity of **demonstrating faith through** the conduct of their lives, through practical **Christian living.**

OUTLINE OF THE EPISTLE

I. James instructs **believers on facing trials, hearing and doing the word,** impartiality **and faith that works.** Chapters 1—2

II. James warns of **the dangers of the tongue,** true and **false wisdom, worldliness and** pride, inconsideration and **unchristian conduct.** Chapters 3—4

III. James exhorts the believer to have **patience in affliction and** to save **an erring brother.** Chapter 5

CHAPTER 1

■ 1. **James,** a servant of God and of the Lord Jesus Christ,

■ **to the twelve tribes** which are **scattered abroad,** greeting.

■ 2. **My brethren, count it all joy when ye fall into divers temptations;**

■ 3. **Knowing** *this,* **that the trying of your faith worketh patience.**

■ 4. **But let patience** have *her* perfect **work, that ye may be perfect** and entire, wanting nothing.

■ 5. **If any of you lack wisdom,** let him **ask of God,** that giveth to all *men* liberally, and upbraideth not; **and it shall be given** him.

■ 6. **But let him ask in faith,** nothing wavering. **For he that wavereth** is like a wave of the sea driven with the wind and tossed.

7. For let not that man think that he shall receive any thing of the Lord.

8. A double-minded man

■ *is* **unstable in all his ways.**

■ 9. **Let the brother of low degree rejoice in that he is exalted:**

■ 10. **But the rich,** in that he **is made low: because as the flower** of the grass **he shall pass away.**

11. For the sun is no sooner risen with a burning heat, but it withereth the grass, and the flower thereof falleth, and the grace of the fashion of it perisheth: so also shall the rich man fade away in his ways.

■ 12. **Blessed** *is* **the man that endureth temptation: for** when he is tried, **he shall receive the crown of life,** which the Lord hath promised to them that love him.

■ 13. **Let no man say** when he is tempted, **I am tempted of God:** for God cannot be tempted with evil, neither

tempteth he any man:

■ 14. **But every man is tempted,** when he is drawn away **of his own lust, and** enticed.

15. Then when

■ **lust** hath conceived, it **bringeth forth sin: and sin,** when it is finished, **bringeth forth death.**

16. Do not err, my beloved brethren.

■ 17. **Every good gift and every perfect gift is** from above, and cometh down **from the Father** of lights,

■ **with whom is no variableness, neither shadow of turning.**

■ 18. **Of his own will begat he us** with the word of truth, **that we should be a kind of firstfruits** of his creatures.

■ 19. **Wherefore,** my beloved brethren, let every man **be swift to hear, slow to speak, slow to wrath:**

■ 20. **For the wrath of man worketh not the righteousness of God.**

21. Wherefore lay apart all filthiness and superfluity of naughtiness, and

■ **receive** with meekness **the engrafted word, which is able to save your souls.**

■ 22. **But be ye doers of the word, and not hearers only,** deceiving your own selves.

■ 23. **For** if any be **a hearer** of the word, and not a doer, he **is like** unto **a man beholding his** natural **face in a glass:**

24. For he beholdeth himself,

■ **and goeth his way, and** straightway **forgetteth what manner of man he was.**

■ 25. **But whoso looketh into the perfect law** of liberty, and continueth *therein,* he **being** not a forgetful hearer, but **a doer of the work,** this man

shall be blessed in his deed.
26. **If any man** among you
**seem to be religious, and
bridleth not his tongue,**
but deceiveth his own heart,
this man's religion *is* **vain.**
27. **Pure religion** and undefiled
before God and the Father
**is this, To visit the
fatherless and widows**
in their affliction,
and **to keep himself
unspotted from the world.**

CHAPTER 2

1. **My brethren, have not the
faith** of our Lord Jesus Christ,
the Lord of glory,
with respect of persons.
2. **For if there come**
unto your assembly
a man with a gold ring,
in goodly apparel,
and there come in
also a poor man
in vile raiment;
3. **And ye have respect to
him that weareth the gay
clothing,** and say unto him, Sit
thou here in a good place; and say to
the poor, Stand thou there, or sit here
under my footstool:
4. **Are ye not then partial**
in yourselves, and are become
judges of evil thoughts?
5. Hearken, my beloved brethren,
**Hath not God chosen the
poor** of this world
**rich in faith, and heirs of the
kingdom** which he hath promised
to them that love him?
6. **But ye have despised the
poor. Do not rich men
oppress you, and** draw you
before the judgment seats?
7. Do not they
**blaspheme that worthy
name** by the which ye are called?
8. **If** ye fulfil the royal law according to
the scripture,
**Thou shalt love thy
neighbour** as thyself,
ye do well:

9. **But if ye have respect to
persons, ye commit sin,**
and are convinced of the law
as transgressors.
10. **For whosoever shall
keep the whole law, and
yet offend in one** *point,* **he
is guilty of all.**
11. For he that said, Do not commit
adultery, said also, Do not kill.
**Now if thou commit no
adultery, yet** if thou
kill, thou art become
a transgressor of the law.
12. So speak ye, and so do,
as they that shall be judged
by the law of liberty.
13. For he shall have judgment without
mercy, that hath shewed no mercy;
and mercy rejoiceth against judgment.
14. **What** *doth it* **profit,**
my brethren,
**though a man say he hath
faith, and** have
**not works? can faith
save him?**
15. **If a brother or sister be
naked, and destitute of
daily food,**
16. **And** one of
you say unto them,
Depart in peace,
be *ye* **warmed and filled;
notwithstanding ye give
them not those things which
are needful** to the body;
what *doth it* **profit?**
17. **Even so faith, if it hath
not works, is dead,**
being alone.
18. Yea, a man may say, Thou hast
faith, and I have works:
**shew me thy faith without
thy works, and I will shew
thee my faith by my works.**
19. **Thou believest that there
is one God;** thou doest well:
the devils also believe,
and tremble.
20. But wilt thou know, O vain man,
that faith without works is dead?
21. **Was not Abraham**
our father

■ **justified by works,**
■ **when he** had
■ **offered Isaac**
his son upon the altar?
■ 22. **Seest thou how** faith wrought
■ **with his works,**
and by works
■ **was faith made perfect?**
23. And the scripture was fulfilled
which saith,
■ **Abraham believed God,**
and it was imputed unto him
■ **for righteousness: and he**
■ **was called the Friend**
■ **of God.**
24. Ye see then how that
■ **by works a man is justified,**
■ **and not by faith only.**
25. Likewise also was not Rahab the
harlot justified by works, when she
had received the messengers, and
had sent *them* out another way?
■ 26. **For as the body without**
■ **the spirit is dead, so faith**
■ **without works is dead** also.

CHAPTER 3
■ 1. **My brethren, be not many**
■ **masters,** knowing that we shall
receive the greater condemnation.
2. For in many things we offend all.
■ **If any man offend not in**
■ **word, the same** *is*
a perfect man, *and*
■ **able also to bridle the**
■ **whole body.**
■ 3. **Behold, we put bits in the**
■ **horses' mouths,**
that they may obey us;
■ **and we turn about their**
■ **whole body.**
■ 4. **Behold also the ships,**
which though *they be* so great, and *are*
driven of fierce winds, yet
■ **are** they
■ **turned about with a** very
■ **small helm,** whithersoever the
governor listeth.
■ 5. **Even so the tongue is a**
■ **little member, and** boasteth
great things. Behold, how great a
matter a little fire kindleth!
6. And the tongue *is* a fire, a world of

iniquity: so is the tongue among
our members, that
■ **it defileth the whole body,**
and setteth on fire the course
of nature;
■ **and it is set on fire of hell.**
■ 7. **For every kind of beasts,**
and of birds, and of serpents, and of
things in the sea, is tamed, and
■ **hath been tamed**
■ **of mankind:**
■ 8. **But the tongue can no**
■ **man tame;** *it is* an unruly evil, full
of deadly poison.
■ 9. **Therewith bless we God,**
even the Father;
■ **and** therewith
■ **curse** we
■ **men,** which are made after the
similitude of God.
■ 10. **Out of the same mouth**
■ **proceedeth blessing and**
■ **cursing.** My brethren, these things
ought not so to be.
■ 11. **Doth a fountain send**
■ **forth** at the same place sweet *water*
and bitter?
12. Can the fig tree, my brethren, bear
olive berries? either a vine, figs?
so *can* no fountain
■ **both** yield
■ **salt water and fresh.**
■ 13. **Who** *is* **a wise man**
and endued with knowledge
■ **among you? let him shew**
■ **out of a good conversation**
■ **his works**
with meekness of wisdom.
■ 14. **But if ye have bitter**
■ **envying and strife in your**
■ **hearts,** glory not, and lie not
against the truth.
15. This wisdom descendeth not from
above, but *is* earthly,
sensual, devilish.
16. For where envying and strife *is*,
■ **there** *is* **confusion and**
■ **every evil work.**
■ 17. **But the wisdom** that is
■ **from above is first pure,**
then peaceable, gentle, *and* easy to
be entreated,
■ **full of mercy** and good fruits,

■ **without partiality, an**
without
■ **hypocrisy.**
18. And the fruit of righteousness is
sown in peace of them that
make peace.

CHAPTER 4
■ 1. **From whence** *come* **wars**
■ **and fightings** among you?
■ *come they* **not hence,**
■ **even of your lusts**
that war in your members?
■ 2. **Ye lust,** and have not: ye kill,
and desire to have,
■ **and cannot obtain:**
ye fight and war,
■ **yet ye have not, because**
■ **ye ask not.**
■ 3. **Ye ask,** and receive not,
because ye ask
■ **amiss, that ye may**
■ **consume** *it* **upon**
■ **your lusts.**
4. Ye adulterers and adulteresses,
■ **know ye not that the**
■ **friendship** of the world is enmity
with God? whosoever therefore will
be a friend
■ **of the world is the enemy**
■ **of God.**
5. Do ye think that
■ **the scripture saith** in vain,
■ **The spirit that dwelleth in us**
■ **lusteth to envy?**
■ 6. **But he giveth more grace.**
Wherefore he saith, God resisteth the
proud, but giveth grace
■ **unto the humble.**
■ 7. **Submit yourselves**
■ **therefore to God. Resist the**
■ **devil, and he will flee**
from you.
■ 8. **Draw nigh to God, and he**
■ **will draw nigh to you.** Cleanse
your hands, *ye* sinners; and purify
your hearts, *ye* double-minded.
9. Be afflicted, and mourn, and weep:
let your laughter be turned to
mourning, and *your* joy to heaviness.
■ 10. **Humble yourselves**
in the sight of the Lord,
■ **and he shall lift you** up.

11. Speak not evil one of
another brethren.
■ **He that speaketh evil of** *his*
■ **brother, and judgeth**
his brother,
■ **speaketh evil of the law,**
and judgeth the law: but if thou judge
the law, thou art not a doer of the law,
but a judge.
■ 12. **There is one lawgiver,**
who is able to save and to destroy:
■ **who art thou that judgest**
another?
13. Go to now,
■ **ye that say, To-day or to-**
■ **morrow we will** go into such a
city, and continue there a year, and
■ **buy and sell, and get gain:**
■ 14. **Whereas ye know not**
■ what *shall be* on the
■ **morrow. For** what *is*
■ **your life?** It
■ **is even a vapour, that**
■ **appeareth** for a little time,
■ **and then vanisheth** away.
■ 15. **For that ye** *ought* **to say,**
■ **If the Lord will, we shall**
live, and
■ **do this, or that.**
16. But now ye rejoice in your
boastings: all such rejoicing is evil.
■ 17. **Therefore to him that**
■ **knoweth to do good, and**
■ **doeth** *it* **not, to him it is sin.**

CHAPTER 5
1. Go to now,
■ *ye* **rich men,**
weep and howl for your
miseries that shall come upon *you.*
■ 2. **Your riches are**
■ **corrupted,** and your garments
are motheaten.
3. Your gold and silver is cankered;
■ **and the rust of them shall**
■ **be a witness against you,**
and shall eat your flesh as it were fire.
■ **Ye have heaped treasure**
■ **together for the last days.**
4. Behold, the hire of the labourers
who have reaped down your fields,
which is of you kept back by fraud,
crieth: and the cries of them which

have reaped are entered into the ears of the Lord of sabaoth.

5. **Ye have lived in pleasure** on the earth,

and been wanton; ye have nourished your hearts, as in a day of slaughter.

6. **Ye have condemned** *and* **killed the just;** *and* **he doth not resist** you.

7. **Be patient** therefore, brethren, **unto the coming of the Lord.** Behold, **the husbandman waiteth for the precious fruit of the earth,** and hath long patience for it, until he receive the early and latter rain.

8. Be ye also patient; stablish your hearts: for **the coming of the Lord draweth nigh.**

9. **Grudge not one against another,** brethren, lest ye be condemned: behold, the judge standeth before the door.

10. **Take,** my brethren, **the prophets,** who have spoken in the name of the Lord, **for an example of suffering affliction,** and of patience.

11. **Behold, we count them happy which endure.** Ye have heard of the patience of Job, and have seen the end of the Lord; that the Lord is very pitiful, and of tender mercy.

12. **But above all things,** my brethren, **swear not,** neither by heaven, neither by the earth, neither by any other oath: **but let your yea be yea; and** *your* **nay, nay;** lest ye fall into condemnation.

13. Is any among you afflicted? let him pray. Is any merry? let him sing psalms.

14. **Is any sick** among you? **let** him call for **the elders** of the church; and let them **pray** over him,

anointing him with oil in the name of the Lord:

15. **And the prayer of faith shall save the sick, and the Lord shall raise him up;** and if he have committed sins, they shall be forgiven him.

16. **Confess** *your* **faults** one to another, **and pray one for another,** that ye may be healed. **The effectual fervent prayer of a righteous man availeth much.**

17. **Elias** was a man subject to like passions as we are, and he **prayed earnestly** that it might not rain: **and it rained not** on the earth **by the space of three years and six months.**

18. **And he prayed again, and the heaven gave rain,** and the earth brought forth her fruit.

19. **Brethren, if any** of you do **err** from the truth, **and one convert him;**

20. **Let him know, that he which converteth the sinner** from the error of his way, **shall save a soul from death,** and shall hide a multitude of sins.

THE FIRST EPISTLE OF PETER

BACKGROUND INFORMATION

Author – Peter, an Apostle.
Date Written – probably
between 60 and **70** A.D.

Number of:
Verses - 105
Chapters - 5
Total Words - 2,482
Scan Words - 1,201
Scan Words represent 48 %
of Total Words.

Theme – written to show
believers that
**in spite of persecution,
there is** living hope and
**ultimate triumph in Jesus
Christ.**

OUTLINE OF THE EPISTLE

I. **Peter explains** that
salvation is wrought by
the Father, the Son and
the Holy Spirit
and he
**gives a call for
Christian dedication.**
Chapters 1—2:10

II. **Peter outlines** the
nature of
Christian social
relationships,
sufferings, rewards,
**and explains the
ministry** of the elders and
the flock.
Chapters 2:11—5

CHAPTER 1

■ 1. **Peter,** an apostle of Jesus Christ,
■ **to the strangers scattered**
■ **throughout Pontus,**
■ **Galatia, Cappadocia,**
■ **Asia, and Bithynia,**
■ 2. **Elect** according to the
foreknowledge of God the Father,
■ **through sanctification of**
■ **the Spirit,** unto obedience
■ **and** sprinkling of
■ **the blood of Jesus Christ:**
Grace unto you, and peace,
be multiplied.
■ 3. **Blessed** *be* **the God**
and Father of our Lord Jesus Christ,
■ **which according to his**
■ **abundant mercy hath**
■ **begotten us**
again unto a lively hope
■ **by the resurrection of**
■ **Jesus Christ** from the dead,
■ 4. **To an inheritance**
incorruptible, and undefiled,
and that fadeth not away,
■ **reserved in heaven**
■ **for you,**
■ 5. **Who are kept by the**
■ **power of God through faith**
■ **unto salvation** ready to be
revealed in the last time.
■ 6. Wherein ye greatly rejoice,
■ **though now for a season,**
if need be,
■ **ye are in heaviness**
■ **through manifold**
■ **temptations:**
■ 7. **That the trial of your faith,**
■ **being much more precious**
■ **than** of
■ **gold** that perisheth,
though it be tried with fire,
■ **might be found unto praise**
and honour and glory
■ **at the appearing of**
■ **Jesus Christ:**
■ 8. **Whom having not seen,**
■ **ye love;** in whom,
■ **though** now
■ **ye see** *him* **not, yet**
■ **believing, ye rejoice with**
■ **joy unspeakable**
■ **and full of glory:**

■ 9. **Receiving the end of your**
■ **faith,** *even* **the salvation of**
■ *your* **souls.**
■ 10. **Of which** salvation
■ **the prophets** have
■ **inquired** and searched
diligently, who prophesied
■ **of the grace** *that should*
■ *come* **unto you:**
■ 11. **Searching what,**
or what manner of time
■ **the Spirit** of Christ which was in
them did signify, when it
■ **testified beforehand the**
■ **sufferings of Christ,**
and the glory that should follow.
■ 12. **Unto whom it was**
■ **revealed,** that not unto
themselves, but unto us they
did minister the things, which
are now reported unto you
■ **by them that have**
■ **preached the gospel**
unto you with the Holy Ghost sent
down from heaven; which things the
angels desire to look into.
■ 13. **Wherefore** gird up the
loins of your mind,
■ **be sober, and hope**
to the end
■ **for the grace** that is
■ **to be brought unto you at**
■ **the revelation of**
■ **Jesus Christ;**
■ 14. **As obedient children,** not
fashioning yourselves according to
the former lusts in your ignorance:
15. But as he which hath called
you is holy, so
■ **be ye holy in all manner**
■ **of conversation;**
■ 16. **Because it is written, Be**
■ **ye holy; for I am holy.**
17. And if ye call on the Father, who
without respect of persons judgeth
according to every man's work, pass
the time of your sojourning
here in fear:
■ 18. **Forasmuch as ye know**
■ **that ye were not redeemed**
■ **with corruptible things,**
as silver and gold, from your vain
conversation *received* by tradition

from your fathers;
■ 19. **But with the precious**
■ **blood of Christ,** as of a lamb
without blemish and without spot:
■ 20. **Who verily was**
■ **foreordained before the**
■ **foundation of the world,**
but was manifest in these last times
for you,
■ 21. **Who** by him do believe in
■ **God, that raised him up**
■ **from the dead,**
and gave him glory;
■ **that your faith** and hope
■ **might be in God.**
■ 22. **Seeing ye have purified**
■ **your souls** in obeying the truth
■ **through the Spirit**
unto unfeigned love of the brethren,
see that ye
■ **love one another**
with a pure heart
■ **fervently:**
■ 23. **Being born again,** not of
corruptible seed, but of incorruptible,
■ **by the word of God, which**
■ **liveth and abideth for ever.**
■ 24. **For all flesh** *is* **as grass,**
■ **and** all the glory of man
as the flower of grass. The grass
■ **withereth, and**
the flower thereof
■ **falleth away:**
■ 25. **But the word of the Lord**
■ **endureth for ever.**
And this is the word which by the
gospel is preached unto you.

CHAPTER 2
■ 1. **Wherefore** laying aside all
malice, and all guile, and hypocrisies,
and envies, all evil speakings,
■ 2. **As newborn babes,**
■ **desire the sincere milk of**
■ **the word, that ye may**
■ **grow thereby:**
3. If so be ye have tasted that the
Lord *is* gracious.
4. To whom coming, *as unto* a living
stone, disallowed indeed of men, but
chosen of God, *and* precious,
■ 5. **Ye also,** as lively stones, are
built up a spiritual house, an holy

priesthood, to
■ **offer up spiritual**
■ **sacrifices, acceptable to**
■ **God by Jesus Christ.**
■ 6. **Wherefore also it is**
■ **contained in the scripture,**
Behold,
■ **I lay in Sion a chief corner**
■ **stone,** elect, precious:
■ **and he that believeth on**
■ **him shall not be**
■ **confounded.**
7. Unto you therefore which
believe *he is* precious:
■ **but** unto them which be disobedient,
■ **the stone which the**
■ **builders disallowed,**
the same
■ **is made the head of**
■ **the corner,**
■ 8. **And a stone of stumbling,**
and a rock of offence, *even*
■ *to them* **which stumble at**
■ **the word,** being disobedient:
whereunto also they were appointed.
■ 9. **But ye** *are* **a chosen**
■ **generation, a royal**
■ **priesthood, an holy nation,**
■ **a peculiar people;**
that ye should shew forth the praises
of him who hath
■ **called** you out of darkness
■ **into his marvellous light:**
10. Which in time past *were* not a
people, but *are* now the people of God:
which had not obtained mercy, but
now have obtained mercy.
■ 11. **Dearly beloved,** I beseech
you as strangers and pilgrims,
■ **abstain from fleshly lusts,**
■ **which war against the soul;**
■ 12. **Having your conver-**
■ **sation honest among the**
■ **Gentiles: that,** whereas they
speak against you as evildoers,
■ **they may by** *your* **good**
■ **works,** which they shall behold,
■ **glorify God in the day**
■ **of visitation.**
■ 13. **Submit yourselves to**
■ **every ordinance of man for**
■ **the Lord's sake: whether it**
■ **be to the king,** as supreme;

14. Or unto governors, as unto them that are sent by him for the punishment of evildoers, and for the praise of them that do well.

15. For so is the will of God, that with well-doing ye may put to silence the ignorance of foolish men:

16. As free, and not using *your* liberty for a cloak of maliciousness, but as the servants of God.

17. Honour all *men*. Love the brotherhood. Fear God. Honour the king.

18. Servants, *be* subject to *your* masters with all fear; not only to the good and gentle, but also to the froward.

19. For this *is* thankworthy, if a man for conscience toward God endure grief, suffering wrongfully.

20. For what glory *is it*, if, when ye be buffeted for your faults, ye shall take it patiently? but if, when ye do well, and suffer *for it*, ye take it patiently, this *is* acceptable with God.

21. For even hereunto were ye called: because Christ also suffered for us, leaving us an example, that ye should follow his steps:

22. Who did no sin, neither was guile found in his mouth:

23. Who, when he was reviled, reviled not again; when he suffered, he threatened not; but committed *himself* to him that judgeth righteously:

24. Who his own self bare our sins in his own body on the tree, that we, being dead to sins, should live unto righteousness: by whose stripes ye were healed.

25. For ye were as sheep going astray; but are now returned unto the Shepherd and Bishop of your souls.

CHAPTER 3

1. Likewise, ye wives, *be* in subjection to your own husbands; that, if any obey not the word, they also may without the word be won by the conversation of the wives;

2. While they behold your chaste conversation *coupled* with fear.

3. Whose adorning let it not be that outward *adorning* of plaiting the hair, and of wearing of gold, or of putting on of apparel;

4. But *let it be* the hidden man of the heart, in that which is not corruptible, *even the ornament* of a meek and quiet spirit, which is in the sight of God of great price.

5. For after this manner in the old time the holy women also, who trusted in God, adorned themselves, being in subjection unto their own husbands:

6. Even as Sara obeyed Abraham, calling him lord: whose daughters ye are, as long as ye do well, and are not afraid with any amazement.

7. Likewise, ye husbands, dwell with *them* according to knowledge, giving honour unto the wife, as unto the weaker vessel, and as being heirs together of the grace of life; that your prayers be not hindered.

8. Finally, *be ye* all of one mind, having compassion one of another, love as brethren, *be* pitiful, *be* courteous:

9. Not rendering evil for evil, or railing for railing: but contrariwise blessing; knowing that ye are thereunto called,

that ye should inherit a blessing.

10. **For he that will love life,** and see good days, **let him refrain** his tongue **from evil,** and his lips that they speak no guile:

11. Let him eschew evil, and do good; let him seek peace, and ensue it.

12. **For the eyes of the Lord** *are* **over the righteous, and his ears** *are open* **unto their prayers:** but the face of the Lord *is* against them that do evil.

13. **And who** *is* **he that will harm you,** if ye be followers of that which is good?

14. **But and if ye suffer for righteousness' sake, happy** *are* **ye:** and be not afraid of their terror, neither be troubled;

15. **But sanctify the Lord God in your hearts: and** *be* **ready always to** *give* **an answer to every man that asketh you a reason of the hope that is in you** with meekness and fear:

16. Having a good conscience; **that,** whereas they speak evil of you, as of evildoers, **they may be ashamed that falsely accuse your good conversation in Christ.**

17. **For** *it is* **better,** if the will of God be so, **that ye suffer for well-doing, than for evil-doing.**

18. **For Christ also hath once suffered for sins,** the just for the unjust, **that he might bring us to God, being put to death** in the flesh, **but quickened by the Spirit:**

19. By which also **he went and preached unto the spirits in prison;**

20. **Which sometime were disobedient, when** once the longsuffering of **God waited in the days of Noah, while the ark was a-preparing, wherein**

few, that is, **eight souls were saved by water.**

21. The like figure whereunto *even* **baptism doth also now save us** (not the putting away of the filth of the flesh, but the answer of a good conscience toward God,) **by the resurrection of Jesus Christ:**

22. **Who is gone into heaven, and is on the right hand of God; angels and authorities and powers being made subject unto him.**

CHAPTER 4

1. **Forasmuch then as Christ hath suffered for us** in the flesh, **arm yourselves** likewise **with the same mind: for he** that hath suffered in the flesh **hath ceased from sin;**

2. **That he** no longer **should live the rest of** *his* **time** in the flesh to the lusts of men, but **to the will of God.**

3. **For the time past** of *our* life may suffice us to have wrought the will of the Gentiles, when **we walked in lasciviousness,** lusts, excess of wine, revellings, banquetings, **and abominable idolatries:**

4. **Wherein they think it strange that ye run not with** *them* **to the same excess** of riot, speaking evil of *you*:

5. Who shall give account to him that is ready to judge the quick and the dead.

6. **For** for **this cause was the gospel preached also to them that are dead, that they might** be judged according to men in the flesh, but **live according to God in the spirit.**

7. **But the end** of all things **is at hand:** be ye therefore sober, and **watch unto prayer.** 8. **And above all things have fervent charity** among yourselves: **for charity shall cover the multitude of sins.** 9. Use hospitality one to another without grudging. 10. **As every man hath received the gift,** *even so* **minister** the same one to another, as good stewards of **the manifold grace of God.** 11. If any man speak, *let him speak* as the oracles of God; if any man minister, *let him do it* as of the ability which God giveth: **that God in all things may be glorified** through Jesus Christ, to whom be praise and dominion for ever and ever. Amen. 12. **Beloved, think it not strange concerning the fiery trial which** is to **try you,** as though some strange thing happened unto you: 13. **But rejoice, inasmuch as ye are partakers of Christ's sufferings;** that, when his glory shall be revealed, ye may be glad also with exceeding joy. 14. **If ye be reproached for the name of Christ, happy** *are ye;* **for the spirit** of glory and **of God resteth upon you:** on their part he is evil spoken of, but on your part he is glorified. 15. **But let none** of you **suffer as** a murderer, or *as* a thief, or *as* **an evildoer,** or as a busybody in other men's matters. 16. **Yet if** *any man suffer* as **a Christian,** let him not be ashamed; but **let him glorify God** on this behalf. 17. **For** the time *is come* that **judgment must begin at the**

house of God: and if *it* first *begin* at us, **what shall the end** *be* **of them that obey not the gospel** of God? 18. And if the righteous scarcely be saved, where shall the ungodly and the sinner appear? 19. **Wherefore let them that suffer according to the will of God commit** the keeping of **their souls** *to him* in well-doing, **as unto a faithful Creator.**

CHAPTER 5

1. **The elders** which are among you **I exhort,** who am also an elder, and a witness of the sufferings of Christ, and also a partaker of the glory that shall be revealed: 2. **Feed the flock of God** which is among you, taking the oversight *thereof,* **not by constraint, but willingly;** not for filthy lucre, but of a ready mind; 3. Neither as being lords over *God's* heritage, but **being ensamples to the flock.** 4. **And when the chief Shepherd shall appear, ye shall receive a crown of glory** that fadeth not away. 5. **Likewise, ye younger, submit** yourselves **unto the elder.** Yea, all *of you* be subject one to another, and be clothed with humility: **for God resisteth the proud, and giveth grace to the humble.** 6. **Humble yourselves therefore** under the mighty hand of God, **that he may exalt you** in due time: 7. **Casting all your care upon him; for he careth for you.** 8. **Be sober,** be vigilant; **because** your adversary

■ **the devil,** as a roaring lion,
■ **walketh about, seeking**
■ **whom he may devour:**
9. Whom resist stedfast in the faith, knowing that the same afflictions are accomplished in your brethren that are in the world.

■ 10. **But the God of all grace,** who hath called us unto his eternal glory by Christ Jesus, after that ye have suffered a while,

■ **make you perfect,** stablish, strengthen, settle *you.*

■ 11. **To him** *be* **glory** and dominion for ever and ever. Amen.
12. By Silvanus, a faithful brother unto you, as I suppose, I have written briefly, exhorting, and testifying that this is the true grace of God wherein ye stand.
13. The *church that is* at Babylon, elected together with *you,* saluteth you; and *so doth* Marcus my son.
14. Greet ye one another with a kiss of charity. Peace *be* with you all that are in Christ Jesus.

■ **Amen.**

THE SECOND EPISTLE OF PETER

BACKGROUND INFORMATION

Author – Peter, an Apostle.
Date Written – unknown.

Number of:
Verses -   61
Chapters -   3
Total Words - 1,559
Scan Words - 758
Scan Words represent 48 %
of Total Words.

**Theme – written to urge
believers to defeat false
teachings** by practicing
Christian virtues
and to
**prepare for the coming of
the Lord.**

OUTLINE OF THE EPISTLE

I.   **Peter's salutation,**
    advice for growing in
    grace, and being
    grounded in the
    truth.
    Chapter 1
II. **Peter's warning** about
    false teachers.
    Chapter 2
III. **Peter's admonition** as to
    how believers must live
    **in hope of the second
    coming** of Christ.
    Chapter 3

CHAPTER 1

■ 1. **Simon Peter,** a servant and an apostle of Jesus Christ,

■ **to them that have obtained** like precious

■ **faith with us through the**
■ **righteousness of God and**
■ **our Saviour Jesus Christ:**

■ 2. **Grace and peace be**
■ **multiplied unto you through**
■ **the knowledge of God,**
and of Jesus our Lord,

■ 3. **According as his divine**
■ **power hath given unto us**
all things that *pertain* unto life and godliness, through the

■ **knowledge of him that hath**
■ **called us to glory**
■ **and virtue:**

4. Whereby are given unto us exceeding great and precious promises:

■ **that** by these
■ **ye might be partakers of**
■ **the divine nature,** having escaped the corruption that is in the world through lust.

■ 5. **And** beside this, giving all diligence,

■ **add to your faith virtue;**
■ **and** to virtue
■ **knowledge;**

■ 6. **And** to knowledge
■ **temperance; and**
to temperance

■ **patience; and** to patience
■ **godliness;**

■ 7. **And** to godliness
■ **brotherly kindness; and**
to brotherly kindness

■ **charity.**

■ 8. **For if these things be in**
■ **you,** and abound,
they make *you that*

■ *ye shall* **neither** *be* **barren**
■ **nor unfruitful in the know-**
■ **ledge of our Lord** Jesus Christ.

■ 9. **But he that lacketh these**
■ **things** is blind, and cannot see afar off, and

■ **hath forgotten that he was**
■ **purged from his old sins.**

■ 10. **Wherefore**

the rather, brethren,

■ **give diligence to make**
■ **your calling and election**
■ **sure:** for if ye do these things, ye shall never fall:

11. For so an entrance shall be ministered unto you abundantly into the everlasting kingdom of our Lord and Saviour Jesus Christ.

12. Wherefore I will not be negligent to put you always in remembrance of these things, though ye know *them,* and be established in the present truth.

■ 13. **Yea, I think it meet,**
as long as I am in this tabernacle,

■ **to stir you up by putting**
■ *you* **in remembrance;**

■ 14. **Knowing** that shortly
■ **I must put off** *this* **my**
■ **tabernacle,** even as our Lord Jesus Christ hath shewed me.

15. Moreover I will endeavour that ye may be able after my decease to have these things always in remembrance.

■ 16. **For we have not**
■ **followed** cunningly devised
■ **fables, when we made**
■ **known unto you**
■ **the power and coming of**
■ **our Lord Jesus Christ,**
■ **but were eyewitnesses**
■ **of his majesty.**

■ 17. **For he received**
from God the Father

■ **honour and glory, when**
■ **there came such a voice to**
■ **him** from the excellent glory,

■ **This is my beloved Son, in**
■ **whom I am well pleased.**

■ 18. **And this voice**
which came from heaven

■ **we heard,** when we were with him
■ **in the holy mount.**

■ 19. **We have also a more**
■ **sure word of prophecy;**
whereunto ye do well that ye take heed, as unto a light that shineth in a dark place, until the day dawn, and the day star arise in your hearts:

■ 20. **Knowing** this first,
■ **that no prophecy**

of the scripture
■ **is of** any
■ **private interpretation.**
■ 21. **For the prophecy came**
■ **not** in old time
■ **by the will of man: but holy**
■ **men of God spake** *as they*
■ *were* **moved by the**
■ **Holy Ghost.**

CHAPTER 2
■ 1. **But there were false**
■ **prophets** also among the people,
■ **even as there shall be false**
■ **teachers** among you,
■ **who** privily shall
■ **bring in damnable**
■ **heresies, even denying the**
■ **Lord** that bought them,
■ **and bring upon themselves**
■ **swift destruction.**
■ 2. **And many shall follow**
■ **their pernicious ways;**
by reason of whom the way of truth
shall be evil spoken of.
■ 3. **And through**
■ **covetousness shall they**
with feigned words
■ **make merchandise of you:**
■ **whose judgment**
now of a long time
■ **lingereth not,** and their
damnation slumbereth not.
■ 4. **For if God spared not the**
■ **angels that sinned, but**
■ **cast** *them* **down to hell,**
and delivered *them* into chains
of darkness, to be reserved
unto judgment;
■ 5. **And spared not the old**
■ **world, but saved Noah**
the eighth *person*, a preacher
of righteousness,
■ **bringing in the flood upon**
■ **the** world of the
■ **ungodly;**
■ 6. **And turning the cities of**
■ **Sodom and Gomorrha into**
■ **ashes** condemned
them with an overthrow,
■ **making** *them* **an ensample**
unto those that after
should live ungodly;

■ 7. **And delivered just Lot,**
vexed with the filthy conversation
of the wicked:
8. (For that righteous man dwelling
among them, in seeing and hearing,
vexed *his* righteous soul from day to
day with *their* unlawful deeds;)
■ 9. **The Lord knoweth how to**
■ **deliver the godly out of**
■ **temptations, and to**
■ **reserve the unjust unto the**
■ **day of judgment to**
■ **be punished:**
■ 10. **But chiefly them that**
■ **walk** after the flesh
■ **in** the lust of
■ **uncleanness, and despise**
■ **government.** Presumptuous *are*
they, self-willed, they are not afraid to
speak evil of dignities.
■ 11. **Whereas angels,**
which are greater in power and might,
■ **bring not railing**
■ **accusation against them**
■ **before the Lord.**
■ 12. **But these,**
as natural brute beasts, made to be
taken and destroyed,
■ **speak evil of the things that**
■ **they understand not;** and shall
utterly perish in their own corruption;
13. And shall receive the reward of
unrighteousness,
as they that count it pleasure to riot in
the day time. Spots *they are* and
blemishes, sporting themselves with
their own deceivings while
they feast with you;
■ 14. **Having eyes full of**
■ **adultery,** and that cannot cease
from sin; beguiling unstable souls: an
heart they have exercised with
covetous practices; cursed children:
■ 15. **Which have forsaken the**
■ **right way, and are gone**
astray, following
■ **the way of Balaam**
the son of Bosor,
■ **who loved** the wages of
■ **unrighteousness;**
■ 16. **But was rebuked**
for his iniquity:
■ **the dumb ass speaking**

with man's voice forbad the madness of the prophet.

17. **These are wells without water,** clouds that are carried with a tempest; **to whom** the mist of **darkness is reserved for ever.**

18. For when they speak great swelling *words* of vanity, they allure through the lusts of the flesh, *through much* wantonness, those that were clean escaped from them who live in error.

19. **While they promise them liberty, they themselves are the servants of corruption:** for of whom a man is overcome, of the same is he brought in bondage.

20. **For if after they have escaped** the pollutions of **the world through the knowledge of** the Lord and Saviour Jesus **Christ, they are again entangled therein, and** overcome, **the latter end is worse** with them **than the beginning.**

21. **For it had been better for them not to have known the way of righteousness, than,** after they have known *it,* **to turn from the holy commandment** delivered unto them.

22. **But it is happened** unto them **according to the** true **proverb, The dog** *is* **turned to his own vomit** again; and the sow that was washed to her wallowing in the mire.

CHAPTER 3

1. **This second epistle,** beloved, **I now write** unto you; in *both* which I stir up your pure minds by way of remembrance:

2. **That ye may be mindful of** **the words** which were **spoken** before **by the holy prophets, and of the commandment of us the apostles** of the Lord and Saviour:

3. **Knowing** this first, **that there shall come** in the last days **scoffers,** walking after their own lusts,

4. **And saying, Where is the promise of his coming? for** since the fathers fell asleep, **all things continue as** *they were* from the beginning of the creation.

5. **For** this they willingly are ignorant of, that **by the word of God the heavens were of old,** and the earth standing out of the water and in the water:

6. **Whereby the world** that then was, **being overflowed with water, perished:**

7. **But the heavens and the earth,** which are now, **by the same word are** kept in store, **reserved unto fire against the day of judgment** and perdition of ungodly men.

8. **But,** beloved, be not ignorant of this one thing, that one day *is* with the Lord as a thousand years, and a thousand years as one day.

9. **The Lord** is not slack concerning his promise, as some men count slackness; but **is longsuffering to us-ward, not willing that any should perish,** but that all should come to repentance.

10. **But** the day of **the Lord will come as a thief in the night; in the which the heavens shall pass** away with a great noise, **and the elements shall melt** with fervent heat, **the earth also and the**

■ **works** that are
■ **therein shall be burned up.**
■ 11. *Seeing* then *that* all
■ **these things** shall be dissolved,
■ **what manner** *of persons*
■ **ought ye to be in** *all*
■ holy conversation and
■ **godliness,**
■ 12. **Looking for** and hasting unto
■ **the coming of the day of**
■ **God, wherein** the heavens being
■ on fire shall be dissolved, and
■ **the elements shall melt**
■ **with fervent heat?**
■ 13. **Nevertheless we,**
■ according to his promise,
■ **look for new heavens and**
■ **a new earth, wherein**
■ **dwelleth righteousness.**
■ 14. **Wherefore,** beloved, seeing
■ that ye look for such things,
■ **be diligent that ye may be**
■ **found** of him in peace,
■ **without spot,**
■ **and blameless.**
■ 15. **And account** *that* the

■ **longsuffering of our Lord** *is*
■ **salvation; even**
■ as our beloved brother
■ **Paul** also according to the
■ wisdom given unto him
■ **hath written** unto you;
■ 16. As also in all *his* epistles,
■ speaking in them of these things; in
■ which are some
■ **things hard to be**
■ **understood,** which they that are
■ unlearned and unstable wrest, as *they*
■ *do* also the other scriptures, unto their
■ own destruction.
■ 17. **Ye therefore,** beloved,
■ seeing ye know *these things*
■ **before, beware lest ye**
■ **also,** being led away with the
■ error of the wicked,
■ **fall from your**
■ **own stedfastness.**
■ 18. **But grow in grace, and** *in*
■ **the knowledge of our Lord**
■ and Saviour Jesus Christ. To him *be*
■ glory both now and for ever.
■ **Amen.**

THE FIRST EPISTLE OF JOHN

BACKGROUND INFORMATION

Author – John, one of the twelve disciples.
Date Written – probably **between 90** and **96** A.D.

Number of:
Verses-   105
Chapters-   5
Total Words- 2,523
Scan Words- 1,234
Scan Words represent 48 % of Total Words.

Theme – written to show that **through** personal experience with **Jesus Christ,** The Word, **one has passed from death to life.**

OUTLINE OF THE EPISTLE

I. **John's testimony concerning Christ,** his tests of fellowship with God and his declaration of the importance of love. Chapters 1—2:17
II. **John's warning concerning Antichrists** and his explanation of righteousness and God's children. Chapter 2:17—3
III. **John's teaching concerning the trying of spirits,** the nature of God and the victory of faith. Chapters 4—5

CHAPTER 1

1. That which was from the beginning, which we have heard, which we have seen with our eyes, which we have looked upon,
and our hands have handled, of the Word of life;
2. (For the life was manifested, and we have seen *it*, and bear witness,
and shew unto you that eternal life, which was with the Father, and was manifested unto us;)
3. That which we have seen and heard declare we unto you,
that ye also may have fellowship with us: and truly our fellowship *is* with the Father, and with his Son Jesus Christ.
4. And these things write we unto you,
that your joy may be full.
5. This then is the message which we have heard of him, and declare unto you,
that God is light, and in him is no darkness at all.
6. If we say that we have fellowship with him, and walk in darkness, we lie, and do not the truth:
7. But if we walk in the light, as he is in the light, we have fellowship one with another, and the blood of Jesus Christ his Son cleanseth us from all sin.
8. If we say that we have no sin, we deceive ourselves, and the truth is not in us.
9. If we confess our sins, he is faithful and just to forgive us *our* sins, and to cleanse us from all unrighteousness.
10. If we say that we have not sinned, we make him a liar, and his word is not in us.

CHAPTER 2

1. My little children, these things write I unto you, that ye sin not. And if any man sin, we have an advocate with the Father, Jesus Christ the righteous:
2. And he is the propitiation for our sins: and not for ours only, but also for *the sins of* the whole world.
3. And hereby we do know that we know him, if we keep his commandments.
4. He that saith, I know him, and keepeth not his commandments, is a liar, and the truth is not in him.
5. But whoso keepeth his word, in him verily is the love of God perfected: hereby know we that we are in him.
6. He that saith he abideth in him ought himself also so to walk, even as he walked.
7. Brethren, I write no new commandment unto you, but an old commandment which ye had from the beginning. The old commandment is the word which ye have heard from the beginning.
8. Again, a new commandment I write unto you, which thing is true in him and in you: because the darkness is past, and the true light now shineth.
9. He that saith he is in the light, and hateth his brother, is in darkness even until now.
10. He that loveth his brother abideth in the light, and there is none occasion of stumbling in him.
11. But he that hateth his brother is in darkness, and walketh in darkness, and knoweth not whither he goeth, because that darkness hath blinded his eyes.
12. I write unto you, little

children, because your
sins are forgiven
you for his name's sake.
13. I write unto you, fathers, because
ye have known him *that is* from the
beginning. I write unto you, young
men, because ye have overcome the
wicked one. I write unto you, little
children, because ye have known
the Father.
14. **I have written unto you,**
fathers, because ye have
known him *that is* **from the**
beginning. I have written
unto you, young men,
because ye are strong, and the
word of God abideth in you, and
ye have overcome the
wicked one.
15. **Love not** the world, neither
the things *that are* **in the**
world. If any man love the world,
the love of the Father is not in him.
16. **For all that** *is* **in the**
world, the lust of the flesh,
and the lust
of the eyes, and the pride
of life, is not of the Father,
but is of the world.
17. **And the world passeth**
away, and the lust thereof:
but he that doeth the will of
God abideth for ever.
18. **Little children,**
it is the last time: and as
ye have heard that
antichrist shall come, even
now are there many antichrists;
whereby we know that it is
the last time.
19. **They went out from us,** but
they were not of us; for if they had
been of us, they would *no doubt* have
continued with us: but *they went out,*
that they might be made
manifest that they were not
all of us.
20. **But ye have an unction**
from the Holy One, and
ye know all things.
21. I have not written unto you
because ye
know not the truth, but

becaue ye know it, and that no lie is of
the truth.
22. Who is a liar but
he that denieth that Jesus
is the Christ? He is
antichrist, that denieth the Father
and the Son.
23. **Whosoever denieth the**
Son, the same
hath not the Father:
he that acknowledgeth the Son hath
the Father also.
24. **Let that** therefore abide in you,
which ye have heard
from the beginning. If that which ye
have heard from the beginning shall
remain in you, ye also shall
continue in the Son, and in the Father.
25. **And** this is the promise that
he hath promised us, *even*
eternal life.
26. These *things* have I written unto
you concerning them that
seduce you.
27. **But the anointing which**
ye have received of him
abideth in you,
and ye need not that any man teach
you: but as the same anointing
teacheth you of
all things, and is truth,
and is no lie, and even as it hath
taught you, ye shall abide in him.
28. **And now,** little children,
abide in him; that,
when he shall appear,
we may have confidence, and
not be ashamed before him
at his coming.
29. If ye know that he is righteous,
ye know that
every one that doeth right-
eousness is born of him.

CHAPTER 3
1. **Behold, what manner of**
love the Father hath
bestowed upon us, that we
should be called the sons
of God: therefore the
world knoweth us not,
because it knew him not.
2. Beloved, now are we the **sons**

of God,
and it doth not yet appear what we shall be: but **we know that, when he shall appear, we shall be like him;** for we shall see him as he is.

3. **And every man that hath this hope in him purifieth himself,** even as he is pure.

4. Whosoever committeth sin transgresseth also the law: for sin is the transgression of the law.

5. **And ye know that he was manifested to take away our sins;** and in him is no sin.

6. **Whosoever abideth in him sinneth not:** whosoever sinneth hath not seen him, neither known him.

7. Little children, let no man deceive you: **he that doeth righteousness is righteous,** even as he is righteous.

8. **He that committeth sin is of the devil;** for the devil sinneth from the beginning. **For** this purpose **the Son of God was manifested, that he might destroy the works of the devil.**

9. **Whosoever is born of God doth not commit sin;** for his seed remaineth in **him:** and he cannot sin, because he is born of God.

10. **In this the children of God are manifest,** and the children of the devil: **whosoever doeth not righteousness is not of God, neither** he that **loveth** not **his brother.**

11. **For this is the message that** ye heard from the beginning, that **we should love one another.**

12. **Not as Cain,** *who* was of that wicked one, and **slew his brother.**
And wherefore slew he him? **Because his own works were evil,** and his brother's righteous.

13. Marvel not, my brethren, if the world hate you.

14. **We know that we have passed from death unto life, because we love the brethren.** He that loveth not *his* brother abideth in death.

15. **Whosoever hateth his brother is a murderer: and** ye know that **no murderer hath eternal life** abiding in him.

16. **Hereby perceive we the love** *of God,* **because he laid down his life for us: and we ought to lay down** *our* **lives for the brethren.**

17. **But whoso hath this world's good, and seeth his brother have need, and shutteth up his** bowels *of* **compassion from him, how dwelleth the love of God in him?**

18. **My little children, let us not love in word,** neither in tongue; **but in deed and in truth.**

19. And hereby we know that we are of the truth, and shall assure our hearts before him.

20. For if our heart condemn us, God is greater than our heart, and knoweth all things.

21. **Beloved, if our heart condemn us not,** *then* **have we confidence toward God.**

22. **And whatsoever we ask, we receive of him, because we** keep his commandments, and do those things that **are pleasing in his sight.**

23. **And this is his commandment, That we should believe on the name of his Son** Jesus Christ, **and love one another,** as he

gave us commandment.
24. And he that keepeth his commandments dwelleth in him, and he in him.
■ **And hereby we know that**
■ **he abideth in us, by the**
■ **Spirit** which he hath given us.

CHAPTER 4

■ 1. **Beloved, believe not**
■ **every spirit, but try the**
■ **spirits** whether they are of God: because many false prophets are gone out into the world.
2. Hereby know ye the Spirit of God:
■ **Every spirit that confesseth**
■ **that Jesus Christ is come in**
■ **the flesh is of God:**
■ 3. **And every spirit that**
■ **confesseth not** that Jesus Christ is come in the flesh is not of God: and this
■ **is that** *spirit* **of antichrist,** whereof ye have heard that it should come;
■ **and even now already is it**
■ **in the world.**
■ 4. **Ye** are of God, little children, and
■ **have overcome** them:
■ **because greater is he that**
■ **is in you, than he that is in**
■ **the world.**
5. They are of the world: therefore speak they of the world, and the world heareth them.
■ 6. **We are of God: he that**
■ **knoweth God heareth us;** he that is not of God heareth not us.
■ **Hereby know we the spirit**
■ **of truth, and** the spirit of
■ **error.**
■ 7. **Beloved,** let us love one another: for
■ **love is of God;** and every one that loveth is born of God, and knoweth God.
8. He that loveth not knoweth not God; for God is love.
■ 9. **In this was manifested the**
■ **love of God toward us,** because that
■ **God sent his only begotten**
■ **Son into the world,**

that we might live through him.
10. Herein is love, not that we loved God, but that he loved us, and sent his Son
■ *to be* **the propitiation for**
■ **our sins.**
11. Beloved, if God so loved us, we ought also to love one another.
12. No man hath seen God at any time.
■ **If we love one another, God**
■ **dwelleth in us,** and his love is perfected in us.
13. Hereby know we that we dwell in him, and he in us, because he hath given us of his Spirit.
■ 14. **And we have seen and**
■ **do testify that the Father**
■ **sent the Son** *to be* **the**
■ **Saviour of the world.**
■ 15. **Whosoever shall**
■ **confess that Jesus is the**
■ **Son** of God,
■ **God dwelleth in him,** and he in God.
■ 16. **And** we have known and believed the love that God hath to us. God is love; and
■ **he that dwelleth in love**
■ **dwelleth in God, and God**
■ **in him.**
■ 17. **Herein is our love made**
■ **perfect, that we may have**
■ **boldness in the day of**
■ **judgment:** because as he is, so are we in this world.
■ 18. **There is no fear in love;**
■ **but perfect love casteth out**
■ **fear:** because fear hath torment. He that feareth is not made perfect in love.
■ 19. **We love him, because he**
■ **first loved us.**
■ 20. **If a man** say, I love God, and hateth his brother, he is a liar: for he that
■ **loveth not his brother**
■ **whom he hath seen, how**
■ **can he love God whom he**
■ **hath not seen?**
21. And this commandment have we from him, That he who loveth God love his brother also.

CHAPTER 5

1. **Whosoever believeth that Jesus is the Christ is born of God:** and every one that loveth him that begat loveth him also that is begotten of him.

2. **By this we know that we love the children of God, when we love God, and keep his commandments.**

3. For this is the love of God, that we keep his commandments: **and his commandments are not grievous.**

4. **For whatsoever is born of God overcometh the world:** and this is the victory that overcometh the world, *even* our faith.

5. Who is he that overcometh the world, but **he that believeth that Jesus is the Son of God?**

6. **This is he that came by water and blood,** *even* **Jesus Christ;** not by water only, but by water and blood. **And** it is **the Spirit** that **beareth witness,** because the Spirit is truth.

7. **For there are three that bear record in heaven, the Father, the Word, and the Holy Ghost:** and these three are one.

8. **And there are three that bear witness in earth, the Spirit, and the water, and the blood:** and these three agree in one.

9. **If we receive the witness of men, the witness of God is greater:** for this is the witness of God which he hath testified of his Son.

10. He that believeth on the Son of God hath the witness in himself: he that believeth not God hath made him a liar; because he believeth not the record that God gave of his Son.

11. **And this is the record, that God hath given** to **us eternal life, and this life is in his Son.**

12. **He that hath the Son hath life;** *and* he that hath not the Son of God hath not life.

13. **These things have I written** unto you that believe on the name of the Son of God; **that ye may know that ye have eternal life,** and that ye may believe on the name of the Son of God.

14. **And this is the confidence that we have in him, that, if we ask any thing according to his will, he heareth us:**

15. **And** if we know that he hear us, whatsoever we ask, we know that **we have the petitions that we desired of him.**

16. **If any man see his brother sin a sin** *which is* **not unto death, he shall ask, and he shall give him life** for them that sin not unto death. **There is a sin unto death:** I do not say that he shall pray for it.

17. **All unrighteousness is sin:** and there is a sin not unto death.

18. We know that whosoever is born of God sinneth not; but he that is begotten of God keepeth himself, and that wicked one toucheth him not.

19. *And* **we know** that we are of God, and **the whole world lieth in wickedness.**

20. **And we know that the Son of God is come,** and hath given us an understanding, **that we may know him** that is true, **and we are in him** that is true, *even* **in his Son** Jesus Christ. This is the true God, and eternal life.

21. **Little children, keep** yourselves **from idols. Amen.**

THE SECOND EPISTLE OF JOHN

BACKGROUND INFORMATION

Author – John, one of the twelve disciples.
Date Written – probably **between 90** and **99** A.D.

Number of:
Verses - 13
Chapters - 1
Total Words - 303
Scan Words - 151
Scan Words represent 49 % of Total Words

Theme – written to show **the importance of** Christian **truth and** the necessity to practice Christian **love.**

OUTLINE OF THE EPISTLE

I. **John's greeting.**
Verses 1—3
II. **John's teachings on love.**
Verses 4—6
III. **John's warning concerning deceivers.**
Verses 7—11
IV. **John's final greeting.**
Verses 12, 13

CHAPTER 1

1. The elder unto the elect lady and her children, whom I love in the truth; and not I only, but also all they that have known the truth;

2. For the truth's sake, which dwelleth in us, and shall be with us for ever.

3. Grace be with you, mercy, *and* peace, from God the Father, and from the Lord Jesus Christ, the Son of the Father, in truth and love.

4. I rejoiced greatly that I found of thy children walking in truth, as we have received a commandment from the Father.

5. And now I beseech thee, lady, not as though I wrote a new commandment unto thee, but that which we had from the beginning, that we love one another.

6. And this is love, that we walk after his commandments. This is the commandment, That, as ye have heard from the beginning, ye should walk in it.

7. For many deceivers are entered into the world, who confess not that Jesus Christ is come in the flesh. This is a deceiver and an antichrist.

8. Look to yourselves, that we lose not those things which we have wrought, but that we receive a full reward.

9. Whosoever transgresseth, and abideth not in the doctrine of Christ, hath not God. He that abideth in the doctrine of Christ, he hath both the Father and the Son.

10. If there come any unto you, and bring not this doctrine, receive him not into *your* house, neither bid him God speed:

11. For he that biddeth him God speed is partaker of his evil deeds.

12. Having many things to write unto you, I would not *write* with paper and ink: but I trust to come unto you, and speak face to face, that our joy may be full.

13. The children of thy elect sister greet thee. Amen.

THE THIRD EPISTLE OF JOHN

BACKGROUND INFORMATION

Author – John, one of the twelve disciples.
Date Written – probably **between 90** and **99** A.D.

Number of:
Verses -   14
Chapters -   1
Total Words - 299
Scan Words - 154
Scan Words represent 51 % of Total Words.

Theme – written to show that **error must be challenged to maintain Christian purity** and fellowship.

OUTLINE OF THE EPISTLE

I. **John offers greeting,** tells believers to serve others, and rebukes Diotrephes.
Verses 1—10

II. **John implores believers to have a good testimony.**
Verses 11—14

CHAPTER 1

1. **The elder unto**
the well-beloved
Gaius, whom I love in the truth.
2. **Beloved, I wish**
above all things
that thou mayest
prosper and be in
health, even
as thy soul prospereth.
3. **For I rejoiced** greatly, when the
brethren came and testified
of the truth that is in thee,
even as thou walkest in the truth.
4. **I have no greater joy than**
to hear that my children
walk in truth.
5. **Beloved, thou doest**
faithfully whatsoever thou doest
to the brethren, and to
strangers;
6. **Which have borne**
witness of thy charity
before the church: whom if thou bring
forward on their journey after a godly
sort, thou shalt do well:
7. Because that for his name's sake
they went forth, taking nothing
of the Gentiles.
8. **We therefore ought to**
receive such, that we might
be fellow-helpers
to the truth.
9. **I wrote unto the church:**

but Diotrephes, who loveth
to have the
preeminence among them,
receiveth us not.
10. Wherefore, if I come,
I will remember his deeds
which he doeth, prating against us
with malicious words: and not
content therewith,
neither doth he himself
receive the brethren,
and forbiddeth them that would,
and casteth *them* out of
the church.
11. **Beloved, follow not**
that which is
evil, but that which is good.
He that doeth good is of
God: but he that doeth evil
hath not seen God.
12. **Demetrius hath good**
report of all *men*,
and of the truth itself: yea, and we
also bear record; and ye know that our
record is true.
13. **I had many things to**
write, but I will not with ink
and pen write unto thee:
14. **But I trust I shall shortly**
see thee,
and we shall speak face to face.
Peace *be* to thee.
Our friends salute thee.
Greet the friends by name.

THE GENERAL EPISTLE OF JUDE

BACKGROUND INFORMATION

Author – Jude, probably the brother of James.
Date Written – probably between **70** and **100** A.D.

Number of:
Verses -   25
Chapters -   1
Total Words - 613
Scan Words - 288
Scan Words represent 46 % of Total Words.

Theme – written to warn Christians **against false** teachers and their **doctrines.**

OUTLINE OF THE EPISTLE

I. **Jude offers** a salutation and a **warning against false teachers.**
Verses 1—16

II. **Jude presents exhortations to** Christians and a benediction.
Verses 16—25

CHAPTER 1

1. **Jude,** the servant of Jesus Christ, and brother of James, **to them that are sanctified by God** the Father, **and preserved in Jesus Christ,** *and* called: 2. Mercy unto you, and peace, and love, be multiplied. 3. **Beloved,** when **I** gave all diligence to **write unto you of the common salvation,** it was needful for me to write unto you, **and exhort *you* that ye** should earnestly **contend for the faith** which was **once delivered** unto the saints. 4. **For there are** certain men crept in unawares, who were before of old ordained to this condemnation, **ungodly men, turning the grace of our God into lasciviousness, and denying** the only Lord God, and **our Lord Jesus Christ.** 5. I will therefore put you in remembrance, though **ye once knew** this, **how that the Lord,** having **saved the people out** of the land **of Egypt, afterward destroyed them that believed not.** 6. **And the angels which kept not their first estate,** but left their own habitation, **he hath reserved in** everlasting **chains** under darkness **unto the judgment** of the great day. 7. **Even as Sodom and Gomorrha,** and the cities about them in like manner, giving themselves over to fornication, and going after strange flesh, **are set forth for an example, suffering the vengeance of eternal fire.** 8. Likewise also these *filthy* dreamers defile the flesh, despise dominion, and speak evil of dignities. 9. **Yet Michael** the archangel, when **contending with the devil** he disputed **about the body of Moses, durst not bring against him a railing accusation, but said, The Lord rebuke thee.** 10. **But these speak evil of those things which they know not:** but what they know naturally, as brute beasts, in those things they corrupt themselves. 11. **Woe unto them! for they have gone in the way of Cain,** and ran greedily after the error of Balaam for reward, and perished in the gainsaying of Core. 12. **These are spots in your feasts of charity,** when they feast with you, feeding themselves without fear: **clouds** *they are* **without water,** carried about of winds; **trees** whose fruit withereth, **without fruit,** twice dead, **plucked up by the roots;** 13. **Raging waves** of the sea, foaming out their own shame; wandering stars, **to whom is reserved** the blackness of **darkness for ever.** 14. **And Enoch** also, the seventh from Adam, **prophesied** of these, saying, **Behold, the Lord cometh with** ten thousands of **his saints,** 15. **To execute judgment upon all,** and to convince all that are ungodly among them of all their ungodly deeds which they have ungodly committed, and of all their hard *speeches* which **ungodly sinners** have spoken against him. 16. **These are**

murmurers, complainers,
■ **walking after their own**
■ **lusts;** and their mouth speaketh great swelling *words*, having men's persons in admiration because of advantage.
■ 17. **But, beloved, remember** ye the words which were spoken before of the apostles of our Lord Jesus Christ;
■ 18. **How that** they told you
■ **there should be mockers in**
■ **the last time,** who should walk after their own ungodly lusts.
■ 19. **These be they** who separate themselves, sensual,
■ **having not the Spirit.**
■ 20. **But ye,** beloved, building up yourselves on your most holy faith,
■ **praying in the Holy Ghost,**
■ 21. **Keep yourselves in the**

■ **love of God, looking for** the mercy of our Lord Jesus
■ **Christ unto eternal life.**
■ 22. **And of some**
■ **have compassion,** making a difference:
■ 23. **And others save with**
■ **fear, pulling** *them* **out of the**
■ **fire;** hating even the garment spotted by the flesh.
■ 24. **Now unto him that is**
■ **able to keep you from**
■ **falling, and to present**
■ *you* **faultless** before the presence of his glory with exceeding joy,
■ 25. **To** the only wise
■ **God our Saviour,** *be* **glory**
■ **and majesty,** dominion and power,
■ **both now and ever. Amen.**

THE REVELATION OF JESUS CHRIST TO JOHN

BACKGROUND INFORMATION

Author – John, one of the twelve Apostles.
Date Written – probably **between 90** and **99** A.D.

Number of:
Verses -   404
Chapters -   22
Total Words - 12,000
Scan Words - 5,973
Scan Words represent 49 % of Total Words.

Theme – written to reveal that in spite of adverse world events,
Jesus Christ will triumph over all the enemies of God.

OUTLINE OF THE REVELATION

I.   The revelation of the Son of Man, **the letters to the seven Churches and** the open door in heaven. Chapters 1—5

II. The revelation of the **seven seals, the seven trumpets and the war in heaven.** Chapters 6—14

III. The revelation of **the seven vials and the fall of Babylon.** Chapters 14—19

IV. The revelation of **the millennium and the Holy City.** Chapters 20—22

THE REVELATION OF JESUS CHRIST TO JOHN
The Conclusion Of History

The first book of the Bible,

- **Genesis, is a revelation of**
- **the beginnings of history,**

both the beginning of the created order, and human beings. The final book of the Bible,

- **Revelation, is a revelation**
- **of the conclusion of history**

– the end of time, the created order as we know it today, and of man in his fallen state.

- **Revelation,** in essence,
- **shows what will occur**
- **when** God in
- **Christ concludes** human
- **history and ushers in a**
- **New Order.** For centuries now,

Bible scholars have studied the Book of Revelation. There has been a wide variety of interpretations.

- **Some Bible students give a**
- **literal interpretation to**
- **the Revelation.**
- **At the other extreme,**

there are

- **scholars** who
- **attempt to show that the**
- **Revelation is totally**
- **symbolic.** There is, of course, a

great deal of symbolism in the book,

- **but for the** Bible
- **student** who is
- **committed to the Scripture**
- **as the** authoritative, written
- **word of God, the**
- **symbolism points to**
- **a deeper reality.**
- **That reality,**

regardless of one's interpretations of specific verses or chapters in the Revelation,

- **is that** God in
- **Christ will** ultimately
- **triumph over all the**
- **enemies of the truth** –

sin, satan, political systems,

- **and all** that stands
- **in opposition to the**

purposes and

- **will of God. Evil will be**
- **defeated,** the saints of God

will be sustained,

- **persecution** and tribulation
- **shall end, and a new**
- **creation,** a new heaven

and a new earth –

- **without sorrows,**

tears, suffering, heartache,

- **and death – shall be**
- **established by** a direct act of
- **God.**
- **The Eden** which was
- **lost** by the first Adam,
- **shall be restored** by the

second Adam, Jesus Christ.

- **What seems plain**

in the Revelation

- **is that man, through his**
- **own** ingenuity or
- **effort, cannot solve**
- **his problems,**

he cannot save himself individually, socially, or politically.

- **But God in sheer grace,**
- **shall finish all that was**
- **accomplished in**
- **the death and resurrection**
- **of His Son, and in**
- **that new**
- **beginning, He,**

the Alpha and Omega,

- **shall be All in All.**

CHAPTER 1

■ 1. **The Revelation of Jesus**
■ **Christ, which God gave**
unto him,
■ **to shew** unto his servants
■ **things which must shortly**
■ **come to pass; and** he
■ **sent** and signified
■ *it* by his angel
■ **unto** his servant
■ **John:**
2. Who bare record of the word of
God, and of the testimony of Jesus
Christ, and of all things that he saw.
■ 3. **Blessed** *is* **he that**
■ **readeth, and they that hear**
the words of
■ **this prophecy, and keep**
those
■ **things** which are
■ **written therein:**
for the time *is* at hand.
■ 4. **John to the seven**
■ **churches** which are
■ **in Asia: Grace** *be* **unto you,**
and peace,
■ **from** him which is, and which was,
and which is to come; and from the
seven Spirits which are before
his throne;
5. And from Jesus
■ **Christ,** *who is* **the** faithful
witness, *and* the first begotten of the
dead, and the
■ **prince** of the kings of the earth.
Unto him
■ **that loved us, and washed**
■ **us from our sins in his**
■ **own blood**
■ 6. **And hath made us kings**
■ **and priests** unto God and his
Father; to him *be* glory and dominion
for ever and ever. Amen.
■ 7. **Behold, he cometh**
with clouds;
■ **and every eye shall see**
■ **him,** and they *also* which pierced
him: and all kindreds of the earth shall
wail because of him. Even so, Amen.
■ 8. **I am** Alpha and Omega,
■ **the beginning and the**
■ **ending, saith the Lord,**
which is, and which was, and which is

to come, the Almighty.
■ 9. **I John,** who also am your brother,
and companion in tribulation, and in
the kingdom and patience of
Jesus Christ,
■ **was in the isle** that is
■ **called Patmos,** for the word of
God, and for the testimony of
Jesus Christ.
■ 10. **I was in the Spirit on the**
■ **Lord's day, and heard**
behind me
■ **a great voice,** as of a trumpet,
■ 11. **Saying,** I am Alpha and Omega,
the first and the last: and,
■ **What thou seest, write**
in a book,
■ **and send** *it* **unto the seven**
■ **churches** which are
■ **in Asia;** unto Ephesus, and unto
Smyrna, and unto Pergamos, and
unto Thyatira, and unto Sardis, and
unto Philadelphia, and unto Laodicea.
12. And I turned to see the voice that
spake with me.
■ **And** being turned,
■ **I saw seven golden**
■ **candlesticks;**
■ 13. **And in the midst**
of the seven candlesticks
■ *one* **like unto the**
■ **Son of man,**
clothed with a garment down to the
foot, and girt about the paps with a
golden girdle.
14. His head and *his* hairs *were* white
like wool, as white as snow; and
his eyes *were* as a flame of fire;
15. And his feet like unto fine brass,
as if they burned in a furnace;
and his voice as the sound of
many waters.
■ 16. **And he had in his right**
■ **hand seven stars:** and out of
his mouth went a sharp two-edged
sword: and his countenance *was* as
the sun shineth in his strength.
■ 17. **And when I saw him, I fell**
■ **at his feet as dead. And he**
■ **laid his right hand upon**
■ **me, saying** unto me,
■ **Fear not;** I am the first
and the last:

18. **I** *am* **he that liveth, and was dead;** and, behold, **I am alive for evermore,** Amen; **and have the keys of hell** and of death. 19. **Write the things** which thou hast seen, and the things **which are, and** the things which **shall be** hereafter; 20. The mystery of the seven stars which thou sawest in my right hand, and the seven golden candlesticks. **The seven stars are the angels of the seven churches: and the seven candlesticks** which thou sawest **are the seven churches.**

CHAPTER 2

1. **Unto the angel of the church of Ephesus write;** These things saith he that holdeth the seven stars in his right hand, who walketh in the midst of the seven golden candlesticks; 2. **I know thy works,** and thy labour, and thy patience, **and how thou canst not bear them which are evil: and** thou **hast tried them which say they are apostles, and** are not, and hast **found them liars:** 3. **And** hast borne, and hast patience, and **for my name's sake** hast laboured, and **hast not fainted.** 4. **Nevertheless** I have *somewhat* against thee, because **thou hast left thy first love.** 5. Remember therefore from whence thou art fallen, and **repent,** and do the first works; **or else I will come** unto thee quickly, **and** will **remove thy candlestick** out of his place, except thou repent. 6. **But this thou hast,** that **thou hatest the deeds**

of the Nicolaitanes, which I also hate. 7. He that hath an ear, let him hear what **the Spirit saith unto the churches; To him that overcometh will I give to eat of the tree of life,** which is in the midst of the paradise of God. 8. **And unto the angel of the church in Smyrna write;** These things saith the first and the last, which was dead, and is alive; 9. **I know thy works, and tribulation,** and poverty, (but thou art rich) **and** *I know* **the blasphemy of them which say they are Jews,** and are not, **but** *are* the synagogue **of Satan.** 10. Fear none of those things which thou shalt suffer: behold, **the devil shall cast** *some* **of you into prison,** that ye may be tried; **and ye shall have tribulation ten days: be thou faithful** unto death, **and I will give thee a crown of life.** 11. He that hath an ear, let him hear what the Spirit saith unto the churches; **He that overcometh shall not be hurt of the second death.** 12. **And to the angel of the church in Pergamos write;** These things saith he which hath the sharp sword with two edges; 13. I know thy works, and where **thou dwellest,** *even* **where Satan's seat** *is:* **and thou holdest fast my name, and hast not denied my faith,** even in those days wherein Antipas *was* my faithful martyr, who was slain among you, where Satan dwelleth. 14. **But I have** a few **things against thee,** **because thou hast** there

them that hold the doctrine of Balaam, who taught Balac to cast a stumblingblock before the children of Israel, **to eat things sacrificed unto idols, and to commit fornication.** 15. So hast thou also them that hold the doctrine of the Nicolaitanes, which thing I hate. 16. **Repent; or else I will come** unto thee quickly, **and** will **fight** against **them with the sword of my mouth.** 17. He that hath an ear, let him hear what the Spirit saith unto the churches; **To him that overcometh will I give** to eat of **the hidden manna, and** will give him **a white stone, and in the stone a new name written,** which no man knoweth saving he that receiveth *it.* 18. **And unto the angel of the church in Thyatira write;** These things saith the Son of God, who hath his eyes like unto a flame of fire, and his feet *are* like fine brass; 19. **I know thy works,** and charity, and service, **and faith,** and thy patience, and thy works; and the last *to be* more than the first. 20. **Notwithstanding I have** a few **things against thee, because thou sufferest that woman Jezebel,** which calleth herself a prophetess, to teach and **to seduce my servants to commit fornication, and to eat things sacrificed unto idols.** 21. And I gave her space to repent of her fornication; **and she repented not.** 22. **Behold, I will cast her** into a bed,

and them that commit adultery with her into great **tribulation, except they repent** of their deeds. 23. **And I will kill her children** with death; and all the churches shall know that **I am he which searcheth the** reins and **hearts: and** I will **give** unto every one of you **according to** your **works.** 24. **But** unto you I say, and **unto** the rest in Thyatira, **as many as have not this doctrine,** and which have not known the depths of Satan, as they speak; **I will put upon you none other burden.** 25. But that which ye have *already* hold fast till I come. 26. **And he that overcometh,** and keepeth my works unto the end, to him **will I give power over the nations:** 27. **And he shall rule** them with a rod of iron; as the vessels of a potter shall they be broken to shivers: even as I received of my Father. 28. **And I will give him the morning star.** 29. He that hath an ear, let him hear what the Spirit saith unto the churches.

CHAPTER 3

1. **And unto the angel of the church in Sardis write;** These things saith he that hath the seven Spirits of God, and the seven stars; I know thy works, that **thou hast a name that thou livest, and art dead.** 2. Be watchful, and **strengthen the things which remain, that are ready to die: for I have not found thy works perfect before God.** 3. Remember therefore how thou hast

received and heard, and hold fast,
■ **and repent. If** therefore
■ **thou shalt not watch, I will**
■ **come** on thee
■ **as a thief, and thou shalt**
■ **not know what hour**
I will come upon thee.
■ 4. **Thou hast a few**
names even in Sardis
■ **which have not defiled their**
■ **garments; and they** shall
■ **walk** with me
■ **in white: for they**
■ **are worthy.**
■ 5. **He that overcometh,**
the same shall be clothed in white
raiment; and
■ **I will not blot out his name**
■ **out of the book of life, but I**
■ **will confess his name**
■ **before my Father,**
and before his angels.
6. He that hath an ear,
let him hear what the Spirit
saith unto the churches.
■ 7. **And to the angel of the**
■ **church in Philadelphia**
■ **write;** These things saith he that is
holy, he that is true, he that hath the
key of David, he that openeth, and no
man shutteth; and shutteth, and no
man openeth;
8. I know thy works: behold,
■ **I have set before thee an**
■ **open door,**
and no man can shut it:
■ **for thou hast a little**
■ **strength,** and hast kept my word,
■ **and hast not denied**
■ **my name.**
9. Behold, I will make
■ **them of the synagogue of**
■ **Satan, which say they are**
■ **Jews, and are not,**
but do lie; behold,
■ **I will make** them
■ **to** come and
■ **worship before thy feet,**
and to know that I have loved thee.
■ 10. **Because thou hast kept**
■ **the word** of my patience,
■ **I also will keep thee from**
■ **the hour of temptation,**

■ **which shall come**
upon all the world, to try them
that dwell upon the earth.
11. Behold, I come quickly:
■ **hold** that
■ **fast** which thou hast,
■ **that no man take thy crown.**
■ 12. **Him that overcometh**
■ **will I** make a pillar in the temple of
my God, and he shall go no more out:
and I will
■ **write upon him** the name of my
God, and the name of the city of my
God, *which is* new Jerusalem, which
cometh down out of heaven from my
God: and *I will write upon him*
■ **my new name.**
13. He that hath an ear,
let him hear what the Spirit
saith unto the churches.
■ 14. **And unto the angel of the**
■ **church of the Laodiceans**
■ **write;** These things saith the Amen,
the faithful and true witness, the
beginning of the creation of God;
15. I know thy works, that
■ **thou art neither cold nor**
■ **hot:** I would thou wert cold or hot.
■ 16. **So then because thou**
■ **art lukewarm,**
and neither cold nor hot,
■ **I will spue thee out**
■ **of my mouth.**
■ 17. **Because thou sayest, I**
■ **am rich,** and increased with goods,
and have need of nothing;
■ **and knowest not that thou**
■ **art** wretched, and miserable, and
■ **poor,** and
■ **blind, and naked:**
■ 18. **I counsel thee to buy of**
■ **me gold tried in the fire, that**
■ **thou mayest be rich; and**
white raiment, that thou
■ **mayest be clothed,**
and *that* the shame of thy nakedness
do not appear;
■ **and anoint thine eyes with**
■ **eye-salve, that thou**
■ **mayest see.**
■ 19. **As many as I love, I**
■ **rebuke** and chasten: be zealous
■ **therefore,** and

repent.

20. **Behold, I stand at the door, and knock: if any man hear my voice, and open the door, I will come in** to him, **and** will **sup with him,** and he with me.

21. **To him that overcometh will I grant to sit with me in my throne,** even as I also overcame, and am set down with my Father in his throne.

22. **He that hath an ear, let him hear** what the Spirit saith unto the churches.

CHAPTER 4

1. **After this** I looked, and, behold, **a door** *was* **opened in heaven: and the first voice** which **I heard** *was* as it were of a trumpet talking with me; which **said, Come** up hither, **and I will shew thee things which must be hereafter.**

2. **And immediately I was in the spirit; and,** behold, **a throne was** set **in heaven, and** *one* **sat on the throne.**

3. And he that sat was to look upon like a jasper and a sardine stone: and *there was* a rainbow round about the throne, in sight like unto an emerald.

4. **And round about the throne** *were* **four and twenty seats: and** upon the seats I saw **four and twenty elders sitting,** clothed in white raiment; and they had on their heads crowns of gold.

5. And out of the throne proceeded lightnings and thunderings and voices: **and** *there were* **seven lamps of fire burning before the throne, which are the seven Spirits of God.**

6. And before the throne *there was* a sea of glass like unto crystal: **and** in the midst of the throne, and **round about the throne,** *were* **four beasts full of eyes** before and behind.

7. **And the first beast** *was* **like a lion,** and **the second** beast **like a calf,** and **the third** beast **had a face as a man, and the fourth** beast *was* **like a flying eagle.**

8. And the four beasts had each of them six wings about *him*; and *they were* full of eyes within: **and they rest not day and night, saying, Holy, holy, holy, LORD God Almighty, which was,** and **is, and is to come.**

9. And when those beasts give glory and honour and thanks to him that sat on the throne, who liveth for ever and ever,

10. **The four and twenty elders fall down** before him that sat on the throne, **and worship him that liveth for ever** and ever, and cast their crowns before the throne, **saying,**

11. **Thou art worthy, O Lord, to receive glory** and honour and power: **for thou hast created all** things, and **for thy pleasure** they are and were created.

CHAPTER 5

1. **And I saw in the right hand of him** that sat on the throne **a book** written within and on the backside, sealed **with seven seals.**

2. **And I saw a strong angel proclaiming** with a loud voice, **Who is worthy to open the book,** and to loose the seals thereof?

3. **And no man in heaven,**

■ **nor in earth,**
neither under the earth,
■ **was able to open the book,**
neither to look thereon.
■ 4. **And I wept much,** because no
man was found worthy to open and to
read the book, neither to
look thereon.
■ 5. **And one of the elders**
■ **saith** unto me,
Weep not: behold, the Lion
of the tribe of Juda,
the Root of David,
hath prevailed to
■ **open the book,**
and to loose the seven seals thereof.
■ 6. **And** I beheld, and, lo,
■ **in the midst** of the throne and of
the four beasts, and in the midst of
the elders,
■ **stood a Lamb as it had**
■ **been slain,** having seven horns
and seven eyes, which are the seven
Spirits of God sent forth
into all the earth.
■ 7. **And he came and took**
■ **the book** out of the right hand of
him that sat upon the throne.
■ 8. **And** when he had taken the book,
■ **the four beasts and four**
■ **and twenty elders fell down**
■ **before the Lamb,** having every
one of them harps, and golden vials
full of odours, which are the
prayers of saints.
■ 9. **And they sung a new**
■ **song, saying, Thou art**
■ **worthy to take the book,**
and to open the seals thereof:
■ **for thou wast slain, and**
■ **hast redeemed us** to God
■ **by thy blood**
out of every kindred, and tongue,
and people, and nation;
■ 10. **And hast made us unto**
■ **our God kings and priests:**
■ **and we shall reign**
■ **on the earth.**
11. And I beheld,
■ **and I heard the**
■ **voice of** many
■ **angels** round about the
throne and the

■ **beasts and** the
■ **elders:** and the number of them
was ten thousand times ten thousand,
and thousands of thousands;
■ 12. **Saying with a loud**
■ **voice, Worthy is the Lamb**
■ **that was slain to receive**
■ **power,** and
■ **riches,** and
■ **wisdom,** and
■ **strength,** and
■ **honour,** and
■ **glory, and blessing.**
■ 13. **And every creature**
which is in heaven, and on the earth,
and under the earth, and such as are
in the sea, and all that are in them,
heard I
■ **saying, Blessing,**
and honour, and
■ **glory, and power,** *be* unto him
that sitteth upon the throne, and
■ **unto the Lamb** for ever and ever.
14. And the four beasts said, Amen.
And the four *and* twenty elders fell
down and worshipped him that liveth
for ever and ever.

CHAPTER 6

1. **And** I saw when
■ **the Lamb opened one of**
■ **the seals, and I heard,**
as it were the noise of thunder,
■ **one of the** four
■ **beasts saying,**
■ **Come and see.**
2. **And I saw,** and behold
■ **a white horse: and he that**
■ **sat on him** had a bow; and a crown
was given unto him: and he
■ **went forth conquering,**
and to conquer.
■ 3. **And when he had opened**
■ **the second seal,** I heard the
second beast say, Come and see.
4. **And there went out**
■ **another horse** *that was*
■ **red: and** *power* **was given**
■ **to him** that sat thereon
■ **to take peace from the**
■ **earth, and that they should**
■ **kill one another:** and there was
given unto him a great sword.

5. **And when he had opened the third seal,** I heard the third beast say, Come and see. And **I beheld,** and lo **a black horse; and he that sat on him had** a pair of **balances** in his hand.

6. **And I heard a voice** in the midst of the four beasts **say, A measure of wheat for a penny, and three measures of barley for a penny; and** *see* thou **hurt not the oil and** the **wine.**

7. **And when he** had **opened the fourth seal,** I heard the voice of the fourth beast say, Come and see.

8. And I looked, and **behold a pale horse: and his name that sat on him was Death, and Hell** followed with him. **And power was given** unto **them over the fourth** part **of the earth, to kill** with sword, and with hunger, and with death, and with the beasts of the earth.

9. **And when he had opened the fifth seal, I saw** under the altar **the souls** of them that were **slain for the word of God,** and for the testimony which they held:

10. **And they cried** with a loud voice, saying, **How long, O Lord,** holy and true, **dost thou not** judge and **avenge our blood** on them that dwell on the earth?

11. **And white robes were given unto** every one of **them; and** it was said unto them, that **they should rest** yet for a little season, **until their fellow-servants** also and their brethren, that **should be killed as they were,** should be fulfilled.

12. And I beheld **when he** had **opened the sixth seal,** and, lo, **there was a great earthquake; and the sun became black** as sackcloth of hair, **and the moon** became **as blood;**

13. **And the stars** of heaven **fell** unto the earth, even as a fig tree casteth her untimely figs, when she is shaken of a mighty wind.

14. **And the heaven departed** as a scroll when it is rolled together; **and every mountain and island were moved** out of their places.

15. **And the kings** of the earth, and the **great men,** and the **rich men,** and the **chief captains,** and the **mighty men,** and **every bondman, and** every **free man, hid** themselves **in the dens and** in the **rocks of** the **mountains;**

16. **And said to the mountains and rocks, Fall on us, and hide us** from the face of him that sitteth on the throne, and from the wrath of the Lamb:

17. **For the great day of his wrath is come; and who shall be able to stand?**

CHAPTER 7

1. **And** after these things **I saw four angels** standing on the four corners of the earth, **holding the four winds** of the earth, **that the wind should not blow on the earth,** nor on the sea, nor on any tree.

2. **And I saw another angel ascending** from the east, **having the seal of** the living **God: and he cried**

with a loud voice

■ **to the four angels,**

to whom it was given to hurt the earth and the sea,

■ 3. **Saying, Hurt not the earth,**

neither the sea, nor the trees,

■ **till we have sealed the**
■ **servants of our God in**
■ **their foreheads.**

4. And I heard the number of them which were sealed:

■ **and there were sealed an**
■ **hundred and forty and four**
■ **thousand of** all
■ **the tribes of** the children of
■ **Israel.**

5. Of the tribe of Juda *were* sealed twelve thousand. Of the tribe of Reuben *were* sealed twelve thousand. Of the tribe of Gad *were* sealed twelve thousand.

6. Of the tribe of Aser *were* sealed twelve thousand. Of the tribe of Nephthalim *were* sealed twelve thousand. Of the tribe of Manasses *were* sealed twelve thousand.

7. Of the tribe of Simeon *were* sealed twelve thousand. Of the tribe of Levi *were* sealed twelve thousand. Of the tribe of Issachar *were* sealed twelve thousand.

8. Of the tribe of Zabulon *were* sealed twelve thousand. Of the tribe of Joseph *were* sealed twelve thousand. Of the tribe of Benjamin *were* sealed twelve thousand.

■ 9. **After this** I beheld, and, lo,
■ **a great multitude,** which no man could number, of all nations, and kindreds, and people, and tongues,

■ **stood before the throne,**
■ **and before the Lamb,**
■ **clothed with white robes,**

and palms in their hands;

■ 10. **And cried**

with a loud voice, saying,

■ **Salvation to our God**

which sitteth upon the throne,

■ **and** unto
■ **the Lamb.**
■ 11. **And all the angels** stood round about the throne, and *about* the elder and the four beasts, and fell

before the throne on their faces, and

■ **worshipped God,**
■ 12. **Saying, Amen: Blessing,**

and

■ **glory,** and
■ **wisdom,** and
■ **thanksgiving,** and
■ **honour,** and
■ **power, and might,** *be*
■ **unto our God for ever**

and ever. Amen.

■ 13. **And one of the elders**
■ **answered,** saying unto me,
■ **What are these** which are
■ **arrayed in white robes?**

and whence came they?

■ 14. **And I said** unto him,
■ **Sir, thou knowest.**
■ **And he said** to me,
■ **These** are they which
■ **came out of great**
■ **tribulation, and have**
■ **washed their robes,**

and made them white

■ **in the blood of the Lamb.**
■ 15. **Therefore are they**
■ **before** the throne of
■ **God,** and serve him day

and night in his temple:

■ **and he** that sitteth on the throne
■ **shall dwell among them.**

16. They shall hunger no more, neither thirst any more; neither shall the sun light on them, nor any heat.

■ 17. **For the Lamb** which is in the midst of the throne
■ **shall feed them, and** shall
■ **lead them unto living**
■ **fountains** of waters:
■ **and God shall wipe away**
■ **all tears from their eyes.**

CHAPTER 8

■ 1. **And when he had opened**
■ **the seventh seal, there was**
■ **silence** in heaven about the space of half an hour.

2. And I saw

■ **the seven angels**

which stood before God; and to them

■ **were given seven trumpets.**
■ 3. **And another angel**

came and stood at the altar,

■ having a golden censer;
■ and there was
■ given unto him
■ much incense, that he
■ should offer *it* with the
■ prayers of all saints
upon the golden altar which was
before the throne.
■ 4. And the smoke of the
■ incense, *which came* with the
prayers of the saints,
■ ascended up before God
out of the angel's hand.
■ 5. And the angel took the
■ censer, and
■ filled it
■ with fire of the altar, and
■ cast *it* into the earth: and there
were voices, and thunderings, and
lightnings, and an earthquake.
■ 6. And the seven angels
■ which had the seven
■ trumpets prepared
themselves
■ to sound.
■ 7. The first angel sounded,
■ and there followed hail
■ and fire mingled
■ with blood, and they were cast
■ upon the earth: and the
■ third part of trees
was burnt up,
■ and all green
■ grass was burnt up.
■ 8. And the second angel
■ sounded, and as it were a great
mountain burning with fire was cast
into the sea:
■ and the third part of the sea
■ became blood;
■ 9. And the third part of the
■ creatures which were
■ in the sea, and had life,
■ died; and the third part of
■ the ships were destroyed.
■ 10. And the third angel
■ sounded, and there fell
■ a great star from heaven,
burning as it were a lamp, and it
■ fell upon the third part of
■ the rivers, and upon the
■ fountains of waters;
11. And the name of

■ the star is called
■ Wormwood: and the third part
of the waters became wormwood;
■ and many men died of the
■ waters, because they were
■ made bitter.
■ 12. And the fourth angel
■ sounded, and the third part
■ of the sun was smitten, and
the third part of
■ the moon, and the third part of
■ the stars; so as the third part of
them was darkened,
■ and the day shone not for a
■ third part of it, and the
■ night likewise.
■ 13. And I beheld, and
■ heard an angel flying
■ through the midst of
■ heaven, saying
with a loud voice, Woe, woe,
■ woe, to the inhabiters of the
■ earth by reason of the
■ other voices of the trumpet of the
three angels, which are
■ yet to sound!

CHAPTER 9
■ 1. And the fifth angel
■ sounded, and I saw a star
■ fall from heaven
■ unto the
■ earth: and to him was given
■ the key of the
■ bottomless pit.
■ 2. And he opened the
bottomless
■ pit; and there arose a smoke out of
the pit, as the smoke of a great
furnace; and the sun and the air
were darkened by reason of the
smoke of the pit.
■ 3. And there came out
of the smoke
■ locusts upon the earth:
■ and unto them was given
■ power, as the scorpions
of the earth
■ have power.
■ 4. And it was commanded
them
■ that they should
■ not hurt the grass

of the earth, neither any green thing,
■ **neither any tree; but only**
those
■ **men which have not the**
■ **seal of God in**
■ **their foreheads.**
■ 5. **And** to them it was given that
■ **they should not kill** them,
■ **but** that
■ **they should be tormented**
■ **five months:** and their torment
was as the torment of a scorpion,
when he striketh a man.
■ 6. **And** in those days shall
■ **men** seek death,
and shall not find it; and
■ **shall desire to die, and**
■ **death shall flee from them.**
■ 7. **And the shapes of the**
■ **locusts** *were* **like** unto
■ **horses prepared unto**
■ **battle; and** on their heads *were* as
it were crowns like gold, and
■ **their faces** *were*
■ **as** the faces of
■ **men.**
■ 8. **And they had hair as**
the hair of
■ **women, and their teeth** were
■ **as** *the teeth* of
■ **lions.**
■ 9. **And they had**
breastplates, as it were
■ **breastplates of iron; and**
■ **the sound of their wings** *was*
■ **as** the sound of
■ **chariots** of many horses
running to battle.
■ 10. **And they had tails like**
unto
■ **scorpions, and** there were
■ **stings** in their tails:
■ **and** their
■ **power** *was*
■ **to hurt men five months.**
■ 11. **And they had a king**
over them,
■ **which** *is* **the angel of the**
bottomless
■ **pit, whose name in** the
■ **Hebrew** tongue
■ *is* **Abaddon, but in** the
■ **Greek** tongue hath *his* name

■ **Apollyon.**
12. One woe is past; *and*, behold,
there come two woes more hereafter.
■ 13. **And the sixth angel**
■ **sounded, and I heard a**
■ **voice** from the four horns of the
golden altar which is before God,
■ 14. **Saying to the sixth angel**
which had the trumpet,
■ **Loose the four angels**
which are
■ **bound in the** great
■ **river Euphrates.**
■ 15. **And the four angels were**
■ **loosed,** which were prepared for an
hour, and a day, and a month, and a
year, for
■ **to slay the third part**
■ **of men.**
16. And the number of
■ **the army of** the
■ **horsemen** *were* **two**
■ **hundred thousand**
■ **thousand:**
and I heard the number of them.
■ 17. **And thus I saw the**
■ **horses in the vision, and**
■ **them that sat on them,**
having breastplates of fire, and of
jacinth, and brimstone:
■ **and the heads of the**
■ **horses** *were*
■ **as the heads of lions; and**
■ **out of their mouths**
■ **issued fire** and smoke
■ **and brimstone.**
■ 18. **By these three was the**
■ **third part of men killed,**
by the fire, and by the smoke, and by
the brimstone, which issued out of
their mouths.
■ 19. **For their power is in their**
■ **mouth, and** in their
■ **tails:** for their tails *were* like unto
serpents, and had heads, and with
them they do hurt.
■ 20. **And the rest** of the men
■ **which were not killed**
by these plagues
■ **yet repented not**
of the works of their hands,
■ **that they should not**
■ **worship devils, and idols**

of gold, and silver, and brass, and stone, and of wood: which neither can see, nor hear, nor walk:

21. **Neither repented they of their murders,** nor of their **sorceries,** nor of their **fornication, nor** of their **thefts.**

CHAPTER 10

1. **And I saw another mighty angel come** down from heaven, clothed with a cloud: and a rainbow *was* upon his head, and his face *was* as it were the sun, and his feet as pillars of fire:

2. **And he had** in his hand **a little book open:** and he set his right foot upon the sea, and *his* left *foot* on the earth,

3. And cried with a loud voice, as *when* a lion roareth: **and when he** had **cried, seven thunders uttered their voices.**

4. **And** when the seven thunders had uttered their voices, **I was about to write: and I heard a voice** from heaven **saying** unto me, **Seal up those things** which the seven thunders **uttered, and write** them **not.**

5. **And the angel which I saw** stand upon the sea and upon the earth **lifted up his hand** to heaven,

6. **And sware by him that liveth for ever** and ever, who created heaven, and the things that therein are, and the earth, and the things that therein are, and the sea, and the things which are therein, **that there should be time no longer:**

7. **But in the days of the voice of the seventh angel,** when he shall begin to sound, **the mystery of God should be finished,** as he hath declared to his servants the prophets.

8. **And the voice which I**

heard from heaven spake unto me again, and **said,** Go *and* **take the little book** which is open in the hand of the angel which standeth upon the sea and upon the earth.

9. **And I went unto the angel, and said** unto him, **Give me the little book.** And he **said** unto me, **Take** *it,* **and eat it** up; and it shall make thy belly bitter, but it shall be in thy mouth sweet as honey.

10. **And I** took the little book out of the angel's hand, and **ate it** up; **and it was in my mouth sweet as honey: and** as soon as I had eaten it, **my belly was bitter.**

11. **And he said** unto me, **Thou must prophesy** again before many peoples, and nations, and tongues, and kings.

CHAPTER 11

1. **And there was given me** a reed like unto **a rod: and the angel stood, saying, Rise, and measure the temple** of God, **and the altar, and them that worship** therein.

2. **But the court** which is without the temple leave out, and **measure it not; for it is given unto the Gentiles: and** the holy city shall they tread under foot forty *and* two months.

3. **And I will give** *power* **unto my two witnesses, and they shall prophesy a thousand two hundred** *and* **threescore days,** clothed in sackcloth.

4. These are the two olive trees, and the two candlesticks standing before the God of the earth.

5. **And if any man will hurt them,** fire proceedeth out of their mouth, and devoureth their enemies: and if any man will hurt them,

■ **he must** in this manner
■ **be killed.**
■ 6. **These have power to shut**
■ **heaven, that it rain not**
in the days of their prophecy:
■ **and** have power
■ **over waters to turn them to**
■ **blood, and to smite the**
■ **earth with** all
■ **plagues, as** often as
■ **they will.**
■ 7. **And when they** shall
■ **have finished their**
■ **testimony, the beast**
that ascendeth
■ **out of the** bottomless
■ **pit shall make war against**
■ **them,** and shall overcome them,
■ **and kill them.**
■ 8. **And their dead bodies**
■ **shall lie in** the street of
■ **the great city,** which spiritually is
called Sodom and Egypt,
■ **where also our Lord**
■ **was crucified.**
■ 9. **And they of the people** and
kindreds and tongues and nations
■ **shall see their** dead
■ **bodies three days and an**
■ **half, and shall not suffer**
■ **their** dead
■ **bodies to be put in graves.**
■ 10. **And they** that dwell
■ **upon the earth shall rejoice**
over them, and make merry, and shall
send gifts one to another;
■ **because these two**
■ **prophets tormented them**
that dwelt on the earth.
■ 11. **And after three days and**
■ **an half the Spirit** of life from God
■ **entered** into
■ **them, and they stood**
upon their feet;
■ **and great fear fell**
upon them which saw them.
■ 12. **And they heard a great**
■ **voice from heaven saying**
unto them,
■ **Come up** hither.
■ **And they ascended** up
■ **to heaven** in a cloud; and their
enemies beheld them.

■ 13. **And the same hour was**
■ **there a great earthquake,**
and the tenth part of the city fell,
■ **and in the earthquake were**
■ **slain** of men
■ **seven thousand: and**
■ **the remnant were**
■ **affrighted, and gave glory**
■ **to** the
■ **God** of heaven.
14. The second woe is past;
■ **and, behold, the third woe**
■ **cometh quickly.**
■ 15. **And the seventh angel**
■ **sounded; and there were**
great
■ **voices** in heaven,
■ **saying, The kingdoms of**
■ **this world are become** *the*
■ *kingdoms* **of our Lord, and**
■ **of his Christ;** and he shall reign
for ever and ever.
■ 16. **And the four and twenty**
■ **elders,** which sat before God on
their seats, fell upon their faces, and
■ **worshipped God,**
■ 17. **Saying, We give** thee
■ **thanks, O LORD** God Almighty,
■ **which art,** and
■ **wast, and art to come;**
■ **because thou hast taken**
to thee thy
■ **great power, and**
■ **hast reigned.**
18. And the nations were angry, and
thy wrath is come, and
■ **the time of the dead, that**
■ **they should be judged, and**
■ **that thou shouldest give**
■ **reward unto** thy servants the
prophets, and to the saints, and
■ **them that fear thy name,**
small and great;
■ **and shouldest destroy**
■ **them which destroy**
■ **the earth.**
■ 19. **And the temple of God**
■ **was opened** in heaven,
■ **and** there was
seen in his temple
■ **the ark of his testament:**
and there were lightnings, and voices,
and thunderings, and an earthquake,

and great hail.

CHAPTER 12

1. And there appeared a great wonder **in heaven; a woman** clothed with the sun, and the moon under her feet, and upon her head a crown of twelve stars: **2. And she being with child cried,** travailing in birth, and pained **to be delivered.** 3. **And there appeared** another wonder in heaven; and behold **a** great **red dragon,** having seven heads and ten horns, and seven crowns upon his heads. 4. And his tail drew the third part of the stars of heaven, and did cast them to the earth: **and the dragon stood before the woman** which was ready to be delivered, for **to devour her child as soon as it was born.** **5. And she brought forth a man child, who was to rule all nations** with a rod of iron: **and her child was caught up unto God,** and *to* his throne. 6. **And the woman fled into** the wilderness, where she hath **a place prepared of God,** that they should feed her there a thousand two hundred *and* threescore days. **7. And there was war in heaven: Michael and his angels fought against the dragon; and the dragon** fought and his angels, 8. And **prevailed not;** neither was their place found any more in heaven. **9. And the great dragon** was cast out, that old serpent, **called** the Devil, and **Satan, which deceiveth the whole world:** he **was cast out** into the earth, **and his angels were cast**

out with him. 10. And I heard a loud voice **saying** in heaven, **Now is come salvation,** and strength, and the kingdom of our God, and the power of his Christ: **for the accuser of our brethren is cast down,** which accused them before our God day and night. **11. And they overcame him by the blood of the Lamb, and by** the word of **their testimony;** and they loved not their lives unto the death. 12. Therefore rejoice, *ye* heavens, and ye that dwell in them. **Woe to the inhabiters of** the **earth and** of the **sea! for the devil is come down** unto you, **having great wrath, because** he knoweth that **he hath but a short time.** 13. **And when the dragon** saw that he **was cast unto** the **earth, he persecuted the woman** which brought forth the man *child*. **14. And to the woman were given two wings** of a great eagle, **that she might fly** into the wilderness, **into her place,** where she is nourished **for a time,** and times, and half a time, **from** the face of **the serpent.** 15. **And the serpent cast** out of his mouth **water as a flood** after the woman, **that he might cause her to be carried away** of the flood. 16. **And the earth** helped the woman, and the earth opened her mouth, and **swallowed up the flood** which the dragon cast out of his mouth.

17. And the dragon was wroth with the woman, and **went to** make **war with** the remnant of **her seed, which keep the commandments** of God, **and have the testimony of Jesus** Christ.

CHAPTER 13

1. And I stood upon the sand of the sea, and **saw a beast rise** up **out of the sea, having seven heads and ten horns,** and upon his horns ten crowns, **and upon his heads the name of blasphemy.**

2. And the beast which I saw was like unto a leopard, and his feet were as *the feet* of a bear, and his mouth as the mouth of a lion: and the dragon gave him his power, and his seat, and great authority.

3. And I saw one of his heads as it were **wounded to death; and his** deadly **wound was healed: and all the world wondered after the beast.**

4. And they worshipped the dragon which gave power unto the beast: and they worshipped the beast, saying, Who *is* **like unto the beast?** who is able to make war with him?

5. And there was given unto **him a mouth speaking great things and blasphemies; and power** was given unto him **to continue forty** *and* **two months.**

6. And he opened his mouth in blasphemy **against God, to blaspheme his name,** and his tabernacle, and them that dwell in heaven.

7. And it was given unto **him to make war with the saints, and** to **overcome them: and power** was given him **over all** kindreds, and tongues, and **nations.**

8. **And** all that dwell upon **the earth shall worship him, whose names are not** written **in the book of life of the Lamb slain from the foundation of the world.**

9. If any man have an ear, let him hear.

10. He that leadeth into captivity shall go into captivity: he that killeth with the sword must be killed with the sword. Here is the patience and the faith of the saints.

11. And I beheld another beast coming up out of the earth; **and he had two horns like a lamb, and he spake as a dragon.**

12. And he exerciseth all the power of the first beast before him, and **causeth the earth and them** which dwell **therein to worship the first beast, whose deadly wound was healed.**

13. **And he doeth great wonders,** so that he maketh fire come down from heaven on the earth in the sight of men,

14. **And deceiveth** them that dwell on the earth **by** *the* *means of* those **miracles** which he had power to do in the sight of the beast; **saying** to them that dwell on the earth, **that they should make an image to the beast, which had the wound** by a sword, **and did live.**

15. **And he had power to give life unto the image of the beast,** that the image of the beast should both speak,

■ **and cause that as many as**
■ **would not worship the**
■ **image** of the beast should
■ **be killed.**
■ 16. **And he causeth all,**
both small and great, rich and poor,
free and bond,
■ **to receive a mark in their**
■ **right hand, or** in their
■ **foreheads:**
■ 17. **And that no man might**
■ **buy or sell, save he** that
■ **had the mark, or the**
■ **name** of the beast,
■ **or the number** of his name.
■ 18. **Here is wisdom.** Let him that
hath understanding
■ **count the number of the**
■ **beast: for it is** the number of a
man; and his number *is*
■ **Six hundred threescore**
■ *and* **six.**

CHAPTER 14
1. And I looked, and, lo,
■ **a Lamb stood on** the mount
■ **Sion,** and
■ **with** him
■ **an hundred forty** *and*
■ **four thousand, having his**
■ **Father's name written in**
■ **their foreheads.**
■ 2. **And I heard a voice from**
■ **heaven,** as the voice of many
waters, and as the voice of a
great thunder:
■ **and I heard the voice of**
■ **harpers harping**
with their harps:
■ 3. **And they sung** as it were
■ **a new song** before the throne,
and before the four beasts,
and the elders:
■ **and no man could learn**
■ **that song but the hundred**
and
■ **forty** *and*
■ **four thousand, which were**
■ **redeemed** from the earth.
4. These are they which were not
defiled with women;
for they are virgins.
■ **These** are they which

■ **follow the Lamb** whithersoever
he goeth. These were redeemed from
among men,
■ *being* **the firstfruits unto**
■ **God** and to the Lamb.
5. And in their mouth was found
no guile:
■ **for they are without fault**
before the throne of God.
■ 6. **And I saw another angel**
■ **fly** in the midst of heaven,
■ **having the** everlasting
■ **gospel to preach unto**
them that dwell on the earth, and to
■ **every nation,** and
■ **kindred,** and
■ **tongue, and people,**
■ 7. **Saying** with a loud voice,
■ **Fear God,** and give glory to him;
■ **for** the hour of
■ **his judgment is come: and**
■ **worship him** that made heaven,
and earth, and the sea, and the
fountains of waters.
■ 8. **And** there followed
■ **another angel, saying,**
■ **Babylon is fallen,**
is fallen, that great city,
■ **because she made all**
■ **nations drink** of
■ **the wine of** the wrath of
■ **her fornication.**
■ 9. **And the third angel**
■ **followed** them,
■ **saying** with a loud voice,
■ **If any man worship the**
■ **beast** and his image,
■ **and receive** *his* **mark**
in his forehead, or in his hand,
■ 10. **The same shall drink** of
■ **the wine of the wrath of**
■ **God,** which is poured out without
mixture into the cup of his indignation;
■ **and he shall be tormented**
■ **with fire** and brimstone
■ **in the presence of** the holy
■ **angels, and** in the presence of
■ **the Lamb:**
■ 11. **And the smoke of their**
■ **torment ascendeth up for**
■ **ever** and ever:
■ **and they have no rest**
day nor night,

who worship the beast and
his image, and whosoever
receiveth the mark
of his name.
12. Here is the patience of the saints:
here *are* they that keep the
commandments of God, and the faith
of Jesus.
13. **And I heard a voice**
from heaven
saying unto me,
Write, Blessed *are* the dead
which die in the Lord
from henceforth:
Yea, saith the Spirit, that
they may rest from their labours;
and their works do
follow them.
14. And I looked, and
behold a white cloud, and
upon the cloud *one* sat like
unto
the Son of man, having
on his head
a golden crown, and
in his hand
a sharp sickle.
15. And another angel came
out of the temple,
crying with a loud voice
to him that sat on the cloud,
Thrust in
thy sickle, and reap: for the
time is come for thee to reap;
for the harvest of the earth
is ripe.
16. And he that sat on the cloud
thrust in
his sickle on the earth;
and the earth was
reaped.
17. And another angel came
out of the temple
which is in heaven, he also
having a sharp
sickle.
18. And another angel
came out from the altar,
which had power over fire;
and
cried with a loud cry
to him that had the sharp
sickle, saying,

Thrust in thy sharp
sickle, and gather the
clusters of the vine
of the earth;
for her grapes are fully
ripe.
19. And the angel thrust in his
sickle into the earth, and
gathered the vine of the earth,
and cast *it* into the great
winepress of the wrath
of God.
20. And the winepress was trodden
without the city,
and blood came out of the
winepress, even unto the horse
bridles, by the space of a thousand
and six hundred furlongs.

CHAPTER 15
1. And I saw another sign in
heaven, great and marvellous,
seven angels having the
seven last plagues; for in
them is filled up the wrath of God.
2. And I saw as it were a sea
of glass mingled
with fire: and them that had
gotten the victory over the
beast, and over his image,
and over his mark, *and* over the
number of his name,
stand on the sea of glass,
having the harps of God.
3. And they sing the song of
Moses the servant of God,
and the song of the Lamb,
saying, Great and marvellous
are thy works, Lord
God Almighty;
just and true *are* thy ways,
thou King of saints.
4. Who shall not fear
thee, O Lord,
and glorify thy name? for
thou only *art* holy: for all
nations shall come and
worship before
thee; for thy judgments
are made manifest.
5. And after that I looked, and,
behold, the temple of the tabernacle
of the testimony in heaven

was opened:

6. And the seven angels came out of the temple, having the seven plagues, clothed in pure and white linen, and having their breasts girded with golden girdles.

7. And one of the four beasts gave unto the seven **angels seven golden vials full of the wrath of God,** who liveth for ever and ever.

8. And the temple was filled with smoke from the glory of God, and from his power; and no man was able to enter into the temple, till the seven plagues of the seven angels were fulfilled.

CHAPTER 16

1. And I heard a great voice out of the temple **saying to the** seven **angels,** Go your ways, and **pour out the vials of the wrath of God** upon the earth.

2. And the first went, and **poured out his vial upon** the **earth; and there fell a** noisome and **grievous sore upon** the **men which had the mark** of the beast, and *upon* them which worshipped his image.

3. And the second angel **poured out his vial upon the sea; and it became as** the **blood** of a dead *man;* **and every** living **soul died in the sea.**

4. And the third angel **poured out his vial upon** the **rivers and** fountains of **waters; and they became blood.**

5. And I heard the angel of the **waters say, Thou art righteous, O Lord,** which art, and wast, and shalt be, **because thou hast judged thus.**

6. For they have shed the

blood of saints and prophets, and thou hast given them blood to drink; for they are worthy.

7. And I heard another out of the altar say, Even so, Lord God Almighty, true and righteous *are* thy judgments.

8. And the fourth angel **poured out his vial upon the sun; and power was given** unto **him to scorch** men **with fire.**

9. And men were scorched with great heat, **and blasphemed** the name of **God,** which hath power over these plagues: **and** they **repented not** to give him glory.

10. And the fifth angel **poured out his vial upon** the seat of **the beast; and his kingdom** was full of darkness; **and they gnawed their tongues for pain,**

11. And blasphemed the **God** of heaven **because of** their **pains and** their **sores, and repented not** of their deeds.

12. And the sixth angel **poured out his vial upon the** great river **Euphrates; and the water** thereof was **dried up, that the way of the kings of the east** might **be prepared.**

13. And I saw three unclean spirits like frogs *come* **out of the mouth of the dragon,** and out of the mouth of **the beast, and** out of the mouth of **the false prophet.**

14. For they are the spirits of devils, working miracles, *which* **go forth unto the kings of the earth** and of the whole world,

to gather them to the battle of that great day of God Almighty.
15. Behold, I come as a thief. Blessed *is* he that watcheth, and keepeth his garments, lest he walk naked, and they see his shame.
16. **And he gathered them** together **into** a place called in the Hebrew tongue **Armageddon.**
17. **And the seventh** angel **poured** out **his vial into the air; and there came a great voice** out of the temple of heaven, **from the throne, saying, It is done.**
18. And there were voices, and thunders, and lightnings; and there was a great earthquake, such as was not since men were upon the earth, so mighty an earthquake, *and* so great.
19. **And the great city was divided** into three parts, **and the cities of the nations fell: and great Babylon came in remembrance before God, to give** unto **her the** cup of the wine of the **fierceness of his wrath.**
20. **And every island fled** away, **and** the **mountains were not found.**
21. **And there fell** upon men a great **hail** out of heaven, *every stone* about the weight of a talent: **and men blasphemed God because** of the plague of **the hail;** for the plague thereof **was exceeding great.**

CHAPTER 17

1. And there came **one of the** seven **angels** which had the seven vials, and **talked with me, saying** unto me, **Come** hither; **I will shew** unto the **judgment of the great whore** that sitteth upon many waters:
2. **With whom the kings** of the earth **have committed fornication, and the inhabitants of the earth have been made drunk with** the wine of **her fornication.**
3. **So he carried me** away **in the spirit** into the wilderness: **and I saw a woman sit upon a scarlet** coloured **beast, full of names of blasphemy, having seven heads and ten horns.**
4. And the woman was arrayed in purple and scarlet colour, and decked with gold and precious stones and pearls, having a golden cup in her hand full of abominations and filthiness of her fornication
5. **And upon her forehead** *was* a name **written, MYSTERY, BABYLON THE GREAT, THE MOTHER OF HARLOTS AND ABOMINATIONS OF THE EARTH.**
6. **And I saw the woman drunken with the blood of the saints, and** with the blood of **the martyrs of Jesus:** and when I saw her, I wondered with great admiration.
7. **And the angel said** unto me, Wherefore didst thou marvel? **I will tell thee the mystery of the woman, and of the beast** that carrieth her, which hath the seven heads and ten horns.
8. **The beast** that thou sawest **was,** and is **not; and shall ascend out of the bottomless pit, and go into perdition:** and they that dwell on the earth shall wonder, whose names were not written in the book of life from the foundation of the world, when they behold the beast that was, and is not, and yet is.

9. And here *is* the mind which hath wisdom.

The seven heads are seven mountains, on which the woman sitteth.

10. **And there are seven kings: five are fallen,** and **one is,** *and* **the other is not yet come; and when he cometh, he must continue a short space.**

11. **And the beast** that was, and is not, even he is the eighth, and **is of the seven, and goeth into perdition.**

12. **And the ten horns** which thou sawest **are ten kings, which have received no kingdom as yet; but receive power** as kings **one hour with the beast.**

13. **These** have one mind, and **shall give their power** and strength **unto the beast.**

14. **These shall make war with the Lamb, and the Lamb shall overcome them: for he is Lord of lords, and King of kings:** and they that are with him *are* called, and chosen, and faithful.

15. **And he saith** unto me, **The waters** which thou sawest, **where the whore sitteth, are** peoples, and **multitudes, and nations,** and tongues.

16. **And the ten horns** which thou sawest upon the beast, these **shall hate the whore, and** shall **make her desolate** and naked, and shall eat her flesh, and burn her with fire.

17. **For God hath put in their hearts to fulfil his will,** and to agree, **and give their kingdom unto the beast,** until the words of God shall be fulfilled.

18. **And the woman** which thou sawest **is that great city, which reigneth** over the kings of the earth.

CHAPTER 18

1. **And after** these things **I saw another angel** come down from heaven, having great power; and the earth was lightened with his glory.

2. **And he cried** mightily with a strong voice, saying, **Babylon** the great **is fallen, is fallen, and is** become **the habitation of devils, and the hold of every foul spirit, and a cage of every unclean** and hateful **bird.**

3. **For all nations have drunk** of the wine of **the wrath of her fornication,** and the kings of the earth have committed fornication with her, **and the merchants** of the earth **are** waxed **rich through** the abundance of **her delicacies.**

4. **And I heard another voice from heaven, saying, Come out of her, my people,** that ye be not partakers of her sins, and that ye receive not of her plagues.

5. **For her sins have reached** unto **heaven, and God hath remembered her iniquities.**

6. **Reward her even as she rewarded you,** and double unto her double according to her works: in the cup which she hath filled fill to her double.

7. **How much she hath glorified herself,** and lived deliciously, so much **torment and sorrow give her: for she saith** in her heart, **I sit a queen,** and am no widow, and shall see no sorrow.

8. **Therefore shall her**

■ **plagues come in one day,** death, and mourning, and famine;
■ **and she shall be utterly**
■ **burned with fire: for** strong *is*
■ **the Lord** God who
■ **judgeth her.**
■ 9. **And the kings** of the earth, who have committed fornication and lived deliciously with her,
■ **shall** bewail her, and
■ **lament for her,** when they shall see the smoke of her burning,
10. Standing afar off for the fear of her torment,
■ **saying, Alas,** alas that great city
■ **Babylon,** that mighty city! for
■ **in one hour is thy**
■ **judgment come.**
■ 11. **And the merchants** of the earth
■ **shall weep** and mourn
■ **over her; for no man buyeth**
■ **their merchandise**
■ **any more:**
12. The merchandise of gold, and silver, and precious stones, and of pearls, and fine linen, and purple, and silk, and scarlet, and all thyine wood, and all manner vessels of ivory, and all manner vessels of most precious wood, and of brass, and iron, and marble,
13. And cinnamon, and odours, and ointments, and frankincense, and wine, and oil, and fine flour, and wheat, and beasts, and sheep, and horses, and chariots, and slaves, and souls of men.
■ 14. **And the fruits that thy**
■ **soul lusted after are**
■ **departed** from thee,
■ **and all things** which were dainty and
■ **goodly are departed** from thee, and thou shalt find them no more at all.
■ 15. **The merchants** of these things, which were
■ **made rich by her, shall**
■ **stand afar off for the fear of**
■ **her torment,** weeping and wailing,
■ 16. **And saying, Alas, alas**
■ **that great city,** that was clothed

in fine linen, and purple, and scarlet, and decked with gold, and precious stones, and pearls!
■ 17. **For in one hour so great**
■ **riches is come to nought.**
■ **And** every shipmaster, and
■ **all** the company in
■ **ships, and sailors,** and as many as trade by sea,
■ **stood afar off,**
18. And cried when they saw the smoke of her burning, saying, What *city is* like unto this great city!
■ 19. **And they** cast dust on their heads, and
■ **cried,** weeping and wailing,
■ **saying,** Alas, alas
■ **that great city, wherein**
■ **were made rich all that had**
■ **ships** in the sea by reason of her costliness!
■ **for in one hour is she**
■ **made desolate.**
■ 20. **Rejoice** over her, *thou* heaven, and
■ **ye holy apostles and**
■ **prophets; for God hath**
■ **avenged you** on her.
■ 21. **And a mighty angel took**
■ **up a stone** like a great millstone,
■ **and cast** *it* **into the sea,**
■ **saying,** Thus
■ **with violence shall that**
■ **great city** Babylon
■ **be thrown down, and** shall be
■ **found no more** at all.
22. And the voice of harpers, and musicians, and of pipers, and trumpeters, shall be heard no more at all in thee; and no craftsman, of whatsoever craft *he be,* shall be found any more in thee; and the sound of a millstone shall be heard no more at all in thee;
23. And the light of a candle shall shine no more at all in thee; and the voice of the bridegroom and of the bride shall be heard no more at all in thee: for thy merchants were the great men of the earth; for by thy sorceries were all nations deceived.
■ 24. **And in her was found the**
■ **blood of prophets,** and of

saints, and of
all that were
slain upon the earth.

CHAPTER 19

1. And after these things
I heard a great voice of
much people in heaven,
saying, Alleluia;
Salvation, and
glory, and
honour, and power, unto
the Lord our God:
2. For true and righteous
are his judgments: for he
hath judged the great
whore, which did corrupt
the earth with her fornication, and
hath avenged the blood of his
servants at her hand.
3. And again they said, Alleluia. And
her smoke rose up for ever and ever.
4. And the four and twenty
elders and the four beasts
fell down and
worshipped God
that sat on the throne,
saying, Amen; Alleluia.
5. And a voice came out of
the throne, saying, Praise
our God, all ye his
servants, and ye that fear him,
both small and great.
6. And I heard as it were the
voice of a great multitude, and as the
voice of many waters, and
as the voice of mighty
thunderings, saying,
Alleluia: for
the Lord God
omnipotent reigneth.
7. Let us be glad and
rejoice, and give honour to
him: for the marriage of the
Lamb is come, and his wife
hath made herself ready.
8. And to her was granted
that she should be arrayed in
fine linen, clean and white:
for the fine linen is the
righteousness of saints.
9. And he saith unto me,
Write, Blessed *are* they

which are
called unto the marriage
supper of the Lamb.
And he saith unto me, These are the
true sayings of God.
10. And I fell at his feet
to worship him. And he
said unto me,
See *thou do it* not: I am thy
fellow-servant,
and of thy brethren that have the
testimony of Jesus:
worship God: for the
testimony of Jesus is the
spirit of prophecy.
11. And I saw heaven
opened, and behold a
white horse; and he that sat
upon him *was* called
Faithful and True, and in
righteousness he doth
judge and make war.
12. His eyes *were* as a flame of fire,
and on his head *were* many crowns;
and he had a name written, that no
man knew, but he himself.
13. And he *was* clothed with
a vesture dipped in blood:
and his name is called The
Word of God.
14. And the armies *which were*
in heaven followed him
upon white horses,
clothed in fine linen,
white and clean.
15. And out of his mouth
goeth a sharp sword, that
with it he should smite the
nations: and he shall rule
them
with a rod of iron:
and he treadeth the winepress of
the fierceness and wrath of
Almighty God.
16. And he hath
on *his* vesture and
on his thigh a name written,
KING OF KINGS, AND
LORD OF LORDS.
17. And I saw an angel
standing in the sun;
and he cried
with a loud voice, saying

to all the fowls
that fly in the midst of heaven,
Come and gather
yourselves together
unto the supper of the
great God;
18. That ye may
eat the flesh of kings,
and the flesh of
captains, and the flesh of
mighty men, and the flesh of
horses, and of them
that sit on them,
and the flesh of all *men,*
both free and bond,
both small and great.
19. And I saw the beast, and
the kings of the earth,
and their armies, gathered
together
to make war against him
that sat
on the horse, and against
his army.
20. And the beast was
taken, and with him
the false prophet
that wrought miracles before him,
with which he deceived them that
had received the mark of the beast,
and them that worshipped his
image. These
both were cast alive into a
lake of fire
burning with brimstone.
21. And the remnant were
slain with the sword of him
that sat
upon the horse, which *sword*
proceeded out of his mouth:
and all the fowls were filled
with their flesh.

CHAPTER 20
1. And I saw an angel
come down from heaven,
having the key of the
bottomless pit and a great
chain in his hand.
2. And he laid hold on
the dragon, that old serpent, which is
the Devil, and
Satan, and bound him a

thousand years,
3. And cast him into the
bottomless pit, and shut him up,
and set a seal upon him,
that he should deceive the
nations no more, till the
thousand years should be
fulfilled: and after that he
must be loosed a
little season.
4. And I saw thrones, and they sat
upon them, and judgment was given
unto them:
and *I saw* the souls of
them that were beheaded
for the witness of
Jesus, and for
the word of God, and which had
not worshipped the beast, neither his
image, neither had received *his* mark
upon their foreheads,
or in their hands;
and they lived
and reigned with Christ a
thousand years.
5. But the rest of the dead
lived not again
until the thousand years
were finished. This *is* the
first resurrection.
6. Blessed and holy
is he that hath part in the
first resurrection: on such
the second death hath no
power, but they shall be
priests of God and of Christ,
and shall reign with him a
thousand years.
7. And when the thousand
years are expired, Satan
shall be loosed
out of his prison,
8. And shall go out to
deceive the nations
which are in the four quarters of the
earth, Gog, and Magog,
to gather them together
to battle: the number of whom *is* as
the sand of the sea.
9. And they went up on the breadth
of the earth, and
compassed the camp
of the saints

about, and the beloved city:
■ **and fire came down from**
■ **God** out of heaven,
■ **and devoured them.**
■ 10. **And the devil and fire**
■ **came down from God**
out of heaven,
■ **and devoured them.**
■ 10. **And the devil**
that deceived them
■ **was cast into the lake of**
■ **fire** and brimstone,
■ **where the beast and the**
■ **false prophet** *are,* **and**
■ **shall be tormented**
day and night
■ **for ever** and ever.
■ 11. **And I saw a great white**
■ **throne, and him that sat**
■ **on it,** from whose face the earth and
the heaven fled away; and there was
found no place for them.
■ 12. **And I saw the dead,**
small and great,
■ **stand before God; and the**
■ **books were opened: and**
■ **another book was opened,**
■ **which is** *the book* **of life:**
■ **and the dead were judged**
■ **out of those things** which were
■ **written in the books,**
■ **according to their works.**
■ 13. **And the sea gave up the**
■ **dead** which were in it;
■ **and death and hell**
■ **delivered up the dead**
which were in them:
■ **and they were judged**
every man
■ **according to their works.**
■ 14. **And death and hell were**
■ **cast into the lake of fire.**
■ **This is the second death.**
■ 15. **And whosoever was not**
■ **found written in the book of**
■ **life was cast into the lake**
■ **of fire.**

CHAPTER 21
■ 1. **And I saw a new heaven**
■ **and a new earth:**
for the first heaven and the first earth
were passed away; and there was

no more sea.
■ 2. **And I John saw the holy**
■ **city, new Jerusalem,**
■ **coming** down
■ **from God** out of heaven,
■ **prepared as a bride** adorned
■ **for her husband.**
■ 3. **And I heard a great voice**
out of heaven
■ **saying,** Behold,
■ **the tabernacle of God** *is*
■ **with men,** and he will dwell with
them, and they shall be his people,
■ **and God himself shall be**
■ **with them,** *and be*
■ **their God.**
■ 4. **And God shall wipe away**
■ **all tears** from their eyes;
■ **and there shall be no more**
■ **death,** neither sorrow, nor crying,
■ **neither** shall there be any more
■ **pain:** for the former things are
passed away.
■ 5. **And he that sat upon the**
■ **throne said,** Behold,
■ **I make all things new.**
And he said unto me,
■ **Write: for these words are**
■ **true** and faithful.
6. And he said unto me,
■ **It is done. I am Alpha and**
■ **Omega,** the beginning and the end.
■ **I will give unto him** that is
■ **athirst** of the fountain of
■ **the water of life freely.**
■ 7. **He that overcometh shall**
■ **inherit all** things; and I will be his
God, and he shall be my son.
■ 8. **But the** fearful, and
■ **unbelieving,** and the abominable,
and murderers, and whoremongers,
and sorcerers, and idolaters,
and all liars,
■ **shall have their part in the**
■ **lake which burneth with fire**
and brimstone:
■ **which is the second death.**
■ 9. **And there came** unto me
■ **one of the seven angels**
which had the seven vials full of the
seven last plagues, and
talked with me,
■ **saying, Come** hither,

■ **I will shew thee the bride,**
■ **the Lamb's wife.**
■ 10. **And he**
carried me away in the spirit to a
great and high mountain, and
■ **shewed me** that great city,
■ **the holy Jerusalem,**
■ **descending out of heaven**
■ **from God,**
■ 11. **Having the glory of God:**
■ **and her light** *was* like unto a
stone most precious,
■ **even like a jasper stone,**
■ **clear as crystal;**
■ 12. **And had a wall**
great and high,
■ *and* had
■ **twelve gates, and at the**
■ **gates twelve angels, and**
■ **names written** thereon,
■ **which are** *the names* **of the**
■ **twelve tribes** of the children
■ **of Israel:**
13. On the east three gates; on the
north three gates; on the south three
gates; and on the west three gates.
■ 14. **And the wall** of the city
■ **had twelve foundations,**
■ **and in them the names of**
■ **the twelve apostles**
of the Lamb.
15. And he that talked with me had a
golden reed to measure the city,
and the gates thereof,
and the wall thereof.
■ 16. **And the city lieth**
■ **foursquare, and** the length is
as large as the breadth: and he
■ **measured** the city with the reed,
■ **twelve thousand furlongs.**
■ **The length** and the
■ **breadth and** the
■ **height** of it
■ **are equal.**
■ 17. **And he measured the**
■ **wall** thereof,
■ **an hundred** *and*
■ **forty** *and*
■ **four cubits,**
according to the measure of a man,
that is, of the angel.
■ 18. **And** the building of
■ **the wall** of it

■ **was** *of*
■ **jasper: and the city** *was*
■ **pure gold, like** unto clear
■ **glass.**
■ 19. **And the foundations**
of the wall of the city
■ *were* garnished with all manner
■ **of precious stones.**
The first foundation *was* jasper; the
second, sapphire; the third, a
chalcedony; the fourth, an emerald;
20. The fifth, sardonyx; the sixth,
sardius; the seventh, chrysolyte; the
eighth, beryl; the ninth, a topaz; the
tenth, a chrysoprasus; the eleventh,
a jacinth; the twelfth, an amethyst.
■ 21. **And the twelve gates**
■ *were* **twelve pearls:** every
several gate was of one pearl:
■ **and the street of the city** *was*
■ **pure gold,**
as it were transparent glass.
■ 22. **And I saw no temple**
therein:
■ **for the Lord God** Almighty
■ **and the Lamb are the**
■ **temple** of it.
■ 23. **And the city had no need**
■ **of the sun, neither** of
■ **the moon, to shine** in it:
■ **for the glory of God**
did lighten it,
■ **and the Lamb** *is* **the**
■ **light thereof.**
24. And the nations of them which are
saved shall walk in the light of it: and
the kings of the earth do bring their
glory and honour into it.
■ 25. **And the gates** of it
■ **shall not be shut** at all by day:
■ **for there shall be**
■ **no night** there.
26. And they shall bring the glory and
honour of the nations into it.
■ 27. **And there shall in no**
■ **wise enter into**
■ **it any thing**
■ **that defileth,** neither *whatsoever*
worketh abomination, or *maketh* a lie:
■ **but they** which are
■ **written in**
■ **the Lamb's**
■ **book of life.**

CHAPTER 22

1. And he shewed me **a pure river of water of life,** clear as crystal, **proceeding out of the throne of God and of the Lamb.**

2. In the midst of the street of it, **and on either side of the river, *was* there the tree of life,** which bare twelve *manner of* fruits, *and* yielded her fruit every month: **and the leaves** of the tree **were for the healing of the nations.**

3. **And there shall be no more curse:** but the throne of God and of the Lamb shall be in it; **and his servants shall serve him:**

4. **And they shall see his face; and his name *shall be* in their foreheads.**

5. **And there shall be no night** there; and they need no candle, neither light of the sun; **for the Lord** God **giveth** them **light: and they shall reign for ever** and ever.

6. **And he said** unto me, **These sayings *are*** faithful and **true:** and the Lord God of the holy prophets sent his angel to shew unto his servants the things which must shortly be done.

7. **Behold, I come quickly: blessed *is* he that keepeth** the sayings of **the prophecy of this book.**

8. **And I John** saw these things, and heard *them.* And when I had heard and seen, I **fell down to worship** before the feet of **the angel** which shewed me these things.

9. **Then saith he** unto me, **See *thou do it* not:** for I am thy fellow-servant, and of thy brethren the prophets, and of them which keep the sayings of this book:

worship God.

10. **And he saith** unto me, **Seal not** the sayings of **the prophecy** of this book: **for the time is at hand.**

11. **He that is unjust, let him be unjust still:** and he which is filthy, let him be filthy still: and he that is righteous, let him be righteous still: **and he that is holy, let him be holy still.**

12. **And, behold, I come quickly; and my reward *is* with me,** to give every man according as his work shall be.

13. **I am Alpha and Omega,** the beginning and the end, the first and the last.

14. **Blessed *are* they that do his commandments, that they** may have right to the tree of life, and **may enter** in through the gates **into the city.**

15. For without *are* dogs, and sorcerers, and whoremongers, and murderers, and idolaters, and whosoever loveth and maketh a lie.

16. **I Jesus have sent mine angel to testify** unto you these things in the churches. **I am the root** and the offspring **of David, *and* the bright and morning star.**

17. **And the Spirit and the bride say, Come.** And let him that heareth say, Come. And let him that is athirst come. **And whosoever will, let him take the water of life freely.**

18. **For I testify** unto every man **that** heareth the words of the prophecy of this book, **If any man shall add unto these things, God shall add unto him the plagues** that are written **in this book:**

19. **And if any man shall take away from** the words of the book of **this prophecy, God shall take away his part out of**

the book of life, and out
of the holy city, and *from* the
things which are written in this book.
20. He which testifieth these things
saith, Surely I come
quickly. Amen.
Even so, come, Lord Jesus.
21. The grace of our Lord Jesus Christ
be with you all.
Amen.